Worldly Philosopher

JEREMY ADELMAN

Worldly Philosopher

The Odyssey of Albert O. Hirschman

PRINCETON UNIVERSITY PRESS

Princeton and Oxford

Copyright © 2013 by Princeton University Press
Requests for permission to reproduce material from this work should be sent to Permissions,
Princeton University Press
Published by Princeton University Press, 41 William Street,
Princeton, New Jersey 08540
In the United Kingdom: Princeton University Press, 6 Oxford Street,
Woodstock, Oxfordshire OX20 1TW

press.princeton.edu

Library of Congress Cataloging-in-Publication Data

Adelman, Jeremy.
    Worldly philosopher : the odyssey of Albert O. Hirschman / Jeremy Adelman.
        pages   cm
    Summary: "Worldly Philosopher chronicles the times and writings of Albert O. Hirschman, one of
the twentieth century's most original and provocative thinkers. In this gripping biography, Jeremy Adelman tells the story of a man shaped by modern horrors and hopes, a worldly intellectual who fought
for and wrote in defense of the values of tolerance and change. Born in Berlin in 1915, Hirschman grew
up amid the promise and turmoil of the Weimar era, but fled Germany when the Nazis seized power
in 1933. Amid hardship and personal tragedy, he volunteered to fight against the fascists in Spain and
helped many of Europe's leading artists and intellectuals escape to America after France fell to Hitler.
His intellectual career led him to Paris, London, and Trieste, and to academic appointments at Columbia, Harvard, and the Institute for Advanced Study in Princeton. He was an influential adviser to governments in the United States, Latin America, and Europe, as well as major foundations and the World
Bank. Along the way, he wrote some of the most innovative and important books in economics, the
social sciences, and the history of ideas. Throughout, he remained committed to his belief that reform is
possible, even in the darkest of times. This is the first major account of Hirschman's remarkable life, and
a tale of the twentieth century as seen through the story of an astute and passionate observer. Adelman's
riveting narrative traces how Hirschman's personal experiences shaped his unique intellectual perspective, and how his enduring legacy is one of hope, open-mindedness, and practical idealism"— Provided
by publisher.
    Includes bibliographical references and index.
    ISBN 978-0-691-15567-8 (hardback)
    1. Hirschman, Albert O.   2. Economists—Biography.   3. Economics.   4. Economic
development.   I. Title.
    HB75.A3358 2013
    330.092—dc23
    [B]
                                                            2012046072

British Library Cataloging-in-Publication Data is available

This book has been composed in Garamond Premier Pro

Printed on acid-free paper. ∞

Printed in the United States of America

10 9 8 7 6 5 4

For my children—Sammy, Jojo, and Sadie

*Even when our trust is heavily placed in them, reasoning and education
cannot easily prove powerful enough to bring us actually to do
anything, unless in addition we train to form our Soul by experience
for the course on which we would set her; if we do not, when the time
comes for action she will undoubtedly find herself impeded.*

MICHEL DE MONTAIGNE

CONTENTS

ACKNOWLEDGMENTS

Albert O. Hirschman has accompanied me my whole adult life. As a teenager growing up in Toronto, I spied a small green-covered volume on my father's bookshelf behind his big oak desk. I would look at it while talking with him, intrigued by the title, *The Passions and the Interests*. Following a long tradition of teenage sons, I borrowed it. Permanently. That book now rests on my shelf behind my desk. My children, too, will grow up with Hirschman, though they, unlike me, have no choice in the matter. It is to them that this volume is dedicated because people without choice, especially young ones, deserve to be acknowledged for everything they tolerate when no one asks if they mind.

Writing a life history, I have learned, has meant living with a person for days, months, and years. But there is more: in the moments of maximum intensity, it requires seeing the world through the eyes of one's subject, becoming increasingly aware of what one does not and may never know, for the tacit barriers erected during a lifetime are part of the world-experience itself. To help me piece through this maze over the course of a decade of research and writing, I heard many different Hirschman stories, which of course raises the inevitable question: how does what he seemed to others figure into the tale? The life history has to accommodate the views of those people as well. Some are cited in my notes; some have gone uncited but were illuminating nonetheless in helping me reconstruct the man and his moments. In alphabetical order, the list includes Michele Alacevich, Martin and Daniel Andler, Sheldon Annis, Kenneth Arrow, Paul Audi, Jorge Balan, Carlos Bazdresch, Scott Berg, Samuel Bowles, Peter Bell, Richard Bird, Glen Bowersock, Colin Bradford, David Cannadine, Fernando Henrique Cardoso, Miguel Centeno, Douglas Chalmers, Annie Cot, Robert Darnton, Angus Deaton, Mitchell Denburg, Sir John Elliott, Maria Feijoo, Osvaldo Feinstein, Alejandro Foxley, Alan Furst, Carol Gilligan, Herbert Gintis, Louis Goodman, Peter Gourevitch, Francisco Gutiérrez, Peter Hakim, Stanley Hoffmann, Thomas Horst, Sheila Isenberg, Peter Kenen, Stephen Krasner, Susan James, Elizabeth Jelin, the late Michael Jiménez, Salomón Kalmanovitz, Robert Kaufman, James Kurth, Wolf Lepenies, Kirsten von Lingen, Abraham Lowenthal, Emmanuelle Loyer, Eric Maskin, Anthony Marx, Michael McPherson, Patricio Meller, Mary Morgan, Philip Nord, Sabine Offe, Claus Offe, Gilles Pecout, Jeffrey Puryear, Henry Rosovsky, Emma Rothschild, Michael Rothschild, Jeffrey Rubin, Charles Sabel, Alain Salomon, Thomas Schelling, Philippe Schmitter, Roberto Schwarz, Joan Scott, Rebecca Scott, Amartya Sen, José Serra, Rajiv Sethi, William Sewell, Quentin Skinner, Mark Snyder, Christine Stansell, Paul Streeten, Frank Sutton, Judith Tendler, Miguel Urrutia, Maurizio Viroli, Ignacio Walker, Donald Winch, and Philip Zimbardo. I was fortunate to have been able to interview some before their passing, notably Carl Kaysen and Alexander Stevenson. Others, such as Guillermo O'Donnell and Clifford Geertz, were gone before I could arrange formal interviews. I am grateful to Andrea and Carlo Ginzburg for a very long lunch in Bologna—which did so much to help me understand the multiple Italian influences on Hirschman. Thank you to Eva Monteforte, Albert's younger sister, with whom I spent a wonderful week in Rome going over her memories, letters, and photographs. Katia Salomon, Albert's daughter, was always willing to set aside precious time from visiting aging parents to speak with me and share her father's letters. I appreciate her trust and friendship.

Most of all, it was Albert's late wife, Sarah, who guided me through memories of a life she shared with a remarkable, complicated man, opening their personal letters and diaries for my curious eyes. In many ways,

I have come to see Hirschman through his wife's eyes—itself a challenge to consider. Yet, a biographer could only dream of such companionship; I only hope that it in some way helped her recover forgotten aspects of a life as Albert grew ill and spectral and was increasingly unable to follow the course of our conversations. We made a deal at one point that I would finish this book before she died; it was, I fear, a bit of a one-sided pact, for Sarah read not just one rough draft, but also a second one as cancer was killing her. She died in January 2012, before I could commit final touches to a work she had such a hand and voice in crafting. That she did not live to see this published is more than sad—but it is not a tragedy. While it was not easy to juggle the roles we played for each other, she was to me an invaluable source, a thoughtful reader, and a dear, dear friend.

A book that sprawls across so many continents, archives, languages, and pages in the end required support from Alexander Bevilacqua, Gretchen Boger, Franziska Exeler, Margarita Fajardo, Brooke Fitzgerald, Jeffrey Gonda, Judy Hanson, Debbie Impresa, Sharon Kulik, Joseph Kroll, Allison Lee, Erwin Levold, Daniel Linke, Molly Loberg, Alison MacDonald, Debbie Macy, Anthony Maloney, Martín Marimon, Olga Negrini, Yehudi Pelosi, Elizabeth Schwall, Andrew Tuozzolo, and Bertha Wilson.

Most of this book was written in Paris. I am grateful to my hosts at the Institut d'études politiques for the space and comradeship. Princeton University has been enormously supportive from the start, and the Guggenheim Memorial Foundation bought me some much needed breathing room from the duties of departmental chair.

I received so many constructive suggestions along the way that I cannot do justice to what became a collective effort to study a singular person. Thanks go to friends in Cambridge—England and Massachusetts—Paris, São Paulo, Buenos Aires, Bogotá, New York, and of course Princeton, where bits and pieces of this book were presented. A few valued colleagues and friends went through the daunting manuscript. These include Daniel Rodgers, Arcadio Díaz Quiñones, who introduced me to Albert and with whom I shared many treasured lunches thinking about life history together, Emma Rothschild, and Charles Maier. Each in their own way helped me to see Albert anew, perhaps through their eyes, in large and, importantly, small ways. And how to thank a dream editor, Brigitta van Rheinberg? I keep her red-lined 800-page manuscript as a monument to dedication and amity.

It is tempting to offer to the reader a long list of caveats. But I won't. The seams and speculations that invariably make up a life history I have tried to indicate in the text itself. Just one note of clarification: as Hirschman's name changed several times over the course of the first half of his life, I have used the names according to time and place—in part to exemplify the twists and turns of the twentieth century in the most taken-for-granted gesture of everyday life, the name we go by.

The title of this book evokes Robert Heilbroner's best seller, *The Worldly Philosophers: The Lives, Times, and Ideas of the Great Economic Thinkers*, first published in 1953. A perceptive set of vignettes from Adam Smith to John Maynard Keynes and Joseph Schumpeter, it ends with challenges of depression and war. It is adapted here to denote a worldly figure in at least three senses. Hirschman was uniquely *of* the world, living and working in Europe, the United States, and Latin America and closely observing events around the globe. He was also committed to formulating thoughts *about* the world. His insights about the economy, philosophy, literature, and politics were never forged in the remove of the ivory tower. Indeed, Hirschman would harbor a life-long ambivalence about the professionalizing trend of the American university, and it was by complex good fortune and maneuvering that he climbed the ranks of academia without ever really belonging to it. In this sense, he represented a diminishing species of intellectual.

Never intended as purely theoretical ruminations, Hirschman's ideas were meant as contributions *to* the world. Karl Marx, whom Hirschman studied from the time he was in school, famously noted in his "Theses on Feuerbach" that "Philosophers have hitherto only interpreted the world in various ways; the point is to change it." Meant as a critique of German idealism (in which Hirschman was also schooled), Marx sought to illuminate a practical, empirical, political model of the production of knowledge, theories derived from observations of how historical development actually unfolded. This was, broadly speaking, Hirschman's spirit, though in many respects he imagined himself a dialectical counterpoint to Marx and Marxists and carried the traits of Hegelian influences from the time he was a young man—most especially that world history was the product of opaque and discrete forces, the cunning of reason, whose laws and mechanics one could only imperfectly understand. He was, in contrast to either Hegel or Marx, a kind of pragmatic idealist.

It is the making and life of this pragmatic idealist that is the subject of this book. But as the reader of *Worldly Philosopher* will learn, books themselves have stories and biographies born of ideas. So, too, with this book. *Worldly Philosopher* was my wife's idea. Thank you for starting me on this journey and being my company throughout.

Worldly Philosopher

Mots Justes

In early April 1933, a spasm of anti-Semitic violence rocked Berlin. Thugs beat Jews in the streets. Shops owned by Jews were looted and burned. Hitler slapped restrictions on Jewish doctors, merchants, and lawyers. For the Hirschmann family, well-to-do assimilated Jewish Berliners, the distress paled beside a more immediate shock. The family huddled in a cemetery as a coffin bearing Carl Hirschmann was lowered into his grave. His wife wept. His children did too. Except one. Otto Albert, known to us by a different name, Albert O. Hirschman, concealed his grief as the family bid their farewells to a father and husband.

This was not the only adieu of the day. Otto Albert, a law student at the University of Berlin and a militant anti-Nazi, was in danger. His friends were being arrested; the university was quickly becoming a hive of intolerance. So he decided to go clandestine and then leave for France. When the funeral was over, the seventeen-year-old Hirschmann announced to his anguished family that he was leaving Germany, promising to return after the passing of the storm surrounding Adolf Hitler's ascent to power. Decades would pass before he did. Thus began an odyssey in the making of a pragmatic idealist that would send our subject across continents and languages on a journey over the frontiers of a century's social science.

Albert O. Hirschman detached himself from his family and city, but he never defined himself against them; neither did he mourn the loss or carry his displacement like a badge, a familiar default for exiles. While he never rejected his forebearers, he did not cling to them. Hirschman balanced a life between the inherited and the acquired: he adapted to and learned from new environments while never losing sight of his heritage; without forgetting his past, he did not yearn for "return." In this he had no choice; for over a decade, there was no Ithaca, no wife, no son, no title to go back to. Persecution, intolerance, and war had destroyed the cosmopolitan world that many of his generation had fought to defend.

Hirschman's departure from Germany was the first of many flights. His was a life of repeated departures that began in a Mitteleuropean upheaval, the largest intellectual and cultural exodus the world has ever seen. In France, Spain, and Italy he would toggle between antifascist fights until it was too dangerous to stay, and so he too fled to the United States to contribute to the overhaul of American intellectual life by European émigrés. However, for those in the swelling ranks of the Federal Bureau of Investigation who made a career out of chasing suspects, his track record of political activism tainted him with enough suspicion that he was forced to decamp once more in the heat of the McCarthyite purges. His new destination: South America. There, he would reinvent himself anew—this time as one of the great thinkers of development.

There was a wrinkle in how Hirschman handled his displacements. For someone who meditated over the nuances and tensions between leaving, fighting, and accepting—or as he would later put it, exit, voice, and loyalty—it is fitting that his own exits were hardly clear-cut. Often, he chose to leave as much as he was driven out; he was a willing Odysseus. Hirschman was an unusual exile. Cosmopolitan by choice and chance, he occupied, and to some extent opened, a penumbral space as the insider-outsider—between the establishment and the dissident—to author works that crisscrossed the line separating manifestos from monographs. Uprooting and delocalization placed him outside any single cultural tradition, intellectual genre, or national place—a figure we might consider an antecedent to our more "globalized" intellectual type. Some readers might regard him as the first truly global intellectual, a term that would probably make him wince. Certainly, *his* version of being a global intellectual never cut him off from the multiple roots of his imagination; he was global not because he stood above them but because he could so artfully combine them.

Choice or chance . . . chance with choice . . . At times, I have often felt that making sense of the mixture of forces that compose a life history, especially one so replete with breaks and ruptures, leaves too much to the author. A tempting solution to the problem is to treat them in the subject's own vocabulary; as it turns out, the role of choosing and chance translate into terms familiar to the republican topoi in which Hirschman was steeped and with which he closely identified, *virtù* and *fortuna*. He would recount how Fortune must have smiled upon him when he made his getaway from the police in Marseilles at the end of 1940 or when a surprise letter invited him to Yale in 1957. But he was never lured into believing that there was anything providential at work; he did, after all, have a hand in his own fate—even if it was not always a visible one. Either way, virtù and fortuna entwined to yield one of the twentieth century's most remarkable intellectuals, one who devoted a lifetime to thinking about the role of choice and making the best of chance in human affairs.

The key was to be open to possibilities. More than that, it meant creating them. This is why his exile was not experienced as being severed from home, separating a self from one's past, as Edward Said famously put it.[1] Separation created possibilities for new combinations. Indeed, Hirschman coined a term, *possibilism*, or, perhaps more accurately, adapted it from Søren Kierkegaard's famous aphorism "Pleasure disappoints, possibility never!" to evoke Hirschman's disposition. For someone growing up in the shadow of fascism, war, and intolerance, this upbeat was not an expected point of arrival. In fact, most intellectuals of his generation—and Hannah Arendt, his elder by a few years, comes most readily to mind—worried more than they hoped, saw catastrophe instead of opportunity. But possibilism was more than just a personal disposition; it was also an intellectual stance for his brand of social science. The more familiar search for probabilistic laws based on a list of preconditions for events or outcomes all too often led to the dismaying conclusion that most societies would be unable to solve their problems and break out of vicious cycles on their own. This didn't, in the end, leave much to the imagination and left Hirschman pondering what the point was— ethically as well as intellectually—to being a scholar. He yearned for a social science that reset the imagination of the intellectual to consider combinations that might take anomalous, deviant, or inverted sequences and make them a potential course; to explore combinations that might lay the tracks for different histories of the future.

One way to prevent a life of trouble from becoming one of tragedy was through ironic, humor-laced detachment, a stance that never got in the way of empathy or commitment. Varian Fry, with whom Hirschman worked to get refugees (including Hannah Arendt) out of Marseilles as the Nazis swept across Europe, once recalled how the police finally caught up with Hirschman not because he *had* false papers but because he had *too many good ones,* which made him suspicious. Included in these bogus documents was the certificate that "M. Albert Hermant" was a Frenchman born in Philadelphia and cards testifying that he belonged to a number of associations, including a Club for People without Clubs. His seamless French helped cover his German origins and antifascist tracks. The German sociologist Wolf Lepenies once mused about Hirschman, "We have here a criminal with too many alibis."[2] After an unplanned vascular operation while he was visiting Berlin around the time of the fall of the Wall, Hirschman came out of the fog of the anesthetic, turned to his doctor, and asked in German, "Why are bananas bent?" The doctor smiled and shrugged. Hirschman replied, "Because nobody went to the jungle to adjust it and make it straight."[3]

This was not the only banana joke. In the 1950s, while the Hirschmans were living in Bogotá, Colombia, they made a habit of sending Christmas cards to their friends around the world. In 1952, a friend of theirs, Peter Aldor, a Hungarian cartoonist who had moved to Colombia to become one of that country's great political satirists, drew a card for them. It featured Albert the economist perched in a banana plant clutching a sheet of graphs and figures. Below are his wife and daughters harvesting the fruit,

A holiday card from the Hirschman family,
drawn by Peter Aldor, c. 1955.

whose production Albert is supposedly planning. The caption reads: "An excellent food is the banana. Let's eat it today and plan it mañana." The joke is layered with meanings, one of which was a dig at colleagues who believed in the lofty promises of economic planning.

Humor was central to a literary personality; the form of the argument could not be so easily unraveled from its substance; indeed, late in life he would focus his attention on how people in modern society argue about public affairs. His last major work, *The Rhetoric of Reaction* (1991), tackled the way intransigent arguments threatened to weaken democracy, precisely because they narrowed options and alternatives. At the core of his argument was an observation about how social scientists played with words that had political and economic consequences.

He should know—he was a master player in his own right. Hirschman amused himself with words, their sounds, and their meanings. Adept as he was at double entendres in German, French, Spanish, Italian, and English, his play with words meant careful attention; language and words were to his craft what the scalpel was to his father, the surgeon. Play with words was often a reminder that in the freedom of language one could find light even in dark times. In June 1932, as National Socialists were broadcasting their bile, Hirschman wrote his elder sister to warn her that a long-delayed letter was still being composed. "Do you know why you haven't received this one yet?" he asked her. "Because it is awaiting transportation! Oh the poor one, sometimes at night I can hear it whining, awaiting [*harren*] its transportation."[4]

It was in words that his play came to full fruition. He loved a well-turned phrase, especially when twisting the familiar into the self-mocking. "The dead end that justifies the means! But does the end justify the meanness?" and "I am anxious for criticism as long as you find me seminole" can be found among his jottings. One can find "Metaphors in search of a reality," a formulation he instantly doubted and then swapped for "metaphors in search referent," folded into his notes on the problem of freight rates on Nigerian railways.

Word play was not idle play. The paradoxical, backward, inverted developments one finds in his favorite images and aphorisms mirror the style he brought to bear in his outlook on the world. Like baguettes (with which he became a self-proclaimed world-expert sandwich-maker) that get soft, not hard, as they go stale, Hirschman enjoyed finding meaning from the way History defied "universal laws." Out of the inversions and "wrong-way-around" sequences, came possibilities for things to be different—like the life that springs from what appear to be dead tree branches at the end of each winter. This impression, too, came to him as he gazed out his kitchen window at home in Princeton. As Hirschman joked to Clifford Geertz many years later, too many of their colleagues fell prey to "Law No. 1 of the Social Sciences. Whenever a phenomenon in the social world is fully explained, it ceases to operate."[5]

It was in palindromes that his fascination was realized, and one can detect in his public writings from the 1960s onward a sharp eye for the right phrase: "exit, voice, and loyalty," "the tunnel effect," "the passions and the interests." These were his Flaubertian mots justes. Perhaps his best palindrome—certainly his fondest—was "Senile Lines," composed in a collage of tongues around 1971. It starts like this:

I,

REVOLT LOVER,

FOE OF

PARTY TRAP

EVIL IGNITING I LIVE.

NAOMI, MOAN!

MAORI, ROAM!

HARASS SELFLESS SARAH!

DIE, ID!

NEIN SEIN!

RÊVE: NADA, NEVER.

A world of ideas wrapped in carefully chosen words.

Behind his great books was a clandestine life—not of espionage (though Hirschman did have a brief career as a member of the antifascist underground, and he was once a member of the Office of Strategic Services, the forerunner of the Central Intelligence Agency) nor of secret lovers or double lives. As Hirschman became one of the world's foremost social scientists, he launched a sideline in 1972. With a group of fellow palindrome aficionados, he founded the 4W Club (Where We Went Wrong) to bombard a fictive Dr. Awkward with a letter campaign. It was one of the few international organizations that he was actually glad to direct. Albert's favorite correspondent was the Guatemalan Augusto Monterroso, with whom he shared some *tesoros*. "AMO IDIOMA!" he exclaimed to the famous poet.[6]

Words were to Hirschman what equations were for other economists. Indeed, by the standards of economics, Hirschman was an exceedingly wordy economist. Many in the profession, without knowing that he was once fairly handy with statistics and enjoyed its possibilities, disavowed him as a colleague for it. As Hirschman became a mature scholar, the charge of practicing a social science that did not lend itself to formal, theory-testing rigors or mathematical modeling was a common one. He felt compelled to explain himself to his friend from his Harvard days, Daniel Bell. "The model builders sometimes criticize me," Hirschman explained, "for not putting my thoughts into mathematical models. My reply to them is that mathematics has not quite caught up with metaphor or language—both are more inventive!"[7] To many, this may seem a self-serving defense. But it is true that Hirschman's skill with words always eclipsed his dexterity with numbers, and as the economics profession abandoned the former to pursue the latter, Hirschman was out of step.

Why so much about words? For one thing, they were a sanctuary, a refuge for a man with no country. In the summer of 1944, as he waited anxiously and increasingly depressed in North Africa to join the American Army in Europe, he found solace in words. Despair began to overwhelm him as he thought about the number of people who had suffered on account of the war "or worse, the prisoners in concentration camps." Anguished, he happened upon a verse by Jean Wahl, "Merci mon corps, tu fais bien ton métier de corps." Writing to his pregnant wife (Sarah) in New York, he exclaimed, "Isn't this well said? And so simple! Good poetry produces the effect of great inventions. It is so simple but one must think about it." Characteristically, he concluded with more words inspired by those words: these are "themes to be developed." Behind him, Albert Hirschman left diaries, letters, and marginalia in books filled with "ideas," "themes," and "questions" to mark the trails of his thoughts, verbal routes into his mind's eye.[8]

Language, especially its written form, was a dwelling place for mind and soul. That someone with so many languages should think of its practice as a kind of home may seem strange to us. But it was precisely his Odyssean life, so long unsettled that a physical home was almost an arbitrary one, that enhanced the dominion of words. He was above all a writer, and as Joseph Brodsky once noted, "for a writer only one form of patriotism exists: his attitude toward language."

Words thereby gave solace. But they are also our clues to an intellectual imagination. Words, sentences, prose, and poetry—in effect, literature—were more than embellishments or ornaments to hang on existing social scientific classifications. Hirschman's work represents an effort to practice social science *as* literature. It is what makes him appear so original in style and content now that the bonds between literature and social science have increasingly been severed. Hirschman, and the cultural milieu of assimilated bourgeois Jews of Berlin, sank a taproot deep into the classics, from Kafka the modernist to the *Odyssey*, long portions of which Hirschman could recite from the time he was a child. It is why Flaubert's interiority gives insight into psychology, and it is why La Rochefoucauld plumbs the cunning of self-interest. Good literature, to Hirschman, summons the power of small details and anomalies to uncover something new about the whole. As Fernando Henrique Cardoso, a close friend, collaborator, and future president of Brazil once told me, Hirschman was like a Dutch painter, revealing in the small new ways of seeing the whole. An economist to the end, he was forever conjugating genres, styles, and divisions of the human sciences. As the cursus of his life slowly closed with the century, he made of his style a kind of rampart from which to warn us, without giving up on humor, of the perils of overspecialization, of a narrowing of vision, and of the temptation to fall in love with the image of one's own technical prowess and vocabulary and lose sight of the vitality of moving back and forth between proving and preaching. Appreciating this is crucial for understanding his stance toward evidence and argumentation, why to him rhetoric mattered. He exemplifies at once a disposition that is much broader than the estuary of our social sciences; perhaps for this reason he represents a humanism of social science that may be slowly drying up.

But this would be far too gloomy a reading—and Hirschman would be the first to object to this portrait of his own work. Thank goodness, he would no doubt say, that Fortuna has plenty of tricks up her sleeve.

The affection for writing is what draws our attention to Hirschman; it is his books and articles that have captivated generations of readers and make him unique in the human sciences. But this story is not the story of the works; it is rather the story behind them. By this I do not mean that Hirschman's books and essays should speak for themselves, though their lucidity often left me paraphrasing what was rendered much better in the original. Upon rereading one of Hirschman's essays, the great historian of ideas Quentin Skinner felt compelled to confess that he had been pressing it upon his Cambridge graduate students, "but I find on re-reading it that the points I try to make to them about it are in fact in the essay itself. An unconscious application of a form of dishonesty common, I suppose, among teachers, especially of the harried kind."[9] I agree with Skinner. This study does not seek to explain arguments that are told well enough by the original author, but rather, by illuminating the drama, complexity, tension—and downright hard work of the intellectual labor process—to invite readers to have their own reading experience by telling the biographical backstory of a life's ideas.

But which backstory? These days, biography, especially of the "popular" sort, has become a synonym for private revelation, culled from a stash of secret letters, a hidden diary, or a confession. The presumption seems to be that what is most private is also most revealing, as if the *real* truth about someone is that which is least known, what Louis Menand called "the Rosebud assumption."[10] Leave aside the naïveté of this genre—as if people don't lie in their letters, distort in their diaries, and concoct in their confessions. Hirschman himself was not above melodramatizing the moment. There is also the matter of what is always inscrutable about a life history. In trying to render a vivid sense of the person's likeness from letters, personal notes, manuscripts, and archives from several continents, not to mention the conversations with him and others, I became aware of the multiplying gaps, the unprovable stories, the maddening lack of evidence. Some are the gaps that we know of, such as the death of his dear colleague and close friend, Clifford Geertz, before I could arrange formal interviews with him. The absence of Geertz's testimony will be a lasting fault, and readers should be aware of the absence of his voice here.

There are also gaps of a less accidental kind; Hirschman, though pressed, did not want to revisit his memories of fighting for the Republican cause in the Spanish Civil War. I have often wondered whether his brand of hopefulness and his faith in reform, his possibilism, required covering the tracks of terrible memories. If they did, it is important to know that some details are sometimes more relevant and saddening in their absence because the gap was there for a reason.

Mercifully, biographical uncertainty is something that can now be admitted. It points to something that Hermione Lee has thoughtfully discussed: how a biography amalgamates what is known and what is not known, the present and the absent,—and how it includes the welter of alternatives, accidents, might-have-beens, in a word, the *possibilities* of a life, only some of which can be reconstructed.[11] It is perhaps fitting that Hirschman himself would accent life's possibilities, not just in the way he lived but also for History, and that any social theory worth its weight had to reckon with it. At the core of his possibilism was the idea that people had a right to what he called a "non-projected future." From a biographer's point of view, one might say the same of the past, especially one that traces a subject's uncanny ability to get out of a jam and find reasons for hope and space for reform even when they seem most implausible. It was not an accident that one of Hirschman's favored words was *débrouillard*, from the Old French root, *brouiller* (to mix up), which alludes to artful ways to wiggle out of a convoluted, intractable, or bad situation.

Words met ideas and ideas found their expression in a quest. One might see Hirschman as a latter-day Don Quixote, striving in his books and essays to produce possibilities that can only be dimly seen. Cervantes was, in fact, a favorite of Hirschman's and a source of some of his selected quotes. The very idea of Quixote's *Librillo de memoria*, his book of memories, inspired the kind of note taking and observation that provide grist for the narrative of this book. It was only after several years of research that Hirschman's wife, muse, and, in decisive moments, his life intellectual partner shared with me Hirschman's little brown diaries, in which he jotted some of his most personal notes. Understandably, it had taken time to build confidence in her husband's biographer. These as well as other sources help paint a portrait of an errant knight, a figure often noted for being disconnected from reality. But this is only one mode of reading the character, a mode that became commonplace during the English Civil War, which has warped how we think of dreamers. In Hirschman we find a dreamer—Fry would complain about his invaluable coconspirator that he was too often *dans la lune*—who was most certainly connected to his worlds, connected and committed to the extent that he was willing to lay his life on the line for his cause.

The quest is evident across the writings that would span seven decades. But there is no single idea or topic at work; Hirschman's attention moved along with History. The subjects vary from the economic causes of imperialism and war, the subject of his near-forgotten first book, *National Power and the Structure of Foreign Trade* (1945), to his searing indictment of modern habits of political discourse in *The Rhetoric of Reaction* (1991). One can read any single Hirschman oeuvre as a window onto a moment, and together they make up a kind of intellectual glossary of a century. Certainly, many of his works now rank among classics of the social sciences—one thinks of *Exit, Voice, and Loyalty: Responses to Decline in Firms, Organizations, and States* (1970) or *The Passions and the Interests: Political Arguments for Capitalism before Its Triumph* (1977). To see them as testimonies and products of moments in time and place, to give these books their own history, is one aspiration of this book.

And yet, there are some common traits in this glossary. One trait was style. It can be read at first blush as literary. Hirschman would become one of the greatest *authors* in the social sciences, a division of intellectual life admittedly short on writerly credentials. Many have delighted in his vivid metaphors, memorable images, and poetic turns. But the great prose was in the service of a disposition that urged wariness about big claims, grand theories, and encompassing plans and the certainties that were required to scaffold them—required because social scientists increasingly sought quarry in models, theories, and laws that were meant to be true across time, and thus outside History. Hirschman was a skeptic who preferred anomalies, surprises, and the power of unintended effects, forces that were sometimes easier to see in literature. Whatever prevailed as the orthodoxy—fixing the dollar gap in Europe with austerity, faith in planning in the 1950s, exuberance about foreign aid in the 1960s, Latin American defeatism, and the triumph of free-market ideologies in the 1980s—Hirschman positioned himself as a contrarian. This was because he always feared that orthodoxy and certainty excluded the creative possibilities of doubt, of learning from surprises.

As such, his narrative style summoned readers to question whether History really had to unfold a given way. Schooled as an adolescent in Marxism in one of its hotbeds, Berlin, he came to reject anything that smacked of teleology or historical laws. His early battles with Communist orthodoxy would have a lifelong effect. Sometimes the way out of a jam could come from being more modest, accepting one's limitations, and pursuing strategies that lay before one's nose, if only one could shed the temptation to presume that bigger is better or grander is greater. Other times, it was precisely exaggeration and ambition that was required. Being open to many possibilities meant accepting uncertainty and embracing the fact that one could learn from experience in the world by forfeiting presumptions that one could not know it all. Some of the options included the most counterintuitive. As he would note in *Strategy of Economic Development* (1958), it is where one faces the most resistance that one should press one's pursuits. For this reason, some of his critics have noted that Hirschman had more fondness for understanding complexity in the social sciences than searching for strong predictions. They are right, and they are right to point to his affection for the powerful image over the perfect equation. But there are reasons for this preference that this biography aims to illuminate.

If style was one of the traits, it was connected to the content of his thinking. And the content was deeply rooted in a sense of being in the world. Hirschman's century was one of bad situations, and he found himself repeatedly—indeed, placed himself—at their junctions. Often painted as a hundred years of revolution, war, and genocide, the twentieth century ended with the general consensus that humanity did not dignify itself but rather displayed an ability to perform vast horrors. It is for this reason that Eric Hobsbawm once depicted the long history of the short century as an "age of extremes." The extremes had their intellectuals.

Many intellectuals. And many of these intellectuals worked in the service of the extremes. Just as we are accustomed to see the twentieth century as the age of extremes, we have tended to be more interested in its extremist apostles, from the revolutionaries to the reactionaries.

But between revolution and counterrevolution, empire and nationalism, communism and capitalism, there was also another domain, that of reform. Often beleaguered, beaten, and overshadowed by utopian Titans, this was a realm of purposive and often nonconsensual, and therefore conflictive, change whose pursuit aimed not to perfect humanity, but only to improve it. The pursuit of flawless perfection all too often led to some horrific outcomes—Hirschman would lose family and friends to the century's butchery at the hands of ideologues of the immaculate. What if humans had dared to dream less of humans as perfectible beings than as improvable ones? To Hirschman, it was a shame that the imagination gave so much allure to the former and treated the latter as second-best or simply—and disparagingly—as "acceptable." How boring and undesirable! This was materiel for his struggle with utopians and fatalists from Berkeley to Berlin, who preferred all-or-nothing arguments that invariably left societies delirious with impossible expectations or despondent about their failures.

This book is about someone who thought hard about and dwelled in the neglected, ravaged space between the romance of revolution and the firmament of reaction. It is a personal and intellectual story of a middle ground seen through the eyes of someone firmly committed to its place in the world, partly as a counterpoint to the great ideas that gave rise to grand utopian experiments. But he was not just responding to the charisma of grand schemes; his life was a twisting and gradually developing search for concepts to understand social change with their own integrity, complexity, and one might even say "theory," though this word caused deep ambivalence for Hirschman. Hirschman's life was a personal history of the twentieth century, its epic told through the life of one man who coursed through its most terrible and hopeful moments but never gave up on the ability to imagine life differently, better. Indeed, he would often tell his readers that a solution to the world's problems lay not so much in some technical discovery as in the power of the imagination.

The ensuing story charts a personal history of the world and a global history of an intellectual life.

As we consider the life of Albert O. Hirschman, we might reflect on this place of reform as something more than a residual, a mere afterthought to the loftier utopias that dominate the pages of his century's other thinkers. After all, Hirschman was an intellectual. His lifework represented a commitment to reform, which ranged from rebuilding war-torn Europe, to development in the Third World, and to defending a capitalism made humane by accepting the necessity of being reformable.

Nowadays, we think of reform as fixing, mending what has been broken, but to Hirschman, it was more than a technical exercise in remediation. It was not what we do when we can't imagine doing our best. Perhaps in retracing his life we can begin to piece together a biography of reform itself: the story of Albert O. Hirschman might be read as a collective memory in the form of a personal tale, a reencounter with a social science that finds hope in disappointment, solutions in tension, and liberty in uncertainty, a style of regarding the social world as a source of possibilities that the intellectual can help summon with a different combination of humility and daring.

CHAPTER I

The Garden

You are the task. No pupil far and wide.

FRANZ KAFKA

On August 1, 1914, the German capital erupted in festivities. A glorious war had broken out. The speechifying, recruiting parades, and posters and banners urging the troops to swift victory all celebrated a conflict that promised to end in six weeks. The ensuing armistice would restore a gentlemanly world governed by European monarchs, nobles, and capitalists. This was a welcome war, not a dreaded one. One young doctor applauded along with his fellow subjects. His name: Carl Hirschmann. He was a patriot; he loved Beethoven, Goethe, and the values of the German Enlightenment, as well as the German nation. In the wake of the naval Battle of Skagerrak (known as Jutland in English, May 31–June 1, 1916) he gushed to his wife, "What do you think of our victory at sea? How wonderful it would have been to be there!"[1]

Carl Hirschmann's excitement did not send him to the front or to the high seas. He served the cause behind the lines. A surgeon, a preferred career choice for aspiring German Jews, Hirschmann toiled away at the Charité Hospital in Berlin, tending the sick and mending the war's wounded.

He also became a father. A year before Skagerrak, Carl's son was born. Brimming with national loyalty, Carl named the boy Otto (after the founder of the Great Reich, Otto von Bismarck) Albert (after his grandfather, a banker and patriarch of a well-off family). Carl not only yearned for a boy, he hoped he'd be able to celebrate the birth on April 1 to coincide with the festivities to mark Bismarck's one-hundredth anniversary. Instead, the baby took his time. He was born April 7. Otto Albert Hirschmann, known as OA among family and friends, was a child of war, the loyalties it inspired, and the consequences it wrought for Germany and the world.

The infant Otto Albert was welcomed into a world in which greatness was supposed to await the German nation. But the war baby's parents had to contend with some of the unanticipated effects of the conflict. When it was clear that this would not be a quick triumph, and the troops dug in for a long haul, the German capital began to suffer. Berlin, a metropolis of over two million, was heavily dependent on imported food. To break the German fighting spirit, the Allies mounted a blockade in the first winter, which was one of the reasons why the stakes at Skagerrak were so high. In fact, strategically the German navy never managed to break the blockade. Food stocks dwindled. A few months before Otto Albert's birth, Berlin became the first German city to issue bread-ration cards. The winter of 1916 was called the Turnip Winter—that's all there was to eat. By 1916, egg allocations were down to two per family per month. The next year, the potato crop, a staple for flour and bread, failed. That summer food riots rocked the German capital. And then the following winter was not only bitterly cold, there was no coal to heat homes. Berliners froze to death. Others suffered from severe malnutrition. Hospitals like Carl's Charité were busier than ever. Carl's wife, Hedwig (Hedda), left her two young children in the hands of a nanny while she too went to work, as a nurse. The glitz of prewar Berlin and the pomp of August 1914 had given way to death, shortages, darkness, and endless queues. In desperation, the government flung its remaining resources into two massive offensives in the spring of 1918, bloodbaths that left tens of thousands slaughtered without bringing the country any closer to victory.

When the government finally signed the armistice, a wave of unrest swept the city and brought down Otto von Bismarck's imperial monarchy. While radical workers, inspired by the events in Russia, proclaimed "Red Berlin," and Lenin prophesied that Berlin had now become the capital not of Germany but of the World Revolution, the economy came to a standstill. Factories that had been pumping out war materiel locked their gates. By February 1919, over a quarter million Berliners were without work. Migrants from devastated East Prussia flocked in, creating armies of roving homeless. And then there was disease. In December 1918 alone, influenza killed almost 5,000 Berliners. The pandemic scoured the city and flooded the morgues; the Spartacist uprising a month later ended in savagery. Rosa Luxemburg's body was dumped in the Landwehr Canal, Karl Liebknecht was shot in the back in the Tiergarten Park, and right-wing thugs patrolled the city to stop the Soviet influence from crossing into German lands.

From this mayhem was born the Weimar Republic, the political and cultural setting of Otto Albert's upbringing.

The Weimar years may have brought an end to aristocratic empire, but the republic was also the realization for many Germans of an older dream of greatness, of a model born of the Enlightenment and a vision of the German nation as a tolerant, accommodating political community premised on the integration of the various peoples that lived within German boundaries but who were not necessarily of it: Catholics, easterners, Russian refugees, and above all, the group most invested in the idea of emancipation with integration, secular Jews. Weimar appeared to wipe away the relics that stood in the way of the promise of the German Enlightenment; it invited republican believers to cast aside their doubts. Carl and Hedwig Hirschmann were members of a generation that staked its personal fortunes on this faith. Their three children, Ursula, Otto Albert, and Eva, were of a generation that grew up in the apex of the republican dream. It saw the young Otto Albert through his school days, first loves, first efforts as a writer, and first forays into politics, but with the end of the republic and the rise of the Third Reich, Hirschmann's Berlin collapsed around him, the effects of which provided a basic arc for his life history: his was the last generation to have shared in the German dream and the first to be stamped by its horrific fate. He carried with him throughout his life many of the precepts and values he had inherited as a boy and picked up as a young man in a vibrantly cosmopolitan, civil, bourgeois—republican—upbringing, steeped in the view that things could be made better, that out of the ashes of the old, new worlds could be made.

But throughout his life, he knew equally well just how precarious this world could be.

By the time the postwar dust settled down, the Weimar Republic— that fourteen-year experiment in mass democracy and norm-shattering modernism—had appeared to deliver on its promises to create a new balance of freedom and stability. For a short time, the western world's cultural center moved from Paris to Berlin. Perhaps this was because, un-like either London or Paris, Berlin was a newcomer, a "parvenu among capitals" in the words of another young Berliner, Peter Gay.[2] After all, it had only become the capital in 1871, and even then it still had the hall-marks of a garrison town. So it was freer of the constraints of an age-old urban myth or tradition. Perhaps the old order had more thoroughly crumbled in the German capital so that its residents could more easily devote themselves to novelty. In fact, many Berliners were newcomers: there were some 200,000 Russian émigrés alone. For a time, British poets and writers such as W. H. Auden and Christopher Isherwood called Ber-lin home. Viennese directors, such as Max Reinhardt, relocated from the old Hapsburg center. The Berlin Style was, to a very large extent, made by nonnative Berliners.

Now, Berliners turned to culture. True, it still was the scene of po-litical grandstanding from the Kapp Putsch of 1920 to Hitler's ill-fated 1923 Campaign in Berlin. For a moment, however, the presence of politics faded. In the meantime, Dada artists, Bauhaus architects, Berlin expres-sionists, and avant-garde filmmakers made Berlin their capital. Perhaps best known was the flourishing of a distinct Berlin movement in theater, film, and criticism, especially with the collaboration of Kurt Weill and Bertolt Brecht, whose *Three Penny Opera* presented industrializing Lon-don as an allegory for contemporary Berlin. Berlin's first talking movie, *The Blue Angel*, made Marlene Dietrich famous around the world. But before then, she was already a diva at home. The stage was the setting for her memorable walk down a broad staircase in tuxedo and top hat. In the summer of 1927, the Hirschmann family was vacationing on the Island of Sylt, taking advantage of the new Hindenburgdamm, the causeway that linked the beaches on the North Sea to the German mainland. They went to the swanky Westerland and in a restaurant found the glamorous actress nearby. When she asked a waiter to bring her fur coat, Carl jumped to his feet, took the coat from the waiter, and draped it over Dietrich's shoulders. As she slipped her arms into the sleeves, Carl whispered in her ear, "Meine beste Freundin!" (the name of her hit recording). Dietrich laughed and thanked him.[3]

Especially after the taming of the hyperinflation of the early 1920s, Berlin boomed. It was not beautiful like Paris; it had no great boulevards, had few historic monuments, and was spare in its nineteenth-century classicism. Neither did it have the imperial grandeur and pretensions of London. But it exuded modernity, what Eric Weitz has called "Berlin modern."[4] It was also surrounded by lakes and trees of the Mark Brandenburg, providing weekend getaways for Berliners. Its avenues lined by chestnut and linden trees, Berlin had canals, parks, and an active public culture. Cafes were full. There were three large opera houses, one of them devoted exclusively to modern and experimental productions. Above all, it had theater: three state theaters and four more under the direction of the brilliant Max Reinhardt alone. Even before the republic, Berlin had been the home for expressionist denunciations of social conventions; cultural activity was increasingly seen as a realm for social criticism to lampoon aristocratic buffoonery and lambaste all efforts to censure or curb creative freedoms.

These impressions of Weimar Berlin should not overwhelm the many other ways in which Berliners went about their lives influenced only sparingly by the satiric, the illicit, and the bawdy. For many, the war ended monarchy and empire and humbled some of the old aristocratic grandiosity, but it did not demolish classical traditions. Indeed, the war lifted obstacles against others participating in the marketplace for conventional high culture. This sphere also boomed. Three famous conductors—Wilhelm Furtwängler, Bruno Walter, and Otto Klemperer—had their orchestras in Berlin. Popular highbrow pastimes like rowing had new devotees after the war. The elegant parks, once uncomfortable scenes reserved for the middle classes except on special occasions, were thrown open to social arrivistes. It was the uneasy compromise of the old and the new, the past and the present, the radical and the staid, that coexisted—albeit more tenuously than many recognized at the time—through the republic.[5]

So it was that the city reinvented itself not of wholly new cloth. It had a heritage upon which to build and feel confident in its republican values. Berlin, and Prussia, had a much older history of accommodating, albeit with mixed feelings, newcomers. Its Jews were compelled by the promise of emancipation, and not a few of them—including the Hirschmanns and the Marcuses, the two branches of Otto Albert's family—responded to the calls for assimilation and integration. They could make the enlightened figures of Herder, Kant, Goethe, and Schiller their own. Moses Mendelssohn, the German Socrates, who anchored the Haskala (Jewish Enlightenment) in Berlin, argued for expanded liberties in return for Jews' acceptance of German civic norms. By the time Hitler seized power, the official size of the Jewish community in Germany was half a million, but there were just as many Jews who had converted to Christianity and nondenominational citizens of Jewish descent. Among these were the Hirschmanns. Moreover, Jews were becoming wealthier and more important, and new generations were probing opportunities to engage in science and philosophy—opening a complex spectrum of degrees of integration.

The State itself showed signs of becoming more accommodating. One by one, German states issued emancipation decrees in the late eighteenth century; Prussia's came in 1812. Granted freedom of movement, Jews responded by relocating within and between German states, and as Berlin opened up, it became a favored destination. Then, in 1871, Jews finally got the vote; all formal restrictions on citizenship were lifted. From a population of 50,000 in 1871 when Berlin became the capital, their numbers grew to 170,000, about 8 percent of the population, by 1910. Many of them initially clustered around the massive synagogue on Orianenburgstrasse (a key target during the Kristallnacht of 1938), but they soon fanned out as their population expanded, and many integrated into non-Jewish neighborhoods. If the results were upward mobility, the accumulation of sizeable fortunes, and the construction of palatial homes, another result was a cleavage between those who "made it"—the integrating, prospering, learned Jew—and those who didn't—the "ghetto" Jew, a backward relic affiliated with lowly status, ignorance, and separation from the German mainstream. The ghetto Jew was a reminder of the unfortunate origins that the new Jew often preferred to forget.[6]

The result was, for many Jews, that Jewishness became an increasingly private affair, as what was deemed public or civic acquired a distinctly secular tone. It was no less complex nonetheless, and indeed it is sometimes harder to see how families resolved their Jewishness with their Germanness when so much of this process was going on in the sanctuary of the home. What we do know is that conversion often represented joining a national culture more than a decisive spiritual transformation. In fact, for many it was more a passport to a better future. Whereas many after 1945—led above all by Gershom Scholem—came to treat conversion and assimilation as signs of just how misguided too many German Jews were, we should not lose sight of the fact that before 1933, relinquishing religious autonomy for civic emancipation was a strategy that appealed to more and more Jews.

This is clear in the case of the Hirschmann family. Like so many others, their predecessors drifted from the Jewish community some time in the 1800s and declared themselves without denomination, or *konfessionslos*. Among other things, this had tax implications: no share of taxes went to a church or synagogue. Precisely when this happened to the Hirschmanns is unclear, in part because their integration was so uneven. For all the other ways in which they assimilated, parts of the family were still paying their dues to the synagogue until the late 1920s. Carl wrote to Hedda in 1930 that he finally succeeded in his petition to have her mother, Ottilie Marcuse, exempted from all further synagogue dues (called the community tax). By then, money was tight, so Carl was looking for ways to save.[7]

If one's Jewish identity was a private matter, there were fewer and fewer sanctions against letting it drop altogether, easing the passage from a hyphenated German-Jew to become a German of Jewish background, and thence to becoming a German, which is how Otto Albert would self-identify as he grew up—as a composite of the more general currents flowing under the Enlightenment. Hannah Arendt once wrote controversially of this process, lamenting that "the terrible and bloody annihilation of individual Jews was preceded by the bloodless destruction of the Jewish people." To someone like Gershom Scholem, who grew up in Berlin and witnessed these passages of Jews to Germans firsthand, this was the inevitable result of any commitment to belong to a civic community and give up one's faith in order to do it. While he loved the Berlin of his childhood, adulthood allowed Scholem to see the price that many Jews paid for their assimilation into a society that was much more ambivalent about toleration than Jews were. It would have saddened but not surprised Scholem to know that Carl Hirschmann felt the kind of hypernationalism and mystical exaltation in 1916 that would eventually devour many of his family and kin. By then, a family like the Hirschmanns had moved past the debates that had so divided earlier generations of Jews in Germany, debates between emancipation with integration or the preservation of a separate cultural community. At the time, the perils of the former were not so easy to see. Until then, assimilationist ideals appeared to be making good on their promise. The result was that the Hirschmanns represented syncretisms that were very common among Berliners of Jewish origin. To begin with, they had unmistakably Jewish family names, and there is no evidence that they felt compelled to scrub away the Semitic overtones. The Hirschmanns' aunts and uncles were buried in the Jewish cemetery of Weissensee. Their newspaper was the *Vossische Zeitung*, a slightly leftish, secular daily, which some grumbled was the "Jewish paper."[8]

Time thereby purged aspects of Jewish life and replaced them with secular ones. One sign of becoming un-Jewish was conversion. While we know remarkably little about how this was done, we do know that droves of Jews converted to Christianity: 25,000 in the nineteenth century, and another 10,000 from 1900 to 1933. The Jewish policy in Prussia after 1813 made citizenship rights more accessible. In return, citizens should convert to Protestantism.[9] The Prussian establishment attached cultural conditions to citizenship to ensure that Jews did not simply take on the outer trappings of Germanness while preserving a separate, Jewish identity internally; indeed, it reflected underlying misgivings about the Enlightenment emphasis on secular patriotism and the Haskala notion of public and civic secularity: could these salon-aficionados *really* be entrusted as guardians of a modern Prussian and German state?

Increasing numbers of Jews made the passage nonetheless. We do not know when Otto Albert's parents' families converted, or indeed whether theirs was simply a matter of being *konfessionslos*. Either way, it was far enough in the past that it was not a matter for discussion or reflection. Both parents agreed to take a further step: they wanted their children baptized as Lutherans. The decision seems to have come at the urgings of a friend of Hedda's, who thought this might be a good idea. They "were already distant from Jewish tradition and religion," recalled Albert many years later. "And there was probably a certain level of opportunism involved. My parents wanted to make it easier for the children." Eva remembered that it meant that at school, when it came time for classes in religion, the Jewish girls went with a Jewish teacher, while she stayed with the rest and was thus spared the cloud that hovered over the Jewish girls—that they were "not really" German. Eva herself was so bored of the exercise that her parents, who were utterly secular, gave her permission to be absent from all religious classes. For Otto Albert, conversion had no religious connotation; his main memory of church was seeing stained glass. When he did take religion classes, he read Tolstoy—and became a lifelong admirer of the Russian's spiritualist prose. When asked later by a German interviewer about his baptism, Hirschman replied, "I remember that I refused to be confirmed. I didn't want to. I didn't feel ready to become a confirmed Christian. Even though I had already begun to take private lessons towards confirmation. But somehow I wasn't impressed by the minister, and then I asked my parents to stop." That was it. Conversion and baptism seem to have been more civic rituals, and not very ritualized at that, more gestures of acceptance of a public culture as well as a private belief system that distanced Jews like the Hirschmanns from their Jewish past without making them Christian; they could be modern Germans and Berliners without either. In the end, baptism was so redundant that OA could slough it off with no apparent controversy because he already occupied one end of the integrating spectrum, dropping the "Jew" and the hyphen that once followed a "German" identity.[10]

What this meant at the time to a young Otto Albert is hard to say. The Jewish Question is absent from early letters and manuscripts. Though retrospection is fraught with distortion, we get some sense that assimilation represented gaining access to multiple cultures more than a sacrifice of any single heritage. On Christmas 1982, he spent the day listening to Bach's Mätthaus-Passion and was reminded of concerts in childhood Berlin. That evening he wrote to his daughter, Katia, who was herself becoming more interested in Judaism; he was prompted to reflect on "Jewishness and whether to 'assume' it." He continued to note that "I have tried once or twice in my life . . . but always found that I had too many other roots, beliefs, yearnings, that I just did not want to cut myself off from these other worlds." Several months later, in response to Katia's thoughts about her own beliefs, he had to confess that "I cannot follow you on the Jewish tradition." He did accept that *parts* of it were his, especially "maintaining a certain Jewish identity *outside* of my religious attachment—that is, a certain critical turn of mind, a sympathy for the oppressed, an absence of parochial attachments, a certain sense of humor." But there was much in the Christian faith that he also cherished. "In order to fully enjoy the St. Matthew's Passion or the Cathedral one has to be able to *become* momentarily someone who genuinely mourns for Jesus' death."[11]

Upon one thing the assimilated and unassimilated Jews of Berlin often agreed: the view of the ghetto Jew as someone to be ashamed of. And increasingly, the ghetto Jew was associated with the *Ostjuden* backlanders, Eastern villagers driven west by the contagion of pogroms in Russia, the Ukraine, and Poland. Indeed, many German Jews disavowed this rabble as being part of the same "race" at all, and not a few worried that the influx of these Jews would stoke anti-Semitism at home. In 1912, the year Carl and Hedda were wed, the Jewish leaders of Berlin convoked a symposium to deal with the threat of the Ostjuden. Out of it came a declaration that the newcomers were a menace to the enlightened principles of integration. Albert could recall "criticizing the Eastern Jews," though he added that his parents applied equal scorn to "Jews who flaunted their furs, their wealth." In general, it was not a good idea to draw too much attention to oneself.[12]

Asserting an assimilated ideal meant a decorum for the outside world to see while at the same time performing rituals for the inside world, rituals as reminders that the path upon which these people were progressing was a better one. Outer respectability helped to signify acceptance of German national culture, to reciprocate for the granting of civic and political rights. Yiddish, the ghetto tongue, was frowned upon as a debased, vulgar German; if one were going to pray, at least let it be in Hebrew. Otto Albert's younger sister Eva once used the word *nebbich* in front of her father, whose family lineage was less firmly rooted in the Enlightenment assimilation ideal and who was all the more conscious of being seen to violate it. He slapped her. The young girl, having picked the word up on the streets, was shocked: she had no idea that it *was* a Yiddish word.[13]

For the most part, the code for the inside world was not repressive. Christmas, for instance, bore all the symbols of a Christian occasion but none of the substance—and was thus something they could all celebrate with no evident stigmas. It was above all an occasion for family members—especially the un-Jewish Jews of Hedda's side—to congregate for a dinner and to lavish gifts on the children. The preparation took much of December. Cookie-baking involved elaborate doughs that were kneaded with spices and dried fruits and then had to age weeks before going into the oven, filling the apartment with seasonal aromas and making prize foraging-targets for the children and their cousins. On the twenty-third, Carl would come home with a large, live carp and place it in a bathtub of cold water for the next twenty-four hours. The Hirschmann children would squeal in horrified fascination at the whiskered fish and then watch as their father pulled it from its bath and prepared it to be cooked on the twenty-fourth according to a special Polish recipe favored by wealthy Berliners. That night the family feasted and covered the Christmas tree with perfumed beeswax candles, cookies, apples, and jewels, while Hedda played the piano and family and guests sang Christmas hymns.[14]

If Christmas held a special place in the family's memories, so did their apartment and its location—another signature of the importance of decorum and an announcement of the family's successful ascent to the assimilated idyll. Right after the war, the Hirschmanns found an apartment in the posh Tiergartenviertel, a district just south of the immense Tiergarten Park (which was larger, for instance, than New York's Central Park). It was a convenient walk for Carl to reach the Moabit hospital, to which he had shifted his practice. But it was also the right kind of setting for upper-middling folk, those leaning slightly leftward in their politics yet concerned to enjoy the comforts and safety of an urban bourgeois life. Once the setting for summer homes for wealthy Berliners in the eighteenth century, with the park serving as the private hunting grounds for the Prussian king, the land was bequeathed by Frederick the Great to the city for recreational purposes, and its surroundings were gradually parceled out to developers. It was here that the characteristic nineteenth-century urban-villa style (large row houses, homogeneous yet boasting an ornamental façade) got a strong foothold—and it was to a floor in one of these expansive townhouses that the Hirschmanns moved.

The Tiergarten was a favored area for many ascending Jews in their last stages of integration; indeed, it was a fully integrated neighborhood with a lot of assimilated Jews. About one-fifth of its population was Jewish in 1910. One reason is that it was where members of the free professions (law, medicine, education) could rub shoulders with high government officials and the well-heeled. Tiergartenstrasse (the cross street for Hohenzollernstrasse) was known as the Street of Millionaires, and one block down was the street, if not for the rich, certainly for the famous, especially the stars of the silent silver screen. This included Tilla Durieux (née Ottilie Godefroy), the flamboyant stage actress who had married one of Hedda's cousins, the art dealer Paul Cassirer, whose salon (also nearby) was the first to introduce Berlin Successionists and Postimpressionists to discerning Berlin buyers. Durieux had posed as a haunting Circe in a famous 1913 painting by the great Symbolist artist Franz von Stuck. The public union with the Hirschmann clan ended badly: the couple quarreled and then agreed to divorce. When Cassirer went to meet Durieux at her nearby lawyer's office, he shot himself and died a few hours later.

In among the showy and scandalous was also the staid. The Tiergarten was a neighborhood of consulates and embassies; the Greek consulate was next door to the Hirschmanns home, and Otto Albert frequently had to dash into its backyard to retrieve errant balls. It was the ample second story of a villa-style house addressed Hohenzollernstrasse 21 that was home. The street ran between the Landwehrkanal and the park; at its top was Hedda's mother's house. Ottilie, "Öhmchen" to her grandchildren, insisted that they dutifully visit her on their way to the park with their nanny.

Respectability was thus sown into the very fabric of Hedwig's family, and it went back several generations. Her parents, Ottilie Aron and Albert Marcuse, formed an alliance of successful Jewish Frankfurt financiers (the Arons) and Berlin magnates (the Marcuses). Success in finance and business had created a platform for later generations to join the professional ranks. Hedda's brother Joseph loomed large in family lore. Having fought with distinction as a major in World War I, he was an exalted citizen until he died at a young age in 1931. He embraced his Lutheranism, befriended the Kaiser, owned a house with a small stable in the tony sector of the Tiergarten, and enjoyed wearing his military uniform draped with medals. His marriage to a beautiful, tall, blond singer with whom he had been having an affair for some years may have prompted his sister to warn her children that this kind of behavior was not entirely appropriate, but his money, virility, and style were the envy of many. Much less is known of Harry, a successful neurologist who died very young in 1927, all but unmemorable to his nieces and nephews. Franz, the youngest, was manqué. He did not "make it," literally. With no career and dependent on Ottilie until her death, he was a bit of a sponge. Bearing chocolates, he would visit his young nieces and nephew to play cards, midway through suggesting that they play for money, and would occasionally ask to borrow pocket change. After 1933, as the family began to pull up stakes from Germany, he stayed behind, only to die in 1940 in a Nazi concentration camp, the victim of a decree that converted whole swaths of the assimilated into Jews in order to rid the world of them.

The pursuit of respectability often comes with slips—and in the case of Otto Albert's mother, a potentially catastrophic one. Hedwig was born in Berlin in 1880. Her family lived on Magazinstrasse, in a middle-class neighborhood, where upwardly mobile Jews could gain a toehold. Her religion was registered as nondenominational, with "----------" before the entry on her birth certificate. (As a sign of the times, when the Nazis issued her a passport in April 1939, it bore the blazing stamp of "J", for *Juden*.) Her parents were of means enough to provide a good education not just to the boys, but also to Hedda, who spent time at the university. The slip came with her first entry into the marriage market, which went badly. She married a lawyer from Nürenburg named, by pure coincidence, Hirschmann. The story behind this ill-fated match is unclear. Rumors had it that he was impotent, though a subsequent marriage brought him several children. Other rumors had him the victim of a mental disease. "Not normal" was the consensus. Either way, Hedwig left him, secured a divorce—much to the shame of her mother—and left Berlin to finish her studies in Munich and later in Strasbourg, at first to study medicine and then history of art. Beyond the reach of gossipy circles, the cloud of scandal could pass.

Hedwig thus carried a stigma, which she labored to disguise. This campaign motivated an effort to cover the tracks of a less-than-respectable past with a second marriage, to Carl. Hedwig and Carl's concern for appearances reflected inner desires and aspirations for themselves and their children. The outward search for respectability could also cover inner complexities and was not completely successful at cloaking the family's seams—through them some of the tensions and conflicting memories would occasionally show through. Not long after Carl moved to Berlin, he met Hedwig at a philharmonic concert and immediately struck up his courtship. Carl was an ambitious doctor from out of town; she was a well-educated divorcée, no longer so young, with all the connotations and rumors this might carry with it. Accompanied by her wealthy aunt, Hedda must have seemed several social rungs above him. But they coincidentally shared a last name—the pretext for an initial, if slightly awkward, banter. Within a short time, Hedda was on her way to her second engagement.

Besides, if Hedda did her best to cover her stigma, Carl did his best to obscure his own. In a fashion, Carl and Hedda came to love and need each other in equal measure—Carl in order to join the proper ranks, and Hedda to have the proper family that a fräulein of her class and culture would have needed to remain in her rank.

The marriage of Carl Hirschmann and Hedda Marcuse contained within it some of the hopes and rewards, as well as some of the compromises and frictions, that accompanied the urge to join the ranks of successful, assimilated Jews. Theirs was an alliance bound by love, shared ambitions, and some common values. After a month apart, Carl wrote his vacationing wife, "Every day I look forward more to see you all again and to be reunited with you all, but most of all I am looking forward to seeing you, to breathe in your sphere, to talk to you. Against that, even meeting the daughters again pales, and that is saying a lot."[15] Nietzsche and Wagner were sources of enthusiasm; from the first encounter, classical music, opera in particular, was a shared passion, and they became avid patrons of Berlin's burgeoning performance halls.

But as with any alliance, this one had differences to resolve. Carl and Hedda did not differ so much on what they wanted for the future; their divides were about the past. There is a reason why we know much more about Hedda's family. She was only too proud of her heritage, something she relied upon to erase the memory of her own first marriage. Carl had access to no such remedy.

Carl preferred silence to surround his past and was willing to let Hedda's noise crowd in. At Christmas she would wail openly during ritual performances of Bach's arias and choruses. When the children got older, this display would make them cringe. Her wardrobe was determined to keep up with the times, which in the 1920s sketched a new outline around the female body. Harry's wife, Mimi, set the standard of the "new woman," cutting a profile of elegance with refinement, independence with fashion. She cropped her hair; so did Hedwig. Her fashion preferences were more firmly for modern tastes affiliated with the greater prominence that women of Hedwig's generation and respectability would enjoy in public.[16]

The ways in which women across Weimar Germany were crossing into the public sphere only raised the pressure on Hedwig, which was coming not just from new fashion or consumption; it also came from older, internal family norms. The Marcuses set the social bar high, and Hedda had to struggle to reach it. She had two cousins, Leonie and Estella, who in turn married Max and Ludwig "Lutz" Katzenellenbogen, cousins from a very rich magnate's family. It was a tight world, sociable and yet invidious. Leonie and Estella sent their only sons, Stephan and Conrad, to the same school as Otto Albert. Yet Otto Albert was always aware of the invisible class barriers and differences in values that contrasted his modest, bookish ways with those of his wealthy, playboy cousins. His mother's status anxieties were hard to avoid. One day he came home from school and complained that a teacher had slapped him. Enraged, Hedwig ("Mutti" to her children) stormed to the school to protest. When she met with the guilty teacher she was told "Madam, your son is like a race horse, and he has to be hit once in a while to perform even better." Hedda returned home elated; "My son is like a pure bred horse," she gushed. OA was a little disappointed that his mother had forgotten his smarting cheek.[17]

Her status extroversion could make Mutti a somewhat oppressive mother. When asked about his relationship with her, an otherwise discreet Albert would confess that she was not easy. "The relationship with my mother was not as good as that with my father," he recalled. "We always had difficulties."[18] When he was asked to describe her as a mother, "overbearing" is how he put it. In the end, however, most of the pressure did not land on her son's shoulders. It was Otto Albert's sister Ursula who bore the brunt, and she would later fill her memoirs with resentment. To Ursula, Otto Albert's knack for staying out of trouble, his good grades, and his nonconfrontational style meant that he was Mutti's favorite.[19] If he was the pet, however, he did not indulge her. She asked him to call her by a more tender name, Mumula. He resisted, calling her Mutti, like the other children did. He was also not above standing up to her: when Mutti caught the children horsing around after bedtime, she barged into the room, pulled the blanket away from Eva, lifted her nightshirt, and spanked her; when she turned to her son, he stood up and looked her in the eye as if to dare her to lift her hand. Instead, words of reprobation followed, and then she left. The sisters watched enviously. There is little doubt that Ursula was probably right: Mutti did have special affection for her son. A portrait was commissioned of a twelve-year-old Otto Albert and hung prominently over the living room mantel. There is a photograph of stylish Hedda wearing a kimono that was the rage among wealthy, European urbanites, her hair coiffed in bobbed fashion, her head titled slightly with arms raised in a vaguely self-sacrificial pose. She is standing under the portrait of her son, whose eyes gaze away from the camera into the horizon.[20]

The difference between Ursula and Otto Albert did not reflect a gap in values. They both shared an aversion to Mutti's pretensions. But they

Hedwig Hirschmann, c. 1924.

differed in how they dealt with their aversion to them. Otto Albert, a son, enjoyed some latitude to escape to be with his schoolmates. As a boy, he learned to keep his cool. He refined the art of avoiding a drama, which only added to his family reputation as unflappable. Ursula could not, and did not, keep her cool. The result was sometimes volcanic, especially when the delicate balance on Hohenzollernstrasse was upset by external misfortunes.[21]

Carl Hirschmann's background is more obscure, and what little is known would only become clear to his son in piecemeal fashion. There appear to be reasons for this. His birth certificate tells us that he was born in 1880 in Kölln, of "mosaic" religion, the son of Fanny (née Caspary) and Samuel Hirschmann. "Mosaic" was purposefully vague. Kölln was a village in a German belt ceded to Poland (and was thus known as Kielno) after the armistice—in effect an eastern frontier, not far from Danzig-Gdansk, close to the border with Lithuania. This was deep into *Ost* territory. Indeed, Carl's father was born in Kovno (renamed Kaunas), Lithuania, confirming Carl's undeniable Ostjuden heritage. Considerable energy went into covering this up—indeed, it was kept hidden from the children. It was only many years later, when Hirschman was applying for US citizenship and anxious to have his papers in order, that Mutti disclosed the truth of Carl's birthplace. It is not known what his parents did for a living; some say they were farmers, others say the father was a merchant. At some point, Carl accompanied his family to New York, where many poorer German and East European Jews headed at the invitation of a relative who had struck it rich. He picked up enough English to become proficient but never adapted; emigration did not go well. There is some sense that the American branch of the family was involved in shady affairs.[22]

Carl had higher aspirations for himself. He returned to Germany, worked his way through medical school in Hamburg, and eventually moved to Berlin in 1911. Medicine was a preferred field for Jews, less constrained than other professions, such as law or academia, but which had the aura of being reserved for the wellborn. It was also a profession in which Jew and Gentile worked side by side and in which Gentile patients would submit to the care of a Semite. Fritz Stern, also of assimilated Jewish parents and the son of a successful doctor in Breslau, recalled that "in Imperial Germany, the physician's white coat was the uniform of dignity to which Jews could aspire and in which they could feel a measure of authority and grateful acceptance."[23] Besides, Carl had large but delicate and beautiful—a surgeon's—hands, which once reminded his son of Flaubert's depiction of his own father (also a physician), "brawny hands—very beautiful hands, and that never knew gloves, as though to be more ready to plunge into suffering."[24]

The road to success at the operating table was not an easy one for Carl—and we know little about how he traveled it. He made it clear to the children that his past was an unwelcome subject of conversation, steering talk to matters of the present, a story by Franz Kafka, or a patient's stubborn condition. They learned not to ask questions. Hedwig was as complicit as Carl in obscuring his background from her children and the rest of her family. But Carl played an active role in this and was certainly more than just willing to go along with the more-Marcuse-oriented family life; when he did divulge accounts of his past, he told his children stories of growing up with a pony and riding in a carriage, as might befit a landed family.

The children were not the only consumers of Carl's obscured heritage. So was Hedwig, until it was too hard to ignore. This murky past was a source of shame for which she bore a deep grudge. One day, while Hedda was scolding young Ursula for having fibbed, Carl entered the room, took one look at the scene, and fled. Hedda, by now enraged, lashed out at her daughter and hissed at her that "lying" was a vice that had "deep roots" in this family. Later, Ursula would discover what her mother meant, for in Carl's eagerness to woo Hedwig, he was less than forthcoming. Indeed, he had peddled the same tales of ponies and carriages and ensured that Hedwig could not follow the genealogical trail. Perhaps because he sensed that his "eastern," small town, humble roots could not live up to Hedda's haughty expectations for any prospective suitor, his stories were embellished. When Carl paid his obligatory visit to Ottilie, to win her approval the story became more elaborate about his family's estates. Ottilie even tested Carl's etiquette, inviting him to lunch and serving him roast pigeon to assess his manners; fortunately, the surgeon was skilled with a knife and passed with flying colors. At no point did Hedwig meet her future in-laws, and she does not seem to have asked to. How complicit she was in the cover-up is hard to say, but it became even more elaborate. When Carl and Hedwig got married, Carl arranged for someone from Kölln to send greetings and congratulations to Ottilie. On the wedding day, apologetic telegrams arrived explaining that it was impossible for Carl's proud parents to attend the ceremony. Everyone fell for the ruse; everyone wanted it to be true. In moments of marital stress, it became known as "The Lie," which gave the union troubled foundations.

Ultimately, there was a limit to how long this cover up could last—and we do not know when Hedwig had to face facts she would have preferred to ignore. The absence of the parents would eventually have elicited probes. Certainly, by 1927 the truth was out: one day Carl's only sister, Betty, showed up from New York with her husband, Herman Lurie. They came bearing gifts, playing the expected part of distant "American" relations. But it was a short visit and left a malodorous impression: this was not a delegation that reflected especially well on the Berlin Hirschmanns' status. Behind the scenes, the déclassé New York connections, the Yiddish-speaking forebearers from the east, would all have come out.[25]

The tension over The Lie hung over the family like a nimbus. It shaped the family memories, whose commonalities and discrepancies remind us of what Albert O. Hirschman would repeat over the course of a prolific lifetime—that the beholder's eye had a role to play in what one made of the landscape of opportunities and constraints that surround us, that we could choose, to a point, the narratives that make us. It is perhaps revealing that Ursula's memoir of her youth (which was published in French and Italian) discloses the tension over the lie, which she considered fundamental to her parents' complex marriage and helps explain her mother's zeal to belong to the opera-going, fur-clad, Berlin establishment. By contrast, Albert—who translated the work into English, although it never got published—glossed over some of the passages that refer to the lie in his redaction, either because it was not a history he wanted dredged up, or because he thought his sister overstated the east-west divide within the marriage. They thus differed even on how to have their parents remembered: Ursula wanting to reveal the tensions she felt explained her own rebellious streak; Albert preferring not just discretion but the possibility of a less tormented, more hopeful story of the family's improvability.

The burden of the lie could be borne as long as Carl was better at delivering on the promise for a brighter future than reminding his wife of his "east-Jewish" past. Much, therefore, depended on career advancement as a sign of achievement and a source of higher income. Accordingly, Carl was ambitious. He rose quickly up the surgeon's ladder of success. By 1920, he was the head of surgery at the Municipal Hospital-Moabit, a rambling clinic in a working-class district on the other edge of the Tiergarten, a site of much agitation in the late imperial years. That same year, he entered the annals of local medical history when he assisted Otto Mass, the lead doctor at the Hospital Berlin-Buch, in a successful operation on a relapsed brain tumor. Otto Albert's father was best known for his collaboration with Dr. A. Simons, a neurologist. Together, they figured out a way to get access to the pituitary gland, whose malfunctioning could lead to the disease acromegaly (enlarged feet, hands, and facial features); the trick was to proceed not through the cranium but through the nose. This procedure yielded a series of medical sketches, which a proud Carl brought home to show his son. Otto Albert was probably impressed, but the drawings made him want to vomit.[26] Carl worked hard, putting in long days at the hospital before coming home for *Abendbrot*, a supper often served cold, with the rest of the family, and then going to his home clinic to greet patients and make phone calls. The telephone figures prominently in the adult Hirschman's recollections of his father. In the evenings it rang frequently. Albert could recall his father stepping out of concerts to make an emergency call—sometimes leaving a note that he had to rush to the hospital, thus missing the second half of a performance. Indeed, he passed up many family vacations to stay in Berlin to minister his patients.[27]

Hedda's extroversion was a contrast to Carl's quiet, studious, and slightly sad disposition. There is an especially moving photographic portrait of Carl, taken some time around 1930 by the well-known photographer Gertrude Simon. He is dressed in a dark suit; his head is heavy boned and provides the setting for large, thoughtfully melancholic eyes. In his home office there hung a print of a nineteenth-century Symbolist painter, Arnold Böcklin. It was a famous 1872 self-portrait of the artist at work with death leering over his shoulder playing a violin (the original hung at the National Gallery). Böcklin was best known for his Island of the Dead series. Much later, the son could recall shuddering at the sight of the image and could not fathom his father's interest in representations of the morbid. It depressed him, and he wished his father would replace the picture with something more uplifting. Both Albert and Eva recall their father, especially after a long day at work, and more commonly after 1929, going into his home office and sitting there in silence, his head in his hands, gazing downward. "He depressed easily," remembered Eva. Otto Albert, in particular, worried; his sister remembers repeated attempts by the son to cheer the father up with chess games, talk about books, or light banter. He had few personal friends, though plenty of family acquaintances emanating from Hedda's affiliations. His closest friend was Ulrich Friedemann, a pediatrician and fellow assimilated Jew whose family was a frequent guest at Hohenzollernstrasse.[28] There were times in which the life of hard work appeared to take its toll on the father. In the summer of 1930, he once more forfeited the family vacation, tending to his mother-in-law and caring for Tilla Durieux (recently wed to Lutz Katzenellenbogen). One patient in particular (called Löwenburg) was causing no end of grief, and he did not feel ready to pass him on to the doctors of the Charité Hospital. "It's dreadfully hot here again and the day with its worries and 1000 petty concerns is wearying, but all I can say is that I'm bearing up well and since I have resolved to keep my head up, I'm feeling well." The fatigue of self-sacrifice is clear: "I'm so full of worries about others, I don't let it come up any more that I hide myself in myself, but instead want to live busily and actively, and both especially strongly for you all," he wrote to his vacationing family. Two days later, Carl sounds as if he is reaching his rope's end. Ground down by the conflict between Tilla Durieux and Lutz Katzenellenbogen and trying to keep the newsmaking actress at arm's length while the Löwenburg case was causing "mental agitation," he confessed: "I'm tired and worn down."[29]

Hirschman's own memories of his father are filled with portraits of kindness and seriousness. There were the occasions for fun: Carl and Otto Albert would occasionally do exercises on the gymnastics bar, swings, and trapeze out in front of the villa. Carl was no absent father. Though he left early every morning for the hospital, he returned every day to dine with the family. He lavished attention when he could on all three children. He was also dutiful in minding the affairs of Hedwig's sometimes high-maintenance relations. Carl ministered to the health of his mother-in-law, occasionally giving up vacations to stay in Berlin to look after her as she got older. He was also charged with accompanying Hedwig's cousin Lutz Katzenellenbogen on a cruise to Egypt, the purpose of which was not only to keep the wealthy kinsman entertained, but also to talk him out of divorcing his wife, thereby avoiding a family scandal. The latter task was a futile one. Lutz left Estella and created a major dustup with the family, made worse a bit later when he struck up an affair and then a marriage with the scandal-prone Tilla Durieux.[30]

The trip to Egypt did yield one side benefit: on the way back, Carl arranged for Hedwig and Otto Albert to meet him in Paris, where they would spend a week together. It was not the twelve-year-old's first trip to another country, but it was the first to Paris, and it left a permanent impression. The boy was awestruck by the city's beauty, the open boulevards, the parks, the Louvre, the expanse from the great museum to the Étoile, the mammoth Père Lachaise acropolis for famous deceased citizens as well as the Communards' Wall. It was the entwined beauty and history that fascinated Otto Albert; he never forgot his first sight of the Gothic stained glass of Sainte-Chapelle. Carl was committed to showing his son the world; what is more, he encouraged him to see it for himself.[31]

Between Carl and his son was also a shared, mutually respected intellectual world. The father took a keen interest in the boy's education; he taught him chess (a game for which Albert bore a lifelong affection; later, in his own travels, he would carry with him a portable set so he could explore openings and pursue lines on his own). Carl read Kafka's short stories,

Carl Hirschmann c. 1928.

explained Nietzsche to his son, and engaged in long discussions about the incompatibility of Nietzsche and Marx. "Investigations of a Dog," one of Kafka's posthumously published stories, was one of the favorites of both father and son. The tale of a dog's pseudorational method to arrive at incongruous explanations for his existence was not just absurd, it also pointed to some of the foibles that accompany closed certainties, a style that would yield a lifelong imprint. Carl also welcomed the son's own discoveries. On one summer climbing trip to the Sudetenland, a teenage Otto Albert somehow procured a copy of a book by Max Adler, one of the founders of Austro-Marxism, and presented it to his father. Carl, otherwise not an avid reader of openly political tracts, appreciated Adler's eclecticism and sympathized with the leftish yet firmly anti-Leninist message. Many years later, Hirschman remembered the conversations between father and son about Max Adler as characteristic of the warmth and consideration that Carl brought to his fathering style—a reprieve from Mutti's nonbookishness and suspicion of radical political ideas, a stance that would create conflicts and divides in the household as OA and Ursula became more active. For the time being, the love of literature and the affection between father and son were tightly bound. In 1925, Carl could not join the family on summer vacation on the North Sea beaches. There was too much work with patients at home. But he clearly missed the time he would have spent with Otto Albert. "I would love to join in," he lamented, "bathing, gymnastics, playing with the ball or chasing after it, flying a kite, making a noise, romping about, all that would be right up my alley, provided that you join in everything and people then say, when father and his son go to the North Sea!" There was room in Carl's letters to his son to complement affection with advice: "I also ask you kindly not to overexert yourself." There were also important matters to consider: "so gifted a student as you has no need to work in the holidays." The letter closes with a poem by Heinrich Heine from the section on the North Sea in his *Book of Songs*:

> The storm rages now
> And whips the waves,
> And the waters, boiling and furious,
> Tower into a moving waste
> Of white and flowing mountains.
> And the ship climbs them
> Sharply, painfully;
> And suddenly plunges down,
> Into a black and yawning chasm of flood.
> O Sea!
> Mother of Venus, born of your quickening foam.

Before signing off, Carl concluded, "You will know who is 'born of quickening foam.'"[32]

Carl himself had moderately progressive views (as did Hedwig, but she kept these to herself) and tended to vote Social Democratic in German elections. His sensibilities were not, however, the expression of a strong ideological disposition. Quite the contrary. He reserved judgment, avoided proclamatory styles, and raised skeptical questions when faced with his children's youthful hubris, often asking his son and daughters *their* thoughts on Kafka or Goethe. One day, Otto Albert asked point blank about his father's convictions, and when Carl concluded that he had no guiding principles, Otto Albert bolted down the hall exclaiming to his sister "Weiss Du was? Vati hat keine Weltanschauung!" (You know what? Daddy has no world view!).[33]

If he was the model of open-mindedness, Carl was not endowed with irony, and one is tempted to ascribe his son's own sense of humor and ironic detachment to his reaction to his father. So, while Carl labored on his career, doted on his wife's family, and welcomed his children's own peregrinations, he was unequipped to deal with some of the harshness of life in Weimar Berlin when times got tougher. For one thing, the dream of assimilation and acceptance was not easily defended from resilient anti-Semitism without raising some awkward doubts about the promise of assimilation. And there was plenty of evidence of anti-Semitism all around. Carl Hirschmann sported a scar across his forehead—the legacy of a fencing duel. A fellow student had made an anti-Semitic slur, which led to a fight. Carl wore his scar like a badge of honor, his *Schmiss* a testament to his self-respect. The slights did not go away after the war. But what Carl did—a tactic shared by many others who preferred to avoid challenges to their dreams or the discomforts of racial conflict—was to shut it out. He hushed up signs of intolerance, either to shelter his children or in the hope that time would let it all pass. Or both. In the summertime retreats to the North Sea, Carl would help his children build sand castles. Some of the beachgoers would hoist little makeshift flags—red, black, red and gold—all innocently signifying the party loyalties of the Weimar spectrum. For the Hirschmanns, the flag was black, red, and gold—for the republic. On one vacation in the early 1930s, the children woke up and returned to the beach to find the flags down, many of the castles wrecked, and swastikas planted on the beach. Carl preferred to move to another beach and quietly enforce a consensus that this was not something to discuss. The summer of 1931 was the last for the German beaches; thereafter, Carl took his family to Holland, Switzerland, or the Dolomites.[34]

The Hirschmanns lived well, though not opulently or luxuriously, at the cusp of Berlin's upper-middle class. There was money enough to pay for maids and nannies. The maids lived in the back of the apartment in a small room with a toilet. One of the nannies, Fräulein Wolf, who went by the name Aunt Hete, was responsible for tucking the children into bed each night, "annoying us immeasurably with the phrase she repeated each evening: 'Closing time at the Bosporus.' "[35] When Otto Albert was ten years old, a demoiselle came to the house to teach French to the children, and she lived with them for several years. Later, an au pair came from Paris and tutored the children in their teenage years before moving back when the Great Depression deepened and the Hirschmanns had to tighten their belts.[36] English may have been a useful language—even in those days—for business, and Carl certainly would have been aware of the doors it might open. But French was the language of high culture. If there was a discussion between Hedda and Carl, the choice of foreign language was incontrovertible.

The apartment on Hohenzollernstrasse was also well apportioned. There was a gramophone and a collection of opera records—themselves a sign that the Hirschmanns were keeping up with the times, although the latest breakthrough, a phonograph equipped with an amplifier (devised in 1925), was beyond their reach; they had to hand crank their music machinery. Music lessons were obligatory: Eva and Ursula learned to play the piano. OA was proud to carry around his impressive cello. There was also money enough to buy art—and to be seen in the right places buying art. They procured a Signac from the Tannhäusers, who became family friends and whose gallery on the ultrafancy Bellevuestrasse shared a block with elegant restaurants, wine stores, and other galleries and was a ten-minute stroll from Hohenzollernstrasse. They also hired painters to make portraits of family members. The most important, and most prominent, was the portrait of Otto Albert that hung in the living room. And there were the vacations to Pontresina in Switzerland to ski, to the North Sea and Holland for summer beaches. But none of them could be said to have been the highest end: Pontresina did not have St Moritz's snows; Kampen did not have Westerland's showy beaches.

Within this context, Otto Albert had a supportive, generally loving, comfortable upbringing. His parents had enough confidence in him to let him take extended vacations with friends. Some excursions were organized by his school. In June 1930, Hedwig had taken Ursula and Eva on vacation to Switzerland. Carl had to stay in Berlin to work. Otto Albert hoisted a backpack—arranged with the help of two maids—over his shoulders and left with friends for the train station for a week's camping. Carl assured his wife that OA had left with the right kind of undershirt, though he had to lighten his load by taking out a bulky tin of food.[37] Six months earlier, OA had gone skiing in Switzerland with a different group of friends. "Don't be afraid," he admonished his parents. "Today we went somewhat higher, though not much and the sun burned so much that I do not look so anemic." The previous night had brought a fresh coat of powdered snow, so the skiing was great; his main attention was focused on the New Year's celebration. For the costume ball, OA and his friends dressed as girls, with bodice, stockings, and mock dresses and ribbons in their hair. They all danced until two in the morning, "tipsy from champagne and punch." There was also the occasion for flirting with girls, as well as games involving light kissing. Otto Albert described how the boys and girls lined up in pairs; he was stuck with Frau D, "but actually I would rather have gone with Lolo." The next day, they all took the day off from the slopes and slept in. A subsequent letter explains how OA did manage to make his way into Lolo's graces by offering her math tutorials.[38]

Otto Albert did not feel ashamed to let his family know of his nascent interest in girls. There was the innocent, organized, chaperoned sort, such as the dancing and flirting on vacations. But if he was interested in girls, he was neither anxious to prove himself nor compelled by curiosity. Certainly, he was no match for his cousins the Katzenellenbogens, who had reputations like their father's to keep up. OA's first "love" came via a friend and classmate, Peter Franck. The Francks, like the Hirschmanns, were well-off, assimilated Jews (the mother was Jewish, the father was not), but they lived in the less posh outskirts, near Heerstrasse. Otto Albert would venture out there to spend time with Peter, though increasingly his real reason became clearer and Peter learned to get out of the way and let his sister, Inge, and OA take walks in the neighboring woods. OA confessed to his sister that his affections for Inge were as powerful as hers for a mysterious French teacher with whom Ursula had fallen madly in love. In the end, the friendship with Peter outlasted the love for his sister. Otto Albert does not appear to have had his next amorous involvement until he joined the Socialist Youth movement in 1932, but that relationship was so saturated by the political atmosphere in which both adolescents had plunged themselves that there was little time to devote to romance, even more so as Germany and the Hirschmanns careened toward the upheavals of early 1933.[39]

For the time being, OA's "girls" were his sisters. He had an affectionate relationship with both. Eva, five years his junior, was very much the little sister, admiring her "Söhni's" (her term of endearment) achievements and dependent on him for an alchemy of fun and protection. In the days in which they shared a bedroom, once the lights were out, the leg wrestling would begin, or OA would launch into narratives about history. Eva listened attentively to the exploits of Alexander the Great. She also giggled at jokes such as, "Charlemagne pees in his pants, Pippin the Short washes them" (our first-known of OA's word games, this one playing with the German *pipi* and Pippin). OA would also grill his little sister on what she'd retained from his nighttime sermons. He also took her bicycling, but they were under strictest orders to push their cycles if they were to cross the busy Tiergartenstrasse, a rule honored only in the breach. Eva would accompany her brother to the park and watch him pop wheelies; they would speed their bicycles over jerry-rigged ramps and play chicken. OA was also a loving tease; on one of his trips, he sent a postcard to his little sister: "Perhaps you would take 5 minutes less to clean your room and write me this time. And make sure you handle my books well! I talk a lot about you and I mention especially your bad sides—a very rich topic of conversation that lasts for 5 dances, while your good ones would last at most one." The appetite for mischievous fun was a trait; decades later, Albert would pull pranks on his wife, such as short-sheeting the bed so he could snicker as Sarah wrestled with the linens before a night's sleep.[40]

The relationship with Ursula was at once more intimate and more fraught. A year and a half his senior, Ursula felt the pressure of a younger, overachieving sibling; close enough in age to be paired, they were not easily separated, even when Ursula might have wanted some daylight between them. When she was first sent to school, so was her brother, with the argument that he could do whatever she could. If Otto Albert went to a high-end French *Gymnasium*, Ursula's was more practical and English-oriented. If she excelled at music and art (as, in a sense, she was encouraged to do as a girl in a bourgeois household), OA was the academic. And the signals as to which of these two orientations was the prized one were explicit. His ability to deflect opprobrium was also a source of envy. He rarely got in trouble and could stand up to Mutti; Ursula's relationship with her mother was often seismic. She never got the freedoms that her brother could take for granted—to travel, to study, to spend time with friends well beyond the neighborhood. She accompanied her mother to Switzerland while her brother went on expeditions with classmates. In penning her memoirs, Ursula made the distinction between the two of them quite stark: OA—the darling, achieving, driven, athletic, agreeable, handsome, celebrated by both parents—was the antithesis to the ill-tempered, combative, frequently ill (prone to fevers, exhaustion, which compelled her mother to subject her to endless tests and exams, often to discover that the spells were related to her emerging menstrual cycle), and less academically inclined Ursula. It seems likely the parents did little to obscure this disparity.[41]

But sibling rivalry did not stand in the way of a deep and very basic intimacy. They shared each other's secrets. When Ursula began her furtive, but intense, passions for men—and not a few of them had crowded onto the scene by the time she was seventeen—it was to her brother that

Otto Albert and Ursula, c. 1919.

she turned as a confidant. OA found himself trying to console his sometimes distraught sister, creating a supportive cocoon to shelter her anguish. When Ursula fell headlong into an obsession with an unavailable
man, OA stroked her with his words: "Ursel, oh Ursel, my very, very dear
Ursel! How right you were to fall in love with him. How stupid of those
fogeyish people who demur at words! Don't they understand that it is
about so, so much more?" He did, however, try to bring her to reason:
the man was older, lived far away, and was a devout Catholic: "In the long

run he would be unbearable for you," he warned. "I think that the urge to be a 'little girl' has become less pronounced for you [she was seventeen at the time]. And I have to say, don't start again with an exchange of letters, don't let him get into the suffering again as before—not out of questions of decency, but rather because he would be talked into it and become *dishonest*."[42]

While the Hirschmanns enjoyed many of the elements of an upper-middle-class standard of living, there was not quite enough money to cover large items that would have represented having made it with surety. They lived at the cusp of the establishment, not in it. Perhaps this is why Hedwig could not dispel her anxiety, especially when she compared herself to other members of her clan and their high lifestyles. There was no automobile at a time when a vehicle was within reach of members of the Hirschmann class and was certainly an icon of arrival for anyone who wanted to join the ranks of the *haute bourgeoisie*. Though the family lived in a good location, they took trams and subways to visit Hedda's numerous and scattered relatives. Birthdays were, for instance, important gatherings for the extended kin and the Hirschmann children would have been counted among those who would arrive by public transportation. It would seem likely that Hedda winced at the thought of her relations watching her children stepping from a tram.[43]

More significantly, the Hirschmanns did not own their home; they rented. In the late 1920s, as Carl's career blossomed, the parents would go apartment hunting. But there was either not enough savings, or the prospect of moving into tighter quarters was a deterrent to leaving their floor on Hohenzollernstrasse. Then, when the Depression hit, financial troubles put an end to the fantasy of home ownership. Otto Albert could recall the winter scene at Pontresina in late 1929, watching the hotel guests interrupt their après-ski dinners to call Berlin to find out the latest casualties on the stock market. Little did he know, his father was one of them.[44] Carl had placed most of the family savings in the Ostwerke, which collapsed in the autumn of 1931. A powerful holding company for which Lutz Katzenellenbogen had served as president while overseeing a number of dramatic, if scandalous, buyouts and takeovers in the 1920s, Ostwerke went down with the financial system. The scandal landed Hedwig's cousin in prison. Katzenellenbogen came to symbolize the era of speculation and monied frenzy laced with overtones of conspiracies by Jews who peddled themselves as loyal Germans. In a public trial, the courts found him guilty of borrowing money from several banks without disclosing his liabilities and for falsifying the prospectus sent out to investors for one of his major mergers. Tilla, whom Carl had brokered into wedlock with Lutz, smuggled pills to her husband to help him commit suicide (which was also botched).[45]

That melodramatic summer, while travelling and climbing in the Alps, Otto Albert was astute enough to be aware of what was going on, personally as well as financially. The Reichsmark was plunging in value, the government having abandoned the gold standard, a pillar of stability since 1924. Lake Geneva was beautiful, the Château de Chillon spectacular. But "overall one notices (as well by you, as I know you) a general Fascistization [*Fascisierung*] of the spirit. The sudden nationalism everywhere is amazing," he wrote to his father. A week later, the news was not so impersonal. He wrote an alarmed letter in July after reading about new strictures blocking large withdrawals from bank accounts. "Do you have at your disposal [sufficient reserves]? If you would at once inform me about the situation and especially about you I would be glad. It interests me colossally," he wrote his father.[46] A week later, his fears mounted— "One hears only the darkest news out of Germany"—and he began to take measures to economize on travel expenses. The appeal of Katzenellenbogenesque aristocratic pretensions was wearing thin.[47]

Financial strains, palpable to the adolescent OA, coincided with the tightening of quarters in the flat. When the children were young, it was easier to have them bunk together. Ursula, the eldest, had her own room; but young OA and little Eva shared the same quarters. At some point (probably around his fifteenth birthday), Otto Albert had to get a space of his own, and he was moved to the waiting room of Carl's home office. Its sofa was converted to a night bed; OA, never above turning a virtue out of necessity, was happy to sacrifice privacy in order to sleep surrounded by bookshelves. Then, as the financial woes shook the fortunes of the extended family, Hedda's mother moved in. Ottilie's own wealth, along with the extended family's, some of which had been invested in some rather dubious ventures, had evaporated. Two of her sons were gone, and there was only Franz, a complete dependent. Carl had until then been the custodian of Öhmchen's health. Now he was saddled with her lodging needs. By the end of 1932, the apartment on Hohenzollernstrasse was getting overcrowded for a family that once aspired to an haute bourgeois lifestyle; but two things they did not skimp on was support for the children's expensive schooling and the recreational travel that punctuated it.[48]

The tension that hung over the family finally erupted in 1931, revealing not just the limits of assimilationist ideals and their outward cruelties, but also the family's vulnerability to inner cleavages. Until then, only subtle signs of trouble had appeared: the abandoned search for a house, the need to keep working through vacations. But otherwise Carl and Hedda could keep up the appearances they both wanted. Behind the scenes, there was evidence of marital strain. Carl worked harder than ever, and his recessive propensities at home seem to have grown. In the summer of 1930, while Hedwig had taken Ursula and Eva to Arosa, Carl clearly yearned to join them. At one point, he called her to say that he was going to leave Berlin for the mountains. The phone conversation did not go well, indicating that the two had grown apart and knew it. The next day, he quickly tried to make amends: "You know, this time I'll come to you like in old times, fresh in spirit and not bad in body. Hold on, I still wanted to say, if it's any trouble finding a single room for me, or if it's much dearer or—and that's the main thing—if it's more pleasant, more agreeable to you—if we both sleep together . . . then arrange it that way. I must confess, it was a bit of a relapse, when I told you on the phone that I wanted a room for myself."[49]

Then the strains on Carl took a turn for the worse. He applied for a position as head of neurosurgery in a major Berlin hospital. The stakes were high, for not only was it an important step for Carl's career, especially now that he was into his early fifties, but it was also a condition for his being able to teach medicine at a university—a crowning achievement in the medical hierarchy. Instead, he was passed over in favor of a younger candidate with impeccable Christian credentials. To compound matters, he then applied to fill a vacancy for the surgical chief at the Jewish hospital, only to be turned down, evidently because his children had been baptized. Carl was feeling the squeeze of having committed to the assimilation ideal when anti-Semitism and Jewish self-defense were on the rise.[50]

Carl's failure to be promoted was devastating. Not only did it mean there would be no boost in income at a time when resources were getting tight at home, it was also a blow to the family status. Much later, Eva was to recall that, while she was too young to know exactly where the malaise was coming from, Mutti "was very upset" about the news: "according to her, he was not ambitious enough or didn't do enough." Things got worse as her relatives began to whisper. The tension was always latent: Carl was, after all, an eastern Jew. Now he was an unsuccessful one, which only confirmed his deficiencies. His credentials as a surgeon were now cause for suspicion. Why did he minister to ordinary patients? Why not the elite? Maybe he botched a procedure?[51] For Ursula, who was by now more aware of the drama unfolding around her, what was as striking as the growing bigotry was "my father's incapacity to defend himself, his vulnerability to the big blows in life."[52]

Maternal preening and bourgeois self-consciousness, combined with paternal pity, eventually did not go down well with Ursula, the eldest, powerful, vocal, and often combative child. In her teenage years, she started to scorn her parents'—and especially her mother's—efforts to emulate, if not catch up with, the likes of the Katzenellenbogens. The ostentatious behavior, the parties, the organization of fêtes for children in which the rich cousins danced with other rich cousins and quietly but deliberately left those like the Hirschmanns to stand on the side—all fueled Ursula's confrontations with her mother and the rising tension in the household. Carl went more silent, Ursula and her mother grew more combative, Eva, the youngest, was the bystander; the son, meanwhile, created a carapace of invulnerability out of his immersion in books, schooling, and eventually, politics.[53]

The history of the Hirschmann family is one of ascent, of social mobility and outward display of the successes of the bourgeois, assimilated Jewish world it thrived on. It had its ambiguities—there were family scars that refused to heal, a marital union subject to more than the normal pressures, and the scourge of anti-Semitism that could not be completely shut out of the cosmopolitan milieu of the Tiergarten. By the early 1930s, the clouds that passed occasionally over the Hirschmann family began to thicken and darken—and the temptation to liken the Hirschmann family fortunes to that of the republic they all believed in is almost too hard to resist. An example of the Enlightenment-assimilationist ideal, Otto Albert's upbringing was shaped by the optimism of the republic, a well-mannered home life, and a heritage that exuded an assurance that, with hard work and proper dedication, better times lay ahead. That the cause for such confidence was more fragile than realized was certainly easier to see in retrospect. But as Hirschmann entered the fourth decade of the century and he passed through his adolescence, few could have anticipated how truly dark were the days that awaited him.

CHAPTER 2

Berlin Is Burning

The world will present itself to you for its
unmasking, it can do no other, in ecstasy it
will writhe at your feet.

FRANZ KAFKA

A photo of Otto Albert at nine years old cuts a profile of a thin, delicate figure with soft, sensitive, brown eyes, a full, but not wide, mouth,
dressed the part of the child of Berlin's professional elite. To these features
would be added, as he matured, an unruly shock of hair and an impish,
playful, grin; his eyes would evolve into knowing, ever-attuned instruments; what his father's hands were for the surgeon, OA's eyes were for the
observer of the world. He was by no means a formed being, but some basic
traits were there. The son of an upper-middle-class family of assimilated
Jews from a city that was a symbol of tolerance, he was self-assured, he could
boast—but didn't—achievement, and he possessed an uncanny ability to
charm those around him. With the charm came a remarkable skill in deflecting personal difficulties and avoiding trouble. The combination earned
him the confidence of his parents, teachers, and mentors. Multiligual as he
already was, to his good looks must also be added his sheer intelligence,
ingredients that would have foretold a brilliant career, a model son.

But it would not be so. The republic that had buoyed the world in which
the Hirschmanns prospered came apart, and came apart dramatically, shattering the comforts and status of the household on Hohenzollernstrasse.

None of this was foretold in the mid-1920s. On the contrary: for the
Hirschmanns as for Berlin, there was prosperity and promise. For devoted
parents like Carl and Hedwig, their children were spared no expense:

Otto Albert, 9 years old.

holidays, music lessons, weekend outings, birthdays, and fine educations. When it came to Otto Albert's schooling, there were choices; the parents of bright young Berliners tracked their sons either into classical or practical schools. OA's parents perceived—and thus promoted—a scholarly orientation. They were also intent on making him a worldly creature. Otto Albert was sent to the Französisches Gymnasium (or Collège Français), where he would spend nine years and from which he would graduate in the spring of 1932. Established after the Edict of Potsdam (1685), it threw open the gates for fleeing French Huguenots. As an emblem of Prussian tolerance and a definition of accommodation, the school promoted a cosmopolitan spirit among its students and alumni. By the second half of the nineteenth century, it began to take in larger and larger numbers of Jews: between 1834 and 1933, over one-third of the school's one thousand graduates were Jewish. To sneering anti-Semites, it was known as the Franco-Jewish Gymnasium. It undoubtedly appealed to the sons of educated parents, or to those who were keen to have their sons enjoy a more academically inclined education. This was a school that prided itself on intellectual rigor: its classes were small (Otto Albert's graduating cohort was eighteen fellow students), its professors demanding. Otto Albert rewarded his parents by winning book prizes and special mentions, to Ursula's chagrin. While French was the language of instruction, the curriculum was resolutely classical, rigorous in languages (Otto Albert was proficient in Greek and Latin and would read to his younger sister from *The Iliad*) but less inclined to scientific or technical subjects. This is not to say that science was completely ignored; Professor Otto Nix, a mathematician, introduced his students to Einstein's theory of relativity. But for the most part, languages, the humanities, and mathematics absorbed most of the students' time.

In a day and age in which well-educated young men, especially those inclined to writing, treated traditional rote learning as something on which one had to cut some teeth, Otto Albert was spared some of the wider social rigidities. The school, like the republic, was adept at allowing teachers and pupils to mold what might have been an oppressive classicism to a more modern form. For while there was no shortage of rigor at the Collège, there was also room for unorthodoxy. Otto Albert's most memorable teachers were Professor Lindenborn, who taught religion and ethics and introduced the young Hirschmann to Tolstoy as a way to teach Christianity, and Professor Levinstein, who embellished his classes on Goethe by sitting down before his piano and singing Wagner. Evidently, his singing took up too much time to get through all of *Faust*, so Otto Albert and his classmates had to convene in Professor Levinstein's home at nights to catch up on what got missed in class. Many years later, Hirschmann would recite pages of Goethe's *Faust* to his new wife and would read it to his young

Otto Albert's class at the French Gymnasium,
1926. Otto Albert is on the top row, far left.

daughters at night, a reminder that the memory of a German culture did
not have to remain imprisoned by the ghosts of fascism.

When Otto Albert stood for his *Abitur* (his final exam and thesis),
on January 29, 1932, his assigned topic was an analysis of a quote from
Spinoza: "One should neither laugh nor cry at the world, but understand it." It was, in the scheme of things, a remarkably appropriate line
for what would characterize a leitmotif of his own, much later, composi-
tions. Written under exam conditions of a half day, the young man's commentary summarized much of what Otto Albert had learned of Hegel,
the tradition of German idealism, and Greek literature to treat the quote
as a moral injunction for the present. As befitted the school's aims of creating thoughtful young men for a cosmopolitan republic, the examiners

cared less about his command of Spinoza's own writings (which the young Hirschmann had read but did not imbibe with quite the same determination reserved for Hegel) than the soon-to-be-graduate's values he would carry forth into the world. The sixteen-year-old's exam script ended with a plea for an open mind: "Finally, the maxim calls upon us not to mock or fight something at first sight, but to consider, to understand, to penetrate. It is thus directed against the increase of catchphrases. Against this state of affairs, in which—as Goethe put it—a conceptual lacuna is soon filled by a word, Spinoza's maxim deserves to be defended as an ideal."[1]

More important to Otto Albert's educational experience than what transpired in the classroom was what the school offered on the side. It was in the quasi-formal reading groups, or tutorials (*Arbeitsgemeinschaften*), on topics ranging from art history to classical philology and led by faculty, alumni, and upperclassmen that Otto Albert thrived. The idea was to have the students create a parallel curriculum of their own design, one that would reflect their interests beyond the core of languages, humanities, math, and natural science. Otto Albert and his classmates reached out to a Collège Français alumnus, Bernd Knoop, who took Otto Albert under his wing for intensive reading of Hegel's *Phenomenology of Spirit* once a week over the course of one school year, 1931–32, culminating in the next summer's writing assignment on one of the introductory paragraphs of Hegel's monumental work, which focused on reason and consciousness. Otto Albert parked himself at a great desk in the Staatsbibliothek for weeks, poring over the text and writing his very first independent essay, a dense, twenty-eight-page exegesis. At the time, Hegel was the departure point for any serious student of contemporary German philosophy and social theory, and *Phenomenology* was the ur-text that any ambitious student had to master (or think he was mastering). In the dialectical escalation from spirit to consciousness to self-consciousness so much could be explained—and yet it was not easy; OA's friend, Helmut Mühsam—the nephew of a famous anarchist—quipped: "I understand every word, but not their connection!"[2]

Still, Hirschmann was determined to show his mettle and fathom the ties between Reason and History—and their surprising turns. He did so by tackling a passage of *Phenomenology* dealing with Hegel's concept of ethics and consciousness and how the two are grounded in the nation and in the family—and from which an "ethical order" for human reason emerges. As happens so often in analyses of Hegel's work, the young Hirschmann's prose is as dense as that he tried to decipher; indeed, it does not differ very much from the subject. One might suspect that he grappled with Hegel's opacity by being opaque himself, an inclination that would change dramatically and yield to his trademark clairvoyance. But for a seventeen-year-old making his first steps into philosophy, not to mention Hegel, distance might be too much to ask. This exercise was already something of a tall order. But Hirschmann does offer some sense that he not only understood but also sought to lend an original reading to the great text when he dealt with Hegel's understanding of the family. What was the "ethical" bedrock of the family? Not the husband and wife relationship, "which is clearly natural." Nor was it the tie between parents and children, because "it does not display that identity between subject and object requisite for an ethical relationship." The condition of an ethical relationship rested upon the exercise of free will, which required an exchange of "free individuality unto each other." Accordingly, the ties that most conform to a "truly ethical relationship" are those between brothers and sisters, bound by blood but divided by sex. Hirschmann went on to explain how Hegel viewed brothers (for whom "spirit becomes individualized" as they move through the world, passing from subjects of divine law to human law) and sisters (who become wives and preservers of the home, and thus the preservers of the realm of divine law). It was the braided relationship between siblings that caught his eye and called for reflection. Sticking close to the Hegel text, he surmised that "in this way both sexes overcome their merely natural being, and become ethically significant, as diverse forms dividing between them the different aspects which the ethical substance assumes." How much Hirschmann truly absorbed of this is hard to say. "At the time," he recalled, "everything seemed very opaque to me." Yet, one has a sense that his reference was not just *Phenomenology*, but also his dialectic with Ursula, with whom he was reconstituting a close bond (now as young adults) forged in the heat of the Weimar Republic's decomposition.[3]

He was enormously proud—of both the exercise in writing *and* of having tackled Hegel! That he had "something worthwhile" to say added to the sense of achievement. While it is tempting to identify in this writing on Hegel the seeds of something that would later grow—a sense that humans carried with them larger, logical, and ethical purposes inscribed in Reason and its manifestation in History—this impulse should be resisted. It is true that at the time he imagined himself as the heir of a German idealist tradition, but there is no sense that philosophy was capturing his imagination. Beyond this essay, Hirschmann would steer clear of Hegel until the 1970s, when he would stumble back to *Philosophy of Right* to wonder whether Marx had really revealed the cunning of capitalism's history. In that subtle dig at the certainties of the social sciences, he used Hegel to turn excessively abstract theorizing on its head. Hegel, in fact, was a touchstone in his lifelong reservations about "the characteristic tardiness of theoretical understanding of reality." These are Hirschmann's words. And they are followed by Hegel's hallowed metaphor about the Owl of Minerva who "spreads its wings only with the falling of the dusk."[4]

For the moment, however, the commitment to study Hegel reflected a young man's search for basic intellectual moorings for other interests and the belief that Hegel was a necessary departure point. It was more his developing interest in Marxism that cued his curiosity about dialectics; for any self-respecting dialectical thinker, one had to start with the source himself: the author of *Phenomenology*. This was, after all, Berlin, and Hegel was the city's philosophical icon; any effort to acquire a Weltanschauung had to start here. At the time, there was not yet any recognition on Hirschmann's part that there were various ways into the mysteries of *la raison universelle*, and it would take decades to circle back to Hegel to find in German idealism some foundations for his assault on "mindless theorizing."

Hegel may have absorbed a lot of Hirschmann's attention, but it was not the only reading group he joined. Johannes Strelitz introduced the students to Marx, and Heinrich Ehrmann, an influential mentor, guided the students through current socialist debates involving readings of Lenin, Kautsky, and the Austro-Marxists Otto Bauer and Max Adler. Born in

1908, Heinrich (Henry) Ehrmann would go on to a career in political science at the University of Colorado, Dartmouth College, and McGill University, but at the time, he was an emerging socialist bright light. He had graduated from the Collège several years earlier, and from there went on to study law and political science at the University of Berlin, from which he graduated in 1929.

Books filled the young Hirschmann's days, and his reading habits and tastes provide a backcloth to his life history. Shuffling around the house, he always had his nose in one. Often, he would detain a sister, or his father, to read a choice passage and end with an earnest, knowing invitation to share the pleasures of a well-turned phrase or a pithy insight. Between his father's indulgence and his school's orientations, he was not only well read in the classics, he devoured contemporary fiction like Thomas Mann's *Buddenbrooks*. Mann had won the Nobel Prize in Literature, not quite the headline news it is today, but it added to his allure, and this first novel, an epic about several generations of a bourgeois clan centering on self-sacrifice, delusions, and family decline, was often read as a metaphor for Germany's own national narrative. Another favorite was Fyodor Dostoevsky, who also meditated on religious and philosophical concerns through marriage, inheritance, and familial love triangles. Nietzsche enjoyed almost cult status among Otto Albert's friends—a passion OA shared with his father. But it was, above all, history that he consumed: biographies and epics especially. One author stood above the rest: Emil Ludwig, the German-born journalist, who began his best-seller career in 1920 with a portrait of Goethe, followed by studies of Bismarck, Napoleon, Jesus, and others. What distinguished Ludwig's books was the combination of historical fact, fictionalized filler, and psychological analysis, so that the drama did not just unfold in the outer world; history was about the internal experiences of great figures as well. Not surprisingly, in an age of Freud, Jung, and early existentialist writing, there was a turn inward, an exploration of the personal psychology of heroism, triumph, and tragedy. For young readers, gone was the allure of "selflessness," of History with greatness built into it by the structures of the outside world. Echoes and elaborations on these obsessions could be seen outside the gymnasium in the New Objectivity (Neue Sachlichkeit) movement flourishing in music, photography, and architecture. It is unlikely that the younger readers of Hirschmann's circle were au courant with these trends, but they were part of the more general turn away from outward stylistic embellishments of Romanticism and Expressionism. Of the turn to a deepening concern with inner lives, Hirschmann was more than aware. He was captivated by its mysteries.[5]

What can be said of this early learning? One is that from a very early age, the German language may have been his mother tongue (*Muttersprache*), but it was not his home (*Heimat*). He spoke German among his family and with his friends, but he was at a fundamental ease, and developed a love for, other languages and their literatures from youth; starting with French, he became fluent in English, then Italian, and eventually Spanish and some passable Portuguese. Another is that Otto Albert was walking through doors—even as a teenager—that his parents deliberately opened for him even though they could not share in the discovery of what lay beyond. In some respects, this is just another reminder of the endless sequence of intergenerational gaps that have shaped humanity. But unlike so many other cases, for Otto Albert the gap was not a source of friction; there is no evidence that the son and his parents fought over central values. Some credit for this goes to his parents, and especially Carl, who encouraged OA's explorations. In not getting in the way, they emancipated themselves from becoming the target of his separation. When the rupture came, it was not a shock, nor did it require a repudiation of what the young Otto Albert inherited; he did not have to reject his personal past in order to move forward, another theme that would resonate in his writings decades later.

And yet, there was an underlying continuity with the German tradition of *Bildung*, which was especially appealing to upper-middle-class urbanites determined to claim that their achievements and successes in life were the result of education and self-creation and less of inheritance. It conformed well to the spirit of Weimar Republicanism, even if it created an odor of self-importance and arrogance, which irritated the republic's critics.[6] There was a hodgepodge to the mix of Weimar cosmopolitanism,

New Objectivism, and traditional Bildung values, which reflected many of the crosscurrents and compromises within Weimar republicanism. But for the sons of the city's meritocrats, consistency was probably not the goal; this was a generation coping with the challenge of living with the hangover of industrial-scale violence and mass democracy while preserving some sense that individual improvement and the personal development had something to do with containing the conflicts around them. They were too young to be so profoundly marked by the Great War, as were the Brechts or the Manns, or even to contemplate the psychoanalytic dimensions of mass society, such as the up-and-coming affiliates of the Frankfurt School.

OA and his mates were too young to catch the edge of the avant-garde and move with it, yet old enough to be clear-eyed witnesses to the destruction of the world in which it thrived.

The Collège Français was more than an intellectual hothouse. It was a social one too, and for Otto Albert, an escape from family. Otto Albert made close friends among his classmates. Wolfgang Rosenberg met OA in the Hegel study group, and they became fast friends and rowing partners. A photo of the two boys, probably when they were around fifteen years old, has them climbing rocks on one of the school's frequent outings. A centerpiece of the boys' social lives was the frequent rowing trips in the autumn, at Easter, and on summer vacations. Some of these lasted for over a week. June 1930 was a blazing month; the family had gone to Arosa, Switzerland (increasingly, a preferred alternative to the German beaches) to escape the thirty-plus degree (Celsius) heat. There was a rowing tournament involving schools and clubs from around Germany. OA went with his teammates, sharing a tent with Peter Franck, Wolfgang Rosenberg, and Helmut Mühsam. While not competing they took side trips to farms and went climbing. There were also academic obligations; Otto Albert assured his parents that Professor Levinstein "gave us until after the vacation for the French essay," though he did require them to read a German essay, "What makes Coriolan (a Beethoven composition based on the play Coriolanus) become enemy of his Fatherland?, so I will still have a bit to do."[7] Teams became the centerpiece of school social life and required some amount of investment, not just of time but also of money. Crews shared the ownership of three, four, or five boats—depending on their competitive ambitions. One autumn ritual involved graduating the rowers from the previous year's lowerclassmen to the upper-class ranks before taking to the water—presumably to row more like men. This world of masculine play also included long hikes and bicycle trips, all shepherded by the faculty who would make sure that the students were sure to learn their medieval history by studying cathedrals and castles en route.[8]

The summer of 1930 was hot in more than one sense. It was also a summer of intense electioneering, in which, as Hirschman later put it, "speaking of politics" became an irreversible process, culminating on September 14, when voters shocked the country.[9] With the country reeling from depression, the numbers of jobless rising, and the government unable to contain the crisis, the ruling Social Democrats were pummeled.

Club Riedervelein rowing team, 1929.
Otto Albert is in the middle row, far right.

While remaining the single largest party, their share of the vote sagged to a quarter. Meanwhile, the number of Nazi seats in the federal parliament soared from 14 to 107, and the party swept more than 18 percent of the vote to become the country's second-largest electoral machine. The young Hirschmann was not yet directly involved, but these were the first elections that he watched and discussed closely, especially with his closest schoolmates Franck, Rosenberg, and Mühsam. It was a dramatic event with catastrophic effects as the government gambled on the belief that it could gain more popular support in the midst of a worsening economic crisis and with louder and louder spoilers on its heels.

One reason the boys were so engaged was because the Nazi expansion was also evident at school. Otto Albert's physical education teacher—a gay man who was eventually evicted from the gymnasium for cavorting with another, fascist, student—was open about his affection for Hitler and wore a swastika around his arm. Yet, he liked Otto Albert; though a Jew, he was good at sports. Initially, the swastikas seemed innocuous; it was only with Otto Albert's political awakening that he became aware of the symbolic menace. Nazis were not just *his* political enemies; he was *theirs* too.[10] This realization did not, however, come overnight. Indeed, the school was a kind of sanctuary for the boys to explore their interests and make fun of authorities. Alfred Blumenfeld made plans to sabotage the Abitur-award ceremony. During intermissions between classes, the boys gathered outside to plot and joke at the teachers but always in a register that would not affront their sensibilities. During the ceremony, one ringleader would call aloud the first line of a famous ballad by Goethe, "Erlkönig," which reads:

> Who rides, so late, through night and wind?
> It is the father with his child.

Instead of replying with the original, the chorus of boys would bellow, "Natürlich wieder die Juden!" (Once again the Jews, of course!), followed by an uproar of adolescent laughter.[11]

Such pranks were youthful expressions of what in other settings was escalating into a full-scale confrontation. In Berlin's crowded working-class neighborhoods, the hardened world of tenement houses and dawn-until-dusk workdays, Communist and Nazi gangs were slugging it out for control of the streets—and more so as the republic crumbled. For the gentrified folk, the arguments, for the time being, were still more polite affairs. It would quickly change. Many years later, when Hirschman returned to Berlin with his wife and one of his daughters, they paid a visit to the White Rose Museum to see an exhibition about Count Claus von Stauffenberg and the officers who conspired to assassinate Hitler. They gazed at the displays of documents, read the texts to each other, and pointed at artifacts. Albert explained to Sarah and Katia the distant history to which he had been witness. Nearby, there was a group of school children escorted by a teacher. The teacher, overhearing Albert's accounts, could not resist the opportunity to ask him if he would be willing to "say a few words to the students because it would be so fascinating to hear someone from that time." Albert's German was not what it once was, but he accepted. The children sat down in front of him, and Albert shared a few early details of his life at school, his teachers, and the politics of the time. Then came the questions: "Did you know any Nazis?" Albert, slightly surprised, replied, "Of course, in my class there were lots of Nazis." The students were shocked: "And did you talk to them?" "Well, of course," Albert replied. "We were all the time discussing, trying to convince each other." A half century later, it was not easy for German children to understand that, before the Nazi triumph, in some quarters there could be conversations and athletic tournaments with pariahs.[12]

Still, the divisions at school, restricted to pranks and schoolyard taunting, were the shadows of much greater danger outside the sanctuary of the Collège. Beyond its walls, the radicalization of young men like Otto Albert reorganized their sense of the world. So, while still part of their parents' orbits, they were becoming more critical of them, or at least finding themselves removed from them. Nowhere was this clearer than the reception and influence of Marxist thinking. It was, of course, not uncommon for the scions of the Berlin professional elite to embrace a philosophy that trumpeted the cause of the German working class. In order to appreciate its significance for this generation, it helps to put the circulation of Marxism into a specific time and place: the beginnings of the Great Depression, the spread of authoritarian responses to it, and the crumbling of the precarious postwar order. "Crisis" was not the overused buzzword that it is today. In the early 1930s it had a special valence. It was not mere coincidence that the summer of 1930 also saw Heinrich Ehrmann take Otto Albert under his wing at a summer reading group and presented the fourteen-year-old with a copy of Marx's *Das Kapital*. This was not the kind of work that OA rushed off to read; he did not begin systematic reading until the following year, by which time the *Communist Manifesto* and two volumes of *Der Historische Materialismus* were also on his bookshelf.[13] But it marked a turning point, nonetheless. Marxism offered to Hirschmann and his classmates a new key, an "exciting" way to make sense of the confrontations unfolding around them. For Hirschmann, it provided a Weltanschauung he sought but which his father had disavowed, an intellectual compass, not unimportant for a young man studying the history of German idealism and the fate of its republican progeny.

But the extra thrill came from a worldview's political relevance. Marxists not only had sturdy bookshelves, they also had a party—several parties in fact, some of which had tentacular reach in the Collège through active alumni or teachers. Like the republic, the gymnasium could accommodate seemingly irreconcilable currents. In this sense, Otto Albert was under no pressure to choose the classics over Marxism; immersion in one did not require the rejection of others. Home and school provided havens for a certain learned eclecticism, which was especially significant in light of the polarities developing in Berlin's political sphere.

The recruitment of Otto Albert, and then Ursula, into politics came in 1931, by which time a verbal war between Left and Right was in full swing. But not just between Left and Right. So too was a clash between Socialists and Communists, who were in the advanced stages of enmity, with the Communist Party (KPD) hurling charges of *Sozialfaschismus* (social fascism) at the Social Democratic Party (SPD) rivals. Socialists, went the charge, were as loathsome as the bourgeois they consorted with in the Weimar governing coalition. It was Ehrmann who told Otto Albert about the Workers Socialist Youth (Sozialistische Arbeiterjugend; SAJ), an organization that had branches in all Berlin neighborhoods immersed in the block-by-block struggle for power on the left. Not a few SAJs despaired at the pragmatic moderation of their party leaders, but they were not willing to give up their faith in a parliamentary road to revolution. The Tiergarten had a chapter of the SAJ, though its working class members were in short supply. It was connected to a larger network that convened for giant assemblies at the Sportpalast, Berlin's largest meeting hall, located on the Genthinerstrasse in the working class area of Schöneberg. Here, the left-wing vertical mosaic of Berlin's social classes would gather. Indeed, the Sportpalast was emerging as the central stage of Berlin's political theater. Hitler delivered his first official speech there to enraptured crowds in September 1930. Otto Albert's political engagement was not only induced by a mentor. On his own, he, like many of his generation, was developing a sense of concern about the survival of the republic; the devastating September 1930 elections revealed its fundamental weaknesses. Thus began OA's militancy. His SAJ group was firmly committed to the SPD and was meant to rally the support of youth, especially as the electoral climate began to heat up. But as with so many such efforts, the mobilization brought internal fissures and debates within the party. Political debate in small gatherings or mass rallies was therefore concerned about the fascist menace on one hand and the relationship between the republic and socialism on the other.[14]

With his homework done and supper finished, Otto Albert would slip out of the apartment to attend meetings at the Sportpalast. One evening, Otto Albert and Ursula left to attend a lecture by the Austro-Marxist Otto Bauer. Having read some of his tracts in one of the gymnasium reading groups, OA was discovering a fascination for something called economics. Bauer delivered a spellbinding lecture about Kondratiev long cycles—the theory that economic systems were vulnerable to extended periods (about forty years) of ups and downs associated with spurts and declines of technological breakthroughs. At the time, it was for many a compelling explanation of the Depression, though it landed Nikolai Kondratiev in the Gulag; it raised fundamental concerns about

Stalin's planning theories. What Bauer did that evening was explain the cycle to his audience. A great boom that had begun in the middle of the nineteenth century had long since crested. Now it was in crisis. A new economic model was imminent, and socialists had to be sure to ride the forthcoming cycle. The data-filled presentation was an intellectual tonic as well as a political one. Here was a leader of the Austrian Socialist Party discussing books, economic patterns, and political implications. Here was an analysis that combined them, and a man whose charisma conveyed it. This was unlike anything Otto Albert had heard from his own party leaders or from his teachers. If there was a single event that convinced him to study economics, it was that night at the Sportpalast; five decades later, Hirschman could still close his eyes and reconstruct Bauer's performance.

These encounters with captivating intellectual figures, reading the theoretical analyses of the calamity, and the pressing sense of crisis motivated Otto Albert to explore the connections between thought and action. This preoccupation pushed him further beyond the Collège and into the circles of SAJ militants. The explosive election of 1930 at the end of the summer, whose results blared across Berlin's headlines—Nazi Victory!—added drama to the theory. While Otto Albert was reading Marx and Marxists for the first time, the Social Democratic Party, with which he and his parents were aligned, was undergoing an ever-deepening party *crise de coeur*. Discussions and debates reflected the growing political unease around the country, especially in Berlin, which shifted from the world's capital of avant-garde modernism to the global epicenter of crisis thinking and the frantic search for alternatives.

Among socialists, these anxieties spilled into a vibrant internal debate and growing calls for change of tactics and new visions. Weekend excursions by militants were devoted to discussions of important tracts, workshops in political tactics, and plans for future meetings. On Sundays, OA and sometimes Ursula, who would later affiliate with the Communist Party, donned their blue shirts and red kerchiefs and took the train to assemblies in the countryside. Youth hostels became the meeting grounds for leftist students and young workers from around Berlin. Erich Schmidt, the charismatic head of the SAJ chapter in Berlin, steered the group further to the left within the Social Democrats and argued for the creation of a coalition of Social Democrats and Communists. In this, he was taking on the SPD establishment, incarnate in the Reichstag faction of the Brüning (of the Center Party) government, which was desperately trying to cope with a growing crisis and focusing on the older party line. Figures like Erich Ollenhauer and Rudolf Hilferding "tolerated" the bourgeois parties and put their trust in Brüning until he dropped the remaining Socialists from his coalition and brought in Nazis as part of his botched electoral gambit. In the meantime, the SPD leadership stuck with a government that had swung to such deflationary, antilabor, pro-military, pro-clerical, and even increasingly anti-Semitic standpoints that it made a mockery of whatever the republic's reformists and moderate socialists had envisioned. Rudolf Hilferding wrote to the elder SPD leader and intellectual, Karl Kautsky, on December 1 that "the situation is certainly unpleasant. The fascist danger still threatens and the increase [in support] for the Communists disturbs our people even more. Indeed, a further advance in this direction would certainly bring the greatest danger that the attraction of the Communists would increase powerfully as soon as they surpassed our numbers. It is not a pretty scene, but adventurous stupidities would only make matters worse." As if to mock the SPD leader's cautionary diagnosis, two months later Hindenburg named Hitler Chancellor of Germany.[15]

This kind of blindness to imminent dangers drove younger militants to distraction. For Schmidt, the 1930 elections revealed that old rivalries on the left had to be set aside to confront the common enemy. At stake was parliament itself. Something different had to be done to rescue it, and it was clear to those of the SAJ that the extremes of the Left and especially the Right had no interest and the Center had no ability. Along with Walter Löwenheim (aka Kurt, who had been evicted from the KPD for "right-wing deviationism"), Schmidt called this movement the Circle, and later ORG; sometimes it was known as LO, or just O, for Gruppe Leninistische Organisation. It would become the incubator for the Neu Beginnen movement in 1933, a self-described Leninist vanguard within the Socialist camp devoted to a full-throated analysis of the economic crisis and the practical necessity of a left-wing alliance. Only socialism could rescue the republic. But for the time being, Schmidt's crusade focused on mobilizing the movement to treat the Nazi threat as not just a momentary political blip (which is how the overconfident SPD leadership tended, condescendingly, to dismiss it), but rather the expression of a structural shift in German capitalism with decisive political realignments. Hirschmann later recalled Schmidt's powerful speeches and presence before audiences of politically awakening youth, drawing inspiration from Lenin for organizational discipline to push the party onto a new track. Enchanted by Schmidt's ability to formulate in words what he was beginning to divine in observation, Hirschmann met with Schmidt several times during SAJ activities and fell under the spell of his learned activism. "He was one of those men who thought while he spoke," remembered Hirschman. It was in the spring of 1932 that Schmidt and the ORG leaders sponsored a months-long series of intensive workshops on revising Marxist theory, the history of the German labor movement, discussions of tactics, and exegesis of Lenin's pamphlet *What Is to Be Done?* Lenin was truly "captivating." While other Marxists focused on the stages of historical transformation and were understandably obsessed with what was seen as the inevitable crises of capitalism, Lenin presented an altogether different kind of reading. His prerevolutionary writings actually defended the creative cunning of capitalism. Anything that accented the mysterious role of History's hiding forces drew the young militant's attention. But it was especially Lenin's political writings that gripped Otto Albert. He devoured the April Theses, Letters on Tactics, and the notes that would appear in *The State and Revolution*. Lenin's analysis of the creative possibilities for new forms of action put the accent on what Hirschmann immediately appreciated as "a great subtlety for tactics." The "fascination" with *how* change is effected—not presuming it was so automatic or predestined—started here; not until the young Hirschmann read Machiavelli would he encounter a similar political theorist of the practice of change and the politics of the possible. One of his favorite Lenin tracts was the injunction to the Second Congress of the Communist International from 1920, in which the Bolshevik fixed his sights on the "infantile disease" (Lenin's words) of the rebel's "mindless theorizing" (Hirschman's), with no attention to the subtle cunning of events. Lenin decried dogmatists' affection for blind spots about History's infinitely forking paths in order stick to their line. The traditional Communist faith that a crisis would resolve itself only one way—with a revolutionary triumph—was at best naïve. There was always more than one way to get out of a jam. "Revolutionaries sometimes try to prove," wrote Lenin, "that there is absolutely no way out of a crisis [for the ruling classes]. This is a mistake. There is no such thing as an absolutely hopeless situation." Hirschmann savored these words; one can hear them echo through his prose a half century later.[16]

Nocturnal and weekend activism involved exegeses of Lenin and debates about Socialist tactics and eventually became overlaid with a patina of romance. The circle of Otto Albert's friends moved him beyond the confines of his school or his sister's classmates. It was within the SAJ that OA came to know the family of Rafael Rein, a prominent ex-Menshevik and leader of the Bund, the Jewish Workers' Union under the Russian Empire. Rein had gone to Petrograd in 1917 in the second sealed train from Zurich and played a leading role in the fall of the tsar, then went on to lead the parliamentary faction of the Mensheviks in the Duma. He fled to Berlin and from there became a marked man as a writer for the Russian underground paper *Vestnik*, which circulated into the Soviet Union via Poland. Two of his children, Mark and Lia, were also SAJ activists of roughly the same age as Ursula and OA, and the acquaintances quickly gave way to attractions, OA for Lia, and Ursula for Mark. Lia's gymnasium seethed with violence, for teenagers were semiobliged to sport their partisan colors under their uniforms, only to peel off the top layer when school was dismissed. For the pugilists, this kind of color-coding helped separate allies from targets. Lia thought herself as mobilized as the boys. It would have been hard for any "pure" romance to flourish in an environment so saturated with politics; instead of going dancing together, Lia and OA marched together, which, in Hirschman's memory, did have the advantage of making the sometimes tedious and repetitive exercises more pleasant. If there was any kissing, it had to be done while walking home— already exhausted—from a long meeting or rally.[17]

For all the inspiration and romance that accompanied Hirschmann's political turn, his increasing engagements coincided with, and to some extent were stoked by, an increasingly rancorous debate within the party. The SPD began to tear itself apart. The Sozialistische Arbeiterpartei split off in opposition to the party's unrelenting support for Chancellor Brüning. Other radical factions opted to stay. Hirschmann was decidedly in the "stay" camp and saw no point in fracturing the movement any further; it was more important, he felt, to meet the challenge than to content oneself with an intellectually pure or politically "sound" position; his pragmatic streak was already showing through the fabric of his radicalism. In this, he was joined by another young militant, Willy Brandt, who was a member of the same group and the same age; both insisted that the cause would be better served by disagreeing from within the structure than defecting from it.[18]

The big question was, how far should one collaborate with the Communists? After Moscow, Berlin was the world's biggest Communist polis, with a quarter million members and twenty-five newspapers. Since the Comintern's leftward lurch in 1928, Communists had followed an intransigent line. For many, the loathing of the republic began early—with the killing of Rosa Luxemburg and Karl Liebknecht, the KPD's founders, at the hands of cavalry guards doing paramilitary duty. The doctrine of social fascism, invoked to defame the already vulnerable ruling SPD, argued that there was little to distinguish the Nazis and the government when it came to upholding the basic structures of capitalism. If anything, the Nazis were easier to contend with because they did not bother to mystify the oppressive content of boss rule with the allure of bourgeois, gentlemanly electoralism. In the shared disdain for procedural, parliamentary norms—Hirschmann observed—the Communists and Nazis mirrored each other, in their conviction at having gotten to some basic "truth" about the world and sneering at anyone who urged caution, advocated complexity, or preferred reformist civility. Otto Albert did not have to go very far to reach this conclusion, for the Communist sloganeering for "Red Unity" and "Antifascist Struggle" was steeped in the same militaristic style as the fascists: martial parading, belligerent rhetoric, *aktion* over deliberation. Since the pluralist and reformist values of the republic were such anathema to extremists, they could agree to treat them as doomed. Hirschmann recognized a conveniently circular way of agreeing to destroy all hope of reform. During the transportation strike of November 1932, Goebbels, who envied the Communists' organizational machinery, and Walter Ulbricht, the scheming tool of the Comintern, joined up at the same demonstration. The strikers were so appalled at the spectacle of a Nazi-Communist march that they dissolved the stoppage. Then, that night, Communists and Nazis tore at each other to create a growing list of rival martyrs: knives slashed faces, beer mugs cracked skulls, and bullets pierced the night from the tops of buildings. In the morning, the trails of blood could be seen from where comrades dragged away the dead or injured.[19]

These were scenes that Hirschmann witnessed but conspicuously preferred not to discuss for the rest of his life. But they left their indelible marks on everything he wrote; one cannot help but detect in his defense of moderation and open-mindedness in *The Rhetoric of Reaction* his alarm at Communist and Nazi tirades and certainties. But for the moment, while the KPD clearly loathed the republic, both its principles and its politicians, there were many in the socialist ranks who shared Otto Albert's sense that they were necessary allies; the only hope for socialism, and thus the republic, was a new alliance, for it appeared that the Center and Right were prepared to cave into the Nazis. The hope was that some flexibility and accommodation might yield to a progressive ruling coalition to lift the republic from its troubles.

In the end, these were pipedreams. There was no Left coalition; indeed, KPD militants took to the streets as much to beat up Socialists as they did Nazis. While the electoral scene became more intense, some youth and neighborhood movements vented their rivalry with fisticuffs; indeed, the collapse of the Reichstag's power fueled the militarization of the streets. In 1931, the Social Democrats formed a self-defense front called the Iron Front. Otto Albert did not follow those activists who went from campaigning and doctrinal debates to their paramilitary outfits, the Schutzbund, which argued that "force had to be met with force." These tended to operate more out of union halls and working-class sports clubs. But because the SPD was loath to confront the government with mass strikes or armed resistance, most of the violent activity was restricted to political gang warfare, which escalated dramatically and blurred the line between civic and violent action. The establishment fervently tried to defend civility. Still, some meetings got rough. Those who left the meeting halls could not ignore the prowling gangs of angry Communists and Nazis. For this reason, it was important to escort women to their homes after assemblies, and Hirschmann's bicycling skills came in handy when he was alone. One evening, while Lia, Mark, Otto Albert, and Ursula were at a meeting trying to convince Communists to bury their grudges and doctrinal purity, the argument degenerated into a fist fight. Mark, who was more and more to Otto Albert the archetype of the *engagé* idealist, emerged beaten and bruised. The others escaped unscathed. They all withdrew to the safety of home—to ready themselves for another round the next day.[20]

The plunge into politics created a rift with the parents. At first, the suspicions were more about the suitability of some readings and whether the children were hanging around the appropriate crowds. Both parents took a dislike to Ehrmann and his influence. Writing to Hedwig in mid-1930, Carl exclaimed, "How hard it is to build up childrens' souls! Hereto, to this question, it is necessary that Ehrmann get out of her [Ursula] and the boy's [OA] lives. I'd prefer a jiu-jitsu champion." When the nanny discovered that Ehrmann had given Ursula a German copy of Agnes Smedley's *Daughter of the Earth* (*Eine Frau allein*), Carl was livid: "I find this intolerable and grounds for taking firmer action with him."[21] Smedley, the American writer and radical, was known for her promotion of birth control and her affinity with Chinese Communists, not to mention her service as a Soviet spy. *Daughter of the Earth* was a semi-autobiographical novel about a heroic, self-made, independent woman—who became radical. It is hard to know exactly which of Smedley's causes was more of an affront to Ursula's protective parents. The poems of Erich Kästner and Brecht's *Threepenny Opera* were also proscribed, though Kästner's essays figured prominently in the family newspaper, the *Vossische Zeitung*. The entire New Objectivity movement was altogether too dark and sobering for either Carl or Hedwig, who preferred not to have their children ruminate on the hypocrisy of the establishment.

The weight of the clash between parents and children landed on one parent's shoulders in particular, Hedda's, and one child's, Ursula's. Relations with Mutti had never been completely harmonious, and frictions with Ursula simply worsened, as did the tension with OA, who had been immune to her fussing until then. They were faced with a stark choice: conform to Mutti's pride or defect to street politics. Ursula had no skill in avoiding filial conflict; OA did, in spades. The result was that while OA had always been adept at carving out some autonomy from Mutti's overbearing embrace, he now raised his skill to a higher form, defusing the conflict by avoiding its source. In the year leading up to January 1933, he would be gone for days on end and most nights, largely unnoticed now that his bedroom was positioned with direct access to the apartment's front door and he had his studies to hold up as a fig leaf.

If Mutti projected her anxieties, even at the price of alienating her two eldest children, Carl turned his inward and became more withdrawn and taciturn than ever. With his career stalled, the family fortunes in decline, and the republic unraveling, mounting tension over OA's and Ursula's militancy enhanced his recessive proclivities. Ursula's memoirs may overstate her father's prescient sense that their world was ending, but the point is: the republican dream was dying along with his personal aspirations, and the two were indissoluble. Resigned and melancholy, he spent his time reading poems by the introverted nihilist, Gottfried Benn (from a little anthology, aptly called *Morgue*, published in 1912), and rereading his Kafka, perhaps searching for solace in tales of unfathomable bureaucratic agonies, which he no doubt recognized as his own. Retrospectively, Ursula also knew that the image of death hanging over his desk at home was casting a shadow over the republic and the family.[22]

In 1932, Otto Albert Hirschmann graduated from the Collège. His gymnasium degree was a major accomplishment and an index of status, especially coming from one of Germany's best schools. With his grades, Otto Albert had a ticket to pursue further studies. The question was, where and what? Medicine was ruled out; Carl may have wanted his son to follow in his footsteps, but he could see in his preference for courses at the gymnasium that Otto Albert's passions lay elsewhere. It is likely that Ehrmann helped shape his choices, if only by example. He had studied law and economics. What Hirschmann could not count on, for the first time in his life, was parental approval. The decision to study economics was not greeted with much enthusiasm. They explained that it was "a breadless art"—to which their son replied, with his tongue already in cheek, that it was precisely the power to explain shortages and abundances of bread that made it such an important discipline. For the time being, the conflict could be muted, for economics was taught within the law faculty of the University of Berlin, and Carl and Hedwig could hope that their son would emerge a talented and successful lawyer.[23]

Moreover, the Depression was on Hirschmann's mind; it was hard to avoid, and Otto Albert was, if nothing else, already a fine observer. Not only did the jobless rate hit one-third when he graduated, but his family's own finances, while not ruined, were crippled. The buoyancy of the 1920s, admittedly floating on an influx of American dollars and bank lending, gave way to a profound slump and thus destroyed the legitimacy of the republic. To Hirschmann, economics had the appeal of explaining the crisis around him while offering a more analytical distance from politics; he preferred to keep his politics contained to his, admittedly demanding, involvements with the SAJ. If economics was his inclination, where to pursue this interest was beyond doubt: the University of Berlin. Eventually renamed the Humboldt University of Berlin in 1949, partly to give it a new lease after years of complicity with the Third Reich, it had been the paragon of Enlightenment pursuit from Hegel and Schiller to Einstein and Max Planck. Its large buildings with classical façades, open squares, and stacked libraries captivated the young Hirschmann, and its peerless status removed some of his parents' reservations. That students could wander past the windows from which Hegel once gazed only added to the institution's aura.

But by the time he started his new pursuits, the university was roiled by conflict. Already, universities around Germany were becoming hotbeds of support for Hitler, with fascist students harassing liberal and left-ist professors, and not a few faculty heralded them. The German Student Association (Deutsche Studentenschaft) rampaged against signs of "un-German spirit" and welcomed Nazi speakers to their rallies. It was these students who stormed the University of Berlin's magnificent library in May 1933 and proceeded to ignite tens of thousands of volumes at the Opernplatz, in front of the law faculty and around the corner from He-gel's old office. It is hard to say how much actual "studying" Otto Albert conducted during his sojourn at the University of Berlin. It was extremely brief, affiliated with the Institute for Political Science and Statistics under the wing of the School of Law and Political Science for one semester, the winter of 1932–33. This was, to be sure, a fairly esoteric and probably quite isolated unit within the university's general focus on law, the humanities, and the natural sciences. Still, Hirschmann sought it out. His courses focused on classical political economy, under the aegis of "Political Science Tutorial." He was applauded for his oral and written reports, "The Critique of Smith's Doctrine of Money and Capital through Marx" and "The Limits and Scope of Ricardo's Labor Theory of Value." Beyond this, we know little of his studies, which appear to have focused on deep background readings in classical political economy and on the pamphlets he was reading in the SAJ study groups.[24]

Whatever career he initiated at the University of Berlin was over-whelmed by the demise of the republic. The underlying compromise that held the Weimar regime together did not just collapse. It was destroyed by those who never believed in it and those who lost faith in it. The Hirschmanns could not be counted in either camp.

Nor did they see the catastrophe coming. There has been a debate among historians about just how predictable the Third Reich was. The current thought is that Hitler's triumph and consolidation depended as much on the shrewdness with which he played the political system as on the haplessness and denial of his democratic opposition before then. To be sure, there were plenty of explanations for the crisis of both the econ-omy and the political system, but few could anticipate the brutality of what came later. Increasingly, the votes went to the extremes. The Communists inched into Socialist support. Germans went to the polls in a flurry of chaotic and highly mobilized elections that did less and less to resolve the impasse and more and more to convince onlookers that the old order was beyond repair. In 1932, with Hirschmann in his final year of study, Germany endured two Reichstag elections, two presidential run-offs, and a welter of local elections and watched three chancellors come and go. In July of that year, when the young Hirschmann had graduated and was devoting himself to full-time militancy and left-wing study, the Nazis took 37 percent of the vote to become the largest party, with 230 delegates, in the Reichstag. This was a staggering blow to democrats. It heightened the internal feuding among Socialists and crippled the resistance to martial law.

In the spiral that swept Otto Albert into political life, the family also had to grapple with undeniable signs of rising right-wing intolerance. Still, there was an effort to buoy the faith of assimilated Jews who were committed to the republic's pluralism. Hitler may have invented nothing in his reactionary ideology, but for the Hirschmanns, poring over their newspaper, listening to the news, or gossiping among friends, his performance at the polls was seen as ephemeral. Everything was happening so fast. Seen from the sanctuary of home, the Nazis were, if anything, risible. The rotund Hermann Goering, covered with medals, was called "roly-poly." The shifty, promiscuous, club-footed Josef Goebbels was a favored butt of jokes. But hopes that this would all pass became even stronger after January 1933.[25]

Behind the scenes, the manipulation and posturing between factions on the Right brought to the fore persistent doubts about whether Germany should be a tolerant meritocratic nation as well as the reserve of hatred for the reforming republic. Socialists were paralyzed by the pace of events and the cynicism with which conservatives abandoned republican principles; to Communists this merely confirmed the fundamentally autocratic nature of capitalism, so now steps should be taken to prepare the proletariat for revolution. On January 30, Paul von Hindenburg, the president and World War I hero whose own commitment to Weimar constitutionalism was little more than a formality, brokered the creation of a new cabinet of conservatives with Hitler to serve as chancellor; while the coalition members despised each other, they did agree to collude in the demolition of the republican state. Hitler rushed to his headquarters and told Goebbels with tears in his eyes, "Now we are on our way." The accelerated collapse of the Weimar era only compounded the confusion for a young militant trying to keep his bearings. Upon hearing the news of Hitler's ascent to the chancellorship, Otto Albert put on his uncle's old green suit, grabbed his bicycle, and rode into the rainy Berlin night. Desperate to find out what the left-wing parties were doing to shore up the republic, he raced to the main SPD and Communist headquarters. Was there going to be a general strike? Would the Social Democrats abandon the policy of "tolerance?" Ursula caught up with him at the Communist headquarters, the Karl Liebknecht Haus, and remembered the look on his face as he leaned on his bicycle looking up at the brightly lit top floor of the building where the central committee was gathering: "He looked at the imposing building hoping for a sign of what to do next, and I was there, watching him, and now loved him more than any other person in the world. I understood that he suffered and that he had a more profound sense than me of the seriousness of the moment."[26]

What the teenagers witnessed were shock and paralysis. The vaunted Red Berlin was a paper tiger. That night, the new era came upon them with massive torchlight parades down Berlin's avenues, huge rallies of triumphant fascists, and the throb of Nazi chants. Troopers in their brown shirts and Schutzstaffel (SS) men in their black leather marched through the very heart of the Tiergarten itself to the Brandenburg Gate and stopped before the Reichstag, where Hitler greeted them from a balcony.

When Hindenburg asked Hitler to form the new government, many thought it would last no more than a year. But History being what it is, Hitler's maneuver broke the cycle, though only hindsight enables the observer to see that the National Socialists were a very different breed than the hapless reactionaries who had colluded to share power with them. Nazis dominated the screaming headlines, and their thugs patrolled the streets and broke up rallies, keeping Carl and Hedwig up all night fearing for OA and Ursula's safety. On February 27, the Socialists had called for a mass rally at the Sportpalast. It was to be the largest—and last—such gathering. Otto Albert and Ursula went and watched as the seams of the Socialist movement came apart: wait or confront, let the government implode or bring it down, let the threat pass or resort to armed resistance? The leadership dug in its heels: Hitler was a mere demagogue, it insisted; he was doomed to fail. More-radical militants jeered and bellowed from the seats: they must take action! When the rally was over, despondent Socialists filed out of the arena only to be greeted by columns of police and storm troopers. By that time it was evening. As Otto Albert, Ursula, and friends made their way home, shouting broke out in the streets, the crowds pushed and yelled. Over Berlin's rooftops, something lit up the night sky. Otto Albert looked up to see smoke plumes rising against the crimson horizon. Then came the flames, creating dark silhouettes out of the mounted policemen.[27]

Soon came the riptide of rumors: the Reichstag was burning!

"Things did not change fundamentally," recalled Hirschman, "until the Reichstag fire, which really marked the beginning of the political horror."[28] The next day, the chancellor, alleging a Red uprising, issued emergency decrees abolishing fundamental rights and promising harsh punishments for anyone threatening the health of the Reich. Four thousand Sturmabteilung (SA) troopers scattered across the city to begin roundups. Eventually, all opposition parties were banned and assemblies forbidden; left-leaning newspapers closed shop. In one night the pretext was laid for abolishing the political culture and institutions in which OA and his mates had immersed themselves. Not surprisingly, such a radical change to the rules of the political game was utterly bewildering to those on the ground, no matter how much "theoretical" reading they had done.

The stage was set for a final campaign by Socialists. With Communists by then out of the chamber and Catholics caving to Hitler, it fell to the hobbled SPD to try to stop the Nazi juggernaut. Hitler proposed a law that would allow him to govern for four years without constitutional constraints, legislation needing a two-thirds majority from the parliament. Socialist activists met in homes, union halls, and universities to debate how to get the message beyond private circles in the absence of a free press or public assemblies. Duplicating machines were the tool of preference, but they posed an additional question—where to keep them? For Hirschmann's SAJ group, the solution presented itself in the form of an Italian philosophy student, Eugenio Colorni, who had spotted the attractive Ursula at the library of the University of Berlin. At the time, he was working on a thesis on Leibnitz with a well-known Leibnitz specialist, Erich Auerbach, at the University of Marburg. Ursula and Otto Albert plucked up the courage to ask Colorni to keep a printing machine in his room in a hostel in Charlottenburg. There they could compose their broadsheet; since he was a foreigner, the Nazis would not suspect his involvement. Thus began a formative influence; for a short while, until Colorni returned to Marburg, his hotel room "became a nerve center for antifascist activities and publications" in the final weeks of the new regime's consolidation.[29]

Socialist militants fanned out to the streets, their bags full of leaflets, urging people to rally to the opposition of the new bill. Otto Albert joined small cells of activists for safety. They would go the top of apartment buildings and work their way down floor by floor, leaving leaflets under tenants' doors and talking to whomever they could. Working from top to bottom made it easier to flee in case they were sighted by the police or brownshirts. Amid paranoia about moles and break-ins, Hirschmann's group worked furiously to embolden the party to resist the legislation, hoping they could spoil the gambit. On March 23, the parliament met in the Kroll Opera House. Outside, storm troopers surrounded the building, taunting and threatening Socialist Deputies who dared enter. The police intercepted and even arrested some of the deputies, one was pummeled, and others started packing their bags in preparation to flee. That night, 448 approved of Hitler's request; only 94 Socialists were able to stand up and have their negative votes counted as storm troopers patrolled the aisles barking at them.[30]

In a matter of weeks, fear replaced confusion. Bristling with their laws, the Nazis ravaged the opposition. Arrest campaigns followed. There were so many detained that the government opened its first concentration camp at Oranienburg, 35 kilometers north of Berlin. Nazis seized

Bertolt Brecht's personal address book and used it as a guide to expand their net. Otto Albert's rowing partner, schoolmate, and brother to his first amour, Peter Franck, found himself arrested and also had his address book confiscated. One by one, Peter's friends and associates were rounded up. Everything had now changed for OA.

Meanwhile, Carl had a sense that matters were getting much worse, but he kept his worries to himself. Some of his friends were feeling the pressure. Among them was René Kuczynski—a demographer and avid pacifist—whose name appeared on the SA's list, which led the troopers to Kuczynski's house. In the end they withdrew because the police and the storm troopers got embroiled in a dispute over who had claims to seized properties and detainees. But Kuczynski was rightly petrified. In early March, Carl clandestinely arranged for him to hide in his clinic (located in an asylum for the insane where, presumably, no one worth worrying about would live) and set about making arrangements for his friend to escape, eventually to England, where he would teach demographics at the London School of Economics.[31] It took five decades for OA to learn of his father's private heroism. Only then did he learn from Kuczynski's son, Jürgen, of Carl's sanctuary. Jürgen produced the original full-sized Gertrude Simon portrait, which the family had been safeguarding, as a gesture of gratitude; for half a century, the photograph of Carl had hung on the wall as a tribute to the family's secret savior.[32]

Carl was concealing another secret: he knew he was about to die of cancer. In January, he grew visibly unwell. The children were told he had ulcers. Then one day he returned home from the clinic with X-rays of his stomach and clinically pointed out the growths to his confused, and then upset, children. Some time around March 20, shortly after Kuczynski's hiding, an operation removed the cancerous tissue; but it was too late, the disease had metastasized. Carl lived only another ten days. The children were not encouraged to see him—the decay was so swift and awful that Hedwig did not want them to remember their father in this condition. Instead, she paced the Hohenzollernstrasse apartment repeating to herself, "I must remember him, I must remember him."[33] His friends and associates, mostly doctors, ministered to him and were at his bedside

constantly. Carl was pronounced dead in a hospital in Charlottenburg
on March 31, 1933. The next day, the first wave of government-sanctioned
violence swept Berlin, with assaults and boycotts on Jewish shops and
businesses.

The funeral brought out a crowd of doctors, friends, and family.
There were memorial speeches. Ulrich Friedemann, Carl's closest friend,
gave the longest of the tributes. Thirteen-year-old Eva was inconsolable
as the wreath was laid before his coffin. Carl's body was laid to rest at the
Heerstrasse Cemetery, a handsome interconfessional burial site, which
the Nazis, knowing Jews were buried there, later slated to raze for the
Berlin Olympics of 1936. After the funeral, the family retreated to the
apartment on Hohenzollernstrasse with the closest relatives and friends.
There, Hedwig's grief burst in great fits of sobbing. Friends and family
tried to comfort her. By contrast, Otto Albert was a model of unfeigned
stoicism. The three children retreated down the hallway to the back of the
apartment to one of their bedrooms; there they cried together and shared
a few words. As evening approached, OA emerged from the bedroom to
inform the guests and his mother that he would be leaving very soon for
Paris. With all the grief in the room, it was hard to hear this quiet but
decisive message. Most, including his sisters, figured it was a going to be a
short vacation. On April 2, he was gone—five days before his eighteenth
birthday. These were his final hours in Berlin; he would not return until
1979.[34]

Otto Albert had clearly been weighing his options. In the days before his father's death, news of Peter Franck's arrest had driven him into
hiding; by then, people were learning that address books were invento-
ries of suspects. There was talk that the government would throw Jewish students out of the country's universities; that became law on April
1. There were also rumors that Jews would be banned from the legal profession; that decree came a week later. Faculties of law were thus gutted
of their Jewish students. Antifascist activity had come to a halt "by fiat,"
Hirschman noted, shaking his head as he recalled his final days in Berlin,
and the Nazis had won. It was clear that fighting within the system (what
Hirschman would later call the practice of "voice")—at least for the time

being—was not just futile, it was suicidal. It was time to open new vistas (what he would later call "exit").[35] "Those of us who left at the time," Hirschman told an American documentary filmmaker years later, "left with the hope that this would be a regime that would somehow break its neck very soon, and that somehow there would be some . . . action on the part of some section of German society that would prevent this regime from taking root."[36]

It is possible that this decision to flee was a way of deflecting other sources of pain. It is hard to say for sure since Hirschman was tight-lipped about his final months in Berlin, preferring to layer his traumatic experiences with a heavy armor of silence. We get a rare glimpse into his grief, and his efforts to make something of it, from a letter to his mother written in Paris a year after his father's funeral. "The calendar tells me that a year has passed, otherwise I wouldn't know if it has been a month or three years. I have experienced so much joy and so many new things. On the other hand, everything that we experienced and suffered stands so near, insistent, and physical before my eyes." The rush to embrace the new somewhere else did not succeed in obliterating the grief of the past. While the young émigré uprooted himself in part to allow the challenge of the present to crowd out old sorrows, they did not disappear. "It was the first great pain in my life. I did not have time to think out this pain because after three days the reality of the Paris trip demanded my thoughts. And so it happens that the pain always emerged in the quiet hours."[37] For the rest of his life, the quiet hours of Easter would summon memories of the loss of his father, the first of a series of losses that would sear his memory of the 1930s.

Distance and recollection did afford Otto Albert an opportunity to find in a father's life some significance for a son who was embarking on his own. On September 8, 1933, the day before what would have been his father's fifty-fourth birthday, the eighteen-year-old fatherless son sat down to muster some rare words of sorrow in a letter to his mother. Characteristically, he also felt compelled to cheer his mother up and thus remind her of the good times. "When I try today to imagine Daddy in spirit I always automatically see him working at his desk in a scientific discussion with a colleague or in the white operating apron at the clinic. In this way, I respected, admired, and loved him best." But it was not the professional achievement that motivated this admiration: "The truly great thing about his demeanor, which was so unique and worthwhile, was that he put himself *behind* his work." In keeping with the Bildung principles with which Carl and his class had legitimated the republican system and instilled in their sons' education, the teenage Hirschmann embraced the effort to thwart the viral despair among progressive reformists. But the uplift was jumbled with other memories. That of the failed promotion still stung, bitterly: "When he applied for the direction of the hospital, he did this because he knew that he could fill this post better than any other. The direction was everything to him in his judgment and that of others." OA scribbled in the margins of this letter, "Given that it must have already earlier strongly oppressed him that a person is not treated according to his achievements but instead according to his relationships, how the present system would have affected him!" It was his father's pursuit of "this human ideal," of not working for himself but living for his work, that most inspired the young son: "The work was its own purpose, this self-creation through work seems to be the one right, fruitful, sensible, and noble mindset, from which every human activity should emanate." It was in this "resistance of the 'ego'" that I preserve him in myself and in this way he lives on for me." Here was a way—through work, self-improvement, resisting despair—to keep nostalgia and narcissistic regression at bay. In an age of abandonment, of failed gods and dashed hopes, the young OA did not so much feel violently separated from a loved one than bonded to his example. OA's was not the vengeful father; Carl's spirit was nothing like Hamlet's phantom. But like Hamlet's, Carl's example was the invention of the living, and throughout OA's life one can occasionally glimpse a son haunted by tragedy. In this epistle, however, we see a man looking forward, not backward, searching for solace, not sadness, as he stepped into the world beyond a traumatized Berlin.[38]

CHAPTER 3

Proving Hamlet Wrong

How can one take delight in the world
unless one flees to it for refuge?

FRANZ KAFKA

Days after Hitler became German chancellor, Hirschmann's former French tutor wrote to him from Paris: "In case you desire to come to France, please do not hesitate to stay with us." As his train pulled into Paris, it was to his demoiselle's address that he headed, hoping to get his bearings. To his surprise, his hosts were not French-speakers at home. They, too, were émigrés—from Salonika, Ladino-speaking Jews and veterans of Balkan intolerance—one more family in a city that was becoming the world's refuge from European tyrants. Hirschmann's shelter among Ladinos was the first step into the world of stateless people.[1]

As with many émigrés, Hirschmann was not without contacts that might open doors. Henri Jourdan, the director of Berlin's Maison Académique Française, with intellectual aspirations of his own in France, had met Otto Albert through the Collège Français. Jourdan recommended him to old friends, Pascal and Monique Dupuy. The Dupuys were of high Third Republic stock. Protestants, Monique's father had been a senator and former governor of Morocco and occupied other high offices in the republic, while Pascal's father, a magnate in the coal industry, was a director of the intellectually aristocratic École normale superieur. When Hirschmann arrived in Paris, he dropped the Dupuys a line; they invited the young German to their apartment on the opulent rue de Medici, overlooking the Luxembourg Gardens. Otto Albert must have made a good

Otto Albert and Ursula in Normandy, early summer, 1933.

impression because the Dupuys offered him a job as a German tutor to their two sons, Michel (eleven) and Jacques (thirteen). For the rest of that spring, he worked on the boys' German and bided his time, considering his options and hoping the Nazi storm would pass. He must have grown on the parents because they invited him to join the family for the summer at their house in Normandy at St. Aubin-sur-Mer. With nowhere better to go, Hirschmann happily accepted. The summer at the beach must have reminded him of his younger days. He became friends with neighbors, especially the Cabouat family from Nîmes, also Protestants, whose house bordered on the Dupuys. Their teenage son, Jean-Pierre, joined the circle. Between German tutorials, playing tennis, swimming in the ocean, and walking the Normandy beaches, the dangers of Berlin were far away.[2]

But not out of mind. In mid-July, a telegram caught up with Otto Albert—from Berlin. His sister had also fled and followed his tracks to Paris. Otto Albert explained the situation to the Dupuys, who extended their invitation to Ursula as well. While she had fled with her boyfriend, Ernst Jablonksi, she agreed to leave him in Paris for a few days while she went to visit her brother. Otto Albert was anxious for some news from Berlin. Was the storm finally passing? Should he return? Ursula's news was bad. Since Peter Franck's arrest, there had been more detentions. More friends had either gone underground, fled, or were in detention. Indeed, the police appeared at Hohenzollernstrasse demanding that Hedwig reveal the whereabouts of Otto Albert and Ursula. Mutti urged them both to stay away from Berlin until further notice.[3] For the next three days, Otto Albert and Ursula talked and talked, replaying the recent past and considering future options. A photograph of the brother and sister reunited in Normandy is a reminder of just how young the fugitives were.

Hirschmann's future was decided not just by the repression meted out to Hitler's leftist opposition. Hirschmann found himself a Jew by decree. He could not go back to the University of Berlin even if he wanted to. Six decades later, he quipped to Sabine Offe in the midst of an academic brouhaha over identity politics, "Well, when I was young, we did not have problems with our identity, we had problems with identity-papers!" At summer's end, he decided to return to Paris and moved into a flat with Ursula and Ernst in the fifteenth arrondissement, where many from the first wave of German refugees were starting to congregate. There were always new guests arriving in this "collective apartment," mainly Germans bearing the latest news from the political front. There were also unwelcome guests: swarms of cockroaches and bed bugs. The plague was so bad that Otto Albert contrived a system to place the legs of the beds into cups of kerosene; this flammable solution appears to have kept the armies of insects at bay. Like so many of the expatriates, Ernst, a Communist militant, spent his days anxiously waiting for the news of an uprising, ready to return to join the valiant struggle. But even Ursula could see the limits of her companion's Communist dogma and vain hopes; after a while the brew of love and historical materialism soon lost its appeal and the couple broke up. Otto Albert, who found Ernst's party line a deterrent to conversation, was pleased to see him go. This left Otto Albert and Ursula together in the squalid flat, where they became especially close. Having bonded as activists and shared the discouragement of their parents, they still had their differences: Ursula had joined the Communist Party, whereas Otto Albert never regarded it more than a necessary, if distasteful, ally in the common front against fascism. But party affiliation did not get in the way of what blossomed into "a beautiful friendship." "We lived," Hirschman was to recall, "without having secrets from each other, in any case very few. We talked about everything that concerned us, my relationships with other women and her preferences for other men."[4]

Meanwhile, Hirschmann had ideas for himself. Though he spent the first months wondering how long he would have to wait to return home, it did not take him long to move on. Indeed, there were early indications that he was considering staying in France for a while. In early 1933, as another gray winter was lifting, he wrote a letter to his former girlfriend, Inge Franck, Peter's sister. He had to apologize for leaving Berlin without saying goodbye and for not having written yet. She replied: "I believe you will always be pressed for time."[5] She was prescient. In the next few years, there would be a sense of restlessness in Hirschmann's choices and commitments, a waning appeal of return but no clear sign that he wanted to go anywhere else in particular. Hirschmann was neither a cast-away Odysseus struggling to get home nor an immigrant determined to make himself anew in another place. There is more of a wandering quality; one that would detach him gradually from inherited ways of thinking about the world.

The Paris that greeted Hirschmann in 1933 was in some ways not unlike Berlin a few years earlier. The Great Depression had eviscerated the prosperity of the 1920s. France's slump was less precipitous than Germany's; it was delayed. By 1933, when Germany, Britain, and the United States were showing inklings of recovery, France was beginning to suffer seriously. Businesses were collapsing, factories shutting down, and the protectionist cycle on the rise. By 1935, one in six workers was unemployed. Wages were cut drastically. Everywhere people tightened their belts and did with less—less food, less coal, less everything. In early 1934, the Théâtre de la Michodière opened its doors to Édouard Bourdet's *Les Temps difficiles*; factory closures were as much the backdrop as the stage on which the actors performed. Among the options that Hirschmann had, finding a real job with career prospects was not, in these circumstances, in the cards. Aside from tutoring the Dupuy boys in German, he would have to find his sustenance, and fill his days, doing something else.[6]

This did not bother Hirschmann; he had a quarry in mind. His brief time at the University of Berlin had piqued his interest in economics. The question now was how to pursue his studies in Paris, where Hirschmann did not have at his disposal the same code of understanding he enjoyed in Berlin. One of his first destinations in Paris was the Librairie Gibert Jeune on Boulevard Saint Michel; he emerged with a copy of *Le livret de l'étudiant*, a bulky compendium of information about Paris's schools. He began to pore over it and found just the place: the École libre des sciences politiques, known as Sciences Po. This is where he wanted to study. At this point, another contact influenced the course of Hirschmann's decisions. Ulrich Friedemann, his father's best friend, had given OA the name of a distinguished French pediatrician, Robert Debré. Hirschmann plucked up the courage to approach him, and Debré invited him over to his home, a capacious villa on the Left Bank, to hear the young German's story. When Otto Albert explained that he wanted to study economics at a place described in the *livret*, Sciences Po, Debré summoned his son, Michel Debré (later a prominent Gaullist), who was at the time enrolled at that institution. Only a few years older than OA, Michel Debré also listened to Hirschmann's story. But when he got to Sciences Po, Michel dissuaded him from considering it because "you are a refugee, you can *never* become a diplomat or a civil servant," and Sciences Po was tailored only for that kind of career. Why not consider another grande école, such as the École des hautes études commerciales de Paris? Better known as HEC, this école was more oriented to people with a business career in mind and still qualified, at least on paper, as one of France's elite schools. This seemed like sensible enough advice; after all, the stateless Hirschmann was barred from most liberal professions. The elder Debré was keen to see Otto Albert pursue his interests and agreed that his son's advice probably made good sense. Whether there is a whiff of anti-Semitism in the advice to study business and accounting, not economics and statesmanship, is impossible to know, though Sciences Po was not known for its hospitality to Jews.[7]

The option for HEC had its appeals, but it had not jumped out from the pages of the *livret*, for the fact was, Hirschmann had little interest in being a businessman. It had no affinity with the liberal arts that he had been raised to value. As a result, Sciences Po would always gnaw at his soul because he hadn't pursued it more fully; he nurtured a sense that the education he might have gotten there would have better satisfied his academic curiosities, not least because the education that he did get at HEC was miserable. Every time he neared rue Saint-Guillaume, where Sciences Po's main building was located, an inner wave of lament would sweep over him; in general not a man to nurse regrets, this was a misfortune that was difficult to forget. The main advantage of HEC was that it enabled him to move to the Cité Internationale Universitaire, a cluster of dormitories on Boulevard Jourdan for foreign students and French citizens from outside Paris, and by a stroke of luck, he found lodgings in the Maison des Étudiants Arméniens.

Getting through the dispiriting routine of HEC testifies to Hirschmann's determination and to his sense that he should make the best of his limited options. Among HEC's first appeals was that it was perceived as an elite, discerning, place to study. The École des hautes études commerciales was one in a constellation of grandes écoles, selective institutions of higher education designed to train France's elite to rule the country. And yet, from its opening in the 1880s, it never quite gained the status of its predecessors and was regarded more as a "petite grande école" or for snootier commentators, a "*super-lycée*." Attending HEC was a way for well-to-do young men to reduce their military service from three to one year by, in effect, taking accounting and banking courses. By 1923, after the upheavals of the war, the HEC directors set out to upgrade the curriculum, and even borrowed examples of the Harvard Business School—with few results and no dent in its reputation as a "wannabe" school. Through the 1930s, it had chronic "empty classrooms and [a] disconnected attitude regarding the life of enterprise." Admission standards collapsed, thus aggravating the sense that the school did little for elites to perpetuate their status; and with low enrollments, the school's revenues slumped; and without tuitions, professors' pay was miserly, and many quit or ignored their duties.[8] For Hirschmann, the heart of the problem at HEC was basic: it did not teach economics. Even in Berlin he was aware that economics was more than the study of how businesses functioned, as if the mysteries of supply and demand could be reduced to routine practices of double-entry bookkeeping and rudimentary engineering. But that is precisely what HEC offered. One of Hirschmann's courses was on "technology," which amounted to excurses into various aspects of industrial processing, with special emphasis on *concassage* (crushing). This was a far cry from David Ricardo, Adam Smith, or the analysis of the causes of the Great Depression that dominated his reading in Berlin. OA found it mind-numbing.

There were a few exceptions, but they more often proved the general rule about HEC faculty. Albert Demangeon gave "brilliant lectures" in economic geography, enlivened—rare for an HEC professor—with large, colorful maps. A specialist in the study of how economic sectors were located in particular places and the role of natural resources in industrial development, Demangeon introduced Hirschmann to the notion of interregional commerce and trade between geographic zones as precepts of global traffic. A lecture on the competition between Antwerp and Rotterdam provided a dramatic illustration of how underlying structural forces shaped economic rivalries. Another of Demangeon's lectures dealt with Russia's dependence on foreign trade before the First World War: the "black soil" of the Ukraine was a breadbasket for the rest of Europe and a source of hard exchange for the tsar. As Moscow joined the war, Russia's minister of foreign trade was fond of exclaiming, "Let's die of hunger," though adding, "but let's be sure to export!" Demangeon included his own addendum: "And the minister was the more ready to say that *he* was not the one about to die of hunger!" Hirschmann was rapt. Demangeon was not just making fun of a tsarist official, but also making a point about the dilemma that some countries *really* faced. For the first time, Hirschmann, the progeny of a political economy hinged on the labor theory of value, began to think about conflict in terms beyond the prism of social classes, about sources of world disequilibrium lying outside the tension between bosses and workers. Demangeon laid some very preliminary grounds for Hirschmann's thinking about trade and economic development. It was also a very pragmatic, empirical sensibility that liberated Hirschmann from the abstract Marxism of the 1930s—or for that matter, planners and Keynesians in the 1950s whose elegant but grandiose mechanisms never appealed to Hirschmann's real-worldliness.[9]

The Académie pour étudiants étrangers, where he was required to enroll as the portal to HEC, seems to have taxed his stamina. He had no friends. The courses consisted mainly of accounting, which could not have been more distant from his readings of Otto Bauer or Hegel the year before. At the end of the year, Hirschmann took the comprehensive examinations, which would determine his eligibility to enter the main école. He sailed through and passed into the mainstream of the HEC curriculum, only to discover that it was only a notch above his first year's studies. The courses were old-fashioned, dictated recitations of accounting, business, and legal matters that students were then expected to memorize for exams. There were no discussions, no readings beyond the basic manuals. Most students "were very nationalistic." "We noted what the professor said, and that must be committed to memory. That was really horrible." For all intents and purposes, there was no teaching of economics. "Today the HEC started again," he wrote to his mother in April 1934, trying to strike an up-beat tone, "and it's all about Statistics without interruption (with only 3 days for Pentecost) until July." He managed to find some silver on the lining: "I work now more often in the—cute, small—library of the current National Statistics Office and spoke recently with the director there, who, in a very friendly manner gave me information about the exam and about a few things I didn't understand from his lectures."[10]

Hirschman's life can be tracked by the ways in which he handled disappointment and idleness: the first was bearable, the second he loathed. Faced with HEC drudgery, he turned to what, for lack of anyone to tell him otherwise, he considered to be real economics, like that of Rosa Luxembourg and Rudolf Hilferding. Unfortunately for Hirschmann, these Marxist works were losing their appeal. But there was no one to instruct him on what he might read instead. Solace was found in long novels by Russian and French writers, thus inaugurating a habit of tacking between the masterworks of fiction and hard-nosed political economy, and as so many of his readers have noted, finding the relations between the two. As his final exams at HEC approached, disheartened by the routine of memorization, he rediscovered Dostoevsky. He had asked his mother to send him his copies of *Crime and Punishment* ("and I repeat my request for more volumes," he pleaded more than once). He had to study, "but now I must get to know more Dostoevsky." He buried himself in *The Brothers Karamazov*. Instead of preparing for exams, he got lost in the epic drama about family, betrayal, religious doubt, and madness. This would cost him the top spot in his graduating class; Hirschmann blamed the brooding, Russian novelist. "I then received the diploma. That was the only thing that had any value, a diploma from the École des Hautes Études Commerciales."[11]

There is a question of how he supported himself while he was a student. In the first few months, he was clearly dependent on remittances from Mutti. His letters to her in that first year acknowledge the receipt of transfers. What happened thereafter, especially as the Nazis plundered Mutti's resources, is less clear. But among the few clues is a document in Hirschman's personal papers from the Comité français de l'Entraide universitaire internationale that gave scholarships to students from around the world to attend French universities. This typed letter of glowing reference from R. Arasse, secretary of the Comité français, noted how O. A. Hirschmann "immediately called attention to us, for the titles that he possesses and the *notes élogieuses* that he has received in his examinations." Clearly, the performance at the Collège in Berlin, a credential that would have called attention on its own, paid off. The letter, however, continued. It noted the baccalauréat, the fact that Monsieur Hirschmann was the "author" of a work on Hegel's philosophy, with some sense that the Comité had received some kind of endorsement from one of his tutors, his *maître* (possibly Bernd Knoop), as well as his preliminary course work in political economy at the Institute of Political Science and Statistics at the University of Berlin. The letter refers to his two reports on classical political economy. The result: "We have therefore decided to help M. Hirschmann for the duration of his studies in France. He has not disappointed us. After having successfully passed a certificate at the Institute for Statistics, he was accepted at" HEC. This letter is undated but appears to have been written prior to his having completed his studies at HEC, for it notes that Hirschman was currently ranked fifth in his class of 220 students, with reference to grades from two previous years of studies and preliminary results for his Easter examinations. There is an indication that he also made some money "by giving numerous lessons" and that he earned "each time, *des cerificats élogieux.*" Was this a letter recommending him for further scholarship—for instance to go to London? The timing might suggest so. But what it does imply is that the scholarship and part-time teaching covered his living.[12]

Between the care packages with shirts and cookies from Mutti, some family money at the outset, tutoring German, and winning a scholarship, Hirschmann scraped by. But these were tough years. The staple of his diet was a baguette with butter. He would later jokingly claim that having eaten so many he deserved some fame for having discovered this unique culinary combination which he baptized "un sandwich au pain." It is revealing that privilege did not make of him an inert man once it was gone. Indeed, the new circumstances brought out an inner reserve of resourcefulness and a stock of hope that would motivate him to seize opportunities when they appeared—or to make them if they didn't.

As the news from home went from bad to worse, he worried about his mother and sister in Berlin. "Wonderful for you these days," he wrote to Mutti, "means above all peaceful, without the external agitations that have been so many in the last years and especially in the last year." He exhorted her to enjoy her new work: wonderful "does not mean dull; to the contrary, I hope that you find a position to fill that makes you still useful to society and that you also let yourself feel this." With Carl's income gone and the family finances in ruins, Hedwig Hirschmann had to leave the apartment on Hohenzollernstrasse. This must have been a difficult choice, and it no doubt inspired a wailing letter from Mutti, which explains Otto Albert's chirpy tone. With the large furnishings and extensive dishes and cutlery, Mutti, who was apparently not without some skill in eking out opportunities on her own, set up a boardinghouse. At her new quarters she began taking in lodgers, filling rooms with Jews whose stores and occupations were being shut down in the anti-Semitic rampaging. With the help of donations from an American Jewish ladies' charitable organization, Mutti hired a cook and several maids and was soon able to feed not only the boarders but other needy guests as well. She managed to put sweets, rice puddings, and other plates on the table, providing a decent fare for persecuted neighbors.[13]

If Hirschmann was trying to move forward with his life, troubled memories of that final year in Berlin were an undertow. The letters that have survived to his mother are replete with efforts to come to terms with the family's past. "I wish for you," he noted, "that you should not and cannot resent me—that you learn somewhat better to understand the life and efforts of your children and don't call them a 'disappointment' when they sometimes don't take the exact path that you thought out as the ideal path for them." Hedda's disapproval of Otto Albert's militancy, his choice for something as apparently déclassé as economics, and his more general reluctance to live up to her expectations of success had been so fraught. Her son was also trying to come to terms with his own choices—and here possibly revealing some of his own misgivings about his decisions. Either way, he was insisting that she hear him now: "The most important thing for mutual love is that we understand and appreciate each other. The bible says: God made man in his own image. Maybe. But man definitely can't do the same." Nor did distance appear to heal old wounds. Two years after his departure from Berlin, the question of "return" was still plagued by memories of unresolved, and unresolvable, conflicts. April was always a difficult month, entwining his and his mother's birthday with the anniversary of his father's death and his sudden flight; he was subject to yearnings, "blissful at the idea immediately to return." In 1935, the occasion triggered memories of his Hegel paper and his thinking about parent-child dialectics from *Phenomenology*. Not even the meeting with "a very nice pretty Norwegian girl" could dispel his mood. "Such cruelty," he wrote to his mother in Hegelese, "which for parents certainly will be felt as painfully as a disappointment, which the children could not spare them and should not in my opinion, which they can only make in form as inoffensive as possible, such a cruelty comes about each time that the parents (which is exceptionally natural and understandable), out of their wishes, out of their development, out of their imagination, demand something of their child, which is justified neither in the wishes, nor the development, nor the world of thoughts of the child." He tried to clarify himself to Mutti: "I only want to say that parents with reasonably independent-minded children, especially in the years of their decisive *Bildung*, must simply be disappointed because they, for example, demand togetherness precisely when another use of time will appear as much more valuable to the child." The passage from *Phenomenology* about the dialectics of the master-serf relationship (in which the former depends on the latter's recognition as a condition of his full consciousness, while the latter possesses only the power to deny this) had of course been the subject of endless scrutiny in Berlin. But now Hirschmann was finding in it an explanation for his current malaise and a way to expiate some of his guilt about leaving his family behind. "You will wonder why I write you all this so suddenly? These thoughts have been living with me for a long time and I had barely started writing a page (of the description of my departure), and they (the words) all came out without me knowing or wanting it. I fail to see why you should not know it."[14]

One decision that Hirschmann was making did bear on his HEC studies: he concluded that they were, for the most part, useless. If they were meant to prepare him for the business world, this was not a world he cared to join. This choice, he feared, might compound his mother's disappointment: "I don't have the norm of the gross-bourgeois in me, I see it in others, am uncertain and unoriginal. . . . What are the practical ramifications of this? This is not yet clear to me, I see only a few things that I won't go after: some kind of apprenticeship position in a bank or a business, where it would be assured, I could not work my way up."[15] At the time, one of his options was to go overseas with a French bank. There were few jobs to be had in Paris, and even fewer in Berlin. But some opportunities were opening in South America, where the industrialization of Brazil and Argentina was luring European bankers. The Banco Italo-Frances was considering Hirschmann for a position.

Paris also meant solitude. Unable to make friendships at HEC and queasy about émigré affairs, he spent more and more time on his own. He took solo trips. The seclusion also affected his relationships with women. Early on, he rekindled his relationship with Lia Rein, whose family had similarly fled to Paris. But the relationship did not endure; Lia was determined to pursue a career in medicine, while Otto Albert wanted a companion in his restlessness, someone who could adapt to what was becoming a more and more peripatetic life. Once the affective ties with Lia were broken, no one filled this gap. As if to cover the subject that he knew was on his mother's mind in order to dispense with it, he informed her pithily: "I haven't been able to manage a lasting girlfriend yet." He did, however, find refuge in Paris's chess cafés, which had been—like the Café de la Régence—important salons in which the world's champions had gathered from the eighteenth century. There was one near the Palais Royale where Otto Albert enjoyed playing and watching games.[16]

Meanwhile, Paris was filling up with refugees. At first there were the Russians. Then the Italians. After 1933, thousands of Germans began to flood Paris, looking for cheap hotel rooms and work of any kind. For most, the grip of statelessness tightened over their despairing quest. Without proper papers, they could not get decent work, and without work, it was harder to cover the expenses of getting the right papers. Nativism hung heavy in the air. In late 1933, a scandal erupted involving a shady businessman of Russian-Hungarian-Romanian origins, Serge Alexandre Stavisky, whose money-dealings contaminated ruling party circles all the way to the top—and led to a general outcry about the pernicious influence of foreigners on the French state. Social unrest compounded the hysteria. In February of the next year, mass rioting and police brutality tore Paris apart; on February 6, fascistoid Croix de Feu militants marched down the Champs-Élysée toward the National Assembly, where the Communists were staging their own rally. They converged, with nervous police huddled in formation, at the Place de la Concorde—until the gendarmes opened fire, killing fifteen and leaving hundreds wounded. The new prime minister, Daladier, had to resign in disgrace. The Third Republic had never been a model of stability; from 1924 to 1931, fifteen cabinets came and went. The Depression only accelerated the revolving doors along the Quai D'Orsay. There was a general sense that foreigners made things worse. To an observer like Hirschmann, this must have been déjà vu, but he managed to avoid much of the tension because, unlike many of the émigrés who flocked to Paris, he was so young. At seventeen, he could simply restart his studies; armed with a student visa he avoided the vicious cycle that drove other, especially older, émigrés to distraction.[17]

Statelessness affected Hirschmann's intellectual development in more ways than one. Statelessness can make people *more* political. It did for Hannah Arendt and others, for whom the displacement occasioned by German bigotry and intolerance directed them toward new Jewish identities, especially Zionism. But these were Jews whose upbringing provided anchorage in Jewish culture and ties to a community upon which to build a new political faith and commitment. "The question of a 'return' to Judaism never came up for me [ne s'est jamais posée pour moi]," he explained many years later to his grandson Grégoire on the occasion of his Bar Mitzvah. "First of all, it was never instilled in my upbringing . . . and above all I would have sensed that an embrace of Judaism as a *reaction*, as something history imposed on me which I then had to live (persecution), and for me the question was how not to submit to this miserable history created by Historic Laws (because there are none)."[18]

There was, of course, an alternative appeal, to Communism—whose internationalism gave its militants satellites in most of the world's major cities. This secular faith was even less enticing. Hirschmann groped for his own way without a guiding ism. He did not feel particularly burdened by this lack; indeed, in many respects he did not even consider himself an exile, but rather a "foreign student." Therein lay another important difference between Hirschmann and many of the other familiar names we associate with the émigrés in Paris who wore their intellectual heritage like a badge of honor, hanging on to it, possibly because there was so little else to hang on to. For elders such as Hannah Arendt or Walter Benjamin, Paris was a new setting for working out older problems. They had come to Paris already formed, with intellectual projects and concerns to which exile gave new poignancy. In contrast to a younger Hirschmann, unformed by the German university system, already multilingual, and never quite as smitten by German philosophy, they were decidedly more connected to their pasts, and in a sense therefore more despairing. When pressed by a German interviewer about the "disappearance of hope" that afflicted many Germans in France, Hirschmann resisted: "It never really was the disappearance of hope for me."[19]

But did these efforts mean that he was not an exile? Not quite. Exile was more of a stage than a condition. At the outset, return was the expectation. "Everybody had, as, I think Brecht put it in one of his poems," Hirschman later recalled, "a suitcase always packed. It was the idea that the day may come very soon in which we might go back." When Nazi infighting erupted in 1934 around the Ernst Röhm affair, many, Hirschmann included, thought the time for return had come. Instead, the botched overthrow gave Hitler free rein to slaughter rivals within his party. "It turned out to be a consolidation of the regime," not "the beginning of the end," thought Hirschmann retrospectively. It reminded him that History had a way of betraying those who stored too much confidence in it, and its pseudo-laws. It was not just Hirschmann who watched Hitler consolidate his grip by wiping out rivals; Stalin, too, admired the Nazi purges and SS murders of hundreds of SA storm troopers. A few months later, a gunman shot Sergei Kirov, the Leningrad party boss, ushering in a wave of Bolshevik cleansing and inaugurating a duet between Hitler and Stalin that culminated in the pact to divide Poland six years later.[20]

Having started as a refugee, a citizen of another country stripped of his basic rights, Hirschmann was on his way to some other, still undetermined, status. One sign of this shift was his effort to cover the tracks of his own origins: his accent. Keen to erase where he could the outward markers of his foreignness, to pass as his forefathers had from Jew to German without a public trace, he was determined to make his French indistinguishable from a Parisian's. When he rode the Metro, he ground off German inflections from his French by reading the station names or advertisements posted on the sides of the carriages out loud, practicing rolling his *r*'s, softening his consonants, exercising the nuanced range of *u*, *eu*, *ou*. The efforts paid off: his French was soon impeccable and accent-free. There would be no passing for French so long as he spoke like all the teeming émigrés, many of whom were beginning to encounter the increasingly hostile face of the French state. Indeed, Hirschmann took pride in his ability to walk up to a policeman and speak with him as a test of his "passing" skills.[21]

Aside from some remarkable linguistic skills, credit for this transition must also go to the ways in which statelessness gave him new intellectual coordinates, coordinates he was prepared to orient to. One formative source of new coordinates was in fact an old contact from Berlin. Ursula had found a place in the servant's quarters of the Rein family's apartment in the fourteenth arrondissement, near the Porte d'Orléans. The Reins had fled the German capital a few months earlier, in February. Lia, OA's old flame from the SAJ, had enrolled in the Collège Sévigné, to complete her studies before moving on to the medical school of the Sorbonne. In the meantime, Ursula and Mark (who had completed his education as an engineer) had also become romantically involved—a much more intense and volatile affair than Lia and Otto Albert's fleeting romance. The foursome, redoubled by the travails of making their way as refugees in Paris, composed a tight unit of displacement, friendship, and love, which brought Otto Albert into close contact with Lia's formidable father, Rafael Rein.

More publicly known as Rafael Abramovitch, Rein was only too glad to welcome the magnetic Ursula and pensive Otto Albert into the family. He was less a paternal surrogate for Otto Albert than a presence in a moment in which the Marxistoid ether in which Hirschmann had been educated in the last years in Berlin was thinning out. Rein kept up his activism. If anything, he was considered more and more as a pariah to those in power in Moscow. As a leader of the Russian Workers Social Democratic Party in exile, a prominent person in the Labor and Socialist International, and a journalist for several papers, including the American *Jewish Daily Forward*, he lent his voice to the campaign against the Menshevik Trial in 1931—for which he would earn a privileged place on Stalin's hit list and eventually pay a truly awful price.

Hirschmann, who had his own mounting concerns about Communism, tuned in to Rafael's frequency. Leavened by Russian cordiality, the

Rein apartment was a "gregarious kind of place," full of visitors and an air thick with discussion and debate. While his wife, Rosa, kept the teapots hot and full and toiled in kitchen to feed the constant turnover of visitors, there was always someone with whom the sometimes lonely Otto Albert could talk. The Rein apartment was a refuge from the anti-intellectual and right-wing milieu of HEC, and for all that the family had witnessed, it abounded with generosity and affection. Otto Albert would come to respect Rafael's political judgment and see him, increasingly, as a sage; for Rafael's part, the convulsions of the Russian Revolution and Hitler's rise had taught him a few things, and he was protectively skeptical of his children and their friends' political naïveté. After the Röhm incident, which sent German exiles pouring over the news in search of evidence for Hitler's imminent downfall, Rafael warned them prophetically that this was Hitler's consolidation; the Bolsheviks had done the same. Mark tried to temper his father's condemnation of Communism. With the wall of his room in Paris covered with photos of Viennese workers killed in the struggle for socialism, Mark still nurtured hopes for a common front and yearned to return to Berlin to rejoin the struggle, a prospect that no doubt petrified the father. As the divide opened in the Rein apartment, Otto Albert sensed that he leaned more toward Rafael's realism than to Mark's idealism—which did not always make it easy to accept: "Sometimes one is angry at people who are always right," he said, looking back.[22]

Things were not, as a result, always so smooth in the quartet of Otto Albert and Ursula and Mark and Lia. For one, while Mark was not as critical of Communists as his father, he was not a fellow traveler. But Ursula was. Indeed, at one point, an agent of the Comintern, which had its eye out on bothersome exiles like Rafael Rein, asked Ursula to spy on the "counterrevolutionary" family for Moscow. Then they offered her money to steal documents related to *Vestnik* from the flat. This suggestion that she violate her own personal affections, plus the stormy discussions with Mark, had their effects; within months of her moving in with the Reins, she began to sever her ties with the Communist Party. This was a difficult break, which Mark helped cauterize. When Ursula finally told her Comintern handler that she would not do their bidding, she was icily accused of "petty bourgeois prejudices." This was the beginning of the end of her romance with the party. The Rein's familial love helped her handle what was for many militants an abyss. Otto Albert, never affiliated, had no need; he was losing any affection for Marxist certainties all on his own.[23]

Loneliness and displacement may have fractured some of his bearings, but not all of them, and not completely; Marxism's appeal did not simply vanish just because Hitler's opponents had to flee, thereby discrediting claims about the ineluctable power of Theory. Indeed, there was a diasporic movement that sought to rally the defeated scattered around European capitals and breathe new life into radical thinking. The letters to Mutti reveal a young man still understanding himself according to the coordinates of German idealism. And when it came to his political vocations, Marxian social democracy also retained its purchase. In the evenings, after his studies, Hirschmann joined his sister and friends in reading and discussion groups, debating doctrine and prospects for their return. The debates at the congress of the Labor and Socialist International in Paris in late August 1933 focused on the "German question." Kurt Landau, a charismatic Austrian Marxist, tarred as a Trotskyite (for which, in the end, he would pay with his life at the hands of Stalin's death squads in Barcelona), had moved to Paris in early 1934 and from there blasted away at the German Communists' fundamentalism, calling for a new paradigm for the Left. He "had an impressive way of arguing," recalled Hirschman, who admired the ability "to deduce quite precisely what is to be done and in which phase we happen to find ourselves. . . . This typical political-revolutionary capacity for analyzing the situation, recognizing the parallelogram of forces and then to make a decision . . . that seemed very impressive to me."[24]

This was not the first time Hirschmann had a brush with figures like these. The repression of 1933 broke up the old SAJ, pushing its remnants underground or into exile, where it subsisted in semiclandestinity. It was in these circles of displacement that Hirschmann nurtured a soft spot for men who applied intellectual prowess to political situations to fathom creative possibilities for the future. Landau's captivating ability to contour his historical analysis to the crisis was on display more generally in the writings of German émigrés circulating in the diaspora. These included Erich Schmidt—who had mentored Hirschmann, Willy Brandt, and others in the campaign to forge a pan-left coalition against fascism—and Walter Löwenheim (aka Miles), the founders of the ORG. When Löwenheim had to make a fast getaway in the early months of Hitler's government, he fled to Prague; there he penned a small book that would connect the strategy of alliance-building with a Marxist theory of history by making sense of the world that had been so shattered by the events of 1933. Called *Neu Beginnen: Faschismus order Sozialismus* and inspired by Lenin's *What Is to Be Done?*, the book was widely read among German exile groups. To Hirschmann, "Löwenheim formulated the first truly serious analysis of national socialism, especially because he distinguished himself from the orthodox Marxist versions in which Nazism appears only a new expression of late capitalism."[25] *Neu Beginnen* was the first tract to break with the schematic style precisely because it pointed to a crisis that was much more than a logical, inevitable residual of capitalism. The pamphlet was a centerpiece of a raging debate among Socialists. After the Popular Front period, initiated in 1935, and the start of Moscow's show trials, it folded into a ferocious debate that transcended theoretical issues. As the fate of the Spanish Republic would show, the stakes were deeply political as well.

The standard Communist line was altogether too unidimensional and dogmatic for Hirschmann's tastes. What he had liked so much about Lenin's 1917 writings was the grappling with actual political events and the seizing of opportunities. *Neu Beginnen* had the same appeal and became a touchstone in an increasingly acrimonious debate among émigrés. Indeed, as Otto Albert, Ursula, Lia, and Mark discussed the work and identified with its injunctive style, it added fuel to the debates in the Rein household; Rafael was not at all swayed by its voluntarist message. Though well intended, the view that Social Democrats and Communists could bury past enmities was condemned to crash against Stalin's Manicheanism. For Mark and Rafael, son and father, *Neu Beginnen* was the source of much discussion.

It is worth dwelling a bit more on the text because for Hirschmann it was more than a strategic manifesto. It was also an analytical template that reappears with similar overtones in his later writings about crises—his own effort to come to terms with the origins of fascism in Germany, explanations of authoritarianism in Latin America, and his analyses of the crisis of the welfare state. *Neu Beginnen* was a remarkably astute appraisal of the crisis and at times devastatingly honest criticism of the Left. In many respects no less Marxist than the orthodoxies it sought to challenge, it called upon readers to abandon the pipe dream that Nazism was just some momentary blip of capitalism en route to revolution. Rather, Nazism, as a variant of fascism, was a full-blown model that sought to resolve the underlying contradictions of capitalism, which the Depression laid bare. The result: all hopes for a "spontaneous" uprising of the working classes and a reopening for the refugees to go home were starry-eyed. They had to deal with some realities: Hitler's regime was pulling capitalism from the crisis, which the Weimar Republic could not. Miles went further, suggesting a "tendency"—evidenced in Hungary, Spain, England, and France itself—to replace democratic forms of the state with fascist ones. This wave had to be taken seriously in order to stop it. The opposition had to start by putting aside all fundamentalist convictions that History was on the side of socialism. It had to defend democracy and restore socialism's working-class agenda. "Fascist capitalism," like the "democratic capitalism" it was eclipsing, had to be overthrown; it would not fall of its own accord.[26] Scarcely a few months since Hitler's seizure of power, here was an effort to do more than take stock; it was to take responsibility for a crisis that left progressives far worse off than they were before it began. They could not console themselves with bromides about History being on their side.

The manifesto was more important to Hirschmann as a model of analysis than as a roadmap for political practice. The organizational following of ORG was never very large (its numbers probably never surpassed 300), though it had chapters in most main German cities; those were eventually exterminated by 1935. Thereafter, ORG survived mainly in exile—Prague, Amsterdam, London, and Paris—and without ballast in Germany, becoming better known as the New Beginning movement, after the foundational booklet. For all the ferment and excitement, politics remained an abstract vocation; there was no party, no militancy for it to sire, and no way of putting this new "theory" into practice. That would change with the outbreak of the Spanish Civil War in the summer of 1936. But for the time being, politics was confined to intriguing about what to do next and with whom to do it; to Hirschmann this "debate" was almost as sterile as his HEC courses. Meetings, especially where Communists were present, invariably began with the ritualistic pieties: "Comrades, let's talk first *sachlich* and then *persönlich* (first objectively and then subjectively)." Invariably, "whether and how to align with Communists" became the end point of many discussions, which spun in circles as long as one side of the new coalition saw the others through the epigrams of "bourgeois," "deviationist," "Trostkyist," "counterrevolutionary," and countless other forms of opprobrium.[27] The debate was one-sided and endless. In a way, this suited Hirschmann, not because he was fond of being tarred, but because he was already yearning for a new intellectual repertoire. He was tiring of the circularity of émigré ways and obsessions. The language that once seemed so illuminating was starting to feel incarcerating. When it came time for his eighteenth birthday, Paris' famous *grisaille* parted to let the sun beam through; Hirschmann preferred to enjoy it alone, finding a spot in the Luxembourg Gardens to remember his father, to digest a letter from Mutti, and especially to read some Dostoevsky "in peace." He ate lunch by himself at a student bistro on Saint Michel, walked back to the gardens until dinner, when he picked up Ursula and they splurged at a restaurant on the Champs-Élysées.[28]

What shaped the disenchantment with old ways of thinking was above all the growing sense that Communists made more than just uncomfortable bedfellows; they made bad ones. He had seen enough duplicity and tolerated enough dogma; Rafael Rein's wisdom was seeping through. But so was Hirschmann's recognition that Communists were happy to live with a yawning gap between their claims to revolutionary purity and their ability to muster resistance. Ursula's memoir recounts that her brother had less and less patience for the party's hard line. Hugo, a fellow student in her Parisian cell and a Stalin devotee, depleted everyone's forbearance with his ad hominem and ritual tales of heroic deeds by the true believers in Germany. One day, a slighter older man—also a German émigré—met with the cell and witnessed one of Hugo's performances, as well as Otto Albert and Ursula's skeptical queries and criticisms. After the meeting, this man introduced himself as Heinrich and asked them about their "bellyaches" (the euphemism for doubts about the party line). Otto Albert, familiar with the expression, feigned ignorance; he had no interest in pursuing the discussion further. So, Heinrich indulged the teenager and asked point blank if both of them had difficulties with the party. They both replied, "Yes." Heinrich nodded charitably and explained that he could "help comrades" restore their faith in the party with "prolonged conversations." He was one of the party's intellectual fixers. Ursula was less bothered by the patronizing attitude and was still at that stage of struggling with her beliefs. Her brother, however, was never retrievable, and the supposition that he was a young, impressionable naïf, struck him as offensive; thereafter, he referred to Heinrich disdainfully as The Man.

The Man persisted, so the siblings agreed to accompany Heinrich on long walks and endured his sermons on the Russian Revolution, Lenin, the role of exile militants. Otto Albert's patience eventually ran out—and he stopped appearing, sending in his vote of no confidence in absentia. This, as it turned out, suited The Man fine, since he was more interested in Ursula anyway. Alone with her, he was prepared not only to share his party pieties but also to profess his love for her. Once again, Ursula got herself caught up in an awkward romance of entangled love and ideology, which ended, like so many precursors, with a distraught, heart-broken suitor. Many years later, Heinrich surfaced once more in New York, as Heinrich Blücher, the husband of Hannah Arendt; the years had passed, but the outward affection for didactic certainties had not. In Paris, Blücher had succeeded in confirming many of Hirschmann's doubts about Communism; three decades later, it struck Hirschman that the air of conviction that hovered over Blücher and Arendt, and to which Americans were flocking in search of answers, had still not lifted.[29]

At this point, a determinate force entered his life. It came via Ursula, who, as Otto Albert turned more reclusive, became more and more his sole source of companionship. In the spring of 1935, two years into Otto Albert's sojourn in Paris, Ursula was clearly at a fundamental crossroads. Her romance with Mark Rein had never been a stable one, and it eventually gave way to a close friendship, though Mark himself never quite relinquished hopes of a rekindled love, which made Ursula feel awkward living under the same roof. Then the affair with Blücher was knotty and short-lived. Through friends, Ursula was introduced to Renzo Guia, a flamboyant and ebullient leftist from Turin, who in turn was introduced to OA. Guia became their tutor in Italian. But it was more than language he taught; Guia immediately disarmed Ursula with his humor and irreverence. He made fun of her Communist pieties, which brought forth his peals of laughter. This infected her—and she could not go back to the sobriety and certainty of her cell meetings and their rituals without smiling and shaking her head. Guia also told her about his own political affiliations, which he also conveyed to Otto Albert, who found them much more appealing than the old Germanic wardrobe he was shedding. At first, Guia struck Ursula as unserious—but Otto Albert found the humor—the dismissal of leftist conventions of highbrow moralism, "false activism," and sterile polemics—instantly liberating. When Ursula once insisted that individual acts of resistance violated the norms of being "useful to the movement," that it was better to wait for "objective conditions" to be ripe for action, Guia laughed back: "How important your language is for you! There is more value in one who rises and speaks out than in all your wise net of illegals [referring to refugees] who don't open their mouths but murmur the news into each other's ears." Then came a fatal jab. When Ursula explained that the working class was defining the premises of revolutionary actions, he reminded her of the history of passivity wrapped in theory: "To hell with your working class! It seems to me the moment has come to lose a bit of faith. . . . Twelve million organized Socialists and Communists, the most powerful working class movement in Europe . . . then comes Hitler and all stand still, nobody moves! Is that your discipline? What is it worth?"[30]

Otto Albert did not need a direct challenge to be moved by Guia's action-oriented philosophy. Though Guia's voluntarism would lead him to the tomb of the Spanish Civil War, where a Falangist bomb would kill him, there was a whole philosophy and movement behind it, called *Giustizia e Libertà* (Justice and Liberty), founded by Italian exiles in Paris in 1929 and whose intellects would soon occupy the space for Hirschmann that was once reserved for German idealism. But it was not Guia himself who would prove the determining influence.

To begin with, what prompted this interest in Italian? It was Ursula. Stuck in a morass of romantic and ideological impasses, she was withdrawing from the émigré circles. The prospects for returning to Berlin were dimming completely. At least her brother could immerse himself in Dostoevsky and his studies. These were not options for Ursula. In the spring of 1935, she wrote a confessional letter to Eugenio Colorni, in whose Berlin hotel room she and Otto Albert had composed their clandestine broadsheet in their final days of resistance to Hitler. Colorni was now in Trieste, a professor in a lyceum for women. This afforded him the time to write his major work on Leibnitz while frequenting the city's cafes to join in the discussions with antifascist friends and colleagues, such as Bruno and Gino Pincherle and Giorgio Radetti. Behind the scenes, he was also active in the Italian Socialist Party, which was having some of the same kinds of debates as its German cousin. He was also engaged to marry the daughter of a well-to-do local Jewish family. Ursula's letter, whose precise motives remain unclear, was potent enough to overturn Colorni's plans. He replied with an invitation for her to visit Trieste, which she accepted immediately. By April, she was on his doorstep; within days they were in love and Colorni's wedding was off. Ursula eventually returned to Paris, and from there a torrid exchange of letters ensued; Colorni visited Paris and introduced Ursula and Otto Albert to his exiled friends. OA was swept away by Eugenio's warmth, liveliness, and the fresh air he brought to what was becoming an increasingly stultified milieu. Ursula wrote Eugenio upon his return to Trieste to convey how much "OA would like to be with you, it is strange how he says this and not I."[31]

Colorni quickly became the colligative force in the Hirschmanns' lives—Ursula's, Otto Albert's, and even the young Eva's. Attractive, full of joy, a dispenser of uplifting and positive advice, a contrast to the gloom that prevailed over German exile circles, he was *the* person to whom they turned, as Eva put it.[32] That summer, Ursula and Otto Albert joined Colorni at the family resort at Forte dei Marmi on the Tuscan coast, a two-story villa with marvelous gardens, tennis courts, and giant fig tree under which siblings, cousins, and their children would gather to eat and talk. There were also a lot of meetings: friends—as well as political coconspirators—would converge from Milan. Some of these gatherings would retreat from the fig tree to meet behind closed doors. Eva also joined the vacationing circle briefly, seeing her brother and sister for the first time after so many years apart. A photograph shows a teenage Eva shouldering her beaming brother. It was over the course of the summer vacations, on the Tuscan beaches and in the town's small cafes, that Otto Albert and Eugenio would spend hours in conversation. Around the same

Otto Albert on Eva's shoulders, Forte di Marmi, 1935.

time, Colorni proposed to Ursula; they were married in Milan in December. The family was acquiring a new centripetal force. In the course of a few months, Colorni gave the Hirschmanns a whole new set of personal, political, and, for Otto Albert, intellectual coordinates.[33]

Colorni vastly expanded the horizons of his brother-in-law. For Otto Albert, Eugenio was to be the single most important intellectual influence. It began with the particular spirit of Colorni's political convictions. Born in 1909, Eugenio Colorni was a son of Milan's assimilated upper-middle-class Jews. He went to a distinguished lyceum and was enraptured by the liberal philosopher and historian, Benedetto Croce, who had published several monumental books about the nineteenth "century of liberty" and its legacies for the present. After entering the Faculty of Philosophy and Literature at the University of Milan, Colorni began a career of writing essays on aesthetics, ethics, psychoanalysis, and the philosophy of science. It was his interest in Leibnitz that led him to the University of Marburg, where he studied under Erich Auerbach, the brilliant philologist who had recently translated Giambattista Vico's *The New Science* into German and authored a celebrated study of Dante. In Marburg, Auerbach had turned to French authors of the seventeenth to the nineteenth centuries to prepare his classes, and one can presume that much of this rubbed off on the young Colorni, for his reading preferences bear important resemblances to the core of what was emerging as Auerbach's magisterial effort to connect written texts with lived experiences and to treat people and writers as Historical creatures. Auerbach would himself be driven by Nazis to Istanbul, where he would compose his masterwork, *Mimesis: The Representation of Reality in Western Literature*, a work he had begun in Marburg. Later, he would become a professor of literature at Yale, where Hirschman would finally meet him several decades later, shortly before Auerbach's death. "This afternoon we met a Polish friend of ours who teaches French here," he told Ursula, "and we got to know Professor Auerbach there. After some talking it turned out that he was the one who let Eugenio come to Marburg—he was a full professor there for Romanic languages and then later went to Istanbul. He passed through Trieste in the year 1937 (with his wife) and they met you then. . . . He seemed very nice, lively and intelligent, his wife apparently less so (and hard of hearing!)."[34] It is one of the ironic features of the century of massive, involuntary social dislocations that Hirschman had no idea how indirectly Auerbach had influenced him. It is "a very beautiful and famous book," he would tell Ursula many years later, when she was laboring on her own memoirs and wondered if her brother might help identify the mysterious Professor Auerbach to whom her Eugenio had gone for tutoring.[35]

Upon his reading *Mimesis*, there is no indication that Hirschman could see his own intellectual genealogy passing through Colorni back to Auerbach. It is hard enough for us to see—for there are only strong coincidences and notable echoes in the place of a direct, evidentiary paper trail. The critical link, Eugenio Colorni, would be killed by fascist thugs before he could leave behind a testimonial of his influence. It is not a stretch to observe a tie, however hidden, between Auerbach and Hirschman, for it was Auerbach who bequeathed a penchant for finding in classical works the origins of the present. To Auerbach, it was the divide between the Old Testament and Homer that set the stage for divergent traditions of literary realism. There was also the essayist style of criticism that Colorni adored and adopted, and his affection for long quotes as the basis for his *explication de texte* (which readers of Hirschman can find most developed in *The Passions and the Interests*). There was the great affection for the French novelists of the nineteenth century—Flaubert, Balzac, Stendhal—whose work was the apotheosis of a brand of literary realism that would become a touchstone for Hirschman for the rest of the century. But above all, there was a kind of serene erudition that nowadays seems as remote as the classics that shaped it, a style that owes itself to a particular perspective. "One must be aware, it seems to me," wrote Auerbach in 1953, "of regarding the exact sciences as our model; our precision relates to the particular." The great breakthroughs in the "historical arts" were the result of a refined "perspectival formation of judgment, which makes it possible to accord to various epochs and cultures their own presuppositions and views, to strive to the utmost towards the discovery of those, and to dismiss as unhistorical and dilettantish every absolute assessment of the phenomena that is brought in from outside."[36] This eye for particulars and their meanings imprinted itself on Hirschman, who was already questioning History's "laws" and searching for a spirit that was more epic because it was open to chance and to choice.

The full effects of this inheritance would not take effect immediately; the picking up and devouring of the literary canon would have taken time away from other callings. As it was, Auerbach was about books, habits of reading them, and the passage of intellectual traditions. But for the younger generation of Colorni and Hirschman, there was another reality in the mix: the political present. Colorni did not write much about politics per se, but he was intensely political and very involved in clandestine activities. It was impossible to immunize even his wedding in Milan from clandestine activity. On the evening before the ceremony, in the midst of the rehearsal dinner, Eugenio pulled Otto Albert aside and explained that "you have to accompany me to the Central Station. We can pretend that we are observing the old custom of 'burying the celibate's life.'" They slipped out of the proceedings. At the station, Eugenio asked Otto Albert to wait for him—and if he didn't return he was to notify "certain people." A perplexed future brother-in-law stood by while Eugenio disappeared into the crowd to make sure his cousin Emilio "Mimmo" Sereni boarded the train for Paris. Sereni, a brilliant, prolific author, and one of Mussolini's most trenchant Communist critics, was condemned to exile in Paris but had snuck back to Milan for the wedding and now needed to get out. Eventually, Eugenio returned from the platform, mission accomplished; the pair then dashed back to the wedding rehearsals.[37]

Paris became an active outpost for Italian exiles and their enemies, to the chagrin of French authorities. Thousands of Italian Communists fled to Paris, many of whom joined and became active in the French Section of the Communist International. This made Paris the site for expatriate political dueling. Between 1923 and 1933, twenty-eight Italian fascists were murdered.[38] For Italians, fascism's resilience was all too clear, and they could not help but shake their heads at German-exile expectations of Hitler's imminent fall. Many had been in Paris since the mid-1920s. Some, such as the literary scholar Leone Ginzburg, the writer-painter Carlo Levi, and the political theorist Norberto Bobbio, worked underground in Turin, Milan, and Trieste and would form the backbone of a resistance movement and the Party of Action when Mussolini was finally toppled, though Ginzburg himself would be tortured to death by Nazis in early 1944. Others, such as the Rosselli brothers, who staged a sensational getaway from prison on the island of Lipari, made Paris their base. They founded the *Giustizia e Libertà* movement as a cover for all progressives who were committed to ridding Italy of its despot.

The indomitable force of Carlo Rosselli brought together an alliance of liberals, socialists, republicans, Mazzinian nationalists, to imagine a postfascist order and to conspire to topple Mussolini. Bombings, audacious flights over Italian cities to shower leaflets, schemes to assassinate Il Duce, smuggling illegal newspapers like *Giustizia e Libertà*—there was no end to the clandestine praxis of liberty—and so long as the coalition was oriented to action, there was less cause for theoretical, internecine feuds. A stark contrast to German leftist handwringing would be harder to find. This was the movement that Colorni joined in 1930, in Milan, and he subsequently worked closely with the circle in Turin, led by Leone Ginzburg, though his engagements were often cut short by his travels to Germany to study. When the Turin group—as well as other domestic cells—was rounded up in March 1935, Eugenio Colorni searched out other affiliations; he joined the Centro Interno Socialista (CIS) in Milan, directed by the doctor Rodolfo Morandi, just as Socialists and Communists were engaged in heated discussions over a broad coalition that would culminate in the Popular Front. In 1936, Colorni became the head of the CIS, which sponsored the Paris-based publication *Grido del Popolo*. He would eventually meet up with Rosselli at the Ninth International Congress of Philosophy in Paris and get intimately involved in the discussions over the ties between the Italian Socialist Party and Justice and Liberty.[39]

The spirit of action was intimately bound up with a way of thinking. Italian exiles were not averse to Theory, or *un' idea forza,* to justify, to explain, and to motivate antifascist praxis. Indeed, at the outset, the influence on Hirschmann was very much intellectual. According to Ursula, Colorni was set on helping "cure" the Hirschmanns, as if they were patients. For Ursula, Eugenio's gentle but tireless persuasions were like

Renzo Guia's, a relentless breakdown of her Marxist sophistry, by the end of which she'd relinquished her faith in dialectical materialism. Unfortunately, this political cure did little for the romance between Ursula and Eugenio, and before long, their marriage ran into difficulties.[40] Ursula's brother worried that she did not fully appreciate her own husband's gifts. Indeed, many years later, Albert had to clarify Eugenio's turn of mind to his sister. Her memoirs had described him as a *maitre à penser*. Albert thought this reflected a misunderstanding. "Sartre, Lévi-Strauss, Foucault are 'maitres à penser.' Eugenio was actually the opposite: a constant critic, questioner, stimulator. That he was *homme d'action* and *penseur critique* at the same time was maybe his special trait. . . . Maybe you should change the title here to '*Pensatore critico e uomo d'azione*' or simply '*pensamiento critic e azione.*'" She did not.[41]

What her brother considered a "special trait" was too much for Ursula, who tended to lean on the *azione* side of the scales. But it captivated OA. Colorni's restless, ecumenical style and concern to let the observations of everyday life shape one's outlook would leave an indelible, permanent, and probably the most decisive mark. This also made Colorni a slightly undisciplined thinker. Often, his curiosities got the better of him. When he was infatuated with psychoanalysis, he devoured Freud. He would then skip almost instantly to Einstein and theoretical physics. Publishing the work on Leibnitz kept drifting into the future as new ideas crowded in. But his omnivorous curiosities threw open doors for Hirschmann. Free of the theoretical formalities of Germanic Marxism, Colorni eschewed the obscure and often circular language of its abstraction. His outlook grew from an early encounter at his *liceo* with the giant figure of Italian liberalism, Benedetto Croce; what fascinated Colorni was the aesthetic dimension of liberty, *libertà*, and the richness of positivism, the belief that actual experience and observation were the bases for authentic knowledge. Take a look around you, he told Otto Albert. Notice the world and let ideas be summoned from it. He exposed taboos. He espoused a kind of voluntarism, free of the inexorable course of History. People did not have to conform to the necessary sequence of social development, to wait for the "objective conditions" to ripen before taking action. This is what Guia meant when he laughed at Ursula's constrictive language. To Otto Albert, the conversations with Eugenio drew his attention "to what we call the small ideas, small pieces of knowledge. They do not stand in connection with any ideologies or worldviews, they do not claim to provide total knowledge of the world, they probably undermine the claims of all previous ideologies." These *petites idées* really stuck for Hirschman, who for the rest of his life would jot down observations on scraps of paper or notebooks hoping they might evolve from insights into ideas. "They are like aphorisms," he explained, "very astonishing remarks, perhaps of a paradoxical nature, but which are perhaps true because of it." Since these little ideas lay all around like leaves, the skill was in figuring out how to "gather them up" and make them into "a great idea." It was not for an abstract system to define the significance of daily experiences and choices, but, rather, the other way around.[42]

Like petites idées themselves, the turn away from abstract theory to observational practice took time to germinate. It did not immediately re-integrate fragments of what was once a fairly coherent intellectual style anchored in a particular place, Berlin, into a new one associated with another place. Yet, with time this alchemy of an exploratory intellectual sensibility and voluntarist political dispositions would be one that Hirschman could cultivate and refine over the rest of his life—in many ways *because* it was so itinerant; it was an intellectual temperament that complemented a restless spirit. The petites idées was "a really key thing throughout Albert's life," according to his wife, Sarah, "that he told me almost on the first day I met him, when we talked about Eugenio." This was six years and several wars later, in early 1941—but it was as if he was still sitting beside his brother-in-law the previous day. In that first conversation with his future wife, Albert "taught me not to think in big theories or big things, but to treasure small ideas." Thereafter, the affection for petites idées was also a bond, transmitted from Eugenio Colorni, between Albert and Sarah. "In our life we have had these things that you say to each other, like all couples, and for us it was our petites idées: 'Wow, this is wonderful. It's small, but it's wonderful.' And his letters have a lot of petites idées. He will see a picture, a painting, and he would get a petite

idée. He would see something going on in the street; he would get a petite idée." Small things could provide big insights without being reduced
to them. The Big Idea, which Hirschman associated with the "claim to
complete cognition of the world," claimed "to explain multi-causal social processes from a single principle." The alternative was "the attempt to
come to an understanding of reality in portions, admitting that the angle
may be subjective."[43]

Biographers—indeed their subjects—often latch onto a formative
moment, a turning point, an éclat after which the subject has changed
and whose future consists of its direct effect. This can be a trauma, a
book, an external event. The tendency can easily oversimplify a story.
Hirschmann's encounters with Colorni were a formative moment. But
to identify them as such should not imply that this was the moment that
made the man; it would take him much longer to transcend conventional
academic boundaries, to assemble a distinctive style from an exposure to
different intellectual currents which, thanks to exile, Hirschmann was
stockpiling along with his petites idées stashed in notebooks and scraps
of papers.

Some exiles hung onto their Marxism for security; Colorni reinforced Hirschmann's sense that it was a false source. But what Colorni
did not do was try to convert his brother-in-law to some new system. On
the contrary, what Colorni conveyed was a sense that certitude need not
be a precondition for constructive action or purposeful thinking. Eugenio, six years older than Otto Albert, had an intellectual style that took
nothing for granted—with only one exception, his doubts. It was "the
only sure thing." Doubt is not the same thing as uncertainty, though it
sometimes passes for it. Uncertainty means that you think you may be
wrong; doubt means you are not sure you know. The first makes you less
confident; the latter does not. Colorni believed that doubt was creative
because it allowed for alternative ways to see the world, and seeing alternatives could steer people out of intractable circles and self-feeding
despondency. Doubt, in fact, could motivate: freedom from ideological constraints opened up political strategies, and accepting the limits
of what one could know liberated agents from their dependence on the

belief that one had to know everything before acting, that conviction was a precondition for action. Few things were more frustrating to Colorni, already a veteran of Italian opposition infighting, and to Hirschmann, who had lost his tolerance for doctrinal posturing, than theoretical arguments that masked apathy. One day, sitting with the Italian journalist Franco Ferraresi, an older Hirschman explained his debt to Colorni and his circle: "Those people did not consider their participation in a highly dangerous political activity as the price they had to pay for the freedom of thought, but rather saw it as a simple, natural, spontaneous and almost joyous response." It was freedom of thought that mobilized dangerous political activity. Hirschman looked at the reporter and said: "I have always found this an admirable way to conceive of political action, and to unite public and personal life."[44]

Between them, Eugenio and Otto Albert shared a little saying: that they should "prove Hamlet wrong." If the Shakespearean figure was the archetype of immobilizing doubt, Colorni's ideas were intent on demonstrating that doubt could propel deeds.[45]

Colorni's influence was particular, but he was also part of a broader, Italian, current. By the time Colorni engaged Hirschmann in long conversations, he represented a generation that was trying to stand on the shoulders of two powerful Italian intellectual currents, one liberal through Benedetto Croce and Piero Gobetti (whose *Liberal Revolution* pointed the way to bridge individualism with social concerns into a political theory of action), and the other an inheritor of Marxist philosophy, Antonio Gramsci. These two great trajectories, according to Carlo Rosselli needed to be recombined. This was the message behind his manuscript, *Socialismo liberale*, which he published first in French in Paris in 1930 (the Italian edition did not appear until after the war). As the title itself denoted, Rosselli advocated a way of thinking that combined the liberal tradition's emphasis on the importance of free will with the Marxist tradition's stress on social justice into one brand, fused in a commitment to democracy. Renounce the quest for certainty, abandon astrological searches for the inevitable laws of History, and get past the sterile abstractions of past debates. This was all inscribed in a fundamental skepticism about historical laws, and the need to admit that one can act, learn by acting, reevaluate, correct one's opinions, act once more—in the service of liberty and justice for their own sake.[46]

It would take years for this amalgamation of ideas and influences to form the new chemical balance of Hirschmann's thinking. For the moment, while he was moved and inspired by his conversations with Eugenio and drifted into *giellisti*, Rossellian socialist-liberal circles, with Renzo, he was also nearing the end of his studies at HEC. By the spring of 1935, as Ursula was reaching out to Eugenio, Otto Albert began to make plans for the next uprooting; in early April, he wrote to Mutti asking for her to send him original certifications from the Collège Français and notarized documents confirming her own nationality and status. He was applying for a fellowship to go to the London School of Economics (LSE). HEC had been a disappointment. This made Hirschmann all the more determined to make the next step the right one. If Paris had not satisfied his curiosity to learn economics, Hirschmann hoped that London would. The letter of support from the Entr'aide Universitaire Internationale must have helped clinch the opportunity to open new intellectual vistas; he was accepted to the LSE and given one year's scholarship. In early summer, he finished his final exams at HEC, reading *Brothers Karamazov* to the last, and escaped to Forte dei Marmi for a vacation with Ursula and Eugenio. Then he was back in Paris, packing his bags, getting ready for London.

CHAPTER 4

The Hour of Courage

From the true antagonist boundless courage
flows from you.

FRANZ KAFKA

Over the course of the next three years, Hirschmann shuffled between four countries, enlisted to fight in a civil war, joined an underground resistance, and got a doctoral degree. The languages changed—from French to English to Spanish to Italian and back to French—but his commitment to fight fascism remained the same, no matter the language or land. Uprooted from country yet loyal to cause, Hirschmann found a way to make this an intellectually fertile period, especially after the disappointments of HEC. It was in these years that Hirschmann got his first exposure to real economics at the London School of Economics, which he had long been seeking. His relationship with Eugenio Colorni and the influence of his style of thinking came into full bloom in Trieste. Between the books of London and Trieste was a searing political and military experience in the Spanish Civil War.[1]

These were pendular years. Hirschmann swung between countries and languages, as well as from esoteric reading to self-sacrificing struggle, from *homme de lettres* to man of action, suggesting an erratic, reactive, or unpremeditated quality to his moves. No doubt, in the volatile years from 1935 to 1938, the highly fluid settings in each country clearly affected his choices; there was a great deal of restlessness to his decisions, as his former girlfriend, Inge Franck, had noted presciently, and the volatility of European popular fronts and their right-wing foes account for part of Hirschmann's swings as he moved around the continent searching for new coordinates.

But he was not just reacting to external shifts. His personal will was at stake as well. The difficulty is, it is not easy to figure out what was going on in his mind as his road forward kept forking. This is largely because keeping these two Hirschmanns, the combatant and the thinker, in the same frame runs up against the dearth of sources. He did not leave the trails of this chapter of his life littered with paper—letters, diaries, journals, or manuscripts—precisely the materials that biographers hoard to make sense of their subjects' choices. For some people the proliferation of personal choices is what sparks the flurry of letters and personal confessions. But this is not the case with Hirschmann, who has kept his thoughts to himself to this day. What is remarkable is how tight-lipped he remained about these years of searching, of hope, and of terrible loss. They summoned some of his best and worst memories, which go to the heart of his reluctance to imagine himself in any heroic register. After all, proving Hamlet wrong implied an open flow between thoughts and acts, theory and practice; self-doubt should motivate hazardous political involvements, almost as a counterheroic stance in the world. And yet, one cannot help but see Hirschmann's efforts to live simultaneously as a man of action and a man of letters, a part of a long tradition of heroic volunteers in other peoples' struggles; true to his divided but untorn self, Hirschmann did both.

Another way to see these apparent schisms as parts of a piece is to observe his quest for a certain independence of mind. Quitting Berlin distanced him from earlier faiths. Moving around Europe exposed him to more—and cued him increasingly to the need to forge his own style out of these compound influences. Some kind of inner drive was at work, one that helped him embrace some influences and shrug off others, but a drive that is sometimes easier to see in his deeds and movements than in his scarce words. Only later does it become evident that he had been summoning writerly aspirations and professional ambitions for himself; it is dangerous to push this back in time too hastily. It was by no means clear in 1936 that intellectual passions would gain the upper hand. Even less clear is what kind of intellectual he would become.

Still, a drive appears to be at work from the very start of his sojourn in London. According to his fellowship, he was not required to follow a program of study, because he already had a degree. He was free to do as he wished—take more courses, enlist in a degree program, join a research team. He did none of these. Instead, "I decided to study for my own account."[2] This decision, in retrospect, seems a strange one—especially given the meager learning he had gleaned at HEC. Hirschmann could certainly have benefited from more rigorous instruction. It would not be the last time he passed up the opportunity to be "trained." There were a few exceptions at the LSE, people he did search out for their influence. For instance, he discovered the young Russian-born East Ender, Abba Lerner, who had left rabbinical school to place himself in the hands of the LSE's formidable Lionel Robbins. Lerner was a brilliant, original thinker and was at work on a series of pioneering papers on concepts of international trade and the factor price equalization theorem. He had also spent six months in Cambridge and was one of the few from outside the circle surrounding John Maynard Keynes that grasped the implications of what was happening to economics. Hirschmann could spot an opportunity. He attended Lerner's course on economic theory, which was the foundation for his knowledge of economic principles. He also had an empirical nose, so he registered for a course in international economics with Professor P. Barrett Whale, who would take Hirschmann under his wing. Throughout his time at the LSE, what is revealing was his decision *not* to be forged by the heated debates going on around him; the dominant tones of the intellectual milieu in which he came of age were not necessarily those that most influenced him. If we tend to think of the 1930s as the age in which the great debates over Keynesian economics were being hashed out, for someone of OA's age and ilk it is remarkable that he pursued his interests elsewhere, intrigued more by the quieter undertones of economic controversies that were drowned out by the noise surrounding Keynes and his critics.

By the time Otto Albert Hirschmann arrived at the doorsteps of the LSE's crowded buildings off Aldwych Circle, it had long since given up its mantle as the training ground for social scientists committed to Fabian socialism or to a social-engineering approach to modern problems and was well on its way to being one of the world's great intellectual capitals, full of scholars from a plethora of persuasions. The founding anthropologist Bronislaw Malinowski, the sociologists T. H. Marshall and Karl Mannheim, and political scientists like Harold Laski and economic historians like R. H. Tawney towered over their fields and taught their courses in cramped lecture halls.

Best known at the time as the intellectual counterpoint to the teaching at Cambridge University, where Keynes held forth, the LSE, under the leadership of Lionel Robbins and Friedrich von Hayek, boasted a more free-market approach to economics. Robbins gave the gateway course for all economics students, The General Principles of Economic Analysis; he was determined to combine the rigors of the Austrian school of precise hypothesis testing within "the science which studies human behaviour as a relationship between scarce means with alternative uses" into a British classical tradition.[3] This set the stage for Robbins and Hayek to join forces in Economic Theory, for all students preparing for their second-year final exams. To graduate in economics from the LSE meant running these gauntlets. Both courses were also highly recommended for graduate students. There is no evidence that Hirschmann attended, though they certainly dominated the air of the school. There was also a younger generation of iconoclastic economists coming up through the ranks—such as John Hicks, Nicholas Kaldor, Tibor Scitovsky, R.H. Coase, and Abba Lerner—who cut their teeth on the masters to become "continentals" (a term meant to distinguish them from Cambridge-style economics) and original thinkers in their own right.

In early February 1936, a long queue began to form outside the LSE bookshop. Hirschmann joined the line. It was the day that Keynes's The General Theory of Employment, Interest, and Money was hitting the shelves. Most of the buyers were students. They plunged into the book—though Hirschmann could not help but notice that most of it passed over their heads "because it was a very difficult book."[4] The General Theory intensified an increasingly bitter contest between Cambridge Keynesians and LSE free marketers, led by Robbins and Hayek, who were already on record for disputing Keynes's theories of money and advocacy of state intervention. Some Keynes defenders included younger faculty and students, who were less inclined to dig in their heels, and some like Lerner, were receptive to the revolution. All of this was eye-opening for Hirschmann. Keynes was, for all intents and purposes, unknown in France. Some left-wing economists, such as Charles Spinasse and Georges Boris (Léon Blum's economic advisor), were Keynes admirers. But the notion that deliberate public deficits could reverse a business cycle was far from having any influence on Paris's ministers. *The General Theory* was itself only published in French under the Occupation in 1942.[5]

It was not just what economists were arguing *about* that intrigued Hirschmann, it was the fact that they were arguing about *ideas*. At first blush, this may seem odd. After all, he was coming to the LSE from a Marxist political economy tradition, so laissez-faire economics was subversive. Moreover, books were to be read like the New Testament, to imbibe as doctrine and recite as dogma, not as a set of propositions that functioned as hypotheses that might be tested in the real world; there were no real alternatives to consider or wrestle with. To Hirschmann, his old debates were not about economic concepts, but about political positions. In this new hotbed in London, he was prepared to hear all sides; it was all new. The result is that he did not necessarily see the Robbins-Hayek position as "old hat" in the same way many of their students did. Indeed, Hirschmann took Hayek, in particular, seriously and appreciated the rigorous individualism after his previous diet of "lumpy" collective categories like social class. The accent on what would become known as methodological individualism (a term that came from the Austrian Joseph Schumpeter)—which Robbins and Hayek argued was at the core of the discipline's approach and which premised that social choices were the aggregation of individual choices—blew away old verities. Society was just a composite of individuals, a sum of atomized parts: any self-respecting theory had to reckon with personal preferences and psychology to ground its explanation; societies or classes (not to mention the inferences about their consciousness) are not enclosed, self-sustaining decision-makers. In this setting, the arriviste would pick and choose; that he would treat the setting as an opportunity to try amalgamating parts in new ways was a sign that his eclecticism began early. But it would also sow enduring tensions. The injunction to pay attention to individuals' psychologies and preferences was a lasting influence, but Hirschmann was not so keen to depose the idea of a composite society larger than a mere sum of parts capable of bearing its own ontological weight. He thrived on the "lively" atmosphere: economics was the subject of the debate, empirical methods in dispute, ideas impassioning. "The scales fell from my eyes when I came to England. . . . Only there did I really discover what economics actually is."[6]

The LSE, certainly by contrast to the milieus of Berlin and HEC, where nationalism and nativism ran rampant, was also extremely international and cosmopolitan. Of the 3,000 students at the LSE, 721 were foreign, and of these, 353 were considered "occasional" (that is, not registered for a degree) including Hirschmann. Germany accounted for 84 students, a large cohort, just behind China, India, and the United States in numbers. It was a world in which Hirschmann found it much easier to find friends, some of whom had similar backgrounds as involuntary émigrés and exiles. Two fellow economics students became life-long intimates. One was Hans Landsberg, whom he knew vaguely from Berlin. The other was George Jaszi, the son of Oskar Jaszi and scion of a family of well-known Hungarian émigré artists, who would become one of Hirschmann's closest friends. Both Landsberg and Jaszi were, however, full-time students enrolled for degrees and thus on a different track than Hirschmann the newcomer. Still, they formed a tight bond. With the ruckus around Keynes's revolution, the three trekked up to Cambridge together to hear Keynes lecture; Jaszi and Landsberg were smitten; Hirschmann walked away with his doubts—some of them by now reflecting a growing distrust of anything that smacked of grand theory.[7]

Hirschmann did not follow an intellectual trail that saw him abandoning old ideas and picking up new ones, reinventing himself on a dime. His transitions were more complex and faltering. He did not simply discard Marxism and embrace Hayek, leave behind class analysis to tout Keynes.

There was much more processing, inner deliberation, selection, and adaptation than a standard "conversion" story. While reading up on the Keynesian-Austrian debate, he never gave up his interest in an older heritage of political economy; indeed, the sojourn at the LSE afforded him the first opportunity to delve into the history of economic thought, having left David Ricardo behind in Berlin. It was in London that he was able to pick up currents that did not reduce themselves to the labor theory of value. Most important were John Stuart Mill's *Principles of Political Economy* and Alfred Marshall's *Principles of Economics*. Nor did he forget his interest in David Ricardo, and found a way to rekindle it by making a pilgrimage to Cambridge on his own, not to see Keynes, but to visit Eugenio Colorni's cousin Piero Sraffa, who had also fled Italy, leaving behind his own Marxist antecedents. With a letter of introduction from Eugenio, Hirschmann boarded the train from Liverpool Street Station to visit Sraffa, who was then consumed in his editing of the complete works of David Ricardo at the behest of the Royal Economic Society. Sraffa ranked among the most biting critics of Hayek's Austrian economics and his relentlessly pessimistic logic. But behind the scenes, he was hard at work on the origins of political economy. Ricardo's theory of ground rent was the pretext for what became an afternoon spent in "a long and *belle* conversation" with the shy, bookish, Italian economist in his office at Trinity College. There are no records of the meeting. We can of course speculate on the topics: catching up on family gossip, perhaps thoughts about the duel between Keynes and his critics. It is also possible that they talked about the Italian scene, for Sraffa had been the purveyor of pens and paper for the incarcerated Antonio Gramsci and had authored a little-known study of inflation in Italy during the First World War. He was also a fierce critic of banking practices under Mussolini. These topics fascinated Hirschmann, who was determined to follow Sraffa's example of weaving sophisticated economic analysis together with political commitment. In his retrospective on intellectual life in London in 1935–36, the private afternoon with Sraffa looms as large as the much noisier public clashing over Keynes's *General Theory*.[8]

While there was plenty of economic theory and history of economic thought to go around, it was empirical work in international economics that summoned most of Hirschmann's attention and brought him under the caring fold of Barrett Whale. It was with Whale that Hirschmann got his bearings in basic concepts and empirical sensibilities in international economics—and one has to marvel at how much he must have taken in this abbreviated exchange; what Whale offered buoyed Hirschmann through many years of research and analysis. His course International Trade and Foreign Exchanges laid the basic theory of comparative advantage, factor movements, and the functioning of the gold standard; it ended with considerations on contemporary problems. The reading list was compilations of classics, from David Ricardo and John Stuart Mill to Bertil Ohlin's and Gottfried Haberler's recent books on international trade.[9] Whale, a scholar of German banking systems, was best known for his text *International Trade*, which would go through multiple editions, and he would later become a great figure in the building of economics at the University of Liverpool after World War II. At the time that Hirschmann was working with him, Whale was writing a long essay on the prewar gold standard, which was published in *Economica* in 1937. One can only conjecture about how much of Whale's preoccupations with international trade and finance, and concern with central banking, rubbed off on his pupil.

Whale was also instrumental in a second way: he encouraged his German student to use some of his new skills on a subject that was close to home and to take his first stab at writing. One of his assignments involved a set of readings and a research paper on the franc Poincaré, an emblem of the Third Republic's economic anemia. Created in the 1920s as a unit of account convertible to gold, it was used as the anchor for the convertibility of the French franc, and thus the stabilization of the French economy after the postwar upheavals. Fearing resurgent instability, government after government struggled to defend the franc Poincaré, even at the cost of worsening the Depression by deflating prices and sticking to balanced budgets at a time in which many western governments ushered in deficit spending and counter-cyclical policies—until finally, in September 1936, the Popular Front government ushered in a belated, and tumultuous, devaluation. It says something of the HEC of those days that Hirschmann was present during the heated debate about whether to let the overvalued franc fall and abandon the gold standard, but he understood little. That changed under Whale, with whom discussions veered toward the idea of writing a research paper—Hirschmann's first—on the topic. We do not have a record of what Hirschmann wrote at this time for Whale's course, though an elaborated version would materialize a few years later. But Whale must have been impressed by the result: he concluded his advising of Hirschmann in the form of a letter of recommendation in late May 1936—which is all the evidence we have of Hirschmann's sojourn at the LSE (it issued him no transcripts)—praising Hirschmann's "engagement in writing a memorandum on French monetary problems in which he has shown considerable capacity in marshaling evidence and both soundness and independence of judgment. Altogether, he has impressed me as being a highly intelligent and capable student." Whale clearly saw in Hirschmann a knack for research, for the letter especially "recommends him for employment—for any employment, but more especially for 'economic intelligence' work." Whether Hirschmann had spoken to Whale of this interest, or whether Whale's words sparked an idea in Hirschmann's head, we cannot know. But this is precisely where Hirschmann would try to make his first mark in the field.[10]

As Whale typed his letter of recommendation for the twenty-one-year old, the news from across the English Channel was getting worse by the day. The London press conveyed lurid accounts of Mussolini's invasion of Abyssinia in late 1935, including the deployment of bombs and flamethrowers against troops on camels, and tracked the fruitless debate in the League of Nations over sanctions against the aggressor, until it was too late: by May the African kingdom was occupied. At the same time, Hitler's armies marched into the Rhineland, though the African-American athlete, Jesse Owens, spoiled Hitler's Aryan chest-thumping in June at the Berlin Olympics. Fleet Street was kept busy. Meanwhile, in France, bitter elections were fought in April and May 1936. The Right made decisive inroads on the middle-of-the-road parties. But a coalition of a Popular Front composed of socialists, radicals, and Communists helped ensure that France's political instability would not go the way that

Germany's had in 1932–33. After a second round of ballots, the Dreyfu-sard Léon Blum became the French premier. Anti-Semites of the Action française and the fascist Cagoule went on the war path. Blum's govern-ment, wracked by strikes, reactionary mobilization, and attempted assas-sinations on the premier, brought back bad memories.

It was impossible to sit still; as gripping as his research and courses were, Hirschmann had a dilemma. He later confessed to his French trans-lator that he was restless: "It is true, I wanted to study, but at the same time I sensed that fascism was progressing and that I could not stand back and watch events unfold without doing anything."[11]

In June 1936, with the final term of his fellowship over, Hirschmann packed his bags once more and returned to Paris. He had had a thrilling year and came away with an idea of himself as an economist, though still not fully "trained." As equally unformed, but emerging, were research and writing ideas. The trouble was that he had no sense of how to work on them, no job, no income, and no prospects. He once referred to the hiatus after his LSE studies as very "personally difficult times." "Psycho-logically, I was quite inconsistent and disquieted." He wrote to his old mentor, Heinrich Ehrmann, who had also taken refuge in Paris and was active in the Neu Beginnen movement, that he wanted to participate in something. But what?[12]

The question of what to do was determined by events on the other side of the Pyrenees. In Spain, as in France, a Popular Front government came to power in 1936; but unlike France, Spain more quickly and dra-matically polarized. The cast of detractors, starting with the Catholic Church, was more powerful; so were the pressures from below, pushing to break down the relics of feudalism. The government, heeding trade-union and peasant pressures, quickly began to accelerate its reforms to break the hold of the Church and landlords—until the feared reaction. The military rose up against the Republican government on July 17, 1936. It failed; many in the army refused to join the rebels. The uprising might have fizzled there. But the decision on the part of Hitler and Mussolini to send weapons, reinforcements, and above all airplanes, enabled Gen-eralísimo Francisco Franco, Caudillo de España por la Gracia de Dios, to airlift supplies from the Moroccan colony to the mainland and slowly push the Nationalist frontier forward. The British Conservative government persuaded the Blum government to stand off, though Blum would find indirect ways of trickling aid to the Loyalists. One effect of this refusal to support the Spanish government was to throw it on the mercy of Moscow—for Stalin saw as shrewdly as Hitler did that this proxy conflict was an opportunity to expand his own influence despite the puny size of the Spanish Communist Party. What ensued was a bitter civil war that started as a botched coup d'état.

The precipitous internationalization of the Spanish conflict drew the world's media attention, and by mid-July, it was splashed all over newspaper headlines. This coincided with Hirschmann's return to Paris, where the debate about how to help the Loyalists was breaking open, especially given the dithering stance of the Blum government. Indeed, there was a not minor fear that the civil war would spread to France itself, with the extreme Right rattling its sabers by forming a "blackguard front," while the Communists could not resist the temptation to proclaim the need to form self-defense units of its own. The line in Spain had become the symbolic front line in a pan-European conflict. Finally, there was a "main theater" for the fight against fascism.[13] Hirschmann rushed to see Mark Rein, ever a source of advice and a model, who told him that he was thinking of going to Spain to join the Loyalists. Mark had never distanced himself from German socialism; in fact, he remained involved and had a list of contacts of Neu Beginnen sympathizers who were planning to go to Barcelona. The Spanish Civil War provided an important immediate cause for German socialists, and Hitler's backing for Franco made Spain an opportunity to resist fascism on another front. For Germans in particular, the sense was: no repeat of 1933 defeatism. Indeed, the Spanish Civil War reignited a militant spirit that had faded since the spring of 1933. Neu Beginnen chapters in Prague, Amsterdam, and Paris came back to life to enlist volunteers. Mark told OA of this revival; finally there was an opportunity to redeem despairing radicals.

For similar reasons, Italian exiles also joined the crusade. "Today in Spain, tomorrow Italy," intoned Carlo Rosselli, the leader of the Justice and Liberty movement from Paris. By 1935, Rosselli was more captivat-

ing as a proselytizer than as a planner. As the 1930s unfolded, Justice
and Liberty had moved progressively to the left, partly in response to
the integration of more socialists, and partly in response to Mussolini's
Ethiopian "adventure." Prolonged exile left Rosselli chomping at the bit
for a direct assault on Mussolini. The outbreak of the Spanish Civil War
several months after Mussolini's victory in Africa gave Rosselli his crusade. Echoing Machiavelli, he declared that the "prophets are no longer
disarmed." Scarcely days after Franco assumed command of the Moors
and Legionnaires of Spanish Morocco and launched his attempted coup
d'état on July 17, 1936, the G-L (Giustizia e Libertà) leadership caucused
in its offices on rue Val-de-Grâce; Rosselli rallied the *giellisti* to form a
volunteer brigade for Spain. Not everyone was convinced that this was a
good idea. But they could not stand in his way. Arriving in Barcelona in
early August, he struck a deal with local anarchists and trade unionists to
create the Ascaso Column (named after the anarchist Francisco Ascaso,
who died in the first day of fighting in Barcelona against the rebels) composed of *giellisti* and Italian anarchists. Rosselli took command of this
group of 130 volunteers and then returned to Paris to enlist more fighters.
One of them would be Renzo Guia, Hirschmann's former Italian tutor,
who would die early in the conflict, the victim of a Falangist bomb.

Spain was, according to Rosselli, where the line against totalitarianism would be drawn; it was here that a "motorized revolutionary force"
could also cut its teeth in preparation for an assault on Mussolini. Rosselli
waxed eloquent about the nature of the uniforms that soldiers would wear
for *this* war: "The intellectual who dons the overalls for the first time feels
an ineffable sentiment of joy. Here, I slough off my past, my bourgeois
habits and wants, to consecrate myself to the cause of the workers. I enter
the revolution with only blood and soul. We will be brothers, comrades in
overalls."[14] This declaration of a permanent war on multiple fronts sealed
his fate: Mussolini took aim at Rosselli and his brother, who were later
stabbed to death in June 1937 at the hands of fascist assassins. Paris was
shocked. The funeral brought out 200,000 mourners. In the ensuing grief
and uproar, two days later, on the twenty-first, Léon Blum resigned as
premier of France, bringing an end to the Popular Front.

This was the environment in which Hirschmann enlisted, finding himself doing things he did not fully understand but felt compelled to do anyway. We do not know exactly on which day, but we know that he took the train to Barcelona with the very first German and Italian volunteers. By 2009, this was a detail that had long since slipped from his memory. But what was not hard for him to forget was the reflex. Colorni had spoken to him of moments of courage, a topic upper most on his mind, not least because of Mussolini's tightening grip. Shortly after his brother-in-law went to Catalonia, Eugenio felt compelled to explain the need to write and act in defiance of those who used power for immoral ends. But in characteristic fashion, he insisted that the courage of one's words depended on their sincerity and the readiness to be self-critical, "to be always on guard against oneself."[15] What Spain presented to Otto Albert however, was not a moment for words; he did not go down to "report," as Arthur Koestler did, but for action. It was clear to Hirschmann that this was his moment for courage. Simply put: "when I heard that there was even a possibility to do something, I went."[16]

He spent almost three months in Catalonia, from July to the end of October 1936, part of the first wave of volunteers. This is important to underscore because the initial fight against Franco was not so much mounted by the Republican government, which was too weak to pose a real counterthreat to the military, as by the trade unions and peasant leagues, which had responded to the coup with general strikes and a rush to form spontaneous militias. Indeed, by the time that Hirschmann's train pulled into in Barcelona, the city was in the hands of the workers. Socialist and anarchist talk dominated the atmosphere. Until late October, when the USSR began to ship arms and its envoys began to seize control, a fervor of revolution for and by the commoner prevailed in Catalonia; one must imagine a twenty-two-year-old German socialist walking the streets of Barcelona where tipping was banned because it was considered demeaning; where the words *Don* and *Señor* were outlawed in favor of *comrade*; where cathedrals, deemed citadels of Reaction, were desecrated or burned; and where giant red-and-black banners announced which factory was now owned by which trade union. For a brief moment, here was the socialist revolution that Germans had failed to mount to save Weimar.

In those early months of the war, furthermore, there was little organizational structure and a constant improvisation of command. This would also change when the Communists muscled onto the scene in autumn. Until then, the Italian and German émigré battalions, including Rosselli's Ascaso Column, aligned under the general umbrella of the Partido Obrero de Unificación Marxista (POUM), which were marched off, after a peremptory rifle training, to the front.[17]

To the volunteers, the POUM was just one of a plethora of movements, one in a "plague of initials," as George Orwell put it. Orwell himself would arrive in Barcelona just as Hirschmann was leaving; there is no evidence that they met. While it is possible to reconstruct a sense of what was transpiring in and around Barcelona in those initial months, Hirschmann's precise whereabouts in the mayhem cannot be confirmed. The POUM amalgamated a broad, unstable spectrum. Formed by Spanish Communists, led by Andreu Nin, strongly influenced by Leon Trotsky's notion of the permanent revolution (which had influenced the Neu Beginnen group as well), the POUM defied Moscow directives. From its formation in 1935, it was at odds with Moscow and leery about sacrificing its autonomy under the Popular Front. It was friendly to anarchists and non-Marxist radicals and thus far outscaled Spain's official Communist Party and its Catalonian wing. Orwell, who joined the POUM ranks six months after Hirschmann, noted a growth in its membership from 10,000 to 70,000 between July and December, months of radicalizing euphoria that coincided with Hirschmann's. The POUM story would end, as is well known, in internecine bloodshed when the increasingly Communist-controlled Catalan government arrested Nin and much of the POUM leadership in July 1937, torturing and executing many of them under NKVD (Narodnyy Komissariat Vnutrennikh Del) supervision. It was Orwell's witness to this kind of butchery and betrayal that motivated his *Homage to Catalonia*.

Hirschmann's Spanish Civil War was a different one. He was there when the POUM headquarters at the Hotel Falcón on La Rambla became the epicenter of a rush to defend republicanism and workers' control. This spurred the hastily organized militias to hold the line against Nationalist advances. Until the Communists began to assert leadership, most international volunteers had room—and took risks—to fight alongside and under the command of Spanish socialists and anarchists, many of whom thought that foreigners knew more about war than they did. This made for mayhem. There were no uniforms, at best corduroy knee britches, which were about the only gesture toward uniformity. Black or red handkerchiefs around one's throat gave away one's anarchist or socialist affiliations. Training consisted mainly in marching drills with some basic instruction on how to fire rifles, which jammed in the dust and mud. Most militiamen did not get a weapon until they reached the front, often taking a gun from the soldier they were relieving. Such was the chaos that when the main Catalan anarchist column left for the Aragonese front by train on July 24, they were several hours from the station when they realized that they had forgotten their munitions. Command at the front, if it can be called that, was in utter confusion. Bereft of training and supplies, what the volunteers lacked in preparation they made up with enthusiasm, a resource they would come to rely upon to endure the summer heat and dust, fleas and lice, and the comradely boredom of filthy and chaotic barrack life.[18]

These were the conditions under which Hirschmann went to war under the POUM flag. The Italian and German volunteers cut their initial teeth at the Battle of Monte Pelato. On August 28, 1936, after weeks of dithering and reorganization, the Ascaso Column, formed only ten days earlier, went into battle along the Aragonese front. Outnumbered and underequipped, it held the line against advancing Franco forces. Given the scorching heat, firing began in the relative coolness of dawn and ended before 10:00 a.m. to allow troops on both sides to scramble for water and food. When the smoke cleared, the Freemason commander, Mario Angeloni, and several other *giellisti* were dead; Rosselli was also shot, but alive. Was Hirschmann at Monte Pelato? We cannot be sure, but it is likely. This was the sector that was the only one conducted by an independent, mainly Italian fighting force during the time he was in Catalonia, and it was under the affiliation to which he naturally gravitated. His most detailed disclosure, from an unnamed US government agency around the time of his 1943 petition for naturalization, was a signed declaration that places him in the Zaragosa sector of Aragon from August until October 1936 and that says his units "suffered enormous losses" and "engaged in heavy fighting" before the remnants were sent back to Barcelona.[19] What he recounted subsequently of the nature of the fighting and the enemy is also consistent with what occurred at Monte Pelato. He recalled that his enemies were Black Francoists from the Moroccan divisions. He also remembered the endless crawling in the Aragonese dirt. After a chaotic exchange of screaming and bullets and tumbling about in trenches, he looked down at his trousers and found them soaked. At first he thought he had been hit—only to discover that his wine flask had broken and that he might have involuntarily relieved himself in fear. It could have been wine, urine, or both for all he cared; he was alive—slightly injured, but alive.[20]

While the column lost 10 percent of its fighters, it gained in reputation. In Paris, among the émigrés, the battle was heralded as a triumph against fascism; in Barcelona, the Italians' commanders were invited to the war councils. This may have been a decision the Spanish Loyalists came to regret, for Rosselli, in spite of his injury, was keen to play a leading role and quickly got into a tussle with Spanish and Italian anarchists over control. It was not just that the adrenalin of war, especially after so many years of waiting, had gone to Rosselli's head; there was a vacuum in the whole structure of the Catalan command. This would worsen in September, as Communists entered the scene. But for the time being, Monte Pelato stood out in what was then still a low-intensity war as both sides got organized and began to stockpile weapons and dig trenches.[21]

This is as much as we know about Hirschmann's experience on the battlefield. On the whole, he was reluctant to discuss the Spanish Civil War after he left Catalonia. His wife Sarah—who met him years later—found him silent on the topic, and sensing his unease, she didn't press him for details. Once, when they went to a film together about the Spanish Civil War, as they left the theater Sarah turned to Albert and asked him:

"Was it like that?" He replied evasively, "Yeah, that was a pretty good film." When I asked Sarah about this reserve—on both their parts, his to speak, hers to press—she was somewhat philosophical: "You know, I've always felt through these long years perhaps that that's *my* secret: how I could stick with one person for that long [and not know]. I think every-body has a right to their own memories." Tightly guarded recollections were part of a pattern when it came to bad memories, which he preferred to keep to himself: "I felt this kind of reticence [sometimes] in Albert," she confessed. "He's had quite a few areas like that. I never tried to force him [to talk]." Still, the scars on his neck and leg made it impossible for her to forget.[22]

One reason why Hirschman preferred silence was because Spain was a source of sorrow, of disenchantment with an ideal. It was not his pro-pensity to fret about utopias destined to fall short of peoples' high hopes. Nor was he one to hang onto miserable situations that had no solution; "*Lascia perdere,*" he often said of pointless efforts, let it go. But Spain was different. The endless debate rehearsed in Berlin and Paris over left-wing tactics was more than a farce, it was a tragedy of epic proportions, one which left the discrete hero wordless. He watched the ideological harden-ing as the Communists moved into the fray; he witnessed the first inter-necine fighting and initial fear of reprisals. Hirschmann grew frightened that the Catalan coalition would not be able to remain independent of Communist controls; he was by now hardening his stance on Stalin. It was not something he had full insight into, as he later recalled, nor was the extent of the cruelty and cynicism yet on full display, as it would be for Orwell, but it was most certainly in the air. Within the POUM there were heated discussions about how much to fold into the Communist-led front; some leaders echoed Rafael Abramovich's skepticism about Stalin's intentions, a position with which Hirschmann increasingly aligned.[23]

It was hard to stop Stalin, especially once it was clear that the war would not end quickly and that Loyalists desperately needed his weapons and support. The price they paid was to cede autonomy. In September, the Loyalist forces were being reorganized into volunteer divisions under Communist command. Within months, the NKVD had its agents across the Loyalist territories and was beginning to assert control, fueled by the arrival of Communist militants or sympathizers from around Europe and North and Latin America. The French Communist Maurice Thorez and the German Willi Münzenberg proposed in September that the Comintern order the formation of International Brigades for the foreign volunteers like Hirschmann. At the end of that month, Italian and French Communists were folded into a column, putting pressure on other leftists to join the better-trained and better-supplied forces. It was decided that Hirschmann should go to Madrid to join the International Brigades. He was having misgivings about the politics behind the lines and was appalled at the manipulations and controls of Communists; fearing that the brigades would become another of Stalin's pawns, he refused. This was a decisive move—for while he still believed in a left-wing coalition, he was not willing to submit to Communist authority and give up his autonomy. Beside, among his Italian friends in Barcelona, he was told that the antifascist movement in Italy was also ramping up its activities and that Eugenio was taking a leading role in Trieste. As Rosselli had prophesized, a new front was opening up against fascism elsewhere. The *giellisti* were on the move. Leaving Spain, therefore, was like joining another antifascist struggle, freer of Communist machinations.[24] Hirschmann decided to decamp, his wounds mended, at the end of October; he took a train from Barcelona along the Mediterranean coast, bound for new activist horizons.

Hirschmann's departure coincided with an influx of new international volunteers, who walked into the midst of deteriorating relations behind leftist lines. While the brigades fought heroically in the defense of Madrid, the atmosphere in Barcelona, where the POUM had its stronghold, was venomous. One of the new arrivals was George Orwell, who stumbled into the struggle almost by accident, only to leave behind a memento of heroism and betrayal. Another arrival, albeit less famous, was Mark Rein, who had tipped off Otto Albert in the first place with his list of Neu Beginnen contacts and whom OA had hoped would catch up with him in Catalonia. Mark's saga was less well known than the somewhat self-dramatizing account of Orwell. Mark arrived on March 4, 1937, began to work as an electrical engineer in a radio factory, and followed his father's footsteps as an activist journalist, serving as a correspondent for the Swedish *Social-democraten* and Abramovich's New York–based *Jewish Daily Forward*. Some of his articles criticized the Communist trade-union manipulation. He did not fight; his work was as a journalist and technician. But his writings created a paper trail to a target. A little over a month after his arrival, he vanished from the Hotel Continental while he was on a trip to Madrid—lured, apparently, by a woman who'd offered him inside information on the Communists and invited him to an interview. Given his father's prominence in the Socialist International and close contacts with the Léon Blum government in Paris, Mark's disappearance soon became an international cause célèbre. Inquiries by the French police, the young German journalist and former associate of Hirschmann's in the Berlin SAJ, Willy Brandt, and Richard Löwenthal and the Neu Beginnen militants and desperate efforts by Rafael Abramovich, who immediately moved to Barcelona to spearhead the investigation, yielded nothing more than rumors. In all likelihood, Mark was captured by Stalin's agents, determined to exact revenge for Rafael's publicity of the terror in the Soviet Union. One fellow prisoner testified that Mark was still alive as of May 22. He was probably executed in the following few weeks. We know also that the NKVD went on a high alert in May in Madrid and Catalonia, taking out Communist militants it did not like and anarchists and socialists it mistrusted, using them as cannon fodder in untrained militias in Huesca and Zaragoza in the effort to gain control over the Spanish Republican cause.

Ursula and Otto Albert were in Trieste when the news arrived of Mark's disappearance. Sitting in the Piazza Unità, OA had bought a newspaper, was having his breakfast, and happened upon a small notice about the disappearance and presumed death of Mark Rein. He went white and read the note aloud to Ursula. They were crushed, shaken. But even their grief got entangled in the internecine scheming. Soon, their thoughts turned to Rosa in Paris, a surrogate mother. Desperate to convey their sympathies, Ursula asked one of the militants who was shuffling back and forth between Paris and Trieste to take flowers of condolence to

Rosa. This was Eugenio Curiel, a militant Communist, asked to now trespass into the home of the "enemy." Oblivious of Abramovich's standing in Stalin's eyes, Curiel expedited the favor but soon found himself caught in the fog of suspicion that swirled around all Communist circles in Paris, but most especially among the Italians whose leanings were fuzzy. Having spotted him outside the Abramovich flat, in late 1939 the Comintern ordered that Curiel be secretly investigated as a disguised "Trotskyist." This file—now declassified—is yet another glimpse into the paranoia that saturated the Comintern. Among Curiel's primary sins was his association with Otto Albert Hirschmann—"a scoundrel" and a "Trostkyist." Look, the report urged accusingly, at the fact that he traveled all over Europe with a German passport! He was a close friend of Abramovich and "his scoundrel son" as well as the "boyfriend" of his daughter! Hirschmann was toxic; Curiel got infected.[25]

For Hirschmann, the shock was more personal than political; by then he was well aware of the lengths to which the Comintern would go to assert control. Show trials were in full force in Moscow. Later, when he got back to Paris, he went immediately to visit Rafael to share his condolences; over dinner they pieced together the clues—all of which pointed to the arms of Stalin's persecutory machine. Sophocles once said that the worst tragedy is when parents have to bury their children; the Reins faced the rest of their lives not knowing if Mark was alive in a gulag or dead. To Hirschmann, it brought an end to any faith or trust in Communism. "It was no surprise that the Nazis were awful," he noted. "But to see people whom one expected to contribute to one's own struggle turn into the opposite was in some sense worse." Hirschmann had to struggle to make of his painful loss a spirit to guide by example, not a phantom to haunt him.[26]

The wounds went deep, but there was now some time to recover. Trieste, a city of over a quarter million on the borderlands with the Balkans and the old port for the Austro-Hungarian Empire, had become part of Italy after World War I. Built on a series of slopes, it looked over a beautiful Adriatic harbor. Sunny, filled with open-air markets brimming with fresh produce and pastry shops on nearly every corner, Trieste was a far cry from Catalonia's shortages. Its central square, with the elegant Verdi

Theatre on one side and Lloyds Bank on the other, was lined with coffeehouses looking out on the sea and was a contrast to Paris' somberness. Another big difference was that it was a fascist city; Mussolini enjoyed enormous support in the old ethnic borderland between Italy and the Balkans. When Hirschmann's train pulled in from Venice, the city was enthralled by the news of Italian troops' conquests in Abyssinia; having driven Emperor Haile Selassie from his realm, Mussolini proclaimed the nascence of a new Roman Empire. Hirschmann had to ignore all this and head to his sister's apartment; the first thing was to write to Mutti and let her know he was fine. "Back from Spain!" he said. But he left everything to his mother's imagination. "I just now arrived healthy and happy at Ursul's and Eug." "That was certainly the most interesting trip that I have ever taken," he ended vaguely. At this point in the letter, Ursula seized his pen to add: "He just moved to the table to eat, sweet bread, tea, apricot marmalade. He looks marvelous. He is only a little tired from the trip. . . . Now I will properly fatten him up first thing." Then he took a

Ursula, Silvia, and Eugenio, Trieste, 1937.

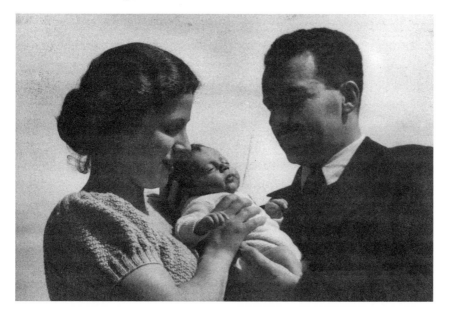

nap. Eugenio, who had been at work, went to see his sleeping brother-in-law. When OA awoke, he found Eugenio standing over him; his "heart stopped"—and then he leaped into a fraternal embrace.[27]

Ursula and Eugenio's marriage was already in trouble by the time Otto Albert arrived. Ursula has left readers with a revealing memoir about a highly intellectual and political union, often lacking in personal romance or affection and afflicted by sexual frustration. Eugenio left no such disclosure. Matters worsened in the summer of 1936, when Ursula was pregnant with their first child, Silvia. Her terrors about labor, her moods, and her sense of being trapped in a city isolated from friends drove them apart. When Silvia was born, she was frequently ill, which aggravated the stress.[28] Eugenio was not without some skill at handling the situation, which gave the marriage a lifeline. He consoled her. He cared deeply for Silvia, doing what he could in the midst of his escalating political involvements and his plunge into theoretical physics and the philosophy of science. And he took a fascination for the baby's every development, finding, characteristically, in the observations of his little daughter a source for larger questions. "Has nature arranged its laws to fit the needs of man or is it rather man who has taken advantage of a certain number of things in accordance with his needs and has arranged them for his convenience? And then, after so arranging them he has said: 'Here are the most perfect laws of nature as they have been arranged by Providence for my use.' With these laws of his own making, man has built up his own concept of nature." He closed his musings with the kind of aphorism that would become a hallmark of Albert Hirschman's own writings: "Nature, believe me, is like a mirror that reflects the image of him who scrutinizes it. And man, the most intelligent of all animals, substitutes his own image for the mirror."[29] Otto Albert was almost certainly aware of the difficulties Eugenio and Ursula faced as the winter of 1937 saw the marriage sink to its nadir. He and Ursula shared everything, and Eugenio had grown into the older brother that Albert never had. It must have been painful to witness.

In the meantime, however, Trieste was a hub of antifascist sedition—which helped smooth over some of the fissures at home. But for Otto

Albert, arriving in Trieste not only opened a new front in the war against despots, his head was still brimming with ideas about pursuing his research interests in recent French economic history. How many of his notes from his work with Barrett Whale he had with him, we do not know. Nor do we know if he carried with him his copy of Keynes's *General Theory*. It is most likely that he managed to gather them during one of his courier operations to Paris. Either way, with Eugenio's help, he was put in contact with a group of statisticians at the Istituto di Statistica at the University of Trieste, led by Pierpaolo Luzzatto-Fegiz, to deploy one skill that Hirschmann did have from his years of statistics and accounting at HEC—how to conduct fairly sophisticated counting measures. Luzzatto was en route to becoming an influential social scientist, but his math was not as strong as his background in jurisprudence, and so Hirschmann could compensate; he went to work on a study of Italian demographics, a discipline for which he developed a lasting fondness. Poring over censual data to measure fertility and child mortality rates, and from them to develop more accurate estimates of population growth rates, Hirschmann drew insights from the pioneering British demographer George Knibbs, who argued that the wrong meanings can be derived from the same data. Knibbs insisted that population growth had to consider age and complementarity between the sexes (to get beyond the standard "neuter" approach), so Hirschmann tabulated the fertility rates of Italian "Donne" by age of marriage and numbers of offspring—to show that women played a distinctive role in Italian fertility. The consequence was an ironic finding that warmed Hirschmann's heart: fascist pronatalist policies, which rewarded women for reproducing, could lead to higher fertility rates *and* higher child mortality rates. As under Whale, Hirschmann made some basic insights go a long way. Knibbs' massive *Mathematical Theory of Population* was Hirschmann's guide in developing a more nuanced model for Italian demographers, and one can detect already at this stage a fondness for paradoxes produced by human behavior.[30]

His work at the Istituto di Statistica afforded a lot of autonomy. It led to his first publication, in *Giornale degli Economisti*, a technical essay stemming from his reading of Knibbs about how to correlate matrimony, mortality, and fertility rates in a way that would reveal celibacy patterns (choices governing when, who, and how men and especially women would have sex).[31] But he also became a specialist in the Italian economy, building on what he had already learned under Whale about France. As fascist rulers controlled the official press, it became harder and harder to figure out how the economy was really faring. Hirschmann was one of the few to be able to understand—and read between the lines of—official fascist data. To this he added a habit of stockpiling data from quarterly reports and the financial press (*Il Sole, Ventiquattro Ore*). In developing his own tables of industrial output, real salaries, and balances of foreign trade, he "took pleasure in this kind of detective work," especially when it "revealed patterns that the fascist authorities tried to hide."[32] His findings came to the attention of several French economists, who solicited Hirschmann's second publication for the Société d'études d'informations économiques. A descriptive account of Italian public finances, monetary policy, prices, and commercial balances, it showed that the Abyssinian war, rearmament, and the recent shift to autarky and the closing of international trade were putting enormous strains on the fascist political economy. Already in 1938, Hirschmann described the signs of spending deficits, creeping inflation, borrowing from private banks, and government controls to contain consumer prices. He revealed a façade of "prodigious techniques" to hide the impression of Italy's "breathlessness." Crafty uses of reserves and the expedient of bank borrowing got the fascist economy thus far—"but the future is coming under auspicious clouds." This was Hirschmann's first stab at "economic intelligence," which Whale had predicted he would be good at, in the service of stripping the economic robe off the Emperor in Rome.[33]

The University of Trieste also afforded him the time to return to his interest in the French balance of payments and the franc Poincaré. He found a way to register at the university to receive a *laurea* (formal doctoral programs came into existence only after the fall of Mussolini). Several research papers—an analysis of the Philippines balance of payments problems, a short analysis of Italy's monetary policies, a brief on the devaluation of the French franc—entered his file of accomplishments. Mussolini's Milizia Ferroviaria may have gotten the trains to run on time, but when it came to regulations on doctoral training at the University of Trieste, the rules were hardly strict. From what we can tell, Hirschmann labored on his own in these shorter papers and on the eventual doctoral dissertation, a 160-page (a standard length at the time) expansion on his study of the ill-fated franc Poincaré. In this portrait of French public finances, the mixed success of monetary controls, and the end of the gold standard, Keynes makes no appearance. Nor do contemporary debates about international economics. Hirschmann was more interested in the futility of traditional state controls in increasingly interdependent economies. It would satisfy the requirements for a Trieste *laurea* degree, which Otto Albert Hirschmann was awarded in June, 1938—and which he would later translate as a doctorate.[34]

Delving into economics and demography felt more and more like a way to make good on his commitments to social improvement without having to be too concerned with the chronic pressure to account for one's "position." By dumping the illusory quest for ideological consistency, which dominated much of the left-wing debating, he gained some freedom to search for something else—more analytical coherence and observational insight. This is what he honed as he turned the figures of the Italian economy inside out. Helping him to refine this sensibility was Eugenio. When Franco Ferraresi interviewed Albert Hirschman for *Corriere della Sera* in October 1993, he broke into the journalist's depiction of Colorni's "rigorous ideological coherence." His correction: "Coherence yes, but not ideological."[35]

What Colorni had, and which Otto Albert had pined for since his departure from Berlin, was books—many books, which Hirschmann was at liberty to borrow. Colorni's personal library was supplemented by the shelves at the famous antiquarian bookstore on Via San Nicolò operated by the Jewish poet Umberto Saba, where the city's literati would gather—to procure their books, read, and discuss in a secure and friendly atmosphere. Saba's was the unofficial center of unofficial cultural life. After the Spanish crucible, Eugenio appreciated Otto Albert's need for new intellectual directions and so fed him a steady diet not of social science (which Hirschmann picked up more on his own), but of literature. It was in Trieste that the full literary impact of Colorni's influence came to bear. Flaubert's *Correspondences*, his *Education sentimentale* and *Madame Bovary*, Saint Simon's *Mémoires*, Laclos's *Liaisons dangereuses*, Benjamin Constant's *Adolphe*—all of these OA started to read after leaving Spain. If Hegel had been his rite, the Flaubert was now an elixir. Hirschmann became fascinated by his attention to the particularity of each word in his prose and correspondences; the search for the right word, *le* mot juste, was as worthy as a political cause.[36] Eugenio added Croce and Leopardi's poetry. It was a long list whose unity lay in the microscopic view of psychologically motivated plotlines about the making and unmaking of romantic and familial unions. Hirschmann immersed himself in the inner lives of actors and authors, the relationships and the worlds they spun from their mind's eye. Sarah recalled the discovery of his fascination for how protagonists, placed in particular circumstances, engaged in cognitive and emotional processes that motivated their decisions and actions. A foundation was laid, especially by the French masterworks, for Hirschman's interest in the psychological processes lurking behind individual and group behavior. "He admired," recalled Sarah of his encounter with Colorni's reading suggestions, "how [authors] contrived these situations to bring out psychological outcomes rather than the other way around."[37]

If there was one author who captured Hirschmann's imagination, it was Michel de Montaigne. The highly personal vignettes, meditations, and moral reflections shook Hirschmann to his core. He immediately grasped the power of the essays—Montaigne questioned absolute forms of knowledge by submitting everything to the interrogating eye of the observer, starting by looking at himself, turning himself over and over to capture the multiple points of perspective or the multiple forms of the self. "We are never 'at home': we are always outside ourselves," Montaigne wrote. "Whoever would do what he has to do would see that the first thing he must learn to know is what he is." The roofbeams over his library were painted with Pliny the Elder's words:

> Only one thing is certain: that nothing is certain
> And nothing is more wretched or arrogant than man.

Montaigne's affection for the aphorism, for accumulating quotes, rubbed off on Hirschmann instantly, and he began to stockpile his own, starting with a mantra from Montaigne; "observe, observe perpetually."

Montaigne's ode to humility and the spirit it shaped rang so true for the young Otto Albert, whose patience with the ideological certainties and blindness that had warped the Weimar Republic into oblivion, and were now tearing Spain's republic apart, had long since run thin. Doubt was in fact the reason why Eugenio pressed the *Essais* on Otto Albert; Montaigne the jurist had been witness to the brutality of sixteenth-century religious conviction and strife in the same way that Hirschman was becoming witness to twentieth-century bloodshed in the name of ideological certainty; Montaigne's "forlorn France" presaged Hirschmann's "forlorn Europe." The tales of personal experience, which filled the *Essais*, recounted a fascinatingly complex and playful challenge of the absolute distinctions between the subjective and objective worlds. After Hirschmann procured his own copy of the *Essais*, either from Umberto Saba or during one of his trips back to Paris, Montaigne's ironic detachment corroded what was left of his obsession with outer truths and realities. "Except you alone, O Man, said that god, each creature first studies its own self, and according to its needs, has limits to his labors and desires. Not one is as empty as you, who embrace the universe: you are the seeker with no knowledge, the judge with no jurisdiction and, when all is said and done, the jester of the farce."[38]

According to Montaigne, nothing was too trivial for consideration, for what we lose when we give up certainty we gain with clarity. Conversations about Montaigne and Machiavelli led to what Colorni called *piccole idee* of jottings and aphorisms inscribed in what Montaigne would have called commonplace books. These evolved into Hirschmann's own petites idées, the materials for worldly reflections deposited in his memory bank of observations and insights; he opened a file for his "favorite quotes." Three decades hence, the principle was still alive; in writing a complicated book about World Bank development projects around the world, he told Ursula that he recognized this as his style and could return to it as a touchstone. While "everybody is now working on the year 2000—that completely paralyzes me," he confessed. What beckoned him were the problems of everyday life in the present and writing a "'real Hirschman' as Lindenborn or Levinstein [two of his Collège teachers] once wrote in the margins of one of my essays. I very much like the expression that Machiavelli used in one of his letters for his own constructions: 'castelluzzi' [little castles, as easy for reality to destroy as for a fecund imagination to construct]—that is probably what Eugenio called a piccole idee and the only thing I can really do."[39] He would later describe the practice thus: "We can be distracted and diverted and divested by small things, since small things are capable of holding us. We hardly ever look at great objects in isolation; it is the trivial circumstances, the surface images, which strike us—the useless skins which objects slough off." There were multiple implications from this brand of thinking: the notion of the playful imagination at the core of one's exposition would be a model for his own writing and the proposition that the human imagination affected world affairs by shaping peoples' beliefs, and beliefs actions, redoubled his interest in psychology and personal motives. Finally, the idea that doubt could invite moral reflection and action rather than thwart them finally emancipated Hirschmann from the obsession to premise all thought and praxis on understanding the totality of History. Montaigne had not sought to plot any basic scientific verities. But his power of the imagination and its compositional form in essays was a decisive influence on the method, style, and content of Hirschmann's approach to social sciences. As of Trieste, Hirschmann and Montaigne's *Essais* would not be parted.[40]

Under Il Duce's shadow, the sojourn in Trieste pulled together some of the intellectual pieces laid down in other parts: literary masterworks that turned the understanding of behavior inward, the discovery of international economics, and the passion for sleuthing for data that tell stories contrarian to the ones peddled by dictators. And of course there was personal experience. The recombinations of Hirschmann's thoughts were not pendular swings between praxis and theory. Living in Italy meant dealing with fascism cheek to jowl; reading in Saba's bookshop already represented the taking of a dissident stance, especially as Mussolini's gendarmes snuffed out what was left of independent intellectual and political activity. Colorni was actively involved in the formation of an underground resistance movement, spurred by the 1935 arrest of the Turin circle of the *giellisti*, with which he was attached; by now there was more active discussion of a popular front of democratic forces and socialists with Communists. With the *giellisti* abroad, publishing a storm in Paris and flocking to the Spanish front, Colorni was one of the opposition's principal contacts behind the lines, running an underground distribution network, the Centro Interno Socialista, to circulate seditious publications smuggled in from Paris. Colorni collaborated especially with two: Angelo Tasca (alias Rossi, alias Leroux), a socialist, and Mimmo Sereni, his cousin, a Communist and head of the Centro Estero section of the party, whom Colorni and Hirschmann had helped usher from Milan several years earlier.

The "moment for courage" had not come to a close in Spain. If anything, the resistance had to grow lest the power of dictators spread and consolidate. Hirschmann enlisted for his next cause. With an unblemished German passport, and now student credentials, Hirschmann could pass across borders much more easily than Italians, who were in any event prominent on the list of suspects held by Mussolini's OVRA (Organizzazione per la Vigilanza e la Repressione dell'Antifascismo) secret police. Otto Albert procured a special suitcase to carry letters and documents back and forth from Paris to Colorni's group, which would find a way to put them into underground circulation. When it became clear that false-bottom suitcases were devices well known to the border police, he got a replacement, this time with false covers, so that materials could be hidden in the tops; Sereni had contrived this device in Paris and gave it to Otto Albert to carry back on the train to Trieste. How many trips he made with the valise is unclear, but it appears they increased with frequency in 1937 and 1938. Because trains were vehicles for communication and escape, invigilating them was a way of choking the opposition; indeed, OVRA had its origins in clamping down on rail workers who held up schedules to attend political meetings or paralyzed them in the chronic strikes after the First World War. Its agents prowled the rail corridors linking Italy to the rest of Europe. Hirschmann's valise was one humble part of a vast cat-

and-mouse operation for importing and circulating news and analysis to buoy an independent citizenry.

There is something characteristic in the image of Hirschmann riding the night train with his Montesquieu and extra socks in his suitcase while hiding illegal newspapers, the old German schoolboy (literally his role in this game) hanging on to old habits. But it also speaks to the nature of *his* war as it moved him back and forth across the lines, precisely because words had become weaponry. By now, his motivations were complex. No doubt being a secret courier was a continuation of his political engagements since his Berlin days and allowed him to keep up his ties with Paris. But there was another motive at work—he was quite anxious to be as close to Eugenio as possible. Eugenio's overwhelming intellectual energy had by then immersed him in Freud and was about to switch to theoretical physics, while the younger Otto Albert thought he was still at square one with Flaubert and Montesquieu, feeling somewhat like a younger brother struggling to keep the pace. Then there were Eugenio's political dealings, which were also increasingly ornate and enigmatic. Otto Albert desperately wanted to be "in" the secretive crowd. When Eugenio Curiel, who was also a brilliant young physicist, returned to his home town of Trieste in 1937, he immediately won his way into Colorni's aura. Curiel was critical to Colorni's emerging passion for the study of theoretical physics. What's more, Curiel then actively shuffled back and forth between Paris, Trieste, and Rome, until his arrest in Trieste in June 1939; it was he who had taken the bouquet of flowers from Ursula and Otto Albert to Rosa Rein after Mark's disappearance. Curiel's politics brought him close to Mimmo Sereni, which gave the clandestinity more of an air of an extended family affair, cutting into Otto Albert's special place. Curiel emerged as precisely the kind of engagé intellectual that Otto Albert aspired to be; the two had a frosty relationship and competed for Colorni's favor. "To tell you the whole truth, I was perhaps a little jealous of Curiel, because he seemed to have developed the close intellectual-emotional relationship with Colorni to which I myself was always aspiring (and was occasionally achieving)." It did not help that Colorni kept chirping to his brother-in-law that the physicist was an "interesting and intriguing figure."[41]

It is important to see Hirschmann's ideas and actions as parts of a more general sensibility that would usher in a more decisive break with his Berlin origins. The old stress on a firm ideological worldview as a condition for action was long gone. But the years of reading economics and literature and following the example of Eugenio and others' informed voluntarism, freed from the straightjacket of having one's "analysis" right as a condition for "praxis," began to fill the void, enabling him to recombine ideas and action in a much more open and free-spirited way. This was not an automatic conversion, and the years 1937 and 1938 saw Hirschmann working his way through it. As he recalled five decades later, "by 1937, at age 22, I had myself lost some of my earlier certainties, but with my German upbringing, I still sensed it as a real defect not to have a fullfledged Weltanschauung." Nonetheless, the freedom from any particular ideology but the strong commitment to politics as an antifascist was a compelling one. There was an "intimate connection between intellectual posture," which stressed the absence of a "firm ideological commitment," *with* "the commitment to perilous political action." Proving Hamlet wrong not only motivated action; events gave democratic resistance to fascism its urgency.[42]

At some point, Eva visited her brother and sister in Trieste, probably in 1937. It would be their last reunion for many years. Eva recalled that her brother was absorbed in his studies with a determination that seemed unprecedented. He did take a few days off from his work to take her to Venice, a few hours by train from Trieste, and they wandered around the Renaissance city, with OA telling her stories about European history, guiding her through the alleys and canals. As their trip wore on, he grew ever more "sage," dispensing advice and good cheer to indulge a younger sister's adoration. The day she had to leave Trieste to return to Berlin, Otto Albert took Eva to the station; they hugged and she boarded. From the window of her train she watched him walk away, then turn around and return. She leaned out toward him to ask him, "What is it?" He beckoned her forward and whispered into her ear, "Don't ever forget to brush your teeth at night," smiled into her eyes, then backed away into the crowd.[43]

This was the last time he would see her for almost a decade. By the end of 1937, Italy was aligning increasingly with Germany and Japan; expansionists all, they marched out of the League of Nations. In April of that year, the Milan leaders of Colorni's CIS—including its founder, Morandi—had been arrested. Colorni assumed directorship of the clandestine movement. As Communists asserted more and more control over the Spanish government, Rosselli reconciled himself to bringing the *giellisti* into a common "unity of action" pact until he himself was stabbed to death. In March the following year, Otto Albert was summoned by the Prefecture of Trieste to register and provide additional documents of citizenship under orders of the Political Police Division of the Ministry of Interior. Two months later, Hitler visited Italy to inaugurate a series of summits—and visit a few art galleries along the way. May 3 was declared a holiday in honor of the Führer, and the proceedings were broadcast by radio across the country. As part of a more widespread campaign to segregate the "national character" of Jews from those of Italians, in July a group of Trieste scientists endorsed the "Manifesto of Racist Scientists," which attested to the biological races and "proving" the Aryan origins of the Italian "race." The university administrators began to make ominous sounds about putting the institution at the service of the nation's purity and security. Young Blackshirts attacked a synagogue and began to harass Slavs in the city. That summer, one of the economists that had taken Hirschmann under his wing, Giorgio Mortara (of the *Giornale degli Economisti*), warned him that the situation in Italy was bound to get much worse: "this cholera" will need much time to pass. Mortara recommended that Hirschmann not publish any more essays that questioned fascist data and policies so long as he remained in Italy—and indeed urged him to consider returning to Paris and offered to put him in contact with several of his colleagues there; Mortara himself would soon flee to Brazil, where he would modernize Brazil's census system.[44]

Then came a series of decrees, which were all too familiar to Hirschmann, stripping Jews of rights to access to schools and universities, or working in them, and prohibitions on marrying gentiles. In July, Ursula, OA, the toddler Silvia, and Eugenio went for a short vacation to the Dolomites; Ursula was pregnant once more. No doubt the conversation dwelled on what to do. By then, Eugenio had made his commitment to the underground. Everyone was telling Hirschmann that he could be more useful in France than in Trieste. When they returned from the mountains, OA went on one of his trips back to Paris with the infamous valise and began to look for jobs, not sure if he would return to Trieste. On September 3, Eugenio wrote to Otto Albert to tell him that he was happy that he got back to Paris safe and sound, for they had been very worried. The letter, written elliptically to elude the Italian censors, implied that they did not expect him to return: "I do not despair—and I hope—that some day we will meet again and maybe forever. . . . There are affinities between us, as well as a mute sympathy which is not easy to find." He continued: "In the meantime, you should probably have seen your Russian girl [Lia Rein] again." Colorni gave him some brotherly advice: "You should absolutely marry that woman." Also, "Try to do your best and—above all—to find a stable job and to earn a lot of money, so you will be able to host me."[45]

These were Colorni's last words to his brother-in-law as a free man. On September 9, 1938, Eugenio was arrested for his "activities hostile to the Fascist State," interrogated by OVRA agents, and transferred to a prison in Milan. The considerable evidence of his involvement in the circulation of clandestine materials from antifascist groups in Paris was trotted out to justify a penal commission's condemnation that he be "interned" for five years on the island of Ventotene. His own trip in 1938 to a philosophy congress timed to coincide with the Paris International Exhibition was also used as evidence—and prosecutors presented his mathematical notes as code for antifascist communiqués. That he was a Jew only added to his guilt. Less harsh than a prison sentence, he still had to survive with payments from his family; when the war finally broke out, he and others were reduced to starvation rations. Eugenio was among the first to be interned in the Bay of Naples; he would be joined by Communists like Luigi Longo and socialists and "Actionists" such as Altiero

Spinelli, Sandro Pertini, and Ernesto Rossi; Curiel arrived in 1940. By the end of 1938, the anti-Semitic decrees ordered Umberto Saba to sell his bookstore; the hub of Trieste's unofficial cultural life closed down. Saba fled to Paris with thousands more refugees.

Ten days after Colorni's arrest, the reasons for cleansing Trieste became clear: ever the dramatist, Mussolini disembarked from the warship *Camicia Nera* in the city's harbor to address an organized crowd of 100,000 supporters gathered before the city hall. He came to announce that Italy would pledge its support and resources for Hitler's claims in Czechoslovakia in the event of a European war. It was Il Duce's first visit to the city, and he used it to deliver one of his most important texts— not only to vouch for the legitimacy of German expansionist demands, but also to announce a new development in his own policies, to explain his recent campaign against Jews, for "the world of Hebrewism has for sixteen years been an irreconcilable enemy of fascism." Italian Jews who have "proven military or civil merit" will be treated with "comprehension." For the rest, "a policy of separation" would be applied. Italy was squarely on the side of a European civilizational campaign to purge itself of the unwanted.[46]

This included Hirschmann, who, for the second time, was destined to stay in Paris by racial decree. Unlike the first flight, however, this one was less of an exodus. Despite his affections for Italy and his family in Trieste, Paris was the city "where I had always maintained my residence. I was . . . and considered myself when I was in Italy sort of as on leave from France." The question now was how to make of his residence a home.[47]

CHAPTER 5

Crossings

Test yourself by mankind. It makes the
doubter doubt, the believer believe.

FRANZ KAFKA

The Paris to which Otto Albert Hirschmann returned in the late
summer of 1938 was not the same as the one that had greeted him
in April 1933. The Depression clung to the city, the Popular Front had
crumbled, the signs of war were all over, and the flood of refugees fed
growing nativism. Paris was no longer the open city it had been five years
earlier. Nor was Hirschmann the same man. He had a doctorate, had refined some tools in the social sciences, and came equipped to practice his
craft of economic intelligence. Indeed, his July publication on the Italian economy for the Société d'études et d'informations économiques had
opened doors to influential people who wanted to know more about the
economics of fascism. He was also keen to establish himself. It was during
his second Parisian sojourn that Hirschmann began to imagine himself a
writer. The possibility of research and analysis had been planted by Barrett Whale. Reading Montaigne and conversations with Eugenio revealed
a creative space between the writer and the world around him, one he
now wanted to explore.

A veteran of struggles against despots in three countries, at the age of
twenty-three Hirschmann was experienced beyond his years.

To see Hirschmann in France from 1938 to its conquest in 1940 is to
see him finding his own way to becoming an intellectual from a "median
state" of half attachments and half detachments, separated without being

cut off from one's origins or one's hosts. This was Hirschmann's condition as he planted roots in Paris while exploring the option of leaving. With nativism and war in the air, it was not clear how long he would be allowed to call Paris home, whether the city could be the place from which to hatch his intellectual aspirations. War, revolution, and dictators had already ripped so many people from their place in the world. Hirschmann's solutions were, as a result, somewhat provisional, full of crossings—it was his ingenuity to discover that this condition, too, could be a location from which to draw a perspective.[1]

There was no city in the world more full of crossers than Paris. By 1938, the city was less and less a sanctuary and more and more a stop on the way somewhere else. Paris was the crossroads of Europe's problems. By fall of 1937, the city had received a flood of illegal refugees, especially eastern European Jews, mainly Poles on tourist visas ostensibly to visit the world's fair. The minister of defense, Édouard Daladier, argued that unemployment and the mounting cost of feeding and housing refugees were driving the country bankrupt.[2] By 1938, almost 200,000 refugees were in France. On April 10, 1938, Daladier became premier, right on the heels of the Anschluss, which annexed Austria to the Third Reich. Now there was an exodus of refugees from Vienna and other cities. On May 2, new laws imposed heavy penalties on those who assisted illegal migrants and gave the police extra powers to deport. The following month, a decree restricted foreigners' rights to engage in commerce. And that summer, at the Evian Conference (July 6–15), France announced that it could no longer be a haven for the world's oppressed. Then came the "concessions" over Czechoslovakia, and the flight of more refugees from Prague and elsewhere. Throughout that summer and fall, there were home invasions, harsh interrogations at the French borders, and efforts to drive out Czech and Austrian refugees or stop them from flooding the country. When Barcelona finally fell under the fascist heel in January 1939, Spanish Republicans poured across the Pyrenees. On January 21, the first camp (called an assembly center) opened in southern France to pen the unwelcome—immortally called the "scum of the earth" by the French police tasked to patrol the barbed wire fences.[3]

While Paris was becoming a city of refugees fleeing Europe's proliferating dictators, it was also a capital of intrigue and espionage. The French Sûreté nationale had to keep up with the secret service agents of the British Secret Intelligence Service (SIS), the Italian OVRA, the German intelligence branch of the SS (the Sicherheitsdienst, SD), and Stalin's NKVD. Assassins and kidnappers made a swift business as their mercenaries, with relative freedom to swim in Paris's refugee-stocked waters.

If the climate for newcomers was decidedly hostile, for Hirschmann, with a degree from a grande école, with perfect French, and having nurtured his Parisian contacts over the years, it was easy to go undetected and legal. He found a comfortable room in a small hotel on the rue de Turenne, in the middle of the Marais, a crowded medieval neighborhood in the fourth arrondissement populated above all by Jews. Living in the Marais gave him his first opportunity to live cheek to jowl with Jews, and it could not have helped but remind him of the dangers facing Jews in Germany.

This raised the question, especially as Hitler's anti-Semitic decrees made life increasingly miserable for those who stayed behind, of what to do about his family in Berlin. Characteristically, Mutti insisted that Eva complete her *Abitur*, or she would never find a suitable husband. With this finished and Eva now eighteen, she took advantage of an agreement between Germany and Britain that gave visas to girls who signed a four-year commitment to work and study as a nurse. In July 1938, she embarked for London and was sent to a hospital in Dover. The timing of Eva's departure was fortunate, for shortly thereafter it became more and more difficult to escape as Britain, France, and other countries threw up barriers to entry for refugees and Germans slapped greater passport controls on Jewish subjects. On November 7, 1938, a crazed Polish Jew, whose parents had been deported from Germany but were refused reentry to Poland, assassinated a German diplomat in Paris. Goebbels and Hitler unleashed a spasm of organized outrage and destruction—Kristallnacht, November 9. Mutti counted among the thousands of Jews who were forced to turn over valuable possessions to "compensate" for the diplomat's killing. In March of that year, Jewish passports were confiscated or marked "valid only within the country." Later, they were stamped with a *J*. Fortunately,

Eva's status as a nurse allowed her to sponsor her mother's legal entry to England; her brother scraped some money together to help cover the fare. Mutti left Berlin in July, though she dithered to the last minute over her silverware, porcelain, and furniture. Then it became Eva's turn to feel the screws turn. No sooner did many of the survivors from Dunkirk wind up in Eva's hospital to be tended by German nurses, than the government ordered the internship of thousands of German refugees, most of whom were Jews. The men were ordered to a camp on the Isle of Man; nurses, suspected of extracting military secrets from anesthetized soldiers, were peremptorily dismissed from their stations. Eva and Mutti found help from a Jewish-American philanthropic group. Their escape to Britain had an ironic twist, for Eva and Mutti teamed up to recreate their Berlin soup kitchen, this time in London for the jobless German-Jewish nurses.[4]

Eva and Mutti's exodus from Berlin allowed Hirschmann to breathe a sigh of relief. But the news from Italy went from bad to worse. In January 1939, Hirschmann received word from Eugenio, written in German to filter through the Italian censors who read all the outbound letters from Ventotene. "I can't tell you how often during these years I had an over-whelming desire to be with you." There was good news: Otto Albert's second niece was born on the island. The conditions were bleak, but Eugenio found a way to dispel the gloom. "Notwithstanding the hardships, life here gives us a certain intimacy and at times we have lived profoundly happy moments. For total harmony only you are missing." This was exaggerated; in fact, the marriage between Ursula and Eugenio was deteriorating once more. Eugenio's health was also bad; for a long time he suffered from a severe nervous ailment that prevented him from being able to read and drained him of energy. Slowly recovering, he rekindled his interest in mathematics and was now branching out into psychology in order to write "antiphilosophical thoughts." "You must read right away," wrote Eugenio, always pleased to add to his brother-in-law's reading list, "Robbins' *Essays on the Significance of Economic Science*, which has suggested to me many ideas which give me the desire to discuss them with you."[5]

Eva and Mutti's departure for London and the arrest of Ursula and Eugenio must have given Otto Albert a sense that France may not be the eternal safe haven for foreigners, especially Jews. Hirschmann, like many refugees feeling the imminence of war, probed his own exit options. One was to leave for South America. Colorni had a cousin who worked for a bank that channeled investment funds to the industrializing societies of Argentina and Brazil. Hirschman, intrigued by new frontiers in Rio de Janeiro, applied for the position, was accepted, and proceeded to submit his documents to the Brazilian embassy to get a work visa. By the time this opportunity came through, Hirschmann had developed alternative means of existence, which allowed him to stay in Paris working in economic intelligence. He decided to stake a gambit on France.[6]

There was also the idea of moving to the United States. Some time in the fall of 1938, Hirschmann wrote to Max Ascoli, the Italian Jewish writer who had taught philosophy and jurisprudence at the University of Rome until fleeing in 1931 to become a vocal antifascist in the United States, and who was lecturing at the University in Exile of the New School for Social Research. How Hirschmann came to Ascoli's attention is not clear. It may have been Colorni's doing; it may have been that Ascoli read one of Hirschmann's essays. Either way, Ascoli, who was actively trying to get as many Italian dissidents out of Mussolini's clutches as possible, turned to Eugenio's case. Otto Albert assured Ascoli that the evidence against Eugenio had been flimsy: "The only pieces of evidence to convict him are some correspondences and mathematical manuscripts that the police have presented as subversive documents."[7] Ursula warned that "no great publicity [should be made] about his case because this might make matters even worse." Hirschmann inquired if Eugenio could come to the New School; but getting the family out of Italy and settled in New York was going to be costly, and Ascoli was trying to muster resources to sponsor other families. Hirschmann himself could contribute only a small amount because he was also pulling together money to get his mother out of Germany. He suggested that Ascoli approach his old friend, Peter Franck, who had already moved to New York, "and he has written saying that he might be able to find funds." Some of the urgency evaporated once Ursula joined Eugenio on Ventotene, and Otto Albert suggested that he and Ascoli wait a year to see if the situation might improve "so that we might be able to agitate more usefully."[8]

In the meantime, he had begun to explore his own departure for New York. While he did not raise the issue directly with Ascoli, his case was back-channeled through distant Hirschmann relatives, Otto Albert's cousin Oscar, the son of Carl's sister Betty. Otto Albert had written to Oscar explaining that his research commitments in Paris would only tie him down until August of 1939, and according to Oscar's message to Ascoli, "He looks forward with keen anticipation to immigrating to this country at that time and that it would be wise for him to precede his mother here, arranging, in the meanwhile, to have her go to England, where his sister resides." In the late winter and early spring, Oscar and Max Ascoli considered arranging for Otto Albert to come to the New School, only to hit the rising walls against Jewish refugees in the United States. Hirschmann, like so many others, was turned away by the gate-keepers of American visas.[9]

While all this was going on, Hirschmann was settling into Paris. Indeed, he was beginning to enjoy some fruits of success. This took the wind out of leaving for New York or Brazil. So did a torrid relationship. Not since Lia Rein had Hirschmann had a serious girlfriend. In the fall of 1938, he met a distinguished French woman, Françoise, with whom he had much more than a casual affair. Her apartment on Pont Neuf gave them the privacy he had lacked in the past. The relationship went as far as discussions of living together and marriage—certainly according to Hirschmann's memory. "As regards my mood," he wrote to Ursula, "I am still in a state of completely unexpected rapture from what I might call my first love." He confessed to "having given up all hope of having this sentiment when suddenly the whole edifice suddenly burst." Unfortunately the relationship ended badly when Françoise replaced OA with a new soul mate. "The whole story is impossible to describe in this letter," he sighed to Ursula. Still, not one to let a silver lining go by, he found in his misery some broader consolation: "I am beginning to have success with women," adding that he was not missing the opportunity to turn the *affaire* into a learning experience by "deciphering" the "feminine psychology."[10] Here was a sign that Paris might be home. He applied for French citizenship.[11]

Despite the hardship and the restrictions on foreigners, Hirschmann cast some professional lines. At first, he picked up odd jobs as a tutor to French economics students preparing for the *aggregation* exams to become school teachers. They would receive their questions twenty-four hours in advance and have to cobble together oral presentations. Hirschmann was their coach.[12] More and better opportunities came along. He sought to capitalize on his expertise on the Italian economy as the demand for insight, thanks to the looming war, was growing. His knowledge of what was going on behind the fascist curtain brought him to the attention of Charles Rist and Robert Marjolin, the editors of a quarterly economic bulletin of the Rockefeller Foundation–backed Institut de recherches économiques et sociales of the Sorbonne. Rist, the senior of the partnership and a more conservative economist, aligned with Lionel Robbins and the anti-Keynesians. Marjolin, only four years older than Hirschmann, had studied sociology and economics at Yale with a fellowship from the Rockefeller Foundation and would go on to a storied career after the war; he became something of a mentor to Hirschmann.

Writing for the Institut bulletin was a thrill. For the first time Hirschmann was paid for work he enjoyed and for which he had prepared. What emerged was a series of reports on the state of the Italian economy focusing on the hidden disequilibria of Mussolini's autarkic industrialization and militarization. Carrying over his earlier work, Hirschmann explained how state spending was leading to inflation and budget deficits. "We might ask," he wrote, "why the Government has revealed this year that the ordinary budget has a considerable deficit while last year they had tucked it all away in the extraordinary budget. The reason is probably that it wants to prepare the public for future sacrifices." It was this kind of shrewd analysis of Rome's deceptive handling of the economy that drew, in particular, Marjolin's attention. He was also keen to place Italy into the context of a more open economy—and tracked the ways in which the despot's fiscal habits and protectionism had the perverse effect of worsening the country's balance of payments, making it more dependent on imports of crucial raw materials, especially energy, and machinery. The invasion of Abyssinia, Hirschmann argued, was not just a political gambit; expansionism was driven by Italy's perceived need for more colonies to make up for its dependency on imported raw materials and petroleum. "With these measures *la mise sur pied* of war by the entirety of the Italian economy has made more advances," warned Hirschmann.[13]

The bulletin essays reveal some early traits. The first is his ingenuity in using sources. To gauge the level of gross domestic economic activity beyond the dubious official figures, Hirschmann kept a careful record of monthly freight shipments on Italy's rail system; he tracked the imports and exports of particular commodities, such as cotton or olive oil, rather than rely on the government's aggregated figures. When it came to discussing Felice Guarneri, the fascist technocrat who rose to become the minister of foreign trade, and his claims that the Italian economy's commercial balances were in fine shape, Hirschmann tallied the declining occupancy of beds in Italy's hotels to show that tourism was in crisis, raising basic questions about the veracity of the official line. He sought the economic story behind the story. A "freelance economic journalist" is how he later thought of his first forays into publishing.[14]

There was more to Hirschmann's developing style. He also now had the time to reconcentrate his attentions on squaring Keynes's *General Theory* with his interest in international economics; by now the book had been lugged back and forth between France and Italy, and his concentrated work for Rist and Marjolin afforded the time to figure out his own position. Hirschmann began to see himself more and more in an area ignored by Keynesians, though not by Keynes himself. If many Keynesians tended to think of national economies as closed entities, Hirschmann saw them as open ones—and the intersections of foreign trade and national policy, which first came to light in his study of the franc Poincaré, was looming ever larger as a compelling field of research interests. His kind of analysis, and the regard from his mentors, relieved him from the pressures of figuring out whether Keynes had all the right answers. Hirschmann drew readers' attention to the fact that Mussolini's model of autarky meant that it had to cover its dependence on imports from some places by accumulating and forcing surpluses from others, notably its "colonies." Second, Hirschmann emphasized the need to understand an economy against the background of a political system; "macroeconomic" policy making could not be so easily severed from the ideological commitments of a regime—a right-wing dictatorship, a socialist government, or a pluralist liberal one. From the start of his thinking about economics, Hirschmann never let his eye stray much from underlying political concerns—less because he had his own ideological agenda than because ideology stamped the decisions of policy makers in ways that escaped the attention of much economic analysis.

Working for the Institut de recherches économiques et sociales gave him his first taste of success. It also opened more doors. Henri Piatier, one of France's leading statisticians read the essays, met Hirschmann, and brought him to the attention of John Bell "Jack" Condliffe.[15] It is likely also that the Rockefeller Foundation's contacts with the Institut also helped, for Condliffe was also a grant recipient. Condliffe, a New Zealander who'd studied economics at Cambridge, had become a leading figure in the Institute for Pacific Studies, based in Honolulu, and from there joined the economic secretariat of the League of Nations in 1931, where he wrote the first *World Economic Survey*. He was a vocal proponent of policies that favored a liberal, multilateral trading system as a necessary bulwark for global peace. As far as he was concerned, protectionist responses to the Depression were a return to the dark ages. One scourge was the tendency for countries to resort to "bilateral" deals favoring signatories at the expense of everyone else: the end of the gold standard and the cycle of competitive devaluations compelled more and more countries to two-way clearing systems and exclusive trade pacts.

To economic liberals, this was a menace. The intellectual crusade to reveal its dangers afforded Hirschmann his first opportunities for paid research—and commissioned writing. They came thanks to the coattails of the practical, easy-going, and well-connected Condliffe, an important figure at the International Committee on Intellectual Cooperation, a fund-starved network of academics who were committed to working across national borders toward solutions for global conflicts, and an intellectual arm of the League of Nations. While it never lived up to its architects' hopes of creating a global class of scholars committed to pooling their talents to solve problems, it did sponsor meetings and research. Some of these sowed the seeds for later partnerships. One meeting was the Conférence permanente des hautes études internationales, dedicated to the study of "economic policies of peace," which was scheduled to meet in Bergen, Norway in 1939. The Rockefeller Foundation set aside funds to support research in areas of public policy that Condliffe considered as hurdles to peaceable international economic relations. One such hurdle was the controls slapped on exchanges of currencies, a device relied upon more and more since the collapse of the gold standard. In this practice, Mussolini's policy makers had been creative artists since their exchange control system was devised in 1934. Condliffe asked Hirschmann to prepare a report for the Bergen meeting to analyze Italy's policies and its consequences as well as a statistical profile on the tendency toward bilateralism. Delighted, he plunged into his research and drafted the memoranda. For the first time, he was receiving a regular, and not unsubstantial, paycheck. "I have found good work preparing something for the Conférence des Hautes Etudes Internationales," he gushed to Ascoli. In the meantime, "my article on Abyssinia has just appeared just as I was not expecting any more from the *Europe Nouvelle*. Too bad because it would have certainly yielded ten times more in *The Nation*." This was a little farfetched but reveals a young economist already setting his heights very high in the world of letters. But these were not the only reasons for pride; Condliffe's request for a profile of foreign trade allowed Hirschman to build his first statistical simulation of foreign trade, using his training in Paris and Trieste and applying it to international economics. "Étude statistique sur la tendance du commerce extérieur vers l'équilibre et le bilatéralisme" was the prolegomenon to what would eventually become his first book. It represented the fulfillment of Barrett Whale's prediction about Hirschmann's inclination to economic intelligence.[16]

The looming war forced the Bergen organizers to cancel the event, but for Hirschmann the report was an opportunity to display his talents for Condliffe and to explore further the thorny relationship between foreign trade and economic policy making in a fascist country. Managing foreign exchange favored the importation of only certain kinds of industrial products. It also drove private domestic spending into state coffers. It was a system, Hirschmann showed, that worked. The lira stopped its slide and scarce reserves flowed into the military-industrial project of the government. But there was a price. The model did not solve the underlying riddle of how to square massive militarization and public-works spending when the export sector was too weak to sustain them. And the price was rising. Inflation rose, consumer shortages worsened, and Italy was solving more and more of its imbalances by relying on "clearing" systems (like special notes—*bollettos*—usable only to pay a trade partner its dues) that fostered trade blocs that shut out third countries. At the heart of Hirschmann's analysis was a basic insight: exchange controls were not just technicalities or neutral responses to economic pressures, but also part of a more general tendency to "corporative control by the fascist government to submit all sides of the Italian economy to the State and its multiple para-state organizations."[17] His conclusion echoed Condliffe's reasons to convoke the conference, to show that the model was sustainable at the expense of Italy's trade partners, especially its colonies—which only bent Italy more toward expansionism and aggression. Autarky "inspires, in the first place, military considerations;" economic policy making furnished a premise for empire.

The essay thus pointed to a direct connection between the economics of the Italian dictatorship and expansionism into Africa. It appears in his first articles, but here Hirschmann took his analysis a step further, to argue that Italy was not exceptional. The invasion of Abyssinia was part of a more general propensity for industrial dictatorships to solve their economic problems by oppressing trading partners near and far. In this sense, policies were more than technicalities "provoked by some kind of endogenous tendency for trade controls, [they] were controls to serve as an instrument to realize policies decided outside and above them (*en dehors et au-dessus de lui*)."[18] This analysis of Italy's exchange management system contained kernels he would develop in future years about the monopolies in international trade, national democracies, and world peace—parts of an intellectual bridge between economic thinking and political practice. We also see the early elements of a style—the pursuing of trails of small yet revealing indicators, an affinity for an experiential and practical economic analysis that was never far removed from political and ethical moorings.

None of this took place in a vacuum. With his family scattered in different corners of Europe and harder and harder to reach, political events were hard to miss. In September 1938, when the concessions of the Munich Pact (which allowed Germany to take the Sudetenland from Czechoslovakia) were announced, a pall descended over Paris. At the time, Hirschmann was working out of an office supported by the Carnegie Endowment for International Peace near Vincennes, close to an army installation. Hirschmann remembered listening to Premier Daladier's voice crackling over the radio as he announced the Munich provisions. Outside, the French army seized Hirschmann's office building and ordered all employees to leave. Hirschmann had to sweet-talk an officer to allow him to retrieve his coat, briefcase, and materials; he was then escorted from the premises. As he returned to the center of Paris by train, he gazed out the window wondering what awaited Europe.[19]

The inevitability of war marred the pleasures of personal success. But it was also a development he found fascinating and that pushed Hirschmann to broaden his observations about the economics of dictatorship. The spring of 1939 filled Parisian radios and newspapers with news of spreading fascism. Governments of the Intermarium (the lands between the Baltic and the Adriatic) tried to create a counterweight. The alignment of Poland, Romania, and possibly Yugoslavia could represent an economic and commercial zone that linked the Baltic to the Adriatic, in an alliance of Polish armies, Romanian wheat and oilfields, and Czech and Yugoslav patriotism, to cut Hitler off at the German-speaking frontiers. It was futile. Betrayed by Hungarian expansionists, in late February Hungary negotiated the Anti-Comintern Pact, which included Germany, Italy, and Japan. The Royal Hungarian army invaded Ruthenia, and on March 15, German motorized infantry swept into Prague and barreled on to the Slovakian border. While it snowed on the Reich's invaders, Hirschmann went out in the Parisian rain to buy his newspapers. He was concerned about peace, but he was also watching carefully the unfolding struggle for European trade and commercial power in the middle of continent; as the fate of an economic Intermarium buffer collapsed under the weight of fascist imperialism, the commercial and territorial struggle for the region intensified. Poland became the next target. To reintegrate the Baltic port of Danzig into the Reich and to make room among non-German lands for Hitler's *Lebensraum*, the Führer declared "Danzig or War!" In May, Stalin dropped his long-time foreign minister, Maxim Litvinov, and replaced him with Vyacheslav Molotov. On August 24, Stalin shocked the world and announced a nonaggression pact with Hitler. Included was a protocol dividing northern and eastern Europe into German and Soviet spheres of influence. While the full details would not come out until after the war, the partition of Poland between the two signatories only redoubled Hirschmann's growing interest in the entwined relationship of trade, diplomacy, empire, and dictatorship. It also confirmed his suspicions about Moscow.

France went on alert. On April 12, an act decreed that foreign men between eighteen and forty who had resided in France for over two months were allowed to join French army, as opposed to just the Foreign Legion. The same promulgation subjected "stateless" foreign men from twenty to forty-eight to the same duties as Frenchmen—a two-year term of service. Alarmed at German bellicosity, Hirschmann enlisted in the French army now that foreigners were not restricted to the Legion. He was a soldier in training when German and Russian armies invaded Poland in September, and France and Britain declared war on the Reich on September 3.[20]

He readied for his second war.

This one would prove to be a different experience from the Aragonese front, up to a point. On September 18, he wrote his mother to say that "all is well with me from a physical and moral point of view. The training is moving forward to make us into verifiable soldiers." Two days later, the French government ordered that all male German refugees be interned, with the exception of those serving in the army: it was either a detention camp or a training camp. Hirschmann found himself stationed east of Paris, dispatched to a platoon of German and Italian émigrés, where "I am making some new friends," he wrote to Mutti. His commander was "very nice and intelligent," he added. They were allowed off the camp on Sundays. From London, Mutti sent new copies of *La Statesman*, which the soldiers shared. A photograph of Cadet Hirschmann has him posing with twenty others in his group. The German and Italian *copains*—mainly Jews and intellectuals who had fled fascism to find themselves trained to fight them—are wearing different uniforms, some none at all. They are relaxed and friendly, looking more like a young faculty meeting. OA closed his note to his mother telling her that they will be celebrating Yom Kippur. "I feel just as I used to in the good days of the Collège Français!"[21]

When France went to war, it did so under some strong precepts. Military planners had been above all obsessed with a surprise attack from Germany and had plowed resources into formidable systems of fortification. The result was the famous Maginot Line, named after the war minister in 1932, who had died of typhoid fever caught while eating oysters. After receiving its basic training, Hirschmann's company, a Bataillon d'Ouvriers d'artillerie, was nothing more than a work gang sent off to maintain

Postcard of Otto Albert's French company.

a rail line connecting to a munitions factory in the Loire Valley, "manual labor" that reminded him of his "profound conviction of his ineptitude with this kind of work." Hirschmann remembered that his officers had no sense at all of Germany's military preparedness or strategy; his training resembled the one he had received in Barcelona—their guns did not fire, their boots did not fit, and their overcoats did not match.[22] There was, however, some solace: given the short days of winter, he had plenty of time in the evenings to read Stendhal's *Le Rouge et le Noir* and to plan a "whole literary program ahead of me." His favorite pastime was rereading Montaigne's *Essais*. He told Ursula that "this is perhaps the bedside book—*livre de chevet*—par excellence, the one that would probably be my choice to take if I had to choose only one book."[23]

These were prophetic words.

The high command was unprepared for a new type of war, especially in the rapid deployment of large-scale forces and the use of aircraft. In the end, German forces avoided the Maginot Line altogether and perforated the supposedly impenetrable Ardennes forest. The distinguished historian, Marc Bloch, a captain in the army intelligence, was still thinking about his lectures at the Sorbonne when "the storm of 10 May burst over our heads;" eighty-five German infantry and ten armored divisions swarmed into Belgium and Holland, and by May 13, they were already crossing into France.[24] Two weeks later, they were rolling swiftly onto Paris. The government began to make plans to evacuate the capital; four days later the Germans rolled down the Champs-Élysées. On June 10, smelling an opportunity for spoils, Mussolini declared war against France. The next day, Hirschmann—not knowing just how badly the war was going for his fellow French troops—wrote about the sadness of finding his family divided by enemy lines. "Knowing now that we are completely cut off," he wrote to his mother the morning after Mussolini's announcement, "knowing that these *êtres que j'aime que j'adore* are living in enemy country this leaves my heart broken in ways I cannot even tell you." Completely ignorant of what was happening on the front, he concluded: "I am doing very well here, and I figure I will be staying here for a while longer."[25] A week later came another shock: on June 17, Marshal

Pétain, the new premier, issued a radio address telling France's citizens that the fighting would stop. Then came an endless, apprehensive week of waiting to hear the terms. The armistice took effect June 25 with the Nazis holding 1.6 million French soldiers as prisoners of war. France would be severed into an occupied north and an "unoccupied" south, based in the city of Vichy.

The sudden collapse of the French defenses sparked a mass upheaval. Eight million people took to the road. First came the waves of Dutch, Belgian, and Luxembourg citizens fleeing the German onslaught. They brought with them rumors of German raping and pillaging. Then, as the Reich's troops poured into France, civilians bundled their belongings and fled in advance. Hirschmann and his fellow soldiers stood at the side of the road and watched the waves of frightened families. "Columns of refugees pass us by and we do what we can to relieve them of their lot—but these are sad images." To make matters worse for Hirschmann's company, word arrived that the families of some of the fellow German soldiers were being herded into detention camps. This led to a desperate scramble to get them released.[26] "In this mass of people," remembered one witness, "nobody could find anybody else. Nobody knew where they were going. People just moved on, and that was it. Towards the south, far from the 'others.' They fled."[27] Pétain's speech on the seventeenth sent riptides through the French army, still scrambling to organize itself or conduct an orderly retreat. The war was over, but there were no orders from the high command as to how to proceed. Demobilize? Recongregate? Go home? What home? When it became clear that France was to be partitioned, many soldiers joined the mass trek southward to the unoccupied zone.

Pétain set up his Revolution nationale government in Vichy and proceeded to salvage a bruised national pride, broadcasting pieties about "work," "family," and "national sovereignty." But the realities of the National Revolution were all too clear—this was a puppet government. There was little safety to be had in the unoccupied zone, especially for Jews. Pétain picked up where his Third Republic predecessors left off— herding non-French refugees into detention camps originally erected as pens for Spanish Republicans in 1939. Radio Vichy spewed a bilious campaign against Jews and "traitors" over the airwaves. By September 1940, there were thirty-one detention camps in the southern zone. Then came Article 19 of the armistice agreement—a mockery of Pétain's rhetoric about French sovereignty—which required Vichy to "surrender on demand" all Germans named by the Reich to its officers. The Nazis sent the Kundt Commission to scour the detention camps hunting for their enemies.[28]

An even worse fate awaited the Germans and Italians fighting on the French side. Hirschmann and his comrades convinced their lieutenant to release them with fake military passes. Each got to choose their new avatar. Hirschmann chose Albert Hermant—it stripped away the aura from *Otto* and kept the *H-r* and *man* syllables. Later, this choice became embellished with the fancy that Hermant was a French Romantic poet—if so, he is so obscure that he was unknown. But it had a nice ring and under pressure was easier to sign with a natural flow of the pen. "*Sauve qui peut, il faut se débrouiller*," the commander told his soldiers, and with that they disbanded, blending into the millions heading southward. Hirschmann procured a bicycle in Le Mans, ditched his uniform, and bought some clothes from a peasant. He followed the country lanes en route to Bordeaux. At Niort, he went into a backyard and buried his German papers in a tin can; now he was undocumented except for his bogus military pass—which was not going to get him far. The trick was to get into the Vichy zone, but to do so, he had to get past German checkpoints. A German officer stopped Hermant and ordered him to the nearest POW camp to rejoin his company. Hermant agreed, saluted his captor, and set off in the right direction, only to vanish into a crowd. Slipping out of their hands, he crossed into the Vichy zone, where he reached out to his only contact: Doctor Cabouat, who knew Hirschmann from his summers teaching German on the Normandy coast. Cabouat invited the runaway to take refuge with his family in Nîmes, a small town near the Mediterranean coast.[29]

Huguenots like the Dupuys, with whom they vacationed in Aubi-sur-mer, the Cabouats knew something of persecution. It was, after all, the Huguenots who had founded Hirschmann's Collège in Berlin as a haven for religious refugees. In France, they enjoyed a discreet reputation for tolerance and an ethical commitment to provide shelter for others. The Cabouats did what they could to shelter Hirschmann, sealing his lifelong admiration for the Huguenot spirit. They landed him a job at the local natural history museum, run by a friend of the Cabouats, during which time he plunged into a textbook on paleontology he found on the museum's shelves. Finding this boring and knowing that he could not hide in Nîmes without endangering himself and others, the issue became how to get out. There was also some lingering "feeling that I should comply with some rules." He wanted discharge papers lest he be accused of desertion by Vichy authorities. So, he ventured to the nearest military camp and managed to get his formal discharge. He still did not have a civilian identification that would stand up to any scrutiny. The Cabouats arranged for Hirschmann to get a *carte d'identité*, a much-prized artifact for any refugee wanting to escape the Nazi dragnet. Madame Cabouat testified and signed the carnet issued by the Nîmes Commissaire on July 6, 1940. Hereafter, Otto Albert Hirschmann was officially Albert Hermant, an interpreter by profession, a Frenchman born in Philadelphia; this last twist was devised just in case an overzealous inspector wanted to check a French birth register.[30]

The pause in Nîmes allowed Hirschmann—hereafter known as Albert, the name he adopted permanently, relegating Otto to the initial *O*—to take stock and prepare his next steps. Somehow, he received word from another German fugitive from Paris, his old mentor from their militancy days in Berlin, Heinrich Ehrmann, who told Hirschmann that he was on his way to Marseilles to escape France. So, Albert thanked the Cabouats for their risk-taking generosity and made for the port. When he arrived, the city was teeming with refugees, not just French, but German, Austrian, Italian, Dutch, and not a few stragglers from the ill-fated British Expeditionary Force. Ever since mid-June, the number of refugees had been backing up at the Spanish border. Some wound up ensnared in the French detention camps; many found their way back to Marseilles to find another way out. The cafes and bars teemed with them. Albert walked past the clusters of frantic refugees and checked into the Hotel

Luxe on the Gran Via Canebière, facing the Old Port. Then he went to locate Ehrmann, who was about to leave for the United States, having just secured a visa. He also caught up with the grieving Rein family, sans Mark, who were also about to leave. The reunion was at once profoundly sad and relieving; having lost his son, Rafael did not want to lose one of his closest friends.

Between Ehrmann and the Reins, and their contact with American socialists of the Jewish Labor Committee and the Neu Beginnen activist, Karl Frank, who had relocated to New York, Hermant learned that an American was due to arrive from Spain at the Gare St. Charles on August 14. His name was Varian Fry. Fry was supposed to arrive with visas. When he stepped onto the platform of the Marseilles train station, Fry was greeted by a smiling young, French translator who volunteered to escort him to the Hotel Splendide. They settled into Fry's room and swapped their stories. Fry liked Albert Hermant instantly. Multilingual and impressed by the story of the false papers, Fry noted his knowledge of the German Social Democrats. He found himself taken by Hermant's irrepressible smile and charm—and soon nicknamed him Beamish, after the impish grin. Beamish could be useful. For the next five months, Fry and Beamish worked hand in glove in a remarkable effort to get stateless refugees out of France.[31]

Fry, a thirty-one-year-old Harvard-educated classicist, had been working as an editor in New York when the war broke out. Having been to Germany some years earlier as a foreign correspondent, he had seen the persecution of Jews firsthand. It left him horrified. When stories about the bottlenecks of eminent writers and artists unable to escape France began to circulate, Fry enjoined a coalition of socialists, Jews, Quaker charities, and New York dignitaries, as well as some trade unions, to donate $3,000 to fund the exodus of a short list of worthies facing arrest in southern France, especially the better-known intellectuals and artists who were known to be in danger. The organization was called the Emergency Rescue Committee. When he got to Marseilles, Fry encountered a vastly more complex challenge. There was far more than a handful of refugees. The recent news of the German philosopher Walter Benjamin's death while escaping from France had cast a pall over the city. The Portuguese and Spanish governments were demanding visas for anyone trying to cross the Pyrenees. Marseilles was choking up. What Fry did not lack was nerve; neither did Hermant. Fry also had the cover of being American, still a neutral power, and Hermant was French, but he also spoke impeccable German, and fluent Italian and English to boot. They could both prove Hamlet wrong.

"I was just one grade below Varian Fry in terms of being slightly too confident and imprudent, perhaps," Hirschman recalled. Imprudent, perhaps, reckless even. But their risk-taking saved many, many lives.[32]

Together, Varian Fry and Albert Hermant spent the summer, fall, and bitterly cold winter of 1940 laying the foundations for an escape operation for fascism's enemies. The list of the saved reads like a who's who: Hannah Arendt, André Breton, Marc Chagall, Marcel Duchamp, Max Ernst, Siegfried Kracauer, Wifredo Lam, Jacques Lipchitz, Alma Mahler Gropius Werfel (the serial wife of composer Gustav Mahler, architect Walter Gropius, and novelist Franz Werfel), Heinrich Mann, Walter Mehring... it goes on. In all, over 2,000 refugees got out of France through the Emergency Rescue Committee's network. Hermant's smile and can-do approach to even the thorniest problem earned him the nickname Beamish among everyone involved in the rescue operation. Fry became very attached to his right-hand man. The only irritant was Beamish's habit of drifting off. "I had only one fault with him," according to Fry, "and that was his absentmindedness. When you spoke to him, it was sometimes five or ten seconds before he would show any sign of having heard you. As he said himself, he was *un peu dans la lune*—a little in the clouds. To an impatient person like myself, it was sometimes rather annoying." But otherwise, he depended on the friendly but mysterious young translator for his underground experiences, facility with money, command of languages, and affection for breaking and bending rules. "He came carefully prepackaged, wrapped in false papers in which he was inordinately proud," remembered one of his fellow rescuers.[33] Beamish used to laugh to Fry that he had too many false papers to be really plausible. Along with his fraudulent identity from Nîmes, there was a membership card for the French Youth Hostels, another for the Club des Sans Club (a tourists' association), and a half-dozen other miscellaneous backups—all of which he loved because they were so elegantly false. "There's such a thing as being too *en règle*," Beamish told Fry. "It's like a criminal who has too many alibis."[34]

The problems for the escapees were many: transit visas to get through Spain and Portugal, entry visas to third countries, and exit permits from France were all hard to get. The first could be arranged, conditional on the second. The third was impossible given Vichy's armistice commitment to turn over refugees "on demand." So, the trick was to get out of France illegally, slipping past the French Gardes Mobiles, who grew more vigilant as the Nazis squeezed the Vichy government for more captives, and then brandish third-country visas at the Spanish border to gain permission to "transit." What Fry offered was a mechanism to get a visa to the United States, which made the other permissions easier to secure, except for those from the Vichy controllers, who were determined to round up quotas for the Nazis. What Fry needed was a secret route out of France, a method for printing false documents and visas, and a way to change money on the black market to pay the forgers and stipends for the refugees. Beamish came up with an initial escape plan based on his own crossing at Cerbère after leaving Spain in 1936; his penciled map on a scrap of paper "was to become a crucial document in the cultural history of our times," according to Donald Carroll, whose article on Fry in *American Heritage* magazine would bring belated recognition of the underground operation.[35]

When Pétain's Gardes Mobiles choked off the Cerbère route, another one had to be found. Fry and Beamish scouted the border zone to find a path where the French and Spanish stations were sufficiently far apart so that guards at the latter could not see if crossers made it through French controls. Such a route was like a needle in a haystack. Eventually, Beamish found Lisa and Hans Fittko in one of his prowls through Marseilles's cafes. Berlin socialists who were slightly older than Hirschmann but of the same Neu Beginnen vintage, the Fittkos already had experience at the art of escape, having assisted a number of people cross the Pyrenees with the help of the socialist mayor of the fishing hamlet of Banyuls, Vincent

Azéma, who safeguarded the escape and smuggling route as "la route Lister," named after the Spanish Republican general who used it during the struggle against Franco. Beamish arranged a meeting of Fry with the Fittkos in Banyuls. It did not go well; Fry had some difficulty following the discussion in German. At one point, he offered to pay the Fittkos for their services, to which Hans responded icily: "Do you understand the word *Überzeugung*, convictions?" Beamish, who knew precisely what this meant but also knew Fry, resolved the misunderstanding; the committee would help support the Fittkos in return for their services in getting refugees over the secret pass. The crossing became known as the F Line.[36]

The initial misunderstanding with the Fittkos reflected more than just a linguistic gap; Fry could be naïve and at times flippant, unaware of the dangers of clandestine work. He had a habit of speaking indiscreetly in cafes and restaurants, which made Beamish squirm. He also knew little about "the real political nuances of the German immigration."[37] Fry seems to have been aware that he was out of his depth on this score and thus left the job of "interviewing" the swarms of people who gathered outside the Hotel Splendide, sifting peoples' backgrounds, and screening out imposters trying to penetrate the clandestine network, to others. Fry relied upon Beamish to screen, in particular, the left-wing refugees, notably the Neu Beginnen militants who'd straggled to Marseilles after being driven from Germany, Vienna, Prague, and now Paris. It was a group that Beamish knew well, so he could help sift the interlopers from the genuine cases. A photo of Beamish taken by Fry in the fall of 1940 has him hovered over a lamp-lit desk with a refugee poring over papers. This kind of one-by-one labor was time-consuming but was necessary for the safety of the operation and the refugees alike.

Room 307 of the Splendide posted two stations, a small writing table and Fry's flat-topped dressing table. Fry and Beamish were soon joined by Franz "Franzi" von Hildebrand, a conservative Austrian Catholic, who screened the nonleftist refugees. Their operation ran from 8:00 a.m. until midnight. Then, at the end of each marathon day, they would meet and compare notes. When they got paranoid about police bugs in the room, Beamish, recalling that the Polish ambassador in Berlin used to hold his

Beamish with unknown refugee preparing to escape
France, Marseilles, 1940.

staff meetings in one of the embassy bathrooms, suggested they talk there
so the noise of the running bath could drown out any microphones. From
those meetings would emerge a list of applicants for US visas, which had
to be cabled to New York, where the Rescue Commission began to expedite the applications for the vice-consul to receive in Marseilles. This
was a man named Hiram Bingham IV, who appreciated Fry's efforts and
became disenchanted with the State Department's anti-Semitic say-little
and do-less response; his issuing of thousands of visas, legal and illegal,
would win him the enduring enmity of the American government that
otherwise wanted to restrict entry.

When the operation got too big for a room in the Splendide and the
hotel management started to get itchy about the numbers of refugees
converging on their establishment, Fry and Beamish relocated to an old
leather goods store owned by a Jewish retailer and called it the Centre
américain de secours. They enlisted a few more volunteers. One was Lena

Fishman, who had Beamish's language skills and so became Fry's secretary and took over some of Beamish's job screening refugees at the desk. More screeners were necessary, so two American women joined the little crew—the beautiful and very wealthy Mary Jayne Gold (*la riche américaine*) and the spirited Miriam Davenport, with whom Beamish had a flirtatious on-again, off-again attraction. Gold recalled her first meeting with Fry and Beamish: Fry did all the talking while the other, "a handsome fellow with rather soulful eyes, had been standing there taking everything in, his head cocked slightly to one side. One of those German intellectuals, I thought, always trying to figure everything out."[38]

Expanding the operation meant, increasingly, that Beamish's work was in the streets, bars, and brothels of Marseilles, expanding the illegal tentacles of the operation. If the operation had a fixer, it was Beamish. It was a role he relished. "Beamish soon became my specialist on illegal questions," wrote Fry at the end of the war. Beamish had three basic tasks: finding sources of bogus passports, keeping up a supply of credible identity cards, and contriving ways to funnel large sums of money into France to fund the scheme without the authorities finding out. He cannot have imagined that his study of Italian exchange controls would have prepared him for this. At first, the Czech passports were doing the trick, but as the number of refugees brought under the program grew, Beamish worried that the whole operation would get revealed. So, he sweet-talked the Polish consul into issuing some passports; the Lithuanian honorary consul agreed to do the same. Lithuanian documents were especially coveted because—still at that point—the little Baltic state was neutral; Beamish got himself one of these, thereby becoming a Lithuanian citizen called Otto Albert Hirschmann, since his *carte* did not qualify him automatically for a French passport. Just in case; beside, Beamish prized his multiplying identities.

This was all a bit of a cat-and-mouse game in which Beamish had to stay a step ahead of Portuguese and Spanish authorities who would stop giving transit visas on suspicious passports; when Lisbon suspended visas on Chinese and Belgian Congo passports, the Emergency Rescue Committee turned to Dutch and Panamanian documents. For those who could not get passports, Beamish contrived a system in which the committee would buy demobilization papers from French soldiers for 200 francs, which gave the holder free passage to Casablanca—which itself became a holding center for refugees aiming to get to Lisbon. All the refugee had to do was memorize the details of the soldier's identity and military experience and get some cast-away uniform on the black market (which Beamish arranged). This system worked well until the officer with whom Beamish was dealing was caught and court-martialled in October.

The solution to the money problem was an ingenious deal with Marseilles's notorious mob. "Hermant, that demon of ingenuity with the puckish smile," Mary Jayne Gold tells us, "had already made good contact on the black market money exchange."[39] Like most big ports, there was no shortage of gangsters in Marseilles, but getting to them was a challenge. One way was through women. And "Beamish liked women—there was no getting away from that," recalled Fry. He found his way into the good graces of the bleached-blonde mistress of the American consul, and she introduced Beamish to a friend—a Corsican businessman named Malandri, who despised police of all stripes and was thus especially inclined to dislike the Vichy regime and its allies. Malandri had connections. One was "Jacques"—the owner of a restaurant called Les Septs Petits Pêcheurs, the biggest mobster in Marseilles, and a very rich man—and this led to a short Russian refugee from 1917 who was equally well connected, "Dimitru." Beamish, Jacques, and Dimitru concocted a deal in which Dimitru would introduce Beamish to interested clients. Beamish would take their francs and pay dollars to the committee's agents in New York; Dimitru and Jacques took a commission for each client. For months the system worked brilliantly, fueled by New York monies as well as clandestine transfers from the British government, which needed Fry to get their trapped soldiers out of Marseilles (in return for which, the committee skimmed some of the funds to cover their political refugees).[40]

Beamish's colleagues marveled at his skill; for all his youth he was a font of devious ingenuity and seasoned wisdom. Mary Jayne Gold, after watching Beamish return from one of his expeditions, asked him how the Nazis confiscated Jewish property. Beamish explained that first they would hang a sign outside the establishment announcing "Jewish Enterprise." Then they would take bribes to allow the proprietor to stay open. Then they simply seized the business when it went broke. Gold thanked Beamish for his tutorial in "applied anti-Semitism," and explained that this was like the gangsters she knew "back home" in Chicago. Beamish smiled knowingly and added that in Germany "the gangsters and the government are the same people." Little insights like these amazed the American ingénue.[41]

Meanwhile, the clock was ticking on the operation. Through October, the group would huddle over their radio and listen to the news of the Luftwaffe pounding English cities. The Sûreté nationale was getting stricter, and Franco would periodically shut down the border altogether. Beamish, for one, knew that the conditions could only worsen—despite Fry's brilliant diplomacy. He grew more anxious to get as many out as quickly as possible. One group of refugees that Beamish was entrusted to screen and help get out were the socialists from Austria and Germany, in particular, the veterans of from the Neu Beginnen movement, many of whom were holed up in the port. They were not easy to assist: they were not as famous as the artists and writers and were often penniless. Many were also Jews and militant antifascists. All this elevated them to the top of the Gestapo list of refugees who were supposed to be surrendered to the Sûreté nationale "on demand." And some were already being held in camps and thus poised to be turned over. Their champion in the United States was Karl Frank, alias Paul Hagen, who worked closely with the Jewish Labor Committee to help it usher out socialists and labor leaders. One day, Beamish called a meeting with Miriam Davenport and Mary Jayne Gold at Basso's, Beamish's favorite bar. When he entered Basso's, he ordered three cognacs, apologized that there was no more scotch on the market, and explained that Pétain was about to come down hard on anyone sheltering the unwanted. There were four Neu Beginnen members—Franz Boegler, Siegfried Pfeffer, Hans Tittle, Fritz Lamm—who could not pick up their American visas because they were imprisoned in the Le Vernet camp and were about to be "surrendered." Hagen had cabled Marseilles to plead for their rescue. Beamish went into unusually indiscreet detail about their cases and the situation at Le Vernet. When Gold asked him why he was telling her all this, he replied, "Because we want you to go up to Le Vernet and persuade the commandant to allow them to come to Marseilles." The idea was that once in the port they could slip their guards and fetch their US visas and escape to Spain. What Beamish wanted her to do was go to the camp and explain that she was a friend of their wives and that they merely wanted an overnight together. Mary Jayne Gold protested, "Why me?" Beamish leaned forward and looked her straight in the eye, "Because with that face anybody will believe anything you tell them. . . . Mary Jayne, you have the most innocent face I have ever seen. Anybody will believe anything you tell them." Still, she protested. "You're our best bet," Beamish insisted. "Ils jouent leurs têtes (their heads are at stake)." "Well, okay, Hermant. I'll try."[42]

The scheme worked. Gold got them out for a short *séjour*, and once in Marseilles, Beamish arranged to convene with the "Neu Beginnen four" in a brothel on rue Dumarest to plot their escape. Fry and Beamish huddled with the refugees. While they spoke in German in hushed voices, the prostitutes, who were busy flaunting and caressing, grew increasingly impatient. It became clear that the troupe ran the risk of discovery. Beamish stood up and announced, "Je me sacrifie," and took one of the women upstairs to dispel any suspicion about the real reasons for the drinking on rue Dumarest. Fry recalled that Beamish left the room with a readiness that belied his words. Later, Mary Jayne Gold learned that Beamish's companion told her pimp that he was an odd German client because he had no interest in sadomasochistic sex.[43]

As the route became more congested—and better known—its dangers increased. There was great fear that authorities would discover it and crack down on the operation. Pétain was determined to demonstrate Vichy's sovereignty with the one force with which he was familiar—the police. Since Marseilles was such a sore point, he announced his decision to visit the port with much fanfare and instructed the Sûreté nationale to scrub the south clean. Beamish left for Toulouse to explore alternative routes over the Pyrenees. When his train pulled into the station in one small border town, he saw a guard demanding papers from descending passengers. Beamish hung back, hoping he would move on. Instead, as the last one, he found himself trapped with the guard. His papers were fine, but the guard suggested they walk into town together. Hermant mustered his charm to chat him up. His tactic was too effective, for the guard soon found Hermant easy game for his jokes about weak-kneed Italian soldiers. He insisted that Beamish join him in a bar with some of his fellow guards. With no choice, Albert accompanied his new friend to the bar for a round of drinks. By the time he got away from his louche companions, he had long since missed his meeting with the committee contact. The trip to Toulouse was a waste. The next morning, Albert boarded the train back to Marseilles and headed straight to Fry's hotel, where he found an anxious American. Fry breathed a sigh of relief, quickly took Beamish to a safe location, and explained that while he was gone French gendarmes had appeared at the office asking for "un nommé Hermant." Fry told them that he had fired Hermant and asked why they were interested. They explained that he faced serious charges, "probably a dirty Gaullist!" It was clear to both of them that it was time for Beamish to leave before Pétain's arrival in Marseilles.[44]

By then, his own escape had been secured. One day, when Beamish was talking with Vice Consul Bingham, the American mentioned that he was trying to find a young German named Otto Albert Hirschmann and asked Beamish if he knew him. Beamish grinned, surprised but delighted. "I will tell you a secret. That's me, you know." Bingham was not altogether shocked that Hermant and Hirschmann were one and the same; by then he knew that behind Beamish's smile was an inscrutable past. But he needed a bit of evidence. There was only one hope: Beamish sent a letter by courier to the owner of the little hotel on rue Turenne in Paris and asked her if there was still a trunk with his belongings, and if the trunk was still there, could she send his German birth certificate? Remarkably, she had kept the trunk (after the war, Hirschman retrieved it and still had it in his Princeton home) and immediately sent the precious document to Marseilles. Beamish produced it for Bingham. Bingham pulled out an envelope with a visa, shook Hermant-Hirschmann's hand, and wished him well in the escape.[45]

What accounts for this surprising turn? Unbeknownst, Hirschmann had forgotten about a letter he had written from Nîmes to his cousin Oscar in the United States. It triggered a sinuous effort to get him out of Europe. Oscar had learned that his cousin was in unoccupied France and anxious to get to the United States. By this time, it was clear that the Vichy government was turning German Jews over to the Gestapo. The problem for Oscar was that he could not support him on a tourist visa; beside, it would prevent Hirschmann from getting any work in the United States. Oscar went to the offices of the Rockefeller Foundation in New York "and spoke to someone there about Otto." Oscar was directed to the General Education Board, "a straw to which I eagerly clung." There, however, he was told that any scholarship application had to include a full dossier of scholastic merits, evidence of educational background, and publications. Meanwhile, communications from Albert had gone silent. Oscar felt he was getting the runaround and started to fret that he was going to lose his relative; his pleas for help grew increasingly alarmist.[46] Meanwhile, he approached Max Ascoli, who in turn arranged an affidavit of support signed by Marion Stern—the youngest daughter of Julius Rosenwald (the founder of Sears and Roebuck), an active philanthropist through the Julius Rosenwald Fund, and soon to become Ascoli's wife—to be sent to the American representatives in Marseilles.[47] The Julius Rosenwald Fund had been opening the cases of German intellectuals they would sponsor as refugees and began the process of arranging "a special kind of visa," Ascoli explained to Oscar, "which has been made possible by the President's generosity."[48]

Ascoli and Oscar were being wishful about President Roosevelt; the saga of frustration and dashed efforts to get refugees out of Europe to safe American shores is well known. With the 1940 elections looming and isolationist sentiment on the rise, the White House was anxious not to be seen to take sides. It is hard to say whether the Rosenwald efforts would have worked. Instead, another channel opened up. Oscar, at his cousin's suggestion, had appealed to Jack Condliffe for information to compile the dossier for the Rockefeller Foundation. This prompted Condliffe, who was wondering about the fate of his talented researcher when France collapsed, into action. During one of his visits to Washington, he dined with Leo Pasvolsky, a top aide to Cordell Hull, Roosevelt's secretary of state, to make the case for bringing refugees from Europe. Pasvolsky (who was himself the child of Russian émigrés and who would later distinguish himself as one of the authors of the United Nations charter) sympathized but explained that the climate was hostile to refugees. For Hirschmann, perhaps there was another solution. Condliffe wrote immediately to his contacts at the Rockefeller Foundation. By the time Oscar paid a return visit to the Rockefeller Foundation in early October, its resources and connections were in motion on his behalf. One of the foundation's program officers, Ruth Peterson, had been pulling a file together for Tracy B. Kittredge, who was familiar with the young economist's work as the foundation's chief in the Paris office. Kittredge, who had played an important role in supporting critical German and French social scientists who were being squeezed by nationalist pressures, was back in New York and equally anxious to rescue some of the Rockefeller social scientists. He agreed with Condliffe that Hirschmann was an unusual talent. They put together a fellowship that would sponsor Hirschmann to study and conduct research at the University of California at Berkeley. This was the trick; being a student unblocked the visa. On November 1, a cable from New York landed on the desk of Alexander Makinsky, the Rockefeller Foundation program officer dealing with the flood of refugees in Lisbon, with a fellowship notice and the necessary paperwork to expedite a US visa for one Otto Albert Hirschmann. Makinsky cabled American diplomats in France.[49]

Now it was time for Beamish to leave. Since returning to the Hotel Luxe was too dangerous, a friend went back to his room, got some clothes, paid the balance of his bill, and checked out. Beamish bid goodbye to Mary Jayne Gold, telling her that he was making a habit of skipping town before the arrival of leading fascists. Fry met Albert a bit later and escorted Beamish to the train station, where they got his ticket to Banyuls. As the brakes were released and the train pulled out of the station, Fry grew depressed. "I felt peculiarly lonely after he left," he recalled. "I suddenly realized how completely I had come to rely on him, not only for solutions to the most difficult problems, but also for companionship. For he was the only person in France who knew exactly what I was doing, and why, and was therefore the only one with whom I could always be at ease."[50]

When Beamish got to Banyuls, he reconnoitered with the Fittkos. Hans suggested that Beamish ditch the rucksack he'd bought in Marseilles. They helped him get clothing and espadrilles so he could resemble a worker wandering in the hills to gather herbs. He threw away all his belongings, save those he could fit into a small musette bag—an extra pair of socks and his copy of Montaigne's *Essais*. He spent the night in Banyuls and early the next morning, December 22, was teamed with some fellow crossers—two older German men. One, as it turned out, was a doctor from Berlin who had known Otto Albert's father. Then the three refugees set out on their trek across the Pyrenees. At some point, one of the crossers grew so tired on the ascent, OA had to carry him part way. After seven hours of walking, they spotted some houses and a peasant herding his cows. Hirschmann asked him if this was Spain. "Sí," and he pointed to the little town of Port Bou, where the border control officer sat in his hut. OA offered the herder some money, but the peasant shook his head; he did not help crossers for profit and wished them luck. Hirschmann nervously approached the border guard. The memories of the Civil War were still fresh, and the group in Marseilles grappled with repeated sagas of refugees being turned back at the border. In the end, the border guard joked with OA and asked him why he and his friends had crossed the mountains by cow path and not along the "good roads," then stamped his Lithuanian papers and waved him into Spain. When Hirschmann got to Barcelona, he found the city a frightened shell of its former self. He said goodbye to his two fellow refugees and wandered a bit around the city revisiting sites he'd defended only a few years earlier, then boarded a crowded train to Madrid; it was just before Christmas and families were travelling to Madrid to visit relatives in Franco's swollen prisons. Some of the passengers were clearly frightened and miserable; they cowered or hid under benches. Other passengers covered them with luggage when conductors or policemen trolled the aisles. Spain was even more terrifying that France was. In Madrid, he switched trains the next day to Lisbon; only when he finally crossed the border into Portugal did the fear begin to lift.[51]

Lisbon was Europe's chokepoint for refugees waiting to get out. Having come overland from the Pyrenees or by air or boat from Casablanca or Tangier, they flocked there in the tens of thousands. In tow came the spies and secret agents to keep an eye on civilians and each other. It was said that there were two currencies in Lisbon in 1940 and 1941, escudos and information. Anyone with ears could parlay the latter into the former. And cash was crucial for the one thing the refugees sought above all: a steamship ticket out of Europe. If the streets seethed with rumors and innuendo, they were also, by contrast with the rest of Europe, brightly lit. For the rest of war-torn Europe, nightfall came with orders to extinguish streetlights and draw curtains. In neutral, nocturnal Lisbon, windows glowed and cafes spilled into the streets. Hirschmann spent five weeks wandering the streets filled with refugees and hucksters waiting for his ship to depart.

One person who spent some time with him while he was idle was the Rockefeller Foundation's Alexander Makinsky, who had moved from Paris to the Portuguese capital in early August 1940 to deal with the efflux of artists and intellectuals. On Christmas Eve, Hirschmann cabled Makinsky from Madrid to assure him that he "was coming right through." Two days later, he showed up at Makinsky's offices and the two of them went out for lunch. Makinsky gave him his passage aboard the SS *Excalibur* and a travel advance to get him as far as Berkeley, California, where he was due to take up his fellowship under Jack Condliffe. At the same time, Hirschmann was not only looking westward across the Atlantic; he had his own personal list of refugees still trying to get out. One was Georges Huisman, the former director of the Louvre, who was wallowing in Vichy. Makinsky was interested, and Hirschmann promised to get more information. Within a week, he had tracked him down and was pulling together a curriculum vita for the foundation. At the end of the day, Makinsky wrote in his diary how "H is attractive, intelligent, full of a sense of humor," a contrast to so many of his entries about the despair that saturated the city and its denizens.[52]

As Hirschmann turned his back on Europe to open up a new chapter of his median state, he also took stock of what had transpired over the previous year. He was about to get out—but not without a feeling of bitterness. "I didn't want to leave," he later told Lisa Fittko, "I wasn't interested in going into exile, I wanted to win."[53] At the same time, a whole welter of more confusing personal feelings got knotted inside. Writing to his mother and Eva, he brought them up to date in a few pages. "My 'story' is of course endless," he explained. Some day he promised to relay the whole unexpurgated account. But for now, he joked, "I must say that I have had until now an amazing amount of good luck—but psst, I am seriously beginning to be superstitious as a result of it." From his joining the French army to avoid the detention camps for Germans, he told his story of bicycling to Bordeaux and his good fortune in Nîmes (He confessed that he liked the name Albert Hermant "much better than my real one!"—suggesting that he was already considering a name change from Otto Albert). He summarized the work with Fry and his labors "for the common cause." But he also shared some unusual disclosures, acknowledging the strains. "I felt terribly lonely during the whole period despite my multiple activities and the stream of people—often interesting and fascinating whom I saw." Near the end of the letter he revealed inner turmoil that was less visible to those who were struck by his good humor. "As someone who is drowning I saw one person at least representative of every single period of my life." If Lisbon afforded a moment to look back on a turbulent and trying year, it also promised him a new, but uncertain, future. "You know how reluctant I always was with regard to the States—I loved Europe and was afraid of America. But I realized soon that there was practically no choice, especially if I had any intention to write our family again one day."[54]

The SS *Excalibur* was one of the four combination cargo-passenger vessels of the American Export Lines, capable of crossing the Atlantic in eight days. From the summer, when it was used to carry dignitaries like the Duke and Duchess of Windsor, American ambassadors, and the Baron Eugene de Rothschild, it was retrofitted after the fall of France to take more second- and third-class passengers, replacing luxury with a cargo of depression and relief. The idleness aboard allowed Hirschmann to take some further stock of his median state; it was a rough crossing, and he spent most of it seasick, along with the other 180 passengers. "I am not a very great sailor," he moaned as the vessel approached New York. But he was never one to pass up an opportunity; fortunately, there was a small library aboard the ship, as well as several chess boards and a ping-pong table. Then he met a young Czech woman "with whom I spent most of the time I didn't play chess or ping-pong." As he approached the end of his Atlantic crossing, he concluded the letter to his mother in the same self-detached style of Montaigne: "Examining my sentiments yesterday, I noticed that they were already somewhat Americanized. Indeed, I shall enter this country with the will of getting to something, of showing that I have merited the extraordinary chain of lucky incidents which have led me here. Though I still love France, I am of course disappointed in many ways, and this makes my fourth—or is it the fifth?—emigration easier for me."[55]

CHAPTER 6

Of Guns and Butter

The disproportion in the world seems,
comfortingly enough, to be only an
arithmetical one.

FRANZ KAFKA

SS *Excalibur* was scheduled to dock at Jersey City on the evening of Monday, January 13, 1941. Storms had battered the East Coast and delayed the vessel's last leg from Bermuda. When it entered the mouth of the Hudson River on Tuesday morning, it was a frigid 13 degrees (F); the sky was a slate gray and was about to release its snow. The refugees shivered as they filed through the immigration offices at Elizabeth, New Jersey, and then scattered to their destinations. By the time Otto Albert Hirschmann handed over his documents—his Lithuanian passport and American visa—he had gotten used to the name Albert and was looking forward to reinventing himself on new soil. He asked that his entrance to the United States be registered as Albert Otto. The agent added his own embellishment, a common enough contribution to the Anglicization of new arrivals, by dropping the second *n* from the surname. When he offered to simplify it more by removing the *c*, that was a step too far; the newcomer balked. Hereafter, Otto Albert Hirschmann became Albert O. Hirschman.

Thus renamed, the twenty-five-year-old German refugee ventured into America. Stateless again, he reached out to his contacts or kin. Not knowing it, he owed an immense debt of gratitude to his cousin Oscar, who had been his advocate from New York and had ensured that the Rockefeller Foundation was on top of his case. The train from Elizabeth carried him to Penn Station, and from there Hirschman took the subway to his cousin's apartment on Park Terrace, at the very tip of Manhattan. There was also some business to wrap up. He cabled Fry in Marseilles to tell him that he'd safely reached New York and that he'd paid a visit to the Emergency Rescue Committee offices to defuse some of the tension between the headquarters and Fry over his recurring demands for more money and visas. No one had been able to explain the problems of the French side with such insight. When the meeting was over, Hirschman's cable assured Fry "COMMITTEE FULL CONFIDENCE IN YOU. AVOIDANCE CLASH WELCOME. LOVE: OTTO ALBERT."[1]

While Hirschman was grateful to his kin and shared what news he had of the family's various fates in Europe, he was less keen to make of his New York kin the basis of a life in the New World. While joining the many German intellectuals who would have such a decisive effect on American pastimes like Hollywood and on American science, music, and philosophy, he was less anxious to do so *as* a German; as in his first departure to Paris, Hirschman did not heal the incision from his past by gazing backward, fixated on the "German question." New York was filling with intellectuals with just this obsession. Rather, once more, exile provided grounds for reinvention. Hirschman did not dwell on the traumas he left behind—and was determinedly tight-lipped about it with others. Rather, he sought out new opportunities. In America, he could become the intellectual he'd dreamed of being in Europe.

America would yield mixed results—and not a bit of frustration.

In the meantime, he was eager to learn more about the terms of his miraculous fellowship. A few days after his arrival in New York, Hirschman visited Kittredge at the Rockefeller Foundation. He was delighted to learn that his first stipend payment would be available by the end of the month. He would receive $120 per month for two years, and the fellowship would cover all his tuition at the University of California as well as travel costs getting there. A month later, Kittredge raised the monthly stipend by $50, so that Hirschman could remit funds to his mother, his dependent, in London.[2]

Delighted at his good fortune, Hirschman also began the quest for opportunities beyond his two-year fellowship. Kittredge was only the first of a series of contacts Hirschman would make. This was clearly becoming something of an aptitude, not to say instinct: dealing with dislocation with a flurry of efforts to meet new people and size up the landscape, leaving behind trails of acquaintances he might later pick up; in short, creating opportunities for himself that might later come in handy. He spent three weeks in New York, went to see Washington, and renewed contacts with some Germans who had relocated there. He returned briefly to New York, then set off for California.

The word *opportunistic* can carry the wrong connotations to describe what Hirschman was doing. He was not scoping the landscape preparing to mold to it by seizing the best of his chances. If this is what opportunistic means, it does not capture Hirschman at all. But if opportunism means creating chances, spinning good fortune, this is more appropriate. Some might say that Fortuna was on his side. Hirschman knew Machiavelli well enough to know that good fortune was also something to cultivate. Among other things, Hirschman had ideas for himself as well as ideas of himself, both of which had been gestating for years. None of these were going to bear fruit naturally. By the time he was bound for the West Coast, he had some fairly clear notions of what to do with the precious two years at his disposal. The Rockefeller Foundation budgeted for a second-class ticket to California. Hirschman preferred to make a bit of money by travelling third class and pocketing the difference. In addition, the foundation agreed to give him the kind of ticket that would allow him to get off and on board at will, so that the refugee could get to know the United States better and make contacts. Hirschman's first destination was Chicago. He resurrected ties with Abba Lerner, under whom he had studied while at the LSE. An unorthodox thinker from an unusual background, Lerner was someone with whom Hirschman had a certain affinity; he was eager to get intellectual advice. Most important, he wanted to consult someone he admired about an idea he had been secretly harboring. Lerner was only too happy to oblige. Sitting in Trieste, Hirschman had examined Italian trade balances. He had also been watching German trade with Yugoslavia: Yugoslavia's share of German trade was small, but Germany accounted for a large share of Yugoslavia's. Then, in Paris, he followed the ill-fated attempts of the Intermarium

coalition to thwart Berlin's commercial ambitions. What role did disparities between countries play in international economics? Did large countries
display a preference to trade with small ones, or were they neutral? Was
this—as he implied in his reports for Condliffe before the war—a prede-
terminant of conflict and war? By the time he caught up with Abba Lerner,
his concerns had billowed: was there an effect between commercial trade
and political power? As Lerner listened to these ideas, he nodded. He urged
Hirschman to explore them.[3]

This was a seal of approval enough for Hirschman, who boarded the
train for California. The arrangement with the Rockefeller Foundation
placed Hirschman in International House, a dormitory for foreigners, "a
home for male and female students." He was struck immediately by the
Bay Area's beauty, the hills, the huge bridges, and the lights. Coming from
Europe's darkness, the sparkling lights of the three cities clustered around
the bay were an endless source of fascination. But most of all, what swept
him away were the libraries, especially Doe Library, whose great stone
edifice, magnificent windows, long desks, and reading lamps indulged
Hirschman's years of thirst. Its collection "is stupendously good and complete," and the stacks were open. Hirschman spent endless hours wandering through them, running his fingers on the rippled spines of shelved
books. Interestingly, he did not rush to read the latest. He made for the
classics. There he discovered Adam Smith and Werner Sombart and set
aside time for more Machiavelli. "Of books I have nothing with me except for Montaigne in the beautiful Pléiade edition," he told Ursula.[4] Doe
Library compensated for this sole, prized, possession.

In Berkeley he became a curio, a condition that made him squirm.
At International House, Sunday dinners featured tablecloths and candles;
it was a special occasion at which those in attendance were supposed to
participate in enlightened discussion. At one of Albert's first attendances,
someone asked him to talk about the situation in Europe; soon there was
a chorus of calls "to talk about your personal experiences." The newcomer
sat there, with his handkerchief twisted in his fingers, nervously waiting
for the calls to pass. "Everybody wanted me to tell my story . . . . They
wanted to get out a notebook and began to write down things, you know,"

Albert and Sarah at International House, Berkeley, 1941.

he told an interviewer in 1985. "I moved out of International House right away because I couldn't stand being considered as sort of a wonder of the world or something like that. I just wanted to be myself and . . . not to have too many contacts." California was isolated from the tragedies in Europe. Here was a young man who was not just a direct witness, but a protagonist! "There was so much, too much, wide-eyed wonder about how it was all possible," he recalled. Rumors swirled about the new arrival. He had come from a world of intrigue and plotting and arrived in academic paradise. He wanted to read; others wanted him to talk.[5]

Not long after his arrival at International House, Albert queued up for lunch one day at the cafeteria. He filled his plate with stuffed peppers and went to join a friend who was sitting with a student of literature and philosophy. Her name was Sarah Chapiro. Petite, beautiful, smart, and with a bright, magnetic smile, she immediately captivated Albert. Her charm and intelligence would have been enough to catch his attention. But she was French, Russian, vaguely but irrelevantly Jewish, displaced like him. From that day forward, they were mates, bonded in this new land.

Sarah Chapiro, like Hirschman, had washed up in California an émigré from the same clash that had torn Europe since the First World War. Her route to Berkeley, where she arrived in the fall of 1940, was not quite as winding, but it was not quite American. A transfer student from Cornell, where she had spent a semester studying French literature and philosophy, she was beginning to learn some rudiments of English. While in Ithaca, she learned of Paris's fall to the Nazis. She wept. Other students asked her why? "It's only a city," they consoled. But it was when she watched half of her classmates—a nontrivial portion of the Cornell football team—struggle through their courses that Sarah realized this sojourn was not going to work. She decided to leave the snow drifts of upper New York State for California, in part to be closer to her family, which had resettled in Los Angeles, and in part because she wanted to be in a larger and more diverse setting. Her extended family of well-to-do Jewish merchants had left Kovno, Lithuania, in 1925 when Sarah was four years old, settling in Paris, where she grew up in the lap of the sixteenth arrondissement. Like the Hirschmanns, the Chapiros were completely assimilated into a secular, bourgeois culture. They were part of the affluent Russians fleeing the revolution. Being an only child, there was no shortage of comforts. In the summer, the family went to beach resorts on the Baltic or in Belgium. In winter it was skiing in the Alps. Sarah's parents put a premium on her education. At first she had nannies. When Sarah contracted scarlet fever, her parents hired a nurse, Ekaterina Lioubimovna, a highly educated White Russian who became her closest companion growing up and would supervise her activities and studies. There were also the special tutors, like the Russian literary critic who guided young Sarah though Russian classics and had a great influence on her. When it came to school, Sarah was enrolled in the Lycée Molière, not far from her flat: an institution made famous because it was there that Simone de Beauvoir, not yet the famous author she would become, taught philosophy. Sarah had the good fortune to be one of her few prized pupils. Exciting and charismatic, she rubbed off on Sarah; de Beauvoir bequeathed a lifelong interest in philosophy and existentialism, an influence that would later rub off on Sarah's husband. Sarah was not, however, among those enmeshed in the complex personal labyrinth that de Beauvoir spun around herself. Needless to say, these compound influences widened the generational gulf between an exploratory daughter and her more conservative parents.

Sarah's parents struck a glamorous pose: her mother was beautiful enough to compete in pageants, and her father was dapper. Sarah's father and uncle, business partners and best friends who took their daily stroll through Paris streets, rebuilt the family fortunes, with a special affection for the shady paths of the Bois de Boulogne and the alleys of the Quartier latin. But as war approached, Sarah's father had a premonition; having endured pogroms and war in the Russian borderlands, he did not want to face more. In 1939, he gathered his family and belongings and set sail for New York. He loathed it from the start. All that noise and dirt! All those crowds! This was nothing like the elegance of their apartment and arrondissement in Paris. So he and his brother pulled up stakes again and headed for Californian sunshine; there they found a house large enough to accommodate two families in Beverly Hills. It also came with a swimming pool, where a future son-in-law would practice his headstands. In that quiet suburban paradise they stayed put.

In Sarah, Albert found a kindred spirit. They spoke French with each other, finding in language some refuge from a culture of which they were a part but with which they did not identify. They shared a love of French and Russian literature, and Albert was only too willing to induct her into an appreciation of "the Germans," especially Kafka and Goethe. Between them, they could heal the dividedness of being European in America. He also found a complementary spirit. If Albert was reserved, Sarah was outgoing; if he was "a little in the clouds" (as Fry put it), she was engaged. It did not take long for them to appear as a couple, to become, as one old friend noted, "toujours les Hirschmans!"[6]

Within eight weeks of meeting her, Hirschman proposed marriage. She accepted. They arranged to travel to Los Angeles to meet her parents in April. There was other business to take care of, too. Shortly before the wedding, Hirschman contacted the Rockefeller Foundation to apprise them of the news and inquiring about an additional family allowance, which yielded a further $30 monthly installment to his stipend.[7] He also wrote to Ursula, with pictures of Sarah, and got her endorsement. At first, she refused. Ursula was alarmed that he should so quickly set up a home in the United States and was not just a bit suspicious about this unvetted woman. Determined, Albert sought a rapprochement, slyly observing that "you begged me not to get married with an American woman—the accent it seems to me was rather on the American woman than on married life itself."[8] Luckily, Sarah was not American, a point which he stressed. Ursula was only too pleased to appreciate her brother's distinction: "She has a baby face of such sweetness and kindness and such a surprising grace in her composure that I felt instantly like friends and related to her, and I wish you are always good to her and never make her suffer."[9]

The wedding, held on June 22, 1941, was a modest, civil ceremony. The best man was Albert's old friend from Berlin, Peter Franck, now re-located to the Bay Area. Sarah's parents, uncle, and aunt also attended. They all piled into several cars and headed for the Berkeley town hall. As they drove, they could see the newsstands with papers blaring the latest headlines: "GERMANY INVADES USSR!" Albert pleaded to stop the car so they could get the newspapers: "I just wanted to get out and read the news!" The wedding was suddenly a lesser detail. Sarah was more confused than upset—her parents prevailed upon Albert to focus on the ceremony. When it was over, they all went to dinner at an old inn in Oakland. The next day, Albert caught up with the events in Europe.[10]

Being non-American in America was bonding; their secession from Europe resolved itself not by their imagining themselves in exile, not as castaways, but rather as partners of, and in, the world, who happened to be in America. Though they stabilized and comforted each other, the question of where they belonged in the world remained an open one—and became a current of their relationship. In the meantime, marriage affected how they related to their milieu. The union of these two displaced persons who found themselves almost arbitrarily dropped down in Berkeley reinforced the isolation that Hirschman was creating for himself. "I shut myself off from the immediate contact with the American world by becoming married to a European, and so I associated mainly with other Europeans."[11] "The first weeks of our marriage," Albert told Ursula, "were spent in the most splendid isolation." "With nature, Sarah, and books, I feel very autarkic."[12]

One thing Albert did not do was seize upon their union to disgorge memories of the past. In their isolation, Albert chose not to share many of his trials. Sarah detected his distinct reluctance to talk about his past and quickly learned not to press him hard. One might have thought that the privacy and intimacy would give him the security to open up; he felt no such compulsion. Though Sarah remained curious and mystified, the darker parts of his past were memories he would share—if at all—only with time. Some did, in increments, come to the surface, often prompted by reminders from Europe. When Albert received his first letter from Eugenio since his arrest in September 1938, he was both euphoric and dispirited. Writing to Sarah, who was visiting her family in May 1941, he exclaimed, "What a letter!" and told her of his longing to talk with Eugenio once more: "I have the impression that his intellectual activity has recovered completely . . . and he is formulating his ideas in physics and is sure that he is on a fertile track. . . . He then writes to me about Nietzsche, Kafka, Huxley and also a book on economics [Lionel Robbins] that he wants to discuss with me! Do you understand how much this consoles me, how much this delivers me from certain anxieties and yet revives the pain I feel for being separated from them?" He confessed that he was left feeling "enraged sentimentally and depressed intellectually."[13]

But if Albert was reticent to unload his personal experiences, he was not so about sharing his love of books. Sarah, who was studying philosophy, brought what she was learning to their home. And Albert—while leaving his political economy at the office and library—reciprocated with poetry. He would read or recite Goethe by heart in German and then translate it for Sarah's benefit into French, the lingua franca of their marriage. Sarah had the distinct feeling that this was part of her preparation for being his wife, like the Russian doctor who could not find a wife and so became a lady's man, justifying his dalliances with nurses by claiming that he could only have affairs because none of them had read *War and Peace*. Sarah would laugh, "So Albert took a terrible chance because he got married to me and I had not read *Faust*!" Listening to his adoration of Goethe, she did, however, get the sense that he was sharing a more precious disclosure than self-centered stories of his deeds and dangers. And whether it was Gustave Flaubert's depiction of the curves of Emma's body, or the psychic vocabulary of Pierre Choderlos de Laclos' epistolary *Dangerous Liaisons*, she was also getting an immediate immersion in Albert's fascination with words; not just any word, but rather the mot juste.[14] Among the authors they shared, a special place belongs to Gustave Flaubert; he was in many respects, *their* author. Between the *Correspondences* and the novels, Flaubert's psychological realism and stylistic insistence on the mot juste deepened the exilic bond between Sarah and Albert. And for bringing Flaubert back into his life, Albert was grateful to Sarah. "I acknowledge you," he wrote to his bride on the eve of their wedding, "for having fortified in me a rationalist element . . . for I have returned all your books [to the library] except for Flaubert, who excites me once more." He explained, a bit elliptically to someone reading the epistle decades later, that Flaubert had helped Albert get over a difficult past: "The subject of the eruption of irrational elements (in the form of superstition) in the life of a young man raised in a species of skeptical rationalism (a rationalism that is neither solution nor panacea but the most relatively effective way of orienting), a position towards which one returns, more or less, after the crisis."[15]

Their autarky had a home. Not only did Hirschman bolt from International House, but after getting married, they found a small house on Highland Place at the foot of Charter Hill. Their backdoor gave on to fields—beyond which was the ridge where the physicist Ernest Lawrence was having his famous cyclotron built. In a tiny Arts and Crafts bungalow, edged with bamboo and with a single bedroom and a minute kitchen, they lived at the furthest edges of the Berkeley campus at a gateway to the trails into the hills. Sarah, meanwhile, took up more and more the domestic side. This did not come naturally—in a family with servants, there had been little tutoring at home, and Albert described her labors in the kitchen as "experimental" and "original." "Her duties as a housewife she accomplishes in an impeccable manner," he assured Ursula. When they went to see her parents, he boasted that Sarah had managed to make homemade plum jam.[16]

Sarah may have been an un-American wife, but Albert was happy to have her teach him that most American of necessities: driving. This appears to have strained her composure somewhat. He was a bad driver. Worse, he liked to drive. The same dreaminess that tortured Varian Fry afflicted his skills behind the wheel. "I do it so well that each time I take the car alone as soon as I arrive at a destination I have to call her because I do not know how to put it among two other cars on the sidewalk," he confessed. In this fashion, the experimental cook and the inattentive driver made a life together.[17]

The Charter Hill house was also the hub of a new social life, for neither Albert nor Sarah had roots in Berkeley. But it was very tight; they relied most of all upon each other for companionship. Among their closest friends were William and Ann Steinhoff, who lived nearby and with whom they shared many dinners and outings to concerts at Mills College, where the Budapest Quartet was in residence. That season, it performed the entire cycle of Beethoven quartets. It was the Steinhoffs who introduced the Hirschmans to the world of recorded classical music. Evenings would be spent listening to a mountain of 78-rpm albums. From there, Albert discovered the radio. He became an addict. "On the radio here you can hear every day from 8 to 10 in the evening the best concerts on records," he exclaimed to his sister, "really excellent programs; for this reason we have abandoned the idea of having a phonograph given to us." The radio introduced Albert to a whole world of music that had not been an important part of his cultural life in Berlin. Berkeley tranquility allowed him to "discover a bit late Tchaikovsky and especially Brahms, whose music seems to me particularly mature and conscious." But just to be sure that his preferences were still straight, he emphasized to Ursula that they were "to be compared with Flaubert in literature, for whom I have maintained a predilection." Indeed, what monies they squirreled away allowed them "to reconstitute the beginnings of a library." This rebuilding was something Albert relished as part of his new domestic stability. "It is very difficult to find books not in English, and the hunt for them is very fun." Difficult, but not impossible, for some of San Francisco's first department stores were founded by French owners and had leftover French library collections. Albert and Sarah would troll the secondhand book shops of San Francisco on Saturdays, picking up classics, especially nineteenth-century French literature, Goethe, Kafka—in short the bibliographic amalgamation of their readings from Berlin, Paris, and Trieste.[18]

Making a home together, sharing music and poetry, building a personal library—all helped Albert and Sarah create an integrated life so far from where they had come. The German philosopher, Theodor Adorno, once observed that "for a man who no longer has a homeland, writing becomes a place to live." In this sense, Berkeley was not so much home as the place where Hirschman could write and thereby make a home with Sarah, a home composed of and by words.

Their assembled lives and shared passion for belle-lettriste books gave Albert an intellectual space that he had not known since his conversations with Eugenio. "You must read," he told Sarah, "Julien Benda's *La trahison des clercs*." *La Trahison*—a blistering assault on French and German intellectuals who spurned (in Benda's view) a classical heritage of dispassionate inquiry to become apologists for nationalism, jingoism, and war—struck Albert as "a contemporary document of utmost importance (and *adorable* for its partiality)." It was precisely Benda's lament for a lost world that that reminded Albert of what, intellectually, he had left behind. What Benda thought European intellectuals had abandoned, Albert could revive in miniature, at home. In this setting, Albert began to pen his petites idées. "I have an idea (a little one, to be sure) concerning what we spoke of yesterday," he wrote. "I am struck at the moment by certain parallelisms in modern thought in different disciplines." People have a tendency to consider aesthetics, political economy, ethics, and philosophy as "certain aspects of each person's acts or human behavior." From this comes "the complete separation of the disciplines from the *ends* implied by different human activities." Political economy, as we shall see, was uppermost in his mind and "has no longer any purpose as the *utility* or Material Welfare but is solely concerned with applying the most rational means for ends that are imagined outside it [*désignés du dehors*]." The result was, for Albert, an "absurd" conclusion in which "we ask *politics*, the sciences of *means* par excellence to formulate the ends by which political economy, ethics, etc. will render themselves accordingly as the *serviteurs affairs*." Which brought Albert back to Julien Benda: "Here you have the abdication, the treason of the intellectuals in a new sense, I think, and we can explain it partially by the development of this hybrid position of intellectuals in the modern world: neither masters, nor prosecuted, but technicians." For him, the abdication, the refusal to put politics alongside other human affairs and its study integrated with other disciplines, led intellectuals to recuse themselves from asking basic questions about "the thirst for power and domination" as ends in themselves. "Fascism is *politicaillerie* on a giant scale." "Why dominate? Fascism will not survive the moment in which we have found the leisure [*loisir*] to pose this question." This was the fundamental question he posed to himself in the "leisure" of his marriage as he created a home for his writing.[19]

The bookshelves of the Doe Library, the sanctuary at Charter Hill, and the commitment to prove himself in America affected the ways in which he engaged—or not—with radical circles in Berkeley. Berkeley, by 1941, was a hub for cocktail Marxism. The Bay Area had active militants in the Communist Party: some from the trade unions in the port, some from the faculty of the University of California. It was into these circles that the physicist J. Robert Oppenheimer merged, along with his fiancée Jean Tatlock, as well as many other faculty and graduate students. Many drifted away after the shock of the Molotov–Ribbentrop Pact of August 1939, but many hung on. Hirschman made a point of giving them as wide a berth a possible, but it was hard to seal off the entreaties, especially given the mystery that trailed him, that he was one of the few who had *really* fought fascism. His old friend and his best man at their marriage, Peter Franck, had kept up his affiliation in the party. Albert struggled to keep the personal and the political apart, but Franck made it impossible, and ultimately spoiled their friendship for good. Peter insisted that Albert

come to meet a comrade of his, Haakon Chevalier, a charismatic professor of French literature at Berkeley, known to Sarah and Albert alike. He
was also an active Communist recruiter in the Bay Area. By this point, Albert's experiences in Berlin, Paris, Barcelona, and Trieste had confounded
all hopes for a "common cause" between Socialists and Communists;
the disappearance of Mark Rein had terminated them. The dogmas of
the party had no more allure; Albert had long since embraced the free-
form style of Eugenio's liberal socialism. But one day, Albert unhappily
relented to Peter's pressures and agreed to meet with Chevalier. When
he returned home to Charter Hill, Sarah asked him how the meeting had
gone. Albert's expression said it all: his face was that of a man forced to
smell rancid meat.

This episode may have planted a seed in a file that the Federal Bureau
of Investigation (FBI) opened on Albert, for around the same time, Chevalier had asked Oppenheimer if he would be willing to make technical
information about the work at Los Alamos Laboratory available to the Soviet Union. We cannot know for sure; what we do know is that suspicions
about Albert were awakened by FBI field officers in the Bay Area. The episode also contributed to the end of his friendship with Peter Franck. Writing to Ursula, he noted that "Peter reveals all too often his fundamentally
bad character and is not even (he never was) very intelligent. But as "Best
Friend" he has become an institution. I have still not found a circle of true
friends. In New York I would have some, but not here."[20]

Hirschman may have been isolated, but he was not lonely. With Sarah's companionship, a steady diet of books, and just the right amount of
support from his officemates in the Doe Library, his solitude was precisely
what he wanted to turn to his project—to write a book. He wasted no
time in making himself at home in his writing. No sooner did he arrive in
Berkeley and install himself in one of the gray desks in Condliffe's library
suite, than he went to work. Berkeley was a disarming, but most welcome,
surprise. Indeed, the very nature of American academia was a novel setting. University life in Berlin, London, and Trieste involved a much more
porous—if disruptive, chaotic—relationship with the outer world. In the
context of the rapidly polarizing political atmosphere, universities could

not help but be one of the sites where debates were especially electric. By contrast, Berkeley seemed "totally shut off, in a sense, from something called the real world."[21]

The isolation was strange but liberating. Berkeley afforded time and peace. In seminars and discussions, students "earnestly" (if innocently) debated ideas and problems removed from the relentless pressure to attach them to political positions or confront their ideological ramifications. At the time, the economists at Berkeley were obsessed with whether Keynes was "right or wrong," which struck Hirschman as both less confined than the more immediate—and less academic—need to deal with the social and political crisis, and at the same time quite provincial. Hirschman, by now, was fatigued by what he felt was a false debate between Keynes's champions and his critics, as if *The General Theory*'s significance depended on its victory and defeat.[22] What interested him was a preoccupation drawn from his Marxist antecedents: conflict between organized interests and how bargaining power, shorn of the rigid class structures, actually worked to create systems. Moreover, he wanted to put the analysis on a plane in which it was not social classes, but regions (inspired by his old economic geography classes in Paris) and nations in an international financial and trading system (inspired by his classes in London) that fought over capitalism's spoils. All his accumulated thinking from the franc Poincaré to the Italian imperial economy pointed toward questions of global trade and their effects on national economies—a theme obscured in the debate among pro- and anti-Keynesians on whether markets were self-correcting. At the same time, he was becoming concerned about the reverse process: how the organization of national economies affects international commerce. Fascists were, if nothing else, hard bargainers with neighbors.

What gave him the freedom to explore was his sponsor, Jack Condliffe, who had some sense of what Hirschman had been through and was thus inclined to permit him to roam under the broad umbrella of the Rockefeller-funded Trade Regulation Project. Condliffe had just published *The Reconstruction of World Trade: A Survey of International Economic Relations*, to which Albert had contributed an analysis of exchange controls and which used the lessons of the botched responses to the aftermath of the First World War to recommend a different architecture to follow the Second. To Condliffe, the efforts to restore a pre-1914 gilded age had been naïve. One had to accept the interventionist state endowed by electorates and leaders with a mandate to protect "national" interests engulfed in a "conflict between nationalism and industrialism." The regulation of international trade was the result of this conflict—and it would be best if economists accepted this shift rather than deny it in an effort to retrieve a multilateral, free trade model. The issue was rather what kind of regulation—bilateral bargaining and the formation of big blocs dominated by economic powerhouses, or the creation of an international regulatory order that upheld fairness and impartiality for all trading members? The latter was an economic condition for a durable peace; the former was a recipe for rivalry and friction.[23]

This tension was already on Albert's mind before joining the Trade Regulation Project. Indeed, chapter 4 of *The Reconstruction of World Trade*, on the rise of economic autarky, relied on Albert's unpublished essay, "Étude statistique sur la tendance du commerce extérieur vers l'équilibre et le bilatéralisme," which prefigured how he would fit into Condliffe's plans. With his move from London to Berkeley, the Rockefeller Foundation funded a new project that extended the themes that were supposed to be tackled at the Bergen conference of 1939—how states manage their commercial relations in ways that enhance or thwart cooperation between governments and thus keep peace or fuel conflicts. Housed inside the Doe Library in a large room filled with books and furnished with gray metal desks, this cluster of professors and their European economist assistants toiled away on the crisis of world commerce. Here was where the New Zealander welcomed his protégé with open arms. Condliffe's project contained several branches of research, including the evolution of state trading and the practice of exchange controls in Central Europe. The fellowship that Condliffe had secured for Hirschman was open-ended. In theory, he was supposed to be conducting research on the theme of Italian exchange controls, and to some extent Condliffe did rely on Hirschman for research assistance for the larger project. In practice, this afforded Hirschman an opportunity to work on his own ideas. Condliffe sensed that Hirschman's ideas on autarchy, bilateralism, and the formation of trading blocs embedded in "Étude statistique" were going to be an important part of the overall diagnosis of what went wrong after 1918. He was on his way to writing something innovative, and so Condliffe gave him a wide margin of support and independence.

There was also some sense, hope even, that Hirschman would use the Rockefeller fellowship to upgrade his credentials. It was less an explicit term laid out by the foundation than a suggestion that he should prepare to qualify for an American PhD and thus launch a successful career as an economist in the United States. Hirschman certainly wanted the latter but was not willing to take the route that others prepared for him, and so he eschewed the coursework that would give him any further degrees. In the back of his mind, Hirschman must have known that the decision not to upgrade his Trieste PhD was a risky one. But with a chance to conduct research and write an original book, he wanted as few intrusions as possible.

He did take a few courses—one with William Fellner, a Hungarian expert on business cycles who taught a general seminar on the principles of economics, and one with Howard Ellis, who taught international economics and coordinated the Bureau of Business and Economic Research, which had sponsored Condliffe's grant. For the most part, Berkeley was not a hotbed of economic thinking, and so its seminars were probably not very compelling. By the rapidly changing standards of the time, Condliffe himself was not a very sophisticated economist; it was his pragmatic generosity and open-mindedness that most influenced his assistants. Meanwhile, Fellner and especially Ellis were skeptical of the Keynesian revolution and kept sniping at what they considered a fad—which only licensed Hirschman's decision to sidestep the great economics debate of his time.

What Hirschman did sense was that economics was becoming more and more mathematical, and Hirschman's training was more in advanced accounting, more applied than theoretical. This was already a concern of his by the time he reached Berkeley. In the summer of 1941, he enrolled in a course on mathematics for economists, and the following fall he enrolled in probability calculus, by the end of which he had competent skills, which he used to his advantage. He must have known that this would never be his forte in the field. Still, he tried his hand at developing several statistical indices for measuring concentrations of foreign trade and the incidence of attraction of trading countries with larger or smaller partners. These yielded his first two publications in English, one for the *Quarterly Journal of Economics* and another for the *Journal of the American Statistical Association* in the late summer of 1943, a feat that Condliffe happily boasted about to the Rockefeller Foundation.

It was in the latter publication that he presented his arithmetic model of indices of concentration. Unlike existing measures, which restricted themselves to gauging the inequality of distribution (of, for instance, wealth or income, most famously known as the Gini coefficient), what Hirschman was after was a measure not just of distribution but also of the *fewness* of buyers or sellers as a measure of their market power—the number of firms in a market *as well as* the degree of concentration. The result was a calculus measured by summing the squares of the market share of the largest firms, yielding an index from 0 (a large number of small firms) to 1.0 (a case of pure monopoly by one firm over an industry). This calculus gives an observer a consistent gauge of the size of a firm to a particular industry. Much later, the index became a standard measure for competition and antitrust enforcement. For Albert, however, the measure was less intended for firms' market shares. His concern was measuring countries' trade with other countries. Condliffe was not the only proud one; Albert wrote to Ursula, "I have also built some new indices for measuring certain economic phenomena and the first results are in—I have one of my assistants calculating and it is clear! They are pretty interesting."[24]

Condliffe and Ellis were the "professors" in the project. There were also several assistants, who played, if anything, a more important role than the maestros. Alexander "Sandy" Stevenson, a young Scottish student, became Albert's closest associate in the office. Stevenson had applied to study economics at Berkeley shortly before the war broke out and crossed the United States on a Greyhound bus. Moving into Phi Delta Theta house was an abrupt apprenticeship in one aspect of American university life—but fortunately for Stevenson, he found an alternative. Condliffe arrived from London and hired Sandy, whose fellowship was running out, as his assistant. He created the index for *The Reconstruction of World Trade*. So, well before Hirschman's arrival, Sandy was intrigued to meet this exotic German talent, having helped Condliffe track him down through the Rockefeller Foundation.

Another assistant was Alexander Gerschenkron, whose background was not dissimilar to Hirschman's. The two of them, Gerschenkron and Hirschman, would go on to have notably entwined lives, and at several important junctures, Gerschenkron would have a decisive—if invisible— role in Hirschman's career. Several years Hirschman's senior, Gerschenkron and his family had left Russia for Vienna after the revolution. Like Hirschman, he was to a large extent self-taught; the University of Vienna had become a shadow of its former glory in economics. He came to the attention of the Berkeley circle through Charles Gulick, who had hired him as a research assistant—some would say ghostwriter—for Gulick's *Austria from Hapsburg to Hitler*, an arrangement that left the gregarious Gerschenkron with an enduring grudge. After the Anschluss, he had left for England and thence to Berkeley, funded by the same Rockefeller Foundation grant that supported Condliffe. Gerschenkron's section of the Trade Regulation Project was State Trading. In fact, like Hirschman, he worked on his own ideas, which led to the publication of his first (and only) monograph, *Bread and Democracy in Germany*, published in 1943. Growing out of the common concern with protectionism, Gerschenkron demonstrated the ways in which the great Prussian estate owners, Junkers, made agricultural protection a cornerstone of the "iron and rye" coalition that buoyed the German empire—and how the persistence of Junkerist power was the principal obstacle to modernization and democracy in Germany, prefiguring the crisis of the Weimar Republic. In this sense, it was fully in keeping with Condliffe's abiding concern about the connections between freedom of international trade and liberalism at home.[25]

One might have expected these expatriates to huddle together. They did so, but only to an extent. Stevenson and Gerschenkron became close friends, having breakfast together regularly, sharing the feeling of using

American slang at the local diner when ordering Breakfast No. 4! By contrast, Hirschman kept to himself. From his first day, he struck a profile as a reserved—even deliberately reticent—officemate. Everyone in the office knew he had adventures to tell of from Germany, Italy, Spain, and the fall of France; he had been present, studying economics, in the very countries they were now observing from far away. But no one dared ask. He emitted subtle but unavoidable signals that his past was not a subject of conversation. Nor, indeed, was the present; Sandy recalled how shocked everyone in the office was the day that the door opened and Albert introduced everyone to his fiancée, Sarah Chapiro. No one even knew he had a girl-friend. As concerns Hirschman and Gerschenkron, it is most accurate to say that they worked alongside each other on the big gray desks, thinking in parallel rather than thinking together. Still, there are some remarkable echoes in their first books. While they developed a profound respect for each other, they never became close friends or intellectual soul mates.[26] As far as Condliffe was concerned, this was an ideal team, each helping and reinforcing the other in their autonomous pursuits, and he informed Kittredge that the combination allowed each to realize important and original work while "aiding the other collaborators."[27]

Hirschman had arrived in Berkeley with ideas of his own and a determination to develop them. Why dominate? was a question at the forefront of his mind. To help sharpen his thoughts, he returned to the classic readings, a habit he would refine over the years. As he was wandering in the stacks of Berkeley's library—yet another of the great pleasures of the American academy that he was discovering—he happened upon Machiavelli's *Opere complete*. In Trieste, Machiavelli was one of his staples, and by then he had also developed a fondness for reading epistles, most especially those of Flaubert. Albert flipped to the pages of the Florentine writer to find his correspondences. Therein, he initiated a lifelong admiration for the abundant, roaming letters between Machiavelli and Francesco Vettori. From them, he culled more quotes and aphorisms. One in particular he plucked out: "Fortune has decreed that, as I do not know how to reason either about the art of silk or about the art of wool, either about profits or about losses, it befits me to reason about the state." What to

Machiavelli was so vexing, to Hirschman seemed vital: the connections between trade and power, the ties between economics and politics. Hitler, it struck Hirschman, *did* get what Machiavelli had not. And with this insight, Albert plunged into the writing of his first book. Provoked by Göring's famous line that "guns will make us powerful; butter will only make us fat," he labored from the early spring of 1941 over double-spaced longhand on pads of paper. The script was also written in English, which Hirschman quickly mastered, though he had doubts to the end about his eloquence (and it is true, compared to his later works, it still had the occasional awkward passage).

The effort consumed its author. The newlyweds did not take a honeymoon, though they did find time to take the occasional ski trip in Nevada and went to see Sarah's parents in Beverly Hills. Governing those years was a sense that Hirschman, as he had told his mother, wanted to prove himself in America.[28] While the research and data compiled for the book was something that brought Hirschman to the office he shared with Condliffe, Gerschenkron, and Stevenson, when it came to writing, he retreated to his apartment. Sarah, busy studying, had little to do with the direct composition—a role she would acquire in his later books. Only three people commented on his drafts in early 1942—Condliffe, Gerschenkron, and Stevenson. With encouragement and suggestions, he went back to his desk. In the end, Hirschman only trusted two readers of the manuscript draft, Sandy Stevenson and Fred Bloom, a fellow German with odd mystical proclivities who helped Hirschman on some of the earlier articles and the footnotes. In the meantime, when radios broadcast the news of the bombing of Pearl Harbor, and the United States entered the war, Hirschman stepped up the pace of his work. He could not face a war against fascism in which he was not taking a part. By the end of 1942, it was done, and the manuscript went off to the University of California Press, which Condliffe had recommended. He had developed new quantitative tools, harvested data, sorted out his argument about the world economy, and had written a book in his third language in less than two years.[29]

It was a formidable accomplishment. It was also a mess. The final draft of *National Power and the Structure of Foreign Trade* started with Machiavelli's confession and gave way to a stack of sheets with notes scribbled all over as the author, impatient with his English and keen to be as precise as possible, edited relentlessly. In the rush, the handwriting was so poor that no typist could decipher it. Only Sarah could. "The first book was my first act of great love," recalled Sarah, chuckling. She went to a typist in an office on Telegraph Avenue and read the manuscript verbatim while the typist manufactured the typescript.[30]

National Power sought to cast new light on two prevailing anxieties—how to account for the Nazis' aggrandizing hunger and how to evaluate underlying trends of the world trading system. But he also wanted to connect these concerns. This was unusual by the terms of the social sciences of the day. Depression-era economists were more absorbed in debates about Keynesian macroeconomics or the failure of the multilateral trading and financial system, and less with the connection between economic policy and political regimes. Meanwhile, the authoritarian turn in Germany and Central Europe was cast in purely national frameworks, as if the misfortunes could be laid at the feet of national characteristics. This included Gerschenkron's account. The result, as far as Hirschman was concerned, was not just an empirical gap, but also a conceptual failure. If Göring had provided a blunt statement about the perceived conflict between the social purposes of the state, between war and welfare, well-meaning democrats and reformers were in a state of denial that war and welfare were bound up with each other. They had fallen prey to Machiavelli's separation of state power from any consideration of wealth; the result was a failure to understand the fundamental nature of fascism and its will to dominate others, and therefore turned a blind eye on the problems of the world economy. What Hirschman sought to do, therefore, was to introduce "New [national] Machiavellianism" and the "system of *international* trade" to each other and to illuminate what he called the "intermediate links" connecting power politics with global trade.[31] This was an audacious agenda.

From start to finish, it was a unique contribution to the field. It completely avoided the raging debates of the day. Keynes was neither right nor wrong. And it steered clear of most of the discussions among international economists about how to envision a postwar system that would rebuild and stabilize the payments system. Hirschman was guided by an altogether different set of preoccupations. Imagined against the background of German and Italian economic aggression—Germany's to Central and Eastern Europe, Italy's to Africa—coupled with the more general global trends toward protectionism and state intervention and monopoly, Hirschman wanted to combine all three together to reveal how autarky did *not* mean that nations looked purely inward for their economic pulse. On the contrary, they continued with an outward trade strategy. But instead of free commerce, they opted, when they could get away with it, for a bullying commercial strategy. Observing the intersection of national sovereignty and world trade, Hirschman wanted to show how strong states manipulated foreign trade to bolster state power at the expense of weak states; the breakdown of the world system and the clash between big blocs was hardly an irrational, nationalist pathology. It was an understandable response to a basic contradiction. In this sense, Hirschman was still hanging on to some underlying Marxist sensibility—to see economic relationships as intrinsically unharmonious and inclined to disequilibria. But he distanced himself from his Marxist roots by seeing patterns of exploitation beyond class terms; empire was not—as Marxist economists had been arguing—the result of cyclical capitalist crises, but rather was ingrained in the nature of commercial interdependence. In this sense, he wanted to shake liberal and Marxist tendencies to see aggrandizement as irrational or the expression of reactionary elites (like Schumpeter did) and to bring some "realism" to the understanding of political economy and economic analysis to the study of realpolitik.

Machiavelli may have been mystified, but mercantilists figured out how foreign trade was an instrument of national power. They, unlike their successors, never lost sight of the ways in which butter and guns depended on each other; welfare and warfare were not irreconcilable, they were inextricable. Part of *National Power* outlined the history of economic thought from Machiavelli to late nineteenth-century liberal political economy, detailing the rise and fall of an ability to visualize what the Scottish philosopher David Hume had seen as the harmony of "the greatness of a state" and the "happiness of its subjects." A century later, English economists came to see that interdependence by trade led to peaceful collaboration, as if mutual interdependence defused conflicts and allowed a state to redirect its energies from war making to welfare. All the while, as Hirschman pointed out, not only were European empires going back on the rampage, but by 1900, the rivalries and tensions between them were heating up. The "liberal" moment was precisely that—but only one moment in a broader historical sweep. It was not an appropriate hiatus for contriving general covering laws of history or universal principles of economics, whether Marxist or liberal. Not yet explicit in *National Power*, one can detect Hirschman's first cautionary note against social scientists' appetite for ageless theories derived from observations of one age.

So, what was the relationship between "dependence" on trade to "domination" of others? Here, Hirschman wanted to inscribe his concepts in terms of basic modern trade theory and was indebted to the University of Chicago's Jacob Viner's influential 1937 collection of essays, *Studies in the Theory of International Trade*, which outlined the ways in which wealth and power commingled; although a free trader, Viner was clear-eyed about the connections between the classical concepts of the "gains from trade" and the power concept premised on dependence on trade, and about how states experienced an unavoidable temptation to manipulate the trading system by reducing the dependence in a way that did not compromise the gains from trade. This was especially tempting, Viner felt, in moments of crisis such as the Great Depression. What Hirschman sought to do was develop some formal, testable hypotheses for the connections and then cast them into a series of mathematical formulations outlined as a series of notes on the second chapter of *National Power*.

Other Hirschman traits also appear. He displayed a fondness for the illuminating metaphor or coinage. One challenge, for instance, was to puzzle out the "intermediate links" that held the system together. Hirschman coined two phrases to illustrate two processes. One was the *supply effect*, which alluded to a country's ability to import from a number of competing partners; in effect, more dispersal of sources gave a country more bargaining power. The other was the more elusive *influence effect*, reflecting the ability of a government to interrupt its export and import business; a country that could rely on domestic provisions in the event of a trade crisis had more leverage than one that depended on the exports of its staples or imports of needed consumer goods or raw materials. Greater influence effect gave a country wider room to use military muscle to drive a hard bargain with those having a lower influence effect. The result was that giving up free trade was hardly irrational; strong nations displayed an understandable preference for subjugating neighbors endowed with fewer choices of trading partners or commodities than their behemoths nearby. In this fashion, commerce was an alternative to war as a method of exercising coercion—a twentieth-century model of imperialism that did not require "conquest" to subordinate weaker trading partners.

Another Hirschman trait was a concern with the human behavioral foundations of the system. Temptation lay at the heart of the problem. One can see in this book the underlying fascination with the human motivation lurking behind behavior and the importance that Hirschman would place on psychological factors. When it came to the intersections of foreign trade and national power, any postwar order had to grapple with the means to curb it. "As long as war remains a possibility and so long as the sovereign nation can interrupt trade with any country at its own will, the contest for more power permeates trade relations, and foreign trade provides an opportunity for power which it will be tempting to seize" (pp. 78–79). Seen in this way, Germany's approach to trade—to swing away from commerce with countries with similar or higher GDPs and to concentrate commerce with smaller neighbors to the east and south— was hardly pathological and suggested some "amazing coherence." It may have been extreme, but it was not exceptional. The "bloodless invasion" of Bulgaria, Hungary, and Romania reflected the Nazis' exploitation to the fullest of the opportunities that were "inherent" in international trade, whose precedents were clear from the 1890s in the form of "export dumping"—about which Viner himself had written eloquently. Between the supply and influence effects, Hirschman updated the ancient saying *fortuna est servitus* (p. 12).

If flexing trade muscles was a way to subordinate partners and fueled "economic aggression" that could not be explained away as bad cultural habits, greed, or the entrenched interests of landowners (Gerschenkron's Junkers) or bankers seeking opportunities to invest overabundant capital (a prevailing Marxist theory) but rather was a property *of* the global trading system as long as there was basic asymmetry between trading partners, what was to be done? Hirschman was aware that German aggression was partly a response to the punitive terms of the peace after World War I, although he urged readers to see that it had older origins that the Treaty of Versailles merely helped bring to the fore. There was in fact a larger challenge. "The Problems of Reconstruction," *National Power*'s fourth chapter, argued forcefully against the temptation to see Germany as an aberrance, an exception to a more general rule about trade. Economic aggression had to be seen in more systemic ways—as woven into the very fabric of national sovereignty. A real peaceable order required a drastic overhaul of the multilateral system. It had to confront the source of the problem—a contradiction from which liberal, democratic regimes were not immune. If there was a "natural temptation" to use trade as "an instrument of national power," Hirschman felt it was therefore obligatory to sacrifice the means of national power holders' access to commercial weaponry. The core of his injunction came down to this: "Nothing short of a severe restriction of economic sovereignty" would preserve a world that wanted peace with the gains from trade. The lesson of 1919 was that restraining one side, the Germans, had simply sharpened national antagonisms and created additional opportunities for an even more viral and dangerous form of nationalism.

Hirschman was taking on big figures, though the full extent of this challenge was not so clear, in part because the author rushed his final product without expanding on its conceptual ambitions. He may not even have been fully aware of them. Adam Smith wanted new coordinates for thinking about wealth—not as the purview of states, but rather as the product of societies. Ridding the old doctrine would free the world of "power temptations." In a sense, Hirschman was restating the Smithian formula with data and an eye to a concern about peace. So long as state power depended on control over trade, economics would serve despots.

But what Smith missed, Hirschman felt, was the recognition that there would always be *temptation* so long as there were small and big countries, rich and poor. Hirschman, who pored over the Doe Library's edition of *The Wealth of Nations*, felt that Smith ascribed the problem to a failure to see wealth differently—not to basic inducements and incentives. So long as there was an underlying disparity in scale and income around the world, states—mercantilist, capitalist, or communist—would be vulnerable to the kind of predatory activity that careened the world into war. It would not help just to preach a different conceptual gospel, even though it had more virtues. In this sense, the world economy was always subject to a basic "power disequilibrium."

But there was more to Hirschman's argument. Greater global integration did *not* check predation by making countries more interdependent and, therefore, more cooperative. There was an equal risk that unmanaged, interdependence could aggravate relations and yield to tit-for-tat bullying by the wealthy and the big. Hirschman's endless tables illustrated how countries became more dependent on one or fewer markets and more dependent on one or a few commodities as they specialized and reaped the gains from trade—countries would be prone to dependence *with* power temptations.

The only way out, to achieve peace with welfare, was a wholesale break from the formula that had governed global trade since Machiavelli: "This can be done only by a frontal attack upon the institution which is at the root of the possible use of international economic relations for national power aims—the institution of national economic sovereignty." For its time, this was an audacious argument. But he went further, arguing that "the exclusive power to organize, regulate, and interfere with trade must be taken away from the bonds of single nations" and turned over to "consular services," "chambers of commerce," "export-import banks," international transportation companies, and a list of civic and private agents involved in global commerce, rescuing trade from states whose leaders could not resist the temptations to empower themselves at the expense of others. He threw the whole model of national sovereignty into the air, advocating "the internationalization of power" by giving real teeth to Article 16 of the Covenant of the League of Nations, which gave it direct control of state trade policies. Roosevelt's "freedom from fear" and "freedom from want" could be reconciled only with a dramatic change in the way we think about the international political economy (p. 81). Hirschman's prescriptions grew increasingly unmoored from his analysis and went from the audacious to the Utopian, a move that would lose the sympathy of some of his reviewers and would prove an exception to his preference for small, close-to-the-ground, analysis.

By the time Hirschman reached his final pages, he was boiling down all his convictions about how policy makers might think about their place in history. He reminded readers that they should not presume that any global division of labor was ordained. Many outcomes—good and bad—were possible. The search for covering laws was destined to take explanations from particular times and places and universalize them. One can see a grain of his Hegelian past, and his bow to the cunning of reason, through the lacquer of his economics: it is "highly improbable that any *particular* pattern of the international division of labor will last forever." His readers needed to be reminded that they were living in just one of History's moments. This did not lead him, however, to more meta-laws. Rather, one hears the echoes of Eugenio Colorni. It was how people chose to perceive the world that guided their choices—though it did not determine their options. All transitions in history, therefore, create challenges, but these challenges can be aggravated by the illusion that they are permanent conditions. His final words were reserved for the pessimists. While the nineteenth-century "free trade" moment had passed, and the classical political economy which derived to explain it was now frayed, there was no need to fall prey to "flights of the imagination at the start of which we find a real lack of imagination" (p. 151) Colorni could not have been far from his thoughts when he accented a practical, Utopian turn, a centerpiece of his reformist principles; when he emphasized the role of the imagination in history; and when he cast his eyes beyond the present to formulate policies for the future; the lack of imagination was simply "an incapacity to conceive of a state of affairs radically different from that with which we have been acquainted" (p. 151).

The final, moving, pages anticipated much of what would later flow from Hirschman's pen.

But they also created a problem. It was not always clear with whom Hirschman was jousting. By then, trade pessimists were in the retreat, and the sentiment was swinging—as he no doubt knew from his conversations and work with Condliffe—to thoughts about a global regulatory framework. And while its postwar incarnation fell far short for many idealists, the basic norms—especially in the United States, which would play a decisive and leading role in restoring a multilateral trading system— had shifted decisively. Most of the citations to pessimists were to German writers, starting with Werner Sombart, who worried that German industrialization would lead to self-sufficiency, and commentators on the First World War. There is certainly a way in which he anticipated later criticisms of world trade, from later antiimperialist critics of the 1960s to globalization pessimists of the 1990s. But at the time, it was an odd note to strike and suggested that he was shadow boxing with an already vanquished opponent, and thus driven to advocate a concept of "the internationalization of power" that seemed, if not excessively idealistic, blind to the fact that a transition to thinking about a new global order was already beginning.

If Hirschman harbored any hopes for a cascade of enthusiastic reviews, they were dashed. By the time the book came out, it was read as being out of step with the times. Seeing the defeat of the Axis powers on the horizon, many economists were less concerned with empire and dictatorship, having moved forward to think about elaborate global trading regulations; it was a hot topic at the Allies' financial moguls' discussions at Bretton Woods, New Hampshire, where the postwar economic architecture was designed. *National Power* was almost instantly forgotten. Philip Buck of Stanford University praised the book's "originality in devising a new method of analysis" and for illuminating a central puzzle of the twentieth century. He agreed with the general principle that world trade not be left to the governance of sovereign nation states. Another reviewer also lauded the technicalities of Hirschman's indices. Indeed, in general, reviewers found the measuring devices impressive, but the applications less so. Michael Florinski of Columbia University appreciated the "provocative" nature of the "compact study" and nodded to the "erudition, thoroughness and imagination." The core of the volume on foreign trade as an instrument of national power was "penetrating" but "somewhat abstruse."[32]

There was a more fundamental problem. It got little attention because it was—to many—already obsolete, and the final ruminative passage seemed, to some, downright obscure. If Hirschman advocated a "frontal attack" on "the institutions of national economic sovereignty" with a whole new architecture for managing global trade, one reviewer could not bite his lip: "This proposal, needless to say, has not the slightest chance of being acted upon within any predictable future, if ever." Many years later, Hirschman himself conceded that the book carried the burden of "infinitely naïve proposals" whose ability to solve the world's troubles rested on a deus ex machina of an entirely new order to wish away an "unpleasant reality" he'd uncovered instead—as would become a hallmark of later writings—of "scrutinizing it further for inner modifiers or remedies." But this is the voice of the mature theorist of reform, looking back on the less ironic, youthful, idealist who had not yet developed his antennae for the dialectic of forces and their counterforces whose interstices were the spawning ground for "possibilities rather than certainties."[33] The result was that, as the few reviewers who dealt with it noted, the book's recommendations were, at best, vague, too general, and had "nothing to offer" to those concerned with how to manage postwar commerce. The economic problems of the postwar years turned economists' attention away from the war's causes to its consequences. The book got pigeonholed as a study of "international relations" and was largely ignored by economists. It soon dropped from sight and went out of print as being prewar vintage; its relevance was already past.

This was not the work that Condliffe hoped would make the young German economist's career; far from it. The deeper messages about the underlying dynamics of inherent tensions, disequilibria, and conflict were at odds with an age that clung to hopes that the world's problems had been temporary and were reducible to bad management, poor leadership, and venal tyrants. If Hirschman was drawing on the well of Marxism to say that there was something more fundamental at work in political economy, his tone was at odds with the struggle to anchor the coordinates of a new, liberal, postwar consensus.

One effect of the book's poor reception was that the index over which he labored so hard disappeared with it. In itself, this might not have gotten under Hirschman's skin. But it was when it got picked up and branded as someone else's index that his frustration came to the surface. In 1950, O. C. Herfindahl published a study of the American steel industry that adapted Hirschman's index, albeit footnoting him, to offer measures of concentration in this one business. It was soon picked up by statisticians and regulators concerned with an objective measure of market concentration for their trustbusting work and named the Herfindahl Index. This misnomer was recognized by no one—but it irritated Hirschman to such a point that he felt compelled to set the record straight in 1964 in a small entry to the *American Economic Review* called "The Paternity of an Index." There he laid out the forgotten history of this technical exercise explaining that the measure was being mistakenly named after Corrado Gini, who did not invent it, or Herfindahl, who had simply reinvented it. But rather than lay claim personally, he ended with a laconic and imperfectly disguised index of his feelings about the years as a forgotten figure: "Well, it's a cruel world."[34]

We have gotten slightly ahead of the story. Whether Hirschman was aware of the risks he was running as he frantically wrote, we do not know. What we do know is that the book was a calling, the result of many years of reflection and a determination to prove himself in a new setting. By the time he was applying the final touches, however, an older calling resurfaced. One must remember that he was trying to explain the structural origins of Hitler's empire. The political reality of its extent eventually reached the shores of California's Bay Area. By early 1942, while Hirschman was presenting his initial draft to his officemates, Roosevelt and Hitler were enemies. In the ensuing months, the war dissolved Condliffe's little fraternity in the Doe Library. One by one the fellowships ran out. Gerschenkron went to work as a stevedore in the shipyards. Stevenson followed Condliffe to New York to work at the Carnegie Endowment for International Peace. Ellis went to Washington to work for the Federal Reserve Board.

Albert O. Hirschman enlisted in the US Army.

CHAPTER 7

The Last Battle

A stair that has not been deeply hollowed
by footsteps is, from its own point of view,
merely something that has been bleakly put
together with wood.

FRANZ KAFKA

T hough it was less than a year after his escape from Europe, the
bombing of Pearl Harbor hurried *National Power*. There was competition now for Hirschman's attention, another fork in the road. One
way pointed the way to a *vita contemplativa*, a road he yearned for after
his itinerant and militant years in Europe. Another pointed the way to a
vita activa dedicated to the struggle against fascism, a cause he'd rallied
to like a reflex since 1931. Here was a new opportunity to enlist. He did
so, almost immediately—less than two months after Pearl Harbor. A serious bout of pneumonia and then a tonsillectomy laid him up for weeks,
delaying him. Still motivated by the urge to prove Hamlet wrong, to preserve within himself an idea of an integrated fighter and thinker, there
was another reason for volunteering for a regimented life: having spent
so many years with a dubious legal status, and with internment camps
for enemy aliens filling up around California, he wanted his citizenship
resolved. Necessity and conviction thus prompted him to volunteer for
his third war, fighting under a third flag, for the same cause.

The pendulum, it seems, had swung back to action. But Hirschman
did have a preference for how—not whether—to serve. There was one
way to integrate "theory" and "practice," to deploy his knowledge about
the enemy as an "economic intelligence" agent. Here was an opportunity
to make an old personal ideal real. Once he had recovered from his mal-

adies, he wrote to Kittredge at the Rockefeller Foundation in New York seeking advice and support. He did not think, according to Kittredge's notes, "that he could serve most effectively by becoming a private for the 3rd time."[1] The program officer heard him out and agreed to send a letter to the adjutant general of the US Army testifying to Hirschman's background and abilities. Kittredge did, adding emphatically, that "Hirschman states he is *not* a Communist" to calm the alarms about his service in the Spanish Civil War.[2] Accordingly, Hirschman himself wrote to the adjutant general following Kittredge, explaining that he was Lithuanian (this was still his passport, which no doubt augmented his anxieties about his legal status) but born in Germany, with the hope that "my linguistic knowledge or my professional training in statistic [sic] or economics or both, can put me to some use." He added his expertise in the French and Italian economies, and included, for good measure, that he had worked for the Allies while in Marseilles helping "English and other Allied soldiers trying to escape from France and that the British Embassy in Washington has a record on my activities during this period." He closed his offer on a note of principle: "I fervently hope that you will consider that my record as an active opponent to the Totalitarian countries may compensate to some degree the lack of American citizenship." He prepared to take his medical exam in mid-February and asked the Rockefeller Foundation to defer his fellowship, fully expecting to be called for service in April or May.[3]

A year passed before Hirschman fulfilled his quest. The delay remains a mystery (in part because a fire consumed a section of the National Personnel Records Center in July 1973). The delay did allow him to finish his book, however. In the meantime, the local draft board reclassified married men, which accounts for some of the delay. Then he was reclassified for "occupational reasons," which struck the Rockefeller Foundation as odd because no one had "taken the initiative to obtain this change of status." Because the overture to the adjutant general was going nowhere, he asked Rockefeller to cover a trip east—to the University of Chicago, Harvard, and Princeton—"to discuss his completed manuscript with prominent readers." Mostly, he was keen to meet Jacob Viner. He also wanted to use the trip to make a personal show of interest at the doorstep of the men he thought could most use his skills.[4]

Other than Kittredge, Hirschman had no strings to pull when the American intelligence apparatus was being assembled out of the old boys' networks of Ivy League faculty and graduate students. Hirschman was an outsider. He appeared at the Office of Strategic Services in Washington and the Board of Economic Warfare. Nothing came of his calling cards. Then he took matters into his own hands and enlisted in the infantry as a private.

On April 30, 1943, he was finally called to the Army's San Francisco Reception Center. As he went, he could not put his anxieties about his citizenship aside: to the last minute sending corrections to his dossier lodged at the Alien Registration Division of the Justice Department. And yet, he remained obscure about some crucial details. For one, he left his German citizenship in the dark and preferred to introduce himself as a Lithuanian. We can only speculate on his reasons. Some might see him reversing his father's denial of his Ostjuden roots. Most likely, with Germany being the enemy, he wanted to avoid detention. Either way, none of this appears to have dampened his induction into the army. He took his basic training just outside Berkeley for three months, where marching drills and shooting practice made up for the lack of proper training in the Spanish Republican militias or the French army. Then he was transferred south to Camp Roberts, just north of San Luis Obispo.

The barracks were what Berkeley had not been: an American immersion. The Condliffe group had been an international hodgepodge. Hirschman had married a Russian who had grown up in Paris. He had studiously avoided the classroom and the residence halls where Americans might have invited him into the melting pot. The barracks rectified this isolation. The other soldiers were mainly from California, "ordinary Americans" as he recalled. He liked them, though he could never get used to the food. If Hirschman was supposed to become a soldier, there was one habit the army trainers could never drill out of him: he kept forgetting to tie his boots properly. For this he would be denied passes to visit Sarah, and so she had to come to Camp Roberts to see him. There are two revealing photos of him taken at Camp Roberts. The first, with his company, reveals the disparity between the American army and the French one of several years earlier. Here the troops are all dressed alike, stand in neat formations, and look prepared to march into battle—a sharp contrast to the crew that was sent to repair rail lines in the Loire Valley. The other is of Albert Hirschman alone, tanned from training in the California sun, with his rucksack, rifle, and helmet, looking every bit the soldier. Sure enough, he confided to Kittredge that "I cannot help making all the time comparisons with the French army as to food, clothing, equipment, and treatment and as in every single respect the comparison is overwhelmingly in favor of the American army, my morale is exceptionally high."[5]

Perhaps it was his inability to remember his bootlaces. Perhaps he still had a habit of being *dans la lune*, as Varian Fry complained. Perhaps he was a bad shot. We will never know why, but Hirschman was pulled

Hirschman at Camp Roberts, 1943.

from a combat unit. It is also possible that an officer saw some valuable skills in the private. At Camp Roberts, he was tested for language and interpreting abilities, which must have impressed the brass because he was immediately dispatched to the Army's Specialized Training Program, and there was talk that he was bound for Stanford to learn Japanese. But the idea of having him serve in the Pacific theater soon gave way to another— the Allies were deep into the planning stages for the first assault on Axis Europe, in Italy. He could clearly be more useful there, and his skills recommended him not for combat but for intelligence work. It was roundabout, but Hirschman found himself assigned to the Office of Strategic Services (OSS).

In the fall of 1943 he took the train to Washington for a second time, where he would spend several months hanging around the OSS headquarters waiting for his assignment. Founded in June 1942, the OSS had a mandate to collect and analyze information and to conduct special operations not assigned to other agencies or services. Its director, General William J. Donovan, was still hiring staffers when Hirschman appeared on the doorstep. *This* was a club Hirschman wanted to join. (Eventually the headquarters would be home to eight future presidents of the American Historical Association and five future presidents of the American Economic Association.) Hirschman thought he could be of use two ways. One was the plotting that went into penetrating the Reich with OSS operatives comprising German and Austrian exiled socialists, communists, and labor activists who could conduct operations behind the lines. The other was the Research and Analysis Branch (RAB), directed by Harvard's William L. Langer, who fanned out to recruit top minds from the country's elite universities. This was also a club Hirschman *could* join. By the spring of 1943, Donovan was taking in German refugees such as Max Horkheimer, Theodor W. Adorno, Herbert Marcuse, Otto Kirchheimer, and Franz Neumann, a major figure among German socialists and author of an influential study of Nazism, *Behemoth: The Structure and Practice of National Socialism*. This "community of the uprooted" included Hirschman's natural peers. It had the additional allure of allowing foreigners to join the world of the old school tie.[6]

Wishful thinking brought personal expectations. Presuming he would stay in Washington and having received a travel fellowship, Sarah joined him from California in late fall 1943. They found a small flat near the zoo, a challenge in a capital swollen with the administrators of the war effort. Idleness afforded the couple some time to visit museums, take long walks, and talk of the future. The dreams of a career in economic intelligence and a home in Washington were not—as Albert and Sarah soon discovered—in the cards. Ten weeks after Sarah arrived in Washington, they learned that Albert was to be shipped out in early February.

They were stunned. It was the first of a series of blows. But for the moment, they had to deal with imminent separation. The one thing they did decide was to have a baby. If Albert was going to die in Europe, Sarah wanted his child. They spent their remaining days together in the flat and wandering the streets. In late January, shortly before he was called

Albert and Sarah in
Washington, DC.

to a naval base in Virginia to head out, they paid one final visit to the National Gallery. Standing before their favored paintings, Albert's arm around Sarah's shoulder, they talked about the art, keeping the war at bay. At the end of their visit, Sarah went to the restroom only to discover that she was menstruating. She was not pregnant. She erupted in tears. But with Albert waiting in the foyer, Sarah did not want to compound the mood. She cleaned herself up, wiping away the traces of her anguish; as she emerged she could not tell if Albert noticed. In those final moments together before Albert was sent to his ship, they conspired to be silent about their misfortunes.[7]

Sarah packed her bags and went back to Beverly Hills; uncomfortable there, she decided to go to New York, continue her studies in French literature at Columbia University, and wait for the war to end and her husband to return from the front. She moved into International House and immediately went to work on Denis Diderot's novel, *Jacques le fataliste et son maître*. There was more news: Sarah learned that the last days in Washington had yielded one hope—she *was* pregnant after all. The problem now was that the rules of the residence forbade pregnancy and children—presumably because it set a dubious example to other young women. At the beginning, Sarah dissimulated. Among the other women in the residence Sarah quickly made some friends. When she was too tired she would enlist one to fetch her milk and cookies, until one day one of her companions said "You know, Sarah, you have a really nice face, but really you are getting fat! I mean, this idea of getting milk and cookies every night at midnight is not a good idea." When it became impossible to deny, Sarah and two friends found an apartment near Gramercy Park for a while. As the birth approached, her parents paid a visit to New York to inspect the arrangements; they were not at all pleased at the unusual arrangement for their first—and possibly only—grandchild and prevailed upon their daughter to reconsider. Sarah wrapped up her studies, pulled up stakes, and moved back to Los Angeles to live with her parents. Katia was born in Santa Monica in October 1944. Baby Katia, raised and pampered by the Chapiro clan in a Spanish-style Beverly Hills house, would not see her father for two more years.[8]

Albert's posting brought with it more disappointment. Not only was he not in the RAB, but he would not be working on intelligence on Germany at all. Instead, he was assigned to work with a group of Italians and immediately sent to Algiers aboard a Liberty Ship—by then, the campaign on Europe's "soft underbelly," in Winston Churchill's unfortunate words, had started. Moreover, Private Hirschman found himself laboring as a translator and slipped into a state of undying boredom. There was nothing nail-biting about his service. Hirschman's hands were filled with books, not a gun; instead of fighting, he spent the war years reading. Before his hurried departure from Washington, he did have enough time to locate a copy of Machiavelli's *The Prince*, the sole book he could take with him for his campaign; he thought it a fitting tome for the Allied liberation of Italy—to ruminate on the prospects for a restored republic by reading Italy's greatest republican thinker. The problem was, Private Hirschman stowed his copy of *The Prince* in his "B" bag in the hold, so he had to spend the passage to the Mediterranean riffling through the ship's library, which had been endowed with a collection of tedious detective novels. During the voyage, he also had to put the final touches to the preface of his manuscript, which he did; the hardest part was figuring out how to thank Condliffe with words that conveyed gratitude without "making him the inspiration for my work." He also thanked Peter Franck, though with a wince, "but it is only fair."[9]

Hirschman spent seven months in Algiers, waiting as the US Army prepared to continue its assault on Italy and then inched its way up the peninsula. Whatever excitement had gone into figuring out how to beat the German and Italian armies in North Africa was long gone by the time Hirschman carried his gunnysack down the gangplank. The desert was turned over to the preparations for the Allies' first assault on western Europe. The Italian campaign was a proving ground for the OSS's ideas and practices in the field and were run out of the Secret Intelligence (SI) Branch. Notwithstanding the planning, there was chronic confusion and conflict over the role of intelligence in combat—and it took time, and some fierce fighting on the part of the enemy, for the army to make use of the SI information and analysis—until it hired Max Corvo to coordinate the field operations. The Sicilian-born and Middletown-raised Corvo had a distinct preference for hiring Italian-Americans; field agents had to be Italian to function close or behind the line, he felt. Corvo took few enlisted men into the SI.[10]

By then it was clear what the OSS had in mind for Hirschman: to be an interpreter. During the Atlantic crossing he had been detailed as a French instructor, so he knew that it was his language facility that his officers prized. Hovering around the villa overlooking Algiers where the OSS had set up its base, he devoured Italian and French newspapers and prepared oral reports for his commanders. "I am working pretty well," he told Sarah a month after his arrival, "of my own initiative, and if this is successful I may have a chance that they might let me continue, and I am not asking for more. I am absolutely free to work here as I wish." Idleness afforded some time for petites idées; looking out over Algiers' rooftops from the villa, seeing the city's laundresses drape their wet linens over the line, Hirschman wondered whether "we have been building houses so that there might be some points to hang the laundry to dry."[11] On the whole, however, playful tidbits were rare; waiting was too anxiety-inducing to foster mind play.

The real action was going on elsewhere. The RAB had dispatched units into liberated territories who sent back Field Intelligence Studies to OSS headquarters, which was run by Rudolf Winnacker, Donald MacKay, H. Stuart Hughes, and a group of "applied historians."[12] The inner circle of OSS men did the brain work. Boredom, war's gangrene, soon set in and dominated the months in Algeria. "I am feeling a bit like a moron, because my work is so monotonous after a few days and I am not getting out enough."[13] OSS insiders irritated him: "A young American from Harvard whom I met in Washington has recently arrived and I might wind up working with him a bit. But he's an insignificant guy though convinced enough of his own value. He poses stupid questions that make you want to die (stupid question = questions for which there is no intelligent reply) and rushes suddenly to judge everything with a sovereign tone while ignoring the country around him, its history, and its language."[14]

At first, playing chess helped, and he squared off with a neighboring Austrian sergeant, though by the end of March he complained that "I have lost my chess game, and I absolutely don't know why."[15] He kept trying to find a way out of his limbo, appealing to officers who expressed an interest in finding meaningful work, only to be told the next day that he would have to wait. At one point, he even caught up with his old friend, fellow Nazi-escapee and LSE student Hans Landsberg, who had moved from the National Bureau of Economic Research to the OSS for the Italian campaign. They dined together one night and Albert spilled his miseries. Landsberg promised to do what he could to help, but to no avail. Albert told Sarah that "I was at first angry with him because I thought he was doing nothing to help me get out of this impossible situation. But the truth is that there is little to be done. One must be armed with patience, but it's not always easy." In Montaignesque style he concluded that "I see myself objectively as a 'case' and can understand how this experience is terrible for me."[16]

Restless and irritated, he tried to make the best of a miserable situation. One way to cope was to get away. Aside from Landsberg, Hirschman hunted for as many acquaintances as he could, in part for a ticket out and in part for company. He found a French inspecteur de finances, Jean de Largentaye, who had discovered John Maynard Keynes' *General Theory* on his own, and "while his English is not very good, he translated the book himself," and it had been recently published by Payot. Albert "had a sumptuous lunch" with de Largentaye ("served by an Arab boy!"), and explained to him Abba Lerner's recent insights on public finance; he was so "eager to hear the latest news about economics that I did not have the chance to complement him for the meal."[17] Another economist he tracked down was an associate of Robert Marjolin's, and he spent five hours with "very intelligent and sympathetic" company.[18] And there was also one of France's most famous Algerians, Albert Camus, whose books, *L'Étranger* and *Le mythe de Sisyphe* had appeared in 1942, which Hirschman snapped up at a local bookstore. Camus himself was spending the war years in France; undaunted, Hirschman looked up his brilliant and fiery wife, Francine Faure, who was herself despairing at being separated from her husband. She was the first, but not the last, to note the not unflattering physical resemblance of the two Alberts.

However, his closest associates were Italians exiled in Algiers who congregated at Umberto Terracini's house, where Albert spent many evenings discussing the future of Italy now that Mussolini had been toppled. Terracini, a former Communist and friend of Antonio Gramsci's, had been cooped up with Colorni and others on Ventotene. Freed in 1943, he had left for North Africa.

It was through Terracini that Hirschman filled in some missing pieces about Eugenio. On Ventotene, a group of prisoners including Eugenio, Altiero Spinelli, and Ernesto Rossi went to work on a manifesto for a postbellum Europe that would eclipse the destructive effects of nationalism by creating a federalist superstructure for all the European states. While a group effort, Rossi composed the final draft of "European Federalism," wrote it on cigarette paper, and had his wife Ada smuggle the sheets out in the false bottom of a tin box, but it would not circulate until Eugenio later did an extensive revision.[19] The nation-state—argued the manifesto—had ceased to be an effective way of organizing community life: its "desire to dominate" must now be placed under the guardianship of a federalist system to ensure the "highest level of freedom and autonomy." Finished in late summer 1941, what is remarkable is how three prisoners could spend their energy envisioning a peaceful, democratic Europe when signs pointed toward a fascist victory, especially because Panzer divisions had begun to swarm into Russia in June. It is a testimony to their commitment to finding a source of light in very dark times.[20]

Eugenio was transferred from the island to an ancient and isolated town on the mainland, Melfi. A few were sent with him, such as Manlio Rossi-Doria and Franco Venturi. Here the conditions were even worse. Ursula could not stand the confinement, and her affections for Eugenio were so depleted that she took their three daughters and went north in April 1943 to join Spinelli and Rossi. By then, the Italian underground was swelling and organizing into political affiliations. The summer of 1942 saw the birth of the Partido d'Azione (PA) in Rome. Known as Actionists, the PA's founders picked up the Justice and Liberty legacy of the "third way" (*terza via*) to amalgamate socialism and liberalism. As German police clamped down on the underground, Spinelli left for Switzerland to work with a group of Italian exiles. Ursula joined him there. By early 1944, she was pregnant once more—this time, the baby's father was Eugenio's former coauthor, Spinelli. Albert got word of his sister's paramour and pregnancy from his mother—which left him utterly dispirited. "The old difficulties that you know about," he told Sarah, "have not been resolved, and this depresses me." His mother's letter left him in a "black mood," for "I must now see that in my subconscious I had eliminated everything that we know, and I have been hoping for the reconciliation between her [Ursula] and Eugenio. But this news buries all these hopes."[21]

Terracini filled in the aftermath. Colorni escaped to Rome in the spring of 1943 with a medical permit and slipped into clandestinity, from which he edited the European program for Partido Socialista di Unità Proletaria (PSUI). With Ursula and Altiero now together with his daughters, Eugenio poured his energies into the socialist underground in Rome. He edited the Ventotene Manifesto, wrote its introduction, and took over the publication of *Avanti!* which issued the treatise. This done, *Avanti!* called for a mass mobilization to ensure that a postwar Italy give socialist ballast to European peace. One of his underground tracts, issued in August in 1943, argued that "the Federation must not be a league of states but a republic of all Europeans; the citizens of Europe must participate in its political and administrative activities through direct representatives and not through the medium of their national governments."[22]

Getting this news added to Hirschman's anxiety to get into the field, behind the inching advance of Allied troops. Italy was the bloodiest of the western fronts. German forces under Field Marshal Albert Kesselring dug into the ridges and hilltops of the Apennines and ground down the Allied advance. Between January and May 1944, it took four major offensives to break the spine of the Gustav Line, which allowed American troops to liberate Rome on June 4. Florence was free by summer's end; it took nearly another year for the German armies in Italy to surrender.

Daily dispatches relayed the advance to Algeria. As American forces neared Rome, Albert grew desperate to catch up with Eugenio. On

June 22, Albert went to celebrate his wedding anniversary at Terracini's home. When he arrived, Terracini pulled him aside with devastating news. The Allied liberation of Italy electrified the *resistenza* behind the lines; partisans squared off against fascist bands—such as the Black Brigades, formed in the summer of 1944 to bolster German troops. The distinction between combatants and civilians evaporated. Eugenio became one of its victims. On May 28, 1944, a neo-Nazi gang (the Caruso-Koch band) spotted him on the Via Livorno on the Piazza Bologna as he was en route to a meeting of the PSUI's military command. Two of the thugs approached him and demanded to see his papers; Eugenio shrugged in contempt. The assailants shot him point blank. He died two days later at the San Giovanni Hospital, a week before American troops entered Rome.[23]

Albert was shattered. He staggered back to his room overlooking the city to write Sarah an anniversary letter. Pure pathos came out. "It is pointless to describe to you what I feel—it is a great pain and a great loss." A few days later, he confessed "that I can think of nothing else. I have the feeling that the wound this has caused me will only grow. It is only now that I realize what a fount of hope Eugenio still represented for me—what an example, what an idol I had." Then came the self-incrimination, guilt, and anger at the army for holding him back: "I lacked the imagination I should have used to help him, to prevent him from exposing himself, and at least to find a way to see him again."[24]

His losses were piling up—his father, closest friend, now his brother. Losing Eugenio was like losing a part of himself. "I am completely broken by the news of Eugenio's death," he confided to his diary on June 23. "A large part of any interest life held for me is now lost. I now see how much faith I had in him."[25]

For a moment, the grief released some anger about his sister's role in the tragedy. Albert confided to Sarah, in barely subdued words, that "I cannot prevent myself from feeling a certain bitterness toward my sister." His diary captures a brother more torn between blame and empathy. "I ask myself anxiously what will be U's reaction. Is she responsible? She will be to the extent that she feels responsible." A bit later, the note shifted, albeit in wording that lends itself to more than one interpretation. "This has all the elements of a tragedy. I have no hope for the denouement. I feel that there will be ill-will between her and me, unfortunately." Thereafter, he kept his feelings to himself, withdrawing under the carapace of his silence. An implicit pardon was the price to pay for his sibling affection. On the heels of Italy's liberation, he could finally write to Ursula in Switzerland asking for news of the girls, as well as this man, Altiero. "It is pointless to tell you how much I desire to see you again, and the more the barriers and impossibilities disappear the more this separation becomes insufferable and maddening." Eugenio quietly slipped into the domain of personal memory. Decades would pass before Albert would speak of Eugenio to his sister.[26]

Then some news gave him a purpose. Someone told Albert that Eugenio had been killed with the proofs of *Avanti!* under his arm—and that his last editorial was called "Trust in the German Revolution." "What a contrast to the exacerbated nationalism that is such a fashion now," Albert exclaimed to Sarah.[27] Now, to his search for books to read, he would add the search for Eugenio's final manuscripts, which made him even more anxious to get out of Algeria. In the scorching heat and personal inertia of a North African summer, Albert's life looked increasingly bleak. "All my days follow and resemble one another—I feel myself bit by bit overwhelmed by an African lethargy."[28] "This a great 'check' [*échec*] on my career and plunges me into a complete uncertainty. . . . I hope that you will still love me when I get back."[29] At the end of July, Algeria got the news that Paris had been liberated; the streets erupted in celebrations. Albert ventured to the public square to gather the news and watch the revelers; but he did not rejoice. "I am reading *The Trial* by Kafka," Albert confided. "I am very receptive to this reading because my experience, though without the metaphysics, has a lot of points of contact with the heroes of this book."[30]

No sooner had he finished *The Trial* than he finally got the orders he had been waiting for. As the Italian campaign turned into a direct war with German armies, the OSS found a role for him. "Now I have to learn again how to be a soldier, farewell to the lovely hotel room and all modern comforts," he snickered about his frustration in the American army.

"For me this is like the 3rd time I will have been drafted: May 1943, January 1944, and now. All that awaits me is to be 'dedrafted' for the 3rd time to make this complete!"[31] In early September, a DC-3 transported him to Monte Casserta—"my first flight was prosaic—much less exciting for example than crossing the Bay Bridge with you." He was glad to land, and glad to finally join the campaign. His commanders sent him to Siena, "a most beautiful town" and picturesque location for a holding center for captured German officers at the DeVecchi Villa. When the Allies took Florence and SI moved, Hirschman moved with it. What he was doing was following the front as it inched its way northward against the Wehrmacht. His job consisted in translating for Italians who had crossed the front and could inform the advancing Allied troops about the terrain and position of the German troops. Occasionally, Hirschman was assigned as the interpreter for captured German officers. He was finally finding something to do. "My morale has improved considerably thanks above all to useful and interesting work. The obstacle presented in Africa has perhaps not been entirely lifted, but it has at least been turned."[32]

It did not take long, however, for the ennui to resurface on occasion. The conditions—the winter of 1944 was bitterly cold, and the food was atrocious compared to the markets of Algiers—were bad. "Even with this the work can be even interesting." Once again, he crossed paths with Hans Landsberg. The reunion had a different tone. "I have been able to collaborate a bit with him" here, he told Sarah, pleased, "after so many so many aborted attempts. In this fashion, I have had a chance to get a sense [*toucher de la main*] of some work that I might find even more interesting without those stupid obstacles."[33] By this point, Hirschman clearly had a sense that some invisible impediment stood in the way of his being entrusted with the more serious intelligence work he craved. He tended to put it down to bureaucratic incompetence of the army.[34] "Someone from high up" assured him that "my present work is just provisional and that something much more interesting is in store for me. This has considerably improved my mood, so that even my current work is far from being totally uninteresting."[35] Tips like these invariably led nowhere, and Albert's expectations would be deflated once more; he was certainly not immune to lapsing back into boredom and frustration, especially when he glimpsed the kind of labor performed by other OSS men. Sarcasm occasionally broke through: "I get some satisfaction from work—only 90% of my time is wasted . . . which is not bad for an army."[36] So too did some pent-up rage. On a visit to the Vatican in October 1945, he marveled at the art collection but concluded that the entirety was of "crushing massivity, of solidity of influence and power. While walking in there and upon meeting an abbot, one has as much inclination to be nice to him as to blow up the whole place."[37]

What prevented the boredom from lapsing into depression was his milieu. If the days were idle and evenings free, he could spend them among friends old and new. Wherever he was posted, he sought out the local intelligentsia and artists. Moreover, in contrast to the tensions of Algiers, he felt at ease wandering the streets of Italian towns and cities. And in contrast to the French self-satisfaction, he preferred Italy's rejoicing at being free after two decades of dictatorship, but he acknowledged that there was much to be done by and for Italians to make up for the past. Letters that once complained of heat, lack of bookstores, and French nativism gave way to pointillist depictions of his paces, for despite the army censors' requirements that he omit all references to place, it was not hard to miss that he was in Tuscany. As he wandered the narrow streets of Siena, he marveled at its history and the shops filled with antiques; his letters are filled with the smallest details portraying the precious little "things" that made the city so beautiful. It brought back memories of the National Gallery with Sarah; the local museum put on a display of well-chosen pieces "from this marvelous school poised at a crucial moment in the history of art, still respecting medieval and byzantine conventions and forms yet burning with new ideas and impatience." When his interpreting work at the DeVecchi Villa was done, he'd drive to the house of Piero Sadun or Toti Scialoja, two of Italy's emerging Abstract Expressionists, who were influenced by Soutine and Gorky. Both had been involved in the Resistenza, but by the time Albert happened upon them, politics was a source of fatigue; they were eager to recover the trampled world of art and literature. Bearing cigarettes, chocolates, cans of sardines—supplies he absconded from the Villa's stores—Hirschman became a minor celebrity among a people who had spent years under the weight of wartime rations. When Christmas arrived, his hosts put on a recital of seventeenth-century Italian songs in his honor. And when he left, his bags carried two of Sadun's drawings and a pastel.[38]

Florence could not help but rekindle memories of Eugenio. While working in "a grand Renaissance castle," Albert found lodgings among "very charming peasants," and looked forward to sleeping on a mattress instead of army-issued cots. They gave him the royal treatment by placing his bed near the *prete* pot, full of glowing embers, that hung from the ceiling and by inviting him to special meals. He also happened upon an old friend, Umberto Saba, on the shores of the River Arno, gazing out at the city's ruins. The withdrawing Germans had blown up its famous Renaissance bridges to impede the pursuing Allies; Saba was watching, mournfully, as American engineers were erecting makeshift crossings. By this point, the former bookstore owner from Trieste and famed Italian poet was in a depression. He had been inclined to bouts of deep melancholy, but the effects of war and dictatorship plunged him into a near suicidal state—"he has aged enormously and has passed an awful year here. . . . He is one of the rare people that one senses in his very flesh the foul things that have happened." Saba was delighted to find Hirschman. That evening they dined while Saba recited several of his old poems "that he liked, but in a very pure and beautiful language that evoked his hunger to tell me of everything that would be impossible and inexistent from here on."[39] Saba and Hirschman then shared their grief over the loss of Eugenio. The poignancy of the moment found itself in the opening lines of one of Saba's poems:

> In quel momento ch'ero giá felice
> (Dio me perdoni la parola grande
> e tremenda . . .)

> At that time when I was still happy
> (may God forgive me the great
> and awesome word)

They appear almost five decades later in the closing pages of one of Hirschman's books to remind American readers that the excessive compulsion to be happy deprives the word of its intensity, in part because it obscures the relationship with its opposite.[40]

Saba also introduced him to a group of friends who had taken refuge in Florence, in particular, the writer, Carlo Levi, an old associate of Piero Gobetti and the Rosselli brothers and one of the founders of the Giustizia è Libertà movement, and who had been part of the Italian underground wing, along with Leone Ginzburg and Colorni. Hirschman found himself, therefore, among old friends and occasionally stayed in an apartment on Piazza Piti that served as a kind of nerve center. He spent his days translating for the army, and his evenings with Italian writers discussing the future of Italy, how to build a new democracy, and how to tackle the country's crippling poverty.[41] "These intellectuals are practically all Communists and a few are Actionists. Sympathetic, intelligent, fraternal, and by habit (and exaggerated by necessity, it must be admitted, unfortunately) half conspirators."[42] In the nocturnal discussions, Albert was especially struck by the eloquence of Carlo Levi, who shared a manuscript of a book he was completing called *Christ Stopped at Eboli*, which recounted his own austere experience as a prisoner under Mussolini. On April 12, Albert was reading a passage of the manuscript depicting how impoverished Italian peasants hung two portraits in their houses, one of Christ and one of Franklin Delano Roosevelt; when the news arrived that the American president had died, Florence went into mourning.[43]

In North Africa, it had been hard to come by books. As the war ended, procuring them became easier and easier. Kierkegaard, whom Hirschman was reading during his many idle hours, had coined the expression "passion for the possible," which etched itself immediately into Hirschman's imagination; it would become an aphorism he would use like a thread sewn into his future work: to perceive the range of the possible, to widen the perception, even at the expense of abandoning the pursuit of the probable. Here was a mantle Hirschman could make his own, a petite idée he would cycle back to for decades. His peregrinations around Italy also allowed him to scour the country's bookstores. He found an

Italian translation of Alexis de Tocqueville's *The Old Regime and the Revolution*, "which I am finding very interesting," he told Sarah. "I have always wanted to read this book!"[44] He seems to have read Camus repeatedly. He marveled at this "most acute and militant journalist" and asked himself, "Is it possible that a profound conviction about the ultimate inanity of everything makes you more able (because you are more distant than others) to defend in a most combative way some basic principles of honesty, justice, etc. which are basic to the debate but in reality far from being realized? I believe it."[45]

Hirschman was not just reading whatever he could lay his hands on. There was an underlying current to his selection. For instance, he found Sartre "une intelligence lumineuse" but was clearly more impressed by Camus' style and politics. Kafka captured Hirschman's sense of deep alienation in the army; the nature of the organization oppressed individual creativity and initiative, and all manner of efforts to try to give his service some meaning found poignant echo in *The Trial's* rendition of Josef K.'s struggles to cooperate with a legal process he could never comprehend and a fate he could never escape. Of course, Hirschman could not have guessed at some of the reasons why the OSS dragged him through Italy with little purpose. But it reinforced a drift from German idealism toward a greater accent on individualism that was captured by the Italian crusade for liberal socialism. As the war was coming to a close, Hirschman's suspicions of big theories and all-encompassing explanations of the world—exemplified by the dogmas of fascists and hard-line Communists alike—was evolving into a more skeptical stance toward anything that sacrificed the individual to the group. It is true, his army experience was unhappy, and one should hesitate before magnifying a private's weariness into an intellectual shift. But when he found a copy of Friedrich von Hayek's recently published (in London, in March 1944) *The Road to Serfdom* in a Rome bookstore, a nerve was struck. "Reading this book is very useful for someone like me who grew up in a 'collectivist' climate—it makes you rethink many things and has shown me in how many important points I have moved away from the beliefs I had when I was 18 years old. The experience of the army has also confirmed or rather demonstrated forcefully the advantages of a monetary society, anonymous, and where one preserves at least a sector of private initiative."[46] In the cramped, subaltern life of the soldier, it is not surprising to find someone pining for privacy and choice. But this passage was more than that; it is an important disclosure of how the army experience reinforced deeper intellectual faiths and deepening disenchantment with grand, collective schemas that ignored personal ingenuity.

Even more than a reminder of his skepticism of statist planners, Hayek got at something Hirschman felt strongly: the need to acknowledge the basic limits to the "intelligibility" of our complex world. Leaders were wont to claim complete knowledge when they did not have it and thus to squash the individual's ability to make adjustments "to changes whose cause and nature he cannot understand."[47] Hayek's vision of spontaneous, unguided, and hidden forces at work presumed an inscrutability about life that Hirschman shared, in which its ironies, paradoxes, and the possibilities of unintended consequences provided the underlying engines of change. This did not mean a nostalgia for the free spirit of laissez-faire capitalism; Hirschman's *National Power and the Structure of Foreign Trade* made clear that a will to power and concentration was inherent. What was appealing, rather, was a sensibility that reminded him that Kafka's Josef K or Camus' Meursault were, not unlike him, individuals caught in vises of indifferent systems that made no sense while proclaiming their unbending commitment to the system's abstract meaning. In this sense, Hayek's jeremiad crystallized a premium that Hirschman would place on personal liberties and his deep reservoir of skepticism about perfect knowledge. It was not mere coincidence that Hayek featured an epigram from de Tocqueville's *Democracy in America*, another of Hirschman's staples, that rung true for him as he read it stationed in a war-torn Rome. Here it is, from volume 2, section 4, chapter 7: "I should have loved freedom, I believe, at all times, but in the time in which we live I am ready to worship it."

Books and friends had been Hirschman's solace during the disconsolate Italian campaign. In them he was reminded of his belief in individuals, their courage and their choices, their foibles and fears, as they contended with the demands and pressures of larger, anonymous, and often oppressive systems. Personal grief or frustrations did not become premises for general despair. In this sense, while he shared some of Hayek's concerns about collectivism, Hirschman never opted for the prose of lament for a bygone era. Quite the reverse: his mind remained focused on the intrepid ways in which people could make the best of bad situations (as he did, relentlessly) and of their own activity create foundations for reform. In Italy, he observed this—and participated in it—firsthand. When entering a city, he'd scout the local bookstores. Dollars, rations, and cigarettes were powerful means to get his books. They were also the salve to reconstitute a moral economy around sharing scarcities; Hirschman had been attentive to this side of life since his studies of Italian currency controls. He was watching the system through a private's eye—albeit one with a PhD and a book about global trade and empire—and he could not resist penning some observations. Hirschman translated a short, lovely, eulogy to the black market in Italy. Written by Manlio Cancogni, the Italian writer, the essay echoed Hirschman's mood. The authoritarian state stomped on peoples' freedoms and condemned them to eat moldy, disgusting bread whose "digestion is a feat." The hero was the black market, where, in the face of efforts to extirpate human ingenuity, people found ways to get what they needed or find what they wanted; the state stood for sterility, apathy, a fossilized life; the black market was a refuge for creativity, initiative, and independence. A paean to Hayek, the story was shorn of his pessimism.[48]

Unease about collectivism pursued him through Italy. He worried about France's resurgent patriotism, concerned that it would forget the lessons of the past and drape itself in the glorious mantle of pseudovictory only to repeat mistakes of the past, and thought the Italians' spirit of self-criticism was uplifting. In general, Hirschman worried that nations would move on from the war "as something unpleasant whose boring effects must be circumscribed in order to forget and return to 'normal' life as quickly as possible. In my view, everything that can help engrave in our consciousnesses and of those generations to come of the all the horrors of this war, everything that would not allow people to forget or to deny or console themselves cowardly should be accepted and embraced."[49] But it was for Germany that he harbored the deepest concerns about collectivism. Reading about the bombing of Dresden a month before the German surrender, Hirschman worried that too much of the blame would be placed at Hitler's feet. "This complete defeat of German totalitarianism that appears to be coming may be the most distasteful result of Hitler's policies." This should not be diminished. But there was more at stake: "The way in which Germany has conducted this war leaves it no other possibility for collective rehabilitation for a long period—maybe 1,000 years as once advertized by the 3rd Reich. All that is left is to fold back upon itself in an anti- or a-social individualism pushed to its extreme as a result of the disastrous experience with collectivism. Hitler, who wanted to make nonsense of History will have succeeded only in making nonsense of Germany's history. . . . At bottom, it is the complete emptiness and all is possible that makes me pensive tonight," he wrote to Sarah.[50]

These ruminations about collective responsibilities about the past did not get in the way of some personal thoughts about the future. One of the buoys to his moods was learning that Sarah, despite the sad news at the National Gallery in Washington, was in fact pregnant. On March 10, 1944, he got news from Sarah informing him that she'd passed through the first trimester; "I am overwhelmed," he exclaimed, "and have spent the entire day dreaming with my eyes open." The news happened to coincide with "a decision I have made about my work . . ." He referred to "doubts which I still had," but now "the justice of this decision has been dissipated by your telegram."[51] Exactly what these doubts were is not clear; he may be referring to his career or his sense of a future in the United States. It is unlikely he ever worried about being a good father. Quite the contrary: he had strong feelings about the baby's name. It should be easy to pronounce in many languages and it should not be "fashionable" nor too foreign for Americans, "for we will always be Europeans in America and Americans among Europeans. It is important that the children [note the plural] not be too affected by this hybrid condition of the parents." In the end they settled on Catherine (after St. Catherine, the Sienese scholastic philosopher, as a tribute to the city that welcomed Albert back to Italy),

Katia for short. He also had thoughts about religion given the "hybrid" of Russian Orthodoxy, German Lutheranism, and Jewish origins: Albert urged that the children should enjoy the greatest freedom to choose, no baptism (unlike him) and a nonreligious circumcision if the baby was a boy.[52]

The birth of baby Katia in October 1944, while he was in Siena, shook off, for the moment, self-doubting. Of course, the joys were slightly muted by the fact that he was not there for Sarah's delivery, and he was concerned for the pain and suffering she might have endured without his company.[53] But the combination of Katia's arrival and his presence in Italy conspired to make him think more about the future. A week after learning that he had a daughter, the afterglow filled his letters and shifted his gaze to a new horizon. "My imagination runs wild," he wrote in English, "happily [this time back to French] I am now overloaded with work and for the past two days I have been at the typewriter until late at night—and I am speeding up—look what a wonderful perspective for you after the war, for I will not have any more argument that for you it takes less time to write this letter or that manuscript."[54]

Of one other thing Hirschman was certain: he had no future in academe, and the prospects for working in "economic intelligence" were no brighter. Even as the war came to a close "I have more or less abandoned the idea of a famous 'academic career.'" When Condliffe wrote him to tell him that *National Power* was about to be published, he quipped that "it will always be useful as a *carte de visite*."[55]

Instead, he began to think that Sarah should bring Katia to Rome and they should give up on the United States. "I find myself very happy in this country," he said about Italy, "and I even have a great faith in her in spite of all the baseness and awful ruin. Perhaps it really would be best for you to learn Italian."[56] This was early in 1945. "I am more and more oriented," he told Sarah after Japan surrendered, "toward Italy as a field of future activity without being very precise about what that might be concretely. I dream of 4 or 5 part-time jobs and in each one of them I depend on no one but myself. In any event, you should consider beginning to take Italian lessons, what do you think?" If OSS work was less than he'd hoped for, he still dreamed up projects. One "consists of creating an *Institute for the Determination of National Revenue of Europe*, nothing less than that, with its location in Rome and me as its president of course!" "It would consist of unifying the statistical methods used by different countries and to make them the bases for real European economic planning." Ideas like these swirled around his head, though he very often circled back to the need to establish his credentials in the United States before establishing his footprint in Europe. "It will be important for me to spend some time in Washington to familiarize myself with American methods, and then get some funding from Rockefeller, etc, and that will be it! . . . I suppose that there are better 'goals in life' but that is for another moment."[57]

Germany's surrender found Hirschman stationed in Udine, close to the Austrian frontier. It brought a transformation in his job. No longer was the army trying to get intelligence about the situation on the other side. It was dealing with captured German officers. Hirschman was sent to Rome, where several of the top captive commanders were under detention. By then, Hirschman was anxious to get to the Italian capital, for the death of Eugenio had become an obsession. Somehow, he got hold of some papers while in Florence, "but not all of them." He poured over them like a Talmudic scholar: "There are brief or incomplete essays that illustrate clearly the turn in his spirit and are of a thought that is so refreshing and original, posing new problems in an unexpected way."[58] This only whetted his appetite to find the rest. "I hope I can go to the Capital to see friends and to occupy myself with E's manuscripts."[59] What were Eugenio's final words? At every stop, and with every Italian who might know anything, he would pause to try to find more details about what had happened. In May, he paid an especially bitter visit to Forte di Marmi, the Colornis' summer home. For several months, the town had been the front of the war and had been pounded by the fighting. When Albert got there, he found the old villa had been shelled; all that was left was the ground floor and part of a staircase to the second floor. The maid, whose husband had been carted away by the Germans, had cleaned up and salvaged a few pieces of furniture. Albert gave her his spare change, 3,000 lira. That night, he sat down and wrote to Sarah of his despair "in seeing the house destroyed and the countryside ravaged where I passed some of the most beautiful weeks of my youth most full of hope and enthusiasm."[60]

It was not until he got to Rome, when he caught up with an old friend, Bruno Pincherle, an Actionist and another Jew from Trieste, whose brother was a doctor and very close friend of Eugenio's, that the picture became any clearer—and more disturbing. According to Pincherle, his brother had tried to save Eugenio in the hospital, but to no avail. But he did learn one thing from the dying philosopher: Colorni had been carrying something secret in his bag and was trying to evade capture when he was gunned down. Pincherle introduced Hirschman to someone with whom Colorni had been hiding in clandestinity: Luisa Usellini. She possessed the contents of his satchel he was carrying when he was shot. What Hirschman found were several scientific essays plus a series of literary-philosophical dialogues, one of which captivated Albert: "Fear of Dying," written only a few days before the assassination. There was too much for him to read, so he paid a typist 2,000 lira to make copies and began to make inquiries about publishing the papers posthumously. In the meantime, he got a more complete story of Eugenio and Ursula's separation: that Eugenio had escaped Melfi before Mussolini's fall, that Ursula and Eugenio had definitively split before then, and that while in Rome Eugenio had learned of Ursula's pregnancy with Altiero Spinelli. The estrangement had been complete. Learning this took some of the ire from Hirschman's reunion with his sister.[61]

Ursula, however, remained in Switzerland; their reunion was long delayed by the upheavals of the war, Ursula's serial pregnancies, and the uncertainties of Italy's future. As late as May 1945, while Albert was back in Siena, he asked her to come and meet him in Milan (if he could get a leave from the army) or Siena "as you seem to have great facility in movement." "Let us swear to each other," he urged, "not to reach the seventh anniversary of our separation."[62] Rome, however, united Albert with Altiero Spinelli. They shared many of the same outlooks. But Albert came away with the profile of an activist, not an intellect. He saw in the principles of European "federalism" some overlaps with his own thinking about the importance of curbing national sovereignty. But there was a tone of disappointment. "His thinking," referring to Altiero, "resembles a bit a liberalism that he absorbed as an antidote to Marxism and he has very little awareness of all the thought that has developed in the United States and England about the co-existence of freedom with planning (Manheim, Lange, Lerner)."[63] He could not help but find Altiero wanting, but only in Sarah's confidences did he share his misgivings. Albert respected Altiero as a charismatic man of politics. But beneath the surface of mutual respect, Altiero never measured up to the fondness or intellectual affinity Albert reserved for Eugenio.

No one did.

By early October, the war had been over for months. A commander told him that it was likely he would be discharged within a few weeks, and he began to plan his departure. It was not to be—yet. Hirschman's war would end with a figurative and literal bang.

A lot of grizzly carnage was committed behind the lines. Colorni's killing was only one of around 9,000 executions of Italian civilians, whose story has been dampened by efforts to portray the Wehrmacht as having fought a "clean war" in Italy—and thus mute the war crimes issue in order to consolidate a Western alliance during the Cold War.[64] In March 1943, one SI operational group went out to infiltrate enemy territory around La Spezia to blow up a railway line and interdict traffic at the Stazione Framura; it was supposed to be an amphibious operation involving two officers and thirteen enlisted men. Before landing, a German PT boat sighted their craft. A flood of searchlights poured from the shore. The whole mission was captured and tortured. General Anton Dostler, the commanding officer of Germany's Seventy-fifth Corps, ordered that the prisoners be shot in compliance with Hitler's 1942 diktat that anyone caught sabotaging behind the lines should be summarily killed. His officers, knowing that this breached conventions of war, dithered. It took Dostler several rounds of instructions, but he finally got his underlings to obey. The fifteen prisoners were executed on March 26; the German officer who had resisted the order—Alexander zu Dohna-Schlobitten—was dismissed from the Wehrmacht for insubordination.

The incident was the basis of a celebrated trial—celebrated not because it was exceptional, but because it was the first Allied war crimes trial, and a test for how jurists were going to handle captured commanders. For Hirschman, it was an important event because, as luck would have it, the army assigned him to be Dostler's translator, an ordeal that would leave him distraught. "In principle, I hate the work of interpreting but in this case this might be interesting. I think," he warned Sarah, "that you will read about it in the papers because it will be a big spectacle because it is the first trial of this sort against someone so high up."[65] Albert was right, but he never imagined that he might be part of the spectacle. Dostler was accused of violating the regulations attached to the Hague Convention of 1907 and long-established laws and customs of war. His case lasted from October 8 to 12, 1945, and his legal counselors did their best to test the mettle of Allied prosecutors. It was, indeed, a showcase trial and all sides knew it. The courtroom was packed every day with reporters and onlookers. Flashes went off as the defendant entered and left. "I am the most photographed man in Rome," Albert quipped. If the academy and economic intelligence wouldn't have him, "I may look good enough to pass through all this and be picked up by a studio's talent scout."[66]

It turned out to be an "interesting, but exhausting" ordeal for the interpreter, who had to convey word by word each exchange of the defense and prosecution. Dostler's defense "was incensed" and started by challenging the jurisdiction of the US Military Commission in Rome, a condition of the Geneva Prisoners of War Convention of 1929, which gave prisoners the basic right to be tried by a legally sanctioned court. The proper tribunal should have been a court martial. This challenge was eventually dismissed. Then they argued that Dostler was following Hitler's orders. But prosecutors had detailed evidence and affidavits—thanks in part to the resistance of junior officers ordered to do the killing—chronicling Dostler's command and instructions and pointed out that, unlike Dostler, who sat stoically in a chair before a panel of judges, enjoying defense lawyers and a translator, the American SI agents got no trial and no hearing. Wearing combat uniforms and possessing military identification, they could not be mistaken for anyone other than soldiers and

were thus protected by the provisions of the Hague Convention. Even if
Dostler were following Hitler's commands, they did not apply to soldiers.
The defense claimed that the uniforms could not be so easily identified
and added that as the fifteen were all Italian speakers, these were Max
Corvo's men. Moreover, Dostler could not confirm that they were in fact
US servicemen when he gave the execution order. In the see-saw, the SI
uniforms were exhumed and eye-witnesses testified they knew they were
American soldiers. The case for Dostler's guilt appeared to be sealed. As
the trial neared completion, Dostler elected to testify in his own defense.
He climbed into the witness box to explain that in 1933 all officers of the
German Army had had to take a special oath of obedience to the Führer
and thus had to comply or face their own execution. The translator stood
nearby, mediating words. The prosecution grilled him—did he know of
any case in which an officer was executed for disobeying an order? He
did not. There were some moments that shocked the translator, as when
one of Dostler's witnesses, a fellow German commander, testified that "I
would like to add that the accused, in spite of his outward appearance, is
a soldier with a heart." Hirschman was aghast. But the "absolutely Kaf-
kaesque conceptions on the part of the superiors," did not sway the judges.
The pronouncement: guilty of war crimes.[67]

We do not know what passed through Hirschman's mind as he sat
through the five-day trial. He was, like many court officers, voiceless in
a room that hinged on carefully poised words. His letters to Sarah, on
account of the censorship, are silent. No doubt, he had to focus on getting
the correct translations for the defendant to enjoy the benefits of fairness, so that in the course of the hearings his attention was tightly coiled
with the exchanges between the lawyers, judges, and witnesses. While
the transcripts leave Hirschman out of the proceedings, the visual images
of the courtroom remind us that the two—General Dostler and Private
Hirschman—sat side by side in stiff wooden chairs whispering into each
others' ears like colluders. It seems ironic that the person who did by far
the most talking in the courtroom was Hirschman himself, though the
words he uttered were never his own. Here was a man who had fought his
entire adult life against everything the stern-faced German general stood

for, compelled day in, day out to sit inches apart as the linguistic guardian of his rights. One can scarcely imagine what went on behind his subdued visage. Did he think of the Berlin he had lost? Did he think of the baby daughter he did not know? Did he think of Eugenio, gunned down by fascist thugs nearby?

One record we have of Hirschman's sentiments during the trial is his response to the sentence. Dostler and Hirschman were asked to stand before the judges. The latter wore his dark green uniform and khaki tie; the former wore the full scarlet-trimmed regalia of a Wehrmacht general, his hands slightly clenched as he awaited word. Major General Lawrence C. James read the verdict "with agonizing slowness," observed the *New York Times* reporter at the scene, because "a GI interpreter standing beside him had to translate each phrase into German." The interpreter "turned pale as he had to utter the death sentence" to the German general's face. The courtroom, packed with spotlights, reporters, Allied soldiers, and several hundred Italian observers, watched in frozen silence as he trembled through James' order that General Dostler was to be shot to death by musketry. In the hush, a visibly shaken Corporal Albert Hirschman of Berkeley, California, left the scene without a word.[68]

The next day, *The New York Times* printed a front-page story of the sentencing and featured a photo of General Dostler conferring with his legal counsel, with his interpreter in the middle. Sarah, who knew nothing of her husband's doings was shocked when she unfolded the paper in California to find the grainy black-and-white photo of Albert tête-a-tête with a Nazi general. Whatever international sensation the story was meant to cause was overwhelmed by her personal amazement. As she read how the interpreter went pale, she also breathed a sigh of relief that the war had not destroyed her husband's sensitivity.

A US Army firing squad executed Dostler in the Aversa Stockade in the morning of December 1. He was the first German general charged, tried, sentenced, and executed by the Allies for a war crime.

Hirschman's work was done. Due to ship out from Naples in December, he had about six weeks free from duty. He packed his bags for a voyage to recover the pieces of his shattered European past. This did not in-

Hirschman and Dostler.

clude a return to Berlin; Germany still evoked too many bitter memories. The first stop was Paris, and his old hotel on rue Turenne. To his delight, the owner had kept his trunk, and Albert rejoiced when he found his old copies of Gogol and Kafka—"above all my 3 Pléiade volumes of Diderot, Voltaire and Rousseau." He was delighted to find his favorite coat! Perhaps to remind himself of old times, he moved into the hotel for ten days.[69] The owners had a big party for him with all the maids and doormen. He confessed to Sarah that he felt "guilty" for being in the city they both loved but without her. "Never since our separation have I had such a desire to walk and chat with you. It is not fair, quite simply, that you are not here." Most of his time was spent rekindling acquaintances from before the war, especially should he and Sarah move forward with plans to return to Europe. He paid a visit to his old boss and advisor from the Institute of Economics, Robert Marjolin, who had returned from Washington, where he had represented Charles de Gaulle, and was quickly establishing himself as a major force in the Ministry of Economics in charge of foreign trade. In the little time that Albert had, he and Marjolin had lunch and dinner several times with Marjolin's wife, an American artist. They discussed extensively the problems of postwar economies and the reconstruction and European trade. The conversations helped motivate Albert to return to Washington to play a role in the American side of the reconstruction effort as a kind of transatlantic partner with Marjolin; the gaze returned to the future. He retrieved his mother's jewels he had safeguarded in a bank and paid a visit to the Dupuy boys, for whom he was once a German tutor; they were much grown up by now and on their way to distinguished careers in their own right. He scoured the bookstores of Saint Michel ("without much result"); Sartre and Simone de Beauvoir were "impossible to find," especially Sartre "for whom there is a cult here . . . like Sinatra," he joked, "which illustrates well the difference between the two countries." He also helped himself to the late-fall servings of oysters, "which I adore more than ever."[70]

He sold the bulk of his books to Gibert Jeune, where he had once procured his *livret*, the manual on universities in France in 1933, and shipped the most prized volumes in his trunk back to the United States, said goodbye to Paris, and set off for London to see a mother whom he had not seen since Dostler and the Nazis had seized control of Germany almost thirteen years earlier. There must have been a lot of apprehension; while Hirschman had worried about her and sent regular remittances, his letters had been few and far between, and one of the issues that needed resolution was where Mutti would go. Eva had moved with her husband, Harold Roditi, to New York, and Ursula was presumably going to move to Rome. Albert was still not sure of his eventual whereabouts.

The visit lasted only a few days and confirmed all his worst fears about his mother. Their conversations were strained and degenerated quickly.

Albert with nieces in Rome, late 1945.

"In brief," he reported, "she became intolerable, and I would have liked to strangle her for many reasons." It was decided that Mutti should go to Rome and be with Ursula, though as Albert noted, this was hardly an easy choice because Ursula got on with her mother no better than Albert did. But with four daughters, she could use all the help she could get. With this settled, he bid a sad goodbye to his mother and returned to Rome to prepare to be shipped out.[71]

By the middle of November, Ursula reached Rome; brother and sister finally met. The occasion was filled with joy, relief, endless conversations, as well as endless older-sister advice. There was also a surprise: Ursula was pregnant once more. "It's madness," Albert wrote to Sarah, "but in the end it's like that." Albert took special pleasure in displaying his newfound driving skills (thanks to Sarah) and took his elder three nieces, Silvia, Renata, and Eva, for spins around the Italian capital in his jeep. He also arrived loaded with chocolates and sweets piled in cartons used for packets of Camel cigarettes. This was not a war he wanted to end on a bad note. A photo of Sergeant Hirschman, dressed in civilian clothes, has him playing with his nieces, enjoying the role of the generous American uncle having fun, not the German exiled intellectual, French economist, or Italian resistor.[72]

Behind the façade, Hirschman was not without worries. What would he do back in the United States? Should the family return to Italy as Ursula was counseling? How was he going to support his family? But he was eager to be reunited. "The last few days," he wrote to Sarah from Rome shortly before leaving, "I have been filled with doubts if I can stand not being back in the United States and not being able to see Katia any more.[73] Hirschman's war—which had begun, for all intents and purposes in 1932—was over by the winter of 1945. Almost exactly four years after his first crossing from Europe to America, he went to Naples and boarded a troop carrier. Back in the United States, he was sent to Fort George Meade in Maryland, where he was honorably discharged for reasons of demobilization and awarded the World War II Victory Medal and an Honorable Service Lapel Button for World War II. Hirschman tucked these away for posterity.

When he finally arrived in Washington, he checked into the Rogers Smith Hotel, pulled out a stationery pad in his room, and wrote a quick note to Sarah to say that he was back and waiting to see her. His days alone would soon be over.

CHAPTER 8

The Anthill

The spirit becomes free only when
it ceases to be a support.

FRANZ KAFKA

For many social scientists picking up the pieces of their scattered lives
after years of war, peace meant the return to professional life. American universities, swelling with returning GI students, reclaimed their
academics from Washington. Not a few of the veterans of the Office of
Strategic Services became leading scholars of European affairs. But for
Hirschman, the pathway was paved with anything but clarity. There was
also a fledgling family to rebuild. Around Christmas 1945, Sarah received
word from Albert. Anxious days, and then weeks, passed before she got
the news that he had arrived in Washington and was waiting for her. Two
years of warfare had kept them apart. Not exactly estranged, their lives had
been profoundly altered. Europe, "home," was in ruins. Katia was now a
toddler—and had yet to see her father. When Sarah got Albert's note from
the Rogers Smith Hotel, she packed her bag immediately, left Katia in the
hands of her parents in Beverly Hills, and headed for the nation's capital.

The reunion of Albert and Sarah Hirschman was one of millions for
veterans returning from war to face the challenge of reconstructing lives.
Of the marriage between Albert and Sarah there were no doubts. But
the rest—where to live, what kind of work, how to support a family—
was completely in the air. The itinerant Albert had done this many times
before. But now was he was not alone, and of this he was acutely aware.
There was also the matter of how to launch a long-delayed economist's

career, over which he had idled many hours fantasizing in Europe in the shadow of yet another war.

For the moment, Albert and Sarah focused on renewing their marriage and making the decisions about where and how to live. Sarah waited in the dismal room at the Rogers Smith as Albert made his rounds, depositing his dossier on crowded personnel desks of the burgeoning offices of the federal government agencies, hoping someone might be interested in a talented, published, multilingual economist. Between job searches, the couple looked into lodgings. The housing market was as glutted with home-seeking families as with job hunters. What they found was pricey, uninviting, or had been snatched up. "Even after a month after my arrival here, I still haven't seen my daughter," Albert complained. "I feel that this is getting much too long since by now all we have done in the past few days is wait for a seat on the train."[1] After three weeks of hovering in the capital, they decided to return to California and await news of Albert's job applications. When they got back to Beverly Hills in mid-February, Albert wrapped his arms around Katia, and the two of them launched into a conversation about goldfish in the backyard pond.

Albert meets Katia, 1946.

The Chapiro's home in Beverly Hills provided the setting for Albert to recover from the war. He lounged. He practiced his headstands by the side of the pool and played chess with visitors. With servants and in-laws, there was more than enough help to take care of daily chores. The house, filled with Russian, was not without its diversions. Musicians and performers would treat it as a way station when passing through Los Angeles. New Year's brought out Heifetz, Rubinstein, and Piatigorsky for quartets and celebrating. Katia's verbal skills and toddling about the yard were an endless source of fascination. Katia "is surprisingly affectionate" and "really very cute, not at all too fat," he gloated. Still, parenthood took some getting used to. Katia was well behaved—meaning she "doesn't cry when one leaves her lone, playing for hours by herself." But the dirty work he was pleased to leave to Sarah. "America," he mused, "has not yet invented a machine" when it comes to "bringing up baby." It means "for all mothers here it is total slavery." A natural feature of any domestic setting in Berlin a generation earlier, nannies were rare and expensive—"only for film stars and successful businessmen."[2]

No news from Washington. The city had spurned him before, and he did not want to repeat the experience. So, after a month in the California sun, he packed his bags and returned to Washington, promising Sarah he would find a job and a home. It was now becoming more urgent: Sarah was pregnant again—their second daughter, Lisa, was due in the fall.

Washington was a land of opportunity for an economist with international credentials and knowledge. Armed with his curriculum vitae, fresh copies of *National Power and the Structure of Foreign Trade*, and high hopes, Hirschman resumed his precatory tour of the capital. He wandered the halls of the old Foreign Economic Administration (to which the Board of Economic Warfare had relocated), the new Export-Import Bank, the Department of Commerce, and the Treasury, which was taking a leading role in handling the Europe's crushing debts. His first stop-off was there, where he had arranged to meet one department head. He walked away optimistic. This man, he told Ursula, "offered me, I believe, a quite interesting job relating to the International Monetary Fund and Bank (Bretton Woods agreements). Because of that I submitted a request to be admitted into the Civil Service and I will wait for the answer."[3] But only silence followed. Phone calls yielded promises that positive news was forthcoming. It was not. "Unfortunately the position that had almost offered to me I was unable to get," he complained to Ursula in mid-April, "because of a cut in governmental funds."[4]

As ever, Hirschman relied on contacts. The Board of Economic Warfare (BEW) employed several of them, including Peter Franck and Lia Rein's new husband. The OSS's Economic Section was another; there was Hans Landsberg. It was the BEW, especially its Enemy Potential Division, that looked like the surest bet. After a day of meetings, and a discussion with staff that felt like a Berkeley seminar about the French and Italian economies, Albert spent the evening with Lia and her husband, sure that he would land a job. One of the senior staffers, Heinrich Heuser, the German author of a recent book, *Control of International Trade*, was especially eager to have Hirschman as a colleague, and the two exchanged ideas from their respective books. The division's head, with a recently awarded PhD from Harvard, gave Hirschman an application form and spoke of his starting salary: $3,800 for the first year. Hans later told Albert that he'd left a very positive impression on Heuser. A few days later, he was summoned back to the BEW for a 3:00 meeting, brimming with expectation. Instead, he was informed, icily, that there would be no position. One of the brass pulled him aside and whispered in French, "*ne parle a* personne *de tout çela* [don't mention this to *anyone*]," referring to Hirschman's prewar past in Europe. At this point, Albert began to fret; either the bureaucracy was impenetrable or his background was a stain; his book upon which he pinned great hopes began to feel like a bottle thrown into the sea.[5]

While job hunting, Hirschman also had to find a home. This was not much easier than finding a job. The federal government had swelled since the 1930s. Washington was no longer the seat of a pared-down, laissez-faire national government. The result was a crowded capital. It was Peter Franck—again in the same place at the same time—who suggested that he change his approach and invoke his status as a veteran with an ad in the local newspaper. After a few weeks of futility, Albert followed the advice, with his own touch. One day the *Daily Evening Star* hit the stands with a unique posting. It began with a poem called "Away," composed by a vet trying to find a home for his family. The lyrics worked: the next day one woman in Arlington Virginia read the ad, took pity on the vet, and invited the poem's author—Corporal Albert O. Hirschman—to her bungalow. She offered to move into a large trailer in the backyard while the Hirschmans occupied the house until they could find something more permanent. A grateful Albert seized the offer. In all, the Hirschmans lived in Arlington for a year and a half before finally buying a house in Chevy Chase, Maryland, with the aid of Sarah's parents, who also pitched in with buying the first car, a Ford sedan, to help manage life in the American suburbs.[6]

Settling into Washington also meant taking care of family affairs in Europe. There were immediate needs: with food and medicines scarce in Europe, Albert used his contacts to send care packages of clothes, flour, coffee, sugar, diapers, and medicines for his proliferating nieces in Rome.

Albert, Katia, and Lisa on the beach, North Truro, MA, 1949.

The Cooperative for American Remittances to Europe allowed standard-
ized packages of 49 pounds of "surpluses" per family to be sent for fifteen
dollars. There were also shipments of coats and boots for the grueling
winters of 1946 and 1947. Mutti, meanwhile, was tough. She feuded with
Ursula constantly and refused to move to Italy. Fed up, her son declared
that "her behavior indeed is almost close to that of a mentally ill person
and I am seriously contemplating consulting a psychiatrist in the near
future."[7] Finally, in 1949 she moved to Rome. There was also Eva, who
had married Harold Roditi. Roditi was condemned to a wheelchair after
being involved in violent clashes between left- and right-wing rivals in
Paris in February 1934; which side he was on was shrouded with doubt.
They had moved to New York, and when the Hirschmans set up in Washington, they were occasional visitors. Albert liked Harold, but he had to
admit "that I do not have many common intellectual grounds with him."[8]
That marriage soon dissolved, and Eva, too, joined Ursula in the Italian
capital. One New Year's eve, she met Luigi Monteforte. They were soon
betrothed and would have two children. Rome was becoming the new
hub of the Hirschmann family and the destination for remittances and
packages from Washington.

The job hunting finally came to a close thanks to an old friend from
the LSE, George Jaszi, who was now working at Averell Harriman's
Commerce Department and agreed to put in a good word there for him.
Hirschman wound up at the Clearing Office for Foreign Transactions,
headed by John Shirer. Relieved, in April he could finally look forward
to a regular paycheck. But the work was dull. It kept him away from European concerns, and he was simply overqualified—which was soon apparent to his superiors, who also tried to help him move up, to no avail.[9]
He confessed to Ursula that "it is certainly much harder to have courage
to surmount the daily obstacles of life now than before. Now that die
Träume nicht alle reifen [that all dreams have not come true], at least one
would like to let oneself go, not to have to do superhuman efforts—for
what? Simply to live."[10]

By chance, possibly through Alexander Stevenson, who was also at
the same place at the same time as Albert, Albert's name came to Alex-

ander Gerschenkron's attention in October. "Shura" Gerschenkron had been brought from the docks of San Francisco by Howard Ellis to join the research staff of the Federal Reserve Board—what Sandy Stevenson jokingly called "that old mafia"—and was delighted to join the Ivy Leaguers and foreigners like Fritz Machlup and Gottfried Haberler. Gerschenkron quickly moved up the ranks to become head of the International Section, which allowed him to hire his own staff. He wanted someone to cover Western Europe, and especially Italy and France. Albert was the perfect candidate, and Shura was not going to be held up by procedural niceties. Gerschenkron called him immediately and invited Albert to his office at the Federal Reserve Board. The old colleagues brought each other up on the latest news, and at the end of the conversation, Gerschenkron got to the point: did Albert want to move to the Fed? The answer was an instant yes. He was elated; this might afford the opportunity "to travel to 'my' countries." Just as important was what this meant for his faltering career: "My work is surely going to be very interesting and maybe I might be able to exert some modest influence on 'high politics.'" A bit wishfully, if not naïvely, he told his sister that "all problems of foreign economic and financial policy are brought here before a council of five in which the FRB is one of the five (the other four: State Department, Treasury, Department of Commerce, and Export-Import Bank." Here was a chance to have influence, as well as to enjoy the Board's "independent research and the atmosphere that prevails there is quite like at a university."[11] It would have been hard for his job to live up to such lofty expectations. But for a while, it came close.

Once again, Albert and Shura were colleagues. They divvied up Europe. Albert's research focused on the West (excluding Britain, whose scale of debt and problems had an analyst all its own), while Shura took the East and focused especially on the USSR. Their boss was Burke Knapp, who appreciated the duo as the pillars of his International Section of the Division of Research and Statistics. In those fluid postwar years, this team did not last long. In 1948, Gerschenkron moved to Harvard, and Knapp went to the State Department and thence to become the vice-president of the World Bank. Around the same time, Robert Solomon joined the staff, and it did not take long for him and Albert to become close, coauthoring several working papers and regularly sharing their thoughts, Robert becoming, if anything a closer colleague than Shura.

The Fed offices occupied one of the gray Washington buildings erected during the Depression. Made of Georgia marble in the Beaux Arts style, they conformed to the monumental scale of the capital's public architecture. Facing Constitution Avenue and the Mall, the Fed's headquarters were a statement of restrained ornamentation and imperceptible rupture with convention, with every detail, from the lampshades to the bas reliefs, carefully planned by its makers. It was an appropriate home for a way of thinking about economic affairs governed by caution, which should have rung some warning bells for the more freewheeling Hirschman. The aura of the Fed, and of the whole entourage near and around Foggy Bottom, was saturated with a clubbish in-group style. The F Street Club was the who's who for lunch crowds of the Georgetown Set of journalists, senior officials, and politicians engaged in world affairs. With no access to the old school networks, and uninterested in a political career, Hirschman was not part of this scene; he and his colleagues were happily left in the back rooms, away from the corridors of power.

For the most part, Knapp's approach to his research staff was to give them free reign to work on problems they saw as pressing. For the first few months, Hirschman's work was uneventful, and he stuck to the tasks of reporting to the board. But it took Hirschman little time to embellish his data with a more analytical and more prescriptive voice, especially as it became clearer that Europe was not rebounding after the war. By the end of 1946, he showed why the outgoing finance minister in France, Robert Schuman, could not devalue as a response to France's yawning trade deficit. The difficulty revealed a paradox that lay at the heart of why it was becoming more and more difficult to turn European economies around. For countries dependent on imports, any devaluation would make imports more expensive and thus spark an inflationary cycle, which was bound to make problems worse.[12] Hirschman offered an analysis that ran headlong into conventional economic orthodoxies about self-correcting markets, views that got more and more air time after the November 1946 elections that handed Congress back to the Republican Party for the first time since the 1920s and introduced a new crop of politicos to Washington, such as Representative Richard Nixon from California and Senator Joseph McCarthy from Wisconsin.[13]

At first, Hirschman paid little heed and enjoyed his autonomy; he had plenty to absorb him. Europe was stumbling. Inflation was running out of control. Shortages worsened everywhere. In December, a snow storm rolled across the continent, burying it. This was followed by a deep freeze; the Thames iced up. Around Europe, trains and barges stopped moving—cutting off the flow of coal and fuel. The ice killed off the winter wheat crop, threatening mass starvation. Albert and Sarah stepped up their remittances to Ursula, sending whatever winter wear they could find. Old friends dropped by—such as Carlo Levi, who would stay with the Hirschmans for extended periods while in the United States—who shared the grim news.

The growing crisis in Europe inducted Hirschman into Washington's policy-making backrooms. France and Italy in particular approached the edge of a cliff, as Hirschman catalogued to his superiors.[14] Burke Knapp wanted more than reporting; he asked Albert to write a comprehensive analysis of both countries for the *Federal Reserve Bulletin* in early 1947.[15] For the next several months he labored at the task, excited to be back to publishing. To Ursula, whom he relied upon for a steady flow of newspaper clippings, he wrote that this was not just his first intellectually exciting task, but given its visibility to his superiors—"VIP's (= very important persons)"—it was an opportunity to make an impression.[16]

The essay was Hirschman's first breakout into economic intelligence and analysis in English. An inventory of desperation, rationing, price controls, the collapse of banking systems, mounting inflation, and rapidly deteriorating trade balances, Hirschman explained how, one by one, European countries were resorting to the same policies that got them into their prewar fix: quotas, tariffs, foreign exchange controls, and protective walls. Any idea of a regional trading system was swept away by autarky and bilateral deal making. The world Hirschman depicted was one in which Europeans were bereft of the capacity to produce necessities and the ability to import essentials. When feeble governments in Paris and Rome tried to help consumers, they simply ignited inflation—requiring, therefore, even more rationing. Faced with scarcities and declining wages, they were gripped by strikes and more economic paralysis. Western Europe was not poised for a self-generated recovery. The immediate aftermath of the war could, Hirschman wrote, be "aptly compared to the process that takes place in an anthill that has been disrupted." There were roads to clear, mines to open, debris to remove with ameliorative foreign aid. But, almost two years into peace, this model of recovery was exhausted. Everything was out of balance—budgets, external payments, and the stress of trying to get things right were making things worse. Hirschman was unequivocal: this crisis was *not* a paralysis of production, but rather of trade, especially regional trade; the ants were at a standstill because they had nothing to do with the fruits of their work. It was a grim but incisive analysis but not a hopeless situation: aid could help rebuild infrastructures, but there had to be a drive to multilateral trading so that markets could reactivate the anthill.[17]

What the Fed brass made of the message is unknown. But they published Hirschman's words on the front page of the *Bulletin* at a critical moment in Washington's deliberations over Europe. Certainly, his career lurched forward. When Gerschenkron left for Harvard in the middle of 1948, Hirschman became the chief of the Western European–British Commonwealth Section of the Fed's Division of Research and Statistics. This positioned him as a midlevel staffer at the nexus of a remarkable experiment in creating a new world out of the rubble of war—and initiated Hirschman's lifelong fascination with the possibilities and constraints of policy making for reform. His name did not appear on the famous memoranda that figured so prominently in the way American rulers sought paradigms and models for thinking about the place of the United States in world affairs. Hirschman provided, rather, thinking behind the thinking. He was one of the invisible men behind the Marshall Plan; this chapter of his life evokes the promises and frustrations of a critical moment of American statesmanship from the inside of its inner sanctums, another kind of anthill.

How was the United States going to wield influence in world affairs after the war? Would it use its superpower status (a term coined in 1944 by the political scientist William T. R. Fox) to get deeply involved in affairs abroad during peacetime? American newspapers portrayed a continent sliding out of reach. In Czechoslovakia, Communists had swept 40 percent of postwar votes and led to a year of fierce internal jostling that culminated in a Communist putsch. In June 1946, 40 percent of Italians also voted for the PCI, and in November, almost 30 percent of French voters cast their ballot for Communists; across Europe, coalition governments faced the choice of jettisoning Communist partners, and thus becoming crippled, or lurching leftward. In France, the government evicted the Communists from the ruling coalition, only to face veiled threats of an insurrection; the PCF leader Maurice Thorez alluded to a Soviet invasion. France, warned Hirschman, was at a crossroads. But if one had a choice, it was better for France to have "one big crisis than two separate ones," for it would compel the government to shake things up in a way that separate, smaller crises may not. Years later, as Hirschman reflected on the crises in Latin America, he invoked a similar notion of an "optimal" crisis—deep enough to provoke change but not so deep that it wiped out the means to make it. In the gloom that pervaded the hallways of foreign-policy makers, Hirschman sought ways to convert necessities into virtues.[18]

As it turns out, matters were about to break. While Hirschman had his eye on the sinking French economy, a major diplomatic effort was under way. A council of foreign ministers from the United States, France, Britain, the USSR, and elsewhere, convened in Moscow in early spring of 1947 to discuss how to handle the postwar situation. It quickly broke down into two blocs, East and West. Washington's sphere appeared much more vulnerable. The French foreign minister told the US secretary of state, George C. Marshall, that the West could count on France, but that France was on the ropes and desperately needed "time to avoid a civil war." A deeply troubled Marshall returned to the United States to warn Americans that the war had been won but that "the patient is sinking while the doctors deliberate."[19] Marshall wanted to get beyond piecemeal "aid" solutions, and his undersecretary of state for economic Affairs, William Clayton, was in full agreement. Bromides about laissez faire orthodoxies or the clamor, especially coming from the ranks of leading Republicans, that America had done more than enough for Europeans, were counterproductive. Truman's foreign policy team shared the general sense that the United States had to play an interventionist role in world affairs, on the premise that nationalisms of all kinds had to be held at bay—that democracies could only be rebuilt with a new cooperative spirit between states and even a willingness to forgo cherished principles of state sovereignty. This pitch was loud and clear in *National Power and the Structure of Foreign Trade*; it also rang through the prose of Eugenio Colorni's Ventotene Manifesto. Hirschman relished the chance to be a part of daring new policies that moved beyond cherished principles of state sovereignty. In early June, Marshall addressed Harvard's graduating class of 1947 and laid out a plan for and with Europe.

Deterioration in Europe tipped the scales in Washington and pulled Hirschman's section of the Fed into the effort to prevent the crisis in postwar Europe from exploding. Averell Harriman led the president's Committee on Foreign Aid and stacked it with important businessmen and pragmatic Republicans. Harriman enlisted an MIT economist and seasoned OSS insider, Richard Bissell, as his executive secretary to draft up a plan for Congress. Albert Hirschman came to Bissell's attention. We cannot know for sure why or how, since the Bissell Papers are still not open to researchers; it may be that he was reading some of the Fed insights from Hirschman's pen, which was working overtime. Hirschman delivered two big reports to Burke Knapp about the commercial structure of countries into which Americans were considering pouring over $10 billion. Again, he argued that trade was depressed because European countries had locked themselves into interconnecting bilateral arrangements. The desperation to hoard foreign exchange to redeem war debts made things even worse. If European trade could not revive, the region would continue to record big trade deficits with the United States. And if the net payments kept exceeding net receipts, the United States would be giving "aid" to the "dying patient." Hirschman insisted that this was remediable; this was not a patient afflicted with a "chronic" ailment. The problems were temporary and conjunctural. It is important to note: this was a contentious argument. Many conservatives argued that what Europeans needed was a good stiff devaluation to make their products more competitive in the dollar area. Hirschman dissented. Devaluation would only worsen France's problems because necessary imports would be more expensive, and it would ignite inflation, cause more mayhem at the workplace, and reduce production. This was the trap of the "dollar gap"—conventional remedies would not work; giving aid with one hand and urging market corrections like devaluations with the other hand was self-defeating. France—the neuralgic core of the problem—had to increase exports, and if the dollar area was impossible to penetrate, France had to find alternative markets closer to hand.[20] Italy was an exhibit of why stock-in-trade recipes would only work at a self-defeating price. The country's vice president and minister of the budget, Luigi Einaudi, an advocate of conventional wisdom, responded to the country's runaway inflation with massive cuts in public expenditures and tightening of local credit—which plunged the country into "familiar symptoms of depression." Writing in the *American Economic Review*, Hirschman could not resist pointing out the irony that Einaudi, a priest of "orthodoxy," was forced to step in and rescue several heavy industries that began to close their doors, leading "to more State intervention in, and greater State control of, Italian economic life." Ursula's list for her care packages grew longer and included ever more basics.[21]

Within a month of Knapp circulating Hirschman's reports on France and Italy, Bissell was on the phone to the Fed. He wanted Hirschman on his team. The US Senate had approved by a wide margin the European Recovery Program (ERP) and a "moral commitment" to spend $17 billion from 1948 to June 1952. There was no doubt that Hirschman was waiting for the opportunity. "I am working already for weeks," he wrote in late November, "on the elaboration of the European Recovery Program, in a way I have never worked before: Saturday-Sunday, almost always until very late at night etc.—it's the final spurt, since soon everything has to be put together for the Congress."[22]

From this emerged the Economic Cooperation Administration (ECA), led by an initially reluctant Paul Hoffman, the president of the Studebaker Corporation. He turned to Bissell as the centerpiece of a brain trust that would do the thinking behind the "planners" and be responsible for deep analysis of the recovery program. Hirschman grew to admire Bissell's style of encouraging his staff to think creatively and pragmatically, advocating a style of problem solving that did not rely on an ability to know and anticipate—and plan for—all problems all at once.[23] In fact, there was no "plan" as such, just a mechanism to raise and inject working capital into a system that was paralyzed by a weak financial structure and chronic balance of payments problems. No capital transfusion, Hirschman and Bissell felt, could yield sustainable recovery without tackling the underlying obstacles to the Europe's payments system. The plan was in fact a process of creative, pragmatic deliberation, motivated by a vision of Europe as an active commercial, interdependent region.

Out of the new Miatico Building on the corner of H and 17th Streets, a few blocks from the White House, Hirschman was "on loan" from the Fed to the headquarters of the ECA. The Marshall Plan shuffled him back and forth; he was still reporting to the board of governors of the American central bank and also servicing Bissell's brain trust, which was designed as a "council of five" (with thinking representatives from State, Commerce, Treasury, the Export-Import Bank, and the Fed) in which Hirschman served as the "voice" of the FRB. Hirschman was thereby doubly free. He was spared the day to day work of the ECA—figuring out the sums that had to be transferred to European central banks, where they would be converted into local currencies and loaned out. Nor did he have to conform to the monetary orthodoxy for which the Fed was a citadel. Instead, he had the room, afforded by Bissell, to explore broader questions about whether and how Europeans would cooperate. "His" countries at the Fed—France and Italy—happened to be the front line of the crisis for the ECA. Few economists knew them as well as Hirschman did.[24]

Hirschman buried himself in work. Leaving home early in the morning, he joined a car pool of fellow economists bound for their offices downtown, leaving wives and children in the city's outskirts, and often returning home in the middle of the night.[25] The associates formed the Working Group on Questions and Answers because their notes helped Bissell and Harriman handle the grilling from Congress. It included Theodor Geiger, Robert Triffin, and Harold van B. Cleveland. When the ECA opened an office on the rue de Rivoli, across from the Tuilleries in Paris, the working group enlisted the crafty, energetic William "Tommy" Tomlinson.

With this breakthrough in Washington, the challenge was Europe's. Money and ideas would only go so far. Hirschman warned Altiero Spinelli, an early voice of European federalism, that the early results of aid did not look promising. "Because the coordination of investments did not give results, it is based now more on liberal methods: remove controls on exchanges and on commerce. However there too it is doubtful how far one can go without 'enforcement' bodies and some at ECA realize this very well."[26] Europeans had to coordinate. A big step was the founding of the Organisation for European Economic Co-operation in 1948, which gave European leaders a mechanism to sort out their differences and to consult with each other. Still, it did not untangle one important knot: the multilateral system of payments. As Hirschman noted in a "critical appraisal" of the organization's early track record, there were still tensions over countries that refused to give up exchange controls, barter arrangements, and bilateral trade accords. "More and more I am concerned with the conciliation of Europe," he confided to Ursula; the European states' commitment to national sovereignty was a giant barrier to intra-European trade and permanent recovery.[27]

There had to be new ideas. To that end, Bissell gave Hirschman the nod to peer further into the future to consider what Europe might look like with a properly functioning system to resolve their regional balance of payments and untangle the mess of multiple exchange-rate systems. Bissell wanted a system that would penetrate more deeply into what was holding up the reconstruction—national state sovereignty in Europe—without appearing to endorse a new protectionist bloc. There was also an immediate alarm about France, which by 1948 neared a precipice. Paris spent the summer of 1948 without a government, and by the fall, spasms of violence gripped the city. Many in Washington worried that if France collapsed, the whole ECA would fail.[28] As soon as it was clear that the ERP would get through the Senate, and with France's alarming deterioration, the board elevated Hirschman to chief of the Western European-British Commonwealth Section of the Fed's Division of Research and Statistics. Bissell rushed Hirschman to Paris and Rome to evaluate the scene.

Here was an opportunity to imagine and outline the economic architecture of a postnational Europe. It was also an opportunity to return. In fact, Hirschman had been angling for such an adventure for months, eliciting an invitation to deliver a lecture at the Institut d'économie appliquée in Paris and asking Ursula if she could broker something similar with friends like Paolo Baffi at the Bank of Italy or at the Istituto per gli Studi di Economia in Rome.[29]

The first stop was France. Robert Rosa, an economist working out of the Federal Reserve Bank of New York, accompanied Hirschman on his return to Paris. They made a good pair—and Hirschman appreciated the company. He also quickly settled back into the rhythm of his longstanding relationship with Robert Marjolin, who was quickly emerging as a key figure among Fourth Republic policy makers under Premier Henri Queuille. He no doubt took the opportunity to bend Hirschman's ear to get Washington to support his government's policies. Hirschman and Rosa returned more hopeful than when they left. They found plenty of evidence that there was a "physical recovery." Steel production was up. France could look forward, finally, to a good harvest. The political and financial instability displayed signs of calming down, thanks in part to the first infusions of Marshall funds and the confidence they brought. Inflation was on its heels. Despite the apocalyptic headlines, France was on the right track. This was no time to give up hope in the ability of the new government to manage reforms.[30]

Having watched the Queuille ministry settle into power in Paris, Hirschman then traveled to Rome, where he spent a month. Installing himself in the Research Department of the Bank of Italy, he marveled once more at the ingenuity of Italian officials and the artful responses of citizens. As if to pick up where he left off in 1938, he poured over balance sheets of the Bank of Italy and budget transcripts of the Institute of Statistics. He also plowed through business reports and data of the largest electricity distributor in the country in an effort to get beyond official figures to gauge the pulse of industry. If regulators contrived brilliant, if obscuring, ways to manage exchange rates and to stabilize the lira, Italians citizens were no less creative in their resort to a thriving black market. The result was more economic dynamism than one would expect from the widespread poverty, illiteracy, and maldistribution of resources. If France underperformed, Italy overperformed. Italy, unlike France, had not begun the process of reforming its banking and credit sector and thus ran the risk of releasing the demons of inflation. Italy may not have appeared as crisis prone as France; but, in fact, it was precarious. The planners had to stay vigilant—and urge investment in Italy's bottlenecks.[31]

What the European trip did was affirm Hirschman's basic optimism and help him draw attention to the ways in which authorities were not prostrate, passively waiting for American assistance to bail them out (as some of the press was inclined to report). It also reminded him of the importance of paying attention to details and nuances, the little things: "Europe" was not of a piece, and so the Washington crowd needed to be attentive to the complexities and particularities if audacious reforms were going to maximize their returns.

If Hirschman returned cautiously optimistic about Europe, he was dismayed to find the apostles of orthodoxy gaining the upper hand in United States. Europe's stubborn inflation and economic lethargy led some to warn that the planners were throwing good money after bad: the proof was in the persistence of balance of payments deficits. They urged a sharp devaluation and spending cuts to bring inflation to its knees. Hirschman was appalled; there was no sense at all of the historic moment. Under normal circumstances, there would have been a connection between inflation and balance of payments problems; "it is easily understood," he noted. But these were not normal times, and Europe's needs for imports to sustain the recovery made their demand particularly inelastic. The allure of a "shortcut solution" to exchange shortages—it being easier to decide to "disinflate" an economy than "to bring about basic read-justments of industrial structure and trade patterns"—did not make it right. In a warning that must have rubbed against the grain of some Fed authorities, he dismissed orthodox solutions to complex problems, espe-cially ones so likely to foster "growing public demand for indiscriminate 'reflation' which would reproduce the situation prior to 'disinflation.'" In August, he stepped up his defense of the ECA's diagnosis and remedies in a confidential memorandum to the board that insisted that the ties between inflation and balance of payments involves a *"causal relationship [that] runs both ways."* Inflation was the effect of a deeper transformation that had to be tolerated so that underlying change could run its course. It was not the basic cause. Do not let the "cures . . . be worse than the disease."[32]

Some might see Hirschman as repudiating market solutions to eco-nomic problems. Certainly, his "unorthodoxy" has often been seen as a signature contribution to the history of economic thought. But ascribing his affection for heresy as an aversion to market thinking should not be pushed too far. Though he cautioned against the simplicity of monetary explanations and solutions, he did see the marketplace as the basic motor of Europe's recovery. It can be seen in a small way in his criticisms of those—such as the *The Economist* magazine, which crusaded for controls on the glut of US goods as a necessary stopgap to the trade imbalance—who urged Europeans to "discriminate" against American goods tempo-rarily while regional industries recovered. This was a bad idea and worse economics. Discrimination was like devaluation or austerity, a blunt, oversimplified tool for a complex problem. What was needed was "far greater flexibility and readiness to make adjustments than has been dis-played hitherto by most European economies." And this meant opening, not closing, markets. It can also be seen in a big way in his response to Bissell's request for a panoramic perspective on the future. Hirschman assembled his thoughts, got feedback from two of his closest associates in the brain trust, Charlie Kindleberger and Raymond Bertrand, and culmi-nated his defense for economic union in one line: the integration of Eu-ropean economies would "remove many of the obstacles which have been blocking progress in this direction." Europe had "hidden wealth," much of which thrived in the black market. It needed, instead, an open market. Only with freer flowing markets that could be corrected did orthodox policies make any sense.[33]

Like those above him in the ECA, Hirschman was positioned between two poles. To one side were the advocates of worldwide open trade, who argued against regional blocs as barriers and argued for orthodox measures to curb internal disequilibria; stiff monetary medicine and throwing open the markets would remedy the dollar gap. On the other side were nationalists, who emphasized the need for production and jobs by protecting domestic markets; insulating national demand and pumping it with government spending would lead the recovery. So long as the debate was dominated by universalists on one side and nationalists on the other, nothing would get done, and the United States would have to bail out its allies with no end in sight. How long would American public opinion stay committed to the operation? The fall elections of 1948 were brutal and anti-Communist hysteria reached new highs. A tired, weakened Marshall stepped down. His successor, Dean Acheson, was less immune to the escalating charges that Communists had formed a fifth column at the core of Foggy Bottom. Then the American economy slumped, shrinking Europe's markets and heightening its balance of payments problems. Hirschman worried that it would throw governments back on their nationalist heels.[34]

By early 1949, Hirschman was growing anxious that the larger vision that he and Bissell shared was going to get lost in the malaise; short-term reactions were going to spoil the long-term deep adjustments. In April of the previous year, Europeans had taken the first step with the Organisation for European Economic Co-operation to coordinate the recovery; Robert Marjolin became its first secretary-general. Internal feuding among the countries plagued him. They could not agree upon a common format for working out the complex latticework of debts and payments. Hirschman argued for his higher-ups to support Marjolin in Paris. With Tommy Tomlinson working from the offices on the rue de Rivoli to cycle ideas into the OEEC Council, many of the ideas incubated in Washington wound up on Marjolin's desk—and vice versa. Did Marjolin recognize the prose of his former protégé? It is possible. What we do know is that he skillfully maneuvered the council members to elaborate a plan to make European currencies transferrable among each other, and thus move from bilateralism to multilateralism.[35] American policy makers could put their thumbs on the scales. The ECA, Hirschman argued, was bargaining with each of the Marshall borrowers individually and not compelling them to overcome their internal differences. It is worth quoting the final lines of one of his reports at length: "From a narrowly Machiavellian point of view it has sometimes been argued that the United States has no interest in the emergence of a unified European area. Actually, the current experience demonstrates that, as long as we are dealing with the European area as a whole, our interests can only be served by a consolidation of that area which would assure us equality in negotiations in place of our present position as a minority participant."[36] Washington should deal with Europe *as* a region.

Ideas for greater union, "federalizing" sovereignty in Europe, as Hirschman had been advocating for some time, had been circulating through the agency's working group. Now, the ECA was willing to force Europeans to come up with a sustainable payments plan based on freer regional trade. In October 1949, Harold van B. Cleveland and Theodore Geiger submitted two papers that condensed the thinking within Bissell's working group. Western European economies had to find a way to "integrate." A European union gave "the best hope for a regeneration of Western European civilization and for a new period of stability and growth." The time had come to turn necessity into an opportunity. Several weeks later, Cleveland asked Hirschman to sketch the outlines of a monetary authority for a federated Europe. Scarcely two years after the Second World War, Hirschman rolled up his sleeves to begin "drafting a project for a European central bank and currency." It would take a while to finish. But he was excited: "the ECA finally seems to get ready to exert real pressure."[37]

The convergence of Paris and Washington led to a fundamental shift in the Marshall Plan. Hoffman picked up the brain-trust papers and went on the campaign trail, opting personally to deliver a powerful speech in

Paris to the OEEC Council that explained why a new structure was necessary for Europeans to close the dollar gap for good. The State Department, which felt the ECA was muscling in too deep into its diplomatic territory, howled, but it did not stop Hoffman who was, by now, fatigued at the bureaucratic wrangling in the administration and despondent about the ill-temper in Congress, and thus losing some of his energy. He mustered his clout for one final push. The word "integration" was mentioned fifteen times in his speech. This time, many European leaders were ready; the OEEC under Marjolin responded immediately by proclaiming as its goal the creation of a "single large market in Europe" and inaugurated an aggressive process that compelled its members to slash restrictions on imports from other members. Hoffman, emboldened by the new OEEC spirit, rushed back to Washington to get Congress to apportion more funds, this time making the case, as one would expect from an automobile executive, that loans would help Europe become more efficient because integration would yield greater economies of scale.

Behind the scenes, Hirschman was working on the details of *how* Europeans might cooperate and bury the temptations of bilateralism for good. He himself had thus come a long way from thinking that this temptation was inherent to international trade, a gist of *National Power and the Structure of Foreign Trade*. One idea that Cleveland had invited Hirschman to consider was a common monetary authority. His response laid out the immense difficulties of erecting a supranational agency over the heads of state leaders who were just rebuilding their sovereignty of their countries. But this did not make it unimaginable. "While it may be impossible to tear down the economic and fiscal attributes of national sovereignty by direct assault, it may be possible to coordinate these attributes and to build . . . new institutions in the 'interstices' of the national prerogatives." What followed was a step-by-step guide for how such a process would unfold, from coordinating monetary stability to institutional innovations. The issue for Hirschman was not *whether* Europe should have a common currency, but rather *how* "to think of a monetary and financial organization for Europe that does not ask for the impossible, yet which would result in a closely knit European monetary and financial structure." He did not discount the idea of a common currency but made it clear that it was a goal rather than a means for creating a larger, integrated market. He likened the arrangement to a return to the principles of the nineteenth-century open markets, but without the gold standard whose inflexibility gave way to nationalism and bilateralism. "The 19th century method of allowing coordination of national economic policies to be brought about by their automatic adjustments to foreign development, no matter how drastic, is impossible for governments whose political existence depends on the maintenance of full employment and the achievement of continuously rising living standards." What was necessary was a successor that was more accommodating to governments' needs for political legitimacy while premised on economies that were dependent on trade with neighbors. The blueprint for what he labeled a European Monetary Authority made its rounds through the ECA echelons as a "secret memorandum."[38]

This was a visionary idea whose day had not yet come. In the meantime, Europeans came up with their own plan, the European Payments Union (EPU). Hirschman's brass wanted his evaluations. He applauded it as a milestone for multilateralism: "It really is obvious that the greatest advantages from world trade are realized when every country can buy in the cheapest market." It was a return, he felt, to a system that had flourished in the middle of the nineteenth century. "The choice before us," he insisted, "is not integration or maintenance of the status quo, but rather whether we wish to stop and then reverse the slow process of *disintegration*, which has been taking place in Europe almost uninterruptedly at least since the First World War." Without some kind of general framing agreement of this sort, "at every shock, cyclical or otherwise, the national economies are likely to look to further insulation as a way out." This, he noted in his last line, reminds us that the goal is not just trading for its own sake, but fostering "a healthy Western European society in our struggle for peace."[39]

Looking back, Bissell considered the EPU "the greatest achievement of the Marshall Plan." For Marjolin, it was the framework for "a habit of working together which may perhaps be regarded as the most important political success of the Marshall Plan."[40] Finally, European trade was released from the obstinate intricacies of quantitative restrictions that had flourished in the 1930s. In a lecture he delivered to the State Department, Hirschman tried to dispel the fears that European regional integration would create a bloc that would stymie worldwide integration. There he argued for the need for "multiple approaches" to multilateralism, that worldwide efforts to dismantle barriers to trade could be reinforced by regional unions; lowering the walls of individual countries was by far the toughest hurdle, and if the easiest way to bring them down was with openness to neighbors, then that was a useful expedient and intermediate step. Once they began to fall, the process could build on itself. "I thus believe," he told his audience, "that it is not necessary to choose between the one-by-one and the collective approach." This would be the first time he would advocate that reformers think about multiple strategies and not a single road to change.[41]

There was an irony buried in these reformist years. As they began to yield their fruits, the cause seemed less desperate. The need to think openly became less urgent. So it was that as Europe finally bounced back after a nail-biting reconstruction, the window that was open to Hirschman's thinking began to close. By the end of 1949, the Communists had completed their triumph over Nationalists in China; the following January, Mao went to Moscow to spend a month meeting with Stalin. That same month, Alger Hiss faced convictions of perjury for lying while testifying under oath. Richard Nixon pounced and denounced the State Department as "Acheson's College of Cowardly Communist Containment." Matters went from bad to worse with the arrest of the physicist Klaus Fuchs and disclosures—after the Soviets had detonated their atomic bomb—that nuclear secrets might have been leaked. Joseph McCarthy went wild. In the summer, North Korean forces invaded the South; by August, NATO forces under General Douglas MacArthur were on their heels. Seoul was an occupied city. Three days after the North Korean assault, Congress authorized $4 billion in military spending and cut $200 million from the ERP appropriation. "Mutual security" replaced "economic cooperation."[42]

The Cold War turned the screws on Hirschman's style of open reformism. The partition of Berlin brought the drama close to his heart. The decision to create a new West German currency, the deutschmark, which is what sparked the Soviet blockade, was discussed intensely in his section of the Fed. Writing to Ursula in mid-1949, Hirschman had mused that world peace may require a defeat of the USSR. An irate sister accused him of American warmongering. Albert's response, which coincided with the lifting of the Berlin blockade, was a measure of his ideological development since his socialist days in Berlin. "I, of course, cannot change anything about your judgment of me," he explained, but he felt the need to correct Ursula's "errors of fact" and "misunderstandings in particular regarding my alleged conformism." He did not endorse a "preemptive war against Russia," but rather "a revolutionary struggle against the Stalin regime in Russia itself." One does not have to labor to read sibling disappointment between the lines to his sister; Ursula did not understand him. "I found it outright funny that . . . you accused me of conformism." In fact, his disappointment lay in her failure to read his real mood—of growing isolation. "If you knew how little [my conviction] corresponds with the milieu in which I live!" Surrounded by good "liberal" men bereft of humility or humor who wanted to solve all the world's problems with "far-reaching state intervention in the economy," he was stung that Ursula did not understand that his turn of mind implied unease with *all* simple explanatory models or worldviews. Stung, but not entirely surprised; secretly, he felt that she had not fully appreciated this turn of Eugenio's mind. He was not about to abjure self-doubting in order to cling with Ursula to the purity of youthful beliefs or to concede to Cold War convictions and to fold into the gathering mainstream American thinking about freedom.[43]

A nuance beyond her reach, what Ursula did not understand was her brother's increasing seclusion. The ECA was losing steam and purpose. European reconstruction and integration showed signs of self-sustenance after 1950. The project was never meant to last; doing so would have defeated the purpose. But there were also local administrative problems. The State Department always resented ECA influence. Treasury, by then, was also hostile because it wanted a global free market—and thus scorned regional blocs. The National Advisory Council on Monetary Policy, which watched the Fed's International Section with hawkeyes, was the bastion of worldwide multilateralism and attacked ECA policy vociferously. With the passage of the EPU, Hoffman felt his work was done, could stand no more of Congressional belligerence, and left for the Ford Foundation; in early 1952, Bissell would follow suit. Ted Geiger, one of Hirschman's closest associates in the brain trust, defected to the National Planning Association. The Miatico Building offices were put to another use.

To the outer world, Hirschman appeared the picture of professional success. The outer world might have surmised the same for home life. The Hirschmans finally settled down in Chevy Chase, Maryland. A comfortable suburban, wood two-story cottage near the end of a leafy street, it had the added benefit of not being far from Helen and George Jaszi, Albert's old friend from the LSE who had landed his first job in Washington.

Living in the American suburbs brought its share of pleasures and challenges. Albert was itching to have a larger family—more so than Sarah, for whom suburban housewifedom offered Spartan amenities. He "was the one who wanted right away another child," recalled Sarah. "I wasn't keen on it." "The only argument *against* it," he confided to Ursula, "was that it will delay a bit the point when we are able to travel, but there are many in favor of it." Lisa was born on October 17, 1946, almost exactly two years after Katia.[44] When Lisa was born, he had brought Katia to the hospital to await the baby's delivery. There were no complications with the birth, so the family drove back to Maryland in their Ford with baby Lisa; when Albert returned to work shortly thereafter, he fretted over whether he should be handing out cigars, which he had heard was the American custom. In the end, he did not, but he was left with doubts about whether he had committed a faux pas. This was the most stressful aspect of becoming a new father.[45] In general, Albert loved to return to his two-story home from work, to be greeted by happy, smart, and energetic daughters. On weekends, he took them on excursions. Washington's famous zoo was a favorite destination; so was the Jaszi's house nearby, where there were children of similar ages. For "Papa," the backyard was a setting for endless inventing of games. For one of her birthdays, Katia remembers her father having to be away. While she was romping with her friends in the leaves, she looked up to see an old man walking down the street toward the house with a bulky package. The kids paused, wondering who the strange intruder was. When the old man entered the yard he peeled off the beard and shabby clothes to reveal a father loaded with gifts and goodies for delighted squealing girls.[46]

Still, there was a monochromatic aspect of their lives that was harder on Sarah than Albert—who had his daily escapes to the capital. Compared to life in Berkeley, and even more to memories of Paris, Washington was boring and became ever more so. The suburbs depressed Sarah. While she had help around the house, and there were also some friendly neighbors, it was the environment beyond the front door that she found stultifying. When the weather was good, she would let the girls undress and run around in the yard. Passing cars would slow down, its drivers and passengers frowning at the spectacle. Sarah asked a neighbor why cars would stop in front of her house? "But of course! You have your children stark naked, playing!" Sarah went crimson.[47] Albert had his colleagues and a career. When they, such as George Jaszi and Hans Landsberg, or Paul Baran, the Russian-born economist and friend at the Fed before leaving for Stanford in 1949, came to the house, the talk was over her head. "I couldn't understand a blessed word of what was going on." Even Helen Jaszi, truly Sarah's friend in the United States, was an economist. One day, Albert introduced Sarah to the wife of one of his carpool mates. She was a Russian, a war bride, also at a loss for what to do in the Washington suburbs. She would spend her days at home. "I am so lonely, Sarah, in this house by myself. In Moscow, I . . ." The desperation prompted Sarah to find excursions with her. Then one day the news came that the war-bride had committed suicide in her bungalow, alone.[48] Anxious to find something for herself, Sarah did eventually find a part-time job teaching languages to foreign service officers needed for the diplomatic expansion of a budding empire. It got her out of the house and introduced her to some friends. After a half day's work, she would return to the suburbs when the girls got back from school.

Sarah's difficulties mirrored Washington's problems. In the summer of 1948, the House Committee on Un-American Activities (HUAC) took the Red Scare to new heights. On August 13, Harry Dexter White, who had since left Treasury to become the US director of the IMF (International Monetary Fund), appeared before the HUAC to defend himself from McCarthy's charges. Three days later a heart attack killed him. Rumors of suicide flooded Washington. Things went from bad to worse the next year with Mao's triumph. McCarthy stood up before the Ohio County Women's Republican Club and fulminated that the United States was losing the Cold War and pointed to Dean Acheson's State Department and the legion of traitors in Washington as the culprits. In the fall of 1950, Congress passed the Internal Security (McCarran) Act, which widened the scope for the attorney general to investigate people suspected of subversion; the accused could be prevented from leaving or entering the country, and guilty citizens could be denaturalized. It converted the fear of anyone who felt suspected—as Hirschman by then did—into a panic.[49]

This was the setting in which Albert decided to escape suburbia and the trap in which he was quickly finding himself at the Fed. In the back of his mind, the return to Europe had always been an aspiration, and Albert and Sarah had discussed it on and off. The spoken language at home was French, and they did their best to remain au courant with intellectual developments on the Left Bank. But Hirschman wanted to return with some cachet. "I continue to keep an eye on more permanent European options," he told his sister in early 1948, "such as, for instance, observer for the International Bank or something within the context of ERP. The most important thing is to acquire a small name and then seize a good opportunity." This was one of the motivations for his frenetic work and determination to build up a list of publications. While he received overtures to help set up the ECA office in Paris or join the new Economic Commission for Europe in Geneva, he felt that work in Washington was still very rewarding and promised him the best opportunities for advancement.[50]

The mood was altogether different a few years later. The red-baiting intensified, the interagency working groups dissolved, and Fed superiors curbed Hirschman's autonomy. In July 1950, the ECA underwent an overhaul and the Board of Governors of the Federal Reserve System announced a staff shakeup and the creation of the Division of International Finance. The new director was Arthur W. Marget, the Harvard-educated monetary theorist, vociferous critic of Keynesian doctrines, and apostle for the return to what he called "orthodox" principles of macroeconomics. The Fed, as far as Marget was concerned, was to get out of the business of endorsing unsavory unorthodoxy. The moment of interagency collaboration and pooling of talent was coming to a close. Hirschman became despondent. Returning from work, he would enter the front door, greet Sarah and the girls, and climb the stairs to close himself in his study. Sarah worried but did not know how to intervene. She wanted to respect his right to privacy—but she knew there was something deeply wrong when her otherwise buoyant husband spent hours locked away in solitude.

His reports to the Fed became more and more technical. They were also becoming scarcer. After the EPU, Bissell's group began to dissolve and its members were reclaimed to their departments. After the summer of 1950, almost a year went by before he submitted another report to the board, a short one on the effects of currency appreciations. His memorandum about new criteria for economic lending to Europe in light of the need for rearmament with the outbreak of the Korean War did not circulate.[51] In September 1951, he wrote an analysis of Belgium's surplus with the EPU, shorn of the sweeping advocacy that characterized his language in the lead-up to the creation of the union.[52] This was his last. He apologized to Ursula for not having written in so long and conceded that her intuitions that his silence meant that something was amiss were entirely right. "A series of events have depressed me in such a way that I can only pull myself together to do immediate and routine tasks." Ursula surely recognized veiled allusions to their shared past: "Is this again the start of a period when to live and to create doesn't count for anything, when only survival matters? I assume that the decision is largely that of the individual, but I need time to react, time to adjust." However, ever seeking the silver lining, he found solace by turning inward. His family and his books—he read more Kafka—received attention that had earlier been sidelined by the heady excitement of the Marshall Plan. "It is great that I am on such good terms with Sarah and the children, at least there is no doubt that making them happy is something meaningful, something that makes me happy. I have recently taken to working less at night and on weekends and to spending more time with the family and friends and even books."[53]

What decision was he referring to when he wrote Ursula? He wanted out, desperately. The idea of returning to Paris now became urgent. Hirschman contacted Tommy Tomlinson, who began to explore the possibility of a transfer to the rue de Rivoli offices in Paris, possibly under the aegis of Treasury. In July, Hirschman sent Tomlinson a lengthy letter outlining his thoughts about how the ECA might be reformulated to deal with Cold War realities and the pressure for rearmament. With Hoffman on his way out, Washington, he confessed, was adrift, not least because his closest partner, Bissell, was suffering from the complications of appendicitis, and there were rumors about how long he would last in this climate. "We are beginning to feel," Hirschman told Tomlinson, "that we may miss a historic opportunity for generating a great new momentum for our old goal: a united Continent." He surveyed the landscape in Europe, and especially France, which he felt had to be the leader, and made a pitch to Tomlinson for the idea of creating an integrated European army (Hirschman was not beyond grandiose thinking as a way to change course), hoping that this would open some doors for a transfer.[54]

He must have known this was a long shot, for Hirschman was exploring fallbacks. "Everything seems to be so difficult at the moment. Maybe it is the lethargy before the storm—I am thinking about radically changing my life," he confessed. "But that is of course not so easy anymore, everything needs to be thought through and prepared well in advance." One option was to find a project in Italy. This piqued his interests, and soon Hirschman's imagination went to work. A research trip to Italy "and then look for something more permanent there? It would be of particular interest to me somehow to collaborate on the agrarian reform," and so he considered investing in "a couple of agricultural machines here and in Europe and then put them for lease in an Italian province." As ideas went, this was one of Hirschman's least sensible; he had never liked his engineering courses at HEC in Paris. But at this stage he knew he was groping—"maybe this is all hopelessly romantic, but you have any idea please let me know," he pleaded to Ursula.[55] He also confided to his mother and Eva that "the desire to return to Europe, and especially Italy, becomes stronger."[56]

Then came disturbing news. As Albert prepared a lecture for the American Economic Association meeting in Boston after Christmas, he received word that Tomlinson's application for Hirschman's transfer to the ECA bureau in Paris occasioned a security review. He bundled Sarah and the girls on an airplane for Los Angeles, where they would spend the holidays with Sarah's parents in Beverly Hills. Albert, meanwhile, had to follow up on a telephone call he had received from an acquaintance in another agency. George Willis, a middling figure in Treasury, was given the thankless task of meeting with Hirschman to explain to him that the Loyalty Review Board of the Civil Service Commission would not approve his transfer; he insinuated, moreover, that in this climate, Hirschman would be better off seeking employment outside the federal government. "There are difficulties with your appointment," Hirschman learned. He grasped for potential reasons. His Sozialistische Arbeiter-Juden years? The Spanish Civil War? Working with Fry? Then he grew alarmed. There would be no more pay checks.[57]

The Christmas of 1951 must have been a depressing one. He did not go to California. Instead, he called his old friend Sandy Stevenson, who had moved to the International Bank for Reconstruction and Development (the World Bank), and asked for a meeting. Albert did not fully reveal his difficulties to Stevenson, but he made it clear that he wanted out of the Fed. Stevenson, the head man for Europe-Africa-Australasia, was one of the figures on the inside discussing the internationalization of the World Bank. He mentioned to Hirschman that they were opening a new initiative in Latin America, in particular in Colombia, where the bank had sent a "mission" and was about to embark on its first "development" project in the region. Maybe there would be prospects? He suggested that Hirschman visit the Colombian ambassador, since that country's government was going to staff and run the project out of the Central Bank in Bogotá.[58] Hirschman immediately set up an appointment with Cipriano Restrepo Jaramillo. A somewhat dour and formal man, Restrepo was impressed that such an accomplished economist would be interested in working in the Colombian capital. He offered Hirschman the position on the spot. They agreed that the details could be sorted out later. Hirschman gladly accepted.[59]

He returned to Chevy Chase and called Sarah in Los Angeles to report the news. We are leaving Washington, he told her. But not for Paris—for Bogotá, Colombia. Shocked, Sarah dropped the phone and ran for her parents' *Encyclopedia Britannica* to find the place on the map.[60] Nor was Sarah the only surprised person. Robert Triffin, one of Hirschman's closest colleagues in the Marshall Plan and one of the increasing numbers fleeing Washington (Triffin left for Yale), was also taken aback. Hirschman had long shared his ideas with Triffin about moving to Paris, so when he found out about Bogotá, he wrote, "I was rather surprised to hear of your decision. You seemed so inclined to go to Paris, especially during the pleasant evening I spent at your home, that news was very unexpected." His old Berkeley advisor, Howard Ellis, was equally flabbergasted and also saddened to see the board of governors lose such a talent. But to Ellis the cloud was also silver-lined. He and Norman Buchanan, a colleague in the economics department at Berkeley, were interested in this adventure. "He and I will probably want to exploit your first-hand acquaintance with this highly dynamic under developed area." Stay in touch, urged Ellis. It was this prospect of new discovery that no doubt motivated Hirschman to take the leap; he pocketed this invitation for the future.[61]

In early March, Hirschman flew to Bogotá for two weeks to finalize the deal with the finance minister, Antonio Alvarez Restrepo. When they met, the minister, who would later become one of Hirschman's good friends, was in a cheerful mood, and with a smile produced a copy of *National Power* for him to sign; Hirschman looked down to see that the copy was in Spanish, *La Potencia Nacional*. With this, Hirschman's adventure in Latin America was off to a good start. He especially liked surprises when they were friendly. He returned to Washington, by which time Sarah was reconciled to the big move; she was bored of the Washington suburbs and wanted an adventure. What made it easy was Hirschman's sublime confidence that it would all work out. For a "planner," this was a highly improvised move. Still, as he had come to appreciate in the 1930s and would come to advocate in the years to come, it was not necessary to know everything in advance before making big decisions.

An undated entry in his diary, likely from Washington, reveals a Hirschman still thinking about Hamlet. This time his petite idée was about Hamlet's agony of how "to let be." This was different from the French *laissez faire*, or "letting things go." The Italian wording was especially compelling: *lascia perdere*, which he took to denote "to leave beings alone when they are likely to inflict damage." Is this kind of letting-go "more difficult and therefore more attractive?"[62] A partial answer can be found not in words, but actions. The Hirschmans let America go. They packed, said goodbye to friends, and set off for the unknown.

CHAPTER 9

The Biography of a File

Someone must have been telling tales
about Josef K....

FRANZ KAFKA

From 1943 to 1966, a shadow trailed Albert Hirschman. But unlike most shadows, this was one he never saw. Hirschman did suspect that some invisible force was at work; some things in his life were too unfathomable. He could not understand why the OSS did not make more of his intelligence skills and preferred to deploy him as a mere interpreter; he tended to explain this away as the bureaucratic ineptitude of armies or large organizations, in part because he had less and less affection for them. But there were times when his career ran into inexplicable roadblocks. The Office of Strategic Services had been an exercise in vexation. His job hunting in Washington appeared to be going nowhere until Shura Gershenkron waved away procedures and hired him on the spot. But by 1951, these invisible forces were back.

They also became harder to account for. Someone—he could not recall whom nor when, when I asked him—once told him that suspicions surrounded him because he had helped stragglers from the British Expeditionary Force escape from Marseilles in 1940. This, of course was true, and it is true that en route from Lisbon to New York, he disembarked from the *Excalibur* in Bermuda and "debriefed" with an intelligence agent of the British government. But he never worked as a spook for MI6 (Britain's Secret Intelligence Service), though in Washington's security file on Hirschman such rumors can be found. Far more important were other sources of concern about his "loyalty." It is a paradox that concern about loyalty should hover over Hirschman because he himself would become one of the foundational thinkers of what constitutes it and what depletes it.

In basic ways, there was nothing exceptional about Albert Hirschman's unknown shadow. In the age of state secrecy, especially during the Cold War, millions of lives have been affected or destroyed by the contents of files they had (and still have) no access to. Hirschman's is revealing because of its ordinariness and because one can track the decisions he made as he struggled to conform to the effects of the secret file.

The file, in this sense, has a biography—a "life"—all its own, independent of the person about whom it purportedly reported, in part because it was so inaccurate, a likeness of someone else. Anyone familiar with the rituals of declassifying documents in the United States will recognize the silly, if thwarting, blocking of names and information to protect the privacy of third parties—as if one could not figure out whom "Mr. Hirschman" married in Berkeley on June 22, 1941, or for whom he translated at the pioneering War Crimes Trial held in Rome on 8 October 1945. Both of these—and many others'—names are black-lined out by censors. The file remains nonetheless a sad portrait about the power of innuendo and paranoia that governed some peoples' lives for many years. When I gave a copy of the 168-page file to Sarah, she was, not surprisingly, aghast to discover why their lives had to take such mysterious turns.[1]

Hirschman's dossier was opened in 1943, when in the early summer, the army dispatched him to serve in the Office of Strategic Services. The adjutant general of the army had already been assured by Hirschman and his sponsor at the Rockefeller Foundation, Tracy B. Kittredge, that he upheld liberal and democratic causes and that he was "*not* a Communist." This first round ended in November, with a general recommendation to restrict Hirschman's security clearance; there was reason to believe that he was a risk. It relied exclusively on reports by a field agent who shuttled between New York and San Francisco. We know that a Bay Area FBI field agent, Russel McTwiggan, traveled to New York to pay a visit to Alexander Makinsky of the Rockefeller Foundation. Makinsky, who had met

Hirschman in Lisbon, assured the FBI that there was no reason to doubt Hirschman's loyalty. We also know that a San Francisco FBI agent— probably McTwiggan, who told the foundation that he had been "contracted" by a third party—found an informant who was able to disclose a surprising amount of detail about Hirschman's European background, his affiliations, and activities. McTwiggan, "ingratiating" but "professionally secretive" to Makinsky, alluded to "fragmentary references that some suspicion of Fascist leanings might be involved."[2] Though the FBI could not confirm Communist or Fascist involvements, and all the evidence pointed to the contrary, the extent of activism in Germany, Spain, and Italy set off alarms. It was enough to create doubt about Hirschman's reliability.

But what were the causes for concern? Where did they come from? The sources of the information about Hirschman's European past emerge only if one digs deeper into the file itself—for like so many files, they often tell the history of their own evolution.

The file haunted him from the time Hirschman set up in Washington in early 1946. The file also accrued an inner life of its own, separated from the man it was supposed to record. This was because it was a file embedded in a history of files; secret services all around the world were buying warehouses of cabinets for them. Hirschman's return to Washington came on the heels of the defection of a Russian agent, Igor Gouzenko, in Ottawa, who turned over a cache of files to the Royal Canadian Mounted Police that revealed the extent of Soviet espionage in the West. The RCMP, MI5, and the FBI (the Central Intelligence Agency, CIA, did not yet exist) grilled him and revealed an extensive network of operatives in Canada, Britain, and the United States; it set off a witch hunt of mammoth proportions to root out "disloyal" members of the civil services of all three countries. Meanwhile, unaware of the effects of the defection north of the border, Hirschman was on the lookout for a job in Washington, still nursing ambitions of working in the area of economic intelligence. He submitted applications to the Treasury Department, the Commerce Department, and the Federal Reserve Board and hoped something would come along.

It was the application to Treasury—where he most wanted a posting—that enabled the file initiated by the OSS to build its own career. This was because the US Treasury Department, which was playing a major role in wartime and postwar reorderings, was coming under suspicion when several senior officers, including Harry Dexter White who had collaborated with John Maynard Keynes at the Bretton Woods Conference and laid the basis for the creation of the International Monetary Fund and the World Bank, were accused of passing secrets to the Soviets. At first, Hirschman appeared to be on his way to Treasury at precisely a time in which a cloud of suspicion was gathering over the department. He explained to his sister that he was going to rush to Washington "to meet the heads of the Treasury who offered me a, I believe, quite interesting job relating to the International Fund and Bank (Bretton Woods agreements). Because of that I submitted a request to be admitted into the Civil Service and I will wait for the answer."[3] He was delighted. In February 1946, an agent of the Treasury Enforcement Agency gave Hirschman a clean bill of "loyalty" health; "references regard him as a loyal American of outstanding character." The door appeared to begin to open for Hirschman's appointment to Treasury.

But then the chief coordinator—name blocked—stepped into the case. He observed that the enforcement agencies' consultation with the old OSS records on March 6, 1946, had revealed something fishy and insisted that it be followed up. He told the staff to dig deeper. This double-checking investigation provides further clues about the OSS's background checks three years earlier, and it gave the original, flimsy report a new lease on life. The November 1943 review, probably conducted by McTwiggan and based on an interview conducted with a source in the Bay Area, had yielded an "unfavorable report," and thanks to the chief coordinator of the Treasury's 1946 probing we know why: it was based on Hirschman's membership in the German Social Democratic Party's youth movement, which meant that he had "frequent contact with, and substantially indicated that this organization could have been more readily identified as being communistic rather than socialist inspired." McTwiggan's work also revealed that Hirschman had worked as a courier for antifascist groups in Italy and was heavily influenced by Eugenio Colorni, who had been arrested (and was thus by implication "suspicious") by the Italian government. All of this occasioned doubts about Hirschman's leanings. The OSS therefore had concluded that Hirschman's educational and linguistic background made him potentially useful but that his engagements "had been extremely limited due to the highly classified type of work performed by" the organization. In short, "derogatory information" revealed by the OSS investigation and inscribed in the file "was sufficient in scope to prevent his being assigned very important or secretive work." So, he was brought into the organization, given brief training, and "immediately ordered from the country." No wonder Hirschman felt an uncanny affinity for Josef K, whose arrest for a crime he never knew he committed was the beginning of a litigious bureaucratic nightmare in Franz Kafka's *The Trial*, which Hirschman read—not uncoincidentally—to pass the time while idling for the OSS in northern Italy.

One is tempted to speculate about the provenance of this misinformation. Could it have been Peter Franck, the best man at Albert and Sarah's wedding and a former Communist, who was the only person in the Bay Area with such an intimate knowledge of Hirschman's politics from Berlin and about whom Hirschman had become increasingly suspicious? Or was it Franck's friend, Haakon Chevalier, also a party member, whom Franck had introduced to Hirschman? Chevalier was, by 1943, under FBI surveillance because in the winter of 1942–43 he had asked J. Robert Oppenheimer, the guru of the Manhattan Project, to share scientific findings with an agent of the Soviet consulate in San Francisco. Hirschman certainly knew that Chevalier was trouble from the moment he met him. When he returned home from the rendezvous, his face had the expression of someone who had just smelled rotted meat. Unfortunately, the claim that Hirschman was affiliated not with socialists but with Communists was acidic and hereafter repeated itself over and over as the file thickened.

What is striking is this: what was unsaid by the FBI in its 1943 report now became, thanks to the Treasury's probe, inked into Hirschman's classified profile. In the spring of 1946, as a result, a picture was developing in the mind of the chief coordinator of the Treasury's review as he also noted that Hirschman had fought in the Republican Army in Spain. A memorandum of March 29, 1946, stated that "although most of the appointee's abilities and character" were positive, the Treasury Enforcement Agency "was unable in view of appointee's associations with other Governments to establish that his primary loyalty was to the Government of the United States."

Washington fell in the grip of a Red witch hunt, especially once the "blonde spy queen" Elizabeth Bentley appeared before a Congressional grand jury in early 1948 with a list of "traitors." This included Harry Dexter White and his Bretton Woods deputy, Lauchlin Currie (whose path Hirschman would later cross). She also fingered a spy ring operating in Treasury's Division of Monetary Research. Concerns about espionage inside the state, and especially Treasury, became hysterical. Hirschman had the misfortune of applying right at this time to join the Treasury Department's Office of International Finance. The door was slammed in his face. This time, the law enforcement coordinator concluded that "the appointee is a man who has a 'blind' foreign background which no amount of investigation would ever satisfactorily resolve in such knowledge as we have of him indicates that he is a poor risk, or perhaps a better term is a dangerous possibility. Frankly, I do not see any good purpose of making further inquiry, and to me, it is unthinkable that a man of this type should be put in a sensitive organization like OIF." Then Treasury's loyalty attorney chimed into the file: "This man's background is too obscure for Treasury to risk. There are allegations unresolved and probably unresolvable of both Communism and Organizations with British Intelligence (not to mention other countries). Treasury didn't take him in 1946. The situation is more serious now. We definitely shouldn't take him." The request was denied "because of [the] 'loyalty' question." Did Hirschman know this? When I interviewed him, the details were hard to recall, and this whole aspect of his past was something he had characteristically preferred to forget than to let fester.

Worse was to come in 1951, when Hirschman, seeking once again to leave the Fed for the Treasury Department, applied for a transfer to serve more directly the European Recovery Program (Marshall Plan). The vet-ting process was conducted by the Loyalty Review Board of the Civil Service Commission, an agency created in 1947 by President Truman as a sop to the growing hysteria in Congress that Communists had penetrated the government and were compromising the country's security. Hirschman was one of three million employees investigated, and one of the 200 who were fired or resigned as a result. Now, doubts about his "loyalty" proved lethal to his career in the government. The FBI began to gather background information. It found one source "of unknown reliability" who claimed that Hirschman had been a Communist in France in 1940. It found another that noted that he had been an anti-Communist in Spain in 1936. That this evidence was contradictory did not erase any doubts about his loyalty—quite the opposite in the minds of his investigators! By late 1951, a frightened Hirschman began looking for a way out. But to this day, he has tended to think that his dismissal had more to do with changes in US economic foreign policy than concerns about his loyalty. Many years later, when asked by Pierre-Emmanuel Dauzat, his translator, if he was ever suspected of "un-American activities," Hirschman was perfunctory: "No. Not at all."[4] His declared memory did not include this shadow.

Concerns about Hirschman's disloyalty led to his "exit" from the government. But it did not put an end to the file's career, as if to confirm that the file had grown purposefully autonomous from its subject. After all, isn't that the point of secret investigation, lest the subject be able to tarnish the objective work of its authors? In August 1952, the Board of Governors of the Federal Reserve filed a memorandum from the Civil Service Commission, which advised that it was "taking precautionary measures to prevent appointee's re-employment in the U.S. government at a later date, until the question of his loyalty was established." But because Hirschman had since resigned his post at the Fed, the commission had closed its investigation. (When I asked the Federal Reserve Board to declassify Hirschman's personnel records in order to see this memorandum, I was told that they had not been preserved.)

Then again, in 1954, San Francisco File Number 100-25607 was reopened in response to a search for a witness to Hirschman's naturalization petition of mid-July 1943 for more background information. Why this happened is not clear. The witness's name is deleted because a third party is still covered by the Privacy Act. This source informed the FBI that indeed Hirschman had been a member of the youth movement of the Social Democratic Party in Germany, "which was largely communist and that a source had advised HIRSCHMAN was known as a communist." It is unclear whether this is in fact what the source said or is what the FBI agent inferred from the source; in the ways these files unfold, the distinction is (deliberately?) effaced.

The Army and Navy Investigative Files reveal that the shadow of doubt lingered into the 1960s, even though the McCarthyite paranoia had passed. In 1961, Hirschman was being considered to go to the Army War College for undisclosed purposes. The file says simply, "for his attendance." The secret services were on high alert: the allegedly covert operation of the CIA at the Bay of Pigs was miserably embarrassing. It would have been ironic that Hirschman, by then one of the leading Latin Americanists in the country, was being called upon to talk about the future of American security in the region to its guardians. If he was, his shadowers had second thoughts. This led to a security review, and the FBI passed information on to the army that led the department to decide "not to extend an invitation to the appointee for attendance at the Army War College."

This was the file's last act. Finally, in October 12, 1966, the White House Office of Science and Technology submitted a request for Hirschman's security clearance because they were considering hiring him as a consultant in their efforts to expand into Third World development. In the end, Hirschman never took up the post. Although the 1966 investigation thickened the file, it put an end to its career. How thoroughly the FBI scoured their own material by this point suggests that alarm about Hirschman's past had all but vanished—or at least some caution had come to govern the earlier sources of information. Rather than rely on previous entries to the file (possibly, FBI insiders knew that much of the early history of personal intelligence gathering was tainted), the FBI launched a fresh round of inquiries—and for the first time began with

Hirschman's own statement about his past and current "loyalties." For once, he could represent himself before the FBI. To add a twist to this tale, at this occasion Hirschman was less than entirely disclosive. He had made this kind of false self-representation before, notably when he enlisted in the army as a Lithuanian. This time, his signed declaration of his non–US Army international travels from the time of his birth omitted all reference to his three-month sojourn as a fighter for the Republican cause in Spain. Otherwise, it was a very thorough statement. Why he excluded the reference is unclear—and by the time the FBI declassified the file in 2006, Hirschman could no longer recall such detail—but it suggests that he did feel, after so many years of unaccountable roadblocks, that there was something to hide, and that it had something to do with his fighting in Spain. It may be that his emphatic reply to Dauzat may have been a reflex to cover older efforts to sanitize his past, to purge a shadow he by then suspected was trailing him. We do not know—but it certainly speaks to intractable limits for researchers wanting to rely heavily on oral testimonies to reconstruct the past and the necessity to deal up front with the importance of that biographical uncertainty.

Either way, from July until October 1936, he told the FBI he had been living in France. It did not occur to any officer to double-check this claim against the earlier documented track record that he had been in Spain and that sources had verified his fighting on the Republican side. The only item that elicited any concern in 1966 was Ursula Hirschmann's and her second husband's—Altiero Spinelli—membership in the Communist Party in Germany and Italy, facts disclosed by the State Department in 1963 after Spinelli's visit to the United States on State Department leadership grants (by then, Spinelli was one of Europe's foremost advocates of unification).

The FBI ordered agents to conduct a new review out of its regional offices in Washington, Boston, New York, New Haven, Baltimore, Richmond, Los Angeles, St Louis, and San Francisco for agents "to verify education in Europe and residence of relatives in Europe through records reviewed and persons interviewed in the United States." This yielded thirty-four interviews with "confidential informants," including several who "have knowledge of some phases of un-American activities, including communist activities in the Northern California area." The reports from the field agents came in unanimously declaring that there was no reason to doubt Hirschman's loyalty to the United States. It is not hard to spot the identity of some of these informants. One was based at Yale University and was well acquainted with Hirschman and his wife; he knew them from the time they arrived in New Haven in September 1956 and had ample opportunity to work with him. His evaluation was glowing and assured the bureau that there was no doubt about Hirschman's reputation and reliability. It seems likely that the informant was the well-known political scientist, Charles Lindblom, whose name had appeared as a potential reference in an earlier document. Another report from the Boston office testified to one informant's knowledge of Hirschman since his Berkeley days and that he had worked with him at the Federal Reserve Board from 1946 until 1948, until the informant himself moved to Harvard University; now they were neighbors. This could be none other than Alexander Gerschenkron. His declaration to the FBI is like Lindblom's. Gerschenkron the informant even told the FBI that the University of Stockholm ran a regular seminar in its economics department, and the only readings on the syllabus were publications by Hirschman! Another testimony came from a former colleague from postwar Washington, Yale, and Harvard (where the unnamed source taught at the Kennedy School), also unequivocally vouching for Hirschman's loyalty. This could only be the future Nobel Prize winner Thomas Schelling. Similar reports came in from former associates at the RAND Corporation. Los Angeles agents fanned out to the Santa Monica Police Department, the libraries of the *Los Angeles Times* and *Los Angeles Herald-Examiner*, and even the Credit Bureau of San Luis Obispo (where Hirschman had received his basic Army training and had been naturalized) to check his credit and arrest record. A New York agent, John D. Fleming, went to the newspaper morgue to find that it "contained no derogatory information." He also paid a visit to the Rockefeller Foundation (which is how we know Fleming's identity), where he also learned of Hirschman's unblemished loyalty. On November 15, 1966, the FBI turned over its report to the acting attorney general.

With this inquiry, Hirschman's shadow got separated from his body and was filed away in the archives of the FBI. It only saw the light of day again thirty years later in response to Freedom of Information Act request number 1030518-000 by this author. What should we make of it? The FBI's reliance upon flimsy sources and bad information speaks for itself. So does the alarm posed by a foreigner with a "blind" past. The coiling of nativism with growing anti-Communism hysteria did Hirschman in by the early 1950s, when the Red-baiting reached its frenzied peak during Senator McCarthy's inquisition. In Hirschman's trajectory from loyalty to public service in the fight against fascism before 1945 and the effort to rebuild Europe's economies after 1945 to his exit in 1952, there is also a larger arc. Having recently arrived in the United States in 1943, when he enlisted in the public cause, Hirschman had few contacts or friends in his adopted country who could serve as "informants" or witnesses about his character and work; there were no checks against the powerful inertial forces of suspicion and eagerness to believe sources that confirmed an ungrounded bias to mistrust. Two decades later, in the mid-1960s, the story was very different. A list of famous Ivy League professors, think-tank experts, friends, and associates became the champions he did not have in the 1940s and 1950s, when those charged with gathering information in the name of security were all too willing to rely on their own fallible judgment. As for Hirschman, while his shadow haunted him and at times drove him to despair, in the end he never lost his propensity to find creative ways to make the best of a bad situation.

CHAPTER 10

Colombia Years

You can hold yourself back from the
sufferings of the world, that is something
you are free to do and it accords with your
nature, but perhaps this very holding back is
the one suffering that you could avoid.

FRANZ KAFKA

In 1952, Colombia was in the throes of a terrible conflict. Its capital was emerging from the worst urban unrest and destruction in the hemisphere's history. Marauding gangs and sharpshooters no longer patrolled the streets, but charred buildings and empty lots remained as silent echoes of a spasm of violence that had since spread to Andean valleys and plateaus where guerrillas, militiamen, and the army fought for control. This was an improbable setting for a marginalized economist to make a big difference or a place for his family to make a new life. But, if nothing else, Hirschman's displacement testified to the adage about how life's best rewards come from what is least planned. The years that the Hirschman family sojourned in Colombia were, in many respects, the best of their lives. Adventurous, culturally exciting, and intellectually awakening, this war-torn country gave Albert Hirschman an environment to reinvent himself. Driven from the policy-making sanctum of the United States, Hirschman was quick to spin a virtue out of necessity. Some years later, when a colleague asked him why he moved to South America, Hirschman joked "I was born under Prussian rule, so when the emperor calls, I obey."[1]

The emperor in this case was the World Bank. Known then as the International Bank for Reconstruction and Development, it had been created in 1944 to help fund the reconstruction of Europe after the war. In the end, the scale of the Marshall Plan dwarfed the bank's budget, and

Sarah and Albert in the Llanos, Colombia, 1953.

the bank's role never measured up to its billing. "I think we are going to be driven into a very different field sooner than I thought, into the development field" the bank president, John J. McCloy, told his executive directors in late 1947. The institution cast about for a new role in world affairs. McCloy—who, as the well-heeled Wall Street attorney to the Rockefellers and wartime senior servant in the State Department, epitomized the figure of far-seeing magnate—saw how quickly the world was changing with decolonization of what would soon be baptized the Third World. Here was an opportunity for the lending agency to help colonies lift themselves from poverty and backwardness. The idea was to secure them for free-market capitalism lest they fall into the hands of Communists—paradoxically through ambitious planning. The handmaidens of this conversion were, in Mary Morgan's words, "economic missionaries." One laboratory for this experiment would be Colombia, "the most ambitious undertaken so far by the Bank," as its president noted. This was how Hirschman went from the reconstruction of Europe to development in Latin American, from the US government to a global agency, which gave him a privileged position to observe development close up, seeing warts and all, during its formative years.[2]

Like the groping, improvising way in which world institutions refashioned themselves as the dust of the Second World War settled, Hirschman also sought new bearings. Years later, he reflected on the man he was when he arrived in Colombia. "I looked at 'reality' without theoretical preconceptions of any kind." When he returned to the United States almost five years later, he discovered that "I had acquired a point of view"—one that was at odds with orthodoxies forged in American universities. While playful, this claim to self-enlightenment can be misleading. When he went to Colombia, Hirschman was hardly an ingénue when it came to markets and hidden springs of change. The frustrations as a Marshall Planner had hardened his skepticism of ideological formulae in the drag of abstract theories. What made the Colombian experience so distinctive was proximity: observing so closely, and for enough time, the process and effects of the decisions of which he was a part. The art of learning from doing and then watching closely, a sensibility already encoded from Colorni and Montaigne's personal tutorials, accented his fascination with small things and routine behavior; it would become a cornerstone of a disposition that Colombia brought to fruition. He crisscrossed Colombia, pen in hand and paper handy, examining irrigation projects, talking to local bankers about their farm loans, and scribbling calculations about the costs of road building. He leaned toward what his future colleague, Clifford Geertz, would call "experience-near" knowledge, the insights of an actor, keeping the "experience-distant" concepts of the detached observer at bay, at least for the time being.

Colombia may have been a mess, but it was not Hirschman's first graze with deep civil strife, although it would be his most prolonged. The country's political climate crackled with tension by the 1940s. The assassination in 1948 of the Liberal Party firebrand Jorge Eliecer Gaitán as he walked out of his office in the Agustín Nieto building at the corner of Seventh Avenue and Jiménez Avenue (Hirschman's office would be very nearby) set off a decade of civil war known eponymously as La Violencia. Two hundred thousand Colombians died at its hands until the military finally stepped in to put General Gustavo Rojas Pinilla in power in June 1953. The dictator began the slow process of containing partisan violence, albeit at a cost.

It was in this context that the World Bank decided to involve itself in the Colombian economy. One of the anomalies of Colombia was that it was a political mess, but an economically robust one. Its elites had always prided themselves on pragmatic modernization and openness to foreign ideas—and investments. In late 1948, as the republic was sliding into its political morass, Emilio Toro, the Colombian member of the Board of Executive Directors of the World Bank, approached President McCloy with a list of projects that might appeal to the lender. The upshot was a decision to send a mission, called a "survey," to the fissiparous republic to come up with a master plan. The proposal went to the president of Colombia, Mariano Ospina Pérez, who endorsed it enthusiastically. Colombia would, in the eyes of its developers, be a model for others; maybe "development" could rescue its democracy. Such was the hope.[3]

The survey's history would affect Hirschman's experience and observations. Getting a chief on short notice was not easy. McCloy used all his contacts. He asked several business moguls, then turned to Lionel Robbins, the anti-Keynesian economist from the London School of Economics, pointing out that this was an opportunity for Robbins to play a formative role in bank policy and new "activity in [the] development field." Robbins thought about it for a weekend. Then he declined. In the end, McCloy found his man in a Canadian-born economist, Lauchlin Currie, an influential Keynesian and prominent New Dealer. He might have been slightly at odds with bankers' orthodoxy, but he had a lot of experience in administration and international financial relations. The close assistant to Treasury secretary Harry Dexter White during the 1944 negotiations at Bretton Woods, New Hampshire, in 1941 he had headed the Economic Mission to China. Brilliant and experienced, Currie also had the missionary trademark. Currie did not just have confidence, he exuded it; *he* required no personal conversion. Currie was also suspected of dealing secrets to the Soviets, conveying information to Elizabeth Bentley, a Russian agent, and charged with having undermined the Kuomintang government with his policy recommendations during the war. Investigations into his past began in earnest in late 1949, by which time, for all intents and purposes, Currie was moving to Colombia, where he would settle down. It was one of many ironies of the Cold War that Currie and Hirschman, the "fellow traveler" and the seasoned skeptic, would wind up entangled in distant Colombia, clashing over the future of the whole enterprise of economic development.[4]

Once named as mission chief, Currie expanded the scope of the survey to include designing a master plan to raise the standard of living for the entire country. Bank officials were skeptical; this was not what Toro had proposed, though he was eager to aggrandize. But they acceded, laying the tracks for a problem regarding the place of local knowledge in the business of economic missionizing. The size of the team expanded to fourteen members (none of them Colombian) ranging from experts on agriculture to railways. To help the experts, locals provided the "staff."

If a plan was the goal, Currie was clear about what the plan was to accomplish: "a coordinated attack on the problem of poverty," he proclaimed. He quickly set to clearing the ground for his grand scheme. The mission arrived in Colombia on July 10, 1949, spent four months touring the country conducting its research, and had a draft of its findings available in March 1950. In all, it took a year to assemble a team, conduct research, evaluate alternatives, elicit feedback, and produce a lifeless 600-page tome, impressive mainly in its ability to amass vast quantities of data.[5] The response in Colombia was no less hurried. Within weeks, the government announced the National Planning Council. Whatever one might think about this hurried approach to "planning," there was no shortage of enthusiasm. Eugene R. Black, former chairman of the Federal Reserve Board and the new president of the World Bank, threw his weight behind the mission's recommendations. He extolled the "unbiased analysis . . . by a competent group of independent experts" to Colombian president Ospina and applauded Colombia's swift response in "already taking active measures in line with the Mission's recommendations to obtain expert assistance in the vitally important task of effecting improvements in governmental organization and administration."[6]

The Basis of a Development Program for Colombia was an archetypal document from an age of humanitarian missions. Coded in the scientistic rhetoric of economic missionaries, it argued that the root of the problem was a vicious poverty cycle: the poor were poor because they were unhealthy and illiterate. The result was that too many people produced for current consumption, yielding little savings for capital growth. Colombia not only needed an infusion of capital from abroad, it had to tear down a wide range of intractable obstacles, such as the land tenure system, and make up for others with rural credits and energy and transportation improvements. What was needed was a comprehensive "generalized attack" to break "the vicious cycle of poverty, ignorance, ill-health and low productivity." The emphasis was on aggressive and coordinated improvements on all fronts simultaneously to avoid distortions, bottlenecks, and lags. Nothing piecemeal; this was a mission. What the report echoed was a growing academic current, propounded above all by the Polish-born economist Paul Rosenstein-Rodan and the Estonian Ragnar Nurkse, in favor of "balanced growth" across a variety of sectors simultaneously, of a "big push" to break the trap of underdevelopment, a disposition leaning hard to the "experience-distant" end of the conceptual spectrum.[7] All of this was supposed to emanate from the members of the council planners housed in the Banco de la República.

It was perhaps predictable that grandiose expectations would crash against inconvenient realities. Some were of the missionaries' own making. Within the council, the mission's inflated scale and top-down government planning crossed with personal conflicts. The World Bank urged the council to hire an outside "expert" to assure technical ability and keep decisions from getting embroiled in partisan fighting. Vice President Robert Garner, with Sandy Stevenson's imprimatur, had recommended Albert O. Hirschman "as an economist of outstanding ability and integrity"; both Hirschman and the bank agreed that expertise and outsiders had to be kept to a minimum to simplify internal affairs and that one priority should be to train a cadre of experienced and proficient Colombian administrators. Garner told the council chairman, Emilio Toro, that "we feel strongly that there should be only one 'Economic Advisor' to the board" and that Hirschman would have "final authority" to make recommendations. Hirschman sketched out detailed guidelines for his role in the new council and presented them to Toro, curbing his role to screen investment alternatives and to evaluate projects for the policy makers. Excited, he felt that an effective council with an effective outsider could strike the right balance of influence and integration; planning should not take place in a cocoon, he explained. But Toro had other plans; he had kept close ties with Currie, who'd returned to Colombia as a consultant, and urged him to join the council as an "adviser" to focus on matters of the wooly problem of administrative reform. Currie happily accepted and wasted no time expanding the meaning of administrative reform.[8]

Garner foresaw trouble. He knew of Currie's ambitious penchants and habit of "creating resistance." He warned that Currie "might, despite the best of intentions of every side, embarrass Hirschman." Toro, who seems to have taken a disliking to Hirschman's modest sights, assured Garner that Hirschman was the "top economist" and the "boss." But he was irrepressible, as was Currie. The clash of personalities reflected a more profound collision of ideas. Currie liked big plans, especially when they made administrative reform the condition for everything else; Hirschman preferred projects, even big ones—but the more specific, the better. Aligned with Liberals, Currie tended to create animosity between the council and the Conservative government; Hirschman eschewed partisanship and wanted to focus on problem solving.[9]

To make matters worse, a Belgian economist, Jacques Torfs, also joined the council as an advisor. Torfs and Currie did not see eye to eye; Hirschman too would soon have problems with the Belgian. Between

Torfs' convictions, Currie's ambitions, and Hirschman's growing skepticism, there was plenty of disagreement to go around among the tiny team associated with Colombia's lofty economic plans. Hirschman confided to Richard Demuth in Washington that "this is not only unpleasant (Currie's operating methods do not help matters), but also seems to confuse the Council members." To another he quipped that "the whole episode reminds one of Napoleon's Hundred Days, with the fortunate difference that Currie's comeback lasted only about half as long."[10]

Hirschman, it must be said, was not exactly an obvious choice to advise the president of Colombia on economic policy. Latin America was terra incognita. The closest he got to development was an invitation to attend a conference in 1952 at the University of Chicago organized by Bert Hoselitz, soon-to-be founder of the journal *Economic Development and Cultural Change*, which would be committed to a more interdisciplinary approach to progress. At the time, Hirschman thought of the southern and eastern Europe he'd known before the war and wrote about in *National Power and the Structure of Foreign Trade*. Development was synonymous with industrialization.[11]

The Chicago event was memorable for a more important reason. Alexander Gerschenkron, Hirschman's colleague at the Fed and office mate in Berkeley, unveiled a pioneering work in economic thought, "Economic Backwardness in Historical Perspective." Shura argued that progress was not of a piece; societies did not have to follow the same route toward development or to fail. The Marxists' plodding stages of growth were wrongheaded; so too were counterpoints like "modernization" theory, with each stage eclipsing its predecessor. Backwardness was not a condition that had to be erased as a prerequisite for advancement. It contained some hidden advantages: it could husband a precocious spirit, could foster ideologies of change, and had institutions (like a powerful state) that could pool resources more effectively, and latecomers could skip earlier phases while advanced societies had to labor continually with updating their industrial plants. Backwardness could be an asset, not a liability. At the time, Gerschenkron's arguments were utterly new. For Hirschman, they were eye-openers. Historical lateness was not necessarily a reason to despair or a motivation to grasp for ambitious plans to overturn the status quo. The implications were not yet clear to Hirschman; Colombia brought them to light.[12]

Other than having read Gerschenkron's paper, Hirschman *was* an ingénue. He was not aware of Rosenstein-Rodan's work. Nor was he aware of the stirring controversy about the role that international trade played in national development. Since the creation of the United Nations Commission for Latin America and the Caribbean (commonly known as ECLA), and the famous 1949 "manifesto" written by the Argentine economist Raúl Prebisch, called *The Economic Development of Latin America and its Principal Problems*, there had been a major clash of views. For increasing numbers of Latin American economists, global trade was skewing the pattern of local growth. None of this came to Hirschman's attention until many years later. In effect, he began to think about development in Colombia from the ground up—with a style but with no theory.

Colombia thus promised all the hallmarks of a professional, personal, and intellectual adventure—which started as so many precursors did, with language. Hirschman's Spanish was not very good; he had only ever spoken it extensively during his months in Catalonia in 1936. But this soon passed. Before long, Albert found himself at play with Spanish word games, though he never managed to rid his Spanish, or indeed any other language save French, of a distinct German accent. He was not the only one to master Spanish. The whole family did and with the same spirit of adventure. The Chevy Chase house was emptied, and remnants were dispatched to storage. Armed with a few suitcases, they boarded their flight to Bogotá. When the plane ran into difficulties, they were forced to spend a night in a hotel in Miami. While Albert was digging around in the suitcases to find the girls' pajamas, out came fistfuls of old dresses, pink gauze strips, and forgotten evening gowns from Sarah's mother's wardrobe. As the evening wear came flowing out of the suitcases, Sarah confessed that she had secretly packed away her mother's old gowns so the girls could play their dress-up games. So much for traveling light. The next day, as the plane descended on the Colombian capital, the Hirschmans pressed their faces to the windows to admire the emerald green fields of the valley below and the hem of Andean mountains that surrounded it. At the airport, a delegation of officials was there to greet them. After much handshaking and presentations, someone from the Central Bank piled the Hirschmans into a car. With the girls squealing in the back seat, everyone marveled as the driver wheeled effortlessly around potholes and donkeys to get the family to their new home.[13]

The latitude of his tasks enabled him to tailor a work method to fit his inclinations. A trademark of his later research style, conversing with as many people about as many topics as possible to spot possibilities drawn from everyday practices of problem solving, took shape in Colombian fields and factories. Getting to know the country meant getting near its people: lots of travel to talk to farmers, local bankers, industrialists, and artisans who labored to improve their lot in small, ordinary, and to the lofty-minded social scientist, often imperceptible ways. Rather than concern himself with the state issues and courtly intrigue, Hirschman preferred the micro-foundations of economic development—and became especially intrigued by the role, neglected in the Currie Report, of the private sector. He focused on evaluating firms, industries, and sectors as prospects for major investments, presenting their cases to the council as it sifted the worthy from the unworthy. Perhaps Hayek's warnings of the perils of subjecting people to rules and plans designed for a single (even if enlightened) purpose echoed in Hirschman's ears; either way, his choice was to accent individual activities for evaluation and attention.

This kind of sleuthing posed its share of challenges. Travel was hard. The roads were treacherous. Railroads were few. The airplane was new, expensive, and only carried passengers to major destinations. Beside, it was also not without its hazards, because the Andean mountainsides were famously lethal obstacles for even skilled pilots. Hirschman's preferred mode of transportation was his car. He loved his car, a gray Chevrolet, which he had delivered to the steamy Pacific port of Buenaventura. When the vehicle arrived, Sarah and Albert flew to Cali and then took the train to the port to pick it up. After some wrangling at customs, they liberated the vehicle, hired a driver, and prepared their overland return to the capital. That night, the hotel's orchestra blared into streets while Albert and Sarah sat on rocking chairs drinking highballs and watching the local belles dance the cumbia. The next morning, their driver never appeared. "He must have gotten drunk," surmised Sarah. So Albert plucked up the courage—though it probably required little—and embarked on their maiden road trip up the piedmont from the Pacific, down through the rich plain of the Cauca Valley, passing another Andean ridge to wind through the coffee groves around Manizales, and over more ridges back to Bogotá's valley. This prolonged, winding rollercoaster ride over nosebleed-high gradients was the beginning of a romance with Colombia and Latin America. While the jungle roads and mountain passes, not to mention the fear of bandits, hung over Sarah, Albert's confidence in their Chevy and his own driving prowess would not be dimmed. Sarah found herself captivated by the orchids hanging from cliffs over the roads. Along the way they picked up hitchhikers, an Indian shepherd, and several policemen escorting two prisoners. If there were any concerns for safety, they were waved off in order to meet as many ordinary Colombians as possible. By the time they got home from their adventures, the car and its driver had been broken in. That night, however, Albert had nightmares of falling over every precipice he had managed to avoid.[14]

In his fashion of operating in larger organizations, Hirschman carved out a niche. At first blush, it seemed to work. His relations were especially cordial with the Finance Ministry, the Banco de la República, and especially the Agricultural Bank (Caja Agraria), whose staff solicited his help in evaluating investment proposals for the countryside. In 1953, he also took on contracts with a new lending agency, the Banco Popular, and got involved in low-cost housing projects in Bogotá, Cali, and Medellín in collaboration with a French housing expert from the United Nations, Yves Salaün, ventures that excited a passion for studying private but collective ways to solve problems for the poor in a country where outlays were, at best, beggarly.[15]

The Planning Council was an endless source of fascination and possibility; the latitude it gave him allowed room to improvise, adapt, and create initiatives that were not necessarily envisioned in the original master plan. It could also be frustrating. Howard Ellis's letter of encouragement had alluded vaguely to potential problems. Ellis and Buchanan were curious "whether your appraisal differs in significant ways from what appears to be the excellent recommendations and findings of the Currie Report."[16] Could it be that Ellis knew Hirschman well enough to detect something? Sure enough, the differences soon came to the surface. One source was the vision: a plan drafted by a team of foreign experts armed with impressive, if questionable, statistics but administered and realized by Colombians whose local knowledge was treated as partial, unscientific, or worse, because they were the ones who had to be transformed. Hirschman was caught in the middle—and was an early witness to development economics' peculiar afflictions. Working alongside the Colombians as the "foreign expert" and growing to admire some of the administrators of the Colombian government and private actors, he had to wrestle with his peers and their plans, which were premised on confident algorithms of national savings and the muscular vocabulary of capital-output ratios, growth projections, and investment targets. The three foreign advisors met twice a week in afternoon gatherings at the Banco de la República to report on their ventures. Currie and Enrique Peñalosa (later a friend and moving force behind agrarian reform) authored a rosy prognosis for 1953 and the prospect for a fiscal surplus—and predicted room to spend money. Hirschman was livid. He not only urged caution, he argued that the council was becoming the source of confusing advice to ministries. "You have to be naïve not to know that the preliminary calculations of the Budget Directorate were intentionally low," he fulminated.[17]

Afternoon staff meetings left Hirschman feeling pressured to conform his projects to the original grandiose scheme laid out in the survey. Hirschman's notes and letters overflowed with resentment. We do not know if Currie ever picked up the scent. If not, he certainly got it when Hirschman published an uncharacteristically scabrous review of Currie's 1966 book, *Accelerating Development*, in the discipline's flagship, the *American Economic Review*. Currie was furious and complained bitterly to the editor, Moses Abramovitz, who conceded that it was poor judgment to let an adversary review another's work.[18]

It was not just Currie. Jacques Torfs, drove Hirschman crazy with his overconfidence in an abstract synthetic plan and the dubious figures upon which it rested. Torfs, a firm believer in the elemental formula for development based on minimizing capital-to-output ratios, claimed to have compiled complete tables of Colombian national accounts based on an industrial census from 1944, as well as reports from the superintendant of corporations. "His whole technique is so personal, artificially esoteric but essentially arbitrary and therefore uncommunicable that the idea that he might train someone to step into his shoes one day, is quite utopian." The task of "Colombianizing" the office, which Hirschman understood as paramount, was "a hopeless endeavor," so long as the outsider-expert was the only one who understood the occult. The whole environment became poisoned. Burke Knapp—back in touch now that he'd joined the World Bank—apologized to Hirschman, "You have had a rotten deal and we understand and sympathize with the extraordinary difficulties which you have had to confront." It says something about the grammar of development that the alliance between a World Bank vice president and his deputy in the field could not offset the collusion of a rival expert with local officials bent on making their offices the gatekeepers of the process.[19]

Knapp only got the half of it. Tending to see the problems in terms of personal chemistry, he missed what was inscribed in the very nature of expertise in a developing country. The Marshall Plan, which asked Washington's economists to be "on tap, and not on top," had its own troubles; it was more tolerable because it did not ask the planners to be the source of unquestioned verities. Hirschman now found himself drafting decrees because of his exalted status as *the* foreign expert—a status that made him cringe. A premise of the Currie mission was that only foreign experts could really understand the problem because they were foreign and because they were experts. Colombians themselves were not expected to understand because, as the circular logic would have it, they came from underdeveloped circumstances. These interlocking biases eventually became a cornerstone of his critique of foreign expertise and "aid." It also shaped his sympathetic jibe at Latin American intellectuals to get over their mantras about inferiority and backwardness (Hirschman would invoke the common saying that "aquí en el trópico hacemos todo al reves"—here in the tropics we do everything backward—as defeatist self-scorning.) Hirschman confided to Howard Ellis that he really wanted to learn lessons *from* development and not presume to know its secrets in advance.[20]

Still, he did not throw in the towel. When Knapp offered him a job in the new Western Hemisphere Department, Hirschman declined. "To come back now would be to concede failure, when in actual fact there are even as of now several sides to the picture." He had some good contacts, was developing "a few ideas," and had "quite a bit of work in progress, the completion of which is of interest to me and I hope of some use to the Council." Besides, the family was settling in and starting to enjoy the adventure.[21]

What were these ideas? By 1954, Hirschman was fixating less on the country's pathologies than on what it was doing right. In early March he put the final touches to a research project that he had been mulling for some time. But "Case Studies of Instances of Successful Economic Development in Colombia" never saw the light of day. Almost everything about it was at odds with the expectations of development and practices at the council. The country and its people were moving forward, not wallowing in the lethargy of tradition. Indeed, the proposed research method ran against the grain. Instead of compiling general national statistics, he proposed a study of successful businesses, starting with an analysis of the "personality and background of founders and managers"—their training, decision-making styles, methods of financing—the elements of a different analytical approach. The cases, drawn from the projects he knew from direct observation, included Manuelita, the sugar plantation and refinery in the Cauca Valley; Coltejer, Medellín's big cotton textile plant; Bavaria, the brewer; and Banco Popular de Bogotá, which specialized in small loans to individuals, artisans, and small firms and "which has experienced remarkable expansion recently due to novel methods and political support." Hirschman sounded out some sources of support: MIT's Center for International Studies, directed by Max Millikan, Harvard University's Center for Entrepreneurial Research, and Colombia's National University and the National Association of Industrialists.[22]

The ideas went nowhere, or so it seemed. In the meantime, working for the Colombian government was becoming too uncomfortable. Things changed with the coup d'état of General Rojas Pinilla on June 13, 1953. At first, the overthrow enjoyed some popularity. Like many, Hirschman felt ambivalent about the coup. Among other things, it promised to slash the level of partisan violence. The new Banco Popular and many social reforms aimed at delivering benefits to small producers, artisans, and peasants queued up for more attention. But with time, General Rojas consolidated his power and personalized policy making. Hirschman confided to Washington that the government was immunizing itself from advice and raising taxes on companies, which "is both irrational and excessive in a country in which corporate enterprises need to be developed." Hirschman found himself caught between the cogs of a president determined to do it his way, a Finance Ministry staff wanting independent support, and a council with its own agenda. The minister, Carlos Villaveces Restrepo, asked Hirschman to work with "*him* in my personal capacity," but the council vetoed the idea, thereby shielding the administration from any insider warnings against "a strong 'soak the rich' trend," which "seems to be at work within the new government."[23] In the meantime, the economic situation worsened. The slide in coffee prices aggravated Colombia's trade imbalance and ushered in a period of austerity. The general dug in his heels—and eventually even the World Bank had to suspend loans; by then, the original Currie plan had long since unraveled. Aligned with the Liberals, Currie resigned from the council and became a dairy farmer. Many others also left.[24]

The autonomy and freedom of action that Hirschman yearned for, and to some extent had carved out, was thus constrained on various fronts. As Sarah recalled, "In Bogota he was often very depressed by the multiple difficulties he had." His final report to the council was an inventory of mixed results. The contract for an electrification mission was a good sign, as was the plan for the development of the Atlantic coast and support for deposits in popular housing accounts. But "the general balance is, in my opinion, negative." The lack of coordination, no room to advise a president who, in any event, "never takes it," reports that languish on the shelf—why bother anymore, especially once he realized that he could recreate what was so compelling about the original venture without the aggravation by simply leaving the Colombian government and setting up his own private consultancy?[25]

This is what he did.

In April 1954, as his two-year contract with the Colombian government expired, he emptied his desk and left the Banco de la República building. Hirschman prepared for the day in a way that only he could. He bought himself a comfortable armchair, placed it beside the desk he improvised as a home office, and planned to do a lot of reading. The only regret about leaving the council was losing his devoted secretary, Fanny Durán Vargas, the daughter of a prominent Liberal politico, who had become a close family friend. Burke Knapp sent a personal letter of regret—but understanding; "I dare say you have come to the right decision." Perhaps presciently, probably as encouragement, he closed with, "I feel sure that your work in Colombia, even though it has had its painful aspects, has given you a fund of experience which would be immensely useful in tackling a comparable range of problems in other Latin American Countries."[26]

Money had to come from somewhere. He took a short trip to Washington to explore his options. But as he told Ursula, "I have very little desire to go back to Washington, not to mention that it might be impossible or at least not advisable anyhow because of the McCarthy atmosphere." Still, he needed a livelihood. The frantic days spent in Washington, not surprisingly, yielded nothing—other than long conversations with his old friend George Jaszi. Returning to Bogotá was thus even more depressing. As he told George, "Back here, I am passing through some trying weeks since obviously my heart isn't in this job any more."[27] What to do? Going back to Europe, Italy in particular, was an option—and once again Hirschman appealed to his sister for ideas and suggestions. Should he work "for a big corporation," or find "a research project funded by one of our several foundations," or "completely switch to something else and set up a business, to turn a piece of rainforest into a flourishing cattle breeding farm"? "Albert," Sarah confided to Helen Jaszi, "has several great plans in mind." Not one to let the uncertainties of the future weigh on him, he let the great plans uplift him. We have seen him at this kind of crossroads before, including entertaining fantasies of retreating to the land—a fanciful and not entirely realistic idea from someone who had never used a farm tool. The situation forced him to confront the limitations of his practical but skeptical turn of mind. There was a reason, he intuited, that the Curries of the world enjoyed an advantage: "I am precisely no creator of systems, but I always only come up with small improvements or criticisms, which give me pleasure while I am doing them, but which, upon their completion, always throw me back into a vacuum in which it seems completely impossible to me to ever have a single new thought again. Therefore the need to create something on which I am able permanently to sharpen my intellect."[28]

If he could not create a system and had no inkling how to devise an alternative master plan to solve Colombia's problems, he at least wanted to solve *some* problems. So, he launched a consulting business that would build on the knowledge he had acquired working for the council but that would give him the autonomy from bosses and plans. The decision was an instant success, so much so that Albert had to opt out of a Caribbean vacation with Sarah and the girls. "People here are very impatient and very impulsive—they want his 'economic' advice *now*," Sarah grumbled.[29] When times got especially busy, Sarah pitched in, typing reports on the problem of sewers in Cali, taking phone calls, and gathering data to submit loan applications for municipal utilities. Eventually, Albert teamed up with a colleague also sent by the World Bank to work in the council, George Kalmanoff, whose contract ran out in November, to set up shop in their own offices. Hirschman had a plaque made up, "Albert Hirschman. Consultor Económico y Financiero," which he hung proudly on the door of his small enterprise.

The partnership thrived off contacts from the council; in some respects it created an opportunity to do what Hirschman thought the council *should* have been doing: identifying opportunities and spotlighting solutions on a level at which investors made decisions, but not from the perspective of a glassed office in a downtown building. The consultor's first contracts were with private businesses and banks, such as the Caja de Crédito Agrario, which asked Hirschman to evaluate investment proposals. Some firms, such as Ebasco, a New York–based paper- and box maker interested in expanding to South America to set up a pulp and paper mill, hired Hirschman to evaluate the market. Hirschman and Kalmanoff pored over the data for Ebasco to profile a strong and expanding local demand and also noted the opportunity to converge with several local partners, such as the Institute for Industrial Promotion, as well as several firms such as Cartón de Colombia and Manuel Carvajal's firm. "The creation in Colombia of such an enterprise," he wrote of Ebasco's venture, "is no doubt one of the most important next steps in the country's rapidly advancing industrial development, and we hope our report will contribute to this end." While the consultants had no doubt that they serviced their clients, they were not above smuggling in some ulterior, broader goals.[30]

They took on more contracts with government agencies needing help with proposals for securing funds from the World Bank and other multilateral lenders. Project assessment soon became a staple of his consultancy. Little did he know that this evaluation business would become an instrument in Hirschman's winding career in the social sciences for decades afterward. It also gave him an opportunity to study, and highlight, what was going right, not wrong, in Colombia. When the Central Bank asked him to write a pamphlet for investors, the result was "Colombia: Highlights of a Developing Economy," a long booklet with the traits of Hirschman's forgotten research proposal on cases of successful development. When José Castro Borrero, the manager of Cali's Municipal Enterprises, contracted the consultors for a financial outlook for the municipality for five years, what he got what was a detailed, upbeat index of the ways in which the regional capital could solve its fiscal problems and promote opportunities for enterprise. Impossibility, futility, backwardness—the keywords of pessimism—were not part of Hirschman's lexicon.[31]

Teaming up with Kalmanoff functioned in part because they worked side by side rather than together. The growth of the development business meant plenty of suitors and lots of room for each consultant to do their own thing. Kalmanoff, younger and less worldly, had his own preferences and left Hirschman to focus on investment project analysis. The partnership was never more than a busy, well-positioned professional arrangement. The partners appeared to be happy. Hirschman's list of contacts was widespread and countrywide and included the sugar planters of the Cauca Valley—Rafael Delgado Barreneche (a Conservative of some influence in the early 1950s) and Alberto Carvajal. The Cauca Valley projects would loom large in Hirschman's later writings about Colombian development as a model of local entrepreneurship. He relished the opportunity and feeling of "entering more profoundly in the reality of the country and getting to know a great number of people." Working closely with decision makers in a less paternalistic fashion also had its appeals. Hirschman enjoyed "finding it impossible to take an airplane without rushing to meet such and such a minister whom I knew personally. This was an agreeable and surprising experience for a young man like myself."[32]

And yet, there were signs of restlessness, possibly even fatigue, with the everyday work of consulting. Though he knew he was no system creator, he did yearn for more intellectually oriented opportunities; he not only wanted to help solve problems, he wanted to think about problem solving. When the assistant director for Social Sciences for the Rockefeller Foundation, Montague Yudelman, was visiting Bogotá in early 1956, he got the distinct impression that the team of Hirschman and Kalmanoff was a passing alliance. Each partner came to meet with Yudelman individually. Kalmanoff wanted to finish his PhD and write a dissertation based on some of his Colombian work. "He has strong personal reasons," observed Yudelman, "for wishing to leave Bogotá." Hirschman had something else in mind, but it, too, left the partner out. Ever since his waning days at the council, he had been thinking of a "Latin American Sample Survey Center." He wrote to George Jaszi in early 1954 asking for advice and even prospective partners ("How about yourself?" he asked). But he had not given up hope; indeed, he had run a market study for a local gas utility and found the venture an intriguing one. After all, he thought, isn't it important to know what people actually want from all this guff about development? His fantasies had even led him to think of relocating the family to Mexico City (an idea that Sarah cheered on as an exciting adventure; she clearly had gotten the bug for quests). Another idea was setting up a branch for the consulting firm in Caracas. Yudelman's visit was the time to make the pitch for creating a consumer survey research center with links to the University of Michigan's Survey Research Center and the United Nations Economic Commission for Latin America, though neither appears to have been apprised of the idea. Yudelman told him that the foundation could not assist in profit-making ventures. "The matter was left at that. AH asked that this discussion be treated as confidential," concluded Yudelman.[33]

So it was that Albert Hirschman remained in Colombia and stuck to his consultancy. In the meantime, the Colombian years became more Colombian. His longest trip abroad was to Central America—where he traveled for six weeks from March to May 1955 at the behest of the Commerce Department to write "Guidebook for American Investors," schmoozing his way through hotel lobbies, drinking cocktails with local businessmen and bankers in their suites, and sizing up the opportunities. But he did not just stick to the capitals. When he could, he carried his trademark to Central America and visited as many factories and housing projects as he could identify. In Nicaragua, the manager of the Banco Nicaraguense, Eduardo Montealegre, assumed the role of chaperone; he initially made a good impression. But that wore off as the trip wore on. He "has become far less sympathique to me," complained Hirschman, but, he added tongue-in-cheek, he "is a great patriot. Everything is better here than in Guatemala, Salvador, Costa Rica, not to speak of poor Honduras." Hirschman loved Guatemala, which reminded him of Switzerland, with the added anthropological appeal of Mayan villages.[34]

Adjusting to Colombia took some time, especially for Sarah. The girls went to school at the Colegio Nueva Granada, not too far from home. Meanwhile, Sarah scrambled to learn Spanish. She also had to figure out how to govern a retinue of personal servants and maids—who tutored the Hirschmans in the art of making hot chocolate and melting panela. "The whole idea is revolting," Sarah protested, though she was forced to concede that "it's pleasant not to have to worry about dishes, cleaning and so on."[35]

At first, they rented a quiet but dark house from an Italian landlord on Calle 72. A year later, they moved to a house on Calle 74 nestled in the foothills of the low mountains that hug the capital. Backed by tall eucalyptus trees and a stream, the *monte* was a beautiful setting at the (then) northern edge of the city, composed of modest single-family homes. Up the hills, poorer people built shacks of corrugated metal. The girls watched children who, instead of going to school, cleared the ground and broke rocks, and felt the urge to invite them to their yard to play with their toys and read their books, until Sarah and Albert dissuaded them on account of the lice, tuberculosis, and other potential trouble. Sarah realized they had arrived in a different world when she witnessed the daily ritual of her semirural neighborhood: around noon wives and daughters would emerge in long skirts and dark hats carrying stacked towers of portable metal containers full of hot food for the working men huddled in their ponchos on their lunch break. Sitting on the edge of the grass by the road, the women would serve meals to the menfolk. In the Hirschmans' backyard, the maid raised chickens, which the girls liked to watch from the living room. It took some time to get used to the fact that the morning's clucking fowl could wind up as evening's dinner.[36]

The house on Calle 74 became home. Albert set up a barbeque. Sarah furnished the house carefully, her eye peeled for old furniture and antiques, especially from crumbling colonial churches, procured in little shops in La Candelaria. There were also plenty of hammocks dangling from walls and trees.[37]

It did not take long for the Hirschmans to develop a cosmopolitan circle of friends and acquaintances. In many ways, they acquired the social life they never had in the capital of the United States. Part of the ease was the scale: Bogotá was not a large, diverse, or impenetrable city. And, to a point, its cultural elite welcomed newcomers. *El Tiempo*'s political cartoonist, Peter Aldor, and his wife, Eva Aldor, Hungarian émigrés, were hosts of spirited soirées and meetings of Colombian and international artists, scientists, and writers. The bookstores, often owned by émigrés, served as literary hubs. The Librería Central in the center of the city, owned by the Austrian Hans Ungar, was a popular gathering point for writers and artists. Its selection of European and Latin American art books was an important magnet. Later Ungar expanded the store to include a small art gallery, on whose walls hung the work of a younger generation of painters like Juan Antonio Roda and of émigré artists like Guillermo Wiedemann (who had fled Berlin in 1939) and Leopoldo Richter. The country never ceased to impress. Once, while having stolen away on a trip to the colonial city of Popayán in southern Colombia, Albert and Sarah were awakened in the middle of the night by a band of drunken men singing and reciting epic verse as they staggered home. The next day, the provincial governor promised them a car and a driver to show them around—their chauffeur was the son of Maestro Valencia, one of the country's most celebrated poets and one of the merrymakers the night before.[38]

Sarah, for all the challenges making the personal adjustment, organizing family life, and chauffeuring Albert until the promised bank driver materialized, tended to be the agent of their social lives. If Albert tended to be quiet and observe the goings on at social occasions, Sarah was energetic and lively. It was largely through her efforts that the Hirschmans soon had many friends. There was a circle of Russian émigrés to whom Sarah naturally gravitated. She also had her special friends, Gabriela Samper and Hanka Rhodes. They had only one close American friend, the cultural attaché at the embassy, Hugh Ryan. Getting to know Colombians was a bit harder—gentle and kind, they could be hermetic. Sarah never ceased to be appalled by the way gringos in Colombia looked down their noses at the natives, while Albert was no less irritated by the presumption at work that foreign experts had some magical knowledge denied to Colombians. Maybe the initial difficulty making Colombian friends reflected discrete ways Colombians reciprocated the distance between the expatriates and the locals.[39]

At first, friends tended to be other émigrés, such as the Friedman family. Lore Friedman was the mother of two children of roughly the same age as the Hirschman girls and a teacher at the Colegio. An Austrian Jew who'd left in 1937 with her husband Fritz, Lore introduced herself to Sarah. Their houses were not far away, and the Friedman children would pass the Hirschman house en route to the Colegio and pick up Lisa and Katia. Out of sight from the windows, the kids would remove their formal school shoes and replace them with more seasoned—and cooler—footwear, then dash the rest of the way to meet up with other friends. During the evenings, the two families would often meet to listen to classical records on the stereo. The Friedmans had a piano, so their home became a hub for local chamber musicians as well. In the summer of 1954, Sarah took the girls to visit her parents in Los Angeles. The Friedmans joined them in California for a holiday, and the two families (minus Albert, who remained in Colombia working) drove up the West Coast of the United States.[40]

Though violence wracked the countryside, the capital was going through something of a heyday of visual and performing arts, thanks in part to the number of refugees and émigrés from Europe, who often found Colombia an easier refuge than North America. At the Teatro Colón, concerts brought out the cultural establishment. The Hirschmans began to feel as if the entire audience was full of friends and acquaintances; performances became social occasions.

One cannot help but observe the contrast with life in Washington. The difference can also be seen at home, perhaps because the girls were more independent and active. Outside the girls' bathroom, Albert posted a list of commandments:

Morning jobs:

1. Brush teeth
2. Wash face
3. Brush hair
4. Do *not* quarrel

Evening jobs:

1. Put away clothes
2. Make sure playroom is orderly
3. Brush teeth
4. Wash face
5. Prepare school things for next day
6. Be mischievous

As the girls grew older, Albert folded them into his affection for word games. Katia used to slip into the bathroom to watch her father shave and together they would make up verses. One was called "The Ocean and the Lotion."

I swam in the ocean
With strong swimming motion
I carried a lotion
Which spilled in the ocean.

And this little lotion
Must have been quite a potion:
Ever since the big ocean
Smelt strangely of lotion!

Dust-ups between the sisters could be the source of poetic invention. One Saturday morning in January 1954, Albert helped Katia pen this one in her journal, called "Lisa's Magnetic Eye":

In our hall
We often play ball
We have lots of fun
We play and we run
But once our ball
Had a very bad fall
Straight it went into Lisa's eye
And the poor little girl began to cry,
Her father said her eye was magnetic,
But her mother was much more sympathetic,
And she said in a voice that was quite energetic:
    "We love our Lisa
    Let nobody tease her!"

The years in Colombia coincided with a precious stage in the relations between the Hirschmans and their daughters as they passed through childhood to early adolescence. Over dinner, Albert would tell Lisa and

Horseback riding in Boyacá, December 1955.

Katia stories from the *Iliad* and *Odyssey*. He shared recollections of his own lessons from the Collège while the girls sat in rapture. Weekends were occasions to explore en famille with the Chevy to choice destinations around Bogotá and the breathtaking province of Boyacá. A photograph of the Hirschmans, mounted and covered with woolen *ruanas*, paints a portrait of happy adventurers. The small town of Fusagasuga, nestled in a green valley outside the capital, was an easy day trip. So was the small farm of the Friedman family. Laguna de Tota was a favorite outing. The Hirschmans in their Chevy and the Friedmans in their jeep would set out across dirt roads, through little villages, stopping to visit old colonial churches, explore local markets, and wind their way up the sides of the Andean cordillera to a large, blue lake in a cold, windswept landscape. There the families would go hiking and stay at local *refugios*. There were also longer expeditions to the lowlands, the *tierra caliente* to Bogotanos more accustomed to the Andean altitudes.[41]

By the time the Hirschmans began exploring, the worst of La Violencia had passed. But tension still prickled the air. Most people preferred not to talk about the carnage—it was "hush hush" time, Lore Friedman recalled. Sarah worried for the kids' safety on the streets of Bogotá. Travel on country roads could present dangers. Before visiting friends' country homes or farms, Hirschman would inquire among those who knew more about security issues and the state of the war. Occasionally, he had to deliver the bad news that travel plans had to be deferred. For the most part, partisan violence left foreigners alone—but not always. On one occasion, as the family ate a picnic in a field by the side of a road, a group of machete-wielding men approached. The girls huddled with Sarah as Albert poured on the charm to explain that they were simply sightseers. The men bowed and left. It was a reminder that not all Colombians were spared. More often the threats came from the bad state of the roads than human menaces. The indomitable Chevy would occasionally run into landslides, ditches, and washed-out roads. Passengers would pile out and locals would help the family push the car past the roadblocks. Albert admired Colombian resolution in confronting such obstacles. Daunted but undeterred, they would find a way across. One of Albert's favorite sayings as everyone heaved at the Chevy's bumper was "Échele con todo!" to the driver—"Give it all you got!" as the car bounced over the rocks and plowed through the mud. With the car on the other side of the impasse, the family would shake hands with their local saviors, dust themselves off, and climb back in the car to continue on their voyage.

From Colombia, Europe seemed further away than ever. It was in these years that Albert and Sarah let the idea of returning to Paris go for good. The only real lifeline to the past was Ursula and Eva, with whom Albert kept up a faithful, if occasionally intermittent, exchange of letters. To Mutti, who had moved to Rome, Albert allowed his letters to his sisters suffice; she could get her son's news secondhand—though it was not as if she put herself out as a correspondent, and the one (and possibly only) letter that survives the postwar years is an epistle filled with details about her penury. Albert, however, remained a dutiful son and sent her regular checks.[42]

Europe may have been out of mind, but not so the United States. From the blue came an invitation to participate in a conference at the Massachusetts Institute of Technology sponsored by the Social Science Research Council about scientific solutions to problems of economic planning in the tropics. Five economists with firsthand "experience" in the field were asked to share their thoughts with "scholars." Other than its surprising effects on Hirschman's career, it was an occasion noteworthy mainly for its emblematic dichotomy between field experience and scholarship. At the time, MIT was the hub of a lot of thinking about development, especially by Max Millikan and Walt W. Rostow. Hirschman had come to Millikan's attention when he sent him the draft of his research proposal on Colombian successes in early 1954. Hoping his research idea could be parlayed into a grant, he accepted the invitation to deliver a paper as a consolation; it spurred him to formulate more general thoughts. He plunged into it with a verve he had not mustered since his Marshall Plan days. He read as widely as he could, given his miniscule library. He got his hands on some recent theories on growth and pored over David (Mr. TVA) Lilienthal's history of the Tennessee Valley Authority. "In my free time," he told George Jaszi, "I am now reading mostly background material for the paper I am supposed to write for the MIT-SSRC conference," on which he was pinning more and more hopes. This was a paper he was writing for his "mental health."[43]

Millikan's conference in October 1954 was decisive because it brought Hirschman face-to-face with a scholarly field for the first time, only to discover how "off" he was. At the time, although development was on the lips of so many social scientists, few still had the kind of direct experience that Hirschman had. More often, ideas about development conformed to what was soon called modernization theory and its foreign policy implications, which suffused the pores of MIT's Center for International Studies. An outgrowth of an effort to design counter-Communist models of social change for poor societies—Rostow was committed to promoting ways to roll back the appeal of the "Communist disease" in underdeveloped countries—the center had close ties to the State Department and the Central Intelligence Agency. Eradicating poverty was supposed to diminish the appeals of radicalism. When Rosenstein-Rodan joined MIT in 1952, he brought more economic rigor to the group. His famous 1943 essay about backwardness and industrialization in eastern and southern Europe led Rosenstein-Rodan to urge a Big Push to overcome the entrapments of poverty. A liberal anti-Communist, he believed that a comprehensive and concerted assault was the only way to prevent specific advances from being swallowed up by the inertia of tradition. His thinking was to mark Rostow's later writings and recommendations to various White House occupants.[44]

Hirschman had only a partial grasp of the quickly emerging field. What he did get he found tedious. Beside, there was precious little empirical work of the sort he valorized. Too much of it smacked of more "theoretical" takes on what he was observing in the council. In retrospect, it was perhaps inevitable that the MIT paper was going to run into trouble. But we can see how it would anticipate a much broader debate and controversy about how best to tackle poverty and growth in the Third World, a debate that had precursors in the 1950s. But for now, Hirschman's was a solitary, not fully developed cry for a different kind of key. On hand were some of the gurus of the field, such as Rosenstein-Rodan, Hollis Chenery, and Robert Solow. It is not clear whether Rostow was present. None were impressed. What they heard were doubts about investment planning and the economics of development, doubts that did not shy away from uneasy questions about aggregated analysis and unflattering words about the role of foreign "experts." As career-defining papers go, this one was a flop.

"Economics and Investment Planning: Reflections Based on Experience in Colombia" is the work of an author in a transition of which he was only becoming aware because he was coming from obscurity in the field and had not been stamped by what passed as academic orthodoxy. But these were part of the reason why his thinking was so orthogonal. His opening words must have burned the ears of his listeners as he warned that too little was known to draw big conclusions of the sort the MIT organizers sought. "Our abilities will sooner or later invite reactions of the type 'But the Emperor has nothing on!'" The economist, he noted, suffers from the universal "desire for power" and often fails to "admit that there are limits to his prowess." The result was "an optical illusion that economics as a science can yield detailed blueprints for the development of underdeveloped societies." Hirschman did not disavow the economist; he simply cautioned against the allure of overaggregated analysis and the siren calls of "over-all, integrated development programs" of the type that brought him to Colombia in the first place. They might do better with a commitment to reality content based on observation from the ground up, precise understandings and models instead of a blind faith in general statistics.[45] Doing so might reverse the insidious relationship between foreign experts and their hosts, one which was doomed to compound problems. Like any marriage, the misunderstandings came to light when ideas ran into the messy nuisance of practice. The expert blamed the government for sloth, corruption, and more. The host, in turn, binged on self-incrimination for being unable to live up to the "rigid rules of conduct" and lofty expectations of the planners. It was all doomed because both sides bought into romantic dreams spun of a Platonic plan that could not help but fall short of expectations. Not surprisingly, planning orthodoxies ended in mutual stereotypes about foreign expertise and local futility. Hirschman threw down a verbal gauntlet. Instead of a "propensity to plan," Hirschman advocated a "propensity to experiment and to improvise"—a spirit missing from the council and whose absence deprived all sides from actually learning from experience precisely because the planners were so convinced that it was not they who had to be converted. After all, they were "experts."[46]

With words like these, whose Hayekian harmonics flew over the heads of those present, it is not surprising that Hirschman's foray into the academic world was greeted with icy politeness. But this was no tragedy. Though Hirschman flew back to Bogotá with hopes of future invitations to collaborate with scholars, he was not prepared to abandon his views in favor of more acceptable theories. In fact, the next few years rewarded him with mounting evidence for his dissenting hunches. Sarah captured it most personally in a letter to her best friend. Her father had been hounding them to leave Colombia for a "more civilized place," as he had done when he took the family out of Lithuania for Paris. But Sarah confessed that "I wish we had such clear cut aims. We both realize that you should think of the future—make plans for the children etc. But I think we both somehow feel that it is impossible to know what is best and that the present is so much more important—because if the present is solid and good it will be a surer basis for a good future than any plans that you can make." It does not take much to hear the echoes of Albert's unease about economic planning in Sarah's attitude to family prospects. Beside, and perhaps more important, "we have been very happy here."[47]

CHAPTER 11

Following My Truth

All human error is impatience, a premature
breaking-off of methodical procedure,
an apparent fencing in of what is apparently
at issue.

FRANZ KAFKA

Shortly after moving to Bogotá, Albert and Sarah set up a shortwave
radio to keep up with world news. They huddled over the crackling
set to listen to Adlai Stevenson's acceptance speech at the Democratic National Convention in August 1952, where the candidate gave a memorable
oration about patriotism based on tolerance and humility. It was through
this radio that they followed the ensuing election—one of the most appalling in modern American history. From far away, Albert and Sarah
flinched when the vice-presidential candidate, Richard Nixon, led the
anti-Stevenson crusade, smearing the Democrat with dirt about Communist influences. Senator Joseph McCarthy piled on, armed with FBI
memoranda about Stevenson's alleged Marxism and homosexuality. The
night Dwight Eisenhower trounced Stevenson, the Hirschmans joined
some American friends and the Aldors to hear the election results scratch
through the radio. Albert struggled to put an upbeat spin on the results
as they came in—maybe Eisenhower's victory will fortify the liberal wing
of the Republican Party? Even he knew it was a stretch; the sojourn in
Colombia, while exciting, would be prolonged.[1]

While life in Bogotá was a pleasant adventure, Albert Hirschman's
mind grew restless. Work was rewarding, its practicalities stimulating.
Colombia was also endlessly fascinating. Sarah and the girls were happy.
And yet, the nature of work posed little time to reflect; as a consultant

he was forever on the lookout for new contracts and practical solutions. But he knew that his activities lent themselves to a different approach to development than that emanating from the disciplines of the American academy. As time passed, he could only surmise that his audience before MIT's notables had sealed off any further contact with North American social scientists and condemned him to a career of practice, not theory.

In mid-July 1956, Hirschman went to the office one day and opened his mail. In it was a letter from Lloyd Reynolds, the chairman of Yale University's economics department. "The Department has asked me to inquire whether it would be possible for you to consider an appointment as Visiting Research Professor for part or all of the academic year 1956–57," wrote Reynolds. At such a late date, just over a month from the start of classes, this was a hurried offer. But there was no teaching involved: "Visitors are entirely free to work on any piece of research or writing which they may have on hand." One need not stretch one's limits to imagine Hirschman's reactions. The timing alone is revealing. Albert immediately called Sarah, who was in Beverly Hills with her parents. The call bore an uncanny resemblance to the one that preceded the departure from Washington four and a half years earlier. This time she was less shocked than tentative. She felt at home in Bogotá. The girls were happy. They had a wonderful life. But Albert's career had reached a plateau. Sarah knew, not for the first or last time, that this was a unique opportunity to revive the closeted métier of an intellectual. There does not appear to have been much negotiating: Reynolds had sent his letter to Bogotá on the 13th, and Hirschman accepted within a week. While this meant he would delay opening a branch of his consultancy in Mexico or Venezuela, he was "truly exhilarated." The terms were quickly sorted out, and the Hirschmans began to pack for the year. Albert wrote to Tom Schelling to ask if he and Corinne could help find something to rent in or near New Haven, and the Schellings went house hunting. "It's going to be a pleasure to have you here," wrote Schelling, "and a highly exploitable opportunity. I'm awfully glad you accepted."[2]

Many years later, Hirschman acknowledged the significance of Reynolds's invitation. It arrived as Hirschman was fighting local traffic, dealing with his clients, and "hanging around hotel lobbies trying to land new contracts," he told his first chairman. With the fullness of hindsight, he added that "the letter of yours has turned out to be a principal turning point in my life. For me, it typifies what Machiavelli has called the influence of fortuna on one's fate in contradistinction to that of virtù. Of course, looking at the matter from your point of view, writing that letter and making things work out were part of the daily performance of your work and duties—it was part of your virtù. From which circumstances we can derive an important generalization: one man's virtù is another's fortuna."[3]

Among the steps and contingencies in Hirschman's reinvention, moving to Colombia was one opportunity for a new start. But in no way did it point to a life as an intellectual, though Hirschman was itching to do more than write investment memoranda. The Yale letter thus represents another such step, this time, albeit for just one year, to leap from utter obscurity on the periphery to the heart of the American academic establishment. No wonder hindsight seemed to string each opportunity together with a cord of good fortune; fortuna did indeed appear to be smiling on him. A common biographical device relies on turning points and epiphanies as pivots. But plenty of chances are squandered. Others come with expectations that never ripen. And most acquire significance only after the fact, which reminds us that it is what comes later that makes the turning point visible. As Machiavelli instructed his prince, it is equally important to seize opportunities and align the forces of virtù and fortuna on one's side in order to convert an opportunity into achievement. It was with *this* Machiavellian esprit that Hirschman relocated once more.

The family moved to North Haven, where they would live for two not-always-easy years. Certainly compared to the adventure of Bogotá, leafy American middle-class suburbia, whose social awakening from the blanket of 1950s conformity was still over a decade away, was doomed to be a letdown. By contrast, New Haven, where Albert had an office in the Yale economics department, was an altogether different setting. Such were the clefts between life and work that the Hirschmans had to cope with. But it was clear what this was meant to service: Albert had to write a book. Acutely aware that his previous effort to author a passport to influence, the by-now forgotten *National Power and the Structure of Foreign Trade*, did *not* curry Fortuna's favor, he knew something had to be different about the second effort. One subtle determinant was timing. If *National Power* was written to explain a world whose problems had appeared to have passed, the trick now was to write something to intervene in an emerging problem.

What came of this was his landmark *The Strategy of Economic Development*, written in no less of a fevered hurry than his first book, which thrust him to the forefront of intellectual debates about economic modernization, social change, and policy making in the Third World as it was erupting. France's war in Algeria was bogging down into a savage struggle, and Indochina was the next frontier of Communist expansion. Meanwhile, ninety miles off the coast of Florida, insurrection was spreading in Cuba. Timeliness almost understates how Fortuna pressed her thumbs on the scales for Hirschman this time.

That was one difference. Another was that his first book was written without an intellectual field with which to engage or parry. Eventually, a field would emerge to wrestle with lopsided trade relations, but at the time, *National Power* was an orphan even before it was published. By the time Hirschman settled down to write *Strategy*, an orthodoxy steeped in Cold War anxiety stared him in the face, and he disagreed with it vehemently. The beginnings of the failure of this orthodoxy, combined with escalating international tensions, gave Hirschman's ideas some traction among North American social scientists and policy makers looking for alternatives as Washington found itself bogged down in conflicts in Africa, Indochina, and neighboring Latin America.

Orthodoxy may be too strong a word to describe what was, after all, a new field; but it did enjoy the privilege of some basic consensus among some influential thinkers. With the rollback of Europe's formal controls in Asia and Africa and growing nationalism in Latin America, it became harder and harder to pin the Third World's problems on tropical climate, demographic growth, or inadequate resources, which had variously justified colonial interventions and policies in the first place. Nor, it was clear, did the Bretton Woods institutions of the World Bank and the International Monetary Fund or the safeguards for a liberal trading order under multilateral commercial treaties provide the sufficient conditions for "development." It was one thing to prevent the world from sliding back into depression; it was quite another to lift societies out of poverty. The result was a groping for explanations for backwardness and the search for policies that would lure emerging nations away from radical alternatives, including Communism.

By the mid-1950s, "balanced growth" was becoming a prevailing wisdom in the fledgling field of development economics. Poor countries suffered from a surplus of labor and shortage of capital, and the combination was a lethal, low-level "equilibrium trap"—too much poverty, not enough savings, low investments, emaciated infrastructures, and the resilience of obstreperous traditions. The central issue was "investment criteria"—coordinates for policy makers and lenders to allocate capital to pull societies out of their corner as exemplified in Ragnar Nurkse's 1953 *Problems of Capital Formation in Underdeveloped Countries*. Balanced-growth theorists sketched how the dilemmas facing poor countries were interlinked: obstacles and hindrances transmitting themselves from one part of the system to another; chokepoints in one quarter could stymie advances elsewhere. This was so for two principal reasons. First, favoring one sector or industry would mean a surge in its output without enough demand to absorb it. The other main reason was that underdeveloped societies were short on capital, which had to be disbursed in a way that did not create scarcities in other sectors and industries that would choke off progress. *Balanced* growth was a way of breaking down the obstacles to development by hitting them all simultaneously and strategically to minimize dislocations like inflation or balance of payments troubles. Here was an approach aimed at avoiding as many conflicts as possible while changing the basic features of poor economies.

Balanced growth was also a script tailor-made to feature one particular actor: the foreign economic advisor with panoptic powers. The economic missionary could grasp the larger picture and wield analytic tools to figure out how to calibrate the delicate balance and time interventions to minimize the frictions of an evolving system. There were several figures closely associated with the movement. They did not always see eye to eye, but they agreed on some essentials. One was Walt Rostow, a smart, ambitious, Yale-educated economic historian whose leanings grew more anti-Communist with the onset of the Cold War. At MIT, he cofounded the Center for International Studies as a nerve center for thinking about economic development and its political corollaries. Later he would go on to coin the term *modernization* and have an influence on US policy in Southeast Asia. His 1960 classic, *The Stages of Economic Growth: A Non-Communist Manifesto*, crystallized social scientific influences on Washington's approach to containing radicalism abroad. The book offered a parable about how societies move through phases of development from "backwardness" to "maturity."[4]

The other main figure, also associated with MIT's center, was Paul Rosenstein-Rodan, an émigré from Poland, who shared much of the anti-Communist concerns of his American peers. He too was concerned with backwardness and advocated a "big push" to drive an economy out of the sand of its peasant base by investing in several sectors at once. By the late 1950s, he advocated the use of heavy investment of foreign funds, aid, and investment to spur the process, which dovetailed with the growing sentiment in the United States that foreign economic policy had to do more than rely on a passive liberal trading order to contain the spread of radical anticolonial ideologies. W. Arthur Lewis's 1955 book, *The Theory of Economic Growth*, synthesized the position. Lewis, who was Hirschman's age, had some of the same practical background dealing with policy makers in decolonizing Ghana. His treatise focused above all on the obstacles to capital formation, especially in the restricted pool of savings in proportion to the yawning demand for across-the-board investment. To increase savings required a major overhaul of a society's basic institutions and norms. While Lewis was less a fan of generalized planning than others of the "balanced growth" school, even though he did help blueprint Ghana's first Five Year Development Plan, he nonetheless shared their fear of instability lest the price system throw the entire system into disorder and anarchy.

The spectrum of thinkers among balanced growth advocates agreed on one thing. The crux of the problem lay in what underdeveloped societies were not: they were not developed. The circularity required that they had to be transformed without creating underlying imbalances that might throw a society off course—and fall prey to radical prophets. From one equilibrium state, planners had to create avenues to deliver societies to another equilibrium state. Against this backdrop, it is clear why Hirschman's ruminations in 1954 at MIT did not go over well. Hirschman was skeptical of overarching models, he was less inclined to pathologize backwardness, and he was getting more interested in the role of disequilibria in history. So, it was a surprise to receive another overture from the United States two years later.

At the time, the Department of Economics at Yale was a rebuilding powerhouse, largely the effects of Reynolds' energies and vision—and Ford Foundation support. Once famous in the 1920s as the home of Irving Fisher, it had fallen behind Harvard, Chicago, and MIT. Reynolds was the kind of chairman with an eye for smart scholars with original turns of mind, like Schelling. He also spotted a hot new field, development economics. The institutional match was therefore a good one for Hirschman. Reynolds had secured support from the Ford Foundation to endow the Irving Fisher Visiting Professorship with the idea of promoting "problem-oriented research." This was good for one year. Hirschman was the first holder.

There were also significant affective ties at Yale. Some of Hirschman's old colleagues from the Marshall Plan had moved there, such as Henry Wallich, who had worked on German reconstruction and later became a governor of the Federal Reserve Board and for whom Albert had a special affection; Robert Triffin, a former Fed colleague and soon-to-be critic of the Bretton Woods system; and Schelling, who had also served under the Marshall Plan. Wallich himself had launched Yale's first course in the economics of underdevelopment and so was especially keen to learn from his friend's extensive, firsthand experiences. This group wanted to "rescue" Hirschman from what they regarded as tropical oblivion. Schelling had been present at the MIT conference and was more enthusiastic about

Hirschman's insights than the hosts. The two had remained in touch over the years, swapping holiday cards; one year, the Hirschmans sent the Schellings a card bearing a cartoon of the family with Albert up a banana tree with Sarah and the girls looking up at him, bearing the caption "An excellent food is the banana, Let's eat it today and plan it mañana!" The ironic take on economic orthodoxy was kindred with Schelling's. At the time he was working on his own landmark book, *The Strategy of Conflict*, about bargaining and strategic behavior; never part of the mainstream, Schelling and Hirschman were natural companions—hence the grinning allusion to "a highly exploitable opportunity." Little did Hirschman know that Schelling had played a hand behind the scenes. Intrigued by the MIT paper about Colombia's successes and upon hearing of the last-minute Ford grant for the visiting professorship, Schelling urged Reynolds to contact his friend.[5]

Fortuna struck more than once. By the middle of the academic year 1956–57, it was clear that Albert would not be able to complete his envisioned book. In March, Albert approached Norman S. Buchanan, who had taught at Berkeley when Albert arrived there as a refugee and in 1956 had become the director of the Social Science Division of the Rockefeller Foundation. Buchanan, whose work at the foundation was more and more involved with development issues in the Third World, saw an opportunity. He arranged to fund another year for Hirschman at Yale. Hirschman shared his glee with his sister. "I will be able to continue with this and other kinds of wisdom: about two weeks ago I was informed that the Rockefeller Foundation (I cannot burden Ford any longer) is going to finance my research . . . at the same time I am going to work as a consultant, in particular in connection with the foundation's plan to support and create social science research projects and institutes in Latin America, Europe, and Asia." He was also already aware of problems with his fit in the American academy. "Although the uncertainty concerning my future employment will continue to persist, I do not mind much, since I am still not sure I would really enjoy university life in the long run—although I am now tending toward it more than a few years ago. Still, I don't think I am suited as a professor—not confident or loquacious enough."[6]

So, a one-year fellowship evolved into two years.

In return, Albert agreed to do some consulting work for the Rockefeller, which sent him to Brazil in August 1957 to participate in the International Economics Association meeting in Rio de Janeiro. Henry Wallich joined him. The trip to Rio turned into a formative fortnight because there was another purpose to the trip: the foundation had wanted Albert to spend a month looking into some of their funded projects and the prospects for social science research in Brazil and Colombia. This gave Hirschman an opportunity to get to know Latin American scholars in a way he never had while living in Bogotá and working on the margins of academic research circles. His analytical travelogue of impressions presaged a lifelong involvement with North American foundations behind development projects and social science research in Latin America.[7]

The Rio conference was an eye-opener. Hirschman got his first real exposure to Latin American, especially Brazilian, social scientists, such as Celso Furtado (who was relatively silent, but "was really the éminence grise"), Roberto Campos, the "intellectually snobbish" Alexandre Kafka, and the more elder, "aristocratic," and orthodox Eugenio Gudin, who presided over the Fundação Getúlio Vargas, the event's cosponsor. Kafka's paper at the conference was particularly illuminating for it offered a theoretical critique of economic development from a Latin American perspective, one that flew in the face of northern orthodoxies: it pointed not to vicious cycles of poverty and shortages of capital, but rather to fundamental structural shifts and tensions associated with the changes in capitalism within the region. Latin America was hardly poor and inert, the region's economists insisted. Kafka pointed to the ways in which shocks created growth opportunities, which in turn spawned social inequalities and inflation; growth promoted structural disequilibrium, rather than resolving it. "Imbalance," argued the Brazilian economist, "seems to be an interesting part of the explanation of the successful economic development of important Latin American countries." It was change itself that was the challenge, not the lack of change. Here were eloquent, technically proficient economists who had no trouble seeing the problems of American social science. Rosenstein-Rodan made his case for the "big push" and generalized planning only to run into flak from Furtado, Kafka, and other Latin Americans present. Hirschman took this all in with amazement. This was, Hirschman quickly realized, "a remarkable convergence."[8]

In the wake of the conference, he worked his way through the university and think-tank circles of Brazil. These discussions only confirmed his impressions from the conference. After a long meeting at the Brazilian Institute of Economics with Kafka and others, he concluded that "this is obviously a remarkably competent group of people—almost uncomfortably so, for it is bound to be envied and denigrated by the far more ubiquitous incompetents." Of course, it was a divided scene—largely between a figure like Celso Furtado, left-leaning, nationalistic, and the more conservative Roberto Campos on the other side. Hirschman was impressed by both, though he acknowledged that the latter tended to cluster some of the smarter younger economists. The School of Sociology at the University of São Paulo came in for similar praise. After almost three "fantastic" weeks in Brazil, Hirschman returned to Yale and feverishly rewrote the early, now lost, drafts of his manuscript. Of course, this was a risky move. With one year left on the clock of his fellowship, extensive revisions threatened to prolong the writing beyond his support. But the inspiration from Brazil could not be denied.[9]

His impressions, a source of some loneliness and doubt when they were formed in Colombia, were now confirmed by what he encountered with these charismatic and original Latin American colleagues. They also ushered in a romance with Latin American, and especially Brazilian, social scientists, who seemed less disciplinarily constrained and more eclectic—without being any less serious about their economics.

As he immersed himself, the news arrived that his mother, now 77 years old, had died in Rome in December 1956. It was a sign of how strained their relationship had been over the years that Hirschman was not so troubled by her illness. Indeed, his work had cut into his correspondence with Ursula—which elicited a sharp comment from his sister after Mutti's death. "Many thanks for your letter with the description of Mutti's last days," he wrote contritely. "It was good to know that she was not alone and that she only suffered for a short time. How was it for our and your Eva? Was the relationship to your children in the end better?" Evidently, Mutti had the same ability to alienate her grandchildren as she did her son. But Albert had some patching up to do with his sister. "Please don't be angry with me because I haven't written. I cannot get myself to degrade our relationship to the level of writing post and Christmas cards."[10]

Albert's embarking on a new career at midlife lifted the charmed halo that hung over the Hirschman family. Sarah found North Haven a hub of boredom, not unlike the suburban life she had endured in Washington. It would have spelled hardship had the girls not been enrolled in schools. Sarah could explore new horizons. She took courses at Yale, especially in anthropology. Sidney Mintz, whose pioneering work on Puerto Rico was itself shaping ideas of development from a different disciplinary standpoint, opened up the world of anthropology to Sarah, and thus to Albert. Mintz became a close friend, and he and Albert had affinities in their reservations about the orthodoxies of modernization theory. Another close friend was the professor of French literature, Victor Brombert. With time, Sarah's hesitations about leaving Bogotá began to fade.

It was Katia and Lisa who struggled most in the adjustment. Albert's work would pull him more and more away from home in a way that the Bogotá routine never did; there is no memory of making up poems or weekend adventure. This coincided with the girls' adolescence and their tribulations going to high school in suburban, 1950s America. The girls had had friends in Bogotá and preferred the more relaxed, tightly knit atmosphere of their Colegio, which was a close walk from the house. Now they faced junior high school and high school and the influences of peer pressure on two, culturally displaced girls. Katia, in particular, found the adjustment from the comforts of Bogotá trying. In her first autumn, the North Haven High School put on a dance. Anxious to fit in, she donned her fanciest dress, white socks, and patent leather shoes. The scene was mortifying. The gym was huge, the music loud, and all the girls wore silk stockings, the precursor to panty hose. No boy asked her to dance; Katia glued herself to a chair to wait for her parents to rescue her. Still, the girls tried hard to adjust. One day they returned from school with lipstick on.

And the stockings! To Sarah, they looked dressed for Halloween. "What happened to you?" she exclaimed in horror. There was one consolation: a television in the basement of the rented house, and Albert and Sarah let the girls watch half an hour per day. While they missed their friends and life in Bogotá, they soaked up Zorro, Lassie, and the Lone Ranger. Perhaps it could not be helped, but looking back, Katia and Lisa associated the move to the United States with a loss of family adventure; Albert's journey into an academic career was not one they could join.

Even language became a thorny issue. At home, in Washington and in Bogotá, French was the family tongue. Tensions first surfaced in Washington, when the girls, uncomfortable with the schism between private and public ways, would return from school and ask their parents "not to speak French now." This common-enough plight of immigrant families soon found a variety of compromises. By the time they moved to North Haven, French was the language for driving in the car, and since there was a lot of driving, rust did not develop on the girls' vocal chords. Breakfasts, where, in spite of all the moving about, the Hirschmans always shared a proper meal, were also French time. But as the girls moved through adolescence, English edged out French. Sarah and Albert did not finally abandon French as the nuptial tongue until they moved to New York. One day, Albert returned from his office at Columbia University, having had to lecture in English, to confess "you know, I really feel that it would be good for me to speak English at home." Teaching had been so traumatic that he needed to find ways to alleviate the anxiety. The linguistic conversion began at once. To Sarah, shifting their relationship to English "was the most difficult thing I ever did in my life."[11]

Still, life in the United States was not without opportunities of its own—like schooling. And it was always clear, and accepted, what the underlying purpose of the relocation was: to allow Albert to reset his career through writing. He did not squander his side of the deal; the family's support and Yale's opportunity were gift horses whose mouths he was not about to inspect. Brimming with ideas and determined to compose something that garnered more attention than his first effort to join the republic of letters, he plunged into writing without hesitation. But the project was not, at the outset, a book. He began with a few articles, one on economic policy and another on investment decisions, which he submitted to the *American Economic Review* and *Economic Development and Cultural Change*. "I am under great moral pressure to be 'creative,'" he told Ursula, explaining that he was furiously coming to terms with theories of economic development. "I am even about to create my own and am thinking about writing a book."[12]

In stages he moved toward the idea of a full book; by the spring it had some undergirding principles. One was that it be short on details and more deductive and conceptual in nature, based on Colombian lessons but without making them explicit. This did not mean that he diminished the significance of empirical fieldwork. It may have been that Hirschman worried that a single "case study" would pigeonhole the book. What is an "insight," Hirschman wondered? Here, the influence of Schelling, his most influential manuscript reader, was subtle but important. Schelling, without knowing how prominent he would be, pushed Hirschman from the start to translate the lessons from his Colombian immersion into more general insights, to connect the observations of small, local changes to inform the broad view. Hirschman told his sister, after one of his chats with Schelling, that he found his friend "one of the most intelligent people that I know (almost scary)—he turned away from economics and is now more interested in questions of foreign policy and peace strategy." What helped was a distinction between human *strategies*, a key word for both thinkers, and not *theories*, as motors of social processes. Moreover, they shared an affinity in dealing with the relationship between case studies and general insights. Neither bothered too much that a single case of multiple strategies would constrain conceptual innovation; Hirschman noted that Karl Marx wrote *Capital* based on observations of industrialization in one country without having to add "—A Case Study of England."[13]

There were also immovable practicalities to consider. Even if he had wanted to compose a classical case study, there were certain rules of evidence to follow. In the rush, he'd arrived in New Haven without organized data and had no time to collect any systematically. Beside, if he wanted a career maker, it would be better to be as universal as possible, and he wasted little time striking out in that direction. Freed up in this way, by April 1957, he had three sections written. When he got back from Rio, his drafts went through a major overhaul. Off the library shelves came the works of Latin American heterodox thinking, ranging from the Peruvian Marxist of the 1920s, José Carlos Mariátegui, to Raúl Prebisch, the influential Argentine economist whose 1949 "Manifesto" for the United Nations Economic Commission for Latin America was so definitive for—if hotly debated by—Latin American social scientists. Hirschman was finally tangling with alternative, more radical thinking about development within Latin America, though his more developed thoughts on this structuralist tradition would come out later. For now, they emboldened him to see the balanced growth doctrine as one increasingly troubled standpoint—and one that made a lot of value-laden assumptions about the societies it claimed to want to remedy. As he put it to Buchanan, he "was catching up with the rapidly expanding literature on economic development."[14]

The work was more than an impressionistic brainchild of experience. Its uniqueness lay in its combination, of which experience in the field was a part. The making of *The Strategy of Economic Development*, which appeared in the fall of 1958, reveals a tangle of influences woven of many strands. Economic development may have been a rapidly expanding field, but it was also, at least to Hirschman, narrow and rehearsed the same theoretical and uncomplicated mantras he found so tiresome. Behind the veneer of understanding and smiling tolerance lurked impatience. But Hirschman knew how and when to move to more interesting quarries. Aside from his own observations, he drew from a range of fields beyond economics to inform his economics.

The multiple sources of inspiration can be gleaned from files labeled "Strategy Notes," which were compiled as he composed. One important font was a literary tradition of dissent from the onrush to devise master plans to right the world's problems. The disparate traditions of skepticism about great idealist movements were hardly new discoveries. Hayek, Benda, the defiant Italian antifascists—in various guises these prophets reverberated in his irritation with the planners in Colombia. The claim to knowledge dressed up in grand theories about the world could, as Hirschman would later write, prove a hindrance to understanding it. Edmund Burke was one influential skeptic. *Reflections on the Revolution in France* had been one of Hirschman's favorite works, not just because it challenged philosophers who wanted to play on the political stage with what Burke sarcastically called the "pulpit style" and its attendant conviction that philosophers could do more than merely know the world, they could change it. The pulpit style could also author beautiful horrors. What appealed to Hirschman was less Burke's famed (if misunderstood) conservatism than his skepticism. It was not the "philosopher in action" that was the problem. If anything, Hirschman admired thinkers with an engaged style. Nor was revolution the problem. If anything, Hirschman sought bold, audacious alternatives. Rather, it was the leap from abstraction to prescription that concerned him. Settled at Yale, Hirschman pored over the "Letter to the Sheriffs of Bristol," a pamphlet denouncing politicians who "have split and anatomised the doctrine of free government, as if it were an abstract question concerning metaphysical liberty and necessity; and not a matter of moral prudence and natural feeling." It prompted him to scribble to himself: "Nothing in progression can rest on its original plan. We may as well think of rocking a grown man in the cradle of an infant."[15]

Hirschman's dissent from the rage to plan gave way to a broader cautionary position about the role of governments as mechanisms to rationalize the world. This brought Hirschman back to Hayek, whose *The Road to Serfdom*, a jeremiad against the certainties of grand engineers and the convictions of state socialists, moved him while serving in the American army. He read Hayek more widely, including the musings on Auguste Comte. Hirschman quoted Hayek's dismay about "the demand for unity and systematization" and quoted the Viennese philosopher's observation about Comte that there is "nothing more repugnant for real scientific spirit than disorder of any kind." Hirschman was starting to see that the disordered nature of development, and its fundamental disequilibrium, required specific strategies, not overarching solutions, even Hayek's own great flywheel—the price system. "Strategy Notes" is full of annotated passages about the "fallacy of abstraction" (Harold Laski) and "premature, impatient pseudo-insights" (inspired from reading Karl Wittfogel).[16]

Favorite works of literature fill his pages. He read Dostoevsky's *The Demons*. And there was the touchstone, Franz Kafka. This time he read the short story *The Great Wall of China*, a fictionalized retrospection by a Chinese intellectual who recounts the making of one of the world's great monuments as an example of the folly of grand designs by great "scholars." The immensity of the project doomed it to prolonged incompletion. Meant to defend the kingdom from outside hordes, it had to be seamless, impregnable, encompassing—and therefore impossible. No amount of planning and engineering could compensate for the improvisations and imperfections required to advance the interminable project. And since the great barricade was supposed to be a projection from the emperor's mind's eye, one had to presume that blemishes and flaws were of the ruler's intent. This was Kafka's tongue-in-cheek jab at idealists of all stripes. To Hirschman, the great malefactor was impatience. He transcribed Kafka's words: "all human error is impatience." It was the source of the cardinal sin. "Because of impatience," wrote Kafka, underscored by Hirschman, "we were driven out, because of impatience we cannot return."

The urge to resolve, to rectify, and to remedy in a hurry, Hirschman felt, hindered rather than helped people consider alternatives. Its wellspring was partly the result of an overconfidence in a particular model of knowledge and, as he put it elsewhere and traced later, a "cognitive style" born of the social sciences in the eighteenth century. But part of it was motivated by a different kind of human drive. To this end, Hirschman probed into psychology and psychoanalysis. Compared to reading Burke, Hayek, and Kafka, the behavioral sciences were new hat. Freud had not been discussed at home in Berlin; indeed, there was a strong current of suspicion and discomfort with talking about unconscious, prereasoned impulses and motives. How Hirschman forayed into this field is not known. But he did. What he got was the tail end of a shift away from imagining the behavioral aspects of human change as if they were subject to natural laws. The "scientistic" view that biological and mechanical laws and images provided the best way to understand the world was, by the 1950s, in retreat. The turn toward efforts to understand the self—its constructions and pathologies—that is, an inward gaze, combined with anxieties about the uprootedness and alienation of modern society, had social scientists turning to psychologists. "Look in psychoanalytic theory," he enjoined to himself in his jottings.

In this "theory," he found a burgeoning literature about group dynamics and personal responses and the basic clashes and frictions they involved. He read numerous books on psychoanalytic concepts and took extensive notes, more than from any other set of readings. What caught Hirschman's eye was the importance of one basic trinity: frustration, aggression, and anxiety. The latter, in particular, was most intriguing, especially as digested from Erich Fromm, which reminded him that the modern condition did not absolve people's problems, but rather created a whole new set of troubles out of meeting personal needs in competitive settings—and the attendant anxieties in turn yielded to efforts to avoid them. Extensive notes from D. Hobart Mowrer's *Learning Theory and Personality Dynamics* (1950), especially from chapter 19 ("The Problem of Anxiety") reveals his interest in a basic distinction between "normal" anxiety and "neurotic" anxiety, with the former not being disproportionate to the objective threat, but being instrumental to meeting it. It was precisely this "normal" anxiety that gave individuals and groups a basic psychic resource to overcome their difficulties, as well as the capacity to learn from experience. Notes on another author find Hirschman fascinated with the notion that failure, and learning from it, was a strategy for success; failure and achievement did not necessarily have to be seen as setbacks to each other.[17]

Skepticism and thinking about the microfoundations of behavior had Hirschman thinking hard about development neither as something that could be imposed or introduced from without, nor as something that could be driven by unlocking some special secret force, like a *deus ex machina*. Instead, he fingered social agents overcoming difficulties as the central pieces of his conceptual rebuilding. But how to think about this as a process? Overcoming a difficulty meant not just removing an obstacle, but rather seeing that it began as a perception—that is, that the impediments to moving forward lay as much within human agents' heads; the inner fetters were the hardest to overcome. If this could be applied to how people dealt with the emotive world, why not with the economic one too, just as a therapist might urge a patient to confront an obstacle by apprehending it? Many times this exercise might end in failure and frustration, but over time it would yield a change. "The repeated coming up to it (the obstacle)—you get to know it," he noted. This centerpiece of analytic practice, now transposed to thinking about society, was not altogether new. Characteristically, Hirschman found the classics already mulling these kinds of dilemmas. He found special significance in Burke's line from *Reflections* that "our antagonist is our helper. He that wrestles with us strengthens our nerves and sharpens our skill"; to this Hirschman added his own line about "our evasion of and intimate acquaintance with difficulty."[18]

This all pointed to a different spirit of reform, not one directed at smashing up external obstacles and thwarts as if they were the true chains preventing traditional societies from enjoying modern destinies buoyed by a new equilibrium of rational actors and benevolent institutions. Reform meant embracing tension, internalizing it. "Do we <u>need</u> tension to function, or only adjustment?" he asked, leaving little doubt that his sympathies lay with the underlined, to surmise the following: "In the case of individual: is there such a things as in economies 'optimal tension.'" There was, therefore, a fundamental distinction for Hirschman in approaches to reform. On one hand, reforms were aimed at removing tensions that prevented change, as if change were a frictionless leap from one condition to another. On the other, reforms produced tensions that compelled change, as if change were fueled by conflict and without it would stall. The distinction sheds light on a variety of types of reformer. Two kinds materialize in Hirschman's notes. More would come later. There were "those who want to change things because they *are* wrong." And there were "those who want to change the present because of knowledge that it leads to unbearable or catastrophic future," an addendum from reading Isaac Deutscher in the *Partisan Review* in 1958, "The Jew as Non-Jew."[19]

Finally, among the strands of influence was Shura Gerschenkron's famous essay about backwardness from the 1952 Chicago conference. Implicitly, Hirschman had already begun to gaze out through a Gerschenkronian lens—Colombia's "backwardness" was not necessarily a bundle of self-inflicted fetters to progress. But moving to Yale had Hirschman reading other works by his former colleague, particularly his essays on Russian intellectual history and the influence of thinkers on Russian policy and economic development, which conveyed much the same gist—that Moscow's sense of lagging behind was a strong motivator while an autocratic state had instruments for mobilizing resources that markets were slower to achieve. The sum helped Hirschman see the limits of growth models premised on earlier historical experiences—Walt Rostow, for one, used a stylized history of the British industrial revolution to chart a universal path to "take off." "One of the astounding feats of modern economics," Hirschman later concluded, "is the way in which the analysis of the growth process of advanced industrial countries has yielded an apparatus of seemingly ready applicability to the most primitive economies. . . . [But] the more useful [theories] are in one setting, the less they are likely to be so in a completely different one. An attempt to 'apply' them . . . may turn out to be a lengthy detour rather than a short cut."[20]

The book just "flowed out," especially after the trip to Brazil. One effect of catching up on his economic reading was that he felt compelled to become more technical, and thus upgrade his math. He labored for months trying to convert his ideas into equations. Friends—Schelling, Wallich, and others—disabused him of this eagerness to find the right quantitative expressions; perhaps this was premature, they argued, and that math was not yet able to keep up with Albert's insights. Hirschman was inclined to agree. Now, whether they were right or not is a hindsight judgment, and some economists have felt that this decision *not* to translate his unorthodoxy into precise, arithmetic formulae deprived the discipline of a major breakthrough. There is truth to this, given the sharp quantitative turn of economics. If Hirschman had wanted to influence the broader discipline, he would have had to conform to this new mathematizing norm. But it is worth recalling that Hirschman never saw himself as making a necessary choice between metaphors and math, between trying to capture the richness and complexity of the real world or to produce tightly controlled equations to illustrate a concept. The two, rendering reality and conceptual refinement, were entwined. And in any event, the idiom of metaphors and aphorisms that lace Hirschman's work, starting with this one, was as motivated as the mathematical urge by the need to locate useful analytical keys, not to complete a faithful portrait of the outer world. One of his favorite quotes was from Cervantes's defense of Don Quixote's imagination being untethered from reality: "God forgive you for the damage you have caused everyone in wishing to return to sanity this most amusing fool! Don't you realize, sir, that the benefit that might accrue from the sanity of Don Quixote will never come up to the pleasure he gives us through his follies?"[21]

Hirschman's trouble was perhaps more banal. By the late 1950s, putting his work into the kind of language that was more and more the currency of economics did not play to his strength, and he knew it. With the clock ticking and a career on the line, he made a choice to play to his strengths. The result was a manuscript with technical displays interspersed but never the analytical core of any of its arguments. Resolving these problems were more than an intellectual challenge; they raised personal anxieties about his fit in an American academy bound by disciplinary rituals and norms. Writing to Ursula in October of 1957, as the first draft neared completion, he observed that "this life doesn't come easy to me, I never know how meticulously I have to prepare myself and I therefore feel constantly under pressure. That's probably how it is at the beginning and gradually everything will improve and of course the first year is particularly exhausting. But I am suspecting that the constant presenting, acting as a professor, representing an authority, really puts one's critical abilities to sleep and makes them die off. On the other hand, there is the need to be scientifically up to date, to engage with one's colleagues and to remain intellectually versatile—at our age it is probably important to have such a reliable mechanism at hand that achieves this." He worried that a "reliable mechanism" was beyond his reach.[22]

The original cover of his book was of a jigsaw puzzle, partly assembled, partly scattered—meant to denote the premise of the book that there is little that is especially integrated or balanced about development. Hirschman chose this on purpose. Between the covers he wanted to put his jigsaw together while leaving many parts scattered to denote the unfinished nature of the subject he was exploring. Indeed, his original title was meant to be *Unbalanced Growth*. But he confided to future colleagues at the RAND Corporation, Charles Wolf and Paul Clark, that it "is too provocative and provoking a title and [I] have provisionally decided to call it *The Strategy of Economic Development*." The echo with Schelling's word choice Hirschman kept to himself. One is also tempted to see in the cover a personal representation of a life taken apart and reassembled in pieces—and still incomplete.

The outer surface of the book was a sharp attack on balanced growth advocates. But underneath was a critique of more the generalized preference for abstract model-building in the service of big all-encompassing plans of modernization through top-down reform. While the approach, he argued,

> appears quite general, its principal parameters have been chosen so as to give it maximum relevance within the environment with which it was intended to deal. But the very success of this enterprise make it virtually certain that the model will have minimum relevance in any radically different environment. (p. 33)

In the Sputnik age of outsized plans and "overall assaults" on backwardness, Hirschman wanted to strike an entirely different pose, offer a different vocabulary, for reform—without implying, as conservatives did, that it was all futile. From Hirschman's perspective there was a common problem: the view of development as a grandiose release of tension and blockages so that the economy could put itself on a smooth path to a new, "developed" equilibrium. This was pie-in-the-sky nonsense; the causality was the other way around. It was the very creation of "pressures, tensions and disequilibrium" that had to prime the motion and then unleash more frictions and tensions. There was a "hidden rationality" to the chain of tension-producing constraints or challenges: by creating them, people are lured into solving them. *To hide* was to become a key verb for Hirschman, full of possible significances over a long *vitae* of writing. What he had in mind was playing with Adam Smith's notion of the Invisible Hand. Instead of transparent, self-evident, all-inclusive plans, Hirschman opted for more cunning operations and unplanned consequences. To jump forward a bit in time, within a few years he would be rereading *The Wealth of Nations* to fathom the unintended general effects of individual pursuits. For the time being, he wrote in his diary, "The mystery is the meaning."

If this was the subtext of *Strategy*, its text consisted of themes stemming from his tension-producing, disequilibrium-creating stance. It made the case for fashioning new conditions for decision making; conditions to induce or compel policy makers and investors to have to decide where, when, and how to invest capital by presenting them with opportunities and challenges. The heart of the matter was how to think about investment. To balanced growth advocates the answer was where capital was shortest—these were sectors guilty of throttling growth. Their strong preference was for social overheads, such as ports, roads, and power grids, to eliminate prospective scarcities before the growth cycle began. Hirschman wanted it the other way around. Developing countries were not fragile infants at risk of being choked in the cradle without expanded infrastructures. Better to invest in industries, agriculture, and trade directly; allow them to expand and to create the obstacles and bottlenecks—and therefore create shortfalls in social overheads. Herein lay the idea of spawning pressure points.

This was not just a technical move. It shifted the spotlight to "entrepreneurs" and away from "planners." It also raised fundamental doubts about the experts' convictions about "sequencing" the process before it ever began—as if one could chart history's course in advance with a plan of meeting "prerequisites" and satisfying "conditions." Nothing could be more wrongheaded. To Hirschman, backwardness or lateness afforded opportunities to skip or invert the normal sequence of stages. There was no single route through history.

Shifting from anticipating problems in an overall schema and favoring state-led investments, to favoring private, precipitating problems did not sideline the modern economist, even as "expert." Hirschman still had full faith in the economist, but the "expert's" agency was that of a more discrete, subtle actor in the story. Economists can be most useful by indicating which productive sector or industry deserves investment according to the industry's "linkages" to other economic activities. One might see this as Hirschman generalizing the "consultant's" view. The idea of linkages was one of *Strategy's* most enduring contributions. There were two kinds of linkages—forward (what happens to a product as it gets refined or marketed to yield subsequent economic activity as it rolls to the consumer?) and backward (what sorts of inputs are necessary for the production and handling of the good?). Each yielded different kinds of activities. What was important was that a push in one industry or sector could set in motion tensions or scarcities and thus new opportunities for lucrative ventures in other industries or sectors "linked" to the original push. It was in the very imbalance and the disequilibrium created by the initial shove that the economy might develop. In this schema, the intentional targeting of disequilibria and destabilizers replaces large infusions of capital and the general "big push" favored by images of "balance" and "coordination" gathered under the abstract principles of "development planning."

By the end of *Strategy*, the core of Hirschman's thinking about what was scarce in traditional societies becomes clear. It was not capital. It was not a middle class. It was not "entrepreneurship" or the right kind of cultural bedrock of striving individualism. It was altogether more original: the capacity to problem solve in a capitalist world, the "ability to make development decisions." Balanced growth presumed that core of the vicious cycle of poverty was a shortage of capital. To Hirschman, capital was simply underutilized for lack of perceived opportunities. In fact, what was in short supply was "the ability to carry out cooperatively decisions and activities for development," which was now compounded by development gurus who insisted on an idea of progress as an uphill struggle whose success depended on a concerted, expensive, overall push on indivisible economic fronts. With this as the only way out of the trap, no wonder people in the Third World felt—or were made to feel—incapable of making effective decisions on their own!

Here one can see his debt to psychology and his fascination with frustration and anxiety as the patient "works through" traumas; in development, societies face problems of disequilibria by learning to solve them because they cannot afford not to. The trick was to create just the right amount of tension to enable decision making to serve, as he put it, as a "binding agent" compelling societies to resolve induced instabilities such as inflation, balance of payments problems, and population growth. He recognized the reluctance of people to submit themselves willingly to this trial. It was not just a self-imposed burden; it had the feeling and appearance of something unnatural. "There is something distasteful, hectic about this method. One wants to force nature's hand. One is always on the brink of disaster and disaster strikes if the calling forth is unsuccessful." This passage illuminates not only his principles, but his doubts. With pressures came risks of failure. Hirschman's approach was one that had to accept the full blame for its consequences, for having advocated "foolhardy risks." On the other hand, if we have no latitude to solve an induced problem, "we cannot afford to fail" means being "bound" to solve it. This was pressure. But at least it did not pin failure on the patient, the underdeveloped society that refused to shake off its traditional ways and "resisted" outsiders and their pushy interventions.[23]

The result was an optimistic charter that took aim at the prevailing view that there were so many constraints on development, so many scarce factors, that the enterprise required a totalizing approach to tackle them all in one swoop—or be condemned to fail. Given the proliferation of scarcities and shortages, Hirschman wondered whether such "objective scarcities of specific factors" were quite so central at all. Why not consider "manmade difficulties" in mobilizing resources, like the ability to solve problems? The more Hirschman thought about it, the more he realized that a closer examination "permitted a more sanguine view." The result, in contrast to expensive, expansive, intellectually seductive general plans and combined assaults, was a piecemeal approach targeting the scarcest of all variables. This was the premise of "unbalanced growth," a term he eventually abandoned because he did not want his work positioned only as an alternative to a mainstream. There was also a matter of scale and of what was knowable. Once more in contrast to the all-encompassing big-push-or-nothing standpoint, Hirschman featured modesty. In a phrase he liked to share with readers and listeners, he summarized his view of unbalanced growth thus: "To look at unbalanced growth means, in other words, to look at the dynamics of the development process in the small. But perhaps it is high time that we do just that."[24]

He did not even try to contain the surge of pride as he wrapped up his manuscript. What had grown out of an assortment of insights, petites idées, and readings had evolved, he thought, into a framework for a grand intellectual agenda. As the book was about to appear in the fall of 1958, he shared his sense of triumph with Ursula: "The reason why I would like to force it on you is that for the first time I have the feeling that I have produced or captured more than just a petite idée. The main themes can still be developed and applied, and I already have a couple of pages of thoughts that could possibly become the basis for a general investigation." With completion surfaced a lurking sense that the book was more than sum of his ideas about the world; it was the discovery of a personal truth. "I still remember how Miss Rubinstein once explained to me that I shouldn't worry about love—and she stretched out her arms and then slowly brought her two index fingers together from afar—as sure as that, she said, would the girl that I will love get together with me one day. As it may be, along the lines of this example I think that there exists for each of us a personal (and nevertheless general) truth, we only have to trace it and then follow it deliberately and courageously. And I just had these last months the exciting feeling that I am about to succeed in following my truth."[25]

Strategy, therefore, was freighted with more than a career. Having watched his first book vanish onto library bookshelves with minimal attention, Hirschman was determined not to face the same anonymizing fate again. He would promote the book himself. Upon reading an essay by the All Souls College economist, J. R. Hicks, Hirschman found occasion to point out like-mindedness and sent Hicks a copy of *Strategy* with guideposts to relevant paragraphs. "You will see," Hirschman wrote, "I make, I believe, exactly the same point that you state on page 346, namely that if a country is able to maintain per capita incomes in the face of rising numbers, the stage is set for cumulative growth." Hirschman's pleasure was to be shared. "I am rather happy about the coincidence because up to now I had the feeling that in this section I was the one to climb up a queer tree, for the sake of maintaining the consistency of my general approach."[26] This was a bit of a reach, it must be said, for this concern for population was neither controversial nor important to the book. But it was a convenient opportunity to reach out to a famous colleague.

As fortuna would have it, what gave the book its splash was timing. Development was hot, and readers were looking for guidance. The critique of modernization theory was already starting to form by the late 1950s, but there was still little available that did not swing to the other extreme, of Marxist or radical anticolonial critiques of capitalism. What Hirschman offered was a dissent that was still sympathetic to the power of market forces, a case for reform as the first rays of revolution shone out from the horizon.

Attention came from high circles. Roy Harrod, Keynes's associate and official biographer who had met Hirschman while at the IEA meetings in Rio de Janeiro, procured a copy as soon as it appeared and lathered Hirschman with gratifying praise. "I found it the most interesting book that I have read on economics for years," wrote the Oxford economist. Harrod continued: it is "perhaps the most stimulating book that I have read on any subject in some time."[27]

Other heavy-hitters were less fawning. The harshest critique, published in the *American Economic Review*, came from the Stanford economist, Hollis B. Chenery, who was present at MIT when Hirschman aired his early reservations about the enthusiasm for ambitious master plans in 1954. Chenery's reservations centered on the premise that the main obstacle to development was not so much the supply of capital as the ability to invest. It was a technical distinction of significance. The reviewer cut to the chase: "Hirschman's emphasis on the ability to make investment (or development) decisions leads to a theory of development which is more applied psychology than economics." Since it was not capital that was scarce, "the economist is left with nothing to economize except the elusive quality of decision-making." While he praised Hirschman for addressing "motivational factors" in economic theory, he charged him with "overstating his case," replacing simplifying notions of capital scarcity with new, no-less reductive assumptions about the centrality of decision making as the key. One "overemphasis" replaced another.[28] The Chenery review stung. Shortly after reading it, Hirschman wrote to his friend J. J. (Coos) Polak, at the International Monetary Fund, to share his feelings about the "rather unpleasant review." Hirschman shrugged: "I would have thought that the book should have [given] rise to strong feelings (of like or dislike)." He was actually hiding some pain here. Chenery had sent him a copy of the review before it was published, and Hirschman tried to salvage himself, politely. "Perhaps I have overstated my case, but it seems to me that you in turn overstate the extent of my overstatement," he wrote. More important, he sought to defend the use of psychology in the theory of development and social change: "My principal assumption is that underdeveloped economies are squeezable and my principal contention is that there are special techniques of resource mobilization which are not necessarily the same as . . . the techniques of efficient use of given resources. I do not understand why the former techniques are necessarily the concern of the psychologist and only the latter the province of the economist."[29]

Chenery was not the only reader who wondered about some of the assumptions built into Hirschman's *Strategy*. A young economist, Amartya Sen, wondered if Hirschman had not created something of a false dichotomy between "balanced" versus "imbalanced" growth. Asked by Austin Robinson to write a short note on the book for the *Economic Journal*, Sen normally considered much of what passed for development economics as "exceedingly boring." But *Strategy*, he felt, belonged to a different league—and deserved a fully engaged review. Sen's criticism was that neither balanced nor unbalanced models stand up in their pure form; they differed only in the degree of interdependence each assumes. But he bowed to the pummeling of the orthodoxy and "this cliché-ridden branch of economics."[30] C. P. Kindleberger, an otherwise sympathetic reader, found himself running out of patience with the book after the seventh chapter; so much of the book was organized around illustrating the special twists and hidden dynamics of growth that "paradox is piled on paradox; frequently, however, what is discussed is only a paradoxical aspect of a larger question, with the issue left unresolved whether the paradoxical aspect outweighs or simply modifies the normal analysis." Kindleberger wondered whether Hirschman ever really showed that capital shortages were not the problem to begin with. In the end, he echoed Chenery: "Authorities of developing countries can find warrant for practically any course of action they may choose to take." Still, Kindleberger's review acknowledged the originality of the analysis and where it now stood in the field: "With the publication of *The Strategy of Economic Development*, the scales have tipped against balanced and in favor of unbalanced growth."[31]

There could be no complaint that readers were not taking the book very seriously. It was clear that *The Strategy of Economic Development* would not go the way of *National Power*. Having spent two very productive, highly concentrated years writing and reading, positioning himself at the forefront of a looming debate, Hirschman had succeeded. His book became an instant landmark. But establishing his profile had taken some of the adventure out of life, adventures of the sort that provided the opportunities for travel and observation in Colombia that were so vital to conceiving *Strategy*. The book complete, Hirschman's wanderlust caught up with him. Writing to a friend, Paul Streeten, a Balliol College don who had authored a shorter critique of balanced growth theory around the same time, Hirschman noted that "now that I have emptied my bag, I really feel like filling it up again at some faraway place, but our children being soon 12 and 14, I suppose we should stay put for the next few years."[32] It would not take long for a new opportunity for adventure to come along.

CHAPTER 12

The Empirical Lantern

The decisive moment in the history of
mankind is everlasting. That is why the
revolutionary spiritual movements that
declare all former things to be of no
account are in the right, for nothing
has yet occurred.

FRANZ KAFKA

After *Strategy*, then what? The book had clear, entwined objectives—to recast the debate about Third World development and
fulfill a personal dream of being an intellectual. But basic issues about life
remained in the air. Two years away from Bogotá, where was the family to
live? Tasting the beginnings of success in the United States as an intellectual, Hirschman now wanted to stay. But he was without a job, hustling
for work and contracts. By the summer of 1958, he was on month-to-
month earnings with two teenage daughters. Hirschman, undimmed in
his determination, saw the problem coming. "Nothing is easier," he told
Ursula, "than to pursue a goal if that goal is clearly and convincingly visible. The most difficult thing is to continue to believe that the goal is possible if it has already slipped through our fingers several times or turned
out to be brittle and rotten. The willingness to recognize a new goal (or
rebuild an old one), to continue waiting for the moment where it suddenly might reveal itself—that is the task, together with the willingness
to give it up, if necessary, to 'betray' it."[1]

As Sarah always marveled, Albert exuded confidence that things
would work themselves out; he enjoyed the persona of the improvising,
solving *débrouillard*. But few could play the part with his uncanny skill.
This time, his gambit worked. The success of his publications and his
unique hands-on experience threw open a flurry of opportunities, as he

had hoped. History favored him. *Strategy* appeared just as the pace of African and Asian decolonization gathered speed, and nationalist and radical alternatives to capitalism gained increasing followers. Radical, Marxist appeals for revolution and anticapitalism argued for a complete break with the West and its legion of economic missionaries wielding master plans drafted in Washington, London, and Paris. Hirschman had something different to say about development, which, as the demand for alternatives rose, would send him on voyages that ended with meditations about the soul of reform in a new age of revolution.

Among his suitors were some of America's leading foundations and think tanks. This activity put him in touch with scholars in Latin America at a time in which there were few contacts and even fewer collaborations north-south. As Hirschman became a go-between figure, he not only became more influenced by Latin Americans, he also grew more and more aware that intellectuals themselves played a role in the social changes they studied. He caught his moment: if nothing else, the 1960s was going to be a decade to register the power of ideas, as well as their limits.[2]

No sooner had the ink dried on *Strategy* than Hirschman was summoned by Norman Buchanan at the Rockefeller Foundation. Buchanan's desk was piling up with overtures from Raúl Prebisch and Victor Urquidi from the United Nations Economic Commission for Latin America, the ambitious Jorge Mendez, director of the economics department at the University of Los Andes in Colombia, and the troupe of modernization theorists like Max Millikan and Everett Hagen from MIT, who were keen to promote links with peers south of the border. Buchanan wanted guidance and asked Hirschman to draft a confidential report on how North American scholars were approaching development.

Hirschman offered a census of the field. The early part of the summer of 1958 was spent reading and consulting with colleagues at the World Bank, Harvard, MIT, and other universities. Then he penned his views of the state of the art. "The field of economic development," concluded Hirschman, "is in danger of becoming stale." Though prodigious, it ran the risk of covering everything and therefore saying nothing. Most economists in the field were concerned with taxonomies and definitions, when the conceptual work had to begin elsewhere. The missing piece was rather a "dominating analytical structure, of some 'General Theory' of development which could provide a focal point for theoretical discussion and empirical verification." Second, it needed a lot more description and empirical evaluation. He called for a combination of new theoretical exploration *and* deep familiarity with cases.[3]

Hirschman was positioning himself as an exhibit without making it evident. He concluded by volunteering "Some Suggestions for Research on Comparative Development." In laying the groundwork, in the form of reports to his benefactors, for an extended, ambitious, personal research agenda, he hoped it would guide him through the coming years. If anyone had doubts about what *he* wanted to do, these were laid to rest. The unemployed economist concluded that it would take only one economist and two assistants with "two to three years for a research team" to compile the data and conduct the analysis. "Few universities professors can obtain this kind of leave," he nudged. "Many would consider it undignified to 'bury' themselves for a considerable period of time in any single underdeveloped country."[4] The method appealed to his taste for the heroic field-worker, a character coming into full bloom with the anthropologist who observed processes in the open (as opposed to the closed laboratory).[5]

It the end, it was all mothballed. Hirschman's booster, Norman Buchanan, died suddenly that summer. Still, the field beckoned, at the very least to resist familiar academic temptations of "la rage de vouloir conclure" as Flaubert put it, the urge to theorize and explain all for its own sake.

As the academic year 1958 drew to a close, Hirschman was staring unemployment in the face. It looked like the family would have to pack their bags and return to Bogotá. Instead, they packed their bags for California. At Yale, Hirschman had gotten to know the brilliant, iconoclastic political scientist, Charles (Ed) Lindblom. Lindblom saw a kindred spirit in Hirschman. Not without some hustling abilities of his own, Lindblom had arranged with the RAND Corporation for Albert to join him for the summer of 1958 as a scholar in residence. The Hirschmans installed themselves in a dark apartment with oppressive green walls. At least it was Santa Monica, distant enough from Sarah's parents to avoid familial intrusions but close enough to indulge their passion for the beach and Albert's handstands for his daughters.

Founded after World War II as a research group to advise the Air Force, the RAND was conceived as a means of retaining its intellectual advisors after the war. With a $1 million grant from the Ford Foundation, it became a model private, nonprofit research and evaluation enterprise living off government contracts and based in Santa Monica. The idea was that researchers should devise projects and collaborate to meet a burgeoning market for technical expertise when universities were only slowly shifting to large-scale research and applied analysis in the social sciences.[6]

The horizontal office building surrounded by waving palm trees was open twenty-four hours a day for analysts to work around the clock. Interdisciplinarity was a key factor and a source of some pride, inside and out. Even its detractors, such as Harvard social scientist David Riesman, acknowledged its success at truly interdisciplinary work. As its studies increasingly stressed the complex interplay of factors in Cold War military strategy, the RAND developed a reputation for pioneering systems analysis. Perhaps the most famous work was conducted by Hirschman's close friend, Thomas Schelling, who pushed the use of complex game theory into the field of war and peace and worked on his *Strategy of Conflict* (1963) at the RAND right on the heels of Hirschman's final edits to *The Strategy of Economic Development*. In the era of the organization man, what the RAND could dedicate to research was, compared to most universities, very substantial.[7]

With the globe moving beyond the two-world order, the RAND was quick to keep its edge and moved its sights to the tropics. Hirschman's sponsor, Charles Wolf, a veteran of the Point Four Program ushered in by President Harry S. Truman in 1949 to promote technical assistance in newly independent countries of what would be called the Third World, was given resources and range to spot talent as the institution branched into security beyond NATO and into economic realms.[8] Wolf, who had read drafts of *Strategy*, would go on to head the RAND's Economics Division and author the influential *Insurgency and Counterinsurgency* in 1965, by which time the organization was cleaved between anti- and pro-war groups and acquiring a reputation it could not shake off as a think tank for the government's security apparatus.

For a brief, formative moment, the RAND was the setting for an intense dialogue between Hirschman and Lindblom. This would be a fertile, if at times fraught, partnership. They had begun to work on an essay together in New Haven. What materialized was a curious blend. Hirschman laid out his approach to economic development, and Lindblom outlined his approach to policy making as distinct sections. Then the pair coauthored their converging and diverging views; what they shared were doubts about the quest for the rational and completely informed policy maker as the cure for problems. They wanted to revive ways of thinking and modes of behavior too often dismissed as irrational, "wasteful, and generally abominable." The collage of separate and combined voices first appeared as a working paper for the RAND in the spring of 1960 and later was published in *Behavioral Science* in 1962. A curious work, it is best seen as a bridge to Hirschman's growing awareness of policy making and ideas guiding the development process.

It was a bridge engineered of intellectual influence. What started in Santa Monica continued across an itinerant schedule of trips around Latin America over the ensuing years. Lindblom accompanied the Hirschmans on a long trip to Mexico in the summer of 1960 to conduct research for what would become *Journeys toward Progress*. After this, he found a way to join trips elsewhere, to northeast Brazil, Chile, Argentina, and Colombia, often writing up extensive interpretive impressions en route.

Already famed for defrocking the high priests of the state and their affection for technical components of making a policy or a plan, Lindblom targeted "the widespread tendency to assume that to solve a problem one needs to know its causes." It made policy makers feel confident about their prescriptions but did little for the predictability of success. But it presumed an impossible degree of intelligibility. Like Hirschman's urge "to prove Hamlet wrong" by showing that doubt could lead to better learning, Lindblom argued that the world's problems were sufficiently complex that many could not be fully intelligible as a condition for tackling them—but tackle we must. When Hirschman and Lindblom got to

Albert and Ed Lindblom in Colombia, 1960.

Chile, they got an earful from rival social scientists and policy makers wrapped up in knotted debates over the basic causes of inflation. Solving this big riddle was treated as a necessary step to the "right" policies; in the meantime, the situation worsened and the debate ground to a heated impasse. It was a textbook case of how the grail of complete understanding could make the problem worse.[9]

A "wrong-way-around" style drew the two together. One can see Hirschman, from 1958 onward, complementing his insights about disequilibrium and imbalance with an understanding of the role of perceptions and policies. It helped that Lindblom was as detached an observer as one could find; he had never been to the Third World and he didn't speak a word of Spanish. Inquisitive to a fault, he came to the partnership bereft of preconceptions and eager to soak up what he could—from the profound to the banal. Throughout their trips, Lindblom pushed and prodded Hirschman to step back, to be more analytical, to develop and test hypotheses. Often, on the heels of an interview, Albert would be greeted by an extensive memorandum of analytical insights. Midway through the project, Ed wrote up seventeen "miscellaneous hypotheses" about problem solving in Latin America, bits and pieces of which one can see developed in the book that would emerge from the flow between the two social scientists—one the careful observer, the seeker of surprises; the other endowed with a sharp and restless conceptual mind.[10]

What came of all this was not the once-envisioned book. Lindblom's notes reveal the limits of the partnership. "In my last afternoon and evening here in Rio, we may or may not get around to talking about the overall plan of the book," Lindblom noted, "so let me put down for what it is worth the feeling I now have that five narratives and a concluding chapter, such as you have been proposing, seems to me to underplay the analytical material that would go into the final chapter." What Ed wanted was less storytelling for each case—which had been Albert's preference—and rather a strong opening set of conceptual chapters, with subsequent short portrait chapters, followed again by systematic comparison and analysis. During the Chilean leg, he dictated a running commentary and had his tapes typed up and sent to Albert, urging a theoretical treatment that "free [the chapters] from the charge of being journalistic, how they can engage a social scientist's interest rather than ask him to defer his scientific interest until the concluding chapter."[11] The two eventually parted ways, but not before Lindblom helped Hirschman to think hard on the delusions, illusions, and ironies that riddle the policy maker.

While the pair sorted things out, Hirschman had his own concerns to labor on. One was the on-going effort to convert the principles embedded in *Strategy* into mathematical equations, something he had tried when he first arrived at Yale but suspended. Evidently, he still felt the need to prove some bona fides to his profession. Hirschman's arithmetic was good, but not advanced, as measured by the standards of increasing numbers of his peers, and certainly compared to the way the RAND mathematicians and economists were formalizing propositions about the world in complex formulae. In fact, going to the RAND brought him even more face-to-face with the quantitative turn in the social sciences and revealed this gap. Hirschman consulted his new colleagues for months and experimented but could never satisfy himself that he could capture nuances better in numbers than he could with words. Once again, he abandoned the challenge.[12]

The RAND also wanted Hirschman to contribute more directly to their security concerns in Latin America. Nixon's 1958 "goodwill tour" of the region was an embarrassing fiasco, and the vice president skulked home from Caracas after nearly being lynched. Massive railway workers' strikes paralyzed Mexico. Civilian unrest toppled military regimes in Argentina, Colombia, and Venezuela, giving way to populist and increasingly nationalist governments. Finally, the triumphs of the Cuban revolutionaries over the course of 1958 prompted Wolf to ask Hirschman to return to an old concern: how international trade affected political loyalties, specifically evaluating Soviet trading interests in the region and the implications for US policy. Hirschman submitted his report in September 1959, by which time relations between Havana and Washington were spiraling downward and Khrushchev had opened trade negotiations with Castro. Hirschman urged American policy makers to take the long view: consider the potentially beneficial effects of what looked like setbacks. Why not let Latin Americans trade with whomever they wished and the region's new generation of leaders develop voluntary ties with Washington? Otherwise, Americans would be seen as meddlers. Noninterference would also allow Latin Americans to see Soviet promises and rhetoric for what they were firsthand—inflated. The bottom line was not just antialarmist: gains from trade to Latin America from commerce with the Soviet bloc would promote development, and development would raise incomes and therefore imports from other countries, including the United States.

What looked like a simple loss could be a complex gain. Examine the meaning of *influence* very carefully, urged Hirschman, and see that even an increment of Soviet sway might have the paradoxical effect of augmenting US influence. *Fortuna est servitus,* he concluded.[13]

Seeing his prophesies ignored did little to endear him to American policy makers oozing with bravado. When Kennedy advisors tried to enlist Hirschman to the Alliance for Progress, he greeted them with interested skepticism. After a day at the White House with Richard Goodwin, the man in charge of US relations with Latin America who made the pitch for an Operation Latin America, Hirschman said no; he was wary of its "simplistic optimism." Washington's grand schemes brought back unpleasant memories. "It must be admitted," he told his brother-in-law Altiero Spinelli, "that it is not easy to escape from the Establishment in this country; for example, after my rather critical article on Latin America last year I was flooded with offers to take on this or that job in connection with the Alliance for Progress."[14]

Two weeks later, the CIA uncorked a misbegotten plan to over-throw Castro with a barely clandestine invasion botched at the Bay of Pigs. Hirschman was horrified that the Kennedy administration would offer aid with one hand and covert operations with the other. Worse, the Cuban debacle could not help but make efforts to refurbish US-sponsored reform even more difficult. He sat down to pen his criticisms of the Al-liance for Progress for the *Reporter*, edited by an old friend, Max Ascoli. He argued that the alliance improved on the mindless interventionism of previous years, but it still represented another case of the "misreading of the mood of Latin America." Just as Soviet cozying to Latin America was bound to reveal some truths about Moscow's peddled illusions, so too Washington's lofty rhetoric stood a better chance at tarnishing itself. Do not be surprised, Hirschman warned readers, if Latin Americans are less pleased with a promised "alliance" (whose military overtones did not escape him) than its architects supposed. Faced with a wave of national-ist governments in many Latin American capitals, "we may well have to choose between *alianza* and *progreso*," he concluded.[15]

Before all this, Hirschman's worries about his personal future began to mount. His leads at Rockefeller and Yale were running out. He had worked hard to get *Strategy* into the hands of influential readers, but the book would not appear until the fall of 1958. Now the RAND holding operation was ending. As far as North American universities were con-cerned, he was still a little-known author of a few suggestive essays with an unpublished PhD from an obscure Italian university. With two daughters facing high school and finally acclimated to the United States, he faced the prospect of dashing more than his own hopes.[16]

Behind the scenes, Yale moved slowly to turn his fellowship into an appointment in the Department of Economics. Meanwhile, a prospect opened up at Columbia University. The economist Ragnar Nurkse went on leave from Columbia for the academic year 1958–59. In May, he accepted a position at Princeton, only to die suddenly of a heart attack. In desperation, Columbia approached Hirschman to teach international economics in September. With no other option, he accepted. Never having taught a class, he prepared to take up his first academic appointment with but a few weeks' notice. That fall, *Strategy* appeared, followed by the volley of attention. Without much ado, Columbia rushed to convert his sessional appointment into a permanent one.

One might have thought that this stroke of good fortune would have led to exaltation. It was Montaigne who noted that some of life's greatest pleasures are those for which one is least prepared. Certainly, landing a position at Columbia finally enabled this peripatetic thinker, laboring at the edges of being an intellectual, finally to combine a career and a passion and aim them both in the same direction. Hirschman was delighted. And yet, from the start of his passage into academe, we face evidence that he was not altogether resolved to equate being an academic with being an intellectual. Hirschman greeted his first faculty appointment with deep ambivalence about being the "professor." At best, it was a job. When he got the news he would be going to Columbia for a year, he told Ursula that "I [will be] a visiting professor, but this time I will have to teach—international economics, international capital movements, seminars etc.—at Columbia University. I don't know how that will be. I have never done that before, and I am currently preparing my lectures (Just started with it and think it's utterly boring!)." A few months later, his mood had changed a bit: "I myself am quite excited about life here," he said, confessing to being "still quite worried about my ability to give a lecture every week."[17]

Hirschman made few friends at Columbia, in part because his sojourn there was brief and interrupted by frequent trips. One was Dankwart Rustow, a Middle East specialist interested in democracy. At the time, Samuel Huntington was also at Columbia, and the two of them organized seminars together. Another friend was James Tobin, in the economics department, who, after he learned that smoking cigarettes was cancerous, convinced Hirschman to join him in quitting. Hirschman, not much more than a social smoker, took another decade to kick the habit completely. On the whole, however, Hirschman was marginal to Columbia; there was a miss-match between the institution and their new star. He was hardly mainstream to the discipline, so Hirschman opted out of the economics department's activities; his closest colleagues were in other social sciences units. He did not even like his office; Albert switched styles and began to write at home, setting up a small study in the bedroom of their flat in 350 Central Park West. Though the seventh-floor, two-bedroom apartment was small, it was uncramped because the family had left so much behind in Colombia. But it was bright, cozy, and adjacent to Central Park, perfect for long walks. A photo of Albert taken in the fall of 1961 has him at a cluttered desk with his bibliographic necessities on shelves behind him, a scene of solitary comfort in the nest of a master bedroom.[18]

This marginality was tightly bound to Hirschman's attitude to teaching. It was a necessary but almost entirely aversive task. From the day he took the position, he fretted, "How to do this?" One of his first steps was to find an empty classroom. He locked the door and essayed a dry-run lecture to vacant seats. The result made him groan. Practice makes perfect for some, but not for Hirschman. Teaching was a source of anxiety he would never dispel. There was something insufferable about the sermonic style that dominated the pedagogy of the American academy. The capsule of a one-hour lecture in which one was expected to bundle truths on a topic, leave the hall, and repeat the performance later in the week on some other topic violated his inclination to present students with enigmas, paradoxes, and ironies and to mull them as he did his petites idées. As a largely self-taught intellectual, the very idea of "teaching" was utterly foreign. Try as he might, he never got the knack. And he tried mightily, often rushing to a bathroom before a lecture to vomit his anxiety into a toilet. To students, the angst came across as distraction. He rambled. He mumbled. Mid-sentence he would pause, his right hand supporting his chin, his eyes drifting upward to fasten on a spot on the ceiling. Students would shuffle uncomfortably in their seats for what felt like an eternity. Sarah, meanwhile, knowing of his misery, would wait at home in a gloom she kept to herself.

His lecture scripts provide some insight into what was going on. He would type out long phrases and paragraphs, possibly in the hope that writing out the lecture longhand would spare him the agony of having to improvise—that handy technique of the cocky professor. But then he could not resist the temptation to revise; he filled the double-spacing with scribbled edits, relentlessly striking out words and clauses and wedging his revisions between the lines. If the editing got too heavy, there would be supplemental passages on separate sheets—themselves full of strike-outs and revisions, which would condemn him to flipping back and forth between pages of scrawl. A paragraph of a lecture could be an interminable, winding affair. One of his favorite development examples was coffee as an export crop. After so many years in Colombia he should have been able to explain the case effortlessly. But no, a simple example consumed ten technical lines without a pause, embellished with multiple insertions and modifications. Then came a digression, as if Hirschman were engaged in a private conversation with himself. "True, but: . . ." he continued.[19] All this with an old world accent did not help.

Was this lack of preparation sheer uninterest? To students like Colin Bradford, who did pay close attention, something else was going on. Bradford felt like he was watching someone try to write out loud, editing his words as he delivered them, searching for the right turn, *le mot juste*. Indeed, many of Hirschman's literary hallmarks were in the lectures: the call for new perspectives, the affection for overturning verities, a delight in inverted "stages" and turning liabilities, as students learned about Brazil, into assets. And lots of metaphors and aphorisms. Hirschman was, in effect, trying things out and giving voice to his twists and misgivings, which left truth-seeking students bewildered. Here was a man of letters thrust into the wrong milieu.[20]

Those who saw past the style revered him. Richard Bird, a young Nova Scotian interested in the economics of poverty, took his course in the spring of 1959, devouring *Strategy* in preparation. When he entered the seminar room, a smiling, slightly absent-minded Hirschman greeted him at the front of the table, and it soon became clear that everyone had their copy of *Strategy* and had enrolled in the course to hear from the master of unbalanced growth only to discover that his charisma got poured into his text and not his talk. Perhaps his closest student was Judith Tendler, who entered Columbia in 1961 and would go on to become a close friend and collaborator. Even her experience completes a picture of a boring instructor, but nevertheless a devoted supporter and inspirer with ideas. Her memory was that she and many other students, held Hirschman in awe. They—Bird, Bradford, Tendler—took no time to realize that they were in the presence of a singular scholar with mysterious world experiences who preferred to explain himself with allusions to Flaubert or Brecht. Bradford was so smitten that he wanted to imitate Hirschman's sartorial style. Little did he know that Hirschman himself disliked the button-down shirts and starched collars almost as much as the pontificating professorial bravura. But Bradford went to Brooks Brothers to get a suit of his own. One of his classmates, Robert Packenham, noticed that Bradford was starting to look an awful lot like Professor Hirschman! As Hirschman settled into the profession, he soon found ways to hunt down alternatives to the staid look without giving up any panache.

Awe can distance. Even in the intimacy of a seminar room, Hirschman was a remote figure. His colleague, Peter Kenen, an assistant professor and rising star in the field of international trade, cotaught a graduate course in international economics with his elder and noted that "there was always a curtain—transparent—but nonetheless a curtain" between Hirschman and the rest. Kenen was voluble; Hirschman was not. Kenen spoke; Hirschman nodded, smiled, and let the students fill in the gaps.[21]

The style was also wrapped up in Hirschman's lack of interest in disciplinarity and one of its reproductive mechanisms, "training." Un-"trained" himself, he felt he had little to pass on that was not in his books. Hirschman had no method to instill, no *idée maîtresse* to impart. This would not change with time. As he became more famous, he was downright hostile to the idea that he might be the leader of a Hirschman "approach," much less a school of thought inspired by his ideas. It is possible that the time such a venture would take was not time he wanted to spend; the breakneck speed with which Hirschman was generating research projects and writing suggests that he was more eager to make up for lost personal scholarly time. But there was also a principle at stake, for Hirschman never felt that his ideas enjoyed the properties of an encompassing model or an explanatory theory. At most, they were ideas meant to be mulled, overturned, reconsidered, and even rejected in pursuit of better understanding and keener insight. Some years later, a World Bank director, Robert Picciotto, would write to Hirschman about his encounter as a fledgling economist with the master in 1964 and confessed that "among all the pioneers, the wisdom, elegance and cogency of your writings are unrivaled." Picciotto included a copy of a manifesto calling for a change in the bank to conform to what he called the Hirschman Doctrine. The master, by now in his early seventies and given to accept praise happily, was flattered but clear: "Unfortunately (or, I rather tend to think, fortunately) there is no Hirschman school of economic development and I cannot point to a large pool of disciples where one might fish out someone to work with you along those lines." He could really only count one "student," Judith Tendler.[22]

Meanwhile came the Cuban Revolution, followed by the media circus that accompanied Fidel Castro's visit to the United Nations General Assembly in the autumn of 1959. His detour to Princeton and Columbia brought him to crowds of students and a few professors, including Hirschman. Castro's style, endearing to some, had no charm for the veteran of ideological wars of the 1930s. Ultimately, Hirschman was a reformist. Castro was not. Hirschman was never, despite the folk-hero status of the Cuban commander, a fan of the Cuban Revolution—and it would affect his engagements with Latin American intellectuals. His skepticism was confirmed when he met with Felipe Pazos, a democrat, an influential Cuban economist, and Central Bank president, escorting Castro. Hirschman and Pazos stepped aside for a brief private meeting, probably in Hirschman's office, during the whirlwind. We can only speculate about how much Pazos told Hirschman. What we do know is that shortly after the Cubans returned to Havana, the conflict between Pazos and Castro erupted. Pazos resigned. Castro's brother, Raúl, thought the banker should be shot. Instead, he was allowed to leave for exile. There was no question of Hirschman's sympathies, which redoubled his determination to make a case for reform to defy the rigid, categorical, thinking in Washington as well as Havana.[23]

The same rising tide of revolution in Latin America alerted the Twentieth Century Fund. Created in 1919 from the philanthropy of Edward A. Filene, a successful Boston merchant, the fund was especially concerned with public education and world affairs. By the end of 1957, the trustees were concerned that the fund should raise its attention to Latin America to be on par with that to Asia, Western Europe, and Africa. They had sponsored major projects under a remarkable group of luminaries, such as Gunnar Myrdal, Jacques Maritain, Robert Lynd, and Carl J. Friedrich. By 1959, the trustees were "anxious to submit a project in this field." Hirschman's appointment at Columbia was like manna. Adolf E. Berle, the chairman of the fund's board and former member of FDR's brain trust, arranged a conversation with the new arrival. Berle emerged beaming. Hirschman was the man the organization needed. He had extensive experience in Latin America, spoke Spanish fluently, was a recognized figure, and was brimming with ideas. Berle took his idea of having Hirschman spearhead a new venture to the board, which comprised heavyweights such as Francis Biddle, John Kenneth Galbraith, David Lilienthal, and Robert Oppenheimer. The fund's president, August Heckscher, raised his eyebrows in recognition; he had known the enigmatic Hirschman when they were residents at the International House at Berkeley in 1941.[24]

Hirschman found himself in much demand, shuffling back and forth between New York and Washington to indulge proliferating requests for him to "explain" Latin America to alarmed and underinformed audiences. "His services are widely sought," noted a fund staff report, and his publications have "received widespread and favorable attention."[25] After so many years of obscurity, Hirschman enjoyed the attention—to a point. But it was not very satisfying; he itched to get back to his research program. Now, as Hirschman sought support, his ideas and the fund's concerns matched up well.[26]

What Hirschman proposed was a working group to meet over the course of 1959–60 to think seriously about the region at its crossroads. "Much of Latin America is today in a restless and perplexed mood," noted Hirschman in his memo to the fund, "somewhat similar to that which characterized the United States in the thirties." There was concern about the prospects of democracy, as well as doubts about economic development. Inflation and rural unrest sent policy makers scrambling and improvising. What Hirschman proposed was to explore whether there was a "Latin American style" of policy making. If so, what were its features, achievements, and challenges? How were problems identified, analyzed, and tackled? There was also a discrete goal: to step back from US policy guided by the anxiety to fix the region's problems; instead, Hirschman felt, Americans had to understand how Latin Americans defined and fixed them.[27]

Hirschman's group straddled several divides. He combined the scholarly and policy worlds. The largest cohort represented economists from the World Bank and the Inter-American Development Bank. There was Lincoln Gordon, the ambassador to Brazil during an especially turbulent time in Brasilia and Washington; Joseph Grunwald, the director of the Institute of Economic Research in Santiago, Chile; and David Felix, a young economist from Wayne State University. At an early stage in the discussions, Lindblom was also active. Hirschman was also committed to avoid a syndrome typical of American scholars who talked among themselves about others; it was important to have strong Latin American participation as well. Accordingly, he included the Mexican writer Víctor Alba; Brazil's Roberto Campos, the former director of Brazil's National Development Bank; and Víctor Urquidi of the Colegio de Mexico. The group convened in December 1959 and started meeting monthly until April. Each gathering grappled with drafts of a few papers, concentrating on a few problem areas and leaving extended periods for discussion. The hot topic was inflation—a problem sweeping Latin America and a controversial one because it was the source of bitter feuding between self-styled "structuralists" and "monetarists," precisely a model of how men with ideas framed problems and prescriptions. The debate within the group, especially among Campos, Grunwald, and Felix, piqued Hirschman's interest in the "impatience of the patients," especially with each side arguing for "fundamental" explanations and thus far-reaching solutions, solutions that struck Hirschman as beyond the scale of the original problem. Here, he mused, was a style of thinking and pattern of problem solving that risked compounding things.

The final result was a collection of essays brimming with ideas but not quite adding up to the promise of Hirschman's original goals. The only one to really plumb the question of whether there was a style of thinking about policies and problems in Latin America was Hirschman himself. "Ideologies of Economic Development," his long opening chapter to the anthology *Latin American Issues* (published by the Twentieth Century Fund), was his first foray into thinking that the way development was imagined was critical to how it might unfold. It blurred the hardened lines between economic analysis and the rest of the social sciences. It was also one of the first to pose the question: how did the way Latin Americans understood their problems shape the way they tackled them? If economists were accustomed to thinking of themselves as outside societies looking in, like a doctor examining a patient, Hirschman turned them into the subject.

There was something that was especially intriguing about Latin American economists, and social scientists more generally, he felt. Whereas Europeans and North Americans tended to turn their observations into universal claims about "society," Latin American intellectuals tended to particularize their societies as uniquely blessed—or more commonly, afflicted—with problems of their own making. Self-incriminating explanations for backwardness ranged from racial mixtures, tropical geographies, or Hispanic legacies. More recently, nationalists and radicals were wagging their fingers at European and North American neocolonialism. Either way, imagining reform did not come naturally to Latin America's social scientists, that is, until the formation in 1948 of the United Nations Economic Commission for Latin America (ECLA), which tutored the emergence of a new brand of economist and social scientist, seen by Hirschman as a figure who might break the fatalist lock. Though he was skeptical of the ECLA analysts' accent on unfair international trade as the source of the problem, he nonetheless pointed to them as a new model of social scientist looking for solutions in a region where the only conceivable futures lay in the hands of providence—or revolution. The last words of his essay were for American readers. In Europe and North America ideology had been pronounced dead, and public policy handed over to "sophisticated incrementalists bored with yesterday's ideological bouts." Latin America was different. "We are seriously out of phase with the mood prevailing in Latin America," wrote Hirschman. South of the border, "ideologies are in their accustomed roles, holding men in their grip, pushing them into actions that have important effects, both positive and negative, on economic growth."[28]

Appearing in 1961, *Latin American Issues* was timely. There was little well-informed analysis, in spite of the firestorm of news about events south of the border. It was this book and some nudging from Adolf Berle, who had returned to diplomatic service as head of an interdepartmental task force on Latin American affairs, to put hemispheric relations onto a new track that fueled Washington's eagerness to enlist Hirschman's services. By then, Hirschman wanted to analyze policy, not make it.

Working on *Issues* opened more doors. From the start, the Twentieth Century Fund's board had hoped that this network would become the basis for a larger, "major study" that it hoped Hirschman would undertake. "By this procedure Mr. Hirschman's interests will be brought into line with those of the Fund and his services will be made available on an increasing scale." The fund wanted to sponsor research that would make a difference to policy makers, and Hirschman wanted to study policy making. By then, Hirschman was also itching to return to the field. As he explained to the board, "Social scientists usually analyze problems such as inflation and land tenure from the outside, like certain doctors who engage in a strict minimum conversation with the patient." But how was a problem first "perceived as a problem?" And how did the perception shape the solution? The board was delighted; it named him research director of Latin American Projects and gave him resources to cover three years' field research and salary for a sabbatical for 1961–62.[29]

Projects that yield books about social and economic problems can be divided into two sorts. One gets written "because the author even before sitting down to write has hit on an *answer* or an overriding thesis which *he* at least feels sure is an illuminating insight," Hirschman once observed. Another kind arises because an author "had an unanswered *question* which he wanted to worry with the intensity which only the writing of a book affords." The first helps the mind focus on an answer, but "will easily convince itself that this answer solves not one, but a great many questions." The second starts with a question leading the restless mind to uncover "not one, but a variety of answers." These reflections, written while Hirschman finished *Journeys toward Progress,* leave no doubt as to *his* frame of mind. In completing the work, he realized he'd stumbled onto what would became the element of a personal literary signature—a model for those who liked multiple keys and frustration for those who wanted more black and white. Gone was the search for encompassing theories; clearer was the role of a guiding question or paradoxes leading in multiple directions. Shortly after writing *Journeys* he had to confess, not unhappily, that he found it impossible to summarize the book into "one, two, or even three neat points." Gone was the temptation to distill his aperçus into concise equations; clearer was his preference for narrative analysis. "I took my empirical lantern and examined at close range and in considerable detail the history of three protracted and important Latin American policy problems." This project had become the economist's internal voyage as well.[30]

It was in the book's title: holding up his lantern meant extensive travel. As soon as classes were over, the Hirschmans packed their bags for Bogotá, which would become a base for several years. By June 1960, Colombia was not the same country as the one the family had left four years earlier. The dictatorship was gone, old partisan feuding had yielded to Cuban-style guerrilla *focos,* and the civilian successors were gearing up for major reforms as a way to put the history of conflict and turmoil behind. Bogotá was humming with activity—intellectual, cultural, and political. During the second summer the Hirschmans spent back in Colombia (1961), leaders and policy makers were gripped in a widespread

debate about democracy, reconstruction, and social reform that was unlike anything Hirschman had seen before in the country. The excitement
and urgency of a fast-moving debate in which he felt he could intervene
clearly energized him. Enrique Peñalosa, the scion of a powerful family
and a close friend, fed Hirschman a steady diet of clippings and information about the new agrarian reform institute while commenting on
drafts of the Colombia chapter. In 1962, like a coconspirator, he warned
Hirschman "that the great landowners are beginning to go to war to support the modifications of the [original agrarian reform] decrees."[31]

Neither, of course, was Hirschman the same man. As an accomplished
academic, the author of proliferating numbers of books and articles, and
an increasingly influential figure among foundations and policy circles,
he viewed Latin America from a different angle. Still, there was room for
familiarity. The Hirschmans rented a house from an American family
that, to Albert's delight, had bought his old desk and chair from the Calle
74 residence; he was thrilled to be able to write up his field notes and draft
chapters in his old cradle. There were also occasions to deepen old friendships. Katia and Lisa posed for one of Colombia's most famous photogra-
phers, Hernán Díaz. They spent a lot of time with Maria and Juan Antonio Roda and Enrique Peñalosa and his family. There were weekend trips
to favorite destinations. At times, work and family adventures could be
rolled into one. The girls helped with field research alongside their father.
For all the pleasures of working and traveling in Colombia, the sun was
setting on a phase of all their lives. At 1961's summer's end, the family
packed their belongings in Bogotá and shipped what remained to New
York and bid adieu to old friends, leaving Colombia as their home for
good. Once back in 350 Central Park West, the Díaz portraits were hung
on the walls, and later the Roda painting of Katia and Lisa would be too,
and relics from the churches and furniture from the Candelaria district
became permanent reminders of another home.[32]

Colombia shaped Hirschman twice over: first as a source for alternative thinking about development economics, and now as a cauldron of
reformism. It was a template for the rest of Latin America, which was undergoing similar groundswells of agitation motivated by a new generation

of radical doctrines. Concepts like "dependency" spotlighted the role of unequal exchange in underdeveloping the Third World; only by challenging liberal trade relations could there be hope for development. In the more stratified societies, peasants were seizing estates, and slum dwellers squatted on empty blocks. Insurgencies began to spread. Hirschman felt the pressure on the small, sometimes abstract and evasive, message of *The Strategy of Economic Development*. Suddenly, it seemed there were so many decisions that were being made; they were no longer in short supply. More than that, what were once seen as intractable obstacles that only a balanced technical assault could overcome suddenly seemed more fragile. Radicals, emboldened above all by the Cuban revolutionaries, made these barriers seem vulnerable to acts of great human will. Castro and others promised to wipe away underdevelopment by shattering these structures in a single blow. Latin Americans, Hirschman saw, were hardly recoiling from instability, pressure points, and disequilibria. The challenge was how to tap the fervor for change in a way that did not fall prey to exaggerated fantasies of some developed Utopia.

The answer was to be found in reform. When he returned to New York in September 1962, he informed the fund that "my trip to Colombia was particularly useful, for there a rather forceful land reform law had been passed at the end of 1961, and the first reform project had just been started by the newly organized Colombian Land Reform Institute."[33] This was true elsewhere. In Brazil, another civilian government unveiled an effort in 1959 to tackle massive poverty in the northeast of the country under the umbrella of the Superintendency for the Development of the Northeast (SUDENE). The brainchild of Celso Furtado, whom Hirschman had met while consulting for the Rockefeller Foundation, SUDENE had made the city of Recife a hub of reform. Furtado was its first director and by 1962 had vastly expanded its operations—leading it into budgetary problems. Meanwhile, the government of President João Goulart was running into conservative opposition. "Effective reform is not foreclosed," Hirschman told the Twentieth Century Fund, "but the road to reform is full of unexpected turns." For precisely these reasons, it was vital to keep a finger on the pulse of these changes. Perhaps anticipat-

Albert in Recife, 1960.

ing the conflicts that were to come, he warned that "it certainly is not that smooth, orderly movement led by the vaunted 'non-Communist Left'—a very hard group to lay one's hand on in these countries."[34]

The project was vast. "Close range" and "considerable detail" to the history of fast-moving reform in five complex countries was not just ambitious. It reflected the naïveté of a social scientist who yearned to do field work with little experience. It was one thing to build on concepts from practical experience, the approach in *Strategy*; it was another to organize evidence coherently and derive insights from it. This was a nub of concern from Ed Lindblom and eventually led to two cases being dropped. Mexico was supposed to exemplify reforms affecting foreign investment, and Argentina was an example of oil policy. Argentina in the early 1960s was seared by upheaval, its democratic system shaking in the absence of a Peronist party and Perón, and oil was the subject of a heated debate. Though less turbulent, Mexico was no less complicated as the regime contended with massive labor disputes and the patina of stability of the government was wearing thin. In fact, the whole area of economic nationalism was becoming a vast, highly contentious, and unbounded subject. Part way through the research,

Hirschman abandoned these two most difficult cases and opted to focus on Brazil to examine regional development policy and SUDENE, on Chile to study inflation, and on Colombia to look at agrarian reform.

Journeys was the product of a historic conjuncture, and its author consciously let its energies shape it. Hirschman toggled back and forth between writing and field research, revising draft after draft in the light of new evidence and unfolding debates. One effect of this approach was to allow the passion of reformists motivate his analysis and seep into his prose; Hirschman was hardly an impartial raconteur. As he drafted chapters, he sent them out to the protagonists for their feedback, starting with Colombia, then Brazil, and followed by Chile, the case he found most difficult but perhaps most intellectually challenging. Carlos Lleras Restrepo, the champion of the agrarian reform law who left the country temporarily to let tempers cool, received a draft of the Colombian chapter thanks to Peñalosa, who was leading the countercharge in his absence. Through extensive conversations and commentary, Peñalosa had shaped Hirschman's views—and so he was not surprisingly beaming about the analysis he found in the draft. He and Lleras in turn had a long conversation about it; Lleras asked his lieutenant to convey just how impressed he was at seeing their struggle so illuminated.[35] Celso Furtado, the SUDENE founder, received his chapter and wrote back quickly from Rio with praise, "It seems to me an excellent overview and work of interpretation." He added few amendments. What he wanted—not surprisingly given the glowing analysis of his venture—was a quick translation into Portuguese.[36] President Kennedy's ambassador to Brazil, Lincoln Gordon, a partner in the *Latin American Issues* project also relayed day-to-day unfoldings. He too read a draft of the SUDENE chapter and kept Hirschman abreast of Furtado's clash with the plutocratic governor of Pernambuco. This loggerhead "is true in greater or smaller degrees with several of the Governors," and Gordon suggested that these strains "would be an interesting part of your political analysis."[37]

Emerging in Hirschman's mind was a history whose conclusion remained to be determined and an analysis that pressed its thumb on the scales in favor of audacious reform. In this sense, *Journeys* did more than collapse the distance between the observer and the reformer: it identified with him, gave him a label—the "reformmonger"—and was dedicated to two icons of the spirit—Celso Furtado and Carlos Lleras Restrepo, "masters" of the movement. Eventually the president of Colombia from 1966 to 1970, Lleras was the consummate advocate of daring, destabilizing efforts to redirect the course of the country's history and whose spirit was kindred to Hirschman's own advocacy of risk-taking, unbalanced, and bottom-up approaches to development. His brainchild, the Colombian Institute for Agrarian Reform (INCORA), created in 1961 with Peñalosa as the first director, was a herald for reformers in Latin America and an alternative to more radical models of collectivization. To Lleras this unconcluded history was an opportunity for a kind of social science to affect it. "There is a great need," he implored Hirschman, "to organize peasants to become more politically active outside of the political parties—but rather as interest groups, like business groups are organized."[38]

Hirschman identified with a broader turn among Latin American social scientists. Consider, once more, Colombia. The rural sociologist, Orlando Fals Borda had come to Hirschman's attention in 1957 during the evaluation tour for Norman Buchanan. Fals Borda's work for the Caja Agraria and the Ministry of Labor left a deep impression. Perhaps thinking of his own transition, Hirschman informed Buchanan that Fals Borda "makes an excellent impression, seems genuinely interested in continuing scientific work rather than letting himself be absorbed by consulting activities."[39] On the heels of the Rockefeller report, Fals Borda's *El Hombre y la Tierra en Boyacá: Bases Sociológicas e Históricas para una Reforma Agraria* rolled off the printing press. It was not just a pioneering ethnographic study of one of the country's most destitute regions and one of Hirschman's favorite destinations, it was written with a determined eye toward understanding the social forces behind the pressures for land redistribution. This portrait of a "world in transition," from one still encased in its colonial features to one on the brink of an untold future, depicted a passage analogous to that of seventeenth-century Europe. But this time, the "virus" of "social injustice" came to the attention of the sociologist who could not stand by and document the cries for help from the immiserated peasantry of the highlands. For Hirschman, it would be a touchstone reference; the issue was not whether Colombian rural society would change, but how. And conducting the *how* was the essence of reform. Before long, Fals Borda became a personal friend of the family and a frequent visitor to the house in Bogotá. By then, he too had changed, for the book had made him the social scientist most closely aligned with reforms and one whose own contacts with the peasant movement exemplified a new model of "organic intellectual"—at once observing society and promoting its transformation. One day, Fals Borda appeared at the doorstep with another friend of the same spirit, the brilliant young priest, Camilo Torres, whose own restlessness about the pace of change was creating waves with in the Colombian Church. Fals Borda and Torres, cofounders of the Sociology Faculty at the National University in Bogotá, were committed to a new kind of engaged social sciences. Sarah and Albert welcomed the two into the house and then spent hours discussing the country's problems; both Colombians were eager to share their views of the simmering problems and agitation in the countryside. As if to exemplify what was at stake at the crossroads and the breadth of the choices, Torres's yearnings for change eventually led him to give up hope of working within the system. It was not anguish but rather frustration that pushed him to join Colombia's guerrillas, only to be mowed down in his first skirmish with the military.[40]

With this spirit of widening options and accumulated expectations, driven by the rising appeal of more drastic routes to social change, Colombia cast a shadow on the other "cases." The crisis in the countryside and the violence that ravaged it may have been tragic, but it also presented an opportunity. New groups worked their way into power in part to *find* solutions. This is what brought the idea of agrarian reform before it became a policy. So, a crisis *could* be an important ingredient in problem solving and rally an esprit of policy making around a problem. Whether it was rural unrest, inflation, or a terrible drought, such as the one that visited misery upon the Brazilian northeast in 1958, a problem could summon new ways to think about it and change it. The drought, for instance, was devastating enough to shake up an otherwise flaccid National Development Bank and prompt the Kubitschek government to enlist Furtado, recently returned from Cambridge, to set up a plan. It was "very beautiful, very brilliant, very quick," Furtado told Hirschman in one of their long conversations. From this emerged SUDENE, the northeast development bank, which was placed in Furtado's hands. But it was not just the government that responded, so did the church, with a "bishop's program" of their own and soon began to mobilize parishioners. Northeastern politicos soon climbed aboard the program. The result was a new coalition of forces able to push through reforms in the face of traditional resistance. Hirschman's notes on the chats with Furtado reveal his admiration for the alchemy of policy daring and political maneuvering.[41]

Hirschman's stories did not always point one way; these were not triumphal accounts of reformers overcoming all odds. A crisis could just as well deepen the problem. In Colombia, once the violence settled down, the underlying problem seemed to recede and some reformers turned down the pressure. The result was a groundswell of impatience on the part of peasants and a revolutionary offensive by guerrillas sensing it might be their last opportunity. As Hirschman was putting the final touches to the book, Colombia appeared to be backsliding in this fashion, despite Peñalosa's optimism. Chile, on the other hand, was at a crossroads but veering the other way. After years of floundering, which were on display during the *Issues* discussions, the country had appeared to grind itself into an inflationary impasse. Earlier efforts at stabilizing prices by orthodox measures, such as those advocated by the Sachs-Klein Mission (yet another intervention of "foreign experts" to shake up a local logjam), did little to appease anyone. Clotario Blest, the legendary trade union leader arrested for striking against President Ibañez's economic policies, told Hirschman that a 10 to 15 percent rate of inflation "is a good thing." Others, like the Chicago School envoy, Arnold Harberger, bewailed it as the source of all evil. Chile's inflation crisis at first blush was a diorama of futility. The intractable debate between monetarists and so-called structuralists seemed to reinforce the argument that only an overhaul of the "system" would bring price stability. But Hirschman's tale of frustration and social agitation yielded a very different lesson: the very intractability of inflation led leaders to spotlight problems in the system that might bring on a revolution. When he sat down to talk with the leader of the new Christian Democratic Party, Eduardo Frei, he got an earful about run-amok prices, food shortages, poor infrastructure, and poverty. How inflation caused them all was not quite clear—but Hirschman was struck by the self-evidence with which Frei bundled the problems and argued that inflation made tackling them all the more pressing. The ensuing conversation with the leader of the left-wing coalition FRAP, a mild mannered doctor named Salvador Allende, pointed to a basic cause: the abuse by foreign copper companies and the drainage of wealth from the country. To Allende, the inflationary symptom demanded deep solutions, such as taking on exploitative companies. They may have been rivals, but Frei and Allende shared the tendency to treat inflation as a scourge remediable only with social reforms. By 1963, this was an urgent consensus that set the stage for a dramatic decade.[42]

Throughout the stories, the constructive role of tensions and imbalances and the learning by doing and observing became key elements of the histories of reform and policy making. To American intellectuals and policy makers, *Journeys* illustrated the complexity, and occasional violence and high risk, associated with reform. It was hardly the smooth orderly process that could be managed with expertise and foreign aid. It required shaky alliances and "wily and complex tactics" by a breed of locals who must be at the very least understood if their audacity were to work. Then there was a second audience—Latin American intellectuals and policy makers who treated reform as futile. Some saw reform as petty bourgeois sop; others felt that the obstacles and hurdles were so great that reform would stop in its tracks. For both breeds of skeptics, nothing could change unless everything changed. "In a way," Hirschman mused, "the book provides source material for a 'reformmonger's manual' which is badly needed to offer some competition to the many works on the techniques of revolution, coups d'états and guerrilla warfare." He imagined *Journeys*, not just jokingly, as a counterpoint to Che Guevara's best-selling manual, *Guerrilla Warfare*. His purpose was "to break down the rigid dichotomy between reform and revolution and to show that the changes that occur in the real world are often something wholly outside these two stereotypes." Americans had to accept that revolutionary forces were not a threat to *progress*; Latin Americans had to see that revolution was not the only way to realize it.[43]

Journeys toward Progress caught the pulse of a moment, which made it an immediate sensation. It soon became the reference for an alternative way forward uncharted by extremes, avoiding the national security frame of reform as the lesser evil to revolution while at the same time highlighting the role of the engagé social scientist. Some of Hirschman's fans found this less-than-critical identification a bit much. Lincoln Gordon was one. As the ambassador, he was watching Brazil veer toward a more radical brand of populism, and he was inclined to blame domestic policies and propensities as the source of all the region's woes. While he applauded the long analytical chapter on problem solving and policy making and looked forward to reading the studies on Chile and Colombia while on the plane back to Washington, he found the study of the Northeast "provocative." But, he added diplomatically, "I remain unpersuaded by your intellectual love affair with Celso Furtado and your conviction that SUDENE really is something different from the other experiences," adding prophetically, "I hope you will consider setting some time aside ten years hence to write a retrospective piece of self-criticism." This was September 1963, and little did Gordon or Hirschman know just how tragically events would unfold for Brazil—and for Chile—and how difficult it would be for Hirschman to look back on a decade of reformmongering. Developments in Brazil, warned Gordon, "may well go worse before they go better."[44]

Journeys was also personally enlightening. With the surge of reform, from agrarian change in Latin America to civil rights at home, came its nemesis. The perception of the need for reform also spotlighted resistance to it. For some this meant that reform was doomed, and so another way forward had to be opened. To others, the cost of overcoming hurdles could be so destabilizing that it threatened the whole social order. Accustomed to hearing pessimism in Latin America, Hirschman wrote *Journeys* as a way to counter it. But increasingly, he encountered naysayers close by, at Columbia. One was his friend, Samuel Huntington, who grew alarmed that modernization and reform were going to throw the Third World into turmoil, and Huntington's views, as he moved rightward, began to strain the friendship. But there were also younger radicals, like Immanuel Wallerstein, an emerging expert on African decolonization, who worried that without radical change, the development would fizzle. Hirschman found himself at odds with Wallerstein's increasingly, if understandably, alarming view of the prospects for Africa in the world economy.

Hirschman felt the need to address futilists of all stripes head on. An invitation from François Perroux, of the Institut d'étude du développement économique et social and the Collège de France, invited him to speak to an international audience about "obstacles" to the development process. What came of this was a trilogy of essays that confronted the ways in which social scientists, starting with Wallerstein, perceived change and how these perceptions shaped the prospects for change. His lecture was called "Obstacles to Development: A Classification and a Quasi-Vanishing Act." When he stood before his Parisian audience, he had circled and emphasized the words "Vicious Circles" at the top of the first page of his script. Futilists were circular thinkers: reform was impossible because the conditions were not there to support them, while the absence of the conditions is what made reform so vital. This was unhelpful thinking. Hirschman was not so naïve as to think that all hurdles were surmountable. But there were "obstacles" that could be turned into advantages, like the extended family among cacao farmers in Ghana or the surviving skilled European artisans. To see the difference depended on the attitudes of the observer and meant ceasing to treat the past as nothing but a giant source of constraints. Backwardness was not destiny; there was plenty of room for alternatives as long as one did not feel obliged to wait for the "necessary conditions" or seize the "perfect solution." "Obstacles to Development" was the first installation growing out of *Journeys* and was aimed directly at social scientists, to register alarm about the ways in which they contributed to the problems they sought to explain. In due course, he would grow increasingly impatient with this new patient. But for the time being, he seized the opportunity to cite the Marquise de Merteuil in Laclos' *Les Liaisons Dangereuses*, "Believe me, one rarely acquires the qualities he can do without."[45]

CHAPTER 13

Sing the Epic

To believe in progress does not mean
believing that any progress has yet been
made. That would be no real act of belief.

FRANZ KAFKA

A flurry of books and breaking into the acme of the American academy did not leave Hirschman with an urge to settle down. If anything, he was more restless than ever. *Journeys toward Progress* was barely
out in early 1963 when he issued feelers to the Ford Foundation offering
his consulting services. Why? "The cause is good," F. Champion Ward
wrote apologetically, "but, frankly, we don't quite see why what is essentially a consultant relationship need be independently financed when the
results are to be primarily of value to the committee."[1]

Two things were going on. First, Hirschman's itchiness was in part the
result of his unease with Columbia. One senses that he felt more at home
in Colombia. The university was a congenial place to work; Hirschman
had a few colleagues with similar interests in the Third World, such as
Samuel Huntington, with whom he overlapped until Huntington returned to Harvard (where he had been denied tenure in 1959) in 1963.
He, too, harbored reservations about the Third World modernization
euphoria—though his would veer into a more pessimistic track. While
Hirschman celebrated the increasing disorder of modernization as a virtue, to Huntington it was a menace. But on one principle they agreed:
anyone who thought that the transformations in the Third World could
be planned, balanced, orderly affairs arranged by elites and their tech-
nocrats were deluding themselves—and everyone else. But otherwise,

Hirschman never connected to Columbia, neither its colleagues nor students. A kind of detachment loomed like a nimbus over "Professor" Hirschman, who preferred field work in Latin America and writerly seclusion on Central Park West.

In mid-October 1963, Hirschman's phone rang. It was Shura Gerschenkron. They were not telephone habitués, but over the years Albert and Shura had remained in touch and shared each other's work. A fresh copy of *Journeys* sat on Gerschenkron's office desk. It was this, no doubt, that prompted the call—and an invitation for Hirschman to come to Cambridge to meet with a class on development taught by Arthur Smithies in early December 1963. Behind the scenes, Shura, at the peak of his influence, had been angling for the chair of the economics department, Carl Kaysen, to have Hirschman as a colleague. He was taking advantage of a movement (short-lived, as it turned out) to create more cross-appointments. Hirschman was being considered as the first professor of political economy appointed through the Graduate School of Public Administration (soon to be renamed the John F. Kennedy School of Government) and jointly named to the Department of Economics as a specialist in Latin America. This was a time in which the discipline still made room for regional or national expertise and area studies was on the rise. Smithies and Edward Mason covered development economics, but neither had extensive experience in the field. Between Harvard's anxiety to bulk up on the hot development field and catch up in Latin American studies, it did what it does as a reflex: Harvard went faculty hunting. Hirschman and Samuel Huntington were their two big catches that season; Columbia lost them both.

In those days, the business of being a candidate was a more informal, gentlemanly, and inevitably arbitrary and personalized affair. And fast. It was also one in which Hirschman would easily shine. There was a luncheon organized by the dean, Donald Price, and a lecture followed by dinner with Carl Kaysen, Smithies, Mason, and Shura Gerschenkron. The "deliberation," such as it was, was quick and uncontroversial. Kenneth Galbraith quickly jumped on the bandwagon—and within a week Price was in conversation with Hirschman about the terms of an appointment. Within a few months the offer letter had come through, and the recruitment, Kaysen recalled, was left to Shura. It was not a tough sell. Hirschman regarded himself as "a hyphen between economists and political scientists." He fancied this self-image. Beside, it felt like a step up: Harvard had more prestige, better economists, and more "interesting activities for me." The salary of $20,000 was standard for the day. But he knew he would miss the theater, art galleries, and the foreign films on New York's screens. Still, he scarcely blinked; a week after getting the offer, he accepted; retention efforts by Columbia's Dean Andrew Cordier and Provost Jacques Barzun were pointless. Hirschman was gone.[2]

But there was a second, more important source of his rootlessness. The whole prospect of going to Harvard was nothing compared to the distress of events in Brazil. The coup of April 1, 1964, brought down the civilian government of João Goulart—an exemplar reformmonger—and installed some tight-fisted generals who would augur brutal dictatorships. The northeastern SUDENE reform was rubbished. Goulart's minister of planning, Hirschman's friend Celso Furtado, fled into exile, first to Yale briefly, then to Paris. Hirschman had a premonition that the coup was not just a passing event; a blight was now cast on radical reform. "I have been very depressed these weeks about events in Brazil," he told Ursula, "which reveal the follies and crimes of the Right. Even in underdeveloped states they are at the height of those in industrial countries. It is such a shame because there were so many possibilities that Brazil might find its own and attractive way [*une voie propre et attrayente*], and this has all been ruined, at least for the moment."[3] The Brazilian coup was a sign of things to come. The hope for civilian reform was beginning to wane and seemed to be eclipsed by populist revolution and its antonym, junta. Vietnamese villages were becoming war zones, Brazilian officers patrolled the streets of São Paulo, and a year later President Johnson dispatched over 40,000 Marines to the Dominican Republic to thwart a "second Cuba," while Indonesian generals wiped out the ranks of the country's Communists. The seams of development and reform were starting to show. In places they came apart. Scarcely a few years into a Development Decade launched with such fanfare by the United Nations in 1961, it was coming apart. Suddenly, the rapturous tone of *Journeys* seemed out of key.

It was this concern that motivated the missive to the Ford Foundation. Ford was not the only pool into which he was casting. Hirschman wrote to Burke Knapp, the World Bank's vice president, in March of 1963. He promised Burke a copy of the book—my "highly experimental venture"—when it appeared. But he confessed to now being overwhelmed by the feeling of "what it must be like to retire." There is something vaguely manic in his reaction: instead of savoring accomplishment, "in the ensuing discomfort, my thoughts have naturally come to be occupied with the question: What next? And this is the subject of this letter." He had two years' leave forthcoming. He wanted to combine these into a twenty-seven-month run to fathom some of the troubles behind development. From thinking about how *policies* were made, he turned to their *projects* and their effects. Having thought about models and strategies, he wanted to get close to the ground, to study the giant dams, heroic roads, and massive irrigation plans that were earning pharaonic reputations. The specific question was, how did development projects perform?[4]

Some in the World Bank, an institution at the front lines of the growing criticism, had similar concerns. Knapp replied immediately—and invited Hirschman to Washington for further talks. Eager "to learn a great deal," Knapp asked Hirschman to outline the issues and criteria for evaluating development in action. A proposal was on the desk of Hirschman's old friend, Sandy Stevenson, now head of the Economics Department of the bank. From Sandy's perspective, the organization's mission creep from European reconstruction to Third World development revealed no overall assessment of, or method of assessing, the value of its work. Knapp and Stevenson had allies in the form of Richard Demuth, the director of development services, who would eventually assume stewardship of Hirschman's enterprise. After the summer's travels, Hirschman returned to Washington to hammer out the details of a scheme in Demuth's office. All of this was unfolding as Hirschman was considering the move to Harvard.

Without these self-critical bank insiders, Hirschman's ideas would have gone nowhere. Stevenson and Demuth insisted that something had to be done to remedy the situation—beginning with an external, objective evaluator. They had to override the influential chief economist of the Projects Division, Robert Sadove, a firm believer of "change from within," who had earlier turned the World Bank away from Program Loans (a staple of European financing that conferred more autonomy to borrowers) to Project Loans. Sadove wanted busybodies at a distance. Stevenson, who saw right through the circularity, advocated an outsider and thrust forth his old friend, now brimming with unimpeachable credentials.

From the start, Hirschman's project brought out some seething resentment from some insiders. This was a delicate proposal; it was rare for the bank—by no means unique in this reluctance—to throw open its files for an observer to rifle through them. His backers were a tight-knit group whose influence bespeaks the relatively simple, if cliquish, way in which business was done in Washington in those days. Rather than get gummed up in an internal stalemate, Stevenson stepped outside the bank and consulted an old friend of his from the Marshall Plan days, Robert E. Asher, who was then working at the Brookings Institution overseeing the research on international trade and finance. Maybe Hirschman could do the work under the auspices of the Brookings. Asher liked the idea of Hirschman's autonomy, his independence of mind, and what this would bring to his group. Hirschman's stature, as Asher told the Brookings president, Robert D. Calkins, was sterling; perhaps it would help if Calkins had a word with the chairman of the Board of Trustees of the Brookings Institution, Eugene Black, who had recently stepped down as president of the World Bank and who would not have forgotten his sympathy for Hirschman from the early days in Colombia. Whether backroom conversations or a few phone calls helped grease the wheels, we do not know. By the end of 1963, Sandy called Albert to tell him the project was on.[5]

The Brookings' Foreign Policy Studies Division cobbled together a proposal for the Ford Foundation and Carnegie Corporation to examine a set of World Bank projects with three aims: explore improvements in the selection and evaluation of development projects, illuminate the problems and potential of foreign aid, "and contribute to our knowledge of the process of development." The candidate was touted as one of the world's foremost thinkers of development; Hirschman's experience examining projects was ideal for directing this two-year undertaking. The criteria for the projects under review included those running for at least five years and focusing on the introduction of a *new* activity or facility into a particular region (a highway, a rail line, a hydroelectric dam, or an industrial plant) stretching across Asia, Africa, Latin America, and Europe. Stevenson, meanwhile, lined up bank staff to prepare the case files, with his eye trained especially on the South Asian precedents. As far as he was concerned, the Indian and Pakistani projects were the bank's "problem children."[6] By June, Carnegie stepped forward with $31,340 to foot the bills. By July, Hirschman's travel plans were set, by which time Hirschman was bound to Harvard, where he negotiated a first year's sabbatical to conduct the travel and research for what would eventually become *Development Projects Observed*, published in October 1967. His itinerary and projects would eventually include:

El Salvador—electric power plant
Ecuador—roads in Guayas Province
Peru—San Lorenzo irrigation project
Uruguay—pasture improvement for livestock
Ethiopia—telecommunications and roads
Uganda—electric power transmission and distribution
Sudan—irrigation project
Nigeria—railway modernization and Bornu extension line
India—Damodar Valley Corporation and selected industries in
     Mysore
West Pakistan—Karnaphuli Paper Mills
East Pakistan—Karnaphuli Paper Mills
Thailand—Chao Phya irrigation project
Italy—irrigation in South

The choice raised some eyebrows. About the only coherence was that these were projects. Some found the scale, "the widely scattered" selection "around the fields of activity," potentially superficial. Why not, asked Robert F. Skillings of the International Finance Corporation, a division of the World Bank, adopt "a more concentrated approach," like looking at all projects within a given sector (roads, energy, or irrigation, for instance)? Not only would this be more in-depth, it might avoid "the problems of random factors which unavoidably enter into a very small sample," and it might yield "conclusions of more general applications." Skillings was not alone in worrying about the practicability of any lessons.[7] These questions would subsequently plague Hirschman's findings.

The Hirschmans kept their base in Central Park West. Sarah would serve as an "uncompensated assistant" to the project—but all of her expenses were covered. Once Columbia's classes were over, Albert and Sarah rushed "to work furiously in the files of the World Bank so that we are completely informed about the projects we are going to visit."[8] They partitioned the field work into three phases: the first trip would take them back to Latin America (July–October), the second to India, Pakistan, and Thailand (November–March), with a pause in Washington, and the third to Africa, ending with an Italian leg in the summer. Meanwhile, the girls, now undergraduates at Barnard, would take care of the apartment—which left a few friends wondering if Albert and Sarah were not just a bit too trusting.

Their bags bulging with Pan Am and BOAC plane tickets and folders of complex itineraries plotted out by a small army of staff, Albert and Sarah set off as economic explorers. There was no Kodak, but they had plenty of spiral-bound notebooks for diaries and for most places a guide provided by the bank. It helped that the first leg was the familiar terrain of Latin America, where the field work for *Journeys* had tutored them in an observational method. Beyond, it was all new. Of all the countries they visited, India and Nigeria left the strongest impressions. Travel by rail and Land Rover got them to remote, difficult-to-reach, hot parts, face-to-face with the ways in which big projects in poor countries were churning up social conflict.

There is no cache of postcards to retrace the Hirschman peregrinations, just an abundance of field notes, catalogues of words conveying a strong impression of basic confusion. Hirschman's witnesses, mainly managers—agronomists and engineers mostly, the kind of men who made projects work—spoke of the frustrations and complications in-

Lisa, Katia, Sara, and Albert at Katia's graduation
from Barnard, June 1966.

variably spawned by their works. Their running theme—told in the vocabulary of water that didn't flow the way it was supposed to, regions
that felt relatively deprived, and industries with growing stockpiles—
was that their projects had "failed." How could these poster children of
technocratic change from above, curated by ambitious and empowered
engineers, seem to be turning on their makers? Before long, it was the
awesome hubris and downright naïveté that became the nub of the public criticism. None of the projects generated more unease—great hopes
coupled with prodigious complaints—than the colossal Damodar Valley Corporation in India. Based heavily on the New Deal flagship, the
Tennessee Valley Authority, the DVC had become an umbrella for the
transformation of West Bengal and Bihar. Indeed, it was a symbol of independent India: the DVC and India were born almost simultaneously.
With its high expectations came heightened problems. At first, the plan
was to control flooding. Then irrigation was added to the purpose, then

hydroelectric power, and finally it was expanded to promote inland navigation. The DVC was the archetype of planned, top-down development, which ran afoul because some peasants did not get the water they were promised, the energy went to some customers and not others, and some regions griped that they were cut out. And everywhere, implementation was more complex and costly than had been envisioned. The atmosphere in India crackled with uncertainty. Jawaharlal Nehru, the DVC's fountainhead and political emblem of postcolonial India, had died in May 1964. All of the latent schisms—regional, class, and caste—came to the fore. What had started out as an effort to spare people flooding and create a water source for farmers had become an emblem of all that was wrong with the economy. Meanwhile, India was embroiled in conflicts with its neighbors China and Pakistan. The consensus was growing that India's planned development was a "failure."[9]

Hirschman was no fan of big plans, but neither was he about to go to the other extreme. Never an admirer of strong convictions, especially when they were baseless or overdrawn, he was even more skeptical of the view that development failed if it did not go as planned. As the needle swung from the euphoria of the 1950s to disenchantment by the mid-1960s, Hirschman's temper moved the opposite way. His notes reveal him questioning prejudgements even as he was making observations and recording them. Stepping back from all the noise surrounding the arguments about India's future, what impressed him was how the DVC *was* in a narrow sense a failure. This was how many of the engineers and financiers were starting to regard the overwhelming venture of dams, sluices, canals, and hydroelectric plants. Their most self-incriminating conclusion was of having underestimated the demand for the project's fruits. But in a more general sense, he observed successes—achievements that escaped the technicians' grids. All around the dam he saw activities popping up. What is more, there was evidence of regional rivals undermining the hegemony of the DVC—smaller irrigators and competing power sources creating "a second growing point in Eastern India in addition to Calcutta." He wondered to himself: Maybe a narrow failure was *necessary* for a project to have wider effectiveness? Maybe projects "fail" because

Albert and Sarah in India, 1964.

they induce competitors and imitators? They themselves might not be very efficient, but they stimulated efficiency and entrepreneurship among others. Having created a surge in demand, the project was a constructive "pressure point" sparking more activity. This was exactly the kind of destabilizer he extolled in *Strategy*. The DVC had mobilized people—but not in the ways planners foresaw, never mind wanted. The story of the DVC did not unfold as had been scripted in advance, as the heroic summoner of the nation around one integrative project. Rather, it was the source of turmoil. It was bound to "step on so many toes to get its job done . . . that it inevitably makes enemies," Hirschman noted. Here was a familiar theme: resistances propel further pressure to adapt and change.[10]

Seeing this required an eye for what was unexpected, not what was expected. We also see another facet of Hirschman at work while he was observing. He tended to be more hopeful than his witnesses, looking for evidence of things that did work despite the frustration—and when he could find it, *because* of the frustration. Identifying silver linings was becoming an occupational habit; they sometimes got harder to find when the travel got more difficult and social conflict heightened. His optimism met its match in Nigeria, where travel was bone-jarring. Not only did the Land Rover rides deep into countryside to interview palm oil farmers and mill managers leave Albert and Sarah feeling gelatinous, but the country was seething with discontent. The country scarcely five years out from under British rule, its veneer of postcolonial nationalism had worn off. Cleaved between east and west, north and south, between Igbo, Yoruba, and Hausa-Fulani, one response was to pull the country together with modern transportation systems. One of these big ventures was the World Bank–funded Bornu Railway Extension, which sent a long spur line running north and east toward Lake Chad, pulling the hinterlands closer to the coast and opening up districts to commercial farming. Nation building and capitalist development could move hand in hand. This was the theory. In practice, however, the Bornu Extension drove deep into the seedbed of a conflict that would culminate in a secessionist movement in the southeast and the invasion of the breakaway Republic of Biafra by Nigerian Federal troops in July of 1967, catalyzing three years of horrible civil war between Hausas and Igbos.

Africa per se was not the worry, though the disenchantment with development in the continent was starting to spread. Before arriving in Nigeria, the Hirschmans had been in Ethiopia; Albert was "impressed by the 'enormous progress' accomplished in recent years."[11] He hoped to find the same in Nigeria. What he saw caused him to pause, but not for too long. Quickly, he looked for some organizing principle for the difference in this specific case. Maybe there were differences in the "personalities" of projects. Ethiopian irrigation was flexible. Railways, by contrast, only became economical the longer the haulage and the bulkier the cargo; with high fixed costs, they were rigid and prone to centralization, and thus vulnerable to charges of extortion. To compound matters, a direct competitor to the rail line appeared on the scene: the trucker. More nimble, informal, and bargain friendly, local truckers cut into the overland shipping business, especially getting groundnuts to the railhead. So, farmers hired truckers. Pretty soon they figured out ways to hire the truckers to go all the way to port with their harvest. This left the Bornu Extension, having expanded the groundnut frontier and induced the Mandrides Oil Mill at Maiduguri to process oil cakes, less welcome. The rail operators had to jack up rates to make up for losses, leading to a spiral of grievances.

Hirschman resisted bleak conclusions, perhaps too obstinately. "Instead of asking: what benefits [has] this project yielded," mused Hirschman, "it would almost be more pertinent to ask: how many conflicts has it brought in its wake? How many crises has it occasioned and passed through? And these conflicts and crises should appear *both* on the benefit and the cost side, or sometimes on one—sometimes on the other, depending on the outcome (which cannot be known with precision for a long time, if ever.)." Either Hirschman's optimism blinded him to the simmering tensions, or the evidence of this tension was still muted. The latter is not plausible; Hirschman's notes are filled with the grouchy testimonies of his witnesses. It is more likely that his wish for surprising, positive effects overwhelmed what he saw and heard. Either way, he failed to predict that this was one project that would have disastrous consequences and contribute to the devastating civil war in Nigeria not long after Hirschman toured the region; the war of words soon escalated into an all-out civil war whose carnage took up to three million lives. When it did, Hirschman was shocked—and not a bit humbled. His personal failure to see the disasters of development and evaluate them in his World Bank study was the immediate reason for writing, several years later, his most famous book, *Exit, Voice, and Loyalty* (published in 1970).[12]

As he travelled, Hirschman filled his notebooks with petites idées, insights he accumulated along the way: observe, infer, compare, generalize, and then check these generalizations against new observations—and wherever possible, aphorize. There was a thread in all this: tracing the hidden, unexpected, and sometimes surprisingly positive effects of projects often missed in cost-benefit calculus. Irrigation projects in India and Italy, he noted, induced farmers to install tube wells that carried water far away from its source. By contrast, this was not what he saw in electrical power—with which there were strong incentives to deliver as much energy as possible as far away as possible from the source and stop drainage en route. Hirschman uncovered two kinds of consequences that hardly figured in the project manifestos. The result was a "difficulty appraising the benefits: in case of some kinds of projects, benefits are not easily computed, quantified and hence they take the back seat even though they may be most productive [sic]." Typical of his increasingly recursive style, he found a new variation: "Ignorance and error affecting both income and outgo: You step into something misjudging the *environment* and the trouble it holds in store for you, and you change this environment once you find out about it." And so on.[13] Consider another, typed upon his return to New York:

> Irrigation. As long as nature is in charge of mishaps like floods they are acts of God; when men undertake to remedy *one* of nature's ills, this remedy is expected to cure *all* ills.[14]

There was a general thrust to this mode of following the twisting passage from cause to effects—some intended, some not. Running through his idées are the features and behaviors of projects that lend themselves to creating and reinforcing institutions; his eye was trained on a way of seeing development that inverted the expected story. The custom was (and remains) to think of institutions as the precursors of projects; good institutions promote healthy ventures, bad ones produce disasters. As one might imagine this often led to fatalistic thinking about the Third World, where institutions seemed so irrevocably bad. As we will see shortly, Hirschman considered this kind of fundamentalist storytelling at best unhelpful. For the time being, he concentrated on following the clues to his inverted narrative, one in which projects might shape institutions. And some projects were better at this than others. *This* was the secret key and the powerful underlying argument of his big report for the World Bank.

Here's an example of the story he spun. Irrigation projects, for instance, struck him as institution promoters, in large part because people had to organize systems of water distribution, extension services, and maintenance of the sluices and pipes. A good ditch and some pipes could make "a veritable school for bargaining, adjustment, etc." By contrast, highways yielded minimal institutional dividends. There were few side effects and few fertile tensions. The result: some projects spawned conflicts and tensions that people could learn from. "Are there some projects that permit development of political skills of bargaining, agreement—engineering versus others that merely exacerbate or stimulate or make apparent tensions and conflicts?" This is why, for all the grief generated by the DVC, he resisted the "failure" syndrome. One formulation he invented for himself was the idea of "development through entrapment," which he scribbled down while touring the ICICI factories in India. Then he added: "Dissonance: You step into something that is not congruent with your *personality* and change your personality as a result."[15]

All the flying around and frantic site visits eventually began to take their toll. Hirschman was careful to arrange pauses between interconti-

Albert and Sarah taking a break in East Pakistan, 1964.

nental excursions to rest and gather his thoughts. But midway through the second leg, exhaustion crept in. Part of the problem was the physical displacement, the relentless hotel check-ins, money changing, and visas. The travel bug eventually wore off. While Albert and Sarah found India an astonishing country, it was there that they began to count their days on the road. He confessed to his sister that "I am starting to get a little tired of traveling, or before continuing traveling I'd like to be able to assess at least a bit whether anything useful at all will come of this—but no, I have to take in more and more facts." He consoled himself with the fantasy that they might return from India via Rome. There was a month left on the leg, but "we should be able to depart from here on 1 March and the connections Bombay-Rome are excellent."[16]

But part of the problem was also the accumulation of information across dispersed cases. He struggled to make sense of his observations, wrestling constantly with a useful way to classify. Should they be ranged by revenue production (power generators make money; highways don't), or quantifiable benefits versus nonquantifiable benefits (the benefits of railways can be measured with numbers, the impact of telecom projects are harder to)? By the spring of 1965, he was having difficulty keeping his endeavor clear. So many of the projects were idiosyncratic, and Hirschman was at pains to let peculiarities go in favor of some broad brush strokes. Lindblom had warned him of the perils of this kind of analytical narrative approach using increasing numbers of cases. Occasionally, he found ways to spin patterns out of details, their quirkiness and their ever-present surprises. Consider his observations of road crews in Ecuador: "There is one compulsion in road building and maintenance in the tropics: You have to get through before the rains come—this is a valuable organizing aid."[17]

Nonetheless, a pattern emerged, organized around the problem of how to measure trade-offs. There were several he considered: exchanging quality for quantity, sacrificing maintenance to new construction, and rigidity or malleability of the original plan in the course of construction. Roads, for instance, presented greater opportunities for flexibility and trade-offs whereas electrical power did not; either one got the power with a big dam and a complex grid, or one didn't get the power. It was typical of the way he was laboring through his information that the detail fed the abstraction, and the abstraction would survive only as long as it could help illuminate personalities of the detail.

As with *Journeys*, Hirschman wrote while he made his observations and plotted his insights. It is for this reason that he was able to write so quickly when he did finally plant himself in his study. By the time Hirschman was travelling in Africa, his notes began to take the form of lines that might appear in the narrative itself, and some of the off-the-cuff aperçus look like injunctions to himself about what to write when he sat down to compose the book. "Paraphrase Marx," he told himself while in Uganda. "Mankind only takes up those problems *it thinks* it can solve—and then, once bitten, engagé, solves them—or fails."[18] By the end of the summer in Africa, Hirschman set down to write up some interim observations for the bank's Economic Committee, composed of the heads of many of the main departments.

What came to the fore were the less perceptible, indirect or side effects of development financing. These were so varied and embedded that they often escaped the notice of analysts. They were also often too slippery to fit the uniform criteria for assessment. So his first crack at a report emphasized the role of uncertainty. Some projects simply presented more uncertainty about the range and depths of its outcomes. These shaped their "behavioral characteristics" or "personality profiles." Some, like electric power, were easier to blueprint and envision effects; others, like irrigation, were far less so. With more water available, what kind of crops would farmers choose to switch to? It was hard to say. This is important because a lot of the frustration with development—delays, detours, and doubtful payoff—stemmed from advocates having "an understandable tendency to clothe the prospects of all projects in an air of pat certainty." Here was the big message for the bankers: for an enterprise such as the World Bank, dedicated to putting money into projects that the private sector otherwise would not, there was a need not to "repress uncertainties" but to "acknowledge that some of the projects it finances are more certain and experimental than others." The trick was not to be perfect predictors, but rather to be better at "envisioning" projects beyond the penny-in-the-slot-machine of benefit-cost analysis. It was important to keep specific projects' behavioral profiles, and each project's "voyage of discovery," in mind when doing this kind of task.[19]

This was hardly a gritty analysis gilded with practical recommendations. There were no numbers or tables, no flowcharts or process-tracing timelines; indeed, the data were largely kept in the vaults of his massive files. Hirschman chose a more elliptical set of narratives organized around morality tales with a common theme: have your eye open for unintended, positive side effects of projects, especially the ones that induce behavioral and institutional changes in the milieu. Try to spot projects with these potentials. At their harshest, Hirschman's conclusions called for better monitoring. With a life of their own, long-term projects were the source of mysterious lessons that their planners could not always foresee, which meant watching them closely for the unexpected. So all investments should have "project evaluation" built into them. Compared to the intense heat that he would later train on the World Bank, Hirschman was polite if not solicitous. He could hardly be accused of bashing the bank.

Still, the World Bankers were ungenerous and churlish. Here was a chance for insiders to vent about the outsider's findings—thereby exposing the divide between operations (which is what they thought of themselves conducting) and evaluations (which is what Hirschman was doing—and called for more of). Hans Adler found "that his conclusions have only very limited applicability." He added that, to some extent, "we" have already improved appraisal techniques—and suggested, snidely, since Hirschman had relentlessly asked staff for their memos, that Hirschman have a look at "some of our recent reports." Adler scorned Hirschman's recommendation that the distributional effects of projects be considered in their design and evaluation. Public utilities, he announced without a trace of doubt, should "cover costs," nothing more. Let distribution be the domain of fiscal and monetary policy. Beside, if there were adverse effects on distribution, this might help because the poor don't save. The only point Adler could bring himself to agree with was the inclusion of social and political factors in the success of a project. But even here he could not resist a swipe: "This is easier said than done," adding later that "there is also the danger that we may allow for them too extensively." Mario Piccagli, whose bailiwick included two of the evaluated projects, started his reply by noting that the project in Uganda "was an unfortunate selection as it was hardly representative of anything" (this, despite the fact that Hirschman was in extensive consultation with World Bank staff in the selection process). His second point was even more revealing of the ferocity: "While Mr. Hirschman appeared to have had 20/20 hearing for echoes from the other side [the critics, one supposes, or perhaps the "natives"?], he did not appear to have heard anything at all about the Bank's viewpoints on these matters." Piccagli thought distributional concerns "twisted reasoning. . . . I have lost any hope that anybody who feels this way can be convinced by reasoning that it is not so: this appears to be sort of a religious tenet: either you believe it or do not." A.D. Spottswood, chief of the Public Utilities Division, referred acidly to Hirschman as "the Doctor."[20] Hirschman's reactions are unknown. Endearance was unlikely.

A nerve was struck. The bank's staff was not unaccomplished and had steered the organization into its new business, but they were a clubby bunch. There was a reason for Sandy Stevenson's worries: large sums of money were going into projects whose managers were unaccustomed to letting outsiders be anything more than beneficiaries or, when things went wrong, blameworthy. Hirschman ran headlong into the kind of confident groupthink against which future critics, including former supporters, would hurl their dissent. Had World Bankers learned the art of listening, some of the clashing might have been averted. For the time being, Hirschman was alone in calling for more scrutiny and open-mindedness. He read the griping and returned to Washington in mid-October to meet with Knapp, Andrew Kamarck (head of the Economics Department), and Hugh Ripman (chief of the Industry Division). He was the picture of poise. Writing to Kenneth Bohr of the Economics Department (whom Kamarck had suggested as a high-level liaison), he said he was looking forward to Bohr's role as his "general intellectual critic," especially on the more controversial points. After the hazing he'd received from the staff, "the experience with the above mentioned memo has already shown that one cannot be too careful about these things."[21]

By the scorching summer of 1966, Hirschman retreated to the comforts of his air-conditioned study on Central Park West, where he pored over his notes and the feedback (if it can be called that) on the provisional findings. By then, he knew what he wanted to say, and staying sufficiently above his project details, as with *Strategy*, he kept the prose general without being vague. He had long since given up formal mathematical measurements in favor of a lyrical style. But rather than tell stories about particular cases as he had in *Journeys*, this time he teased out general insights wrapped around an aphorism or an iconoclastic principle. "It turned out to be a strange product," he mused as he sent it to the Brookings, "all these project stories were poured together into a quite 'colorful' system—the method is quite Marxist since I derive the 'behavior' of the projects to a big part from their technology."[22] Technology, he had realized, was one of the autonomous forces conditioning the life history of the projects he'd studied; railways, dams, irrigation pipes, and roads conditioned activity and performance. This nascent interest in the role of technology in development experience he filed away for future reference.

It was the paradoxical features of economic change that he wanted to reveal, which led to the book's most famous metaphor. He began with the premise, confirmed over and over in his managerial testimonies, that World Bankers would have nixed projects had they known in advance all the difficulties they would encounter. But they didn't, and many projects turned out to yield their share of benefits, many of which were not intended. To capture this dynamic, the first chapter coined a term, the Hiding Hand, to convey the elusive dynamics behind the process of "stumbling into achievement" that so fascinated him. Adapting Adam Smith, whose Invisible Hand was a metaphor contrived to represent the mysterious, behind-the-scenes working of the marketplace, Hirschman wanted to draw attention to agentic aspects of the hand's workings. This was especially clear in Third World development, where humans were actively intervening in the course of events in the name of effecting change and promoting development. Hirschman happened upon the idea in Thailand, where he had gone to look at a big irrigation project. After stomping about the fields and listening to his witnesses, it became clear that advocates of the project had overstated its benefits and understated its costs. They simply found it too hard to resist claiming wonders such as being able to "make the desert bloom." So, to promote the venture, they low-balled the expenses; "undercosting" could take the place of "overselling."[23] Whereas the Invisible Hand was casually deceptive, the Hiding Hand was actively so—and stimulated people into action. While a project manager might wind up with ulcers because someone's original calculus was wrong, there were all kinds of benefits, public and private, many of which escaped the trained eye of the cost-benefit calculator because they balanced costs only against planned, expected, rewards. This kind of gaming induced people to do things they otherwise wouldn't. To the developer, the point was not to try to restrain this kind of operation but rather to be open to its effects. What he did not do was signal its perils.[24]

The other big effort of the work was to draw attention to development projects' "traits," many of which were inherent in their techniques. Did they require skills, ease social conflict, or aggravate regional differences? A project capable of changing the constraints surrounding it could be a "trait-maker." If not, they were "trait-takers." Hirschman had been scratching his head over how best to characterize the ways in which some projects induced changes in behavior and institutions while others did not. Price theory gave him the cue, where the distinction between price-taking and price-making, between competitive and collusive conditions, helped explain how buyers and sellers behaved. Transplanted to projects, trait-taking applied to situations where a project fit into a cultural and institutional setting and molded to it; trait-making changed the setting and more actively changed the institutional landscape. The message to developers was to consider these forces, especially in evaluating a project's trait-making potential. Unfortunately, here, too, he tended to presume that trait-making was positive. In Nigeria, however, the truck was a taker and fit better into the complex interethnic milieu and regional rivalries. The train, by contrast, more actively changed its milieu. As he would later see, trait-making in this kind of context was hazardous.

Combined, these observations made the pitch for the "centrality of side effects." This was an amplified earlier recommendation to look out for unexpected rewards from projects. But the gist was, more or less, the same: widen the lens when evaluating projects and look out for those unplanned and hard-to-quantify dividends.

This ran headlong into another orthodoxy—one which Hirschman had in his sights. While the quest for scientific determinants for policy making (like the Planning, Programming, and Budgeting System, which Robert McNamara and the "Whiz Kids" had brought so confidently to Washington) was beginning to take a beating as the Vietnam War escalated, it was still the rage among developers. Hirschman warned, prophetically, that overconfidence in these techniques spawned blind spots to the side effects of big projects. Either projects were condemned to fall short of inflated expectations or failed to appreciate what they did accomplish even if they were not planned. When W. Arthur Lewis, one of Hirschman's alter egos in the debate over balanced versus unbalanced growth, published *Development Planning: The Essentials of Economic Policy* in 1966, he laid out the fundaments of the " arithmetic of planning" and linear programming. Hirschman reviewed the book politely. But some of his words barely conceal his quarrel. He praised the "heroism" of the effort. But Lewis' treatment of "political realities" as intrusions that the economist must get used to was simply "unhelpful." Lewis occasionally got carried away "by his penchant for proclaiming sweeping, universal laws or for issuing precise rules-of-thumb." Hirschman was less restrained in his blast against input-output gurus in a short essay written for *Encounter* magazine eight months after the 1964 coup in Brazil, where he decried "the permanent orgy of misinterpretation and misunderstanding" that was now "heightened by a disparity in thinking about economic development." What applied to Washington also held for multilateral institutions like the World Bank.[25]

The book was not, however, practical. Sandy Stevenson was a bit disappointed. From the start, he wanted to change not just the way his colleagues were thinking but the way they were practicing. "I was sorry to hear that you will not be putting into the published edition a chapter which, I think, would have made it considerably more helpful to practitioners in the field of economic development. I am afraid that, somewhat selfishly, I am most concerned about whether or not they take into account any of the factors you emphasize." But the "gentle push" had no effect.[26]

The reception got worse as the document moved down the World Bank ranks. Part of the problem, as one member of the Economics Department suggested, was exaggerated expectations from one of the great figures in their field. "It is a bit like the frustrations you describe in your section on excess demand." "You may wish to consider," noted Herman G. van der Tak, "whether you could provide a more operational 'summary and conclusions,' possibly as a separate paper, which would provide practitioners with guidelines on the side effects that they should look out for." Kenneth Bohr found that creative responses "induced by difficulty in project execution may be of particular value for development is intriguing." But he also found it "a bit disconcerting. . . . The question that arises immediately is what sort of guidance can we get from it for making investment decisions?" This was fair enough; the bank had to choose between investments, and *Development Projects Observed* gave no guidance. While the book was fascinating, it was also "somewhat disappointing." He wanted more summary statements throughout the text and for the "general speculations on projects' behavior" to be brought down to earth with some advice. Hirschman did not think this was a bad idea. It was just not an interesting one. The task fell to a staffer who braved the manuscript to come up with "50 Points" as principles or tools for project appraisal. It was not an easy task—"I found it impossible," noted the junior economist anointed with the job, "to confine myself to the enumeration of operational questions from the point of view of project appraisal (as is usually understood in the Bank) because the picture of a precise construction of methodology for refining the tolls of 'cost-benefit' analysis . . . is simply missing."[27]

It was true: this book was short on text for the practitioners. There was a deeper reason for this. A how-to-do-it manual for project managers presumed the kind of ex ante certainty that Hirschman was calling into question to help people take risks and *do* things. In this sense, as he came to see it in the course of writing, *Development Projects Observed* was the

third volume of a trilogy. He was moving along a continuum from principles (*Strategy*) to policy (*Journeys*) to projects (*Development*), getting
closer to the ground all the while, even as he was expanding his range
from a single country (Colombia) to a region (Latin America) to a global
sweep. This ambition, hidden to readers, only became clear to himself in
the course of writing. This was precisely one of his arguments: projects
have to be open to follow leads and directions that could not have been
foreseen, and monitored to enhance the beneficial ones and thwart the
malign ones. Seen in this broader context, the trilogy had a latent but
"overriding common intent to celebrate, to 'sing' the epic adventure of
development—its challenge, drama, and grandeur." Of course, it was hard
for the practically minded reader to appreciate the lyrical qualities. As
he complained to Tom Schelling, he was tired of the comments that his
exercise was different from what was once "expected." This, after all, was
one of the goals of development itself. "This book is an exploration, an
experiment, and I need a critic someone who can understand that in the
first place, and *then* tell me where I may have gone wrong."[28]

Academic readers, especially those familiar with Hirschman's oeuvre
(now that he was beginning to accumulate a number of fans), *did* get the
bardic cues. Nathan Rosenberg praised it as "a long step in the direction
of developing a form of economic (and administrative) sociology which
is indispensable if we are ever, as a profession, really to make sense in
the advice we offer on matters of economic policy for poor countries."
He had no trouble seeing the ways in which "the level of analysis" was
going to rise, thanks to the book, and sent Hirschman a very detailed set
of commentaries with this objective in mind. While he was at it, he included an essay he had published on Mandeville and suggested that there
was much more in eighteenth-century political economy on the Hiding
Hand than he was crediting. Here a seed was planted that took almost a
decade to sprout. Walter Salant of Brookings found the essay provocative,
precisely because it was one-sided. Hirschman had really only tackled
examples where the difficulties and abilities to solve them were underestimated. What about the disaster cases where difficulties are underestimated and abilities to solve them overestimated? Salant was not suggest-

ing that Hirschman expand the range of comparative cases. Rather, he urged Hirschman to clarify that this *way* of thinking illuminated the variety of successes and failures that deviate from expectations. Hirschman agreed, but added that he wanted to emphasize unexpected successes to show how the Hiding Hand could check risk averters who would prefer not to act, a behavior, he noted, that stood in the way of letting some projects enjoy greater scope for development. In this sense, "ignorance of risk can offset usefully aversion to risk." Risk averters, by acknowledging the presence of the Hiding Hand, could be risk takers without being the cocky brainiacs who populated the world of foreign expertise.[29]

Pleased with his twist on Adam Smith, Hirschman was anxious to feature his verbal breakthrough to a broader audience. He inquired at *World Politics*, then turned to Irving Kristol, editor of the *Public Interest*, a magazine of crossover essays between political thinkers and high-end journalism slanted to progressive anti-utopianism. "True," replied Kristol, "it does step outside the limits we have hitherto imposed upon ourselves. On the other hand, it might be that it is time to revise these limits." Kristol suggested that Hirschman scrub away references to the World Bank and allusions to a "study," to emphasize that it was a critique of "the problem of economic development and foreign economic aid." Hirschman obliged, and Kristol hurriedly gave it his personal extensive editing and pushed it through the publishing mill. The essay was a hit. In rained plaudits from friends and admirers from around the country and abroad. Members of Washington's Institute for Public Administration read it for insights into how to think about innovation. David Riesman assigned it to his students at Harvard. Goran Ohlin wrote from the United Nations Conference on Trade and Development to say that he was applying the notion to industrial investment. Even within the World Bank, some could now see the point of the whole exercise. Andy Kamarck praised it: "You've helped in part to remove the unease that I have had in reflecting on the fact that if our modern project techniques had been used, much of the existing development in the world would never have been undertaken. It may be that with a further working out of the ideas that you explore in this chapter, we can avoid this future inhibitory role of economists."[30]

One effect of the *Public Interest* story was to widen the gap between Hirschman's aspirations and the bank staff's internal concerns. It also took the sting out of the book's reception. The charge that it was "insufficiently operational" (as one reviewer put it) was irritatingly sticky. Part of the problem was the understandable view that the work was commissioned by the bank or for the bank; that Brookings commissioned more policy-oriented work than academics also added to the impression. In effect, *Development Projects Observed* fell between the cracks. It got neglected as a work of scholarship because it was pegged as a manual, yet it was ignored by practitioners because it was too arch. Hans Singer found the style was "a little recherché" and complained that Hirschman had a tendency to "over-elaborate" in a book that he otherwise found one of the most original in the field. This annoyed Hirschman. When Singer likened Hirschman (in a fashion intended to flatter) to Arnold Toynbee and his theory of challenge-and-response mechanisms in the rise and fall of civilizations, Hirschman lashed out: "My thinking is at the antipodes of Toynbee's." Toynbee's main contribution, in any event, "was nonsense.... The minor idea, that a challenge must be neither too big nor too small, is not Toynbee's at all, but goes back at least as far as Aristotle who said that virtue lies often between the vices (cowardice-courage-foolhardiness). It is not legitimate to label anyone whose thinking can be supposed to contain some such Aristotelian proposition somewhere as a Toynbee disciple unless the proposition is specifically tied up with the challenge-and-response *Quatsch* ["rubbish," in German], which it certainly is not in my case."[31]

Then there was the voice from the other side. A retrospective history of the World Bank recorded *Development Projects Observed* as the most extensive evaluation of the bank's techniques of project appraisal. The authors—one of whom was Bob Asher, and not therefore unsympathetic to the project he had helped sire—concluded that the book "does not lend itself to use as a manual for the instruction of the would-be project appraisers, but the insights it provides could be neglected by such appraisers only at considerable cost." Written in 1973, just as a firestorm over World Bank activities was gathering strength, Asher didn't connect the book to the growing chorus of complaints about the bank's practices in part because, by then, *Development Projects Observed* was all but forgotten beyond a few staffers.[32] It was ironic that 1973 saw the smallish Programming and Budgeting Department finally upgraded into the fully fledged Operation Evaluation Division to monitor projects independently from those who managed them. The men behind this quiet but significant shift cited *Development Projects Observed* as the inciter; by then, many on the outside saw this as too little, too late.[33]

Needless to say, Hirschman was disappointed. He thought that he'd captured some of the mysteries of development, had sung their epic, and had made the case for the World Bank at a time in which doubts and disaffection were spreading fast. Some years later, a young political scientist, Theodore Moran, shared his outrage that the World Bank president, Robert McNamara, declared his intention to focus on income redistribution programs while pumping more money into authoritarian Brazil than into socialist and democratic Chile, whose loan requests were slammed shut. A jaded Hirschman replied that "I am somewhat less excited than you about the inner contradictions of the current World Bank position because I have been through it all before. It's really a replay (in comedy form, to prove Marx right) of all the naïveté and muddle of the Alliance for Progress." Having made constructive criticisms before, he was not convinced that speaking out to McNamara was going to have any effect. Any declaration in favor of reformism is less than pointless, "*especially*," added Hirschman, by now becoming more embittered, "when it is well known that he [McNamara] is tied up in all sorts of ways with the pro-status-quo forces in the to-be-reformed country and has a deadly terror of revolution."[34]

This was not the first time he had authored a work that missed its mark. Nor would it be the last; Hirschman's oeuvre would accumulate big hits and minor disappointments.

But there was not much time to worry. In a sense, by the time the book appeared in 1967, Hirschman was moving on, literally. The academic year 1964–65 had been the time "off" to do the field work. The following year, Sarah and Albert rented a place in Cambridge but were still based in New York, and Albert did most of his writing from Central Park West. They finally moved to Cambridge in fall of 1966 and bought a house, 45 Holden St., in the thick of a community of colleagues, "very close to the University," he told Ursula, "which is very nice—but very expensive." Moving away from New York also meant leaving behind the girls. Missing them terribly, Albert and Sarah accepted any pretext to take the train to New York. Meanwhile, in late 1966, Katia was engaged to marry a student of architecture from France, Alain Salomon. Sarah and Albert were concerned. While "he seems very nice, intelligent, and has talent for what he does," he had not yet finished his studies. Alain himself was no less worried. During Sarah and Albert's peregrinations, he frequently stayed at the Central Park West and was daunted by the art, the books, and the aura of the home of a "great man." One day he traveled up to Cambridge to meet his future parents-in-law; by the time he emerged from the subway station at Harvard Square to walk to the Hirschman's temporary abode in Quincy House, he was in a fit of anxiety, and by the time he rang to doorbell he could barely speak. To break the silence, Albert proposed a game of chess—after all you are a European, thought Hirschman. Albert's friendly gesture only worsened things for Alain, who played miserably and in misery. It did not take too much time for Albert to find a hook, a recent book by Christopher Alexander, *Notes on the Synthesis of Form*, which had recently laid out an agenda for revolutionizing architecture. Alain's eyes widened; an economist au courant with the ur-text for the rebellious, young designers! What he did not yet know was that Hirschman had antennae for clarion calls for the inventive imagination. Alain's intimidation soon passed—and a genuine fondness took its place.[35]

With *Development Projects Observed* off to the printers, Latin America summoned Hirschman back. Part of the motivation was to live up to his Harvard profile as a Latin American specialist: "Je suis accusé être specialiste." But he was also concerned to stay in touch with colleagues and to follow up on the fate of reform. If the World Bank was not a hospitable place for out-of-the-box thinking, Latin America was becoming more so, and Hirschman was anxious to be there at the creation. "I have decided that it is time for me to return to this Latin America," he explained to

Ursula. With his classes done, he hit the road once more—a month in Brazil, a week in Chile, a few days in Lima—principally to visit Lisa, who was on a Fulbright scholarship in the Peruvian capital—and then back to his old haunt, Colombia, for three more weeks, where Sarah was going to catch up with him. These were months dedicated to catching up after five years focused elsewhere. A great deal had happened—not least was the 1964 coup in Brazil, which had so disheartened him. Midway through the trip, he was already imagining a book of essays on the political economy of the region. "I am always very happy to be plunged again into these countries—where one lives more intensely, but perhaps it's not the ideal to pursue? But the truth is, it is difficult to resist."[36]

Chile drew his attention in particular. It was an increasingly solitary holdout for development through democratic reform. Whereas Brazilian and Argentine civilian governments had fallen under the heels of the military, Chileans embarked on audacious reform under the Christian Democratic president, Eduardo Frei, whom Hirschman had met during the research for *Journeys*. In addition, the Economic Commission for Latin America (CEPAL) was based in Santiago, as was the Latin American Faculty of Social Science (FLACSO), a UN-chartered graduate school. This turned Santiago into a Mecca for progressive social scientists from the region, such as Osvaldo Sunkel, Aníbal Pinto, and Fernando Henrique Cardoso—a future close colleague and eventual Brazilian president. Cardoso, recently exiled from Brazil, was laboring on an essay about employment patterns in Latin America, Europe, and the United States. At the time, there was growing concern about the deep, ingrained—and apparently insurmountable—obstacles to development in Latin America. A growing hypothesis was that Latin America was stuck in an economic cul-de-sac, unable to break out of trap of dependency on primary exports and weak industry. One manifestation of the trouble was the growing "marginalization" of the urban poor, who were pushed to the outskirts of the labor market and chances for upward mobility. None of this convinced Cardoso, who sought to disrupt the emerging consensus by pointing to more historical openings and multiple pathways. He passed a draft of his essay to Hirschman—who read it upon his return to the United States and wrote a quick note to the young Brazilian sociologist. "We have similar minds," he observed to a delighted Cardoso.[37]

Sunkel, Pinto, Cardoso, and others each in their own way caught Hirschman's eye because they were poised to challenge the view of ineluctable dependency of Latin American economies and unavoidable marginalization of the poor, what he coined as a "structuralist fallacy." Faced with an ailment, some people convince themselves that there is nothing fundamentally wrong and treat themselves with aspirin to deal with pain. Then there was the opposite—people who prescribe radical cures when only mild treatments will do; this was the mood in Latin America, where many social scientists were concluding that the older growth model of industrialization for the domestic market was exhausted, its populist political pillars of Perón and Vargas likewise spent. The preference for this kind of fundamental diagnosis was especially current in Latin America, where "crisis" was treated as endemic; hence the fallacy that all problems had some deep-rooted cause. It was so pervasive that even Hirschman found himself read as a "structuralist" champion. On a trip to Argentina, at the time under the thumb of a junta, a high-ranking official gleefully told Hirschman that "all we are doing is applying your ideas of unbalanced growth. In Argentina we cannot achieve all our political, social, and economic objectives at once; therefore we have decided to proceed by stages, as though in an unbalanced growth sequence." Hirschman blanched. Here was imbalance and disequilibrium in the service of breaking up what the generals considered entrenched hindrances to Argentine progress.[38]

If this came from the Right, it was the Latin American Left that was especially partial to the "unthinking structuralist reflex." Potential "nonfundamental" forces were dismissed as trivial or boring, even if addressing them increased and broadened the paths forward. A sign of this was the way that progressive intellectuals had swung from believing that industrialization was the miracle solution to underdevelopment, to the malefactor. The dream of car plants and steel mills teeming with modern workers went from being a source of enchantment to disenchantment. The setbacks and problems of the 1960s changed the tune; now the factory became the symbol of all that was off course, hopeless. Social scientists were beginning to conclude that industrialists were as feudal and patrimonial as the old landed classes they were once meant to dislodge; they were just one more member of the ageless, venal oligarchy.

This style of thinking struck Hirschman as doommongering. The only way out of the impasse, for the Right, was a forced capitalist demarche, such as Brazil under its generals. For the left, the same structuralist bent pointed to revolution as the only remedy. There was something déjà vu about this. As Hirschman wandered through the region, he scratched out some notes that would lead to an essay reviving the case for industrialization by giving it a different spin, an epic of its own—one that might salvage the cause for a road somewhere between the extremes. The essay, "The Political Economy of Import-Substituting Industrialization in Latin America," would become a classic in Latin American economic history. Far from being "wrong," the industrial adventure carried certain properties that obtain in countries launching "late-late" industry—in contrast to the portrait of the "late" cases of Japan, Russia, and Germany depicted by Shura Gerschenkron. Far too much was expected from the start; it was practically foregone that industry was condemned to disappoint. Late-latecomers built up light-consumer-goods manufacturing, in contrast to the muscular producer goods of the latecomers. Industrialization was therefore smoother, less disruptive—and yielded less instruction or a "convulsive élan" that dominated the Japanese and German eagerness to catch up to the leaders. But to give up now and throw in the towel, argued Hirschman, was naïve and self-defeating. One option, Hirschman suggested prophetically, was to start exporting manufactures, an insight he had probed long before the Asian miracle became a "model."[39]

The nub of Hirschman's analysis was to show that not all histories had to conform to a single normative account that identified industry with an industrial *revolution* in order to work out. In fact, the sooner Latin Americans could free themselves from finger-wagging histories of their failure as compared to first-world "success" stories, the better. They could free themselves of expecting industry to change the social order when instead all it did was pump out manufactures. The first ideas were unveiled to an audience of social scientists in Santiago to become a touchstone of an alternative economic history of the region, a history less driven by an obsession with what went wrong. The younger generation of social scientists like Cardoso took note; he would partner with another sociologist, Enzo Faletto, to author one of the classics of social sciences in the region called *Dependency and Development in Latin America*, which bore a perceptible Hirschmanian imprint of trying to reveal the multiple trajectories of the history of capitalism.[40]

Thinking about a different narrative of the history of development—how to sing the epic of what was accomplished—sharpened the focus on the idea that what was going on in peoples' minds was important in shaping possibilities. At the time, social scientists tended to dwell on the external limits to what people could do—their place in social structures and the institutions that governed them. No work exemplified this more than Barrington Moore's *Social Origins of Dictatorship and Democracy*, published in 1966. Moore and Hirschman were colleagues and had a cordial relationship, but Moore's book left Hirschman shaking his head. The quest for deep, antecedent determinants of large, encompassing outcomes, like dictatorship or democracy or capitalism, stripped history of politics and the possibilities for thinking about alternative, surprising tracks. When Dan Rustow was putting together a special issue of *Daedalus*, the journal of the American Academy of Arts and Sciences, he asked Albert to say something new about leadership. Hirschman agreed and used the occasion to cycle back to his concern that leaders in Latin America fettered themselves with their own perceptions. Prompted by a well-known anthology of essays edited by the Chilean sociologist Claudio Véliz called *The Obstacles to Change in Latin America*, Hirschman gently chided his Latin American colleagues for leaving themselves—as intellectuals—out of the inventory of fetters. They were as much obstacles as any deep structure. One evening he went to a dinner party in Santiago. Wishing to catch up with Véliz, who'd recently returned to Chile, Hirschman asked his hosts for Véliz's phone number. The host didn't have it and dismissed the telephone book as a list of numbers for people who had died or left the country. Everyone laughed and enjoyed the meal. The next morning, in his hotel, Hirschman spied the phone directory in his room. Curious, he looked up Véliz, dialed the number, and quickly found the voice of his friend at the other end of the line. The tale was an example of the ways in which Latin American intellectuals had a habit of overperceiving the ways in which things remained the same and tended to wave off changes as unoriginal or copied from someone else (preferring to fetishize the "original" version of the breakthrough). Indeed, in some cases intellectuals could not even see that innovations occurred in their own backyards because they presumed that these sorts of things only happened in "advanced" countries.

By shifting the debate about dependency from the familiar problems—with feudal elites, capital flight, and reliance on exports—to the mind, he was breaking new ground. In the 1960s, with the gathering consensus on the Left that change could only be effected through a violent, cathartic explosion, Hirschman was trying to sound a different key—already a shift from his celebration of the "reformmongers" to highlight a "revolution by stealth." More gradual, unspectacular, and not easy to see if one looks obsessively for the original, change was threatened with being throttled by intellectuals looking for—and increasingly advocating—the "loud" style. The perception of hindrances could thereby become its most pernicious obstacle: "The obstacles to the *perception* of change thus turn into an important obstacle to *change itself*," he observed.[41]

Latin Americans were not the only prisoners of paradigms and perceptions. There was little that was furtive about the thinking that governed social scientists and policy makers north of the border. One who was increasingly alarmed was Sandy Stevenson, now the deputy director of the Economics Department at the World Bank. He was increasingly concerned about the development decade's increasing noise about foreign "aid" as panacea or poison. Sandy wanted fresh thinking. Evidently unfazed by the disappointments of *Development Projects Observed*, he appealed to Albert. Albert in turn went to a young colleague at Harvard, Richard Bird, whom he had known when Richard was a graduate student at Columbia and who had recently returned from field work in Colombia. They were both interested in how economic transfers affected growth.

Sandy offered the opportunity to address the ways in which Americans thought about their charity to the Third World.[42] Aid was so fraught with generosity and resentment on all sides that it could not help but cause friction. Hirschman and Bird made a strong case for project lending over program support; program funding was bound to create friction between donor and recipient because it all too often implied that donors' "own judgment is superior to that of the recipient" and overrides local knowledge in areas where projects are more likely to have beneficial impacts. Pay attention to the grammar of aid relationships—and the inequities built into them—between givers and takers. When Albert and Richard were done with an initial draft, it went to Sandy in late autumn 1967. The World Bankers, some of them still twitching from the last Hirschman installment, were not exactly pleased by the suggestion that they might be no less blinded by their way of thinking than their Latin American counterparts. In fact, they were incensed. Sandy wrote to Albert just before New Year's, including several long memoranda from his staff. "As you will see," he warned, "they are somewhat explosive. . . . But I think they are interesting and I hope you will find them useful."[43]

Hirschman found them neither useful nor interesting—except as an index of social scientists' resistance to thinking of themselves as part of the problem. If he was dismayed, he never let on. By the time World Bankers were typing up their reactions, Hirschman was moving on to other frontiers.

CHAPTER 14

The God Who Helped

If it had been possible to build the Tower
of Babel without climbing up it, it would
have been permitted.

FRANZ KAFKA

The late 1960s wrenched major American cities and university campuses with unrest; in Mexico City, Prague, and Paris, they became
battlefields that shook regimes. Coups d'états and civil war spread across
what were once upliftingly called "new nations." The promises of the development decade seemed increasingly empty. How could one defend
reform in this context? This was a difficult question, faced not only with
an establishment looking for manageable answers, but also with radical
sources of dissent coming back to life with an energy unseen since the
1930s. In late 1969, after a trip to Latin America, Hirschman penned a
short essay, "How to Divest in Latin America, and Why," a manifesto
calling for American tolerance for nationalism and reform abroad. He
gave a draft to a younger colleague, Sam Bowles. Bowles's response echoed
the tone of a new generation: Hirschman's essay was a manifesto to make
capitalism palatable. Divestment simply left the terrain of development
to national bourgeoisies so that they "can exercise their class interests."
Left-wingers found Hirschman's reformism too tepid to solve the world's
mounting problems. But he liked Bowles, a lot, so, he paused to clarify
his argument: "I don't think the 'constructive' tone is as counterrevolutionary as you think." Was the choice just between revolution or foreign
domination? Surely this was too limited, especially given the difficulties
facing Latin American rebels—trigger-happy despots, scared investors,

and Green Berets? "What I am doing, perhaps, is to try to increase the number of options, by pointing out the requirements . . . of a strategy that does not have revolution as an absolute prerequisite. I have all along argued against those who lay down such prerequisites for economic development, be they W. W. Rostow or [the Marxist] Paul Baran." There had to be more ways of "moving forward." Without them, people would be paralyzed and caught in an uneven clash of extremes. He ended the letter with a fable about a community of Jews who'd gathered to lament their lot. After much complaining, one of them finally stood up and concluded: "God will help!" A moment of silence passed before another carped, "But how does God help until such time as God will help?"[1]

In fact, "How to Divest" was an epistle in article form written to New York's governor Nelson Rockefeller. Nursing presidential aspirations and wanting to display his foreign policy credentials, Rockefeller had invited the Harvard economist to join him on a tour of Latin America. Hirschman politely said no and gave his reasons in "How to Divest," a proposal to help improve things until God came along, an economist's way of doing more than kvetch in the safer precincts of the faculty club.

Indeed, Harvard seemed at first to be an unlikely setting for a heated clash. Life in Cambridge was lively and social. The Hirschmans were immediately swept up in the Harvard way, living in a modest, wood-clad house on Holden St., a few blocks from Littauer Hall, the columned home of the economics department. The Galbraiths lived nearby, and the Hirschmans were frequent guests at their festive, sophisticated soirées full of the "beautiful people." Across the street were the Gerschenkrons. Albert and Shura were respectful and courteous, and occasionally Shura would seek out Sarah at home to pore over Tolstoy; the two conversed in Russian. But the ties tended to be formal, and with time, increasingly strained. For the first time, Hirschman had a personal study at home, but he had little time to use it. "The establishment here is the only thing that is really exaggerated," he confessed to Ursula. The university was busy with seminars, discussion groups, and conferences. There seemed to be a committee for everything. When a new institute for politics was being created in memory of John F. Kennedy, the bash was all glitz. Jackie

Kennedy made a glamorous appearance. Afterward, the guests moved to the Galbraiths' for champagne and dancing. Hirschman wanted to slink home to his study; Sarah did her best to keep him engaged. "How one is then still supposed to be able to write something, that I haven't quite understood yet," he grumbled. One upside of socializing with the well-heeled was that he dusted off his childhood tennis game. Perhaps it was a discrete source of revenge, for he soon found himself beating most of his colleagues on the court.[2]

But he did not grumble much. If he did, it was mainly on account of the teaching and diplomatic duties of a senior academic figure. Some occasions, like Octavio Paz's frequent visits to Harvard, were redeemable; Hirschman and Paz became friends. But mostly, the public scene was tiresome, and he was only partly successful at inventive excuses to avoid it. Harvard gave him friendships, some rekindled, and some new, especially Stanley and Inge Hoffmann. It was almost a natural convergence. Though Albert and Stanley spoke in English, they shared French backgrounds and their discomfort with the disciplinary narrowness of departmental life. Inge and Sarah also became very close. The couples got together frequently for dinners and movies.[3]

Harvard Economics was studded with big names. Beyond the Ionic columns facing Cambridge Street were some of the profession's iconic names. The most famous was John Kenneth Galbraith. The domineering figure was Gerschenkron. But there was also the ebullient Wassily Leontief and Simon Kuznets, who was about to win a Nobel Prize. Soon Kenneth Arrow was to join the group, also an eventual laureate. There was also a rising generation of brilliant younger economists who spanned the spectrum of methods, such as Michael Rothschild and Herbert Gintis. Samuel Bowles, hired in 1965 after having done his dissertation on Nigeria under Gerschenkron's supervision but who had become more interested in operational research and mathematical modeling, was in awe of his new colleague. This was, in short, a diverse, if rapidly evolving, group of scholars. It was also coming apart at its seams.[4]

Though he was one of Littauer Hall's stars, Hirschman's own place in this assortment was somewhat marginal and became increasingly so.

Not long after his arrival, he was named the Lucius N. Littauer Professor of Political Economy, succeeding his former chair, Carl Kaysen, who had decamped from Harvard to become the director of the Institute for Advanced Study at Princeton the previous year. When the announcement was made public, the *Harvard Crimson* featured a beaming Hirschman in his suit on the front page; he hardly looked the part of the apostle for the dismal science.[5] The ensuing publication of *Development Projects Observed* expanded his global reach beyond Latin America, while the frenetic pace of his publications made him a center of attention he did not always relish. Within the department, his closest colleagues tended to be junior faculty members. They, along with graduate students, were always on the lookout for an elder colleague with more sympathy for their radical ideas. Some, like Richard Bird and Michael Rothschild, became coauthors. In general, however, his outward stature was in inverse proportion to his profile in the department. None of his colleagues could recall him speaking at a faculty meeting. By contrast, he was a prolix grouser in private about endless deliberations.

Nor did colleagues, with a few exceptions, seem very interested in speaking with him. At one of the department's faculty workshops, Hirschman was the featured presenter. He presented some of his views on "obstacles," embellished with diagrams for his colleagues' benefit. While the junior faculty watched in awe, many senior members sat puzzled or indifferent. Political economy seemed old hat, and its newer valences were not yet on the horizon. Hirschman was a curio.[6] So, he made the best of what he called his *trait d'union* position beyond Littauer. While his formal position was in Economics, and his undergraduate teaching was lodged there, most of his intellectual ties were scattered around the university: Hoffmann and Huntington were in Government, Schelling in the Kennedy School. Many of his students were not straight economics majors or economics graduate students; most came from political science. Hirschman's fondest setting was the joint MIT-Harvard Seminar in Political Development, which he co-ran with Sam Huntington. Eventually, there was a fleeting effort to do something institutional to foster a more interdisciplinary climate for economists. Hirschman joined a small bloc of colleagues, including Leontief, Galbraith, and Arrow (who wrote the curriculum report), who called for the creation of a Department of Social Economy. But extensive meetings with Dean Henry Rosovsky and President Derek Bok led nowhere.[7]

One thing Harvard did not do was help Hirschman overcome his aversion to teaching. It was not that he had to reach far to prepare his classes. His undergraduate courses focused on economic development in Latin America, and he contributed some core lectures in Economics 1, the department's gateway. There were some spin-off seminars, such as the one on development projects and a freshman seminar on his next book. There were also the special, topical offerings, such as the seminar "The Economic and Political Aspects of Imperialism," a "large ungainly" affair involving a group of assistant professors (Hirschman was the only tenured one) and politically animated graduate students, whom the senior economists tended to eschew. This was the fall semester of 1970, on the heels of the overthrow of Prince Sihanouk in Cambodia and the massacre at Kent State University in Ohio. Though Hirschman was not always happy about the heavy formulations coming from the students, he agreed to be the faculty sponsor, cautioning, possibly to instill a bit of humility, "I'm one of the few who actually read this in German!" The reading list reflected his diet from the early 1930s: Lenin, Rosa Luxemburg, and Rudolf Hilferding (whom he had failed to save in Marseilles). To drive home the point, the syllabus listed only the German editions. Still, he remained tight-lipped about his own past and never shared his own personal brush with the works. The students did not appear to realize there was a backstory.[8]

The courses may have been close to his heart, but teaching still made him sick to his stomach. He remained, in the memory of one of his admiring Harvard students, "a catastrophically bad teacher" but made up for it with his sheer presence—which is just as well, because that appears to capture most of what students got out of him. Even his devotee, Stephen Krasner, one of the pioneering figures in international political economy whose thesis got its first formulation in a Hirschman seminar, recalls Hirschman's polite passivity and scarce feedback. Another economics PhD student, Mexico's Carlos Bazdresch, approached Hirschman early on but got the distinct impression that graduate students were not going to be the focus of his attention. There is something revealing about the gap between the students' impression of a distant, spectral Hirschman and his own sense of sacrifice. On the eve of his first semester at Harvard, Sarah took the girls to Long Island for two weeks, leaving Albert in the flat on Central Park West. "I feel like a boy before his final exams," he groaned to Ursula. "I have been working like crazy these weeks to learn a few things that I will be teaching. Whenever I arrive improvised like this, I am always tempted to exclaim with Gretchen [thinking of Goethe]:

> Dear God! What such a man as this
> Can think on all and everything![9]

A year later, from the same room, during the last days he would spend there before moving the household to Cambridge, he grumbled that writing *Development Projects Observed* had already inspired some petites idées that he wanted to pursue—"but I have to prepare these damn lectures now."[10] The sleepless nights, churning stomach, diarrhea before lectures— Albert's torments afflicted Sarah. "Well," exclaimed Sarah later, "they told him once to pretend that you believe everything, and that you knew everything." It was perhaps this pretense that churned his insides. Either way, Albert's anxiety took its toll on Sarah: "I was never there, [but] I suffered every time Albert was lecturing, I was at home suffering. . . . I actually had the cramps. It was that bad."[11]

As at Columbia, he proceeded to wiggle off the teaching hook at Harvard. No sooner had the Hirschmans settled down, unpacked, and decorated the Holden St. house and Hirschman completed a semester's teaching, than he began to explore alternatives. As he had done so effectively before, he reached out to the foundation world with a flurry of ideas.

One involved ideas about industrial policy he had unveiled to a group of social scientists in Chile. There was a growing chorus of critics on the Latin American Left and Right that disagreed on almost everything— except the dismal view of the future of manufacturing in the region. It was doomed, either because it was not enough of a revolutionary force (for the Left) or because it held back the progress of capitalism (for the Right). Hirschman, as one might expect, found both extremes too pessimistic. In late 1967, he contacted Kalman Silvert, a political scientist at the time working as a program officer for the Ford Foundation. They met in New York in early December and agreed that Hirschman would outline some ideas. The Ford, at the time, was getting more deeply involved in Chile, and like Hirschman, was trying to shore up more middle-of-the-road, reform-oriented research. Having a figure like Hirschman on board would be a boon in a climate of escalating polarization in Santiago. Hirschman wanted Pinto and Sunkel involved, as well as a young sociologist from São Paulo working on Brazilian industrialists, Fernando Henrique Cardoso. What came of this was a new collaboration with Latin American scholars, but not right away. No sooner were arrangements made than Hirschman got cold feet—and explained to Silvert that he did not want to be locked into a trip to Latin America. He had a huge backlog of work to take care of. Beside, "having written three books on economic development in the past ten years, I should perhaps pause and look around a bit to consider where to plunge next."[12]

Here was a break from the pattern; for a decade, Hirschman had been racing through projects at such a clip that there was little breathing room between them. Each project had been a concatenated outgrowth from questions or ideas remaindered from the one that had been dispatched to the printers. His diary contains a half-mocking observation:

> What keeps me from suicide are, besides cowardice, two matters: 1) the idea that it would be considered a refutation of my own theories of creative imbalances etc. 2) the fact that I always seem to have still one idea to write up—the dangerous moment will come when I'll have my best petite idée all worked out.

Some might have wished that more time be spared for each project, especially as they got bigger and bigger in analytical ambition. But one of the features of Hirschman's explosion onto the social science stage in the 1960s was that to the outside world each book appeared to be such a departure from its predecessor, and yet his notes and manuscripts reveal the umbilical ties between them. Hirschman was clearly trying to keep pace with a rapidly changing world, his petites idées multiplying.

The continuity should not, however, be overstated. After all, the unfolding of the 1960s was quickly breaking up the coordinates of reform—in economic development as well as in the War on Poverty. Hitherto, his pragmatic idealism tended to be positioned as a response to more totalizing appeals of others. But now a fuse was burning at the core of reform. The growing tensions prompted Hirschman to take a second look at some of his own precepts. Indeed, there was another reason why he backed out of the Ford project; he had found a sponsor to help him "look around." Word had arrived from the Center for Behavioral Sciences at Stanford that they wanted him to spend a year in Palo Alto. Hirschman had been to Stanford in November to give a talk, "Competition vs Monopoly in the Fallible Economy," in which he explored some of the residual concerns from *Development Projects Observed*. He started with the case of Nigerian railroads. "Why didn't highway competition help? Or did it perhaps hinder? *With* highway poor performance," read his lecture notes, "of RR is *tolerable* evil, without something might have been done to correct sit'a."[13] The fact was, a ghastly civil war had erupted across Biafra in July and disturbed him. His failure to see that a development project he had so recently evaluated was contributing to savagery was clearly haunting him—and he confessed that economists needed to grapple with the unintended consequences of their thought; they could not wave them away as the results of some external force beyond their framework or control. One of the attendees was Hirschman's future colleague, Kenneth Arrow, who was still at Stanford. Arrow thought the idea of creating problems to solve was an ingenious proposition in *Strategy* but was not very enthusiastic about Hirschman's writings about industrialization. Still, Hirschman being one of the discipline's original thinkers, Arrow wanted to know what he was working on. What he heard "knocked me out," he recalled.[14]

What was clear was that Hirschman's underlying confidence in the prospects for reform was beginning to fray; how could one explain behaviors that could turn some unintended consequences into disastrous ones? The difficulty was, Hirschman was pushing at the frontiers of his discipline while still working within it. The problem on his mind was the apparently technical, or neutral, dilemma of competition versus monopoly. A year earlier, Shura and Albert had had dinner together and spent the evening deep in conversation. They grappled with Albert's festering questions: if there was an alternative to lousy railways, why wasn't the consumer response, to favor the humble truck and force the big bad monopoly to change its inefficient ways, doing the trick? The next morning, Shura typed out a long response, drawing an analogy to the problem of American schools: "It is very likely and intuitively very understandable that the consumers with the highest consumer surplus will be the first to desert public schools and move over to private schools." What mattered was the citizens' "surplus"—what they had to forfeit by staying with a bad system and what they gained from sticking with a good one. Shura and Albert were mulling over a problem that was starting to loom large in America: "choice."[15]

For the moment, their foggy explorations were being framed in the language of relative prices and losses, opportunity costs, and theories of consumption. But the spread of pogroms in Nigeria the riptide of unrest in the streets and campuses at home made monopoly versus competition seem a little banal, and Albert was groping for a way to put his analysis of economic development into a broader perspective—and this started to seep through at the Stanford presentation. It left a deep impression on those around the table, like Gabriel Almond, a major builder of comparative political science and chair of Stanford's department, who immediately started pulling levers to get Hirschman to the West Coast. When the invitation reached Hirschman, it was a complete surprise. Overjoyed understates Hirschman's response. "A really formidable piece of news," he exclaimed to Ursula. "There, we have no other obligation than to sit and think."[16]

This meant breaking the news to Ford. Hirschman explained to Silvert that he felt it most important "to leave that [sabbatical] year wholly free of 'programmed research.'" Silvert was the picture of understanding—

and patience; Ford would be waiting for the right time to team up with Hirschman. "Don't do what you don't want to do," said Silvert. My feeling is that you amply deserve a year to yourself, and that the Stanford opportunity affords precisely that. . . . My corporate feelings for your problem may be easily expressed: we are interested in your project; it follows that we are interested in helping you pursue your interests in whatever ways appear reasonable and sensible."[17] It is important not to drop this little exchange as one of the might-have-beens of a writerly life. Neither Hirschman nor Silvert did. As with petites idées, Hirschman was storing away strategic contacts and latent projects for the right occasion. It had been ten years since Hirschman emerged from Colombia; relations with big social science funders had changed. Hirschman was in the enviable position of having opportunities laid at his feet.

We can get a glimpse of what Hirschman was "looking around" at from a file he opened once he knew he was Stanford bound. "Certain areas one feels uncertain about," he started to catalogue. There was a list of topics and dossier of *New York Times* clippings, ranging from labor unions, to fights over inner city versus suburban schools, Black Power, Martin Luther King Jr., and Japan versus Latin America. And there were "Confessions—Mine." These scribblings, unfortunately for us, were spartan. His notes have a frenetic and emphatic quality to them; one gets the impression of someone straining at intellectual frontiers in search of a way to transcend them. One also gets the impression of the world pressing in on his notes; June 1968 heralded what would become known as the Vietnam Summer and yield to a spasm of unrest. What started with a disturbing problem posed by Nigeria, where truckers and a chorus of disgruntled customers had been forced to "raise hell," was becoming a more generalized assault on the commanders of big organizations—companies, states, churches—from Prague to São Paulo to Washington.

There were hell-raisers in the family, too. It was perhaps foregone that Katia and Lisa would get heavily involved in the student movement. Lisa's return from her year in Lima, en route to Wisconsin, where she was going to start graduate school, occasioned some family reunions. At Harvard, the Phillips Brooks House was a hub for young activists. One was Peter

Gourevitch, a graduate student of Stanley Hoffmann's with a similar family background of Russian social democratic émigrés. He was swept up in the antiwar movement and Sarah arranged for Lisa to meet him at the height of the summer agitation. Years later, Peter and Lisa would get married. When Lisa arrived, Katia and Alain came up from New York, bearing news from the front lines of student militancy. Alain in particular came brimming with hopes about the spreading " 'revolutions,' from Columbia, France, etc. for which he is a follower and extremely and tenaciously convinced." The conversations were sometimes strained, with Katia, Lisa, and Alain decidedly affiliated with protestors. Albert and Sarah would wince when their children referred to policemen as "pigs." Alain had joined a group of alternative architects in New York who sought to reclaim charred real estate and developed a "vest pocket park" on the Lower East Side. Inspired by the work of Herbert Marcuse, it was

Albert visiting Alain's project in Manhattan, 1971.

a salvaged ruin for the city's kids. Albert was not persuaded by the revolutionary ideas behind it, but he admired Alain's reformmongering vision.

It was not easy to bridge the divide. Katia wanted children. Sarah and Albert worried about the money; Alain was making none. Eventually, Alain did land a job, in Boston. But then tragedy struck. Katia gave birth to their first child, Elise—a daughter with serious brain damage. Then their apartment in New York burned down. All was lost. When Alain and Katia relocated to Boston, they moved into the house on Holden St. and struggled with their despair over Elise's health. Albert and Sarah did their best to support the grieving couple. While Sarah ministered, Albert was restrained but not distant; he kept his sorrow to himself. Alain could sense that memories of more distant losses were stirred. Katia, to keep busy, compiled the index for one of her father's books, a collection of previously published essays. One night, Katia and Alain went out to see François Truffaut's *Baisers volés* (*Stolen Kisses*). Paris's bloom seemed exhilarating, and the couple walked out of the theater feeling resolved to return to France. As they packed their belongings, Albert's latest anthology rolled off the printing presses. Called *A Bias for Hope*, it was dedicated to the two struggling parents.

The strain posed by the generational divide should not obscure one thing: fundamentally, Hirschman's heart was with the hell-raisers. He applauded the antiwar senator, Eugene McCarthy, and his decision to speak out against his own party and defy the president, turning the 1968 campaign into a call to America's youth not to confuse "dropping out" over disagreement with Vietnam with "copping out." "The relief was so widely felt" at McCarthy's defiance, Hirschman exclaimed.[18] Meanwhile, events in Paris and Prague were riveting, though there was some concern that the wildcat strikes and pitched battles in the Latin Quarter could get worse before improving. Hoping to find some balm, he speculated that perhaps the resignation of de Gaulle, "too late in my view," might work because it now makes "the improvement seem less profound." On the other hand, he crossed his fingers that they might bring "upheavals within the USSR." Hirschman started to collect clippings about dissident Jews and their demands to be permitted to emigrate to Israel. Across the board, from Washington, to Paris, to Moscow, he scorned insiders who supported "country right or wrong," repudiating us-or-them speak. "A plentiful supply of police dogs and atomic bombs" may be goods to some, but are just as likely to be vile to others.[19]

On top of this was the American election of 1968. The campaign was dispiriting: the murder of Bobby Kennedy a blow, McCarthy prone to self-inflicted wounds, and the clash between rioters and Chicago's police at the Democratic National Convention utterly disheartening. Then there was the outcome. As it approached, Hirschman observed that "depression reigns here." "No one knows how to vote." It was not just the victory of the Californian red-baiter, Richard Nixon, whom Hirschman recalled only too well from his time in Washington. It was also the echoes of extremism beyond student campuses. "For the first time there is a true uprising of the reactionary masses (like candidate Wallace), about which I have always known but which, in a sedative way, had always been deprived of representation, until now." To Ursula, who did not require explanation, he lamented that "this too is déjà vu, and it's not happy."[20]

In the midst of all this, Harvard got roiled. The year before, Katia and Alain had been among the Columbia students who had seized the central administration offices. By January, student strikes had spread to San Francisco State, Brandeis, Swarthmore College, Berkeley, Wisconsin, the City College of New York, Duke, Rutgers, and beyond. At Harvard there had been warning signs: as the secretary of defense, Robert McNamara, left after giving a speech at Quincy House in the fall of 1966, his car was stopped and surrounded by students, who scrambled over it and rocked it until McNamara was allowed to retreat. By early 1969, the Vietnam War pitted students against faculty and administrators; outside the office of the Center for International Affairs, whose eminence, Samuel Huntington, had laid bare the connection between development and security, students chanted: "HEY, HEY, CFIA, HOW MANY COUPS DID YOU PULL TODAY?" The morning of April 9, 1969, saw 300 radicals from Students for a Democratic Society storm University Hall in front of Widener Library. A large black-and-red SDS banner was unfurled from the second story windows to the demonstrators below. The next day, the Cambridge police—whose relations with Harvard students were not especially amicable—rolled into Harvard Square with three busloads of officers; 400 armed policemen lined up before the hall while the occupants passed around wet cloths to cut the tear gas. The police charged, some of them stashing their badges so as to pummel students with abandon, followed by a rampage of police violence as officers chased students through the yards and into dormitories.[21]

The occupation and spectacle of an armed assault in the middle of campus provoked outrage at the hapless President Nathan Pusey. Calling in the police so precipitously and giving them the green light to terrorize was a mistake argued many professors. Students had less polite words. Some students, though not many, came out in Pusey's defense. Faculty meetings degenerated into verbal wars. By then, Hirschman missed the final explosion because he was at Stanford, but two of his closest friends, Stanley Hoffmann and Alexander Gerschenkron, found themselves on opposing sides. Gerschenkron gave a stirring speech in which he denounced radical students as criminals out to destroy the institution. It was a heartfelt, exaggerated index of how polarized Harvard had become.[22]

At the end of the summer of 1968, Albert and Sarah were invited to spend a month with Harry Kahn, an old friend from the Marshall Plan days and a successful New York stockbroker. The Kahns had a summer cottage on Cape Cod. While the world erupted in protest, Albert disappeared; he could have spent the weeks on the beach, which is what Kahn had proffered. Instead, the morning walks were followed by long days at a makeshift desk. Hirschman hunkered down and struggled with his ideas; his thinking "is going in some unforeseen directions," he told Ursula.[23]

Moving to the West Coast was like leaping from the frying pan into the fire. This was no longer the Bay Area where Albert and Sarah had met three decades earlier. Stanford University, like many, was roiled by conflict over Black Studies; in the wake of the assassination of Martin Luther King Jr. in April 1968 and the spasm of violence and grieving that followed, this academic "initiative" acquired a whole new tone.[24] But Stanford was nothing compared to nearby Berkeley. In 1966, Ronald Reagan won the contest to be governor of the state, setting in motion a series of clashes across an array of issues. "Send the welfare bums back to work," he thundered. He also promised to "clean up the mess at Berkeley," that haven for "Communist sympathizers, protestors, and sex deviants." The showdown with students took place over an open field in front of the university, which students dubbed People's Park. Reagan, spoiling for a fight, sent his highway patrol and the Berkeley police to cleanse it. Students turned on the fire hydrants and hurled bricks. The Alameda County sheriff's men opened up with buckshot and tear gas. Hundreds were severely wounded; one student died. Reagan responded by declaring a state of emergency and dispatched several thousand National Guardsmen to occupy Berkeley; protesting girls slid flowers down the muzzles of the guards' rifles. "If it takes a bloodbath," snarled Reagan, "let's get it over with." Meanwhile, TV screens were filled with reporting and images of a bruising mayoral election in which a gloating conservative, Sam Yorty, used race-baiting accusations that the grandson of a slave, Thomas Bradley, would turn the city over to Black Nationalists. Albert and Sarah watched the unfolding with a sadness that reminded them why they could not embrace their children's passions. It's an "impossible war," concluded Sarah and has led to "the famous backlash which has now really arrived. We have spent entire evenings watching the television and listening to the public sessions of the Berkeley Council," admiring the rebels but sensing that their foe had more up their sleeves than could be imagined.[25]

In the meantime, one hell-raiser caught Hirschman's eye: Ralph Nader, who personified the little guy's defiance of corporate America. In October 1968, *Playboy* ran a featured interview with the Princeton-educated gadfly. A month later, the *New York Review of Books* ran Nader's essay, "The Great American Gyp." Hirschman read both; the blend of passionate idealism and uncompromising individualism shook off the remnants of 1950s consensus and put a final end to its silent generation. Nader fashioned himself the Robin Hood of the modern-day peasant, screwed not by greedy tax collectors (that outrage would burst onto the Californian scene some years later) but by the corporate magnates. The little guy was now the consumer, and especially the driver of Detroit's "deathtraps," which were responsible, Nader alleged, for tens of thousands of fatalities a year. Detroit's moguls were deaf to the complaints; worse, they went after Nader himself, a reflex that did them no favors in the public's growing skepticism of big corporations. By 1966, his was a household name, the mouthpiece of a movement to defend consumers against corporations. Joseph Sobeck of Needham, Massachusetts, was a sign of the times. After shoddy service on his "beautiful '65 Ford," he wrote to Henry Ford at corporate headquarters to complain:

> I must say that this is a nice way to treat a guy who has bought Fords for the past twenty years. You can also be assured that I absolutely will not purchase a Ford of any kind no matter what your usual form letter to me will say. Or does Ford now have a policy of not answering letters too!![26]

In early spring 1969, Hirschman reached out to Nader and explained that he was studying how people were responding to the large organizations that shaped market life, which gave him material he aimed to use for a course next year at Harvard. Nader was excited. He replied immediately, sharing his admiration for Hirschman's international work, and volunteered material for the course (including Sobeck's plea), bemoaning how "our system has institutionalized 'exit' into an ideology and a remedy for a wide variety of abuses." Now, as a Chevy man, Hirschman may have appreciated the blast against General Motors (though, he too would soon give up on his brand in favor of the upscale Saab). Either way, his ties to Nader were important for his project. Nader was interesting not just because he ventilated in such an articulate way how Americans were experiencing the corporate oversight of everyday life; he had tapped the disappointments of consumers whose activities had a special appeal for a Hirschman who was seeking to place consumerism into the broader panel of peoples' responses to American capitalism. The fact that Nader's casus belli was a car—the maligned Corvair—only added to the appeal.[27]

"What's good for GM is good for America" was a risible reminder of duped bygone days, as was the image of the straightlaced, obedient "organization man." Indeed, organizations had ceased to be synonyms for order and stability—more and more they were seen as the purveyors of disenchantment and treachery.

Hirschman described the setting in Palo Alto once he'd moved in: each of the roughly fifty visitors at the Center for Behavioral Sciences "occupies a cell in a very beautiful location, with superb views, but without telephones or any contact with the world beyond. If this was a paradise, Hirschman conceded that "there are a number here who appear on the verge of a nervous breakdown in this monastic regime." This was as good as it could get given the accumulation of writing projects. To top off his pleasures, he bicycled from the house through the campus's eucalyptus-lined lanes to his office. "When I close my eyes (very briefly!) I imagine myself on the Tiergartenstrasse chasing a bus." To add to the memories was the rumor that Richard "Rix" Löwenthal, Hirschman's mentor from the ORG days, was due to visit the center from Berlin's Free University. In a curious twist, Löwenthal would help Hirschman apply his thoughts to party systems in decline; one can only speculate whether they talked about Weimar—if they did, the traces are imperceptible in the text or notes.[28]

Albert, Stanford, 1969.

As Hirschman settled into his cell and unpacked his bulging files of clippings and yellow notepads, one aspect of his ruminations in his "Confessions—Mine" was clear: his determination to get beyond the vocabulary that he and Shura had been using over dinner. "Social science is compartmentalized," he noted, adding that "cross connections can be found perhaps best by those who haven't acquired Veblen's 'trained incapacity'" (that is, the acquired incapacity to comprehend or even perceive a problem). What he was now pursuing was a "unity of social sciences—communication across disciplines, economics, politics, social psychology, morality" precisely to overcome what he perceived to be creeping narrowness of disciplines.[29] It was something of a paradox of the age that the professionalization of the social sciences appeared to Hirschman to blinker scholars just as the challenges of modern society mounted. The paradox drilled a dilemma into his sense of purpose: at once Hirschman was seeking to shape the social sciences while trying to transcend the ever-rising boundaries separating the disciplines from each other. It would, as we shall see, account for the runaway success of his new project while at the same time unmoor him from the field of economics.

Where the divide immediately came to the surface was not, however, with his mother discipline, but rather with its cousin, political science. Gabriel Almond had maneuvered behind the scenes to get Hirschman to Stanford in the hopes of forging a collaboration. It did not come to pass. The divergence of their relationship reveals a great deal about Hirschman's difficulties in the quickly shifting landscape of the American social sciences. As a political scientist, Almond saw in Hirschman a rare economist who used the tools of his discipline to illuminate politics while thinking politically about economic matters. Their relationship thinned in part because, by the time Hirschman arrived in Palo Alto, the original questions about technology and choice had veered onto a very different track. Hirschman felt a twinge of guilt that his sojourn did not yield to the collaboration that Almond had in mind. But there was more. Almond was a practitioner of structural-functionalist analysis, which could occasionally get worked up about elaborate explanatory schema that never appealed to Hirschman's interest in paradoxes, inversions, and unexpected side effects. A gap was widening between Hirschman and a growing scientistic trend in the social sciences; economists tended increasingly to enhance their progress by eliminating exogenous forces from their models, and political scientists were doing the same, explaining political change wholly in terms of political categories. Hirschman marveled at, as he put it elsewhere, "the noble, if unconscious, desire to demonstrate the irreducibility of the social world to general laws!"[30] If he found the search for "parsimonious" theories in search of universal explanations a fruitless pursuit, in less charitable moments he called it "mindless," bent on oversimplifying in order to control.

The difference was laid bare when a Berkeley graduate student, the Argentine Oscar Oszlak, invited Hirschman to a conference in Asilomar. Hirschman accepted and proposed the title "The Search for Paradigms as a Hindrance to Understanding." Oszlak's dissertation advisor, David Apter, another prominent political scientist, inquired whether Hirschman had accepted. If so, what was his paper about? When the Argentine explained, Apter smiled and countered with his own paper title, "The Use of Paradigms as a Help to Understanding," to defend his side.[31]

Hirschman did not mince words when it came to the imperialist features of some of the ornate, "theoretical" suppositions of the social sciences. In this, he returned to an old obsession to defrock the expert suffering from "the visiting economist syndrome":

> In the academy, the prestige of the theorist is towering. Further, the extravagant use of language intimates that theorizing can rival sensuous delights: what used to be called an interesting or valuable theoretical point is commonly referred to today as a "stimulating" or even "exciting" theoretical "insight." Moreover, in so far as the United States is concerned, an important role has no doubt been played by the desperate need, on the part of the hegemonic power, for shortcuts to the understanding of multifarious reality that must be coped with and controlled and therefore understood at once.[32]

The new breed of social scientist and revolutionary "experience the same compulsion," argued Hirschman. The revolutionaries now cite Marx without understanding him, arming themselves with "laws of change" to justify the view that interpreting the world is inferior to changing it. This was a not-so-subtle dig at American students and Latin American radicals who denied the possibility of change without revolution. More troublesome and pernicious was a "cognitive style" that was, as he put it politely, "unfortunate." The problem was not which side to be on; it was the "impatience for theoretical formulation." To make his case, he compared two books, John Womack, Jr.'s recently published profile of the Mexican revolutionary Emiliano Zapata and James L. Payne's study of violence in Colombia. Womack, it needs to be said, was an assistant professor at Harvard, and Hirschman liked him immensely—not least because Womack did not hide his affection for Mexico and sympathy for Zapata's cause behind a patina of objectivism. Payne, on the other hand, "exudes dislike and contempt" for the society he studied. Womack's fine-grained narrative—"one might say Flaubertian"—about a redemptive struggle, contrasted with Payne's neutral application of the latest "theories" to explain Colombians' "self-made hell" and to tout a model that could be applied anywhere. Payne was the butt of Hirschman's ridicule, which bordered on the cruel; his "model is as wrong as it is outrageous." Worse, it was banal, "at best [it] leaves us with the proposition, which incidentally is both platitudinous and wrong, that if the politicians are vicious, the ensuing politics are likely to be too!"[33]

Heat like this in Hirschman's prose is rare, and it suggests that he was unhappy about the drift of entire sectors of American social science that he considered ruinous. He scribbled a Payne-inspired diatribe about "the conservative, anti-change chamber of social theories."[34] Testing variables, valorizing parsimony, and seeking generalizability all as ends in themselves had the additional ignominy of being painful to read. There was, of course, the charge that Hirschman valued complexity, which to some of his critics meant messiness, as an end in itself, and there are times when his work is not immune to the charge. But it misses the point of *his* cognitive style, which might be located in an unstable—and squeezed—middle. He was not calling for a grand unified social science, but rather a careful rebuilding from *petits* steps, or "mini-building blocks" that did not appeal to dependence on exclusive categories or magnify the distance between reality and intellectual schema. It was perhaps more elegantly framed by Paul Valéry, whom Hirschman was reading as he composed "The Search for Paradigms": "Tout ce qui est simple est faux. Tout ce qui ne l'est pas est inutilisable."[35]

In the course of penning his diatribe, Hirschman added a little aphorism for himself in response to Payne: "Hope as a principle of action." Another petite idée to stash away.

What Hirschman did happen upon at Stanford was social psychology. Hirschman had always had an eye out for the psychological underpinnings of behavior and had never found the conventional self-interested *homo economicus* an especially revealing subject. *Strategy* had leaned on some social psychology to illuminate the ways in which people made decisions. Ideology and perceptions played a role in the habits of reformmongers. And the boundary between trait-making and trait-taking elaborated in *Development Projects Observed* had required some insight into more than just utility maximizing, which is why Albert and Shura burned the midnight oil. Indeed, we can see the strands of the challenge starting to interlace in the presentation Hirschman made in 1963 to the Institut d'étude du développement, when François Perroux had invited him to share his recent thoughts about the "obstacles" to development with a French audience. Hirschman seized the opportunity to try to shift the debate away from the "objective" constraints such as lack of roads or pervasive illiteracy. He wanted to draw attention to the ways in which perceptions of obstacles were sometimes thornier than the obstacles themselves; they could be intractable products of the beholder's eye and thus get in the way of potential alternatives and reforms. And some obstacles could be turned into an advantage when seen differently. The outline notes to what would eventually become "Obstacles to Development: A Classification and a Quasi Vanishing Act," sported a headline: "VICIOUS CIRCLES."

Soon his desk groaned under the weight of piled-up evidence that people made decisions in complicated and often counterintuitive ways. The effects of experiments by Jack W. Brehm, the late Arthur R. Cohen, and most of all, Leon Festinger—the Stanford psychologist who had pioneered the theory of cognitive dissonance and written a book that Hirschman admired, *When Prophecy Fails*—dominated his reading. The latter, a 1956 classic by undercover psychologists about a UFO cult that predicted the end of the world, piqued Hirschman's interest for its use of a "case study" method drawn from a newspaper headline and applying the new concept of cognitive dissonance—just the kind of raw material Hirschman relished: everyday occurrences that yield new insights. How did believers keep up their faith when the prophecy from the planet Clarion did not materialize in Armageddon? Many, for reasons that went beyond simple dismissals of irrationality, hung on. Cognitive dissonance helped explain how disconfirming information and deep beliefs can be reconciled. The heart of the psychological enterprise inverted the customary (and still-resilient) precept that peoples' attitudes shape their behavior. What psychologists did, which Hirschman took to the core of his own approach, was to flip the equation, to treat behavior as a shaper of beliefs and attitudes. Hirschman sent Festinger a draft of the "Obstacles" paper and asked him to review his treatment of how an economist might draw from his work on cognitive dissonance. Festinger, a notoriously irascible man, was impressed. "The remarks you make about dissonance theory and the implications for the theory are quite correct technically. In addition, I think you make them cogently and interestingly."[36]

Praise like this must have brought glee. But the author of *When Prophecy Fails* turned out to be a recluse and had no interest in reciprocating Hirschman's overture to collaborate. Instead, Hirschman happened upon one of Festinger's young colleagues, Philip Zimbardo, who had just joined the Stanford psychology department and was delighted to team with the distinguished economist. At the time, Zimbardo was working on illusions of choice before people made decisions; how they attached to decisions they found most laborious or identified with groups (like fraternities) they suffered to join (like humiliation rituals). Hirschman loved this kind of work and appreciated the careful parsing of questions such as, How long do loyalties last? When does dissonance become intolerable? How do group dynamics perpetuate or crumble? Hirschman and

Zimbardo, himself an antiwar activist and teach-in organizer, spent many hours over lunches and coffees talking about their respective interests and groping for an understanding of how intentions translate into actions. Along with one of Zimbardo's graduate students, Mark Snyder, the three of them designed an experiment on "The Effects of Severity of Initiation on Activism," which proposed to figure out what people do when they find out a group is less enjoyable or profitable than their expectations. Nothing came of it, in part, ironically, because a wave of revolt finally struck the Stanford campus the following academic year—which made getting human subjects to work on conformity and noncomformity seem a bit beside the point. Eventually, the idea rested in a forgotten appendix.[37]

What had started out as a central premise in Hirschman's thinking about economic development—disequilibrium—was broadening to fathom the reasons for the underlying volatility of the world. This was, after all, the tenor of the times; the happy, all-good-things-go-together mood that had inaugurated the 1960s was quickly dissipating. Confidence in progress and planning was giving way to crises and clashes; finally, the world appeared to be catching up to Hirschman's instinctive search for the unbalanced aspects of social life. At the same time, Hirschman realized, there was a basic difference between creative disequilibria and a complete breakdown. It was a fine line he would later have to identify when the turmoil ceded to a darker mood in the 1970s. For now, what was necessary was a social science that brought out "the inborn tendencies towards instability." It was not enough to preach imbalance or advocate antennae for unintended consequences. Hirschman was groping for something more fundamental, more *internal* to the black box of human behavior, a way to make good on what was still so unresolved but central to *Strategy*: the quest for an endogenous theory of how things changed. It was becoming more important as the shine on reform was quickly wearing off; an endogenous theory would clinch the case that reform was always possible because little about the world was as fixed, entrenched, or intractable as it seemed.

What was becoming clearer was that people were internally mixed, always amalgamating motives and dispositions. Nowadays, with the modernist faiths behind us, this may seem self-evident. But in the late 1960s this was not a widespread acknowledgement. There were others groping around for similar coordinates. Erik Erikson advocated a psychosocial approach to the human ego, which had discrete stages to its development and was vulnerable to "identity crises." An ur-text for radical readers, Herbert Marcuse's *One-Dimensional Man* blasted the view of modern Man as a creature of Reason—an ontological fiction that had to remove "him" from a dialectical relationship with society or nature in order to subordinate "him" to what Marcuse called "technological rationality and the logic of domination." The underlying tone of alienation and crisis, which could be marshaled to justify a range of responses, from defying the draft to hurling Molotov cocktails, never appealed to Hirschman. When students pressed these works on him, he was usually polite but always dismissive. Hirschman was after something that simultaneously embraced instability while still being basically about redeeming the core of human behavior, a way to capture the multidimensional features of modern life. He fastened on two expressions. One was the decision to speak out against misdeeds and wrongdoings; the other was to defect. The first was what he saw in the griping about Nigerian railways, the second was the decision to opt for the intrepid truck; the first was protest against the military draft, the second, flight to Canada; the first was fight in the inner-city ghettos of Newark and Los Angeles, the second was to move up the economic ladder and out of the trap. The first, Hirschman labeled "voice," the second, "exit." This coinage would go on to have an august career of its own.

What mattered for Hirschman was how the words expressed peoples' efforts to mix, negotiate, and *choose* between courses. Perhaps rulers of institutions and organizations might then recognize—instead of suppressing—the need for alternatives and could "improve the design of institutions that need both exit and voice to be maintained in good health." Herein lay the hope for "recuperation," a subtle keyword in the text into which Hirschman would pour his thoughts about the world in an effort to bring to light "the hidden potential of whatever reaction mode is currently neglected." The contrast with the tone of Marcuse cannot be denied. If the German critical theorist wanted to smash the system, the German economist wanted to make it more flexible. Indeed, the last line of the book would eventually register a personal plea for openness to the neglected, angular, hidden forces at work in society. "Such," he concluded, "at least is the stuff writers' dreams are made of."[38]

A two-way flow connected the complex views of people and adaptive organizations. Capturing this was the goal of the book, which would be a milestone in the history of the social sciences and which would catapult Hirschman to academic fame. As with *Strategy*, Hirschman drew upon an eclectic disciplinary repertoire. Whereas Colombia had been the laboratory for *Strategy*, Hirschman was now operating at an entirely different scale: the entire world was his observational oyster.

By the end of 1968, he was prepared to unveil thoughts that were inchoate a year earlier. The Center for Behavioral Sciences had Hirschman culminate their fall-semester seminar; he presented a paper called "Exit, Voice, and Loyalty." "In spite of its length," Hirschman apologized, for he had not taken the time to whittle it down, "it's still incomplete."[39] People crowded into the room to hear the rambling, not very clear, almost demure presentation. It started by explaining his interest in connecting fields, how an idea might grow and open hidden pathways by combining insights from psychology, economic development, and decision making—what he called "cognitive dissonance in action." Then came the customary cites of the writers: Pascal, La Rochefoucauld, Constant, and Octavio Paz. The paper was hardly a draft and could not have been easy to follow, because Hirschman was still moving his pieces around. Still, the exercise forced him to focus on what undergirded the final text: behaviors that were at odds with attitudes and expected theories, followed by potential explanations for "inconsistent" acts. His goal was to undo "ordinary sequences" that made attitude change a condition for social change, and thus the limits of exhortation as a way to effect it.[40]

This was his first iteration. While he was writing, he constantly adapted and refined his ideas. He was also updating with imports of breaking events and headlines: the flow of letters that Ralph Nader gave him from disgruntled customers, new issues of *Consumer Reports*, and the fate of the Black Power movement and its academic analogue, Black

Studies, in Bay Area universities. Indeed, Black Studies was an exemplary case. Its proponents asked students and professors to reject a traditional pattern of upward social mobility on the grounds that "it was unworkable and undesirable for the most depressed group in our society." The old pattern of "exit" of a few select African-Americans into white society, which was meant to promote "collective stimulation" of Blacks and the improvement of the ghetto, did nothing for those who remained. In losing the most promising members, Blacks were deprived of critical voices that might otherwise fight for the lot of the group. The rise of Black Studies represented the surge of a new kind of voice that Hirschman found "strikingly analogous" to the Nigerian railroads and public schools. They were all examples where peoples' exit was ineffective at getting organizations to change their ways while voice "was fatally weakened by exit of the most quality-conscious customers." Evidence of this kind of dynamic was all around him. Interestingly, Hirschman made no mention of his own exits—Berlin, Trieste, Paris, Washington—and there is nothing in his notes that suggested a personal connection.[41] If the seminar performance was confusing, it was because he was still sorting out his ideas for what would become a deceptively simple formula.

The final book, *Exit, Voice, and Loyalty: Responses to Decline in Firms, Organizations, and States*, was an immediate sensation; it had that unique mix of being quickly grasped while exploding in many directions. It explained how a World Bank project in Nigerian railways could aggravate relations between ethnic groups and stoke political exit or secession; it also illuminated how American students' demand for participatory democracy was starting to slip into the countercultural herald to "drop out" of society and locate freedom through exit. And he was going after reigning theories of monopoly, a major set piece of economics. It both illuminated current events while addressing core theories in the social sciences. What made the text all the more stunning was its economy of words; he could cover so much territory in so few pages. There was enough of a draft for Hirschman to send out something "too long for an article and too short for a book," ninety-seven pages. Despite protestations about being "out of my depths," Hirschman was not about to hesitate when he was on to something. And he knew he was on to something. "It's still rough and incomplete," he told the Harvard historian Ernest May, "but I decided to circulate it now in this form, get started on something else and later in the year complete the essay when I shall have gathered some comments and second thoughts."[42] Another copy went to departmental colleagues Ken Arrow and Harvey Leibenstein and to Columbia's Gary Becker, whom Hirschman had met at Cape Cod the previous summer. Arthur Stinchcombe, the Berkeley sociologist, also gave it a read and made some suggestions about the formal models, which later got demoted to the first four appendices of the final work. Hirschman worked furiously with the feedback, elaborated his points, and salted in the day's news. Nothing was going to get in his way. "It has been a book that wrote itself," Albert mused, "with no premeditation on my part." By the end of the summer of 1969, a draft was finished. As they packed their bags and prepared to return to a sundered Cambridge, Albert had to confess that the isolation had allowed him to break his own personal record. Now he had to brace himself for a return home to his cleaved university, friends who were no longer talking to each other, and the angst of teaching.[43]

Nine short but wide-ranging essays explored one of the soon to be most-cited analytical trilogies in the social sciences: "exit, voice, and loyalty." So it was that the petite idée germinated into a panoramic book at the heart of which—nestled in the middle of his manuscript—was the answer to the Nigerian puzzle, a seven-page essay called "How Monopoly Can Be Comforted by Competition." As he put his final touches on the manuscript, he reflected on the way in which this book "of vast scale and ambition" had evolved. It reminded him of the ways in which Eugenio had urged him to think of ideas and their unintended directions. "I have decided," he informed his sister, who may have had mixed feelings about the gesture, to dedicate it to Eugenio, "who taught me about small ideas and how they may grow."[44]

Two general propositions shaped the book. One was that the institutions that arranged public life for at least the previous half century were "in decline." Companies, governments, and organizations like universities, all were included. "Decline" was perhaps a misnomer; some organizations were in the throes of fundamental transformations and were hardly archetypes of sclerosis. At the time, it was not so easy to see this, and so the distempers of the late 1960s were seen as a symptom of demise. Hirschman was not alone in thinking this way, indeed decline and crisis were about to put an end to the flower-power happiness of the 1960s.

The second precept followed: faced with decline, inherited patterns of loyalty no longer kept "consumer-members" in their place. General Motors' loyalists were grumbling; some were defecting to other brands. Young Americans increasingly objected to the draft; some were bolting for Canada, Sweden, and elsewhere. The result was an expanding array of reactions, which Hirschman catalogued into two varieties: exit/desertion and voice/expression. One involved withdrawal in favor of another institution, product, or faith. The other meant that people raised hell at the status quo, arguing opinions, criticizing, and protesting. Each response tended to conform to disciplinary domains. For political scientists grounded in the theory of a social contract, voice was the operative term. For economists and their supply-and-demand laws, exit was likened to the workings of a market.

The brilliance of the book was partly in casting basic, visible reactions in simple, accessible words, but it was also capturing the feeling that people were torn between them, sorting out the relationship of exit to voice. Do I withdraw, or do I speak out? When do I choose between them? Here is where psychology helped sort through the ways in which people and societies wrestled with and justified their choices precisely because real-world choices were not always clear-cut; people were seldom diehard defectors or pure hell-raisers. Reactions sometimes substituted for each other, other times exit and voice were complements, and other times they undermined each other. It was the alchemy of mixing and switching between them that occupied the essays and for which the psychological forces helped account for choices. Thus, what was at first blush a simple book about alternatives quickly became complex; rather than stylize reality with a basic theory, Hirschman proceeded very differently. He deployed everyday words to capture some basic drives and then showed how their activity created a fluid, combined, imperfect reality. The world was hardly governed by pure competition, a fluxing universe of "exiters." Nor could it sustain itself on an unfettered, cacophony of "voice." Hirschman neither touted the exit-market option nor the voice-political one. Everything was computation. There may have been an "optimal" mix, but the blend was not a stable one. Even behind loyalty there was a churning, cognitive process. One of Hirschman's favorite passages was Kierkegaard's famous rendering of Abraham's angst over the sacrifice of his son as a gesture of his fidelity to God. Before Abraham's "infinite resignation" came his journey and choosing, and therein lay his freedom. For Hirschman, the interpretation "makes one realize that, in comparison to that act of pure faith, the most loyalist behavior retains an enormous dose of reasoned calculation."[45]

A final point needs to be made. For a Hirschman who appeared so confident—partly because of the simplicity of the formula, partly because of the grace and accessibility with which he wrote—he was also groping toward a more embracing social science. The two responses, exit and voice, and their disciplinary allocutions, economics and political science, were mixable alternatives not mutually exclusive. They were not polar opposites, one individual, the other collective. It was the interplay and interaction of the responses that was at stake. The citizen's challenge was to be influential and deferential at the same time, a "consumer-member."

The hyphen, his *trait d'union*, applied as well to the disciplines, which required "communication" between them. There was an underlying non-neutral purpose, however, to the communication between politics and economics; his was not a call for transcending disciplines for the sake of some greater objectivity. There is a lingering prophetic tone to *Exit, Voice, and Loyalty*. For all the balancing and mixing of urges and responses, there were dangers. One was that people might forget their deferential obligations and let voice get carried away. The other was the danger that overblown exit options might "*atrophy the development of the art of voice.*" At first blush, this seems a strange worry coming at the end of the very loud 1960s; many social scientists were worrying about the overflow of voice, not its atrophy. Nowhere is there mention that the consumer might eclipse the citizen. But Hirschman had his eye on the hazard and would, within a few years, have to contend with it. For the moment, what was important was for the social scientists to keep their eye on this precarious mix at the heart of the republic.[46]

Exit, Voice, and Loyalty (1970) would be the first of a series of interventions that braided sociological observation with a methodological message for the social sciences. This helps explain why he kept circling back to revisit his triad for the rest of his writing career. The interplay of exit, voice, and loyalty, not their divisibility, had led to an insight that he labored to expand as the optimism of the 1960s gave way to a very different mood in the 1970s.

We might then consider the book that would make him famous as itself a hyphen linking an "early" Hirschman concerned with economic development in Latin America to a "later" Hirschman working from a broadened intellectual palette. The connections emerge if we see them as thoughts in motion, concepts building upon themselves as he pushed at links between economic development and social change, between disciplinary dominions of the social sciences, between social contract and supply-and-demand settings. So much basic social science presented order (for political scientists) or equilibrium (for the economists) as the theoretical premise from which concepts derived. This propensity had the added attraction of propagating ever-more sophisticated versions, explanations, and models; they became so sophisticated that it became harder and harder to see the order-equilibrium principles at their conceptual core. Cases of disorder and disequilibrium were explained as the result of a malfunction inspired from outside—exogenous to—the core principles. Uniquenesses, exceptions, and anomalies were waved away from the basic conceptual settings. Hirschman wanted to turn this way of framing problems on its head, to look at the ways in which instability, disorder, and disequilibrium lay at the heart of the matter, how understanding their operation might provide keys to an endogenous approach.[47]

One advantage of small books, and this one's main published text barely exceeded 120 pages, is that they usually are quick to produce. That was the case here. Harvard University Press sent it to Kenneth Boulding, then at the height of his career at the University of Colorado, for review. It was a curious choice, for although Boulding shared Hirschman's interest in overcoming social science's disciplinary divides, his work was increasingly abstract; caustic reviewers thought him a flake. At least he was, Hirschman conceded politely, "broad-gauged." In a page and a half, Boulding urged a few edits, praised the style as "distinguished and occasionally brilliant," and suggested a different verb from "exit:" it sometimes "gets confused with excite." He also suggested that "re-entry" merited elaboration. It was, for all intents and purposes, a carte blanche recommendation.[48]

In one respect, Boulding was quite right. "In a sense," he wrote, "the ideas which it [the manuscript] contains have been around for a long time, but it represents a felicitous rephrasing of old concepts in new and lively language and a perception of relationships between them which have not been clearly apparent before."[49] Hirschman tapped into vintage debates. The brilliance was in putting them together and casting them in the current parlance of consumption and civic protest. What is more, the enterprise was framed in terms of social responses to the "decline" of firms, states, and other organizations—capturing a Zeitgeist of impatience fueled by corporate malfeasance and a worsening war, not to mention a feeling among many younger scholars who snapped up the book that the archaic ways of the university were crumbling.

In another respect, Boulding anticipated an issue that Hirschman would have to wrestle with in the future. The book was heavily tilted toward voice and exit, nouns that mutated into verbs, in part because they exemplified keywords of the age. Loyalty, possibly what Boulding meant by "re-entry," got short shrift. Loyalty was part of the coinage that was not so easily transposed from noun to verb. Indeed, loyalty all too often denoted no action at all, like a default setting or a background condition that shaped the more active choice between voice or exit; loyalty affected the algebra of whether to exercise voice or to make for the exit. "On 're-entry'—I shall think about it, but doubt that I shall want to do much more," concluded Hirschman. His treatment on the subject was earmarked in chapter 7, "A Theory of Loyalty." In fact, however, the chapter did not offer a "theory" of loyalty, but a precept for everything else.

Where people are more loyal, they tend to favor voice over exit; "as a rule," he noted, "loyalty holds exit at bay and activates voice." Still, even if it was not examined with the same dexterity as voice or exit, loyalty was central; it "is a key concept in the battle between exit and voice."[50]

In the end, Hirschman did no revisions to this corner of his triad, while the other two consumed him. This was a shame. The fact was, articulations of loyalism were brewing below the surface noise of protest and "dropping out." It should have been audible to an otherwise astute observer like Hirschman. For starters, right-wing reactions, from the Latin American despots to the governor of California, Ronald Reagan, vowed to turn back the clock on the rabble-rousers in the name of restoring basic values or rescuing the nation from (disloyal) insurgents and welfare bums. Loyalty was a blind spot in an otherwise enormously influential and illuminating book. It is hard not to imply a relationship between this lapse and the arc of a life made of constant uprootings and displacements—Hirschman could *see* the importance of loyalty, but he could not grasp it in the same way he did exit or voice.

The reception of *Exit, Voice, and Loyalty* was unlike anything Hirschman had experienced. There were the reviews, almost uniformly rapturous. They came from all quarters. Hirschman had finally straddled the divides. A leading journal in economics, the *Journal of Political Economy*, published an extended review by Joseph Reid Jr., elaborating the multiple directions and possibilities of Hirschman's work, treating it as a manifesto for a new political economy. "Rigorous building on Hirschman's new foundation will significantly extend the relevance and scope of political economy."[51] Political scientists had Roger Hanson's evaluation in the *American Political Science Review*, which accented the analysis of voice as the *political* features of the book.[52] The reception, however, was uneven. Though the book was "inter-disciplinary," sociologists and political scientists greeted it with more gusto than cousins in psychology and economics—possibly because it was written *from* psychology and economics *to* other social sciences and thus may have appeared "dumbed down" to the insider. Hirschman was delighted at the reception, though as he told Ken Galbraith, the enthusiasm of political science made the reception by economists look pale. Slightly cravenly, he revealed that the reception among his disciplinary peers was smarting a bit. "Can you tell me some time, in all frankness," he asked of his neighbor, "whether I can tell the Press that one economist has something nice to say about the book, too?"[53]

If this was a tactical effort to elicit influence among disciplinary colleagues, it was unlikely to work; as far as most academic economists were concerned, Galbraith was one in name only. It certainly reveals a yawning divide between Hirschman and his discipline's moorings, which went on full display in a rancorous review by one of the gurus of the emerging field of public choice economics, Gordon Tullock. *Exit, Voice, and Loyalty* burrowed under Tullock's skin; the issue had nothing to do with voice, Tullock insisted, and everything to do with the venality of monopoly. Hirschman's argument in chapter 5 was that a level of competition might induce exit from the monopolist, and thus diffuse angry, vocal customers. Competition, in this scenario, "comforts and bolsters" the flaccid monopolist by ridding it of "its most troublesome customers." So, we get a hybrid world of lazy giants and welcome competition—just the kind of complex, mixed systems made of apparent contradictions. This, of course, had been the enigma of the Nigerian railways, recognized as inefficient but able to soldier on. The US Post Office was another example. These kinds of realistic portraits—and not the fantasies of pure monopoly or pure competition—called for theoretical reflection—for Hirschman. For Tullock, the proposition was an amalgam of the dangerous and the naïve. A real railway monopoly was less likely to yield to voice or a "political" expression to the problem; it would have led to more gouging of taxpayers. Voice would never be an effective response to lousy service as long as monopolists could displace the costs of their inefficiency on hapless users or innocent tax payers; "political" solutions were no alternative to "market" ones. Tullock curled his lip and declared that "clearly there is room in the literature for a 155-page book on the responses of customers to declining efficiency on the part of their suppliers, and on the differences between changes in quality and changes in price. Unfortunately, this is not the book."[54]

This stung. Mancur Olson, the president of the Public Choice Society, tried to patch things up, explaining that the movement had no partisan leanings, that he himself was a Democrat. But he conceded that "perhaps the ideological gap was too wide to bridge. As Gordon would be the first to emphasize, he is at the far right of the old classical liberal or laissez faire conservative tradition, and you are surely not on that side"—though it is telling that Olson could not quite peg Hirschman and for this reason was anxious to keep him engaged: "It would be a real shame if you were to be permanently cut off from the Public Choice Society by the accident of a bad review." To have Hirschman at odds with Public Choice would be "as though Bob Solow had no part in the Econometric Society." This was a courteous stretch. Hirschman knew it. He agreed that he should not cut himself off from anyone "because of the manic writings of Gordon Tullock." Still, he came to the curt conclusion that "as you correctly surmise, I feel that I should not take part" in the society's activities.[55]

The longest, most perceptive critique came from the edgy political philosopher Brian Barry, after a global symposium on the book at the Rockefeller Center in Bellagio, Italy in 1973. The symposium was the idea of the president of the International Political Science Association, Stein Rokkan, and included a cross-section of global social scientists, including Shmuel Eisenstadt from the Hebrew University, Jack Goody from Cambridge, Giovanni Sartori from Florence, and economists Oliver Williamson and Olson from the United States. According to the Bellagio Center director, "Historians and old-fashioned political scientists would have felt quite out of place, if not out of sorts, at this gathering."[56]

Barry treated *Exit, Voice, and Loyalty* as the consummate "in" book at a time in which books by big time social scientists, like the rock album, were starting to be the in thing. The in book was one that combined simple essence with great ramifications. Even before the reviews, word of mouth had turned *Exit, Voice, and Loyalty* into a riptide. As Barry himself marveled, the book was an event in part because it crossed all the disciplinary divides that carved up the modern university, and in part because it synthesized the tenor of its time. It was a "talking point" from the moment it hit the shelves, an instant "model" for application and the immediate subject of dissertations. Barry worried that the book might become a "fad" before it became taken seriously. It was not Hirschman's worry; he lapped it up.[57]

The vocabulary of *exit, voice,* and *loyalty* immediately shaped scholarly discourse. When a group of Harvard professors wrote a collective letter to Henry Kissinger in 1971, urging the National Security Advisor and former colleague to resign from President Nixon's administration, they employed the language of *Exit, Voice, and Loyalty.* When their colleague, David Riesman, refused to endorse the petition, he used the same language. Riesman's reasons were that he feared above all that Nixon's men were considering the use of nuclear weapons and preferred to have Kissinger *in* the upper echelons so that his threat of an exit and public resignation would serve as a deterrent.[58] After all, Hirschman had called for a greater "measure of spinelessness" among opportunistic policy makers lest the governments they serve dispense public evils "of truly ultimate proportions."[59] What Henry Kissinger thought of all this is anyone's guess. Hirschman sent him a copy of the book, and Kissinger thanked him with no mention that Hirschman had suggested that the book might offer insights into exit in the wake of the Cambodia bombings.[60]

With *Exit, Voice, and Loyalty* out of the way and the Hirschmans back in Cambridge by September 1969, Albert plunged back into the world. Harvard did its part. "It's an unbelievable center: everyone comes through here," he noted with mixed feelings. In one week he lunched with François Bondy, who was returning from Buenos Aires, Rix Löwenthal, Henry and Claire Ehrmann; attended a reception with the deposed president of Argentina, Arturo Illia; and had a meeting with Andreas Papandreou, a friend of John Kenneth Galbraith and former economic advisor to his own father, George, another ousted democratic leader—from Greece.[61]

Meanwhile Yale University Press wanted to publish an anthology of Hirschman's essays. The exercise pulled Hirschman back to considering his own thinking about development and the flurry of essays he'd written about Latin America since *Journeys.* These essays were passé, so what to think about them in retrospect? What, as Tom Schelling queried, does one think about oneself over time? "What do you notice about your writing style? Do you recognize the same contemporary Albert Hirschman?"[62]

These were tough questions, and Hirschman labored to contend with them. He made sure that if this was going to be a challenge, he might as well rise to it in an ideal setting. June and July of 1970 saw him in residence at the Rockefeller Foundation's villa at Bellagio. In his application for the residency, he explained that he needed to write an introduction to a new anthology, a paper that would also double as the Harvard Lecture at Yale the next autumn. "I would like to get at the 'system' behind those connections between economics and politics which I keep uncovering in almost everything I write." The concern that was buried in *Exit, Voice, and Loyalty* continued to simmer in his mind. If the villa's director, John Marshall, was looking forward to his famous guest, he was soon disappointed. When Hirschman was not hiding away and writing, he was away from the villa touring the countryside around Lake Como with Ursula and Sarah. Ursula made herself at home in the villa, inviting herself to join Marshall for dinners.[63]

What emerged was probably his most elegant essay, "Political Economics and Possibilism," which brought his aphoristic style to full bloom and subtly introduced himself, perhaps with Schelling in mind, as an exhibit character called the possibilist. This essay was also probably his single most important. Hirschman's notes convey an urge to stake out the ground between revolutionaries who felt there was no change without big structural change and an emerging tide of conservatives who felt all change was structural change. What was needed was a clear statement of reformist principles. "The real criticism of the reformer," he scribbled on a small yellow sheet, "is not that he is ineffective but that he might just be effective and that he may thereby deprive the oppressed from achieving victory on their own terms." Included in the principles was the impossibility of complete knowledge and embracing uncertainty. "Go faster than Popper," he told himself, "Not only is history unpredictable but there can be no change without its unpredictability." It was too bad that social scientists were getting so fixated with the perfection of their prophecies: "We always try to predict change." What Hirschman proposed was a word swap—why not try exchanging *possible* for *probable*? This quest led him back to Kierke-gaard, whom he had read on the Italian campaign during the Second World War, and the distinction between the probable and the possible. "Aren't we interested in what is (barely) possible, rather than what is probable?" The drive for certainty and prediction reminded him of Flaubert's injunction against *la rage de vouloir conclure* as sure to lead us to a world of "pseudo-insights," foreclosed outcomes, and lost paths. This essay was often passed over by scholars who—especially in the context of the early 1970s—tended to consider Latin America as synonymous with turmoil and modernization gone wrong and so then did not look at the compendium in the same light as the more universally minded *Exit, Voice, and Loyalty*. And yet, we can see in possibilism the most lucid statement of a different stance on the so-cial sciences. Rejecting the prevailing concern to catalogue preconditions for successful outcomes or doomed fates, he wanted attention focused in-stead on possible paths, oddities, anomalies, unexpected and unintended effects, and of course his perennial affection for inverted sequences to chart a different way of thinking about social improvement. It was also a very different attitude to social research than one could find in, say Barrington Moore's *Social Origins of Dictatorship and Democracy* (1966), or in Seymour Martin Lipset's famous 1959 field-defining essay, "Some Social Requisites for Democracy." Indeed, had Hirschman's essay not been pigeonholed as an introduction to a volume of essays about Latin America, it might have ranked as one of the great set-pieces of the social sciences.[64]

Hirschman's collection was called *A Bias for Hope: Essays on Develop-ment and Latin America*. He planted a flag against creeping disenchant-ment with reform and development by introducing the world to a figure called the possibilist and to a kind of freedom that Hirschman defined as "the right to a non-projected future," which would serve as the possi-bilist's compass. The introduction was a salvo against revolutionaries who could only envision a post-alienated life as a complete antithesis to the present, as well as to those master social scientists wielding their predic-tive models over those condemned to be unable to understand them.

The composition reveals an author struggling to formulate his own voice, to speak out to the pessimists and the fatalists. We can also see him searching for a political economy of which the microactivity of choosing in *Exit, Voice, and Loyalty* was a part. As the disenchantment with Latin American reformmongering set in, and more and more of his students as well as colleagues in Latin America advocated radical alternatives, he felt compelled to articulate an alternative. On his desk was a manuscript by Judith Shklar, the Harvard political philosopher, a long-awaited study of Hegel's *Phenomenology*. It inspired a scribbled, self-clarifying, note to himself:

> I part company with radicals at point where I believe that un-intended consequences of human action are very powerful, that 'ruling class' is unable to control even by that it will set in mo-tion events that will lead to territory on which it never wanted to step—ie. I believe in dialectics in a very basic sense.

He went on:

> I part company with liberals because I believe that these two changes can come about only through conflict, crises and often that last *bublichik* of violence qu'il faut avoir le generosité de recevoir.[65]

As ever, the word choice was meaningful. *Bublichik* came from one of Tolstoy's fables for children. Feeling hungry one day, a peasant (*mujik*) bought and ate a large bun (*kalach*); still hungry he bought and ate an-other one; still hungry he bought and ate a third bun; still hungry he then bought and ate a *bublik*, a kind of small, round pretzel, and was satisfied. The peasant rapped his head and said: "What an idiot I've been! Why did I eat so many buns for nothing—all I had to do is start with eating one *bublik*!" The *bublik* was the small thing that made a big difference.

Paying attention to the small things could make a difference to polit-ical economy. But how? Change could not be planned, nor did it come naturally: "One can only grope for it," Hirschman argued. But did this mean the groping was all in the dark? Not quite. It meant being open to hidden and hiding connections between spheres, like politics and economics, which compels the social scientist to be more modest about claims and more open to surprise, like history with mixed sequences or the paradoxical effects of perceptions. Instead of grand schemes, he advocated the study of "smaller-scale processes of economic-political development." This was the spirit behind his growing classifications of mini-building blocks for a systematic structure. What is sacrificed in ambition is gained in flexibility and realism. Hirschman's agenda began with a change of vocabulary:

> Social scientists are looking for optimal policies and states, and that generally means that they are looking for optimal combinations of desirable, but mutually antagonistic ingredients of such states. Thus we look for the correct combination not only of contact and insulation, but of central control and decentralized initiative, or moral and material incentives, of technical progress and social justice, and so on.

He suggested that we

> devote at least a portion of our time and efforts to understanding the possible usefulness of alternation and oscillation, as opposed to optimal combination.[66]

"Political Economics and Possibilism" was a lucid and impassioned plea wrapping a fundamental problem. If disorder and disequilibrium shaped his conceptual scheme, Hirschman was still looking for a way to make it the premise for an integrative approach in the social sciences, notably weaving economic approaches to politics with understandings of political dimensions of the economy. He had an approach or style—words that concede that we are still short of anything smacking of a theory—that expanded the spectrum of possibilities because it stressed uniqueness over generality, the unexpected over the expected, and drew attention to the possible over the probable. It did so by widening the limits of what could be *perceived* as possible. "Is there [a] role for the unique event in the social sciences?" he mused to himself. Creating such a role would allow us to write different histories and yield different insights. Did we really have to write as if "everything conspired to bring a certain event (revolution or reform) about," or identify "every single element [that] was needed to bring it about," even if the event was a narrow victory? Herein lay the challenge that would consume the ensuing years of intellectual labor. Making room for small, anomalous events made unified theorizing a difficult, if not futile, task. How could one integrate the social sciences without a unifying theory, an *idée maitresse*? Once again, we see Hirschman setting an agenda for himself—but by now, small ideas were adding up to a big problem.

Hirschman's writings of the 1960s had the cunning ability to be both of their moment, capturing its dreams of progress, while at the same time standing at a remove, questioning its euphorias. It took the crisis of the 1970s, a vicious turn in Latin American politics, and lethal blows to reform in Europe and America to pull the possibilist back from the limb onto which he had climbed in pursuit of new ways to hope. But dark times would not dim his quest.[67]

CHAPTER 15

The Cold Monster

To perform the negative is what is still
required of us, the positive is already ours.

FRANZ KAFKA

No sooner did *Bias for Hope* roll off the printing press than Hirschman
packed his bags. His destination: Latin America. By now, he was
approaching intellectual celebrity. Unable to rival Jean-Paul Sartre, whose
visits to Cuba and Brazil some years earlier were those of a star, he had no
interest in the French philosopher's predilection to preach; fame never
weaned Hirschman from his ironic disdain for the pontificating foreign
expert, "the visiting economist syndrome." Still, the eagerness of major
intellectuals, ministers, and reporters to meet him was a reminder that he
was not immune from the affliction. When in Buenos Aires and assured
by the advisor to the Argentinian military junta that it adhered to his recommendations about unbalanced growth, Hirschman had been aghast.
These embarrassments were the price he paid for influence; they were also
reminders that some insights could lead in unwelcome directions.

When he set off for Mexico City, São Paulo, and Santiago, what
he encountered was a portrait of contrast. Brazil was in the thick of a
hardening dictatorship, the legitimacy of Mexico's one-party state was
cracking apart after the violence of 1968, and Chileans had recently
elected a Socialist president, Salvador Allende, whom Hirschman had
interviewed and liked during the *Journeys* tour eight years earlier. If there
was a region in the world where crisis and hope were interwoven, it was
Latin America.

Crisis and hope gilded Hirschman's message. As people packed seminar rooms to hear the sage of radical incrementalism and the apostle of reformmongering, he told Chileans that "underdeveloped countries" had more "opportunity for voice" than other countries where exit was a preferred response, such as the USSR. Echoing the hopes of the early Allende years, he waxed ebullient: the progressive chorus could enhance "the search *to invent* new channels for voices to be heard," thereby amplifying the possibilities for reform and checking the threat that exit might atrophy voice. The Brazilian dictatorship presented a different landscape. For Brazilians it was important to find the right balance, a "*punto de encuentro*," of less exit and more voice, to scent an invigorated opposition and grow ferment among progressive social scientists. To this point, Hirschman was upbeat. By the time he got to Mexico, he arrived in a country in upheaval. The shadow of the student massacre of 1968 still hung over the capital. His friend, Octavio Paz, had come out in vociferous condemnation. Strikes, social tension, and a "general feeling that the foundations of this regime which have been so stable for so long, are trembling badly" occasioned the need for sober rethinking. At the Colegio de México, one of the country's main intellectual hubs since its founding by Spanish exiles in the 1930s, Hirschman raised some reservations about the optimistic key of the exit-voice-loyalty triptych. Latin Americans were at a crossroads. Tempted by the "illusion" that it was easy to redistribute income to solve all problems, the urge to hit the rich and polarize societies "could damage growth" and "augment disequilibrium." Perhaps what he saw in Chile had planted the seeds of unease that began to germinate by the time he reached Mexico, where he ended his lecture speculating "that it is possible that there might be too many variations of voice—from petition to revolution." Still, Mexico did inspire at least one pun: "Why didn't it ever occur to Mohammed and the Mountain to meet half way?"[1]

It was not just Latin America that gave cause for self-reflection. The economic crisis of the early 1970s was a more general crisis of ideas—and of their institutional brainchildren. Entire paradigms and analytical systems began to crumble.[2] Since the election of Richard Nixon, the United

States was in more upheaval than ever. Ditching the Bretton Woods system made the world economy more turbulent. Inflation began its inexorable creep upward, economic growth slowed, and the war in Vietnam escalated. The gloom of the 1970s reversed what seemed in retrospect a festive, hopeful 1960s. In the summer of 1972, Tom Schelling asked Hirschman to write an essay for a special issue of the *Quarterly Journal of Economics*, prompted by Staffan Linder's book, *The Harried Leisure Class*, a Swedish broadside against the effervescence of consumption, which typified the changing mood. To Linder, affluent societies were caught on a treadmill of their own making. The preference for long courtships, time-consuming cuisine, and monogamous dating was giving way to sex, television, and jeans with ready-made holes. Hirschman questioned Staffan's dismal view. As with the swings he noted in *Exit, Voice, and Loyalty*, he predicted diminishing rewards from "obituary-improving activities" and a return to civic life and old style romance. As with markets, self-corrections might stave off the trap of harriedness. This was a bit abstract; it is hard not to see him struggling to resist disenchantment.[3]

The reelection later that year of Richard Nixon aggravated the more general malaise. In the early spring, Hirschman joined a "professors' march" against the Vietnam War, after which he quipped that there were real problems fighting Nixon: "One always suspects that everything he does is some sort of trick—one can't quite take him at face value." He joined the ill-fated campaign of the Democratic candidate George McGovern, writing a brief on US policies toward Latin America. If the electoral defeat were not enough, the Christmas bombing of North Vietnam unleashed B-52 Stratofortresses to shower Hanoi for ten merciless days. In response to the downing of some of the bombers, President Nixon ordered the extension and intensification of the carnage. Hirschman watched in horror. "I don't remember having been so shaken by a political event," he confessed, "feeling so strongly in my bones the need to do something since the Spanish Civil War broke out." These are revealing words for a man who walked around with wounds from the Aragonese front.[4]

While the world was shaking Hirschman's faiths, he was also increasingly unhappy at Harvard. The passage of time did little to alleviate his anxieties about teaching. By the end of the academic year 1971–72, he was exhausted and complained to Katia about how "everyday a new dissertation" and "two seminar papers [are] plunked down on my desk." His stomach still churned before teaching. "He lived for writing, not for teaching," recalled Stanley Hoffmann.[5]

To this was added a poisoned atmosphere in the university after the upheavals of 1969. Many of his former colleagues and friends would no longer speak to each other. Tensions ran especially high within the economics department. The faculty could not agree to a single appointment for three years. There were also deep methodological divides opening up. It affected Hirschman personally, though not because he sided with one or the other camp. Rather, it was the very existence of the divide that dispirited him. More and more, he found himself at odds with Shura Gerschenkron over student demands. In the spring of 1972, a group of graduate students asked him to open a departmental track in Marxist and neo-Marxist theory. Ever the ecumenical, he agreed, though in short order he confessed that it "has become a lot of work and nerves (and I don't know if anything will come of it). The brittle coalition I think I have put together may well crumble."[6] It did; the idea went nowhere. Increasingly, rather than get involved on either side of the various quarrels, Hirschman withdrew into a polite, respectful silence. He would rather preserve friendships than drop his gloves over a dispute he felt had been blown out of proportion. Henry Rosovsky, his former chairman and eventually influential dean, recalled that Albert "grew rather distant from the affairs in the Department."[7]

If there were colleagues with whom he regularly shared ideas, it was with junior colleagues. Visiting assistant professors such as Philippe Schmitter found in Hirschman one of the rare senior faculty interested in their work and careers. At the time, Harvard Economics was the home to a handful of well-known younger Marxist economists: Herbert Gintis, Samuel Bowles, and Stephen Marglin. While Hirschman seldom agreed with them, their intelligence and creativity engaged him. In an ambience better known for the stratification between tenured and untenured scholars, Bowles found Hirschman "extremely warm" and unusually so-

licitous. When in 1971, the gregarious Herb Gintis gave an opaque talk
to the faculty, many of the senior economists "freaked out." Galbraith, on
the other hand, was delighted to "have someone to my left!" Hirschman
was less extroverted; he saved his encouraging thoughts for a more discreet conversation later. When Hirschman returned from Mexico, it was
with Sam Bowles that he sorted out some of his early formulations about
economic inequality's effects on social behavior. In February 1972, "Sam"
(Bowles) and "Tom" (probably Schelling) joined Hirschman for lunch
at the Faculty Club. In the course of their discussion, Hirschman turned
his receipt into a graph of the "lexicographic ordering" of peoples' preferences between the pleasure they get from others' rewards versus their
own. After the lunch, Hirschman went back to his office and scribbled
his notes down on his yellow pad, giving himself a diagrammatic image
to synthesize his ruminations for what would become one of his most
influential papers, on the tolerance for inequality.[8]

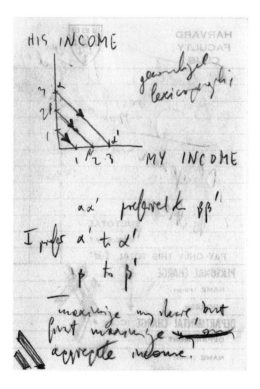

Lexicographic ordering.

Hirschman's was not an ideological affinity; he simply liked colleagues with fresh ideas. In 1969, Michael Rothschild was hired as a junior faculty member as a specialist in the theory of economic uncertainty; he came equipped with a powerful mathematical inclination. Hirschman sought him out. He wanted to know more about uncertainty and shared some of his own ideas with his younger colleague—who found Hirschman "completely wrong" but equally open-minded. Other senior colleagues might have bristled at Rothschild's pointed comments, but not Hirschman, who asked an "utterly charmed" Rothschild to collaborate with him on an essay. Over lunch at the Faculty Club, Rothschild plotted a simple mathematical formulation ("the least mathematical piece I have ever written," he would later confess). Impressed, Hirschman urged him to rewrite the draft so they could publish it together. Meanwhile, he asked a research assistant to help him hunt down a quote from St. Thomas Aquinas and gushed to Katia that "the whole theory is being put into equations by a young mathematical economist!"[9]

The mixture of faith and formulae was not to be. In the midst of all this, Hirschman checked into Massachusetts General Hospital for a heart procedure—so when Rothschild was done, he paid the patient a visit with the revisions under his arm. Hirschman flipped through the pages from his hospital bed, his face going from delight to shock. "This essay is all evidence!" he exclaimed. Rothschild was taken aback. The literary essayist and the precise quantitative analyst came face-to-face with their differences. But to Hirschman the personal relationship mattered too much for a falling out—and the article was eventually published under Hirschman's name with a mathematical appendix by Rothschild. Later, Rothschild came to recognize the problem: Hirschman ran into problems contributing to a field that had long-since made its ballast out of elaborate formulae and definitions.[10]

The mood in the department deteriorated substantially over the decision to deny tenure to Sam Bowles in December 1972. The faculty cleaved. Graduate students accused the senior faculty of ideological bias. Hirschman, a Bowles-backer, was away on leave that year, which meant he was absent for the dispute. But it only contributed to his lack of interest in departmental and disciplinary politics. In the wake of the Bowles vote, he tried to defer his return to Harvard—which generated "all kinds of problems." The chair mollified him with a lighter teaching load, which led Hirschman to remark wryly that "it's good to have some exit possibilities, that makes voice more powerful [sic]." Still, little could assuage him: within the first week of classes he had the feeling that "I'll never be able to get back to my manuscript—there are just too many other pressures and obligations."[11]

One day, he returned from his office and told Sarah that there was "a place where he dreamed of being." It was the Institute for Advanced Study in Princeton. Unlike Stanford's center, it had permanent research faculty who were spared teaching obligations to dedicate themselves to the pursuit of great ideas. Hirschman fantasized being an intellectual without having to be an academic, a model more familiar to his Continental origins than of the United States and its rapidly expanding university midriff. It turned out that his former chairman, Carl Kaysen, had become the institute's director. In November 1971, Hirschman wrote to Kaysen to inquire about a visiting fellowship for the following year. He had several projects going and was intrigued to hear that the respected anthropologist, Clifford Geertz, had recently moved there—"my work on the tropics would probably benefit from his presence." One project was a continuation of his interest in the economic, social, and political effects of technology in the Third World. "I have done a considerable amount of dabbling in this field, which I like to call Micro-marxism," he wrote. At the time, he was reading Fernando Ortíz's *Cuban Counterpoint* and Geertz's *Agricultural Involution*, both of which counterposed cultures organized around agrarian techniques. The project opened up a more conjectural topic, "a curiosity about attitudes and other changes that are entrained by technology although such changes were not visualized and much less intended, when the technology was adopted." Never one to let a useful crisis go by without examining the foundations of ideas that were now in crisis, Hirschman was switching tacks. He had happened upon some writings of Montesquieu and Sir James Steuart about the rise of industry and commerce that piqued his interest. "Both felt," he told Kaysen, "that the pursuit of material gain would keep men from indulging their passions for power, conquest, and domination." The current obsession with the Invisible Hand "justification of individual profit-seeking" had "driven out these earlier richer, though profoundly flawed, ideas."[12]

As with many fledgling ideas, these were still muddled. A sojourn in the wooded comforts of the Institute for Advanced Study, first as a visitor in 1972–73, and then permanently in the fall of 1974, would afford time to explore his multiplying tracks. It also would give him a base from which he could engage in broad conversations with Latin American colleagues, conversations that would shape the history of the social sciences in the region.

The lecture in Mexico was the first sign that his bias for hope was coming in for some self-interrogating. Meeting "half-way," holding down the middle ground, was not as easy as it once was—or seemed to have been. Certainly, what we see is Hirschman's urge to address positions—political as well as intellectual—as they drifted apart. Nowhere was this clearer than on the debate over what caused the gap between haves and have-nots, which was becoming a hot-button issue as development seemed to falter and hopes for social inclusion faded. The list of development disasters was growing; he'd seen some of them, like Pakistan and Nigeria, close up. Inequality had always been on Hirschman's mind; his Marxist background attuned him to class disparities. Conversations with Gintis and especially Bowles may have rubbed some radicalism off on their senior colleague. Certainly, Hirschman was forced to confront a rising left-wing critique of reformism in Latin America. By the early 1970s, his concern with inequality was shifting from a problem to solve *with* development to becoming a problem churned up *by* development—with politically explosive consequences. No book synthesized the disenchantment more than Samuel P. Huntington's *Political Order in Changing Societies* (1968), which assaulted the rosy prognostications of modernization theory that free markets, promoting growth, and expanding democracy were mutually reinforcing. Instead, argued Huntington, rapid development in the tropics made political systems more ungovernable. Hirschman did not agree with Huntington; he had been skeptical of earlier facile theories in which "all good things go together." But there was no reason to throw in the towel and assume the opposite. The development decade now appeared as just one more stage in a much larger saga of the history of capitalism—a "transitory" moment or an "exuberant phase." As he noted, with tongue in cheek, at a Harvard lecture in the fall of 1973, we are faced "unfortunately not with an income distribution explosion, but income distribution literature explosion. Those who would change the social order," he concluded, "oscillate between the illusion of complete powerlessness and the illusion of absolute power." On his lecture script, the final four words were circled. A line connected them to one more: "Chile." What one made of the debate over inequality was clearly tied to the political fate of reform in Santiago.[13]

Rethinking hope was not the same as giving it up. When Hirschman returned to Latin America again in the early summer of 1973—as the socialist experiment in Chile reached its acme—he was more determined than ever to uphold a middle ground, in part because it was caving in. To one side was a chorus calling for more radical solutions because anything else was doomed to fail; to the other were the head-shakers believing that all notions of change were futile, self-defeating, and downright dangerous. Hirschman mused over Octavio Paz's lament about Latin America's "lack of progress" and his frustration that it refused to learn from past mistakes. This type of defeatist thinking was a nub of the problem. Perhaps, Hirschman speculated, the pattern is more complex and its lessons were too easily forgotten. There "*are* periods of learning" alternating with periods of "*forgetting* past lessons." The result only contributed to the sense that nothing could be done incrementally, but rather only through a complete revolution. A potential title to Hirschman's ruminations, he noted in his diary: "The desire for total change as a recipe for disaster."[14]

By this point, Hirschman was trying to fathom the sources of frustration that often accompanied hope and led many to give it up. The lectures, travels, and conversations yielded a milestone essay aimed at querying the reasons to despair. "Very seldom does it happen," he noted, "that a new paradigm about the social world leads to modesty rather than to arrogance. If my paper has a virtue this is it, I believe."[15] In fact, the essay was hardly modest. "The Changing Tolerance for Income Inequality in the Course of Economic Development" was a critique of the prevailing disenchantment as well as a masterpiece about the psychology of epochal transitions. Indeed, he located the shift from elation to desolation in the early 1970s as one moment, one pendular swing, from one set of collective feelings to another. "I am working on a new topic," he told Katia in late 1971. "It's somewhat related to that famous Tocqueville passage, only that in my scheme people don't have to get to be actually better off, it's enough if they see some others beginning to be better off" to make them feel worse. "Envy is such a mean emotion." Worse, it is the "only one of the seven deadly sins from whose practice you don't ever get any fun or enjoyment (as you do initially from gluttony, avarice, adultery)." How could one account for the swings, particularly for people feeling worse off when nothing had worsened for them?[16]

The essay unveiled a famous metaphor, "the tunnel effect," which sought to capture how peoples' sentiments changed from gratification to indignation, as well as the arithmetic of expectations that governed the shift. One day, while caught in traffic at the entrance to the tunnel to Logan Airport in Boston, he watched the reactions of other drivers as well as his own emotional mercury. As the congestion began to give way, he noticed that those in the stationary lane greeted the advance in the adjacent lane with relief—with the expectation that they too would start to move. As they waited, horns started to honk, drivers grew jealous; relief became envy, and envy evolved into outrage because drivers began to feel that someone up front was cheating them. Their mood, as a result, grew much worse *because* they were once gratified and now felt deprived. If the observation of such a daily emotional routine was one source of insight, Hirschman never let the gains from literature drift far from his mind. As he cast about, he stumbled on La Rochefoucauld, a man dedicated to "his systematic attempt to show the pervasive presence of self-interest in all human conduct and feeling." It was La Rochefoucauld who "pointed out that when we rejoice at our friends' good fortune this is not out of friendship but because we expect to extract some benefit from their advance." Judging from Hirschman's preferences, he was likely inspired by

La Rochefoucauld's *Memoirs*, which entwined esteem and enmity in the portrait of his contemporary, Jean François Paul de Gondi, the cardinal of Retz. Now Hirschman was not necessarily endorsing the seventeenth-century French aristocrat; he was trying to expose the apostles of gloominess in the social sciences (like Linder and Huntington) who have "given what seem to me an excessively dominant position to envy, relative deprivation, share-of-the-pie consciousness etc." What he sought was to understand the oscillation between envy and other sentiments, optimism and pessimism.[17]

The *perception* that rewards were being doled out or denied—what Hirschman called "semantic inventions and inversions"—could reverse moods. The tunnel effect represented the first moment of elation; it described the "tolerant" 1960s, which were giving way to the politics of envy and outrage of the 1970s as the tunnel effect wore off. As in *Exit, Voice, and Loyalty*, there was a sliding scale of alternatives, from friendship and amity to rivalry and enmity, whose expression depended on circumstances; it was not necessary, he believed, to invoke dismal laws of human nature to reinforce "revolutions of rising expectations," anger from "relative deprivation," or "mobilization which outruns institutionalization"—stock-in-trade clichés of social scientific gloom. Rather, what was remarkable was the amount of "stability that has prevailed," whose persistence "cries out at least as much for an explanation as the occurrence of rioting, coups, revolutions, or civil wars." Still, in Latin America, what captivated people was the instability; even Hirschman had to conclude that there was reason for "more to come."[18]

The essay on inequality was one of Hirschman's most influential, in league with the witty blast "The Search for Paradigms as an Obstacle to Understanding." Clifford Geertz, who singled out "The Search" as one of the landmarks for what would later be coined "interpretive social science," applauded this one too. "This seems to me a wonderfully vivid metaphor; more valuable than a thousand flow charts linking one ism with another. It also confirms my long held suspicion that the car (automobile!) is the social psychologist's moving laboratory: the one venue in which human nature is revealed raw and undisguised." Geertz must not have known of

Hirschman's delight in driving and high threshold of tolerance for doing it so badly. Quentin Skinner, who read the essay several years later, called it "a fine example of your most delicately ironic manner of writing."[19]

Not everyone welcomed this appeal to understand how perceptions can lead people to abandon hope. Some figures on the Left, for whom Hirschman's thinking was altogether too bourgeois, too accepting of power structures, too reliant on voluntarist solutions, found the proposition an affront. Hirschman sent a preliminary version of the essay to Octavio Paz, who immediately asked if he could publish it in his magazine, *Plural.* When it hit the stands in September 1972, the article elicited outrage from one of Mexico's most prominent sociologists, Rodolfo Stavenhagen. Stavenhagen was irritated by insinuations that if the masses could just wait, they would get their just deserts; the problem was all in the head, which all too often lapsed into a justification for autocratic regimes to handle involuntary emotional switching. The Third World was teeming with indigence. No wonder there was so much contention! He argued that the tunnel effect was actually a "cul de sac," condemned to keep social scientists from focusing on real material inequities. Hirschman countered that it was precisely the relative deprivation theory that he wanted to challenge; his goal was to transcend the oversimplifying precepts about the minds of the poor, their impatience and envy—and, in a typical inversion, he charged Stavenhagen of simply collapsing into the same facile theories about what made people tick and explode. Instead of dismissing the importance of want, he was trying to spotlight precisely why inequality was a more important issue than ever. The pages of *Plural* laid bare two diverging currents in progressive thought that would contend for the heart of Latin American social science: Stavenhagen's strong materialism, which accented the need for fundamental revolution, and Hirschman's agenda for radical reform, which rested on a more subjective understanding of social classes and their struggles. When Guillermo O'Donnell, a skeptic of doctrinaire Marxism, read the exchange, he despaired for the Left. "This appalls me," he confessed, "as an indication of the climate which, I fear, is *in crescendo.* . . . Aside from the real and non-trivial difficulties of mutual understanding there is now an additional decision, an almost explicit and *self-righteous* decision not to understand and use it to issue 'denunciations' to a public that is barely interested in the contents of intellectual debate. That this has reached the ranks ALSO of the Stavenhagens is a very worrying symptom."[20]

What was clear was that if Hirschman had a voice, it was being exercised less in Cambridge, Massachusetts, than in Latin America. Starting with the fall lecture tour of 1971, Hirschman was to return to Latin America with greater frequency than ever. The occasion for his heightened circulation and visibility was not just his essays, which were often immediately translated into Spanish and Portuguese and led to more and more invitations to lecture south of the Rio Grande, but the makings of a network of a new generation of scholars in Latin America who would remap the social sciences and for which Hirschman would serve as intellectual guide and institutional broker. Its seeds were sown in the summer of 1971, when Hirschman accompanied an Argentine political scientist, Guillermo O'Donnell, whom he had met as a graduate student at Yale, to Brazil. Not one to overlook young talent, Hirschman appreciated O'Donnell's efforts to break away from the straightjackets of orthodox Marxism and radical nationalism that dominated progressive thinking in Latin America. Like Hirschman, O'Donnell was trying to bring the analysis of politics into closer dialogue with the study of economic development.

What emerged from their conversations was a lifelong friendship and an important collaboration. Hired by the Ford Foundation, they were dispatched to review CEBRAP (the Brazilian Center for Analysis and Planning), which had been cofounded by the sociologist Fernando Henrique Cardoso in mid-1969 and was dedicated to social and economic research with the goal of supporting democracy under the shadow of the military dictators. Brazilian universities had been purging faculty from its ranks; CEBRAP was a sanctuary for free inquiry, and it quickly became the hub of debate for dissident intellectuals. However, their contrarian stance set them against the idea of American support, viewing it as a pact with the devil, especially after sensational revelations about CIA subventions to the Ford-backed Congress for Cultural Freedom. On the other hand, autonomy from the military regime required resources. CEBRAP's leaders reached out to the Ford Foundation, and especially Peter Bell, a creative and progressive program officer in Rio de Janeiro, for independent support.[21] It was not an easy decision and divided the founders. It also created trouble for the funders, for the Ford Foundation bosses in New York were nervous about becoming so affiliated with rabble-rousing intellectuals. Cardoso and Bell agreed to a review of the organization led by a prominent Latin American social scientist (who could tame the passions of the more radical Brazilian scholars) and a respected North American above the fray (and thus able to appease New York). Hirschman and O'Donnell were the team; the exercise worked. Not only did the review open the spigot for further funding, but CEBRAP soon became a model for social scientists evicted from, or constrained by, universities elsewhere in Latin America. Along the way, Hirschman and O'Donnell engaged Brazilian colleagues in intense but friendly criticism, setting a tone for an opening, eclectic dialogue that would remap the social sciences.[22]

The fate of the Brazilian outpost foreshadowed others'. The question of how to sustain social science research in the age of spreading despotisms sent Hirschman shuffling around Latin America's major cities as an academic entrepreneur. There was also a spirit in the air to support critical voices unwedded to old orthodoxies, a spirit Hirschman was also keen to shore up. It was with these two goals in mind that he emerged as the broker of a network that would alter the region's academic milieu. A hub of this network was the Social Sciences Research Council (SSRC) in New York and its Joint Committee on Latin American Studies, which had been revitalized in the wake of the Cuban Revolution, when Latin America suddenly became a strategic concern for Washington. Under the helmsmanship of Bryce Wood and with generous support from the Ford Foundation and Carnegie Corporation, it promoted innovative research and eventually the formation of the Latin American Studies Association in 1964. Compared to other "area studies," Wood's was also unusual because it integrated distinguished scholars from Latin America. The combination of an active staff, energetic international networks, and resources laid the basis for a generational change in the social sciences. In 1971, Wood enlisted Hirschman to join him at a meeting at Yale along with younger scholars like Louis Goodman, who would eventually replace Wood at the SSRC, to consider the future of Latin American studies. To a promising Ivy League sociologist like Goodman, greeting Hirschman was like meeting an icon. But if Wood wanted a gregarious figure, Hirschman remained reserved and observant. When he spoke, however, all ears perked up: the crisis was an opportunity to open new directions in social scientific inquiry, insisted Hirschman. Bryce Wood saw his opportunity; he immediately brought Hirschman into the Joint Committee.[23]

It was a fortuitous moment in the Joint Committee's history, for its chairman, Joseph Grunwald (Hirschman's friend from *Latin American Issues* days and a prominent figure among reformist economists in Chile), announced that non-US scholars would be eligible for grants. This meant that now the SSRC could direct Ford money directly to the pockets of Latin American researchers. To this end, Ford gave the Joint Committee $1.5 million—a substantial sum in those days—to support scholars. On September 1, 1973, Hirschman replaced Grunwald.

Ten days later, Hirschman learned that the Chilean army was bombarding the presidential palace.

While rumors of a violent overthrow had been flying for months, the scale of the repression had few precedents. Like the news of Nixon's bombing missions, this one brought Hirschman to new lows, not just because so many innocents were perishing, but because the coup was a mortal blow to his hopes for reform. "Besides the horrible news about the current brutalities and suppressions, there is the despondency one feels over *la chance ratée*."[24] Later, as it became clear that the Pinochet regime had come under the influence of the Chicago brand of monetary, sometimes misleadingly called orthodox, economic thought, Hirschman would reserve some pitiless words for what he considered overconfident peddlers of false certainties. They reminded him of the happy planners of the 1950s—only this time more dangerous—and would embolden his concern to challenge the narrowed gauge of Milton Freidman's *homo economicus*.

But this battle came a bit later. Now, there were lives at stake. Old acquaintances, like President Allende himself, were buried in the rubble

of the presidential palace. Other friends and students, such as Jorge Ar-
rate (a Harvard-trained economist and one of Allende's close advisers),
were missing. Dismayed, Hirschman wrote to Guillermo O'Donnell in
Buenos Aires for his help in locating imperiled friends. It was against the
backdrop of the overthrow of Allende that he was asked to appraise his
Journeys toward Progress to celebrate the tenth anniversary of its publication. The ironic twist resulted in perhaps his most somber essay, for
Chile represented a real *fracaso*, not an overperception. He strained to
find in "this sense of shock" some room to "explore, almost from scratch,
the mechanisms of interaction between economy, society and the state."
He had to admit, moreover, that his "return journey" brought him face-
to-face with "negative side-effects" of policies that "formerly could legit-
imately be neglected." Nowadays, they were essential to understand for
any practical understanding of "the singularly Cold Monster that the
State has become in a large number of Latin American countries."[25]

Thus, a triple coincidence of the change in SSRC funding, Hirschman's
stewardship, and the Chilean coup marked an important departure in
Latin American social science and placed Hirschman squarely in the middle of its evolution. Hirschman's commitment to support younger scholars and his eclectic interests impressed themselves immediately on the
functioning of the Joint Committee. There was an additional point: the
Chilean tragedy was instructive for progressive social scientists, and he
dearly wanted to be involved in the makeover. "The hugeness of the mistakes committed by the leaders of the Allende coalition makes one wonder whether the Left is not afflicted with an incurable Death-Wish," he
wrote.[26] This was a disease he was determined to help cure. The Chileans
Osvaldo Sunkel and later Alejandro Foxley, Fernando Henrique Cardoso,
Guillermo O'Donnell, the Peruvian Julio Cotler, and others all had important stints on the Joint Committee, which was staffed by Goodman,
who recalled in particular how Hirschman and Cardoso "were brilliant
together." While they differed in style, in substance they were of a piece.
Without telling anyone about it, Hirschman went back to his Marseilles
experience and used the Joint Committee as a rescue instrument. He
and the others found artful ways to earmark funds for a special, not en-

tirely kosher, fund for writers like Tomás Eloy Martínez, who had to find sanctuaries and salaries. The SSRC, like a latter-day International Rescue Committee, laundered foundation monies. Then, no sooner did he move to the Institute for Advanced Study than Hirschman used its fellowships program as a haven for persecuted social scientists.[27]

Hirschman did not plunge into this adventure without personal misgivings. His interests in the outer world were competing for attention with new directions in his reading and writing. He told Carl Kaysen about a certain "cooperative research project on 'policy making in the sixties' which I thought I might want to coordinate. But the likelihood of this project falling into place and my desire to take it on are both receding fairly rapidly," he wrote in November 1971, with no trace of regret. But a month later, when it became clear that the Ford Foundation was poised to extend major funds to an SSRC project, Hirschman updated his qualms. "Between us, I feel a bit like the revolutionary who has an opportunity to make a revolution at the moment he has lost faith in it, but who in fairness to his followers, doesn't see any other course open to him but to go through with the 'project.'" To Katia he relayed a resolve "to finally bury my Latin American project" after opening "more letters portending difficulties in getting the project back on the tracks." It was becoming a "nightmare" dealing with many people "all wanting to make their own decisions." The only downside was missing the opportunity to collaborate with O'Donnell—"I really regret not being able to work with him." The same hesitation came up a year later, when Cardoso asked him to lead another review of CEBRAP for the Ford Foundation. He tried—unsuccessfully—to beg off. Though "it is one of the most interesting intellectual enterprises I have come across and I feel greatly honored to be called upon to participate in the discussion about its work that you are planning," he was on sabbatical, lost in some remote readings, and was reluctant to travel because he was "deeply immersed in a new project." In the end, though, he acceded; an invitation to be at the table when Latin American social scientists were going to discuss their fate was not something that Hirschman could easily turn aside. "This was too nice and honorable assignment to turn down."[28]

The Chilean coup tipped the scales in favor of involvement. After the sobering trip in 1973, it was all the more important to get beyond the either-or of exaggerated hopes and paralyzing despair. Events only confirmed that free markets were "not a solution" and social revolution is "not available." Hirschman wanted studies of policies that made differences; he wanted to nurture a social science that would liberate Latin Americans from their defeatism and its twin, the application of fancy "theories" derived from someone else's experience.[29] In the meantime, the SSRC had its hands full with a deluge of applications from beleaguered students and scholars in Chile and Uruguay. In the shadow of the Chilean tragedy, the committee gathered at the SSRC offices in New York in November. Hirschman began the meeting by suggesting that the committee support collaborative, thematically driven projects conducted *in* Latin America itself and avoid the tendency for "area studies" to be an American invention. O'Donnell (who was not on the committee) drafted an outline for a collaborative project on "public policy" in Latin America. Given the complexity of personal relations involved, Hirschman tapped a young Columbia political scientist, Douglas Chalmers, who regarded O'Donnell's essay on dictatorships as a landmark. Chalmers penned a memorandum outlining a complex proposal to study "the State."[30]

Getting an amorphous theme like "the State" into an integrative research agenda could not help but mean more discussion, not all of which helped clarify the point of the exercise. Hirschman had to press softly to create a coherent network that still enabled participants to realize their own agenda within it. To this end, Hirschman arranged a follow-up meeting at the Instituto Torcuato di Tella in Buenos Aires and asked Guillermo O'Donnell, the host, and Philippe Schmitter of the Carnegie Endowment for International Peace in Geneva, to plot out for the group a framework centered on something that had concerned him since the 1950s: public policy. The O'Donnell-Schmitter manifesto argued that the project should focus on policy making from the perspective of "the State in action," understood as the making of policies within the structure of the state and between the state and civil society. It was still pretty vague. From Buenos Aires, Hirschman set off on an academic shuttle diplomacy to enlist participants in Santiago, Bogotá, and Mexico City. Chile in the early days of the Pinochet dictatorship was a chilling atmosphere—but Hirschman tracked down a young economist, Alejandro Foxley, who was trying to assemble a group of progressive social scientists under the umbrella of a research center, Corporación de Estudios para Latinoamérica (founded in 1974), at the Catholic University. Foxley, a Christian Democrat, was eager to join the network. "I had an excellent impression of the group Foxley has assembled," who, it so happened, shared his determination not to be overwhelmed by the grisly atmosphere: "They are intelligent, outspoken, determined to persevere and to react to the gloom over what has happened in Chile by hard work and independent thought." Colombia presented a different landscape, for several important figures were joining the newly formed López Michelsen government, which was determined to revitalize 1960s-era reforms. This put some of the obvious partners beyond the reach of a research consortium. In Mexico, he contacted his former graduate student, Carlos Bazdresch, a rising star in Nacional Financiera; he would work with José Luis Reyna to draft a prospectus for Mexican research.[31]

So it was that Hirschman assembled the pieces of a large, multinational collaboration. If the initiative stimulated the beginnings of an important debate, some realities descended on the group. The global economic downturn took its toll on the SSRC's big funders: Ford had to cut back its support of the Joint Committee at a time in which more money was being siphoned to scholars at risk. And, as with any large collaborative venture, this one had frictions to overcome. Some were personal. Not everyone got along; Alfred Stepan appeared to lose interest, so the project lost its Yale moorings. Others were matters of reconciling academic styles: there were some (such as Cardoso and Schmitter) who had theoretical inclinations; Cardoso urged that the group explore alternative conceptual coordinates rather than apply a mechanical application of a model that most of the Latin Americans involved were, in any event, leaving behind. Others (such as Hirschman, and to some extent O'Donnell) wanted more empirical case studies, believing that the new coordinates would come from some careful observations. "A storm has broken out" in the project, Hirschman told Katia. But rather than push his thumb on a scale, Hirschman let the steam blow. He found the tension productive. Cardoso's intervention was "very inspiring;" he "stuck his neck out" by criticizing "middle-level modernization," he noted gleefully to himself. The injunction inspired a little reminder: "What we need is a few shafts of light rather than total illumination."[32]

All this aggravated the intrinsic problem: the consensus over the "concepts" did not make for a research plan that was at once coherent and collaborative—especially one involving several disciplines, countries, and intellectual traditions. One observer complained that the Buenos Aires meeting "got bogged down in highly rhetorical discussions of theories of the state, and that the linkages between these theories and available or future empirical research was not well developed." Hirschman himself had to write to Schmitter with the good news that the SSRC had approved funding for the group to move ahead and draft a "concrete proposal," but he was direct in his concerns about Schmitter's participation. He urged him to write less "for the cognoscenti" and to develop "some positive contributions for the field. The project as presented by you and Guillermo was obviously too vague to warrant the commitment of sizeable funds." Schmitter was drifting off anyway, becoming more interested in the democratic transitions unfolding in the Mediterranean world; as it would turn out, these transitions would have profound implications for how Latin Americans were thinking about the fates of their own despots. To compound matters, O'Donnell was engaged in a prolonged drama over whether to remain in Buenos Aires or take a position at the University of Michigan. Never inclined to lead with gusto, Hirschman was less and less inclined to head this project. He was on to something else. One evening, after a long day of meetings in New York, Hirschman and Goodman bid their adieus outside the SSRC offices. As they shook hands, Hirschman reached into his bag and produced some reading materials for the rest of Goodman's evening. It was not another manifesto on policy making and military juntas, but rather ruminations about seventeenth-century anxieties about markets. Goodman looked at it, stunned to find that his chair of the Joint Committee had been laboring on something so removed from the concerns about despots in Latin America.[33]

The fact was, Hirschman preferred to lead by example, not persuasion. By settling into his new quarters at the Institute for Advanced Study (IAS) in Princeton, which became, de facto, the new home for the project after the Yale ties were cut, he could play a hosting role. But he was not a virtuoso organizer; the "revolutionary who had lost faith" knew it. The project's fruition required someone else's shoulders. These, it turned out, were supplied by the University of Indiana's young political scientist, David Collier, who was visiting the Center for International Studies at Princeton University (which allowed him fluid communication with Hirschman down the road). Collier would fill in for Hirschman, who had once been drawn into providing leadership of the group, albeit ambivalently. The surviving core group met in Princeton in March 1975 and brought in David Collier. This was a partnership that clicked. Hirschman could offer up the IAS as a base without having to alter his personal writing program. The IAS also afforded the network some strategic support through its fellows program—every participant in the network had at least a year there; Cardoso had three years at the institute. And at times, the institute gave cover for beleaguered Latin Americans. After his first year in residence at the IAS, the Brazilian economist José Serra returned to São Paulo in May 1977 for meetings and to take care of some personal matters. Upon his arrival, he was detained and interrogated by the police. He was not tortured but grew more alarmed as he was dragged back to the constabulary three more times, and he began to fret when the police seized his passport; his wife, Monica, still in Princeton, was distraught. Hirschman got on the phone with Joseph Grunwald—who had recently stepped down as President Carter's deputy assistant secretary of state for inter-American affairs. Grunwald put him in touch with a list of prominent State Department officials, including Terence Todman, the assistant secretary of state for Latin America, whom Hirschman had met at previous Washington gatherings. It is not known whether his round of phone calls made the difference, but thereafter Serra had no further problems with the police, got his passport, and folded back into the network without a hitch.[34] As with the operation in Marseilles, Hirschman remained discrete; the invisibility of his intervention maximized its chances of success. Serra never knew of this behind-the-scenes activity.

What he was best known for, as so many visitors noted about Hirschman at the institute, was his part as gracious host, a role he relished. Daily lunches, family gatherings for dinner at the Hirschman home on Newlin Road, and the hallway conversations infected the Latin American visitors. "My constant talks with Albert Hirschman," wrote Fernando Henrique Cardoso to Carl Kaysen, "alerted my mind toward the importance of looking, with passion, at emerging possibilities for unexpected changes in social processes." This was now reflected in the essays he'd written while a member of the institute, a self-reflective preface and postscript to his influential *Dependency and Development in Latin America*, as well as a critique of the ways Latin American dependency theory was being "consumed" in the United States.[35]

Often enough, the most distinguished member of a group is not its natural leader. The decision to step back from his involvement in the SSRC group, to become its *patrón* rather than its coordinator, was precisely what had to happen—and it is to Hirschman's credit that he recognized this and kept the group treading water until a more appropriate coordinator emerged. In October 1975, when the Joint Committee finally unveiled the agenda for the Working Group on the State and Public Policy, it elected to focus on the nature of authoritarianism in the heavily industrialized countries of Latin America. Collier's notes, memoranda, and planning gave it the entrepreneurial skills that Hirschman had lacked—and did not, by this stage in his career, feel any inclination to develop. Looking hard at authoritarianism combined the ethical concerns of the committee with a set of hypotheses about the fragility of democracy in South America. A relieved Louis Goodman was finally able to write to Collier that "since this project was first suggested several years ago, a number of scholars have been interested in it but no one had been able to develop the theme in a way that gave it an adequate intellectual focus or generated enough enthusiasm to make it worth pursuing." O'Donnell likened Collier "to the good *muchachos* of a Western movie that I used to watch a kid. They go through thousands of dangers and as the end of the film approached it would seem there was no hope, but in the crucial moment they find a way to survive, conquer all evils, marry the *chica* and live happily ever after. Really, I congratulate you."[36]

There was another shift, as well. The 1960s era of reform had presumed that civilian rule was the framework. Now the landscape had dramatically and tragically changed. The inner gravity of the collaboration shifted from Hirschman's agenda on possible policies to an examination of the structural constraints on democracy, with an emphasis on the overarching systemic ways in which capitalism had bolted together big social forces to limit or "determine" (a keyword of the day) the paths forward. In the late 1960s, O'Donnell had begun to fathom the economic factors lurking behind the rise of dictatorships to argue that generals were called in to resolve a crisis of economic growth: as industrialization faltered in passing from its "light" to its "heavier," more capital-intensive phases, civilians lost control and despots moved in; as the process of industrial "deepening" ran into trouble, juntas imposed stability. In this fashion, the phases of capitalism in Latin America predicted the type of regimes governing them. His provocative thesis did double duty. It threw down the gauntlet to left-wing anti-imperialist dogmas by drawing attention to the domestic forces behind the new alignments. It also challenged American political science chestnuts about the region's "chronic ungovernability." A lot of the analysis relied upon Hirschman's earlier notion that thickening and deepening the linkages around strategic sectors was the key to growth.

If O'Donnell's original formulation became the unifying hypothesis, Hirschman was exercising his influence on the Argentine to loosen the structural cords of his analysis. It was too deterministic for his tastes. It confused some temporary growing pains of industrialization with a full-blown crisis. And it fell into the very logic that the generals and their social scientific advisors used to justify their harsh measures. One of the rituals at the IAS was for fellows to present their work to the other members. When O'Donnell's turn came around, he presented the draft of a paper that revisited his own original theory of authoritarianism. Hirschman and Geertz went after him. When O'Donnell sent a revised draft, Hirschman "recalled that both Geertz and I were critical of your seminar presentation because of a certain economic determinism. Your paper now shows that the cure for unconvincing economic determinism cannot be less, but more and better economic determinism!" Hirschman tried to impress a more nuanced view of economics that could not be reduced to the imperative to create capital goods industries, as if that were the only logical sequence to earlier stages. This, complained Hirschman, exaggerated the role of backward linkages and overlooked other industrial options and problems. It also did not travel well as a model. What about Pinochet? Chile's industries were in crisis long before Allende. And the Chicago Boys made no pretense about wanting any "deepening," although they did make a lot of noise about price stability. Hirschman enclosed a copy of a paper of his own that revised the notion of linkages that had been so influential on O'Donnell. This is where he made the case for "micro-Marxism." The paper urged readers to examine their copies of *Capital* more carefully: in the oft-cited passage where Karl Marx claimed that "the industrially most developed country does nothing but hold up to those who follow it on the industrial ladder the image of their own future," he suggested that all capitalisms were bound to exhibit the same features no matter how late the start. Hirschman suggested a more extended reading: "One only has to read on in order to realize that Marx had a very acute sense of small and critical differences." The very next paragraph ("which is apparently never read by those who quote the above sentence," admonished Hirschman) has Marx illuminating a very different path of development for Germany than England.[37]

For years, Hirschman had been making the case for the plenitude of historical tracks and no fewer possibilities for moving forward. By the mid-1970s, the quest to understand why social scientists were so immune to considering alternatives had Hirschman fathoming his own intellectual origins, leading him back to formative theories that "by mistaking, or ignoring one of the possible courses events may take" select their own blind spots. Reading *Capital* sent Hirschman back to Hegel's *Philosophy of Right*, and thence back to Marx's extended commentary on Hegel's section on "Civil Society." In this trail, he identified a gap in Marx's reading—or more precisely a failure by Marx to see that Hegel had, by 1821, come up with an economic theory that gave a potential outlet for problems of capitalism, in this case in the form of an empire. Thus, Marx could not profit from Hegel's insight about capitalism's uncanny ability to open up unforeseen solutions to its problems because he committed the error of so many "theorists" who, "in their eagerness for structural change, often fail to appreciate the ability of a 'tottering system' to remedy its worst weaknesses or simply to hang on." Not uncoincidentally, he was tracking Marx's blind spots just as he was writing to O'Donnell. In the midst of this, he reopened his notes on Judith Shklar's manuscript on Hegel's *Phenomenology* and laid them on his desk. Then he went to Shlomo Avineri's recently published *Hegel's Theory of the Modern State* (1972). This prompted him to ask Avineri in Jerusalem about Hegel's economic thinking and tie-ins with Sir James Steuart. Avineri sent Hirschman to the *Jenaer Realphilosophie*.[38]

Reading had become like detective work; following the clues revealed the early oversights and missed possibilities of predecessors. This had consequences for later (sometimes centuries so) social sciences generations. It is easy to skim the arcana that connected Hegel to Chilean inflation as a little pedantic, and some may think Hirschman was turning self-absorbed, withdrawing into ivory-towerish scriptures. But if the social sciences were going to be useful for a democratic Latin America, it had to move from the ground to which the Right and Left had converged—that capitalism was doomed in the region without some radical solution and complete break from what came before.

It was clear enough to O'Donnell, who did not fail to get the point about the Cunning of History, that social scientists were not free from History's traps. By implication, Hirschman positioned himself to O'Donnell as Hegel was positioned to Marx—with the obvious difference that he had the luxury of pointing out the blind spots to his younger colleague. Blind spots not only produced failures to see new patterns, but also blocked ways out of the very structural binds theories were meant to analyze. No wonder the circularity drove Hirschman to distraction. O'Donnell relented, to a point. He accepted that it was "vulgar and mechanical" to have "the productive structure" to explain "all of society." "Of one thing I am sure, between your work and mine there is *something* more in what we are doing. As you can see, you can see what happens to me when I read you and am provoked by you, even if it leads to this waterfall of speculations."[39]

The to-and-fro between Hirschman and O'Donnell revealed a creative tension around which the group organized—to push, test, and recast a hypothesis about the ties between capitalism and democracy, which is what Hirschman had wanted all along. What came of these discrete acts of private tact was one of the keystone anthologies in Latin American social sciences, *The New Authoritarianism in Latin America*, edited by David Collier. When the page proofs were finally done, Collier sent them to Hirschman, Cardoso, and Serra. "This opportunity the past three years [has] been an important period of intellectual growth—and I suspect also of personal growth—for me." As he wrote these lines, he was also in the midst of a move from Indiana to Berkeley. "Reaching this point in the project also leads me to think again of the crucial contribution that Albert has made to our efforts. Particularly through converting the Institute into a center of intellectual ferment for research on Latin America, and through his valued advice conveyed in the course of more phone conversations over the past three years than either of us would care to count, he has played a central role in the project."[40]

In the meantime, the long crisis in Argentina reached its awful climax just as Hirschman planned to leave for South America. The demise of Argentina's civilian regime coincided with efforts, spearheaded by Oszlak, O'Donnell, Marcelo Cavarozzi, Horacio Boneo, and eventually Elizabeth Jelin, to pull together a group of independent researchers in Buenos Aires akin to CEBRAP. In the final months of the Perón government, with his father-in-law named minister of social welfare, O'Donnell was all too aware of the impending explosion. "Here we are with everything moving in sustained fashion towards the final collapse." In the midst of "an incredibly profound crisis," one has to marvel at "the real talent of the government to make it worse and to exasperate everyone it should not, which means, I fear, unlikely that we will reach *tierra firme*." With gratitude and hugs for Albert and Sarah, O'Donnell signed off. Argentine generals toppled the hapless Isabel Perón in late March, which brought the authoritarian question into even more dramatic relief.[41]

It was in this context that Hirschman wrote a series of penetrating essays that took him back to the kind of analysis that influenced him so

much during the dramatic collapse of the Weimar Republic. His sense
then was that analyses of crises had to account for possibilities for escaping them. There were more "roads" to be traveled for a developing society
than many economists admitted; likewise, there were plenty of alternative
political passages. Recovering the contingencies implied "special attention to intervening variables, in particular to the beliefs of ruling groups
about the kind of policies and politics that are required to deal successfully with problems and emergencies in the economic sphere." It was, he
would argue in his contribution to the anthology, in the intervention of
beliefs, perceptions, and ideologies that one might connect economic
problems with political outcomes. Writing to Collier in April 1976, he
explained that "my longstanding interest in ideology and perceptions
makes me want to look at the connections between phases of economic
development and political forms as they are *mediated* by ideologies and
perceptions." As he explained, "It makes a great deal of difference to the
way in which politics are played whether elites perceive a certain cycle of
industrialization as having run out of steam or not."[42] We are back to the
concern to turn *fracasomanía* (the obsession with failure) on its head—
only now the motives were as political and ethical as they were economic.

The summer of 1976 took him on a five-country peregrination
through a troubled region, beginning in Bogotá and ending in Santiago.
In between, the hotels of Medellín, Cali, Caracas, Brasilia, São Paolo, Rio
de Janeiro, and the Gran Hotel Dora on Maipú Street in Buenos Aires
were there to greet him. When he got home, his pockets and suitcase
were bulging with an accumulation of business cards. He rekindled old
friendships, such as that with Aníbal Pinto, and made new ones, such as
Alejandro Foxley and Juan Sourrouille. His notes from the trip bear all
the trademarks of his style, as well as his exuberance about being back
in the field. As usual, he reserved the most time for policy makers. Jorge
García, head of Colombia's Planning Office, told him about the efforts
to direct funds into natural resource extraction and the "disasters" of
government-sponsored investment, such as Renault and Alcalis. Hector
Hurtado, the finance minister of Venezuela, told him about his efforts to
salt more of the country's oil rents away from the *torta* to consumers in

favor of a "special investment fund." From his meetings with businesspeople and engineers, his prose is laden with detailed excitement about their ventures. J. L. Bello, a mechanical engineer, waxed enthusiastic about the developments of Brazil's machine tool industry. Meanwhile, intellectuals were largely a complaining lot. Francisco Leal Buitrago, a student of Colombia's agrarian question, blamed the bourgeoisie for turning "into a bunch of speculators." José Luis Zabala complained about how Pinochet's free trade dogma was decimating local industries.

Throughout his field notes on conversations, Hirschman sprinkled in his petites idées (only some of which appeared later in print) characteristics of his preference to observe, aphorize, and double-check his hunches with follow-up questions. Brazil, especially, captured the paradoxes he found so fascinating. "Rapid economic growth legitimizes or is believed to legitimize. The tunnel effect had actually worn off in 1974 perhaps because there was no progress achieved along political lines. As a result there arose a lack of belief in the reality of expansion. (Remember how Roberto Cavalcanti was booed at the Brasilia Congress for saying real wages had increased during the last year or so: people just could not believe it.)." On the other hand, he noted a few pages—and interviews—later, the government had a self-destructive habit of believing its own growth-promoting myths. "High growth rate makes for white noise that drowns out other noises coming from other problems of society. This isolates the policy makers." This led him to a reprise: "Amendment to the tunnel effect," he noted:

> In the period of rapid growth it is possible for the policy makers to *believe* that everything is in good shape; propaganda and the real worries about the maintenance of the growth rate are then drowning out information about the non-conformity of the 'ungrateful' masses (shades of Churchill after the war). Also the concentration on economic discussions may mislead the government into thinking that the principal problem is economic when what people really want is something quite different. In this manner the government becomes victim of its own manipulation of freedom of expression.[43]

Over and over, he intoned to himself: "Make connections!" Between politics and economics, beliefs and behavior.

The booing of the aspiring politico Cavalcanti referred to an occasion in Brasilia that exemplified the kinds of openings that Hirschman was searching for in the dictatorship. Though the country was in the grip of autocrats, he sensed that there was a prospect for change. In fact, he did not have to look too hard. Strikes were spreading; the government wavered between letting go or repressing. Cardoso himself was sticking his neck out. Hirschman flew to the Brazilian capital to join him at the meetings of the Society for the Progress of Science in time to witness his friend delivery a fiery speech denouncing the government. When Cardoso returned to his seat, Hirschman leaned over to say in grinning admiration, "I never imagined you as a *pamfletario*!" Rumors started to fly that dissidents were about to be rounded up, which filled the meeting with paranoia. Every time a door opened, everyone jerked their heads to see if storm troopers were barging into the hall. "This might be the strangest conference I have ever attended," Hirschman told Cardoso. That night they dined with Severo Gomes, the minister for Commerce and Industry, a moderate within the dictatorship. As long as Gomes was at the table, no one would get arrested. Cardoso noticed Hirschman poke away at his dessert to forestall the end of the meal—and the possible storm troopers. In the end, the meetings were uneventful. The next day, Ruth and Fernando Henrique Cardoso took Sarah and Albert on a long voyage into the Brazilian backlands to visit the old city of Goiás, the home of Cardoso's ancestors. In the governor's palace, a portrait of his great-grandfather still hung. They toured the Baroque city and then bounced along the washboard roads to Fernando Henrique's cousin's rustic ranch near Jaraguá. When they finally reached their destination, Albert was astonished to find a recent edition of the *New York Review of Books* lying on a rickety old table, and they all sat down in the shade to spend an afternoon eating steak and discussing French literature. Such was the diversity of Brazil, and the reminder to Hirschman of his affection for Latin America.[44] After one trip to visit Cardoso in São Paulo and O'Donnell in Buenos Aires, he confessed that "I rather enjoy the position of being the intellectual and personal friend of the people in these centers . . . . In addition to the intellectual endeavor there is involved here a cause one has in common and that makes for a great deal of warmth and friendship."[45]

In the cacophony of griping there lurked alternatives. With the slumping economies and human rights atrocities, it was easier to see cause for despair. This bolstered Hirschman's studious efforts to keep his hopes up. When Gert Rosenthal, the director of the Economic Commission for Latin America, sent Hirschman the proofs of a Spanish translation of one of his articles, Hirschman replied with a fable about the need to exaggerate one's hopes in order to motivate oneself to pressure for change. It is a necessary myth for progressives, Hirschman explained, like the allure of a mirage to motivate a caravan forward through the desert even though it may eventually only find "a tiny waterhole." For without the mirage, "the exhausted caravan would inevitably have perished in the sandstorm bereft of hope." While the results may pale beside the hopes, at least the caravan arrived.[46]

Hirschman returned to Princeton at the end of the summer determined to challenge the sacred cows of ideologists. And none was more sacred than the assumption that it was the nature of capitalism in Latin America that market life required despots. For the Left, the pressures to "deepen" heavy industry by securing the investment climate had called for jackboots to tame unruly citizens. To the Right, the argument was not dissimilar: populists and radicals had the region spinning out of control, and if modern life was to be salvaged, it required some cleansing of public life. It was precisely this agreement—and the circularity of the arguments that buoyed it—that inspired Hirschman's dissent. There was an ethical purpose to his stance: "The more thoroughly and multifariously we can account for the establishment of authoritarian regimes in Latin America, the sooner we will be done with them," he affirmed.[47] A fresh view could point to a multitude of, but not limitless, possibilities and yield stories free of the normative weight that dominated development studies—the "tendency to look for heroes and villains."[48]

There was no more villainous character in Latin America in the mid-1970s than the confederation of economic elites and generals. This fixation was one that Hirschman was determined to break up. One of his implicit aims was to find ways in which economic elites might be salvaged from narratives that depicted them as hopelessly reactionary and bereft of scruples. A strain of his writings from the 1950s had extolled the hidden virtues of the entrepreneur, the doer. The importance of leadership and a heroic coalition of creative *réalisateurs* and intellectuals was one of his underlying themes, and "the polarization and lack of communication between these two types symbolizes, and at the same time renders more arduous, the transition from stagnation to dynamic development." These were his words in *Strategy*. Almost two decades later, as the curtain fell on civilian regimes, one cannot help but sense that Hirschman had the fate of the Weimar Republic in mind, in which business elites had abandoned their pluralist and democratic principles because they felt they had no choice. He admitted that it was hard not to despair. Once upon a time, Enlightened thinkers optimistically affiliated market life with individual liberties, conjuring—as de Tocqueville put it—"a necessary relation between . . . freedom and industry." Now, the affiliation flipped to identify "torture and industry." Both the Left and Right could agree on this—rescuing Latin American capitalism *required* despots to stabilize the investment climate and subdue unruly workers, to break the grip of "exhaustion with inflation." Hirschman wanted to break the iron logic. There was altogether too much reflex to run to extremes. The clarion calls in the 1960s had come from the Left, demanding revolution. Now they came more menacingly from the Right. An orthodoxy had settled in Santiago, one aiming to correct the course altogether with drastic market recipes advocated by faculty from Chicago and their former Chilean graduate students nestled into the highest echelons of various economic ministries to usher in nothing less than "a new economic order," starting with a battery of "shock treatments."[49]

It was the effects of these that Hirschman witnessed during his recent trip and bemoaned. He bemoaned them in part because he was not convinced that they were necessary. The Chicago Boys argued that the old model was irredeemable because of its intractable disequilibria and that it should be replaced with "liberal economic organization." For Hirschman, who'd long since backed off advocating imbalances, the problem was not the model but the difficulty of *"shifting of gears"* between policies, difficulties that were then attributed to the model. At issue was the lack of flexibility in thinking among policy makers as well as social scientists. Authoritarianism thrived in climates in which existed—and again, Weimar was an object lesson—"the generalized consciousness that the country is facing serious economic problems . . . without being able to solve them." The Chicago Boys exaggerated the impossibility of fixing the existing system because they wanted something wholly different.[50]

What bothered Hirschman most was the refusal to take responsibility for the traps that social scientists laid. As he was planning his trip to Latin America, McGeorge Bundy, the president of the Ford Foundation and former dean of the faculty at Harvard, contacted Carl Kaysen, expressing his interest in convening a meeting with "Messrs. Hirschman and Geertz and their colleagues on the question of the Ford Foundation priorities in the area which we have chosen to call 'the hungry, crowded, competitive world.'" The very topic of the gathering expressed the prevailing mood. Hirschman was determined to challenge it by, as he told "Mac" Bundy, showing "that I am less of a mindless optimist than people (and sometimes my closest colleagues and friends) tend to think."[51] On January 27, 1976, an interlocutor from Ford sat down with Hirschman, Geertz, and Cardoso. The conversation began with a dark tone, and Hirschman immediately resisted with a reminder to put social scientific analysis into a broader historical context. The naïve 1950s believed that "all good things go together": increase GDP and get democracy; free people and they will invest. "It was a simplistic model," he recalled. "But now we have come in a sense to the inverse idea, that all bad things go together." Growth is bunk. Human rights are violated. But this "dismal diagnosis" is "probably just as wrong as the earlier one, and I'm also a little bit suspicious of where it leads us." Geertz, who knew Hirschman as well as anyone, and one of the friends who poked fun at the resilient hopefulness that bordered on quixotic, chimed in: "Albert always wants to look on the bright side." "You always say," he added, "truth lies not at the extremes but in the middle."[52]

The divide between hope and hopelessness, between optimism and pessimism, was a false one, Hirschman believed. It was not a matter of whether the overall story was bleak or uplifting, but rather of how it was told, for the epic passage of social change was riddled with chance and choice, and understanding this required humility and a concession to the limits of Reason. From his Hegelian taproots he found the current "correlation" between economics and "the development of torture" as "puzzling" as it was "appalling." He wanted to get at social scientists' mindsets, why they persist "in thinking of having only one thing happen, and everything else will coalesce around it, and we'll come out all right." Why do "we only have one 'new key' at a time?"[53]

Invariably, the question of complexity could not avoid the touchy question of ethics, especially when it came to economics. Hirschman wished that his colleagues felt freer to accept their own limits and uncertainties, but not because their claims were irrelevant. On the contrary. The relevance of economists was limited because "they feel more at home with economic magnitudes" and preferred to settle solely upon them. Hirschman never lost sight of a heroic place for the economist. His trouble was, he found it "intolerable" that a bubble of economists ("a little group of American-trained local economists who think they are still in graduate school") make policy for Pinochet while another bubble of "neo-Marxists" go on about exploitation. Neither orthodoxy was capable of "breaking out" of its hermetic certainties. The irony was, as far as Hirschman was concerned, that feeling at ease with one's limits would allow social scientists to learn about the economy itself. "It turns out it's not all just one black box; there are all kinds of new things churning in there." Even in Chile, "things have not been completely shut down," and he pointed to the important research being conducted there among his beleaguered friends at CIEPLAN. It struck some as starry-eyed, but Hirschman added: "If only there were someone who could bring these people together, it might be possible to create some type of dialogue."[54]

One can think of Hirschman talking of himself here, casting himself in the role of broker for such a dialogue. He invoked his "small study group on Latin America" and the way it was exploring, in the darkness of a despotic age, "interesting passages" through a labyrinth to find light. His conclusions could not help but be hesitant. Weeks later, he prepared to pack his bags and return to Latin America. But his mind's eye was also looking elsewhere, back in time in search of deeper clues to explain how the social scientist learned to think in terms of one new key at a time.

CHAPTER 16

Man, the Stage

The Good is in a certain sense comfortless.

FRANZ KAFKA

Hirschman's life can be recounted as a biography of a reader, recounting stages in the development of a subject's library, from childhood influences to the dog-eared volumes that shaped an intellectual imagination to the books he parried with his own. Such a narrative would arc across familiar categories of an intellectual biography, from formation to contribution, from absorption to creation.

As with any effort to give Hirschman's life history a shape, the story is invariably more complex and not always forward-moving. For one, the books that influenced him as a young man did not retire to the bookshelf. His dog-eared books were worn; the copy of *The Wealth of Nations* had long since lost its binding, though his Pléiade edition of Montaigne's *Essais* remained remarkably intact. Just as he was taken to rethinking his own work, he reread his formative influences, forever finding new meaning in the subtle folds of their prose. During a meeting in São Paulo in 1971, Harley Browning, a sociologist from the University of Texas, turned to Albert and asked him how he came up with such captivating titles. "I always read Flaubert," Hirschman replied.[1]

Flaubert, Montaigne, Smith, Marx . . . and Machiavelli. Reading Machiavelli began when he was twenty years old ("a good time to read M," he once told an audience), living in Paris and making his first steps into exiled Italian antifascist circles "reading Machiavelli and Leopardi."[2] He

489

read M. again in Trieste, with Eugenio. When he got to Berkeley (with Montaigne's *Essays* under his arm), he went to the library and signed out a copy of M.'s correspondences. This was how he started his first book, with Machiavelli's confession to Francesco Vettori that he knew little about the "art" of the economy, which resigned him "to reason about the state." *The Prince* travelled with him as a member of the OSS during the Italian campaign. Hirschman always kept Machiavelli close at hand, not just for *what* he thought about the mysteries of power, but for *how* he thought, how a writer portrayed man—including himself—as a stage upon which competing drives played out their drama.[3] This is one of the reasons why Machiavelli's epistles to Vettori became a refrain. Seven months after confiding his feeble command over trades to the Tuscan diplomat, friend, and hoped-for patron, Machiavelli shared an embellished account of his exile from Florence as a wanderer, hunting for thrushes and gathering firewood, playing cards and backgammon with the local "lice [to] ease my brain from its rot," he would return home in the evenings, cast off his dirty clothes and boots and "put on the garments of court and palace." Properly attired, he went to his study to dine in "the courts of the ancients." There, "I am unashamed to converse with them and to question them about the motives for their actions, and they, out of their human kindness, answer me. And for hours at a time I feel no boredom, I forget all my troubles, I do not dread poverty, and I am not terrified by death." From these conversations with the ancients, Machiavelli explained, he wrote what he learned, a "short study, *De principatibus*, in which I delve as deeply as I can into the ideas concerning this topic, debating what a princedom is, of what kinds they are, how they are gained, how they are kept, and why they are lost."[4]

This was one of Hirschman's favorite passages and he treated it as a dreamscape for himself, an allusion to an idyll where one could meet the ancients; a place free of shame or fear; a place where after a day's hard work in the fields of Third World development one might contemplate princedoms with ancient philosophers. Machiavelli's ritualized encounters with the ghosts of classicism were, in a sense, Hirschman's; he too treated the dialogue with the deceased—through their books—with the proper reverence, down to the sartorial preparations associated with Renaissance custom. In the halls in Princeton, people singled out Hirschman as dapper as he was learned, his garments carefully chosen from a clothier in Paris's sixth arrondissement so that his vestments befit the honor with which he prepared to greet Machiavelli in the sanctuary of the Institute for Advanced Study.

Life with Machiavelli surfaced again in October 1976. Hirschman was rereading *The Prince* and *Discourses* after a long and saddening trip to South America that summer, where the abuse of power was on open display, "and the impact is extraordinary," he told Katia.[5] When it comes to Machiavelli, he said effacingly, "I consider myself a dilettante." But the excitement was back, not least because he found proof that M. had embarked "on a new route, which has not been followed by any one." Like M., Hirschman was wading into the "experience of what it is to think *dangerous* thoughts," to disturb "fearlessness in facing the truth that may be terrible." These are Hirschman's words, not M.'s, but they are premised on his understanding of "Machiavelli as the first big unmasker of [the] Modern Age—[to show] how things *really* happen in politics." But he also recalled that at the age of twenty he had been most impressed by M.'s "search for *regola generale* = generalizations," which he likened to "Marx's law of motion." Almost half a century later, a grown-up Hirschman encountered in M. a skeptic trying to unmask the ironies of "historical *regola*." "Not only is man a rather contemptible creature," Hirschman explained, "but the world is rather poorly (or maliciously) arranged." Repeatedly he found in *The Prince* examples of situations "where for success to be assured one needs simultaneously two ingredients, but only one is usually to be had at one time . . . never both together." So we can find kingly people without kingdoms and kings deprived of kingly qualities. Seldom do they coincide. This is why it was necessary for good men to usurp power (and behave badly) in order to restore liberties (which is good)—the alignment of an "exceptional man" and fortune to "overcome basic conspiracies against success." Here we have Hirschman already pondering how Fortuna might turn her back on reform and force the social scientist—is he referring to himself, one might ask?—to take a different tack: "It struck me that M argues like an economist trying to make the best of scarce resources—you just can't be a paragon of virtue and maintain the state at the same time—so you must maximize morality under constraint of state-maintenance just as a consumer maximizes satisfaction under budget constraint."[6]

One reason why Machiavelli's dream appealed to Hirschman was because he felt increasingly drawn into a dialogue with his intellectual ancestors, forever trying to explain to them the events around him and enlisting their wisdom. A dialogue for the most part conducted in his head, it is manifest in his ramblings, in the file of "favorite quotes," and in his occasional letters. His personal diary reveals him meditating on "two classic paradoxes." They are

> 1. For things to function or to be worthwhile, for life to change to be possible or to prosper, there is need for two contradictory requirements to be fulfilled: e.g. in a state there must be both power and participation, in a marriage similarity and diversity.
>
> 2. The various states of the world are often arranged in a circle, not along a straight line, with the best and worst states close together: that is, maximum participation and mass indoctrination as in a police state touch each other with demobilized, bureaucratic elitist regimes (democratic and otherwise) at opposite sides of [a] circle; or in father-daughter relative closeness is close to incest and both are equally far from coldness-indifference.

"I feel there is a connection between these two principles," he concluded.

The search for insights into the ambiguities and contradictions of his age—heightened freedom coinciding with ruthless abuses, prosperity mixed with terrible want—suggested that these apparent incompatibilities were in fact siblings. It sent him backward to a founding moment in the making of the modern world. Were there currents of thought that could be recovered as historical lanterns for the future now that, as far as Hirschman was concerned, the quest for simplifying yet technically awesome methods was yielding diminishing returns? He folded himself into the problem. In writing to Katia about his preface to a W. W. Norton edition of *Journeys* he felt it necessary to deal with "certain overoptimistic passages of the end of my stories." Looking up "must be understood," he felt, "as a fling to which every writer has a good right at the end of his effort." Ending this way was "part exhortation, part incantation." "After all," he exhorted, "didn't Machiavelli predict the imminent unification of Italy in the last chapter of *The Prince*?" He liked this self-defense: "I really enjoyed that not-so-subtle way of putting myself into Machiavelli's class—one can do that by claiming the same weakness or foibles," with the hope "that one also shares their other attributes."[7]

Moving to the Institute for Advanced Study may have been a dream come true, but for a man whose circuitous career was bereft of the normal professional rungs, it was not just another step. Rather, it was a setting for conversations with the ancients in the search for intellectual pathways, conversations he kept until then only in the precincts of his own mind. In the mid-1960s, the board of trustees of the Institute for Advanced Study began to consider its future when the long-time director, J. Robert Oppenheimer, came down with cancer in 1965. Since its creation in 1930, this shelter for European scholars, especially in the natural sciences and mathematics, had become famous for its string of Nobel Prizes. The goal was to spare great minds the tedium of real-world constraints, to let them mingle with one another, and thus propagate more great minds—and their ideas. So it was that the IAS rested on the precept that some minds teach best by not teaching at all. But thirty years later, it was coming under fire for being altogether too removed from the real world; some lampooned it as a pampered haven for pointy-headed academics freed from the grimy world of undergraduates. Felix Frankfurter, very much a man in the world, had warned the institute's founder, Abraham Flexner, that a "paradise for scholars" need not imply they were angels; "we are dealing with humans."[8] The Supreme Court jurist had a point, and it was one that echoed in the minds of the institute's trustees. The board worried that what it needed was a new "School" alongside the Schools of Historical Studies, Mathematics, and Natural Sciences (Physics). This would be in the social sciences, so that the activities of the institute would be more engaged with the problems of the world. To this end, they recruited Carl Kaysen, the chair of Harvard's economics department and senior foreign affairs advisor to President Kennedy in 1966 to take over from the dying Oppenheimer and to undertake the modernization of the organization nestled in the woods of Princeton. This major departure was not altogether welcome by many permanent members of the other schools. They grumbled but did not get in the way.

Not long after Kaysen moved to Princeton, he began conversations with several of the United States' leading social scientists, including former economics colleagues from Harvard and sociologists such as Robert Merton at Columbia and Edward Shils at Chicago. Merton and Shils urged Kaysen to reach out to the University of Chicago anthropologist, Clifford Geertz, a star in the field of symbolic anthropology, who laid stress on the construction of the social meaning of everyday rituals and symbols to move away from the rather wooly and excessive use of cultural "attitudes." Noted for his pioneering field work in Indonesia, he had just published a study of Islam in Morocco when he got Kaysen's call. Geertz took up the challenge and moved to Princeton in 1970. Geertz and Kaysen became the founders of the new, modest Program in Social Change, established with the notion that it would not seek to replicate university departments. It needed to have its own orientation to contemporary history and current affairs and skirt theoretical and analytic preoccupations of the academy.

Hirschman arrived in the second year of the Kaysen-Geertz experiment, vacating his Harvard office to Amartya Sen, who was spending the year in Cambridge—and who luxuriated in Albert's assortment of literature and history on the bookshelves. Hirschman's first go-around in 1972–73 at the institute was a mixed experience. If he thought he was escaping the turmoil at Harvard, he found himself in the midst of worse in Princeton. There were some upsides. The other visiting fellows, such as David Apter, who had been Geertz's colleague at the Committee for the Comparative Study of New Nations at Chicago, and the French sociologist Pierre Bourdieu, became lasting acquaintances. Hirschman became especially close to Geertz. The project also evolved. As he reported to Kaysen at the end of his visit, the reading and discussion with colleagues has "led me to expand considerably my original project." In fact, he was a little misleading; the original project had long since fallen by the wayside. The real problem was a furor that had exploded over his head. The atmosphere, he wrote to Kaysen, "has been too antagonistic."[9]

What Hirschman was referring to was an upheaval over the expansion of the Program in Social Change. No sooner was Hirschman installed than Kaysen and Geertz submitted the nomination to the institute faculty for a third permanent social scientist: Robert Bellah, a prominent sociologist from Berkeley. Working on religion in the United States and Japan, and well-known for having coined the term "American civil religion" in an essay about the country's moral values, Bellah had been educated at Harvard, along with Geertz, under the mentorship of Talcott Parsons; his coming to the institute would have represented a kind of rebirth of Harvard's interdisciplinary Department of Social Relations, amalgamating sociology, anthropology, and psychology and thus stepping outside the prevailing trend in universities toward disciplinary and departmental structures. Geertz and Bellah did not aspire to transcend the chasm between positivist and hermeneutic traditions, as Parsons had, with a model of their own; they had seen firsthand how Parsons' ambitions led to ornate schemes whose increasingly incomprehensible features were the price he paid for trying to integrate these two large traditions. Still, they shared misgivings about the drift of mainstream social science and agreed that the institute might provide an outpost for an alternative.

The Bellah *Affaire* escalated into the most serious crisis to hit the IAS and threatened to—indeed was partly intended to—halt the social science enterprise in its tracks. Mathematicians considered it soft; the historians thought it all speculative. And Bellah's nominations appeared to confirm their prejudices. André Weill, a member of the School of Mathematics, decried Bellah's work as "worthless," while the philosopher Morton White circulated a critical analysis of Bellah's work among colleagues, calling it "pedestrian and pretentious." In spite of the mounting opposition, Kaysen, who was not blessed with the gift of tact, decided to proceed with the case and recommended it to the trustees, who approved it. This only escalated the tensions as a coalition of outraged historians and mathematicians began to plot Kaysen's fall—John W. Milnor drafted an open letter demanding the director's resignation and replacement by George Kennan. Then, as the trustees felt they had to back their director, some faculty members went after them. Weill, in a rage, confirmed the suspicions of many that the pampered academic elite considered itself above accountability when he declared it absurd that those "absolutely incompetent in the fields of science and scholarship always have the final word." By then the controversy had hit the pages of the *New York Times* and *Time* and *Newsweek* magazines, and the institute cafeteria was filled with a thick cloud of hostility. Weill declared openly to Geertz, who took the blows personally, that he refused to have any further personal relations with him. The unflappable Kaysen, who "never went out of his way to avoid making enemies," took the heat.[10] Hirschman joked among colleagues up the road at Princeton University's Woodrow Wilson School that his sojourn at the institute removed him from "direct contact with development problems," but "not from the passions and rigid ideological positions that often characterize the atmosphere in development." Privately, he wrote that the "uproar . . . was far too complicated and boring to tell . . . but it fills all the small talk at parties."[11]

In the end, Bellah withdrew his candidacy, citing the sudden death of his eldest daughter. But the damage was done. It would take Geertz many years to recover—if indeed he ever did. In retrospect, he had some choice words for Bellah's critics and charged them with treating him "with a cruelty of particular excuisiteness."[12] And Kaysen was aware that his own days as director would have to wind down for the IAS to return to normal. Rumors flew that Geertz was packing his bags. A visitor arrived in the fall of 1974 to find Kaysen and Geertz both "pretty bruised" and "depressed." One day Kaysen entered the office of the newly arrived historian of Spain, John Elliott, to ask his personal opinion of the situation; squirming with discomfort, Elliott was honest—he thought that Kaysen's career at the institute could not go on. But Kaysen did not want to withdraw without making sure that his cause would survive. With

Geertz nursing his wounds, he had to find a new nominee who could help heal the rifts. This time Kaysen created a search committee composed of bridge-builders from the different schools, including Elliott. Kaysen also telephoned his old friend Shura Gerschenkron, who was not known for his fence-mending skills but knew how damaging the institute's failure in the social sciences would be, for counsel. Shura told him that their friend Albert Hirschman was unhappy returning to Harvard and suggested him as a candidate who might be acceptable to all sides. In his recommendation letter, Shura told the story that only a few friends would have known, of Hirschman's rifle assignment in the French army in 1939. When his officer handed him a pre-1914 gun, Hirschman took this as an omen. It committed him "to the invention and introduction of new analytic tools" to fend off the demons of obsolescence. "Nothing is more characteristic of Hirschman's writings than the originality of his mind and the wealth of ideas in which qualities he has few equals in the social sciences in our days." This would thus make it the third time that Shura played Fortuna and altered the course of Albert's life behind his back. Geertz, meanwhile, had grown fond of Albert and felt it wise to consider an economist with heavy credentials as a safe nomination.[13]

After the standoff over Bellah, the Hirschman nomination was, almost deliberately, uneventful and swift. Kaysen called Hirschman in mid-February and asked him if he would be willing to stand as a candidate—a decision that could not have been easy given the firestorm he had witnessed six months before. But he knew this was a once-in-a-lifetime opportunity to free himself from teaching, whose stomach-churning effects had not worn off. He could also plunge more completely into writing. Moreover, he must have sensed that his candidacy was bound to be less controversial. Not only was he one of the world's most renowned social scientists, but, as Kaysen put it retrospectively, his command of "Old World" languages and his "cultural affiliations" made him an appealing colleague for the Europeans on the faculty. There was a whiff of European superiority about the ways in which some had described Bellah's scholarship that could not be directed at Hirschman. He "was the type of scholar that appealed to them." The appointment of Hirschman was a unanimous

affair—he was "so outstanding," recalled Elliott, who was the first to speak
at the faculty meeting. He got up and explained that Hirschman was not
only good for the school, he would bring distinction to the institute; at
fifty-eight years old, his work was becoming more original, more creative,
and he was becoming more productive. The classicists remained quiet,
while the modern historians like Felix Gilbert and George Kennan were
enthusiastic. The vote was 14 to 0, for Hirschman.[14]

Within days, Hirschman had an offer in hand. He accepted almost
immediately. By then, his friend Henry Rosovsky, the Harvard dean,
knew that the case was settled. Everyone knew his mind was made up
the day the offer came through: "No one came to beat down the door to
worry about retaining him," remembered his last dean. His friend and
colleague, Kenneth Arrow, also knew this was a done deal: "Frankly, there
was a recognition that he had no interest in teaching . . . . The Institute
fit his self-image."[15] The chief resistance came from Sarah herself, who
had abundant friends in Cambridge. What is more, she had recently ventured into a public housing project to read a short story by Gabriel García
Márquez, "La siesta del martes," among a group of Puerto Rican women
living there. Inspired by a seminar conducted by the Brazilian pioneer of
adult literacy, Paolo Freire, she was on her way to creating an innovative
network to bring the world of reading and discussing fiction to basic readers and nonreaders. The prospect of moving to the sleepy college town of
Princeton was less than thrilling. But she knew full well Albert's aversion
to teaching and lack of interest in Harvard affairs, as well as his stockpile
of writing aspirations. On May 22, 1974, Hirschman administered the
final examination of his career to his Harvard students in "Economic Development in Latin America."[16] With his grades submitted, he and Sarah
packed their house and, with no formal farewell parties or sendoffs, began
their move to Princeton.

To Albert, the biggest decision was whether to toss out his field notes
from *Journeys* and *Development Projects Observed* while still persecuted
"to read and comment on 2.5 dissertations, deciding which was the best
graduate seminar paper deserving of some silly prize."[17] To Sarah, it was
a much harder process, but she kept her unhappiness for the most part

under wraps. Still, Albert knew of her sadness. As they were unpacking their belongings in Princeton, Albert happened upon a personal advertisement in the *New York Review of Books* that ran LANGUISHING IN NEW JERSEY. "Grist for Sarah's mill," he thought, "although I don't think she was the one who put it in."[18] There were a few in Cambridge who were also crestfallen, such as Stanley and Inge Hoffmann. Harvard was getting busier, more crowded with jet-setting faculty (of which, it must be said, Hirschman was unambiguously one). But Hoffmann was losing the closest colleague he would ever have. "I missed them terribly when they left," he later recalled.[19]

While the summer of 1974 brought the political storm over President Nixon's impeachment to a climax as Hirschman was packing his boxes, it also took him back to Berlin—his first return to his native city and country in over forty years. Why it took him this long is not easy to explain. His sisters had returned and sometimes complained to him that he'd lost the affection they had in particular for the old house, the Tiergarten, and memories of their childhood. In May, as he was preparing to meet up with Ursula, he confessed to Katia that "I do look forward (with some trepidation, *si capisce*) to the Berlin excursion with Ursula." What he took away from this first return trip remains a mystery; it did not, for the moment, kindle much interest in German affairs. And if it did, the physical Berlin of his childhood was wiped out, to be replaced by Weimar memories and values which, it is true, began to streak his writings.[20]

Sarah and Albert bought a house on Newlin Road, a short walk from the grounds of the IAS. They made it their own, unpacking their books, hanging their art—including the Roda portrait of Lisa and Sarah—and placing the antiques Sarah had picked up in little shops in La Candelaria in Bogotá. "It's really a 'livable' house," Albert concluded, "not a thing of beauty or insinuating charm" as the house on Holden Street had been in Cambridge. But it had space for visitors, a magnificent cherry tree in the backyard, and a pair of rabbits who reliably appeared around dinner time as Albert and Sarah would sit down to eat.[21] Newlin Road quickly became an active hub for the social life they would create for the many visitors flowing through the institute. Albert, and especially Sarah, gave the institute a European air of sociability. The icy tension at the institute began to thaw and thereby ease the strain that Geertz was under with his colleagues. With frequent dinner parties and an infinite supply of well-dressed gentility and "small kindnesses," as Susan James recalled, a kind of international intellectual civility bordering on courtliness prevailed over the formative years of social science at the IAS. Albert enjoyed sliding back and forth between foreign languages among guests and visitors and showing the Hirschmans' art. Always ready to share his admiration for the work's formalities, he was equally ready with a story. But visitors were always aware of the invisible line should the conversation drift to more personal territory; it was no-man's-land.[22]

The early days of Social Science saw a congenial and increasingly intimate partnership between Hirschman and Geertz, with polite and respectful faculty meetings at the institute. There was a Plutarchian neatness to the pair. Geertz was a historic pessimist, his partner an "incorrigible optimist." The Marseilles nickname, Beamish, Geertz found perfectly fitting. A gravelly source of outbursts, Geertz was a picture of contrast to Hirschman's smooth, cool, if aloof, mien. "They seemed so different in the way they comported themselves," recalled Robert Darnton, who spent years in the Social Science seminars. According to Darnton, Geertz was a scholar "for whom very few people could command respect." Hirschman was the exception that proved the general rule. Geertz admired him deeply. There was a sense in the combination that Hirschman brought a missing dimension to Geertz's own life, like Kant's Practical Reason, a vast experience in the world and an ability to resolve, through reflection, the questions of what to do, a capacity to think in the service of action. This contrasted with Geertz's own inclination to Theoretical Reason. In this sense, poking fun at the "Beamish" nickname was a cover for veneration, and as the years unfolded, for an ever deeper fondness. On the matter of what kind of social science should be supported at the IAS, there was a kindredness of spirit that is undeniable. Indeed, when the speaker series for the year 1972–73 was arranged, Hirschman was asked to kick it off with his essay about inequality and the tunnel effect (a prospect that made him "a little bit scared once again").[23] He needn't have worried. Geertz loved the paper. It represented precisely the kind of social science the world needed. Along the way, Geertz did add a few little digs at what was going on in universities around them. He found the new trend for laboratory experiments in psychology wanting. "It's dangerously artificial, in ways that render most inferences from laboratory to real life illicit. Hence, I always hanker after some actual social event as my test bed; and in this case the one that nags at me is the one nearest home: the well-heeled student radical. There's something stubborn about that creature that won't fit into what I believe is a most pervasive model. He's relative deprivation personified—but I can't for the life of me see why! The moral, probably, is that he should be ignored."[24]

The caustic words also speak to what Geertz and Hirschman did want: a worldly atmosphere free of provincial students and engaged in serious, cutting-edge discussion of new research. In his first year as a permanent faculty member, Hirschman's visiting companions in Social Science included David Apter, Sidney Mintz, Fernando Henrique Cardoso, John Murra, Guillermo O'Donnell, and Arturo Warman—leaders of the new generation of social scientists working on development in Latin America. Included also was Donald Winch, an economist recovering from his stint as a dean at the University of Sussex during its turbulence. The following year brought Cardoso back and added the younger generation of Americans—David Collier, William Sewell (for several years), Victor Turner, and Orlando Patterson—and by 1976–77 the tilt in the profile of visitors included more historians, such as Michel Vovelle, Quentin Skinner (who would stay on until he was appointed to the chair of Political Science at Cambridge), as well as Hirschman's old friend from Marshall Plan days and well-known economic historian, Charlie Kindleberger. The only Latin Americanist was José Serra, the Brazilian economist, who would stay at the IAS for two years under the aegis of being Hirschman's assistant. What can be said of these assemblies—aside from the absence of women (Natalie Zemon Davis would be the first to join Social Science, in 1977)—was how they represented prominent voices in the two dominant spheres of Hirschman's thinking in the first half of the 1970s: the troubles with development and early modern European history.[25]

While there was not a lot of sustained dialogue across the divide that separated Latin American authoritarianism from eighteenth-century capitalism, they converged in Hirschman's head. The outer world saw one Hirschman: the thinker of development in Latin America who seemed to be hopping incessantly from capital to capital. There was another, one receding into the foundational texts of the modern social sciences, perched in his glassed office on the second floor of the institute's modern wing. The two Hirschmans were, in fact, one. What drove him to history was in part the experience of the more visible Hirschman dealing with the disenchantment with economic growth and "its most calamitous side effects in the political realm": dictators and "wholesale violations of elementary human rights," realities the world propagated in the face of his optimism. As he told a seminar at MIT shortly after returning from Chile and the spectacle of Chicago Boy medicine, he was dismayed by "many economists, cozily ensconced in their ever-expanding discipline and insulated from 'exogenous' happenings, however disastrous" and who "were not particularly struck by the possibility of such connections between economic and political events." Having taken an increasingly vocal stand and urged Latin American social scientists to consider the political implications of their analyses, he was "deeply disturbed by what, so it seemed, we [economists] had wrought or at least helped bring about." So, while the outer world was a source of despondency, Hirschman turned inward by going backward, to the foundations of thinking about capitalism and democracy. His solution was "to withdraw to history"—"to dwell for a while among the political philosophers and political economists of the seventeenth and eighteenth centuries."[26]

In fact, this withdrawal to history was already in train as the hopes for reform and development were waning. The sense that the confident '60s were turning even before the decade was out spurred him to look for deeper patterns, to search for some originary clues about how the first social scientists squared political and economic life as they became separate domains. While working on *Exit, Voice, and Loyalty* in Stanford, Hirschman happened to pick up a book from the shelf in the house they were renting. Called *Economie politique et philosophie chez Steuart et Hegel*, by Paul Chamley, it piqued his interest, not just because it took him back to some of his intellectual moorings, but also because it reopened the gate to classical political economy, where he had begun his teenage forays into the world of economics.[27] Almost half a century later, what had started as an interest in the responses to the industrial revolution—as he had explained to Kaysen—became a voyage of its own. Yellow pads from the years 1972 to 1976 contain notes from Vico, Herder, the Duke of Rohan, Aristotle, the Physiocrats, Helvétius, and of course Machiavelli—and increasingly the figures of the Scottish Enlightenment: John Millar, Adam Ferguson, Sir James Steuart, David Hume, and Adam Smith. The summer of 1973 had him wrestling with Max Weber's *The Protestant Ethic and the Spirit of Capitalism.* "It just happens, he [referring to the German sociologist] was primarily interested in showing [religion's] importance in determining the rise of capitalism . . . while I am trying to go one step farther back & inquire why there was a compulsion for people to look for a new doctrine, there was a problem begging solution, namely how to get away from the desperate plight hence conduct in general . . . in the 17th century." Note taking at the start of any project often reveals initial confusion. This was as true of Hirschman as anyone. But seldom had he started by casting his net so wide. Doing so added to the mystery and intrigue. And ambition. Here was a petite idée with big possibilities. Weber had pointed to the dreams of predestination that wound up yielding "disenchantment with the world." Hirschman was puzzled: but what linked high hopes and disillusionment? "In my scheme," he jotted, "the 'distance that makes one gasp' (the goal of all theory construction) is between the expectations and hopes that helped install & legitimize bourgeois society & capitalist activity, on the one hand, and the desperately disappointing results—so disappointing in fact that we have repressed the consciousness of those expectations & hopes ('*grundlichvergessen*' Freud)."[28]

If he could just figure out the passage between the ways in which capitalism was *initially* understood and reveal its prospectus, he could thereby shed light on why it was seen to fall short. Deriving this kind of "theory," what we might now call recovering a memory of capitalism, might therefore thwart the temptations of the extremes of throwing one's hopes behind the salvations of the pure market or the social revolution.

An intellectual arc was forming that started with Machiavelli's urge to see Political Man "as he really is" and the economic formulations of Adam Smith. A phrase from Montesquieu's *Spirit of the Laws* lodged in his memory and got filed away in his dossier of favorite quotes: "It is fortunate for men to be in a situation where, though their passions may prompt them to be wicked, they have nevertheless an interest in not being so." The phrase would, fittingly, be the epigraph for the manuscript. In it was nestled the foundational paradox that motivated him. While Marxists and romantics alike criticized capitalism for its lack of moral compass, for having demeaned individual drives to narrow and base motives, in fact they denounced the system for realizing precisely what it was originally hoped would happen— turning the "wicked" into men who would have an "interest in not being so." Hirschman discovered that a war was being waged over the very concept of human nature; for several centuries, "man was widely viewed as the stage on which fierce and unpredictable battles were fought between reason and passion or, later, among the various passions."[29] While the essay on the tunnel effect had cued Hirschman to the domains of peoples' emotions— such as envy, the deadly sin that yielded no fun—and their effects on social processes, he was now moving backward in time to confer with his ancients to reckon with their understandings of the passions.

This was new terrain for a development economist and observer of human behavior. As he packed his books for a summer of reading, he confided that "I am a little scared about plunging into a topic which will require a detailed knowledge of social and political thought from the 17th to the 19th century!" But six months later, the fear was giving way to thrill. "I feel that I have never skated on quite so thin an ice, and that's saying quite a lot," he wrote to Katia. In the hands of a different kind of reader, it might have led to antiquarianism or worse; the world of letters is populated by authors who "discovered" the classics for their own, more prosaic, purposes. For a "fox" who knew about many things (and not a "hedgehog" who knew one big thing), Hirschman's conversations with the ancients may have led in new directions, but his manner of pursuing them had not changed. "It's the kind of tension I know of," he observed of himself, "for I really am dying to know what I'll come up with next, and in this particular case I am not even sure how I want things to turn out." Tension, pressure points, and conflict were of course part of Hirschman's theoretical arsenal. But moving into such new territory had also clearly churned it up inside. Few could tell. There were the occasional private confessions to Katia, and of course the long walks with Sarah. It was not lost upon José Serra who, as his assistant with an office across the hall, literally watched Hirschman painstakingly work out his arguments, at once able to cloak himself in self-protective confidence to the casual observer while fretting at his desk, constantly fretting over words with the younger Brazilian. Serra watched one essay on inflation take many months to finish. Hirschman once admitted that he feared talking about his ideas lest "someone might kill them" before they were ready.[30]

The history of ideas was, in some respects, a polar extreme to development studies and its concerns with roads, inflation, and agrarian reform. For Hirschman, however, it was not such a stretch to see the links between these universes; he had always been alert to the ways in which ideologies and intellectuals shaped the thinking of policy makers who fashioned the spectrum of peoples' choices. But there was a way in which the foundations of intellectual history were shifting that brought the classical texts of the past down to earth. Moving to the IAS brought Hirschman face-to-face with new currents. The coming of age in the 1970s of a new school, sometimes dubbed the Cambridge School, shifted the emphasis from the inherent significance of a classic to the meaning of a treatise derived from a reconstruction of the political idiom of when and where it was written. The new turn, associated with Quentin Skinner, John Dunn, and John Pocock and with influential reinterpretations of Hobbes, Locke, and Machiavelli, cleared the ground for recombining ideas with ideologies.[31]

It so happened that the core concern of the new intellectual history was with movements such as republicanism and civic humanism, whose values coursed through Hirschman from childhood. An ideal of an active, participatory citizenship, combined with an ethic of education and learnedness—principles that echoed his father's assimilated Jewish republicanism as well as Eugenio's ethics—the very term *civic humanism* was minted in the Weimar Republic by the historian Hans Baron, one of the republic's assimilated Jews, who, like Hirschman, found himself driven from Germany in 1933. Arguing for an alternative to the nationalist, and ultimately despotic, spirit that was also sired by the First World War, civic humanists traced their origins to Renaissance Florence and through republican theorists like Montesquieu. There were many currents that sprang from it. One flowed through the pen of Skinner, who was to join, upon John Elliott's recommendation, the IAS's School of Historical Studies in 1974, which coincided with Hirschman's arrival. He then moved for three years to Social Science. Among Skinner's large projects was a history of political thought that tried to recover the Renaissance tradition of thinking about freedom and the common good as inextricably bound up with each other. There was, therefore, an important congruence between Skinner's effort to recover a tradition of thinking about political liberty before liberalism and Hirschman's effort to recover lost understandings of personal interests before capitalism.

Was this parallel play? Hirschman was certainly not motivated by a debate among historians. There is no evidence that Hirschman had read either the milestone methodological essays by Skinner or Pocock or John Dunn's classic study of John Locke, when he began his perambulations. He remained, in this sense, the self-guided reader of Montesquieu and Adam Smith, just as he had digested Keynes and Montaigne solo. When Pocock published his celebrated *The Machiavellian Moment: Florentine Political Thought and the Atlantic Republican Tradition* in 1975, it came as news to Hirschman. That spring, he and Donald Winch, who was embarking, largely motivated by conversations with Skinner, on his own study of Adam Smith, agreed that it would be a fine idea to invite Pocock to come for lunch to the institute and talk about his recent book. While this was an opportunity for Hirschman to consider this major intervention, his thinking had already taken shape. There was little engagement with Pocock; Hirschman cited *The Machiavellian Moment* several times with the neutral, if not tepid, recommendation that readers follow Pocock's trail should they be interested in "more detail."

The influence of the new intellectual history was more ambient. For someone with such an observational style, the conversations around him validated "his new project" of making sense of Montesquieu's paradox about wicked men losing their interest in being so. He certainly did not have to feel guilty for his withdrawal. The regular seminars, daily lunches, and routine occasions for scholars to gather and share insights anchored him to an intellectual environment while he was simultaneously interviewing finance ministers and creating think tanks in Latin America. Winch was a regular source of notes for Hirschman's mailbox and would occasionally venture down the quiet hallway to fairly courtly meetings with the quiet, seemingly aloof, senior colleague. There was also a movement, spearheaded by what was regarded as "the English mafia" at the institute, to hold regular informal gatherings to discuss questions of method and historiography. Meeting at Geertz's house, the conversations tended to be dominated by Skinner's energy and deep engagement with the topics as he was wrestling with his own project, which would culminate in the multivolume *Foundations of Modern Political Thought* in 1978.[32]

These occasions were perfectly suited for Hirschman's osmotic style. Forever quietly taking insights from his milieu, his conversations with Skinner and Winch over lunch or a seminar would send him back to his office to reread and write. Winch drew attention to important passages from Adam Smith's *The Lectures on Jurisprudence*, which were in the course of being published for the first time. These revealed a Smith concerned about the ties between the working of the market and public authority, fields that Hirschman thought the Scot had severed in order to invent *homo economicus* and a discipline to illuminate him.[33]

It was Skinner who had the most profound influence, possibly because he was more engaged with the core of Hirschman's enterprise, and possibly because of the shared affection for word games. To the Cambridge School founder, Hirschman's point of arrival, Adam Smith and the dawn of economics, was less the concern than the point of departure, Machiavelli and politics. Skinner teased apart nuances that Hirschman glossed over (for instance, the difference between honor and glory in *The Prince*, which Skinner felt represented quite different ideals in the Renaissance; perhaps Calvin would be a better example than Hobbes as an illustration of someone who imagined the state as a repressor of man's passions?). More importantly, he directed him to an alternative fount for thinking about the ideal of active citizenship and commerce. Hirschman wondered how Machiavelli simultaneously wrestled with "how things *really* happen in politics" while at the same time being attached to the notion that honor and glory were goals of action that could yield socially desirable outcomes—and one cannot help but hear echoes of Eugenio Colorni, the Justice and Liberty movement, and Hirschman's determination to return continually to the antifascist front. To Skinner's eye, this was more fully developed in Machiavelli's *Discorsi*, which was the more influential treatise to moralists of the eighteenth century, than in *The Prince*. There one could find the image of the armed citizen, as Skinner wrote to Hirschman, "ready to fight for his liberties, and jealously guarding them by ensuring that the classes remain pitted against each other and thus that the powers are separated." The hero is "an intensely political citizen," endowed with the leisure to rule and the virtù to fight for his country. This image, Skinner reminded Hirschman, was "immensely influential on Montesquieu, at least when discussing republics." From there, Albert could note the continuity to Rousseau and the strength of the "activist tradition" of thinking about citizenship (in contrast to that laid out by Hobbes, "who commends such inability to meddle"). Hirschman immediately got his hands on a copy of the *Discorsi*.[34]

While all of this was transpiring over lunch and in the hallways of the institute, the trails into intellectual history never led Hirschman far from his concern with the twentieth century, the problems of development, and the shadow of Latin America's despots. As the final picture of his project was forming in his mind, he felt compelled to remind himself of "The Reasons for Undertaking this Project." "So What?" he asked. So what if early modern thinkers saw the coming of capitalism with "extravagant hopes" it "totally failed" to deliver? Writing in the climate of the mid-1970s, "capitalism *was born* alienated and already repressed and repressing." In the gloom of the mid-70s, this was hardly an original observation. Many Latin Americans were telling him this. So were Marxist students and colleagues.[35]

Did it all have to be just so bleak? Smarting after watching his earlier hopes for development and reform run afoul, Hirschman was grasping at an *idea* that "a certain type of economic relations leads to a certain type of politics." But it was far from a simple idea, because he was searching for a way to be "deterministic" (as he had pressed Guillermo O'Donnell in his own search for the links between development and dictatorship in Latin America) and yet contain within his model multiple possible outcomes. In fact, he was dueling with two currents and thus staking a double-edged position. What made the result all the more remarkable was the deceptively simple prose in which he wrapped it. On one hand, Hirschman was after an idea that would illuminate the ties between economics and politics in a way that did not force a narrowed version of the latter to conform to the expanded needs of the former. This, of course, was the prevailing view among *Pinochetistas* in Chile and an emerging brand of "new" conservatives in Europe and North America who thought the rabble-rousing of the 1960s had pushed participation to extremes and made countries "ungovernable." How could an active citizen be kept active in a way that allowed the pursuit of honor and glory, and expanded politics, to yield socially desirable results? At the same time, there was an opposing thrust. He wanted an economy composed of self-interested people capable of wielding power in such a way that imposed "constraints on policymakers" while hoping that their pursuit of private self*ish* goals might yield to the "paradoxical consequences of the introduction of certain institutions"—institutions that could govern countries. In this fashion, unbridled ego-driven individualism might beget individual-liberty-protecting governments.[36]

This meant reckoning with the ancients.

The ancients, like Machiavelli, with whom Hirschman dined and conversed in his head were shrewd observers of what went on around them and detected new meanings in the unheroic activities of Men. Maybe he was "doing an injustice to these thinkers by comparing their fond predictions to the dismal outcomes"? It is often true that realities fall short of tall orders; Hirschman, of all people, could be accused—and many did—of overselling Hope. "But so it is with any perception of the possibility of change!" he exclaimed. "And they at least dared to speculate," he went on. "Nevertheless—what vision!" he exclaimed again to himself.

And, winding himself up a bit more, he could not resist a speculation of his own: "perhaps they increased, by their speculations, the chances of *sometimes* achieving the goal of a more humane polity."[37]

This was a virtuous formulation, a lighthouse for the darkness of the 1970s, a key to Montesquieu's puzzle. It was not original, but rather a recovered tradition into which Hirschman was placing himself in order to declare it still alive. He aimed to recover the idea that "the expansion of commerce and industry is useful because it will deflect men from seeking power and glory, [and] will keep them busily occupied making money which is harmless and perhaps even socially useful." Citing Hegel, he concluded that "the heroic ideal" was now "demolished" and had given way to "change by praxis." "Man can be changed by what he is doing," he scribbled.[38]

The problem became consuming and helps account for why Hirschman was pulling away from his fieldwork in Latin America and his engagement with development economics. There was more. The search for the right mixture of pursuits and constraints, economics and politics, interests and institutions might even provide some clues to help pull development thinking out of the somber impasse into which it had run. The result left him feeling all the more muddled about his own field, and more specifically—and rather melodramatically—torn about the unforeseeable consequences of some of the doctrines he himself had espoused. "I feel incapable of further devoting thought to development until I begin to see a few paths in this foggy landscape for fear that by successful development or even by improving income distribution I contribute to the destruction of the human spirit."[39] For now, the pathway to recasting self-interest in a way that did not make it incompatible with the public good required going back centuries to the founding of its modern meaning.

These visions were the ones that Hirschman set about to recover in *The Passions and the Interests: Political Arguments for Capitalism before Its Triumph*, published by Princeton University Press in 1977.[40] In the examination of discourses, literally arguments, about market life and behavior through the visions of seventeenth- and eighteenth-century political economists, what he revealed was equal parts anxiety about human motives, passions as well as interests, and equal parts homage to the creativity of a language with which to control and channel them into socially useful pursuits. In a sense, Hirschman read Montesquieu and others just as he had "read" the policy makers of *Journeys toward Progress*, examining how they understood the world around them through their vocabulary and word games. At the core of *The Passions and the Interests* was a dynamic of words and arguments getting absorbed or "imposing themselves" to assuage, assimilate, or even anesthetize what was once so shocking about Machiavelli as the first big unmasker of the Modern Age. In his telling, arguments propelled arguments along—constituting an "endogenous process." The sum was intended "to renew the sense of wonder about the genesis of 'the spirit of capitalism.'" For two hundred years after Machiavelli sought to account for "man as he really is," writers grappled with how to think about moneymaking, considering the ways in which selfish wickedness might be thought anew. Mandeville and others argued that the luxury trades and pursuit of "private vices" could be good for "publick benefits" through "dexterous management." In this fashion, personal drives could appear less shocking, and the message about them could be absorbed into "the general stock of accepted practice" by changing the language and rebranding personal passions into interests, first as a substitute coinage, and eventually, as Hirschman told an audience at the Collège de France, into a useful euphemism for self-satisfying activity.[41]

This set the stage for Adam Smith, who took self-interest one step further with the doctrine of the Invisible Hand. The shift was inscribed in the famous line, whose vocabulary laid the tracks for a triumphal formulation: "It is not from the *benevolence* of the butcher, the brewer, or the baker, that we expect our dinner," with Hirschman underscoring Smith's choice of words, "but from their regard to their own *interest*." It was not to their "*humanity*" that society appeals, but to their "*self-love*," not to "*our necessities*" but "*their advantages*." Hirschman underlined the keywords in his copy of *The Wealth of Nations*. Here, Smith famously stripped interests of their "unsavory synonyms" (these now being Hirschman's choice of words) and elevated them to undeniable good thanks to men's "trucking disposition" (back to Smith's words) without a concession to private, hidden vices.

As it happens, there was no historic figure whose legacy would be more contested than Adam Smith as his rivals fought to claim him as their forebearer. If there was one man who would set the stage for a great ideological struggle over how to think about markets and politics, private pursuits and public wellbeing, it was Adam Smith. And Hirschman, anticipating the fight, struggled to create a bridge between the sides by positioning Smith as a man who championed private self-interest but never lost his public moral bearings. Not unlike Hirschman himself.

Now, when Hirschman settled into Smith's writings in the spring of 1973, his first impressions were of an author "contradicting himself in the most *effronté* manner" which "spoilt a neat ideological classification with which I had set out on this whole thing." But in the end, "it makes it of course more interesting." He found, upon reading and reflection that perhaps Smith was not such a jumble; perhaps he was using words differently—and in new combinations—which was one of the reasons why Hirschman came to recognize the power of Smith's rhetoric, leaving him "fairly bubbling over with excitement" at his verbal discoveries.[42] Words like *passion* and *vice* gave way, according to Hirschman, to "such bland terms" as "advantage" or "interest." This was on purpose; by mutating motivations in this way, they could be made more calculable, more predictable, more reliable—a far cry from the bygone rhetoric of unruly aristocratic pursuits. The language of "value" and "production," "waste" and "idleness" had inverted the scourge, culminating in Smith's famous passage on how Towns Improved the Country in book 3, chapter 4, which accented the unintended effects of personal pursuits on "public happiness," for neither "great proprietors" nor merchants ("in pursuit of their pedlar principle of turning a penny wherever a penny was to be got") had public service in mind. "Neither of them," Smith wrote, "had either the knowledge or foresight of that great revolution which the folly of the one, and the industry of the other, was gradually bringing about." One of Hirschman's marked passages, it illustrated the workings of language behind the alchemy of the marketplace. It also carried with it political implications. Smith had no love of merchants, as both Skinner and Winch had pointed out, and the caustic vocabulary about "the pedlar principle" suggests that. "How many people," Smith asked in a passage that Hirschman underlined in his copy of *The Theory of Moral Sentiments*:

> ruin themselves by laying out money on trinkets of frivolous utility? What pleases these lovers of toys, is not so much the utility as the aptness of the machines which are fitted to promote it. All their pockets are stuffed with little conveniences. They contrive new pockets, unknown in the clothes of other people, in order to carry a greater number. (p. 299)

Left to their own devices, interests, not unlike the passions before them, lent themselves to withering depictions and unsentimental views. But from their banality came unintended general goods.

The same kind of force-counterforce portrait that Hirschman drew out of Smith's portrayal of interests extended to his reading of Smith's thinking about states, with Smith bowing to a broadly republican spirit that saw government at the service of the people and its prosperity through self-restraining rules. For while Montesquieu could invoke the bill of exchange as a modest engine of change because he could see no end in sight to arbitrary rule in France, Smith's position was quite different: he could see examples at home of better government. But he was no less concerned about arbitrariness. Now, fear of the personal passions shifted, in a passage that Hirschman marked in his copy of *The Wealth of Nations,* to the menace of "public prodigality and misconduct." The people who compose "the court, the ecclesiastical establishment, such people, as they themselves produce nothing, are all maintained by the produce of other men's labour" (book 2, chap. 3, p. 325). These selections reveal the readings behind Hirschman's writing. The passages of choice, a few of which filtered into the final, spare narrative of *The Passions and the Interests*, point to a Hirschman looking for Smith's key words, drawing out both the evolution of the arguments as well as Smith's own ambivalences as he groped for a way to reconcile republican ideas of virtue with what would soon become liberal notions of rights, civic religion with limited government, the priority of collective life with heterogeneity of interests—the chasm that was beginning to open up between a traditional language of politics among eighteenth-century thinkers and a vocabulary of the later, liberal age. This struggle within Smith fascinated Hirschman, and he wanted to recover it from the sanitized interpretations of later self-interested readers who had lost sight of the Scottish moralist's effort to reconcile civic humanism with capitalism in favor of a Smith as an apostle of self-interest. This version of Smith had, in turn, political implications. The juggling act between virtue and self-interest, power and public good, was elegantly captured by David Hume in one of Hirschman's favorite passages from the 1742 essay "Of the Independency of Parliament."

> Political writers have established it as a maxim, that in contriving any system of government and fixing the several checks and balances of the constitution, every man ought to be supposed a *knave*, and to have no other end, in all his actions, than private interest. By this interest we must govern him, and, by means of it, make him, notwithstanding his insatiable avarice and ambition, cooperate to the public good. (p. 117)

Whereas the original civic humanist code required of citizens that they serve the public interest directly—as active citizens—Englishmen could now be seen, thanks to commerce and industry, to be promoting the public interest indirectly by pursuing their personal gains directly. For all this to function, for the word games to be effective, interest-propelled activity by governments and people required measures of self-restraint. The Invisible Hand was not a heavy one. This is one of the reasons why, as Skinner pointed out to Hirschman, the verb *to meddle* acquired its derogatory currency over the course of the eighteenth century.[43]

Like Pocock, for whom classical republicanism was fundamentally a debate about the fears and perils of self-rule, so too were Hirschman's political economists arguing about the instability and strife associated with market life—anxieties that necessitated a semantic shift: the transmutation of individual passions into interests. The difference was that Pocock's famous study ended in a worrying register about the world to come and the end of a republican political ideal, whereas in Hirschman's account, the semantic moves ended in the "triumph" of a capitalist economic ideal. This artful, unintended, slowly accreted, linguistic turn could then create possibilities for new "discoveries." Interests—by being domesticated, tamed, and softened in the course of what Montesquieu called *doux commerce*—could create a historical consciousness that permitted their moneyed and propertied beneficiaries to enjoy the good regard of sovereigns. Sovereigns for their part could regard self-interested private men as potential stakeholders in a public system known as the modern state—but this presupposed that rulers also subjected themselves to the self-restraining habits and repressions to which the private passions were also submitted. People would become more governable and governments would become more respectful of the autonomy of interests delicately woven from the strands of thousands of transactions. This is why, as Hirschman noted, alienation and repression could yield some positive results, especially, with an unrestrained Pinochet in mind, an authority that refrains from trampling on the liberties of its subjects. The Chilean dictator exemplified what happens when the state does not restrain itself while, paradoxically, claiming to free people for private pursuits.

If Hirschman had autocratic targets in mind, he was also jabbing at those who denounced capitalism as some scheme to oppress man's "true" nature. The crusade of 1960s radicals in favor of the "inalienation" of man to free his inner, self-adoring soul to pursue his passions was no less troubling for Hirschman. There were few, if any, communitarian features of the "civic humanist" in Hirschman's brand of republicanism—which was one that rested on the necessary, creative, and ultimately resolvable and reformable tensions between individualism and the common good. This was reformist ground, not grist for collective revolution. There is a reason why one of Hirschman's own key words in *The Passions and the Interests*, which comports with his republican sense of checks and balances in all affairs, was *countervail*. He wanted disruption *and* repression, harmony *and* disorder—passions *and* interests. Each force contained within it its own tendency to resist it. This did not make them self-correcting, and Hirschman was not meaning to imply, like Hayek, that complex systems have an internal, Archimedean point to which they return unless "meddled with." And from the "countervailing passions" one gets the "countervailing interests," and from this "counterposing force" one derives a set of principles about restraints. This kind of vocabulary pointed not just to the roots of Hirschman's optimism, but also to his sense that there was no need for a single insight, or fundamental Historical Law, to command behavior and policy; it was out of the complex mixing, tension, and dialectic that hope would emerge. Consider his exuberant ruminations on La Rochefoucauld's dissolution of passions and almost all virtues into self-interest:

> A message of hope was therefore conveyed by the wedging [note the agency of words and the role of authorial choice] of interest in between the two traditional categories of human motivation. Interest was seen to partake in effect of the better nature of each, as the passion of self-love upgraded and contained by reason, and as reason given direction and force by that passion. The resulting hybrid form of human action was considered exempt from both the destructiveness of passion and the ineffectuality of reason. No wonder that the doctrine of interest was received at the time as a veritable message of salvation![44]

While the aphorists of the seventeenth-century human condition knew something of the life of the *libertins,* it fell to Smith to draw this realism to some powerful conclusions. And from his conclusions a new line would be drawn in the social sciences. What Smith accomplished in *The Wealth of Nations* that was so revolutionary was to establish an influential *economic* justification for the pursuit of self-interest; until then most thinkers tended to argue in *political* terms, that self-interest would curb the excesses of rulers. This crucial move, in Hirschman's view, set the stage for a splitting of politics and economics and made personal pursuits the basis of a more calculable, predictable order. It was important to set the record straight. Smith's view, according to Hirschman, was "very different from the laissez-faire or minimal state doctrine . . . still widespread today among economists." Rather, Smith viewed politics as the realm of "the folly of men." So Hirschman tried his hand at developing his own metaphor: Smith was not an advocate of a stripped-down state to let the Invisible Hand work its charm, but a state "whose capacity for folly would have some ceiling." This metaphor was among those that never caught on. Hirschman's own view, harkening back to the spirit of Montesquieu's brand of republicanism, was that the same might be considered applicable to the market, which was not immune to follies—as Smith implied in his sneering words about pedlars. But it was only an implication. In the main, Hirschman argued, Adam Smith converted what were once antonyms, "interests" and "passions," into synonyms—so that the whole of society is advanced when everyone is allowed to follow their own private interest.[45]

The Passions and the Interests was an argument for a historic middle ground of a classical republican sort. His struggle was two-fronted. While he wanted to challenge those who saw the self as a utility-maximizing machine, he also rejected the communitarian nostalgia for a world that was lost to consumer avarice and a celebration of "the love of lucre." His was a vision, projected through the prism of ancient discourses that aimed to make it normative, of polite, civic-minded people going about their "business" in ways that enabled self-interest and the common good to coexist in the same sentence, a *Harmonielehre* (study of harmony) that could be both realistic and hopeful. It was a delicate balancing act of restraint and freedom in the service of "a more humane polity." It was also a way of deconstructing the integral self to make him or her more complex yet whole, thereby giving the self a human and humane integrity.

Nowadays, economic actors are considered as processors of information; we have moved from seeing the market as a mechanical arrangement to viewing agents themselves as mechanisms—a view that places economics on the road to becoming a science. This was a turn that Hirschman found unfortunate and is what spurred him to recover the origins of a different, but ultimately doomed, understanding of economic agents.

There were, therefore, two simultaneous arguments being made in *The Passions and the Interests*. The first was a highly original recovery of the classical thinkers' ability to present a combined self, one able to subsume passions and interests within the economic soul while at the same time presenting the autonomy of this recombined self as the bulwark against a trampling, meddling, politically impassioned state. The balancing act cut across a pair of axes: the self and state were each endowed with internally juxtaposing and blending drives, and at the same time there was a delicate equipoise between self-restraining selves and states. The second was about how the broader view of economic man sustained by gentlemanly commercial intercourse was doomed. If these were the arguments for capitalism before its triumph and were original for their prophecies, the very triumph could only degrade them. Adam Smith, in this respect, came across as the hinge in the history of economic thought. By rebranding passions *as* interests, Smith's formulation "destroyed in passing the competing rationale" of the dialectic between passions and interests. Identifying particular interests with that of the whole made interests seem suddenly not so attractive, almost bloodless and mechanical; interests no longer fought with, or defined themselves at odds with, their sibling passions. They simply ruled. What Hirschman wanted was to restore the necessary competition, the rivalry, the tensions and non-synonymous features of human drives that Adam Smith had dissolved in the alchemy of the Invisible Hand. The complex, combined, but uneasy model of selfhood had gotten lost, which is why Hirschman insisted on going back to the passions to retrieve some of the originary anxiety, for the cleansed view of interests split them from man's soul and drained them of normative content. By the end, interests even ceased to be a euphemism at all and gave way to the late twentieth-century's semantic shift to "revealed preferences" and "maximization under constraint," which Hirschman coded as "neutral and colorless neologisms."[46]

At first blush, the war over words might have seemed an esoteric dispute among intellectual historians. It is true that in the history of economic thought, no one had so forcefully combined insights into the simultaneous operations of politics and economics, self and state, by recovering a moment of thinking about capitalism that accepted—indeed, embraced—the idea of the individual as driven by more than the quest for utilities. But there was more going on related to contemporary disputes about how to understand capitalism now that it had triumphed. *The Pas-*

sions and the Interests appeared on the stands as many dismal scientists advocated sparer notions of *homo economicus*, whose striving acquisitive energy had to be freed from the shackles of the state. For those yearning for an expanded view of economics, one that saw through the Milton Friedmans of the world and their iron laws of money, Hirschman's appeal to a more social and political *homonidae* gave some intellectual muscle to challenge the growing "neoclassical" orthodoxy and its influential battery of foundations and think tanks. At the same time, the view that impassioned public life had to take more seriously economic policy making seemed to many a needed coolant; the scourge of inflation in Europe and the United States could not be so easily dismissed, and the Left did so at its peril; the memory of Allende's own political fate fueled by economic misfortunes was still fresh in the mind. The passions *and* interests had to be kept in the same syntax as counterpoints to each other; they were, in Hirschman's mind, codependent. The rule of passions could lead, without checks, to horrible utopias; the rein of interests to soulless pragmatism.

Woven through the many layers of *The Passions and the Interests* was Hirschman's Adam Smith. By the mid-1970s, Smith was becoming a figure rolled out as the great apostle of the new economics with its strident defense of the unfettered market, especially upon the bicentenary of the 1776 publication of *The Wealth of Nations*. Chicago's Milton Friedman, more than anyone, marketed the Scottish moral philosopher as the progenitor of his own convictions. The 1970s would see an intensified political reading of Adam Smith and a mighty struggle over whether to treat him as the prophet of capitalist laws or embrace him as the humanitarian with an eye on moral man. To some extent, Hirschman fell into the trap that Friedman and others had laid: to read Smith as the maker of the bold new world of neoclassical thinking. By terminating "the competing rationale" of interests and passions, Smith cleared the ground for the triumph of the former, whether he meant to or not. This was one of Hirschman's readings.

But there was another as well. At the same time, Hirschman was resisting his own view; he wanted a Smith who thought in his same, bifocal way—seeing economics through a political lens, and politics through an economic lens. The result was a Smith forced to play two roles in the drama of *The Passions and the Interests*. Adam Smith took the blame for heralding a new model of economic man. But there was also a way in which Smith was presented as a transitional, possibly tragic, figure: he was still enmeshed in a moral economy but aware of and even predicting the emerging norms and practices of the capitalist world. Friedman had had his own self-interested reading of Smith; but so too did Hirschman, with Adam Smith the last great economist attentive to the currents and countercurrents of the moral and possessive individualist, the last to imagine the philosopher and the political economist as one—that is, until Hirschman breathed some life into this vision of Adam Smith with air drawn from his own lungs, perhaps with an unexamined view of himself as a prophet of the same sort. Smith was, in Hirschman's eyes not unlike Hirschman himself, poised at a moment in history in which the balance of morals and markets was shifting quickly. Both could not help but struggle to keep alive a complex view of individuals and to promote the idea of a delicate equipoise of society. What Smith saw with foresight Hirschman offered in hindsight.

In the historiography of Adam Smith, Hirschman anticipated what would become an alternative view of Smith as the humanist. Donald Winch's book, *Adam Smith's Politics*, which appeared a year later, made this case. So too, against a broader intellectual tableau, would Emma Rothschild's *Economic Sentiments* (2002). Without the full benefits of these subsequent readings of Smith, Hirschman's view was still ambivalent, and at times confused and confusing, in no small part because he was still struggling—and would continue to do so—to resolve his own quest to moor a humane economics after capitalism's triumph.

Hirschman's version of the intellectual origins of capitalism was greeted by a volley of rhapsodic reviews from quarters in which Hirschman was hitherto unknown. Political theorists such as Alan Ryan sang its praises in *Political Theory*, as did the historian of the eighteenth century Nannerl Keohane in the *Journal of Interdisciplinary History*. Before long, it was being commented upon in Italy, France, Germany, and Latin America. Not even *Exit, Voice and Loyalty* had provoked such a flurry. Stanford's Keohane sent him draft chapters of her first book, *Philosophy and the State in France*, to which Hirschman dedicated a goodly part of his summer vacation in Europe in 1977 to pore over. She replied in kind, with thoughts about his reflections on property as having given men "toes with roots" and thus reducing their mobility. "This is an excellent section, imaginatively linking economics with social attitudes and political possibilities," Keohane wrote. She urged him to have a look at Rousseau's *Government of Poland*, especially the passage in which he saw patriotism and love of country as precepts to strengthen loyalty and to channel more energy into the making of "public goods." While including her revised draft of her introduction, Keohane also had gratifying gossip from the American Political Science Association convention in Washington. "Quite a few people at the convention were talking about your book with interest; I recall particularly discussing it with Pocock, who likes it. And I basked in some of the reflected glory when friends mentioned your footnote on my essay on Nicole; it proves in any case that people are reading the book carefully, if they have got the footnotes by memory." To this Hirschman cheerily replied, relieved to hear that noneconomists were reading his work "as my brethren tend to be totally ignorant of the matters I talk about and are apt to get them wrong as Lekachman did recently in *The New Republic* (even though he meant well)." This capped long comments on her draft and gratitude for the Rousseau tip which "is beautiful and I may use it should I rework my paper."[47]

There were some who acknowledged the two Hirschmans—the development economist and the intellectual historian. But they were rare. One was Bruce Cummings, an assistant professor at the University of Washington working on Korean authoritarianism and Chinese foreign policy, who had read Hirschman's draft essay for the SSRC project and now drew the immediate connections to *The Passions and the Interests*. He appreciated "the difficulty of generalizing from the economic to the political, or establishing the connections between the two," and he could not help but notice the echoes of Perón in Mao "regarding the elasticity of things economic." What Mao called "walking on two legs" (with heavy industry and agricultural assaults pounding at the same time) had created a legacy of rigid thinking that "now appears like Sir James Steuart's states-men, so 'bound up by the laws of his political economy.'" The analysis led, for Cummings, to a clear-eyed view of the responsibility of intellectuals, "another passage I particularly liked." There is the Left, which advances its "revulsion with capitalism" to the point "that they make themselves irrelevant" or a threat, "so that nothing short of a revolution will satisfy them," which "comprises a recipe for repression." Then there's the Right, like Samuel Huntington, who at least "are quicker to accept that responsi-bility." "We all need the heightened awareness you call for."[48]

Awareness was, as it turns out, one of Hirschman's key words, and while Cummings used the term to denote the illumination on the exter-nal world, it also had an internal significance as well. As Hirschman was deep into the writing of *The Passions and the Interests*, Katia was going through a troubled patch in Paris. Albert consoled her with a quote from Goethe: "Childhood is a paradise from which we cannot be expelled." This, of course, was the problem—because aging and changing were in-evitable, so "we're in for a shock" and thus forced to ask ourselves, "Is this still me?" The point about growing up, leaving innocence to join grown-up rough and tumble, is that we are not prepared "for the rough-ness of the games that are being played by the adults of this world." For Albert, this was more than a developmental challenge; he knew this first-hand, for "the biggest shock" was to discover "that *I* can play just as rough as the next fellow." He recalled the moment of "this savage discovery" when he had been released from the French army in the summer of 1940 and was fleeing to the unoccupied zone. It gnawed at him that the bicycle that wheeled him to freedom in Marseilles was one he had stolen. And it clearly continued to bother him; "This was something I did which I had never thought I'd be capable of." To Katia what he wanted to say was that we never get over this elementary duality—our sensitivity to the world and the feelings generated by living in it and the "sacro-egoism" (a term he borrowed from pre-1914 Italian foreign policy—of all places!) that's often required for survival. Moreover, there's never any perfect balance—sometimes the pendulum goes one way, sometimes the other. Perhaps the best preparation "is the awareness, in the back of one's mind, that the time for the other mode of existence will surely come again."[49]

The intention of *The Passions and the Interests* was also this—a reminder of other ways of thinking about our "mode of existence." To think about this awareness could not help but point to our vocabulary and our arguments. It was on this point that Hirschman ended his book: "I conclude that both critics and defenders of capitalism could improve upon the arguments through knowledge of the episode in intellectual history that has been recounted here. This is probably all one can ask of history, and of the history of ideas in particular: not to resolve the issues, but to raise the level of the debate" (p. 135).

This was overly modest. There was in fact more going on than the level of debate. The challenge was not striving for an order that freed some "true" human nature or spirit, the rule of interests or rein of passions, but appreciating their conjoining and fluctuating propensities and the ways that people wrestled with them. Man, therefore, was a stage on which these competing and ineluctably combined drives carried out an epic struggle—one that, in his ever-optimistic turn, yielded to a modern character who could be acquisitive *and* virtuous, self-interested and other-regarding. There was no reason to sever the republican collective good from the liberal private purpose. But this is exactly what modern social theory was doing, worried Hirschman. As he reflected on later thinkers who imagined "that the economy must be deferred to," capitalist societies contrived social arrangements that substituted "the interests for the passions as the guiding principle of human action for the many [which] can have the side effect of killing the civic spirit and of thereby opening the door to tyranny" (p. 125). One side was driving out others. It was Tocqueville, Hirschman reminded, who had some prophetic words for the advocates of a favorable business climate and the benefits of the maxim of *enrichissez-vous!* and who ask merely for law and order. He did not mention Pinochet, but in writing these words as he was travelling back and forth to South America, it is hard to believe he did not have the Chilean commander in mind when he quoted Tocqueville:

> A nation that demands from its government nothing but the
> maintenance of order is already a slave in the bottom of its heart;
> it is the slave of its well-being, and the man who is to chain it can
> arrive on the scene. (p. 124)

Tocqueville had in mind those who yearned for public stability so that private pursuits could be liberated. Perhaps some fundamentals of the sociological imagination had not changed after all. But there is more: it was easier to see the tensions of capitalism in moments of birth or transition, whose uncertainties helped reveal internal juxtapositions at the core of political arguments. The years and centuries to come would obscure the strains and pressures under layers of triumph. Revisiting one's Machiavelli and one's Tocqueville provided a means to recover a memory of a different way to argue about capitalism and thereby to consider anew its possible futures.

CHAPTER 17

Body Parts

If Albert Hirschman were a novelist, the human body might have figured prominently in his writings. Bodies fascinated him, not least his own. His eye for small details—human feelings expressed by a flinch or a discreetly placed hand—is a hallmark of the literary imagination he brought to bear on his social science, but it is only rarely visible through the lacquer of economic analysis and political theory. There was also a fundamental comfort with and confidence in his bodily self, a disposition that was not just coincident with the grace of his prose.

We know the human body was important to Hirschman because of the attention he gave to the gesture. The Gerty Simon portrait of his father, reproduced in the first chapter of this book, was a reminder of a paternal afterlife. But it was not the melancholy of Carl's eyes that stoked Hirschman's memory, but their counterpoint—the strong yet nimble hands of the surgeon. Did these hands rest on the shoulder of a son while reading together? Were they reminders of a father's chess moves? We cannot know for sure; the precise meaning of the memory of these body parts must be included in the store of absences and gaps of a life history. The significance of hands is also clear in Hirschman's favorite passage from *Madame Bovary*, the scene in which Emma's husband, Charles, leans over the dying body of his wife, clasping her hands as she shudders to her end. Emma has chosen to kill herself rather than confront the sordid reality of her affairs and debts. Charles weeps, but the last thing Emma hears is the blind beggar in the street below. Hands are touching, but they do not feel. It was, to Hirschman, a picture image of realism, an echo of the register he tried to bring to his own less narrative style of social science, where the reader might capture the meaning of the whole through a riveting portrait of the small, seemingly insignificant, and almost imperceptible pattern—if not drawn to it by the writer's pen.

Of all human body parts, it was the heart that most concerned Hirschman. Throughout his life, the imagery of the heart divided or pressed to service a one-sided *homo economicus* was what Hirschman wanted to rescue from the social scientist's obsession with rational man. Hamlet's soliloquy on the heart ("Give me that Man / That is not passion's slave, and I will wear him / In my heart's core, ay, in my heart of heart / As I do thee.") reminds us that the heart had to be conjugated in the singular; "heart of hearts" is an unfortunate bastardization. It is being enslaved to passion, not passion per se, that's the problem for a man of reason like Horatio, to whom Hamlet is speaking. Since we have only one heart, it had to be a home for passion and reason, and Hamlet's inability to reconcile this necessary tension helps explain his paralysis. From Hirschman's long days' conversations with Eugenio Colorni, whence they pronounced a shared commitment to prove Hamlet wrong, one might see the heart playing a starring role in his work. Consider the frontispiece of *The Passions and the Interests*: here we have a hand wielding a pair of iron tongs that have clasped a beating and bleeding heart; the pincers have begun to squeeze. The image is from 1617 and its caption, "Repress the Passions!" is a lurid reminder that the heart was the heart of the matter for social science. So too was one of Hirschman's favorite aphorisms collected for his daughter Lisa in June 1967 on the occasion of her graduation from Barnard College, a decade before *The Passions and the Interests* was published: from Vauvenargues he wrote that "Les grandes idées viennent du Coeur."[1]

Hirschman was drawn to the body most of all in the form of a beautiful woman. The ladies of Marseilles were only too happy to forget their despair as the Nazis took over Europe in 1940 and dally with a mysterious young man who could speak many languages. Beamish's grinning and cunning optimism was magnetic in the sleazy bars along the quayside, which came in handy when running money-laundering and document-forging operations. Some of the American (female) volunteers who worked on the rescue scheme marveled at Beamish's skills in seduction. Even Varian Fry would shake his head at the pleasures of his assistant. Hirschman loved to flirt but was discriminating in his choice. The affection for the company of a woman—not to bed but rather to banter, as if the presence of feminine beauty were enough for the senses—was a habit that enabled him to endure cocktail parties and hors d'oeuvres he otherwise preferred to skip. Not a few women remarked to me in interviews that Hirschman was quick to search out the loveliest woman in a crowd and had no difficulty finding a suitable topic for conversation—a painting, a recent book, her project. If there was to be small talk, let it be embellished with aesthetic pleasures.

Without a doubt, his passion for the company of a picturesque woman was one of the many ingredients that bonded him to Sarah. There was so much they shared—books, music, art, politics, and travel—that this dimension of their mutual attraction is easy to skip, not least because among literati the corporal experience is too often treated with some unease. But it is hard to deny that Sarah was a breathtaking woman and she must have struck Hirschman from the moment they met; in that instance, his seductive instincts went into high gear. The posed photos of her as a young woman have a rare combination of glamour and radiance. Nor did age seem to take its toll. The midlife portraits by the great Colombian photographer, Hernán Díaz, do not fail to capture Sarah's striking elegance. So too do Christa Lachenmaier's images (see the portrait in the last chapter of this book), taken in Berlin half a lifetime later. Indeed, the photos of the couple give us a sense of astonishing beauty, as if mutually attracted by each other's good looks. It may well be—though yet again we are in the domain of the biographical unknown—that this underlying magnetism helps explain why a preternaturally flirtatious man who was not above thinking about the centrality of desire in world history was not a womanizer; many people have asked me about Hirschman's infidelity, as if expecting it; because he was so obviously not the uxorious husband, a cloud of suspicion has hung over him. But nowhere in the archives or testimony is there a trace of a paramour. Albert's heart of heart does not appear to have been divided or squeezed: it reserved its passion for Sarah.

And what did he think of his own body? His ailments and troubles were a constant subject in his letters, and there is a slight whiff of the hypochondriac in some of the complaints; he took delight, for instance, in sharing tales of blisters from marching in wool socks during French army training in 1939, and embellished the stories with details of how he lanced them with a spare needle. There were bouts of hay fever as a child and bad pneumonia in Berkeley. But otherwise, it is safe to say that Hirschman was more than a fit man. "Exercise" is too American a term to describe Hirschman's habits of regular long walks, often in Sarah's company, attention to his diet, and vacations that included some form of physical activity. After moving to the IAS, climbing the Alps became a summer's pastime. While not muscular (certainly by the chiseled standards of our air-brushing days), he was strong, well proportioned, and not without a manliness—a manliness of which he was most certainly aware. For as much as he loved to flirt, he was also ready for the right masculine pose. Here again, we are left to wonder about the story behind the pose—what was Hirschman thinking as he propped himself upside down for the camera to capture him in a headstand, or flexing his arms and chest in a semi-jesting (only semi!) bodybuilding stance? Sarah recalled the pride he took at being athletic in his youth. Good grades were a source of self-esteem, but it was his abilities on the rowing team, bicycle trips, mountain climbing, and eventually capacity to endure long marches in soldier training that brought out immodesty. Raised to comport himself properly at old-world parties, he was also a poised dancer; the institute would host annual dinner and dance soirées, and when Albert and Sarah stepped onto the floor, others would cede the center to the ball's most graceful couple.

Families, especially of the well-heeled, nearing-affluent sort, often have their favorite spots for vacations. Sometimes these are the grandparents' home, sometimes a country house. For itinerants like the Hirschmans, there was no single destination. But there was one constant: whether it was Boston, Bogotá, or Bahia, the beach was a favorite spot to relax. This idea of vacationing, drawn from memories of a childhood on the sands of the North Sea, reproduced itself in the Hamptons, on Cape Cod, and in Santa Monica. Once, while Sarah recounted her mixed feelings about family visits to Los Angeles, she was about to catalogue what she disliked about the city when Albert chimed in: "Unless it was to the beach." This was in August 2005, by which point he was all but inaudible and incoherent; yet these words shone through, and to drive home the point, he repeated them. A legacy that allows us to reconstruct some sense of physical self-regard are the family photographic albums, which are filled with records of beach vacations. Because Albert was most often the man behind the lens, we have fewer images than we might like for such an exercise. But it is nonetheless revealing that when he did step out for a focus shot, he did so with performative élan and composure, what they call in German *Haltung*: always keep up a certain poise, never let yourself go or be caught by surprise. The pose, in this sense, was a question of dignity and can easily come across to our eyes as narcissism. Here is more *amour propre* on display than *amour de soi*. By the same token, there is no evidence of an effacing subject caught by surprise with a swollen midriff. Nor do we have evidence of shame or embarrassment about narrow shoulders or spindly legs that a more self-conscious man might conceal with a towel. The fact was, Hirschman did not just have a striking body, he knew it. And not only was he unashamed to put it on appropriate display, he was more than happy to exhibit its abilities. He could hold a headstand, a pose that combined athleticism with playfulness, for an astonishingly long time.

Impressive for a man born a half-century earlier. Hirschman was also not above showing some of the buff of the sculpted figure and would occasionally pose accordingly.

Hirschman knew he was an attractive man. People, starting with his own mother, told him so. Albert Camus' second wife, Francine, told Albert that he reminded her of her (then philandering) husband; Albert was vain enough to know that this should be taken as a compliment. Even by then, Camus was an emblematically photogenic intellectual—made even more famous by the 1947 picture by Henri Cartier-Bresson of the existentialist with cigarette and upturned trench-coat collar. Hirschman was also a smoker, though his was a social habit; perhaps the cigarette was, as in the Camus portrait, another prop for the vanities. The resemblance of Camus to Hirschman is hard to miss: the hairstyle, the lined forehead, clean-shaven with almost movie-star looks.

If he thought well enough of his physique, Hirschman cared as much about what covered it. It's hard to say which part of the letter that Machiavelli wrote to Francesco Vettori in 1513 Hirschman liked more: the idea of conversing with ancient philosophers after a hard day scrabbling for a living, or the ritual of dressing up beforehand. What we do know is that Albert never dressed down, and his refinery made an impression. Perhaps it was the figure on which his clothes hung; perhaps it was the clothes themselves. Either way, his Columbia graduate students admired the fit of the Brooks Brothers shirts and jackets. By the 1970s, he had abandoned that rather staid look for something more casual but no less noteworthy—loose-fitting, silk-blend jackets procured from a clothier behind the Odéon in Paris. The tie was now a thing of the past, but the new combination gave him, if anything, even more flair. In so many of my conversations with old acquaintances, his apparel was memorable—as if a counterpoint to his equally unforgettable pausing, almost murmuring voice, which some took for a stutter. Robert Darnton, himself no slouch when it came to attire, recalled how Albert "liked to cut a figure sartorially" and how much he enjoyed entering a French restaurant appropriately garbed to eat and talk well.[2]

With an attitude to life such as this one, it is not surprising that Hirschman aged without having to give up some of the traits of youth. The degeneration in his features from childhood to mature manhood was at most incremental, and one can still see the uncanny mixture of the twinkling eyes of the curious opportunist and the visage of the dreamer, about which so many people commented, into his seventies; he could still reach an Alpine glacier long after retiring. True, the forehead grew more lined, the swept back hair thinned out. But the breathless grace and easy self-regard remained.

CHAPTER 18

Disappointment

It is only our conception of time that makes
us call the Last Judgment by that name; in
fact it is a permanent court-martial.

FRANZ KAFKA

No sooner did *The Passions and the Interests* come out in 1977 than
Albert and Sarah went to Russia for ten days. These were the waning
hours of détente. Hedrick Smith's prize-winning *The Russians* dominated
the *New York Times* best-seller lists, but East-West relations were turning frosty over human rights. The Hirschmans' trip was an opportunity
for Sarah to reconnect with her native tongue and share the pleasures of
seeing Russian plays in Russian with Albert. Sarah promised to translate.
Their white-night meanderings—through dilapidated churches, days in
the Hermitage Museum, fancy (and overpriced) meals, discrete nudging
of each other to point out the books people were reading, and gazing
through car windows at passing potato farms—eventually took them to
the forests outside Vladimir. One Sunday, they finally asked their driver
about the scattered garden plots in the countryside. He owned one himself, he explained, and invited them to visit his wife and two sons. "Our
driver's lot," noted Sarah, "is a marvel of horticulture." Forty by twenty-
five meters, it was densely packed with vegetables and fruit. The straw-
berries were ripe, and the driver's wife was preparing to make preserves,
taking advantage of her vacation as a nursery school teacher to prepare for
the winter and make some extra jars to sell to neighbors. "What a strange
concentration on a wholly private pursuit for the citizens of a socialist
state!" the diary of their trip concluded.[1] This observation about collec-

tive and "private pursuits" was no casual, offhand remark. It was becoming an obsession.

Part of the obsession was directed at Albert's fellow economists.
Hirschman felt compelled to write to Mac Bundy, the president of the Ford
Foundation, with some thoughts about his creed. Bundy had expressed
an increasingly common disparaging view of the dismal profession: economists enjoyed "the inside track" in thinking about development—and
he was deeply unhappy about this. Hirschman did not disagree with him
about "the preeminence of the economist as a policymaker." The drive
to make behavior calculable and predictable had narrowed the sphere
of what economists might consider economic. But, by the same token,
the other social sciences neglected problems of concern to economists.
Hirschman considered it pointless to get outraged at or exhort economists directly. Economists were too important to the business of problem
solving. Rather, he urged "developing some countervailing power on the
part of other social scientists" in order to enrich economic thinking.[2] He
wore his credentials like a badge, though he knew he stood orthogonal to
his discipline.[3]

In the ensuing years, it became a mission to clear new ground for a
more connected social science. The general sense of crisis and breakup
of intellectual coordinates pushed Geertz and Hirschman to redirect the
concerns of the School of Social Science away from the strong focus on
developing societies to address, starting in 1977, advanced industrial societies. Perhaps Hirschman's return to Berlin played a role as well. For
the first time, European social scientists such as Alessandro Pizzorno and
Claus Offe came to the school. Offe's arrival was a pretext for Hirschman
to dust off his unused German—which struck the young sociologist as
a throwback to his grandparents' tongue; Hirschman's German had fossilized in a bygone era. Also, America's leading liberal philosopher, John
Rawls, joined the assembly for one semester. The group composed of Pizzorno, Offe, Rawls, Martin Shefter, Herbert Gintis, and Robert Cooter
decided to meet Monday evenings in peoples' homes. With a backdrop
dominated by the buzz about the "crisis of the welfare state," spreading
strikes, the meltdown of New York City's finances, and winters of discon-

tent, the Monday-evening group fastened on the hot topic of the "governability of modern democracy." By any reckoning it was an impressive group. Rawls and Offe (a student of the German philosopher, Jürgen Habermas) led an evening's discussion of Habermas's *Legitimation Crisis*; another evening Hirschman and Pizzorno spearheaded a talk of Mancur Olson's *The Logic of Collective Action*.

Having diagrammed his views of the original arguments for capitalism *before* its triumph, and prompted by the Monday-evening gatherings in Princeton, Hirschman sat down to settle scores with Mancur Olson's highly influential 1965, almost prophetic work, *The Logic of Collective Action: Public Goods and the Theory of Groups*, a near-biblical argument for a model of capitalism *after* its triumph. More than any other, Olson's book nurtured the emerging field of institutional economics and popularized coinages such as "collective action problems" and "free-riders." The nuts and bolts had been around for a while; Olson's accomplishment was to pull them together into a single, indomitable, and to some depressing, intervention that anticipated many of the arguments that would gain currency in the gloom of the 1970s. At the heart of Olson's argument was that modern societies create incentive systems that induce individuals to invest their energies in private goods but thwart the pooling of these efforts to create public goods. Moreover, these propensities were bound by an immutable "logic." Efforts to coax people into collective action to provide public goods inevitably lose their steam as defectors respond to the incentives to "free ride" on the backs of others. In contrast, individuals don't free ride when groups support private goods—a conclusion that gave ballast to a rising neo-conservative movement that advocated private solutions to social problems. Olson did not necessarily think that free-riding was driven purely by selfishness; it was the government provision of public goods that made free-riding a rational response. Some neo-cons simply touted the virtues of private greed. Either way, the result was an impossibility theorem about sustained collective solutions to social problems that explained why there could be no real influential mass action.[4]

Olson's book burrowed under Hirschman's skin; the optimism and mystery of his Hiding Hand of the 1960s was losing to the bleak, iron

logic of the Invisible Hand of the 1970s.[5] It did not help that Olson had
written a wrong-headed review of *Journeys toward Progress*, which presented Hirschman's work as a catalogue of corruption, misgovernment,
and hopelessness in Latin America. *Exit, Voice, and Loyalty* was a book
that reviewers frequently set alongside Olson's *Logic of Collective Action*
as a counterpoint: the former explaining collective action movements
while the latter pointed to their futility. One reviewer took *Exit* to task
for failing to take fuller account of Olson's demolition of the prospects of
"voice," which left Hirschman steaming; Hirschman was nothing if not
sensitive to reviews.[6]

Ten years after the publication of these counterpoints in the social
sciences, the mood seemed to have declared Olson the winner. By 1978,
the spirit of '68, which had been so decisive for *Exit, Voice, and Loyalty*,
was looked upon as a rash, aberrant, quixotic outburst. The rising tide of
neo-conservatism was only too pleased to announce its triumph as the
restoration of a natural order. Hirschman took advantage of one evening's
discussions at Cliff Geertz's house to take Olson as Exhibit A for what he
would then spend the next decade and a half trying to expose: the rhetoric and politics of the ideological underpinnings of the Right.

Hirschman picked apart Olson's claims. There were empirical "flaws."
Olson did not deal with entrepreneurship. He ignored leadership and neglected "explosions of public activity." Olson's principal points had been
"well known since Hume"; Hirschman was always pleased to demolish
claims to originality with a nod to the classics (over whom he was accumulating an increasingly formidable command). But none of this was
especially important, and Hirschman knew it; Olson *had* observed a
phenomenon that could not be so easily waved away: the resilience of
private solutions to public problems. Even more: Hirschman did not disavow them. He acknowledged the book's "merits," the chief one being
that he "debunks [the] idea that interest group formation is almost automatic and that one can somehow rely on these groups and their interplay
for [a] public interest outcome." He also applauded the effort to explain
individuals' decisions "not to join" as "not necessarily apathy but the free
ride phenomenon." Olson's was not an argument easily dismissed by in-

voking empirical exceptions or even more a rival ideology. The issue was that Olson presumed a necessary divide, a basic partition between exit and voice, markets and democracy, which left no room for Hirschman's mixed model of Man vulnerable to contingency and possibilities that kept toppling any *logic* (a word that made him shiver) governed by a single, if powerful, drive.[7]

His notes on Olson reveal someone who had lost his customary cool. The "paradox of voting" (why do people bother voting if any single ballot is trivial?) "is a paradox only if it is considered that participation is costly," Hirschman scribbled vigorously. So, he went on: the "act of voting = people exercising sovereignty for one day = feasts of fools." This was, he believed, not just empirically false but a caricature. There are, after all, he wrote to himself, activities whose "striving . . . cannot be neatly separated from possessing [an] object." He brought in Pascal's thoughts on food, play, prayer, and politics where a "cost-benefit calculus becomes impossible." Having seen the distortions caused by over-confident "theories" of development planning dressed in a similar cost-benefit calculus, this must have come across as déjà vu. But this challenge was more daunting—which helps explain the unusually emphatic reactions. "Olson is wrong": he had captured one point, one response, among the several that people could choose. He had contrived a "theory" to make the contingent, the chosen, seem inevitable, converting one possibility into a necessity.[8]

It was a long, heated, evening discussion. Geertz found the Olsonian proposition absurd and huffed at the whole notion of free-riding. Hirschman labored to explain principles he disavowed. Rawls retreated into silence. And Gintis was adamant that there had to be "an answer."[9] In the end, Hirschman managed to conclude with one of his favorite quotes from Rousseau: "What makes for human misery is the contradiction between man and citizen; make him one and you will make him as happy as he can be; give him wholly to the state or leave him wholly to himself; but if you divide his heart you will tear it apart."[10]

This did not satisfy Gintis. Rousseau's plea for the integrated, if unsteady, man-and-citizen was not an "answer" to Olson; but it gave Hirschman some moorings to address ideological responses to declinism of the 1970s. Was there a way to imagine modern life as composed of societies consisting of citizens and consumers who were not forced, or asked, to divide their hearts? The accent had to be on combinations, not separations. Invited to a global conference to celebrate the 500-year jubilee of the founding of the University of Uppsala in Sweden, Hirschman spent the spring of 1977 considering ways to bridge economists' stress on the virtues of competition and exit with political scientists' interest in participation and protest. The path to a recombination began with a return to some basics. Like Rousseau. When faced with the prospect of a fight over a meal, the "savage" featured in *Discourse on the Origin and the Foundations of Inequality among Men* can win and eat, or lose and *va chercher fortune* elsewhere; even the savage had to choose. The point was that the two, talking and walking, were conjoined.

There were, in effect, "polyphonic" solutions and a possible spirit of "problem-solving" between people and policy makers to create complex arrangements that were *understood* as complex. An example was how a country's citizens contrived a fine-grained, local linguistic acumen as an everyday way of coping with the multitude of contacts and demands. To any development observer, as Hirschman recalled of his own experiences in Colombia, this local code was often as mysterious as it was effective in moving things forward. "Understood complexity," as he explained in a letter to the political scientist Robert Keohane. Keohane was engaged in a parallel campaign against "realism" to show how governments cooperated and restrained themselves in the promotion of collective betterment and did not reflexively submit to the temptations of competition and conflict, combined countervailing processes of creation, and corrosion of public goods. The idea of "understood complexity" was one, however, that he left fallow. It is not clear why. Perhaps too much rested on the "understood" part of the formula—did people have to understand their local code for them to function as an effective means to problem solve?[11]

The accent on language and understood complexity does, however, reveal the influence of Clifford Geertz, the traces of which are hard to pinpoint because so much of their relationship unfolded in conversation. Still, from the citations of anthropological fieldwork to the growing emphasis in Hirschman's writings on local knowledge and idiosyncrasies as illuminations of how people made sense of and created meanings out of daily routines, Geertz was helping Hirschman find a way out of the divided social sciences. Geertz, whose own roots in literature dissuaded him from excessively abstract questions about the search for a common humanity or claims about its basic nature, was always far less interested in exploring what people were "really like" *beneath* the surface of it all than he was fascinated by what they were like *in* it all. In the 1970s' rush to come up with universal theories and testable hypotheses that could be transported from place to place, and time to time, Hirschman and Geertz were kindred souls.

They were also two souls on the horns of an institutional dilemma. Their Social Science initiative was still a shoestring operation, dwarfed by the other Schools at the IAS and beginning to run up against funding problems. By 1978, money was scarcer than in Carl Kaysen's day. The new director of the IAS, Harry Woolf, had to impose budgetary restrictions and was constantly urging his faculty to hustle for grants. Hirschman had an ability to defuse tension with a gentle smile and a wry, aphoristic humor, and his interventions at faculty meetings, while occasional, were "always temperate and judicious." He had "a marvelous ability to pour oil on water." But he was no institutional spear-carrier for the longer term project of moving the Program of Social Change to become a fully fledged school within the institute. This was Geertz's enterprise, and he could still get "quite worked up," by the task. In the wake of the Bellah Affaire, it was not one he especially relished, perhaps because he knew administration was not a talent. "It becomes more and more apparent by the day that I was never made to be a bureaucrate [sic]," he confessed to his friend, "which I suppose is a sort of self-complement except that any ass ought to be able to handle our little problems better than I seem to." He apologized to Albert for leaving the school in such hash and signed off one of his notes, "your hopeless colleague."[12]

Hirschman, it must be said, was not a lot less hopeless as an administrator; he'd certainly never kicked the habit of being a bit *dans la lune*. Hitherto, he had left much of the running of the show to Geertz. His international obligations proliferated. The publication of *The Passions and the Interests* led to a flood of invitations to lecture in Europe, where he was suddenly bursting on the academic scene. And institutional work was never, to put it mildly, a forte. He was only too happy to leave the legwork to others; over the summer of 1978 it was William Sewell and Quentin Skinner who cobbled together the beginnings of a large grant proposal. To make matters more complex, Woolf insisted, no doubt to get the institute to comply with Department of Labor norms, that Geertz and Hirschman give up their preference for hand-picking the visitors to the institute and that they place advertisements and conduct a proper selection based on merit, not personal connections. Hirschman was more willing to comply—even though he stood to lose more, since a number of the visiting members had been working on projects more adjacent to his own writing interests, than Geertz. When Hirschman mentioned Woolf's idea of a part-time employee with an "advanced degree" ("for example, wife of a Princeton faculty member"), Geertz erupted. " 'She,' that unemployed, overeducated wife sure as hell isn't going to be making any scholarly decisions (at least, not as long as we're around she damn well won't)." He could not help but bemoan the departure of Kaysen. "Whatever his other faults may or may not be, Carl would by now be contacting Teddy Kennedy, Hamilton Jordan, and Joseph Kraft, but . . . ah . . . , the hell with it." In the face of Geertz's impatience, Hirschman remained unflappable.[13]

Money was one challenge for Social Science. So was broadening the faculty base. When Geertz went on sabbatical to Oxford for the academic year 1978–79, he left Hirschman solo, a Hirschman who was luring invitations to travel. Administratively thin on the ground would be a generous way to describe the state of affairs. Skinner and Sewell, who had stepped into the roles as builders and hosts for the program, were leaving in the spring of 1979. To compound matters, Albert had health problems in the fall of 1978, when one eyelid grew droopy and a pupil contracted, followed by headaches. He grew alarmed when someone mentioned these as the symptoms of Horner's syndrome. His doctor sent him to a hospital for extensive testing, including a spinal tap. What they found was a viral incursion—which meant zinc therapy and waiting for the symptoms to subside. "So as you can see," he wrote to Geertz, "you left our School in rather weak hands." Bill Sewell effectively took over the chairing of the seminars. The affliction was not, however, so severe as to crimp Hirschman's travels to Latin America. A few months later he was off to Bogotá at the behest of the Ford Foundation to evaluate a think tank, where he "met with an uncomfortably exciting atmosphere as there are some danger signals indicating that the country may be going down the path on which Argentina, Uruguay, etc have long traveled."[14]

What the founders lacked in administrative skills or zeal were made up with stature, which they parlayed into a unique intellectual venture. Perhaps it was their common background in literature and philosophy. Perhaps it was their joint appreciation that "Western culture" was not normative when it came to understanding others. Perhaps it was their relative lack of interest in disciplinary conventions. Either way, the shared fascination with language, meaning, and context led them to stake out an identity for social sciences at the institute that would serve as a counterpoint to prevailing currents. While philosophers had long been arguing about the prospects for "a real science of society," it was Max Weber, a touchstone for Geertz and Hirschman alike, who argued that social science's mission was to account for the actions to which social meanings were attributed by the actors themselves. Motives, ambitions, and memories, not to mention passions and interests, had to be freed, as Geertz once put it, from "systems of closed causality."[15] It meant less interest in analyzing how structures determined behavior than how people made sense and understood the world around them—and how they argued about it—as a condition for their actions. They both rejected the ingrained expectation that a modern social science would grow up from its humanistic infancy to maturity as a hard science and leave behind its childhood interests in value, judgment, and personal insight, thereby freeing the scholar from his passions and to deploy the unconstrained use of reason. Geertz and Hirschman were part of, if not leading figures of, the interpretive turn (which is often, mistakenly, associated with post-modernism—which Hirschman and Geertz considered risible). In the 1970s, with social distemper on the rise, with old confidences and certainties on the ropes, a space opened up to pose more fundamental questions, specifically by training a more hermeneutic eye on human society. "Strong readings, (Charles Taylor), "thick descriptions" (Geertz), "deconstruction, (Derrida), and "open cognitive styles" (Hirschman) became key phrases for the movement for an interpretive social science.[16]

In 1978, Geertz and Hirschman, motivated by applications to the Mellon Foundation and the National Endowment for the Humanities for funding, sat down to compose "Our View of Social Science." Because Hirschman was the fledgling school's executive officer, he took the lead initially, with the idea of proposing a three-year program under the heading "Advanced Study of the Process of Social Change." But first, it was felt, "Our View" had to get sorted out; with the help of Skinner and Sewell, they hashed out a vision for an intellectual life at the institute. It is worth quoting them directly, for the choice of words was considered.

> The main focus of our attention is more interpretive: we are mainly concerned, as we always have been, with investigating the meanings of social behavior and the determinants of social change, and continue to be resolutely multi-disciplinary, comparative and international in our approach.

They anticipated the objections:

> We are aware of course that this approach stands in need of some explicit justification, especially as it may appear that we have decided in effect to turn our backs on the mainstream of American social science in order to explore a humanist backwater.

They felt no need to shy away from their alternative formulation to the "mainstream": "Its methods and procedures have resulted in overspecialization, present-mindedness and unwarranted scientism without much compensating capacity to provide satisfactory solutions to the pressing social and economic problems of the day." The text goes on, at times repetitiously—suggesting multiple hands at work on the document—to make the case for an intellectual atmosphere that leaned away from "a tendency to focus exclusively on questions of social causation at the expense of studying social meanings." They piled on their criticism by arguing that "the mainstream" was not only under assault within the United States, but it was hardly mainstream elsewhere. "From the perspective of international social science," and one can hear the echoes of Hirschman's running irritation with American "expertise," it is the mainstream American view which is in danger of becoming a backwater." Their proposal thus aimed to redress the imbalance within the social science disciplines and make American scholarship less provincial.[17]

It is important to underscore the choice of Social Science, in the singular.

"Our View" was persuasive. The Mellon Foundation contributed $476,000 for three years to match a grant from the federal government.

With these infusions, the modest Social Science group expanded its visiting fellows program and began to think about its third permanent member, which would help elevate the initiative to a School. And so the discussion began over who else might be brought in as a third permanent colleague. Hirschman and Geertz went back and forth over the right person and appropriate discipline—which did not always come paired. Geertz and Hirschman agreed on one thing: they wanted Skinner to stay—but he was already in the midst of a return to Cambridge as Regius Professor. Other curricula vitae populated their desks: Shmuel Eisenstadt, Neil Smelser, Suzanne Berger, Amartya Sen. What they were hunting for was someone to come for a year while they figured out if the chemistry worked. One of the problems, as Geertz knew from previous battles, was finding someone to navigate the "History Scylla" and "Mathematics Charybdis." Finally, in 1979, Michael Walzer, a political theorist from Harvard, was nominated and approved with the same acclaim that ushered Hirschman's candidacy. Walzer decamped from Cambridge for Princeton in the summer of 1980.

If Hirschman helped Geertz to get Social Science off the ground with its "interpretive" moniker, he also served as one of the bridges within the IAS. In his second year, the institute faculty chose him to coauthor a general report to the trustees, owing "probably to my fairly successful peace-making activities last year."[18] He was aided by the arrival of other bridging figures. Some were visitors, like Skinner. Others, such as John Elliott, were permanent. In the fall of 1977, he and John Elliott submitted a joint proposal from the Schools of Historical Studies and Social Science. The theme was "Self-Perception, Mutual Perception, and Historical Development," in which one can see the convergence of Hirschman's fascination with the ways in which people looked at the world as a factor in their behavior with Elliott's work on Spanish thinkers' obsession with decline and decay and its imprint on the empire's policies. The three-year proposal sought to formalize the occasional overlapping activities to further a discussion about "the interplay between self-interpretation and action as a generating force in history." The hope was, they pitched to the Mellon Foundation, to "help to break down interdisciplinary barriers both between history and social science, and among the various branches of history on the one hand and of social science on the other." To coordinate this venture they proposed the Princeton University historian, Robert Darnton—already closely tied to Geertz—who could also help build much-needed ties between the university and the institute. To Elliott, the fortnightly evening gatherings at Geertz's house over wine and cheese, which began finally in 1979, and the flow of active, dynamic younger scholars, such as Amal Rassam, Theda Skocpol, and David Cannadine, found in his fraternity with Hirschman a more intellectually lively alternative to the atmosphere governing the School of Historical Studies. For his part, Hirschman played the role as the "effortless, multilingual, cosmopolitan." To Cannadine, Hirschman appeared "very grand"—and was ever the quiet source of "interesting insights from unexpected places delivered with enormous charm." Skinner had the same impressions: Hirschman exemplified what it meant to be the worldly intellectual rather than the obsessive scholar. An intellectual's halo hung over him.[19]

As the years rolled by at the institute, going back to development economics was all but impossible. Several other intellectual fronts now commanded Hirschman's attention. There were the conversations with the ancients about peoples' motives and the pursuit of "a more humane polity." There was the effort to understand dictatorship during the collaboration with O'Donnell and Cardoso. And the prolonged effects of *Exit, Voice, and Loyalty* included continual reformulation and international symposia. By contrast, development economics was on the ropes. The high hopes of the "development decade" gave way to a pile-up of disasters that shattered the confidence of an entire intellectual field. In April 1979, Carlos Díaz Alejandro invited Hirschman to write an essay for a festschrift in honor of William Arthur Lewis, who was retiring from Princeton University and who represented so much of what Hirschman questioned about the field: the commitment of general planning, the defense of large-scale foreign aid, and the depiction of peasant rural economies as mired in backwardness. The two had traded barbed reviews of each others' work. When they found themselves together in Princeton, there was a tacit agreement to share the mutual politeness of an arm's-length relationship. Sometimes, the overlap could not be avoided. When Hirschman presented a paper in Princeton's economics department about his linkages concept, Lewis was openly scornful. It was no secret that the tensions within the field of development economics harbored a personal, and scarcely personalized, rivalry. When Lewis was awarded the Nobel Prize in economics later that year, not a few observers concluded that this doomed Hirschman's chances at the prize; Geertz shook his head and told people around him that it was a sad day. Hirschman himself said nothing, though Sarah must have known his feeling, as she conceded to others that he was crestfallen. While he questioned whether the so-called Third World needed its own peculiar subfield of economics, he did not include himself among those economists who questioned whether "development" even deserved a Nobel (as one economist put it to me, "development was a dog's lunch"). It was clear: if there was going to be a Nobel for a development economist, there would be only one. Lewis got it.

Hirschman opted to write an essay that cannot be read as anything but an elegant obituary on the field. That it was to mark Lewis' retirement was not uncoincidental. As he wrote to the organizer of the Lewis tribute, he was eager to have his essay appear also in his personal anthology— eventually called *Essays in Trespassing: Economics to Politics and Beyond*— "One reason why I am in a bit of a hurry to publish is that, like Sir Arthur,

I am going to be 65 this year. So this will be my own Festschrift, all written in my own hand."[20] And with this, he brought closure on a field about which he had deeply ambivalent thoughts. With its origins in the belief that somehow "underdeveloped" countries needed their own analytical tools—either because they were bereft of the modern features that made capitalism work or because they were the miserable consequences of world capitalism—development economics came up with general models (Balanced Growth), laws of motion (development with Unlimited Supplies of Labor), or basic truisms (Unequal Exchange). To Hirschman's mind, this was all misguided. In the crusade to "slay the dragon of backwardness virtually by itself," the field derived policies from some dubious presumptions about backwardness—that it was mired, static, involuted. Then, the field drew from the wrong historical analogies, like the Marshall Plan, in search of grand solutions. How else to explain how so many people could "entertain such great hopes for economic development" while at the same time living in the "most calamitous 'derailments of history.'" What had once made development economics so compelling in the 1950s—its overconfident ability to comprehend the problems of the Third World, coupled with its delight in drawing elegant, grandiose plans—were shattered. Then, to bury themselves, development economists, instead of dealing with the implications of the political messes to which they had contributed, they performed "a Freudian act of displacement" and "took out" their distress on their subjects and looked for noneconomic explanations for all the problems. In the course of absolving their theories and policy advice of any responsibility in the development game, they put themselves out of a job as the heroes of the day. The contempt that was sown into the view that the Third World was made up of "wind-up toys" that could motor their way through phases of development with the right "integrated development plan" was more than naïve. It was partly responsible for the calamities to which it had contributed. As a crowd filled the seminar room at the institute for members to hear Hirschman deliver his first take on "The Rise and Decline of Development Economics" in the shadow of the Nobel Prize decision, there was a recognition that he was delivering as much a heartfelt statement as an intellectual profile, one that left the air thick with feelings of disappointment, both in the discipline and for Hirschman personally.[21]

If development economics had driven into the sand, economics most certainly had not. As a discipline, it was on a roll by the end of the 1970s, not least because leaders of the world economy were grappling with unemployment, inflation, and scarcity with an energy not seen since the gloomier 1930s. While many—like the president of the Ford Foundation—lamented what they saw as the overweening influence of economists, Hirschman was not among them. He agreed that too many of his peers had narrowed the scope of their queries to elicit the most predictable of answers. But there was a deeper problem. As he had discovered in the misunderstanding with Rothschild over the tunnel effect, the highly developed analytical armature of economics (which yielded to impressively developed tools, which Hirschman admired) made it more resistant to theoretical changes, especially if these changes emerged from outside the discipline. Moreover, the pragmatism of the discipline immunized it from more abstract philosophical thinking. The result was that formative books, such as Lionel Robbins' *Nature and Significance of Economic Science* (which Eugenio Colorni had pressed upon Hirschman on the eve of the Second World War) or Paul Samuelson's influential *Foundations of Economic Analysis*, were profoundly shaped by the positivist philosophy of the 1930s and 1940s. Latter-day economists were not aware of their philosophical moorings borne of a different era.

It was not that the philosophical foundations were wrong; Hirschman admired the positivist and practical streak—and it was this that motivated his against-the-grain appeals to Latin Americans to break out of their elegant, poetic, but defeatist circles. The "good or bad" debate about economics he considered an arid one. But he always knew that the discipline was far more complex than its critics from outside it knew. And it was as much from inside as outside that he sought to pluralize it more and encourage alternative thinking. For several years, he stewarded the ongoing discussion about "new trends in economics" in the School of Social Science, which drew participants from Princeton and the University of Pennsylvania. Most notable were the fortnightly evening workshops aimed at critical appraisals of the prevailing theories of the rationality of *homo economicus* with his stable set of preferences.

Some of what transpired in these evening discussions informed his involvement in projects to tackle the "crisis" of the 1970s. Through the Brookings Institution, Charles Maier put together a working group on inflation that would yield an edited volume. Jean-Jacques Salomon at the Science Policy Division of the Organization for Economic Cooperation and Development (OECD) enlisted Hirschman's advice on the report "Science and Technology in the New Socio-Economic Context." The idea was to respond to some prevailing wisdoms about the nature of the global economic malaise as a cyclical problem or as the conjunctural result of bad policies. Instead, Salomon wanted to index some of the structural and technological shifts that underlay the crisis. This led to some pleasant meetings in Paris—and an eventual long-term friendship with Emma Rothschild, who also became involved. It was a familiar way of framing the problem to anyone tracking Latin American worries about long-term transitions, crises, and employment—that short-term macroeconomic analysis was simply inadequate. But Hirschman was skeptical of some of the alarmist tenor. One OECD call included renewed attention to research and development in new technology "or else." "Or else" what? Research and development made good sense, but surely the world economy was not doomed if it didn't get full attention. Beside, Hirschman noted, some of the thinking about technology was pretty conventional and thus could hardly shoulder the responsibility of thwarting the "else." Tone down the catastrophistic prose, he urged. "Maybe we lacked imagination on this and we should have had a fall-back or fail-safe position of the following sort: more technical progress might be good but if we do not have more we are not yet lost either."[22]

The compound effects of these discussions prompted him to lay out his response to the growing consensus on the Left and Right that the welfare state was in deep, intractable trouble. Not unlike the consensus about the "structural crisis" of industrialization in Latin America, there was a catastrophistic analogue in the postwar arrangement of the developed West contained under the label of "the crisis of the welfare state."

For the Left, capitalism was unable to keep the balance between supporting profits and keeping the system fair and legitimate. For the Right, the diagnosis was not all that different. It was the prescription—decontrol markets and let the bounty of the private sector take care of private, and therefore public, problems—that differed. At Robert Keohane's urging, Hirschman joined a panel at the American Economic Association meetings in 1979, "The Recoil from Welfare Capitalism," at which Hirschman offered his "non-structuralist" interpretation of the malaise. It was much like his appeal to Latin Americans and their obsession about "structural stagnation." Social scientists, ever on the lookout for ominous signs of decline and their "fundamentalist" causes (which social scientists claim as uniquely poised to understand), were overshooting their mark and confusing a "systemic crisis" with "growing pains." The trouble was not a fundamental incompatibility or "contradiction" (a word Hirschman felt was being debased from its original Hegelian formulation) of capitalism, but the complex, often hard-to-fathom, features of transitions and shifts in its history. One cannot help but hear the echoes of the debates of the 1930s over the nature of the crisis and the role of politics—with a teenage Hirschmann squarely in the camp that felt that there were more political and economic options than either the extreme Left, or the Right, would concede. "Being rather bored by both ideological camps," he observed, "I tend to shift from one to the other depending on whom I am talking to. Given the complexity and ambiguity of the real world, a useful function may actually be served by such contrary behavior." As he noted for the Left, where his sympathies lay, the inclination was utterly self-defeating, and *this* mistake he had seen before. Fatalism was "an ideological trap" that in the end would favor the other side.[23]

In this regard, he was utterly prophetic. For all the hand-wringing on the Left, this was a debate they would lose, intellectually and politically.

The determination to resist pessimism and heavily deterministic accounts of the crisis of the late 1970s brings us full circle to Mancur Olson. Early in the series on "new trends in economics" an untenured economist from Williams College who was a visiting fellow at Princeton University, Michael McPherson, joined the informal group. Without knowing it at the time, he was to help Hirschman find an alternative formulation to Olson's "logic," to pick up after the abandoned notion of "understood complexity." McPherson, currently the president of the Spencer Foundation, recalled the day he wandered into the Princeton University bookstore and found copies of the recently published *The Passions and the Interests*; flipping through the pages, he was amazed to find so many of his own concerns being plumbed by the man who was about to be his colleague. But the book was expensive—in those days, junior faculty salaries were so low (even at Princeton) that a single hardback was a considerable investment. He dug into his pockets, bought the book, drove home and devoured it to inaugurate a long history of engagement between the two. Several years later, when McPherson joined the IAS as a visiting member and had an office next to Hirschman, someone knocked on his door. It was Albert, who'd just finished reading a draft of McPherson's paper on ethics and economics, which argued that markets tend to create moral restraints on cooperation *and* on conflict more than people realize. Hirschman was excited; not only did he admire the paper, but it led him to a metaphor to challenge the one that was driving him to distraction, the "free-rider." Hirschman's parry was "oar-pulling": by pitching in together, individuals would move faster with less effort.[24]

Spurred by a metaphor, Hirschman went back to his notes. For the summer of 1978, Albert and Sarah rented a flat on the Île Saint-Louis in Paris, which reunited them with the city that, for all intents and purposes, had remained their spiritual home. Katia and her family lived there, and there were now more grandchildren. There were many friends, and Albert's work was circulating in France. Each had Parisian memories of youth that they now had the time to share.

It was also a period of intense reflection. They tracked the running commentary about how distant the upheavals of 1968 seemed a decade later. Hirschman wanted to place the gap in a larger framework—one that would spare the spirit of '68 from being depicted as exotic and unique. "My dissatisfaction with both Olson and Scitovsky [whose 1976 book, *The Joyless Economy*, was another of Hirschman's antitheses] as a source," began his extended jottings, pointed to two simple alternatives.

To Olson, Hirschman countered that "participation in public life can be something that is desired for itself." To Scitovsky, who calibrated happiness to consumption (even if he thought most of what Americans bought was doomed to displease), he invoked Goethe's idea of *streben*, "striving for something higher," a notion drawn from the nest of his youth. The summer then had him meandering through a potpourri of readings. "Reread N. Ginzburg, *Lessico familiare* [sic] for the joys of dangerous political action in comparison to humdrum everyday existence." What he made of Ginzburg's moving memoir of growing up in a large family of Jewish antifascists in Turin is unclear. Readings meandered from Benjamin Constant and Chateaubriand's *Memoires* (on the idea of the crown as an *intérêt public*) to a full two-page spread of an advertisement from the *New York Times Magazine*—"The Ultimate Driving Machine"—a BMW 528i, with a photo of a man driving through a bucolic setting, his hands wrapped around the steering wheel; the bold text reads: "MEETING THE DEMANDS OF SOCIETY IS NO EXCUSE FOR BUILDING A BORING CAR." The vehicle defied its circumstances: "In a time of lowered expectations, amid increasing mediocrity, the engineers at BMW have actually improved the BMW 528i." Hirschman's fascination with automobiles (indeed, he and Sarah would start buying their cars in Europe, a Citröen one year, a Saab another) dovetailed with his insights on the ways in which people struggle "to hold disappointment at bay"—by washing their cars, simonizing them—in a "desperate attempt to stem normal decline (decay) of elations over having it." Years later, the BMW ad would make a fleeting appearance in his next book.[25]

Conversations with friends also appear in these notes. Hirschman circled back to Amartya Sen. While their families vacationed together in the summer of 1975 in Sabaudia, on the Central Italian coast, Albert was by then the "rich uncle" from America, treating everyone to ice cream. But he also made sure to go on long walks with Sen, who had recently published a landmark essay in *Economica* called "Behaviour and the Concept of Preference," based on his inaugural lectures at the London School of Economics. Already en route to fame for his *Collective Choice and Social Welfare* (published in 1970, which would help earn him the

Nobel Prize in economics in 1998), Sen was hard at work exposing the limitations of the prevailing dogmas about the narrowed self-interested *homo economicus*. A subsequent essay, "Rational Fools: A Critique of the Behavioural Foundations of Economic Theory," was a chattier version of the complex *Economica* paper, but it was more accessible to Hirschman, for whom Sen's mathematics was beyond reach. Albert wanted to know more and plumbed his nephew, Amartya, now married to his niece Eva. By 1978, his reflections on Sen were thickening. Note: "Amartya's meta-preferences come in to play role when there is something wrong with actual preference—it's not necessary to *invent* new set, there is always one waiting in the wings [sic]." Quentin Skinner appears throughout, from his point that Calvin's idea was that "all citizens could do in the public realm was to obey the sovereign—he is not supposed to meddle (action for the public weal becomes meddling)," to, some pages later, "Quentin: In repressive regimes it's up to individual how much he is going to get involved; in open societies it's often a question of his ability, whether he is *asked* to 'run' for this or that office [sic]."[26]

Hirschman was always eclectic in his sources. But the summer of 1978 brought a veritable explosion ranging across languages (English, French, German, Italian) and genres—classical literature to consumer-choice theories. It is no wonder, as he explained to Kenneth Arrow, that he found this the hardest project he had ever tackled. Indeed, to call it a "project" (which was his word choice) exaggerates his sense of direction. *Exit, Voice, and Loyalty* and *The Passions and the Interests* had the virtues of being able to start with a small idea and billow into a book, the first prompted by observations about responses to monopoly in Nigeria, the second to an enigma posed by Montesquieu. What he confronted now was much broader, more diffuse, an intellectual temper incarnate in ideas of "public choice." One has a sense that the whole business was overwhelming him—and that his inability to find a way out was beginning to weigh him down. However, an invitation from the economics department at Princeton University to deliver the Eliot Janeway Lectures on Historical Economics in honor of the Austrian economist Joseph Schumpeter gave Hirschman the right motive to air his alternative to the impossibility theorem that he had ascribed to Olson. While he was wracking himself over "Public vs Private," his tentative title, American television screens were flooded with scenes from Tehran, where radical students had seized the US embassy. That Thanksgiving, Albert and Sarah invited some friends over—the Brazilian literary scholar Roberto Schwarz and the Mexican novelist Carlos Fuentes and their wives—for goose. They were riveted to the television and worried about the government's response with the elections looming. The images of crowds "seemingly so full of hatred against the United States" were utterly depressing. It was not just the hatred on display in Iran, it was the sense of "unity" in America and portents of a "turn inward" that concerned him. "This may well be the end of public interest in development in the Third World—so, from the point of view of my interests, I also see it as the end of an epoch."[27]

With the hostage crisis in the background and long queues forming at gas stations as the United States was struck by a second energy crisis, Hirschman was understandably nervous about his reasons for optimism. Still, in December, he walked before the podium at Dodds Auditorium in the Woodrow Wilson School to deliver two lectures to large crowds of students and faculty at Princeton: "Private and Public Happiness: Pursuits and Disappointments." As with *Passions*, the choice of conjunction was vital for what followed—for Hirschman there was no basic choice between the two; it was not *or* that adjoined public to private; the private and public domains were not exclusive. The point of the lectures was to argue that people were always *choosing* depending on their moods and inclinations. It was this *activity* that Hirschman wanted to draw out. *Exit, Voice, and Loyalty* was a peerless book about *how* people made a variety of choices that changed institutions; the issue now was, *why* did they make choices? Not unlike *Exit, Voice, and Loyalty*, what followed were thoughts based on observations of everyday reactions to peoples' behavior (like the tunnel effect and BMW ads), as well as weaving in lessons from various of the welfare state "crisis" projects and the engagement with Latin American colleagues on dictatorships. Indeed, these were the empirical skeletons of "Public and Private Happiness," although it was impossible for anyone to know. The decision to keep these projects separate from his answer to the impossibility theorem and free-rider problem was probably a mistake. Many would find the eventual book arch, removed, speculative—short of a new model of social science.

This does not mean that the lectures were separated from the world. They were not abstract, but they were theoretical; Hirschman's internal jousting with Olson, and more broadly with individualism, got him closer than ever to his grail, an endogenous model that explained human behavior that motivated social change. A quarter-century after his battles with development planners in the Third World, he was no less insistent that a deeper explanation—and thus a *theory* of reform—had to avoid the *deus ex machina*, the external event or force that would move societies from one place to the next—technological changes, foreign wars, the imported (or imposed!) master plan, external infusions of capital, "foreign aid," disasters, or discoveries that moved history along from one phase to the next. These kinds of providentialist explanations were not only self-limiting, they also did not illuminate possible alternatives to a problem since the trumping breakthrough had to come from the outside. They also tended to point to the agency of outsiders—the well-meaning expert, the foreign capitalist, the enlightened few who looked at societies from the outside-in.

It was time for a different story of modernization. Hirschman offered a theory about "pendular movements of collective behavior," of the dynamics behind swings between happiness and disappointment and between public and private action. He moved from the domain of human experiences to emotional responses, such as anger at educational institutions, self-incrimination for buying a large house and regretting it (buyer's remorse), and the ever disappointing "driving experience," which far from yielding to the lyrical joy ride more often plunged the indebted pleasure-seeker into a traffic jam. This is where the BMW ad came in handy; it promised exhilaration but delivered dissatisfaction (and bills). Everywhere happiness was being dispensed and, behind peoples' pursuits, left trails of disappointment. Disappointment, as he would make clear in the book that emerged from the lectures, was the counterpart to hope, its necessary twin, a force any possibilist had to reckon with. Regret and dis-

appointment were not just the results of mistakes—but of activities conducted "with high expectations *not* to make mistakes." Far from trying to
eliminate a world of disappointment, Hirschman was trying to call attention to its necessity. To search for models that would dispense with dis-
satisfactions and regrets would rid the world of hope; here was an indictment of the Utopian thinking that had laced his skepticism of extremes
throughout his life. "While a life filled with disappointment is a sad affair,
a life without disappointment may not be bearable at all. For disappointment is the natural counterpart of man's propensity to entertain magnificent vistas and aspirations." It was not for nothing that a friend of Don
Quixote (the Knight of the Mournful Countenance) would lament the
curing of his madness, for it now deprived those around him of the pleasures they gained through his follies.[28]

Nothing was fixed. Happiness never lasted and was unevenly
distributed—and thus could not help but elicit its countervailing force,
disappointment. Likewise disappointment was not an equilibrium point;
people were inveterate "project-makers" as well as pleasure-seekers.
Unless depressed—and psychoanalysis was one example of peoples'
search for "exits" from unhappiness and was also invariably a source of
disappointment—people were inclined to swing away from the source
of the diminishing returns to their efforts. These efforts could be either
private-pursuing or public-engaging; the point is that they were subject
to similar propensities. To contrast with Olson's "logic," Hirschman presented a "dialectic" that unfolded within the very self that comprised a
complex amalgam of drives. Man had been a stage for battles between
reason and passion before capitalism; the capitalist experience had not
dissolved this fundamental struggle. Hirschman was returning to his case,
which had been muted by a complex history in *The Passions and the Interests*, for reviving a more complex, "lovable," and "tragic" human subject
for a different kind of epic—a political economy that did not create itself
around dichotomous categories of either-or, which condemned modern
humans to be in a state of perpetually tearing their hearts apart.

Here, then, was an alternative that shifted the accent from mechanisms that pulled societies forward to factors that pushed people to

change. These factors explained changes that went back and forth in two directions—to private- and public-oriented activity as a new model of political economy.

It was an audacious effort. It also overreached.

After Watergate, the coup in Argentina, a crisis of the world economy, and the seeming failure of human-rights-guided foreign policy, it is perhaps not surprising that the motor for the oscillations between private and public activities was disappointment. This "elementary human experience" was the touchstone upon which Hirschman elaborated his meditations on peoples' swings. The accent was now specifically on the role of disappointment, not unlike the diminishing returns a consumer experiences from the purchase of goods, such as consumer durables, or certain services, which were especially "disappointment-prone." Disappointment could then spur public action; it could tender a ladder, Hirschman explained, on which the consumer-citizen "can climb *gradually* out of private life into the public arena," and sometimes it could even lead to the corrosion of the ideology on which the pursuit of happiness was premised. This brought him face-to-face once more with Mancur Olson's analysis of collective action, which by now had become an ur-reference in the muscular drive to decontrol markets with its emphasis on individual cost-benefit arithmetic and the ineluctable problem of free-riding. Of course, Hirschman was not presenting public action as an antidote. It, too, was subject to pendularity. Public action was no less disappointment prone than consumer durables. One hazard was "overcommitment." Hirschman liked Oscar Wilde's quip about socialism as self-defeating because "it takes too many evenings." In societies where "electoral politics are the only politics" and public action is less rewarding than activists hoped, the disappointments can set in early in the cycle of engagement (though often leading to more generalized rage against "the system").[29]

Drifting from consumer theory and Sen's theory of meta-preferences yielded a paradox about modern politics. In democracies, the vote gives every citizen a stake in public decision making. At the same time, it places a ceiling on participation because casting ballots does not allow for the expression of different "intensities" of convictions. The result: voting has a "dual character"—to defend against the "excessive *repressive* state while "safeguarding" it against "excessively *expressive*" citizens. Needless to say, this was a very different way to paint a portrait of the voter's paradox in Olson's simplistic cost-benefit analysis. The story of the lessons learned from France after 1848, after three revolutions in less than two generations, were his case in point. The franchise was an "antidote to revolutionary change" not by stacking the outcome because there was some underlying "structural" distribution of power (as Marxists would argue), but because it stigmatized more direct, intense, "expressive" forms of political action that have the allure of being *both* more effective and more satisfying. "In short," argued Hirschman, "the trouble with political life is that it is either too absorbing or too tame."[30]

This was a case for an unstable middle ground, unstable because it was perpetually leaning people toward contrary impulses, and middling because people never swung fully to private or public activities for long. In this fashion, Hirschman refuted the triumphalism (for the Right) and defeatism (for the Left) of those that asserted that private pursuits have bled public man, as if the idea that creating wealth—the objective of private action—were superior to the pursuit of power, which was now seen as "the exclusive goal of public action." The "ultimate ideological revanche" was to represent the struggle for power as an activity that benefits only the winner, while the pursuit of wealth was "celebrated as a game at which all players can win," so that complete immersion in private activity could be "felt as a liberating experience not only for oneself, but for all society." This is what the rising neo-conservatives, and their odds-on favorite for winning the ticket to lead the Republican Party against the crippled fortunes of President Jimmy Carter, Ronald Reagan, were exalting. Hirschman tried to be optimistically prophetic. "The trouble is that our enthusiastic private citizen is now going to meet with the various disappointments" as the drive to consume one's way to happiness ends in disappointment with consumer durables that people packed into their homes. Gravity dictated that the pendulum would swing back.[31]

The pendular image was an invitation to trouble. Wasn't it just as deterministic as some of the theories he was trying to challenge? Some, like Bob Keohane, tried to dissuade him from emphasizing too much the pushing drive: "It seems to me that you vastly underestimate the attraction of public life to many people." When Hirschman presented a version of the work to colleagues at Stanford, not a few argued back: how could young people at the head of public demonstrations possibly be motivated by disappointment with the pursuit of material goods they never enjoyed? Maybe, as Keohane pointed out, the problem is the search for a "fully endogenous model?" Is there not something intrinsically appealing about engaging in public activity? Hirschman may have conceded too much to the fatalists who saw public pursuits as intrinsically prone to disenchantment.[32]

It was an important comment, and certainly not the first time that Hirschman was questioned for relying on the precept of diminishing returns in his model. One is reminded just how economically Hirschman was thinking in his effort to counter Olson and others in their own terms. Certainly, what he had done was tie private pursuits and public passions together into a rivalrous sibling relationship. They were not autonomous fields; they were not the subjects for ideological interventions. The model's automatic corrective features could not explain how or why behavior could get stuck or, worse, swing much more dramatically to one side. This meant that Hirschman's herald of the return of public man seemed so utterly at odds with the electoral tide. He was shocked at the Reagan victory and even more dismayed by the shift of the 1980s.

It was one of the few times Hirschman tried to be predictive—and it would bear out his reasons for avoiding punditry. But it deserves to be said that he was not just aiming at the ranks of gloating neo-cons. His eye was also trained at notable Cassandras, such as the Canadian philosopher Charles Taylor, whose lament for "the atrophy of public meaning" stood for a more general cry against the mindless consumerism and atomism of the modern world, or Christopher Lasch, whose *The Culture of Narcissism* (1979) was a runaway hit that decried the egotistical individualism of the age. This kind of pessimism was "not only impoverishing in itself" for the same reasons that Olson's impossibilism was, but it also condemned public action "to periodic spasmodic outbursts of 'publicness' that are hardly likely to be constructive." What Hirschman wanted—the "moralizing claim implicit in my story"—was an unstable balance. Not an equipoise of selfless angels or an equilibrium of utility maximizers. He called for more "publicness" injected into everyday living, including work and consumption, "fostering in the private sphere that fusion of striving and attaining that is characteristic of public action." The person who does so is "superior" to the rational-actor of the Republican juggernaut because he or she can "conceive of *various* states of happiness." This "bungler" and "blunderer" was thereby connected to "nobler and richer qualities."[33]

His lectures were clarion calls to resist the climate of despair and summons (from the Right) for citizens to run for the "exits" of public involvement or (from the Left) to shriek about the intractable forces conspiring against collective progress.

The lectures begat a book, one that elicited a cascade of responses from friends, colleagues, and some tetchy reviewers when Princeton University Press's Sanford Thatcher sent it out for evaluation. In retrospect, this is not all that surprising; none of his books had straddled disciplines and fields, from history to cognitive psychology, with such breathtaking scope—and with the same Hirschmanian economy of words. Remarkably, he covered all this ground in 187 manuscript pages, which inevitably meant large patches were on thin ice. Originally called *Public and Private Happiness*, it was later rebaptized to capture the motion at the core of the analysis, *Shifting Involvements: Private Interest and Public Action*. Possibly Hirschman's most ambitious work, he knew he had stuck his neck out. "I have rarely felt so uncertain about a product of mine," he told Katia. "Perhaps this is because, as I say in the preface, what I have written is less a work of social science, than the conceptual outline of one or several novels."[34] Indeed, the preface suggests that there is much more of Hirschman's personal philosophy and life story stirred into the prose. It threatened to become a *Bildungsroman* "with, as always in novels, a number of autobiographical touches mixed in here and there."[35]

The fusion of brevity and breadth was at once the work's immense strength and its weakness. Having covered so much ground, it could not help but do so unevenly and sketchily, and thus, ironically, disappoint.

To some, it contained too little evidence. After the lectures, Skinner, who was immersed in his own work on the origins of humanism in English social thought, composed a long comment about earlier swings from the time that Cicero's moral theory was translated and printed in the 1480s to shape English humanist writers' views of a "conception of the best life for man, and thus of man's highest duties." Man's highest duty was to override his self-love and its pursuits, "in order to pursue 'common weal', ie. the welfare of the whole (weal is for them the synonym for wealth—used interchangeably—and wealth doesn't mean wealth in our sense; it means welfare)." Skinner went on to explain that some, like Calvin, saw private pursuits as a good way to frame man's duties, a view that gathered strength in the sixteenth century, so "minding one's own business" and not "meddling" (a word that Skinner and Hirschman continued to mull over as it acquired pejorative features) were extolled especially by those with interests to promote, such as merchants. Thus, what started as a distinction to help found a moral theory of Ciceronian inspiration, became deformed. Why not dig into these fascinating antecedents?[36] Judith Tendler, his former student, wrote a long letter suggesting that he develop his insights about psychotherapy (and services in general) with its own disappointments. Sex, too, in the age of *The Joy of Sex* and *Playboy*, might make good examples of how people are made to feel that "normal" sexual relations, especially marital ones, are painted as a never-ending shortfall. While the manuscript was "brilliant," she wanted more examples for how the pendularity actually worked. "Because there are so many good ideas," she wrote, "it is like an orgy. It's not just a matter of setting the ms. down for a while, in order to let an idea sink in. One needs, in addition, to have an example to help root the idea—to force you to be with the idea for a little longer, in a way that is less demanding than accompanying the articulation of the idea itself."[37] Writing from Montreal, Lisa also offered her father a few cents about consumer durables (like the Cuisinart), psychotherapy (from her own practice), and the looming referendum in Quebec. A win for the separatists might spell doom for the movement for having lost its "sense of purpose." Like Skinner and Tendler, she called for more detail—especially, thinking about the vogue for referenda around North America, "what you mean by the vote."[38]

The criticism to put more empirical meat on the bones of his analysis was a sign that he had not clinched his argument, even if the style and scope of the work were so captivating. Hirschman's harshest comments came in the form of a lengthy evaluation for Princeton University Press from Robert Lane, a Yale political scientist. While Lane lauded Hirschman's previous works for being "seminal"—transcending fields and disciplines to reframe big debates, he was "dissatisfied" with this one. He found that the manuscript treated satisfaction and happiness insufficiently, and cited works in psychology and on the revolution of rising expectations that Hirschman had missed. Some of the recommended readings were welcome: Hirschman scribbled the call numbers in the margins and promptly got copies from Princeton's Firestone Library. But Lane also raised more serious issues, starting with the tying of public and private activities together. Hadn't Hirschman tried to compare two completely different species, like "elephants and rabbits?" There was also a scarcity of evidence to justify the claims.[39] Lane was not alone in hitting this mark. The historian Joan Scott, whom Hirschman would welcome as his permanent colleague at the IAS, made a similar observation. His "units of analysis" kept shifting from individuals to groups and back again. She also called for more evidence.[40] The consensus seemed to call for a longer, empirically driven book. But this was not one of these. It was an "essay," or series of "essays," an analytical twist on the Montaigne tradition but pressing up against the limits of the genre.

But the problem was not so easily dismissed. The decision to do so would cost him. George Akerlof, of Berkeley, offered a solution to help resolve some of the problems. He got underneath Lane's complaint that private and public domains were simply incomparable and pointed out that "the author mentions, but fails adequately to deal with the problem that most of his motivations concern *individual* motivations and explain an *individual's* cycle but he does not explain the *macro* cycle."[41] One of his proposed solutions was to suggest how individual motivations become contagious through ideology. So, for instance, the ideology of "privatization" speeds the transition from public action to private pursuits. Claus Offe suggested much the same—an intermediating or "third" domain that might help explain the timing and methods of the swings between private and public. This was an old concern of Hirschman's and certainly would have been easy to work into the narrative while keeping the essay form of the book. Indeed, he agreed with Offe, adding that "another very acute critic raised the same point." But it was not one he was prepared to pursue. "My present, a bit evasive defense," he told Offe, "is that I had my hands full making one 'endogenous' transition plausible; and that I merely want to show the possibility of a phenomenological portrayal of such transitions without affirming that the ones I am portraying are the only ones."[42]

Given the ambition of the lectures, which were now en route to becoming a book—to deliver a counterstroke to those who dismissed the possibilities of effective collective action and to usher a social science that did not ask Man to divide his heart—Hirschman's decision not to follow up on the quality and quantity of suggestions is hard to explain. We know that fame now meant more and more travel, and Hirschman showed little inclination to separate the essential from the expendable. In the wake of the Janeway Lectures he was off to Bogotá with Guillermo O'Donnell to review for the Ford Foundation Colombia's premier social science research organization, FEDESARROLLO. Hirschman was also a consultant for the OECD's Committee on Science, Technology and Industry. He had accepted an invitation to Florence's European University Institute to be in residence for a month and to deliver the keynote lecture, "New Approaches for the Study of International Integration," a topic that returned him to his interests of the 1940s. But it required some scrambling. There was, to crowd his calendar further, a commitment to give the lecture "The Crisis of the Welfare State" at the American Economic Association and the "Rise and Decline of Development Economics" paper for audiences at Berkeley, in Mexico City, at MIT, and at Bar-Ilan University in Israel. Meanwhile, he went back and forth to Washington as chair of the Academic Council of the Latin American Program at the Woodrow Wilson International Center for Scholars, and he took part in a conference on agricultural technology in Cartagena, Colombia, an easily declinable temptation if ever there was one. He was selected for the

Frank E. Seidman Award, which involved giving a special lecture. And to cap things off, the prestigious École des hautes études en sciences sociales in Paris invited him—and he instantly accepted—to deliver the Marc Bloch lectures in 1982.

All of this was in the year and a half he had to rework the lectures into a final manuscript. Even for someone as broad-reaching as Hirschman, this itinerary stretched him perilously, and the frequency with which he was travelling surely dug deep into the time that should have been devoted to the manuscript. "Where I agree with Lane is when he says at the end of his letter that I must have a full agenda," he wrote to his publisher. "Nothing could be truer."[43]

The question nonetheless remains, why accept these extracurricular, if obituary-enhancing (to borrow his own *bons mots*), invitations? In some cases, he did try to back out. When Bob Keohane invited Hirschman to appear on a special American Economic Association panel on the welfare state, Hirschman at first declined, citing "over-commitment." But his resistance was lukewarm; he went and wrote a paper (which appeared in the *American Economic Review*, his last for the discipline's flagship)—though he did manage to ward off entreaties from the *Harvard Business Review* to "elaborate" his thoughts on one line from the essay about "the output elasticity of quality." Some of the same resistance-acceptance behavior surrounded his OECD engagement. When the Directorate for Science, Technology and Industry issued its initial invitation, Hirschman explained that he had limited time but that as long as he was only a "consultant" in the drafting of the report, he would participate. But this, too, led to its inflation: recurring requests to "elaborate" or "expand" on this or that insight. And he was constantly squeezing his trips to Paris between other engagements. In the end, it is hard to avoid the conclusion that a certain dose of hubris was involved, which several of his nastier reviewers seized upon. In his defense against Lane to Sanford Thatcher, he described the reviewer as "hostile and aggressive, and this makes it difficult to develop a cool argument." A peeved Hirschman tried to explain that he was trying to transcend surveys on satisfaction to write a "phenomenology of disappointment through the private and public sphere," and found the survey results that Lane pointed to a detraction: "What I am doing throughout the manuscript is theory construction about motivations for changing life-styles—my 'explanations' are obviously meant to become hypotheses in the hands of some economist or political scientist who hopefully will devise some way of testing them." In a move that reveals his yearning to make a mark as a theorist, he added that "this is what has happened with a number of other books of mine."[44] This was not just a heavy card to play, it implied intended theoretical aspirations that previous works did not have. In an age in which books of theory on such large matters were long, complex treatises—John Rawls' *Theory of Justice* comes to mind—Hirschman's revealed a gap between its claims and arguments, a fatal flaw for any theoretical ambition. His responses to the manuscript reviews were cursory, and the weekly invitations to speak at this or that gathering must have seemed like applause. Thatcher, with the success of *The Passions and the Interests* under his editorial belt, no doubt felt he had another winner on his desk and deferred to Hirschman's judgment. Certainly, doing otherwise would have risked touching the nerve of his major author.[45]

What Hirschman did was tack where he faced the least resistance. He elaborated the passages and arguments that were already strong. There were many more quotes from the classics. He added more detail on consumer theory as well as on theory and evidence of the history of political participation. There were top-ups to make up for bibliographic oversights. He did address, albeit in a few paragraphs, the role of ideology in the making of meta-preferences and added a section based on his reading of Harry Frankfurt's distinction between first-order desires and second-order desires (that is, desires about desires). Cicero, too, per Skinner's suggestion, makes an appearance. But little of this was evidence of the kind his readers yearned for. It did not really address the more fundamental issue of how the oscillation between the two connected spheres was supposed to be explained, since this was the internal motion of his endogenous theory. Page 114 featured an image he found in the Bibliothèque Nationale of a worker giving up his gun and bullets to cast a ballot, with the suggestion that universal male suffrage was a way to channel the desires of an "expressive" citizenry and thus give up the notoriously re-bellious ways of Parisian rabble-rousers. Otherwise, there was not much history making the case. Hirschman dug in his heels and called the book "a conceptual novel." The introduction explained that the book was by definition speculative and tentative and acknowledged that there were problems choosing the very term *cycles* to account for the swings between private pursuits and public action. But he soldiered on.

The decision not to address the analytical problems was costly. None of Hirschman's work had elicited such mixed reviews. Indeed, compared to the rhapsodies that greeted *The Passions and the Interests, Shifting Involvements* was a painful letdown. Hirschman himself may have antici-pated this when he flew to Sweden in September 1982 to attend a con-ference to honor *Exit, Voice, and Loyalty* as well as *Shifting Involvements*. After the gala dinner, he was invited to share some remarks. There he confessed that the "shifting" activity was often unsmooth, uneven, and riddled with obstacles. This was at odds with the smooth, gravitational movement of the pendulum swinging away between the covers of his book. The failure to deal with these and the other questions it raised be-came a refrain. A reviewer in the *American Political Science Review* hit the same mark: though it weaves a lot together "Hirschman's theory might unravel if we tug on its dangling threads." The *American Journal of Sociology* found room to praise "the flowing style and flood of new ideas that we have come to expect from Hirschman" but complained that there was a basic asymmetry between private *consumption* and public *action* and concluded that "its major thesis is uncharacteristically strained." The criticisms did not stop at the doors of the disciplines. Robert Heilbroner tackled the book for the *New York Review of Books*, treating the moment as one to introduce the author of *Shifting Involvements* to a wider pub-lic; he too found the evidence for pendular swings so sparse as to make many of the arguments "unpersuasive." The chief merit, as far as Heil-broner was concerned, was in bringing to the fore the great issues of po-litical economy in the tradition of Adam Smith. Jon Elster noted in the *London Review of Books* that Hirschman was in league with the world's leading social scientists and was "at the pinnacle of the profession," but he worried whether Hirschman "had been spoilt by success." Elster found "an element of self-indulgence, sometimes self-congratulations, that prevents him from achieving the same rigour and clarity that characterised his earlier work." The engagement "in a highly speculative sociology of knowledge" Elster found especially bothersome. Skinner rushed to defend: "The modesty of his grasp of your thought seems to me to sit very displeasingly with the astonishing confidence with which he delivered himself of his Olympian judgments."[46]

It was not all so gloomy. In other domains, the book struck an instant chord—and struck hard. Lewis Coser reviewed it for the *New Republic*, using the occasion to add a long biographical profile as a coming-out narrative about one of the country's greats—"America's eclectic economist." Peter Berger called Hirschman "one of our most distinguished economists" in the *New York Times* (which prompted Hirschman to fire off a letter to Katia, gushing that he had finally "made it into *The Times*!" though he added that the review was a little less than he would have hoped for). It was also translated more swiftly than any previous book into French and German—and treated to even more laudatory reviews. Michel Massenet called Hirschman "easily recognized as a true *savant*" in *Le Figaro*. *Le Monde* featured the book on the front page. David Riesman, author of *The Lonely Crowd*, wrote him and called it "an extraordinary experience to read and ruminate about this book." Other friends shared some more critical remarks in a constructive spirit—but in the context of the reviews, they only added to the chorus.[47]

Shifting Involvements may have been a flawed book, but it was a brave one. There was a political argument involved and directed at fellow intellectuals. As people leave the streets and plazas disenchanted with politics to seek happiness in the shopping malls, what will happen to them when consumption yields its own eventual diminishing returns, when the exit option of private pursuits don't work? What will happen if the art of voice has been lost? Public life had its problems—it could be too absorbing and too boring. This was the point of representing actors as neither heroes nor victims, but rather as fallible choosers muddling through imperfect alternatives. The politics of his argument was made explicit at a conference at Berkeley in March 1980, just as he was revising his manuscript. He asked himself, "What was so *moral* about my inquiry?" When he got to the podium, he explained how Princeton students were rather "shaken up" by the original happiness lectures. Students were more accustomed to learning about human nature in terms of "the rational actor beloved by economists." When Hirschman presented Man as "a blundering idealist, someone with interests *and* passions," it sounded to them as a moral observation. Either-or commonplaces made Hirschman's kinds of stories appear muddled and confused. Really, what Hirschman wanted was a human actor "as a more lovable character, somewhat pitiable, but also a bit frightening—hence tragic."[48]

This tragic character sometimes needed some help. It was the job of intellectuals to be constructive, because the existence of public life as a refuge for disenchanted consumers required a practice that intellectuals had played a special role in refining, the art of voice. To throw up their hands now, to concede defeat of "public man," and to give up hope that the citizen still had a pulse within the body of the consumer was, Hirschman argued, self-defeating. Hopelessness would be self-fulfilling. The ethical implication was that intellectuals had a place in all this as the guardians of voice, even in the moments of its atrophy or disfavor. Be ready, Hirschman argued, for day in which the citizen swung back into public action; the ability to deliver rewards for returning to the streets and plazas depended on their capacity to imagine social change, not as total overhauls that were bound to fall short of great expectations—and thus drive the citizen back to private ways. Instead, help the fallible citizen, this imperfect subject, to imagine alternatives without making them impossible. This argument was not so easy to distill from the long excursions through consumer choice and the oscillations of the suffrage. Having missed his mark, uncharacteristically, this was a *big* idea that would consume him for years to come.

In the meantime, Hirschman bristled with disappointment. Insecurities that lurked below the serenity of his outward appearance, a carefully groomed style crafted to rise above the disciplines and precision that now found him wanting, broke through. As the reviews came in, he pored over them, underlining the lines of praise and leaving the criticisms conspicuously untouched. His letters also reveal traces of bitterness. Writing to his friend Reisman, he noted that most reviews reacted to the public-private cycle, "whereas this for me was more like a rod and hangers which for me merely served to lend support to a series of carefully crafted garments. These people criticized the rod and hangers and didn't say anything about the garments."[49]

He lived up to his own model, however: faced with disappointment, find pleasures elsewhere. As he did so often in his life, he set his sights on new horizons.

CHAPTER 19

Social Science for Our Grandchildren

A belief like a guillotine, just as heavy,
just as light.

FRANZ KAFKA

In the summer of 1979, a trio of Berkeley professors decided to organize a conference called "Morality as a Problem in the Social Sciences." Aiming at the functions and malfunctions of a "value neutral" social science, it was dominated by heavy-weight philosophers such as Jürgen Habermas, Richard Rorty, and Charles Taylor. There were other notables, such as Norma Haan and Michel de Certeau. Bellah asked Hirschman to come; Hirschman accepted, on condition that Mike McPherson be included. He felt it was important to have economists in the midst. McPherson welcomed the opportunity as an honor—and then trepidation: when the program came out, he gasped to see that the famous German philosopher, Habermas, was going to be his commentator.

The event stirred Hirschman to stake out a social science that dealt more directly with ethics, not so much the study *of* ethics but rather the ethics of social science. But he was determined to avoid the moralizing tone that hung over the deliberations. He urged the attendees to consider humans as endowed with self- as well as other-regarding propensities. What is more, these urges jostled with each other. Why do we have to choose what kind of self to favor? This was the same complex self that populated *Exit, Voice, and Loyalty, The Passions and the Interests*, and most recently, *Shifting Involvements*. All of these called for a more integrated social science—and indeed one might read them as a serialized manifesto, or an unfolding agenda, for Hirschman and Geertz's ambitions for integration. But it was revealing that none of Hirschman's works offered a unifying social theory. To offer one would undercut the purpose of the IAS school, which favored the study of social meanings rather than causation. At a time in which one was called upon to choose between "rational actors" or some communitarian spirit, Hirschman put the spotlight on humans' happinesses and disappointments and the ways in which they bungled and blundered their ways through choices.

This combined but unstable subject was a cornerstone of an integrated social science. But it was not easily molded to a unifying theory.

Hirschman's effort to be "positive" and value free while smuggling in "some strong moral message" went completely unnoticed at the Berkeley conference. The call for a rapprochement among social scientists of different breeds did not appear to have any effect on the gathering. Rather, the conferees seized the moment to pummel "positive social science" and "empiricism" (these being the aspersions of the day) and whipped themselves into a collective fury against mainstream American social sciences. Hirschman remained silent, observant, filling his yellow pads with notes and doodles. There were points at which he found the one-sided exchange too tiresome to remain silent. Delicately, he offered some constructive criticism of the chorus. At one point, he reminded others of the irony that empirical social science is what had allowed the disciplines to be taken seriously in the first place—with the not-to-discrete inference, surely missed by the ranters, that rejecting empirical research was a passport to obscurity.[1]

His interventions did not appear to have left traces on anyone's thinking. But the event forced him to consider how one might get past what he considered a sterile debate between two kinds of understanding: moralizing and analyzing. He wanted to find a position that was neither mindlessly "detached" nor—unlike some at the Berkeley conference—reverting to social science as moral advocacy. As he explained to the German sociologist Wolf Lepenies, "I would not like to have to say: to restore moral considerations we must *pay a price* in terms of scientific rigor; rather, I like to show that we are losing important insights because of the failure to ask moral questions and in general to spread our net more widely."[2]

The opportunity to spread his net more widely arose when he was awarded the Frank E. Seidman Award in Political Economy, for which he was expected to deliver an acceptance paper. Given by the trustees of the University of Memphis, its previous recipients included Gunnar Myrdal, John Kenneth Galbraith, Kenneth Boulding, and Thomas Schelling. He took up the challenge he had passed up earlier and composed "Morality and the Social Sciences: A Durable Tension," in which he picked up where *The Passions and the Interests* had left off, outlining the origins of the social sciences as a struggle to free inquiry from traditional moral teaching, separating learning from preaching.[3] Machiavelli had wanted to study politics from the premise of man as he really is, not what he ought to be. Montesquieu had warned how useless it was to go on about how much political practice conflicts with morality and justice ("this sort of discourse makes everybody nod in agreement, but changes nobody"). And of course Smith had severed the self-interested "head" from the emoting "heart" with breathtaking effectiveness. Even Marx wanted "cool science" to guide his motion of capitalism. But Marx was a cue to a deeper current in the genealogy of the social sciences, for while he wanted neutral, objective laws to dictate his analysis, he was no less inclined to hot tempered "moral outrage." "It was perhaps this odd amalgam, with all its inner tensions unresolved, that was (and is) responsible for the extraordinary appeal of his work in an age addicted to science and starved of moral values." This particular point elicited a doubt from Daniel Bell, who thought his friend had missed the way in which Marx and Hegel thought about the unity of theory and practice—not as a pragmatic idea whose truth is revealed in use and consequence, but rather as the entelechy of history. So, socialism was "scientific" not in the sense of it being "positive" but because it was necessary and embedded in the order of things; the is-ought distinction was not one a true Hegelian would have recognized. It was not a major issue, but Hirschman tried to clarify: his point was that "Marx, of course, *thought* he had resolved (*versöhnt*, in the Hegel sense) these antitheses, but my point (to which I would stick) is that he hadn't and that his works exhibit a simple juxtaposition of scientific apparatus and moralistic invective, wholly un*versöhnt*."[4]

All this was a prolegomenon to a larger point about the unsettled (one is tempted to say "unresolved") friction between moral and non-moral ways of understanding—not separation, not victory of one over the other, but rather "a durable tension." Even economists, the pariahs of moralists, were turning their sights to examples of nonindividualistic behavior. Some were taking a closer look at altruism. Others pointed to the power of trust in others. Now, it is true, Hirschman lamented, that economists had taken special delight in intellectual expeditions into territories deeply cherished by moralists to apply a "so-called economic approach" to the study of marriage, parenting, and cravings, a world normally said to be governed by "complex passions" of devotion, hatred, betrayal, and love. They derived pleasure—and notoriety—from the shock value of applying cost-benefit calculus to domains hitherto understood only through moral codes. He regarded this kind of "analysis" as silly and self-indulgent, revealing far less than the pleasure it was supposed to deliver in bringing down moralists. But, Hirschman wondered, could it be "that this particular way of achieving notoriety and fame for the economist is running into decreasing returns?" He went on to illustrate the growing interest, first in microeconomics, and more and more in macroeconomics, in a return to the domain of the heart. He cited several of his friends: Kenneth Arrow's work on the role of professional codes of ethics and Robert Solow's recent presidential address to the American Economic Association, which had explained why labor markets were not so smoothly "clearing" as theory would predict because workers paid attention to principles of appropriate behavior among them. (Hirschman wrote to his friend telling him that "I detected not just sociological, but *moral* undertones" to his address.)[5] "Wouldn't you be surprised," Solow had asked his colleagues," if you learned that someone of roughly your status in the profession but teaching in a less charitable department, had written to your department chairman offering to teach your courses for less money?" So, moral-social norms were part of how the market functioned. When Arrow read Hirschman's Seidman lecture, he felt it "really struck home. I have always felt this conflict (this may surprise you) but have tended to repress emotion in favor of the 'cool' head, though not without some considerable feelings of guilt. Your speech has given me some encouragement that it was in the long run the best way."[6]

But the question still remained: how does one practice a "moral social science?" The prescription was somewhat obscure—in itself a revealing contrast to his characteristically lucid description of the problem. It was the very durability of the tension that made this, as he confessed to Mike McPherson, his hardest essay to write. In the first draft, he had concluded that part of the problem among economists was that they had been groomed as "scientists" and thus suffered from what Thorstein Veblen had called "trained incapacity" to such an extent that they could not even "avow to ourselves the moral source of our own scientific thought processes and discoveries." As a result, "quite a few of us are *unconscious* moralists in our professional work."[7]

To exemplify this point, he told a personal story that reflected a latent preoccupation with his own memories, recollections that he had, until the 1980s, kept carefully under wraps. When he sat down to write *Exit, Voice, and Loyalty*, it never occurred to him that there was anything more than his observations of the world at play. It was only when a German publisher asked him to add a special preface for its translation that a memory of his own exit in 1933 was triggered. Summoning the plight of Jews before the Third Reich, he recalled the response of "young and vigorous ones" to the rise of Hitler—by fleeing. The "community" of Jews left behind was gravely weakened by his and others' decisions. His point was that "I was not aware of those deeper moral stirrings when I wrote the book." *Exit, Voice, and Loyalty* had thus benefited as a result of this forgetting; it was more balanced with respect to the relative merits of exit and voice, more general, and more "scientifically persuasive." Hirschman's lesson: "One, perhaps peculiarly effective way for social scientists to bring moral concerns into their work is to do so unconsciously!" This was an odd argument and an odder example, not least because Hirschman never belonged to the Jewish community. It should remind us once more how difficult it is to track the emotional passage of early experiences, for if he felt guilty for having left his family, it was a very deeply buried sentiment. When Quentin Skinner read the passage he found it "disconcerting": "Here you are surely too hard on yourself." It also triggered recollections from old friends, like "Henry" (once Heinrich) Ehrmann, his former mentor in the Socialist Youth, who had fed the teenage Hirschmann an intellectual diet of Lenin and Luxemburg. When Ehrmann read the lecture, he wrote to "OA" about the "guilt feelings" associated with the traumas of almost a half century earlier. "I suddenly remembered," he wrote, "that when 'the Hirschmanns' [meaning OA and Ursel] left, I felt they shouldn't have, convinced as I was that the inaudible whisper in which we were engaged, i.e. the 'underground' was a duty." By the time they were reunited in Paris, "the feelings had already evaporated"—not least because whatever was dutiful about Neu Beginnen clandestinity was being systematically crushed.[8]

The idea that we might be better off as unconscious moralists to resolve the tension between moral and analytical understandings was also an unsatisfying, if not nebulous, conclusion—certainly an odd one for such an avowed social scientist. Several friends told him so. Dennis Thompson, a Princeton political theorist, asked, did it make sense to associate so strongly the head with reason and science, the heart with morality? "On some (perhaps the most respectable) views of morality, it is the head that is the source of moral principles and must control the immoral heart. (Rousseau intends to shock readers in *The Second Discourse* when he blames reason for immorality)." More important, he objected to the proposition that social scientists smuggle their morality into their work unconsciously. While Thompson agreed with Hirschman's concern that moralistic advocacy was not the best way to make moral points, "let alone secure other people's understanding of what you are trying to say," he charged Hirschman with making "a sudden retreat" at the end of the essay. Sure, it was not necessary to come to terms with one's "deeper moral stirrings"—but this did not mean that social science could be ignorant of its moral principles or implications, and still be "moral." McPherson also found the case against self-conscious moralizing puzzling. For one, much of economics was "saturated" with concerns about social welfare or peoples' freedom to choose. So, wasn't the problem not how to make economics more open to moral thought but rather to invite economists "to open themselves to critical reflections on the moral commitments they already have?" This last question elicited a long response from Hirschman, for it had clearly struck a nerve. He would think about it. "I applaud your formulation, not only on diplomatic grounds, but because it opens up an interesting line of inquiry." Also alluding to Thompson's criticism of the unconscious smuggling idea, he promised to give the paper a thorough review before finishing it.[9]

The result was an overhaul of the final pages. The change is worth noting. He did not want moral features of the social sciences to be simply added on as afterthoughts, "like pollution abatement that can be secured by slightly modifying the design of a research proposal." The morality of the social sciences "belongs in the center of our work, and it can get there only if social scientists are morally alive and make themselves vulnerable to moral concerns—then they will produce morally significant works, consciously or otherwise." He concluded on an admittedly utopian note, for having become aware of the intellectual tradition of splitting the head and the heart, and the effects of doing so, a necessary first step toward "healing that split has already been taken." One could then envision a moral-social science "where moral considerations are not repressed or kept apart, but are systematically comingled with analytic argument." The final lines reveal how much his readers had pushed him to go beyond the idea of "smuggling" moral considerations back in to prophesize a social science "where moral considerations need no longer be smuggled in surreptitiously, nor expressed unconsciously, but are displayed openly and disarmingly. Such would be, in part, my dream for a 'social science for our grandchildren.'"[10]

The reception of *Shifting Involvements* revealed one thing: that imagining "a social science for our grandchildren" might be easier to show in practice than to resolve in theory. And it was to that that Hirschman turned: to lead by example. In September 1979, Stanley Hoffmann, chairman of the Committee on Universities and Human Rights for the American Academy of Arts and Sciences (AAAS), invited his old friend to a meeting in Boston to discuss a report that revealed disturbing facts about deals that American universities were making with foreign governments with appalling human rights records. Should there be a stand by the AAAS? The group met in November and floundered on the issue of comprehensive guidelines, never mind suggestions that universities seize the right to tell individual faculty members what and what not to do in their international dealings. Hirschman, with deep experience working with colleagues in Latin America, where human rights abuses ran amok, insisted that forcing Americans to "exit" dealings there would have self-defeating consequences. Still, he urged in a memo after the group dissolved, there could arise times for an arrangement. Some distinctions were also important to keep—between contracts involving individuals versus universities or governments, and between critical and noncritical areas of research. Perhaps there should be a protocol for universities to report their contracts and for the AAAS to circulate information to them about human rights worldwide to help them make better judgments over the decision to exercise exit, voice, or entry? It was important, also, to avoid making a laundry list of don'ts—and to come up with some positive recommendations and insights. Here, his experience in Argentina, Chile, and Brazil working with the Ford Foundation to create independent research centers after university purgings was a precedent, a "story [that] should be told, not just because it is an edifying tale, but because it is important to know of and to seek out such opportunities." In fact, therefore, dealing with institutions and counterparts in settings where governments violated human rights could protect and enhance opportunities for voice. It would be important, he insisted in an essay that would be subsequently published in *Human Rights Quarterly*, to avoid simplistic alternatives and either-or questions propounded by idealists and so-called pragmatists alike, if American universities wanted to support intellectual pluralism in nonpluralist regimes.[11]

His response to Stanley Hoffmann reminded him that it was important also to keep an eye trained on the outer world as a source for guidance. The point was driven home again when Richard Lyman, president of the Rockefeller Foundation, asked Hirschman in March 1982 to join him in a discussion about how the agency "might encourage a more reflective tradition in the social sciences in Third World countries and contribute, thereby, to deepening understanding of the development process."[12] Hirschman had issued some parting words for development when he wrote "The Rise and Decline of Development Economics." He sealed this with a personal retrospective essay for a volume about the "founders" of the field of development economics. "A Dissenter's Confession," as he called it in honor of a lettered tradition of public disclosure, explicitly questioned the treatment of development as something requiring its special brand of social science.[13]

But the field would not leave him alone; indeed, the careers of some of his concepts were now in full flight, which pulled him in multiple directions at once. Guillermo O'Donnell and Philippe Schmitter joined forces with Abraham Lowenthal at the Wilson Center in Washington to explore the idea of transitions to democracy in southern Europe and Latin America, enjoined by Hirschman's "possibilistic" herald to consider potential political tracks and not plod through the list of conditions to make predictions for the future. Hirschman happily joined the discussion but got more interested in the way a graduate student from Stanford, Terry Karl, was applying his notion of economic linkages to explain the fate of big oil-exporting countries. "I was terrified," she later recalled. Surrounded by the famous men (and they were all men) of the field, she now came face-to-face with what she considered the closest human to God. Not only that, this near-deity was her commentator. But instead of picking the paper apart, Hirschman praised its strengths and afterward pulled her aside for a long one-on-one conversation about "getting some of your economic arguments right."[14] Shortly thereafter, CEBRAP brought him back to São Paulo with a young American historian of Cuba, Rebecca Scott, to attend a seminar on the politics of export societies. To economize on his overcommitment, he shared "some further reflections" on his "Linkage Approach"; by this time his returning to popular, earlier innovations was becoming a bit of a habit. Since there were only so many new concepts or findings to discuss, Hirschman was increasingly taking a fresh look instead at some of his older propositions. He followed this with another habit, participating in external reviews of institutions that straddled the world of academia and public policy. Along with Bryan Roberts and Edelberto Torres Rivas, Hirschman was tasked to appraise CEBRAP. By now, the landscape in Latin America was shifting; Hirschman had played an important role in creating a latticework of social science institutions across South America as dictators purged universities. By the early 1980s, political opening was in the air. Now the challenge was not so much how to rescue social science from despots, but how social scientists should balance their passions for democratic transition with more dispassionate distance from the emerging regimes.

If this was a challenge, it was also an opportunity. It reaffirmed the exhilaration he drew from working with Latin Americans. Part of the disappointment of *Shifting Involvements* was that it was the product of internal conversations and fervent arguments with himself and others— mainly conducted in his head and on paper; it was an extension of the dialogues he had had with Machiavelli and Smith, Olson and Sen. What got lost in all the folding inward was his eye for surroundings, the petites idées drawn from watching everyday behaviors. Not a few reviewers made this point and it must have made him wince—for his ability to observe was something of a badge of honor. He could have holed up at the IAS, sheltered by its seclusion and privilege to seek redemption in a new book, or, as many do, used his place in the world as a fortress from which to volley attacks on his critics. Or, he could easily have cut and pasted a new version of old thoughts, another occupational hazard of the scholar. Instead, he opted for an entirely different tack. He left the institute for the world. It was in this context that he decided to take his yearning for a social science for one's grandchildren—one that would transcend the debate between an objective and a normative approach by rediscovering the pleasures and inspirations of looking outward, not inward—to rethink big issues by going back to some of his origins.

The pretext came from yet another routine invitation to review some programs for the Inter-American Foundation. This evaluation became anything but a text for institutional consumption. Created by Congress in 1969 to support popular initiatives to defeat poverty in Latin America, the Inter-American Foundation presented Hirschman with an opportunity to go back to the field, and to the one he knew best, Latin America. Ironically, it would lead to his least well known publication—but one that is arguably his most effective empirical study, the work of the eye of a seasoned observer on a mission to *show* how wrong the rampant individualists were. If *Shifting Involvement* had failed to make the theoretical case, *Getting Ahead Collectively: Grassroots Experiences in Latin America* (1984) made it in a different, and one might argue, more compelling way because it brought out a surer, more confident Hirschman.

Peter Hakim, the recently appointed director of planning and research for the Inter-American Foundation (IAF) had met Hirschman while he was working at the Ford Foundation office in Chile during and after the Allende years; Hakim was then, and remained, impressed by his range and talents. Almost from the instant he moved from Ford to the IAF, he had suggested to its newish president Peter Bell, another Ford Foundation veteran, that the famous development economist be enlisted to their organization's efforts. There was more, however, to the fantasy than just bringing in a great mind. Hakim and Bell wanted to engage more social science in their work. Hakim saw an issue that worried him: as he flipped through the reports on all the grassroots projects in Latin America, it became apparent that there was a pattern—money was going to the hands of beneficiaries and not the brokers or bureaucrats, which was the spirit of the organization. But the expected benefits, when clear, often seemed to fall short. "What is going on here?" Hakim wondered. His first move was to enlist Judith Tendler, by now a brilliant researcher who had perfected, and in some respects surpassed, Hirschman's eye for finding the hidden and unexpected benefits and hazards of development projects. Still, Hakim wanted Hirschman in; he sensed that the organization lacked an overall vision of what to expect and how to assess it. Unlike the more familiar aid agencies, this one was not dedicated to the expensive mega-projects and champagne-bottle-smashing inaugurations Hirschman studied for the World Bank almost two decades before, but rather to asking what poor people wanted and helping them get it. However, the case reports of the Inter-American Foundation assembled from field statements did not add up to an uplifting narrative. They read like a grab bag of stopgap efforts to prevent the poor from getting poorer. Was there an alternative narrative, and therefore purpose, for the organization? Hakim and Bell invited Hirschman to Washington for a conversation in early 1982, just as *Shifting Involvements* was about to appear. Hirschman went and was intrigued by the organization and the problem.[15]

The precise timing of Hirschman's decision to embark on the project is important but unclear. Did the hard-hitting reviews come about before his decision to join the Inter-American Foundation? Did he incline this way even before the disappointment with the book? Was his decision to return to the development world at least one more time, despite his epitaph in "Rise and Decline of Development Economics," a preemption or reaction to the phenomenological world? We cannot know for sure. But Hirschman's zeal and style suggests that there was probably something pendular in his response; after his speculative "conceptual novel," the urge was for something more grounded. Not long after the meeting in Washington, he explained to Hakim that he had a sabbatical from the IAS coming in the spring of 1983, that he wished to undertake a comprehensive, sweeping study—not a formal "evaluation"—of a selection of projects, and that he required no salary, but simply travel expenses for him and Sarah (who would accompany him in the same fashion she had in *Development Projects Observed*, but this time she was much more his muse). After sorting out with one of the IAF staff members, Steve Vetter, which projects to select, Hirschman crafted an elaborate itinerary with precise dates, locations, and a promise to deliver a draft report by the end of June 1983. Vetter likened his task to preparing of a smorgasbord: "Having read some of your earlier publications, I suspect you have a voracious appetite. Will we be able to feed you enough?"[16] He needn't have worried. Hirschman was starving. When Hakim got the plan he was shocked. This seemed far too ambitious and far too carefully choreographed—given the uncertainties of buses, airplanes, and keeping peoples' schedules, was this going to be a nightmare for his staff? He needn't have worried. The Hirschmans made all their flights, all their deadlines—right down to the submission of the final report. Indeed, Hakim's staff "fell in love" with the evaluators. They were undemanding, self-sufficient, and accepted all hardships. After working out a questionnaire with Judith Tendler, off he went with Sarah on a breakneck tour from January until June 1983 of forty-five projects scattered across six countries: Argentina, the Dominican Republic, Colombia, Peru, Chile, and Uruguay.

> Dominican Republic: January 30–February 12
> Colombia: February 13–March 10
> Peru: March 11–25
> Chile (without Sarah): March 26–April 18
> Argentina (without Sarah): April 19–22
> Uruguay (Sarah rejoins): April 23–May 6
> Brazil: May 7–June 5

Field work brought back a Hirschman that had gone dormant since his "retreat" into history and his return to contemporary affairs with *Shifting Involvements*. If reviewers were quick to point out that the book was long on anecdotes and quotes from classical writers but short on the kind of evidence they expected, Hirschman let his observational antennae go to work. While he used the questionnaire that he and Tendler had designed, he was also flexible and adaptive according to each case study and did not let the matrix of questions get in the way of the stories that his subjects volunteered on their own. Indeed, one of Hirschman's skills was to elicit details and minutiae as if they were not evaluators but old friends. One of the foundation's officers, Anne Ternes, accompanied the Hirschmans through Argentina and testified to his aptitude and joy from field work. It was also a learning experience for her as well. "Traveling with Albert Hirschman was particularly helpful for a rep in a new country since he is a persistent, skillful and gentler poser of questions. People see that he is genuinely interested in their experience and respond with thoughtful answers." She followed them around to Quilmes, a poor suburb on the fringes of Buenos Aires, where the IAF was supporting housing projects and which overlapped with a pioneering project designed by a group of social scientists at Centro de Estudios de Estado y Sociedad (CEDES), the think tank established by Oscar Oszlak, Guillermo O'Donnell, and others several years earlier. Critical was Mara del Carmen Feijoó, a grass-roots scholar who had moved to Quilmes in 1971 as a left-wing militant and had affiliated with CEDES in 1978 to collaborate with Jelin on popular coping strategies among the urban marginalized classes—which brought her full-circle to the *barrio* where she had cut her political teeth. Working closely with local priests, Feijoó had integrated into local networks of families who had seized empty lots of land to create ramshackle houses. She became a kind of intermediator for the Hirschmans' entry into the world of activism from below, revealing a world of protagonism among those often seen as bereft of organizing ability. Sarah and María would establish in this *villa miseria* the first Argentine outpost of a movement that Sarah had founded in the United States devoted to adult reading groups among poor communities, People and Stories. María had set up her research-activist program in 1981, aimed originally at erecting a popular church in the neighborhood—if it could be called that—of the Virgen de Luján, and through contacts with People and Stories—Gente y Cuentos—she incorporated an important dimension of popular access to culture. By April 1983 it was poised to launch; María and Sarah would subsequently write a moving testament to the experiment, one that would leave a deep imprint on how Albert would tackle his study of grassroots economic activity.[17]

The mood in Argentina was a mixture of horror and hope, just the kind of setting to whet Hirschman's appetite. The military regime was crumbling in the wake of the debacle of the Malvinas War, and the toll of the human rights abuses was coming to light. Vigils and marches brought tens of thousands of protestors to the street. If the world had a capital of public, it was Buenos Aires. On the other hand, the economy was a shambles. In the name of free market liberalism, the generals had racked up monumental foreign debts and crippled the country's industries. The poor were more afflicted than any. A slum in Quilmes painted a picture of squalor. Albert and Sarah held their noses as they stepped over piles of garbage and steered clear of scavenging dogs. One, whose skin was hanging off in clumps, was hard to distinguish from a small, pink pig. They stumbled on a young man whose back was matted with flies feeding off his open sores. Overhead, spider webs of illegal power lines hung so low over the dirt paths between houses that they worried about getting electrocuted. A fishmonger led his emaciated horse and wagon through the mud. Everywhere, Hirschman noted, the "savage repression" of the dictatorship hung over the barrio; he felt an atmosphere of seething, but disorganized, anger. In spite of the scene, Padre Pichi, the pastor who kept the community development going, soldiered on. He, Albert, and Sarah spent hours huddled in discussions. Ternes was moved by Hirschman's reaction to the scene. He may have been there to collect data—but he was also purveying *esperanza*. When his days in the field were done, he and Sarah accompanied Elizabeth Jelin to a workshop to exchange views about the broader political conjuncture and share their shantytown findings with the CEDES group of Jorge Balan, Enrique Tandeter, Oscar Oszlak, and others. While the situation was saturated with uncertainty, Hirschman urged them, from Padre Pichi to Elizabeth Jelin, not to give up hope. "One last word about Albert," observed Ternes. "Having been witness to a good deal of the World War II and cognizant of the development frustrations of the past three decades, he sustains an outlook of fundamental optimism with a keen perception of peoples achievements, the sequences that learning takes, and how things move forward in fits and starts. He is a subtle morale booster." During the sojourn in Buenos Aires, Jelin took the Hirschmans to the shores of the River Platte for dinner one night. Albert kept observing the waiters, admiring their skill and insouciance. When the bill arrived, Albert fumbled for his glasses; the waiter made a crack about his age—and Albert, captivated by the cocktail of insolent humor and lack of servility, fell into a long discussion with his fascinating waiter.[18]

The searching, divining, exploratory senses are clear enough from the notebooks packed with his and Sarah's handwriting. They record the testimonials of farmers, fishermen, priests, delivery boys, and teachers in mud-floored schoolhouses. Occasionally, Albert paused to record his own feelings: "The sheer reality of these places is overwhelming: one gets totally involved in less than a week. Doom threatens constantly while the possibility of salvation similarly beckons."[19]

Witnessing the have-nots struggle to improve their lives when the state had withdrawn any sense of obligation inspired him to return to some of his perennial concerns, to recycle some of his petites idées. After visiting the Colombian jungle town of Ráquira, where artisans had set up a cooperative to market their handicrafts, he noted how many toggled between tiny farms and their looms to make a living from several activities. The advent of the co-op, however, had induced some to sell their land and go into handicrafts full time and produce for the market "to cash in on the boom of *artisanías*." The trouble now was not just that the market for these goods appeared to be saturated, but that the quality of the work had deteriorated now that the artisans ceased to make handicrafts for their own use. A Marxist would have had no trouble describing this as a classical capitalist change, and the materialist features did not escape Hirschman's eye. But he also put a moral spin on what he saw.

> How to recover good taste once taste has been corrupted is just as difficult as how to restore virtù in republics once they have been corrupted (Machiavelli showed how difficult it is . . .) . . . Perhaps it is easier to maintain the aesthetic attitude & pleasure in doing something traditional & beautiful when this is a part time activity . . . It is more enjoyed for its own sake than when it becomes the main breadearner & therefore acquires an instrumental character.[20]

Moved and emboldened, Hirschman finished his long trip in São Paulo where he settled into an office at CEBRAP. He pored over his notes, reviewed documents, and wrote, furiously. Peter Hakim, by now itching with curiosity, inquired about the state of Hirschman's work. Hirschman offered to send him a copy of the full draft—though warning him that it was all written longhand. Hakim accepted the offer, only to find the script completely illegible. (When I explained how I conducted my own research for this biography, his first reaction was, "But how can you read his writing?") Hirschman consoled him by saying that he would ask his secretary at the institute (who was, by then, literate in his script) to type it up and offered to present his findings to the foundation staff.

The occasion for the presentation of the report set the rumor mill going among the staff. Intrigued that an eminent scholar and his magnetic wife would be interested in poking in their files and looking at their projects, they were eager to hear the results. Some had been reading Hirschman's previous work trying to anticipate his conclusions. Rapt, they gathered in the small auditorium of the foundation's headquarters with Sarah and Judith Tendler present and listened to the stories about the effects of some modest projects they had incubated and supported for so many years. "For us," recalled Sheldon Annis, "this was a big deal; the great man was coming." When Albert stepped up to the front of the small meeting hall, he explained that one of the problems with economists "is that they economize on love." People were astonished. This was hardly what they expected. "It floored us," said Annis. When the flutter subsided, Hirschman observed that one source of the staff's frustration was the feeling that they had to gauge the success of projects in terms that were easily quantified, which had often led them to overlook other variables, like love, civic purpose, and what in Hirschman's childhood would have been called *Bildung*, improvement and self-cultivation for their own sake, development to harmonize the mind and heart, self and society. Sometimes people engage in economic activities for noneconomic reasons or summon noneconomic deeds for economic reasons. The point is: an evaluation had to be open to measures and motives that did not always conform to the prescribed model of costs and benefits. That an economist of Hirschman's stature could give reasons for thinking about development in such expansive ways liberated hard-working staff from the sense that so much of their work was failing because "data" to prove rising productivity were so elusive. Few were more assured than Peter Bell who, unbeknown to those present, was worrying about the organization's future. The debriefing was "an exciting occasion for us all," he remembered.[21]

What Hakim and his colleagues at the foundation learned was that they really were in the development business, even if it was not always easy to see. Indeed, even in failure there could be redemption—redemption through learning, and this is one of the themes he drove home from his narrative. Someone was explaining how it all worked—

"Here it is," Hirschman seemed to be saying, "This is what you are doing." Determined to break the failure complex and show that reforms could work, even those emanating from the most downtrodden under the most inauspicious of political circumstances, Hirschman painted a very different portrait. To Hakim, it was luminous. All the reports that pointed to the shortfalls of each project—shortfalls compared to the grantees' lofty aspirations—had missed the larger point. It had been a point driven home in *Development Projects Observed* (look at side effects!) and again in *Shifting Involvements* (let disappointments produce alternatives!). Consider the following passage from *Shifting Involvements*, which found evidence aplenty among the shantytowns and fishing villages of Latin America:

> We may simply be unable to conceive of the strictly limited advances, replete with compromises and concessions to opposing forces, that are the frequent outcomes of actions undertaken under the impulse of some magnificent vision. Given this propensity of the modern imagination to conjure up radical change, and its inability to visualize intermediate outcomes and halfway houses, the results of public action typically fall short of expectations. (p. 95)

Improvable, not perfectible. Hirschman's complicated, mixed, flawed, imperfect, mistake-prone citizen was on display, in fact more than on display, *working*. All around was evidence of human capacity to imagine social change—perhaps motivated by a magnificent vision but yielding to basic improvements. What was important was not to lose sight of the achievements, even if they were modest. Hirschman kept noting how dairy farmers and housing co-ops put people to work, lending a plebeian twist to *streben*. Projects may "fail" to yield their expectations, but it did not mean they failed to move development along. Hirschman offered them a simple principle—"social energy"—to help illuminate how modest grants could help people create, direct, and expand communities' and associations' efforts to change the world around them. But the change was more evident in the ways that grants forced people to learn how to solve their problems; even if they did not finally solve the problem they set out to lick, they had acquired skills, created movements, and marshaled social energy that they could apply to other problems. This too was an old theme—learning—dating back to *Strategy*. But Hirschman had never lost his acumen for its role in social change. A little, unremarkable experience with his granddaughter led to the following entry in his diary:

> I show Lara (4 years old) how to prepare newspaper for making fire—she learns x from now on will do it *exactly* the same way. Perhaps it is not good to learn too many "useful" things too early in life, for then one will never question the moment one learnt. For innovation to be possible *late* learning may be essential.

The commitment to late learning produced by social energy presented a master narrative the organization needed for itself and a way to think creatively about its mission. Hakim was delighted. "This was all just so exciting to hear," he recalled.[22]

When he finished writing up his notes, Hirschman realized that he had not just presented to the organization a story for itself, he was composing something that belonged to the arc of his own lifework. He returned to some of ideas that had been waylaid by his obsession to answer Mancur Olson. What drew his attention to the stories was how they reminded him of his own past. When he presented his preliminary findings to colleagues at the institute in early 1984, he noted that the venture had required that he have an open mind—"but not a *blank* one." What filled his mind were his own older thoughts. He found himself picking up forgotten strands he had abandoned many years earlier—and it was undoubtedly a self-assuring exercise. "I continue to collect inverted, 'wrong-way round' or 'cart-before-the-horse' development sequences for a simple reason: the finding that such sequences exist 'in nature' expand the range of development possibilities." Free from having to wait for necessary prerequisites meant that people needn't feel paralyzed by mass poverty. In the face of a grinding debt crisis, there was still scope for improvement. What was true of social processes applied to himself as well; even a mature scholar of global repute could rediscover himself and the range of his own possibilities.[23]

In the meantime, he faced the challenge of how to pull together the small details of his disparate projects. They ranged from efforts to give property rights to homes in shantytowns to cooperative schools. As usual, Hirschman did not wade into his evidence with big—or even small—hypotheses to test. It was a strategy that would perplex even the informal methodologist. But with an eye to the balance of competing personal and collective engagements, Hirschman let a pattern appear. What many of the projects shared was an initial thrust to better the private fortunes of families, and doing so led to public activities. One favorite example involved efforts to help *tricicleros*—deliverymen who wheeled around the capital of the Dominican Republic with three-wheeled bicycles with large racks on the front—get out of the trap of chronic defaults on their loans. Local businessmen and nongovernmental organizations contrived a plan to promote groups of seven tricicleros so that they would be jointly responsible for making payments on loans to buy their vehicles. The effect was a surge in ownership. But more than that, this initiative to protect creditors against default by individual borrowers had significant, and unanticipated, social and political effects as the small *grupos* turned into "*grupos solidarios.*" As the *triciclero* organizer beamed, "I can mobilize 500 tricycles to converge on any spot in the city and paralyze everything." And the range of issues that concerned the deliverymen varied from traffic laws to taxes and police enforcement. So, a risk-spreading organization mutated into a "pressure group." This kind of story fascinated Hirschman, and he filled his notebook with calculations about the cost of the vehicles, the insurance scheme, and how much could be saved with accounting precision to end with more than a successful business—a collective movement.[24]

At the end of one of his narratives, he told readers: "Here then is another sequence where the traditional concern with 'bettering one's condition' in the private sense leads over, almost effortlessly and without any clear sense of a break, into public advocacy and participation in public affairs," an insight that returned to Adam Smith. In what would be a small book bereft of detours through theories and concepts of collective action, the only figure to appear was the Scottish moral philosopher. Smith's observation that collective actions were either ignored or "castigated as conspiracies" swept the ground for Hirschman, who sought to examine a spectrum of actions, from the wholly private to the outspokenly public with many intermediate and mixed combinations in between, that came under Adam Smith's rubric: "They are all conceived and intended by the participants as means to the end of bettering their condition."[25]

At the outset, Hirschman considered naming his project "Making it in Groups." He liked the ring. But for a wordplay-man, he did not see the salacious double entendre. But some did. Friends—Mike McPherson, Judith Tendler, and Peter Hakim (who may have wondered how the word-play might go down in Congress)—dissuaded him from this particular heading. McPherson and Hirschman brainstormed and came up with "Getting Ahead Collectively."[26]

It was an unusual piece. The prose was incredibly simple, some might say childlike. This was on purpose. Hirschman wanted the analysis, such as it was, to be accessible, to narrow the gap between the analyst and the analyzed; this was part of the "moral" personality of the book. Hirschman specifically appealed to the publisher (Pergamon Press) for a larger type to make it easier to read. This became something of an issue when the manuscript was sent for review, an exercise unlikely to bring out the best in Hirschman after the scorching he took for *Shifting Involvements*. Sure enough, one of the readers, the Quaker economist otherwise sympathetic to the whole enterprise, Jack Powelson, had the impression that Hirschman was trying to revisit ideas from *Strategy* in light of grassroots findings bereft of theoretical ambition or engagement. It was not unreasonable. But it rubbed Hirschman the wrong way. "The ms. does not want to be, nor does it anywhere pretend to be," he retorted, "a comprehensive evaluation of the experience of grassroots development. It is the report of an eyewitness with a longstanding interest in development issues, but cast deliberately in a non-academic mold, with a minimum of footnotes, references, etc." Striking a defensive pose, he announced that "I believe a scholar should be entitled to write and publish an impressionistic, speculative book provided the book has something suggestive and stimulating to say."[27]

It also contrasted with *Development Projects Observed*, which was organized around analytical claims. In *Getting Ahead Collectively*, he sung the epic by storytelling. Hirschman wrote it "not as a scholarly treatise" but rather as a "reasoned travelogue." But this was a travelogue fixated on the particulars of people speaking to him with some uplifting antidotes to his own recent disappointment. Indeed, he marveled that even in the face of failure and setbacks, people did not swing to private pursuits as *Shifting Involvements* would have predicted. In many cases Albert and Sarah observed, each spasm of organizing was "a stepping stone" to the next, and that the step was upward not down. "The present Latin American generation is not waiting for their grandchildren: they seem perfectly able to resume a 'fight' . . . several times in the same lifetime." He found this a perfect buttress for his indictment of *fracasomanía*, for lack of success could, ironically, help motivate a desire for even more success. And one had to be on the lookout for invisible and intangible benefits such as the dispelling of isolation and mutual trust. As one micro-impresario in the Dominican Republic told him as he scribbled, before "we used to see just each other, but we never knew each other." Now, not only were they personally making it, they had a "change of mentality (*cambio de mentalidad*)."[28]

The decision to tell stories may have reflected the nature of the evidence; though Sarah and Albert had scoured the paperwork for the projects, it was oral testimony that informed the study. Some were performed. Colombian women in La Calera sang about a young woman who had recently married a man who became a lout. "I serve you lentejas & you do not like them—so just leave them." One group of men from San Bernardo acted a play on the dirt floor of a hut to tell the tale of their fathers' dispossession of their land to a rapacious investor.[29]

In contrast to all his other work, the social bottom did the talking in Hirschman's slim volume, which would appear as a special supplement to the journal *World Development* in 1984. Only in a final chapter where Hirschman dealt with intermediaries, the welter of *promoción social* agents, did he move a notch up the social ladder. He avoided ministers, intellectuals, senior bureaucrats; gone are the policy makers that dominated his attention for three decades. Now, Hirschman did not avoid intellectuals; indeed, he met with them throughout the trip. In Peru he happened upon Hernando de Soto, who would later make himself famous as the champion of the informal economy and would become an influential policy maker in the 1990s. That evening, Hirschman noted, "self-made social scientist, interesting, leaning to Hayek?" He also had dinner with Mario and Patricia Vargas Llosa on the Malecón in Lima, and the night before that with Richard Webb, and the night before that with José Matos Mar. In Buenos Aires, Sarah and Albert spent a Sunday with Jorge Balan and Elizabeth Jelin wandering the parks and sculpture gardens and lunching on the shore of the River Plate. Albert devoured a *parrillada* of chorizo, morcilla, and beef while Jelin confided to Sarah some of her personal troubles. There were also the customary visits to the academic think tanks. But none of these are present in the work—despite the fact that as Hirschman travelled through the region he was witness to a raging debate over social movements and the agitation of poor folk.

Part of the explanation is that still in 1983, most policy makers worked for authoritarian regimes or governments with troublesome, if not horrific, human rights records. If anything, the "state" played the role of "aggressor"—bulldozing shantytowns in Argentina or dividing and selling common Mapuche land in Chile—to which civilians responded collectively. Indeed, violence shadowed the two researchers. Some of it came from obvious quarters, the militaries of Argentina and Chile. But persecution transcended the conventional image of state terror. As Sarah and Albert were escorted in a Jeep through the hills of Monte Azul in Colombia, someone pointed out a farm run by a recently widowed woman: "There are many widows around here," one of their guides told them.[30] The trip to Peru brushed Hirschman with the rising Maoist insurgent movement in Ayacucho. He got into Tingo Maria, the high jungle zone to which the expanding coca frontier had reached; the IAF had funded a peasant co-op, but it was wracked by struggles between landed interests, incumbent families, and the landless newcomers, refugees from the very social and political struggles that were sweeping across Ayacucho. What was once a "gem" of a project was now plagued by missing funds, and as Hirschman noted, pleas for more money from the IAF; early success had given way to failure. And, judging from what would come, the coca frontier was a bonanza for some, but not for self-helping collectivism or peace.[31]

One might think that the general sense of upheaval in Latin America would overwhelm the travelogue: the recent explosion of the debt crisis, the growing crescendo of pressures to restore civilian rule, the "big" news that dominated the headlines. These were not absent. Indeed, it was the cold monster of the state that created the gap between the rights of Latin American citizens and policies, into which civic organizations poured their energies to create "safeguarding operations" for the people. But Hirschman's eye was not on the macro. There was another reason for the simple style and close-to-the-ground content. The decision was *not* to write an academic treatise. Even though Elizabeth Jelin (on one side) and Hernando de Soto (on the other) represented emerging poles of what would become a vast scholarly field, and Hirschman was well aware of their research and positions, it was not with them that he wanted to engage in this work. In a sense, he preferred to close the gap between the reader and the subject, thus preferring the genre of the travelogue of development in action. One undoubted influence was Sarah, whose own organization devoted to collective reading and talking about short stories, Gente y Cuentos, was spreading its wings. This effort to talk about literature among groups traditionally marginal from high culture, to bridge literacy and orality and witness what happens, suggested a model for Hirschman's own effort to connect subject and reader.

This left some obvious subjects out. Ministers and intellectuals were absent. But so too was the larger setting. Foreign debt, military dictatorship, and deindustrialization may have been the context, but they were not what captured Hirschman's literary attention because private initiatives for social promotion and welfare came not from elites and educated classes—as was the case for Western Europe and North American before the advent of the welfare state. They came from the grassroots, excluded by definition from the commanding heights that made the big news. Hirschman delighted in the little news. When talking to dairy farmers in Uruguay who, thanks to IAF-financing, had created a cooperative replete with a collection truck, he wrote euphorically, "now a truck from the new plant would collect the milk at the farmer's doorstep thereby saving him 1 to 5 hours every single day of the year!"

This did not mean he was starry-eyed, as if the people he observed happily embraced communal solutions to their problems. His was not a romantic defense of getting ahead collectively. The field notes on Chile captured the degree of infighting among Mapuche parents, some wanting Spanish teaching, others (fathers in particular) hostile to girls' schooling. But the disagreement, he concluded, was good for the community. "A lot of fighting in Parents is healthy," he scribbled, "'Parents' sometimes people who do not have children—Let kids go to school—Boys and girls together. Boys sewing & cooking. Girls castrate animals. Girls' fathers against it—Finally worked." Indeed, across many of the projects Sarah and Albert noted widespread tension between men and women, of latent conflict brought to the fore by the ways in which the hardships of capitalism in the early 1980s sowed quarrels within households.[32]

Many movements were far from "successes" and hung on by threads, surviving only because governments abandoned social services. Many were plagued with problems of staffing. Griping about managers was rampant; sometimes members of cooperatives complained that they didn't enjoy enough "voice" or were afraid of criticizing their friends and neighbors who had become their superiors. After a day of visiting cobblers and carpenters in the Dominican Republic, Sarah wrote: "Problem: one becomes manager-boss the others workers—diff to accept coop."[33] Attrition was commonplace. Albert went hunting for *tricicleros* who did not join the association, only to find one that echoed Oscar Wilde's quip about socialism absorbing too many evenings: "He does not want to spend so much time in group meetings, he does not want to file papers etc." recorded Sarah. Indeed, the *tricicleros'* association had rampant problems collecting dues from members, and not a few let their payments on their vehicles slide into arrears—vindicating Mancur Olson's argument about free-riders.[34] Some successful groups were vulnerable to government predation. An effective and popular soup kitchen in Santiago run by a mother's club got seized by Pinochet's wife, anxious to shore up an image of a caring dictatorship. In

Albert and Sarah at a jewelry workshop, Dominican
Republic, 1983.

this case, the IAF was unhappy but went along with the arrangement until
mismanagement by the state drove the effort into bankruptcy.[35]

Cooperatives were not panaceas; more is not always better; what
works and doesn't work defied any single measure. Between the simple
narrative bereft of formal diagrams or social science claims, and the shortage of obvious take-away points for do-gooders and naysayers alike, it is
no wonder the book got lost in the shuffle.

On the whole, this was no catalogue of corruptions, no inventory
of development disasters. This was progress on the march, thanks to the
collective efforts of poor people who marshaled their "social energy."
Hirschman's field notes were sprinkled with phrases like "remarkable survival," "fascinating to watch," "local group knows what it wants." Out of
the little news emerged a thickening network of activists who made social
relations *more caring* and *less private*" in a broader political setting in

which governments preferred privatization and immobilization. These grassroots stirrings, he speculated in the conclusion, "were an important underlying factor in preventing the social quiescence and introversion that are required for an authoritarian regime to take hold."[36]

In the quest to make the work even more accessible, the IAF program officer coordinating from Washington, Sheldon Annis, approached Hirschman about having the book illustrated to enhance its appeal by making the human dimension literally more visible. Annis contracted a photographer to trail the Hirschmans during their interviews. To follow up, he then dispatched a Guatemalan-based photographer, Mitchell Denburg, to retrace the steps and take more photos to illustrate the grassroots working, *tricicleros* loaded with bananas, a sewing class in Peru's Academy for Women, and farmers milking their cows in Uruguay. Denburg carried the manuscript with him: "It was like a living story as I went along," he recalled. He was struck, like Ternes, at the effect that Hirschman had had on his subjects. "He clearly left an impression with people in Latin America; he had respect for people and their achievements." Some of the photos captured the scenes of research. One example was of San Bernardo del Viento, where the sons of dispossessed Colombian farmers performed the process by which a land-swindler stole their father's property. The impression from the photos was of work and cooperation in action, advancement, and forward motion—to redouble the *aheadness* of the study as an alternative account to the perception of crisis, impossibility, and retrogression, especially for the poor.[37]

With *Getting Ahead Collectively*, Hirschman came up with a partial answer to the problem posed by *Shifting Involvements*. He had gone to the field and there, not among the disenchanted consumers of the fatigued rich countries, he found his public-minded, active citizens. More than finding them, he sought them out. Hirschman's dissatisfaction with his answer to Mancur Olson and the turn of "public" economics was very much on his mind as he travelled through Latin America. After visiting an IAF-supported school in the Dominican Republic, he returned to "the public and the private." "There is a much greater intermingling of these two spheres than in the 'advanced' countries," he noted, "at all levels of society: on top one finds lots of businessmen who are public figures and take positions on public issues, give much time to public causes & agencies. . . . We tend to see only the ugly side of this confusion of public & private, not the way in which it enriches the lives of these people, nor the way in which it is needed to achieve any progress at all."[38] Publicness was not just a solution to market failures. Hirschman saw more; for just as his lovable, pitiable, and tragic human was a combination of reasoned and passionate, so too the functioning of the economy blended the private with the public. Here, Hirschman was stepping away from the mechanical, pendular movement he claimed was at work in society in *Shifting Involvements* and which had elicited so many frowning reviews. *Getting Ahead* was thus more than an empirical counterpoint, a "retreat" back to the field. It helped him resolve his own unease.

The book was, however, more than a self-expiating exercise. It radiated hope at a time in which it was very hard to find sources for any in Latin America. Indeed, it soon became a weapon in a larger struggle over the foundation's very existence, a struggle that would end in defeat—though it would bring Hirschman back into the public eye in its defense. As the Republicans took control of the federal government after the triumph of Ronald Reagan in 1980, they set their sights on agencies like the Inter-American Foundation to have them serve their Cold War foreign policy agenda. One by one they picked off the members of the board of directors (four of whom were picked by the White House), until they mustered the strength to demand Peter Bell's resignation as president of the IAF. In the meantime, they called for a commission to review the agency, chaired by the seasoned diplomat Sidney Weintraub. One day, after a series of meetings at the foundation offices, Hakim suggested that Weintraub come to dinner at his home. "Oh, and Albert Hirschman will be there, too," Hakim added. Hakim knew he was playing a heavy political card, and it worked. Weintraub accepted, and that night they chatted away about the work of the organization, leaving the commissioner duly impressed. The commission's report, submitted in early January 1983, was glowing.[39]

The Republicans were not about to let evidence and evaluation get in their way. The new Reaganite chairman of the board, Victor Blanco, a right-wing Cuban-American businessman, engineered Bell's ouster. Hakim was demoted. Hirschman rushed to Bell's defense and urged that the agency be spared ideological turf wars. He launched a some-what chimerical campaign to get the IAF nominated for a Nobel Prize in economics—using *Getting Ahead* as a testimony to the revolutionary thinking and practice going on under the roof of its staff. The *New Repub-lic* ran an article by Hirschman that charged Republican ideologues with threatening one of the few good signs of US–Latin American relations—support for "pragmatic," problem-solving initiatives to promote nothing less than capitalism from below. Hirschman's title was thus "Self-Inflicted Wounds." Nor was the budget excessive—at \$24 million in loans the previous years, it was miniscule compared to other agencies'. It was, he said, "a precious capital of good will that we have slowly accumulated in Latin America," with important contacts not just with the poor—but, more important for Hirschman, middle-class professionals involved in the basic business of development, school teachers, architects, doctors, and so forth, the constituency that the United States sorely needed in its efforts to improve ties. The Reagan administration "does not need to look for outside enemies," he concluded, "it displays an uncanny knack for self-inflicted wounds."[40]

The stunned and demoralized staff read The *New Republic* essay with relief and felt encouraged that someone was taking up their cause. Peter Bell thanked Hirschman: "I feel doubly honored to have headed an organization so generously praised by a person for whom I have such high esteem. Your solidarity," a keyword of the era, "is enormously important to everyone at the Foundation." But there was no stopping the juggernaut. Fearing his presence would imperil the organization, Bell left for the Carnegie Endowment. Hakim eventually resigned and moved to the Inter-American Dialogue, where he would eventually become its director and make it Washington's premier center for thinking creatively and openly about US policy toward Latin America.[41]

In the end, this little book, a supplement to an academic journal, garnered almost no attention. The editor, Hirschman's old friend Paul Streeten, had suggested that a version appear as an article to give the findings more exposure. He could also include a selection of the graphic images of aheadness. But with little engagement with the burgeoning scholarly concerns with social movements and the so-called informal sector, and with no conceptual pretense unless a reader were to tackle *Getting Ahead Collectively* adjacent to its counterpart, *Shifting Involvements*, it was probably doomed as a scholarly treatise.

There was a way in which *Getting Ahead Collectively* was at odds with Hirschman's drift from development. He had, after all, pronounced the field's demise. The book was intended as a counterpoint to the impossibilists and less as a new argument for progress. One might argue that he had made a break. But it would be a messy one. He was increasingly being asked to guide the future of development. So much for epitaphs. Enrique Iglesias, the executive secretary of CEPAL, asked Hirschman to participate in a workshop on the future of development at the United Nations headquarters. As Hirschman put it cheekily, "I did not mean nor did I say that DE [development economics] is deadly sick, only: that DE cannot handle [the] job of slaying the dragon of backwardness *by itself.*" The problem with economists was that they preach about scarce resources but have "no sense of limit of their prowess." He proceeded to extrapolate a few "lessons" from recent experience and then let the proceedings unfold. Judging from his excited notes, he must have had an impression of a revitalized field.[42]

Though Hirschman had distanced himself from development, he could still be summoned for the right occasion. The Rockefeller Foundation brought him and Cliff Geertz to the Bellagio Villa in late summer of 1985 to participate in a workshop to promote social science scholarship in the Third World "on fundamental development issues." "The luminaries" could not have been entirely cheered by the well-meaning, if conventionally patronizing, format; they were called upon to comment on the younger participants' work—which left them both exhausted, not least because they were constantly challenged "with a vigor," noted the foundation reporter, "that I, for one, had not anticipated." For their part, it must be said, not a few of the participants recorded their gratitude for getting "wisdom of these gurus," and spending a full week "with such giants of the intellectual community."[43]

Ford also came knocking, which stirred up a sense of unfinished thoughts, including remorse about the final days of the Inter-American Foundation at the height of its achievements and its precipitous demise. Ford arranged for Hirschman to visit the Delhi School of Economics in India. Shekhar Shah wanted Hirschman to convene with the leaders of the Center for Developing Societies, the hub of much Indian thinking about development, and to talk with the foundation's staff about relevant debates and practices in Latin America. Hirschman agreed, though he added, "I am quite anxious to reserve some time for *listening*." After checking into Claridge's Hotel, he participated in a conference on the economic history of India and Indonesia, and then Ford Foundation staff escorted him around the capital to hobnob with its leading social scientists. Hirschman enjoyed the role of sage. But it was a side visit to a self-employed women's group in the city of Ahmedabad that captivated him more—and churned him up. On the heels of the fracas over the Inter-American Foundation and the hounding of Peter Bell, Hirschman suffered from some pangs of torment. When he got back to Princeton, he typed up some notes dedicated to Peter Hakim. Perhaps he felt he hadn't done enough to defend the foundation, Hirschman worried. He confessed to a certain *esprit de l'escalier*, the feeling of regret upon descending a staircase of having failed to make a witty remark right after leaving a party. Hirschman wished he had told the IAF stories as a single narrative that arced from one phase to the next, "From Struggle to Development" and "From Development to Struggle." Seeing the embroiderers and wastepaper-pickers of Ahmedabad reminded him that grassroots development "*is* the unity of development and struggle and also the tension between these two components." It was complex, not simple, and "I know that no one will appreciate this more than Peter Hakim."[44]

Getting Ahead Collectively arose from the ground up of a South America emerging from many years of dictatorship. One important feature of the book was to showcase active citizenry solving problems and improving lives when governments turned their backs on them. It tendered a message of hope about everyday people even as Hirschman was playing an active role in the rebuilding of social science research in the dictator-plagued continent, participating in the Ford review of Brazil's CEBRAP, working with Elizabeth Jelin at CEDES in Buenos Aires, and keeping tabs on Alejandro Foxley in Santiago. Indeed as Patricio Meller, one of Foxley's colleagues, recalled, Hirschman's frequent visits were a counterpoint to the flow of Chicago Boys through Pinochet's ministries. He was special "because we could always count on his help." Though they felt isolated and persecuted—their phones were bugged by the police—the conversations could be open and frank in the seminar rooms, where they talked about alternatives, survival, and fear. Hirschman was reassuring; this would pass. He seldom gave details of his own—but the feeling in the room was that there was deep historical experience behind his words. When Hirschman presented his "Morality and the Social Sciences" paper to a tightly packed room at CIEPLAN, his listeners could recognize, despite the mumbling and pauses that increasingly inflected his public speaking, the ways in which their commitment to human rights need not be severed from their concern with growth. Meller asked if he could publish a translated version of the essay in their magazine.[45]

If it could shine light in the darkness, why not? Hirschman's tension may have seemed a little abstract to readers in American academia. But in areas beyond, where the social scientist was less sheltered—and more engaged—the duality of being in the world while analyzing it was an ineluctable condition. The worldliness stored up in a life that stretched across continents and struggles poured forth in words to Hirschman's youngers. Naming the tension was the first step to acknowledging its existence. By identifying its existence, perhaps the social scientist might not feel so compelled to resolve, transcend, or overcome it without losing something precious and important. The social scientist's dilemma could not be cast off like outgrown clothes. Better to admit it than to take refuge in false certainties.

CHAPTER 20

Reliving the Present

Laughable is the way you have to put
yourself in harness for this world.

FRANZ KAFKA

The academic year 1984–85 was Hirschman's last as an "active" member of the Institute for Advanced Study. He was turning seventy in April and was due to retire from his formal commitments. "Rights without duties: the perfect academic life, surely," joked Quentin Skinner in congratulations, without adding that in Princeton's little republic the ratio was hardly tilted toward the denominator. Retirement coincided with international fame. Indeed, it would be hard to imagine a social scientist enjoying more respect in so many corners of the world than Hirschman. Government ministers, presidents of foundations, civic leaders, and scholars from Buenos Aires to Budapest turned to him as a sage. And yet, Hirschman did not embrace the role of advice-dispensing celebrity. If anything, he spurned sermons of certainty more than ever. He scorned those who would peddle their convictions—and none more than the closest thing to a nemesis, Milton Friedman, the Chicago economist who *did* don the mantle of celebrity with breathtaking assurance to become the public guru of neo-conservative ascent. As an antidote, what Hirschman urged was less certainty, more tolerance, and better, forward-propelling arguments. As the Cold War reached its climax, the quality of public conversations and debate at the self-proclaimed center of the democratic world worried him deeply.[1]

Retirement was not without benefits. Hirschman kept his office, his presence in the hallways and seminar rooms at the institute, and a gen-

erous travel and research fund. More and more people came for guidance. Students, such as Anthony Marx, a doctoral candidate at Princeton,
plucked up the courage to ask Hirschman to guide an independent reading
course. Marx, who read whatever Hirschman material he could lay hands
on, thought he'd reached heaven when Hirschman agreed. "He was the
closest thing to an academic God," he recalled. The students did most of
the talking; Hirschman would smile at the occasional hubris of youth.
Many years later, when Marx was president of Amherst College, one of
his fondest moments was hosting Hirschman and the Amherst-alumnus
and Nobel laureate, Joseph Stiglitz, as honorary degree recipients. At the
end of the ceremony, Hirschman and Stiglitz boarded a golf cart. Marx's
son climbed onto the back; Marx watched proudly as Stiglitz whisked
away his God and his son. The Argentine sociologist, Elizabeth Jelin, was
asked to evaluate some neighborhood projects in Chile during the Pinochet dictatorship, a task fraught with ethical problems. How to evaluate
critically without reinforcing someone else's agenda (in this case the military authorities hunting for a pretext to shut projects like these down)?
Hirschman had no answer, but he did convince her that she was up to the
task. "Albert," she recollected, "opened my eyes and made me feel capable."[2]

Retirement posed the question of his institutional legacy. He and
Geertz, joined by Michael Walzer in 1980, had made the IAS a haven for
interpretive social science. Determined to ensure that economics still be
part of the conversation among social scientists—at a time when the discipline's earlier ties to its disciplinary cousins were breaking down—the
issue for Hirschman was, what kind of economics? With retirement pend-
ing, he recommended that the School of Social Science launch a thematic
year to discuss "Toward a Broader Economics" in order to liberate "The
Rational Economic Man" from the straightjacket to which many economists, but not only they, consigned him. This was to inaugurate a three-
year cycle on interpretive social science to open up new directions in social
research—and keep the economists engaged. The determination to "forge
connections" and "foster conversations" dominated the planning material.
In an era that saw the triumph of rational expectations, monetarism, and
an economics increasingly tethered to its self-selected concepts, creating

an alternative—no matter how appealing to some—was a bit like tilting at windmills. Then again, Hirschman was a pragmatist with a quixotic twist, striving for outcomes that could only be dimly seen.

The question of how economics was going to fit in the School of Social Science was not just an institutional, or even an intellectual matter. It was also personal. Behind the scenes, Geertz, Walzer, and Hirschman had forged something unique in modern intellectual life. Over dinner at Albert's retirement party at the institute, Cliff got up to make a speech—"not at all easy," he confessed. Geertz tried to convey to those present that what made Social Science special was not just that each of the trio was wholly involved, but that they were involved in all of the school all of the time. Unlike the increasingly conglomerate university, the members of the school delegated nothing. "We are a company of intellectual friends, the sort of thing that is reputed to have existed in Greece, but is rather hard to find in contemporary academia. For myself," he continued, "I have never had a closer or more admired intellectual friend, or one who has had more impact, both personally and in scholarly terms, upon me than Albert. The Greeks again would have called such a relationship 'love;' but we, now, so far have we come, are precluded from doing that."[3]

Ten years after his retirement, Hirschman was still advocating the creation of a political economy chair at the institute—for an economist with interests in developing societies and *varieties* of capitalism and in dialogue with other social sciences, ethics, and philosophy. Everyone silently understood that this was a tall order. Implied here was a portrait of, if not himself, his understanding of the discipline, one that the discipline did not recognize as its own. Just as his vision was impressively broad, it was singularly implausible. There could be no more Albert O. Hirschman; he was the product of a place, Mitteleuropa, and an intellectual moment that no longer existed. It must be said, however, that Hirschman was not alone in groping for an alternative. The president of the MacArthur Foundation, Adele Simmons, flew to Princeton to confer with Hirschman because she had been "concerned for some time about how economic theory is often used as a barrier to social and economic change."[4]

It would not be up to those outside the discipline to shape its course. The leaders of the IAS did not forsake the commitment to economics, even if they recognized that the conversations that Geertz and Hirschman sustained across the disciplinary borders were not easy to reproduce. The institute assembled a committee to raise funds for an Albert O. Hirschman Chair in Economics to commit the institute permanently to the discipline, for a successor to Hirschman, and to guarantee at least three visiting memberships per year. Several European banks and American notables opened their wallets for the spear-carrier of the campaign, James Wolfensohn, president of the World Bank and chairman of the institute's board of trustees. An impressive 141 friends and colleagues followed suit. The school eventually nominated the brilliant game theorist, Eric Maskin, best known for his work on mechanism design; he moved to Princeton in 2000—and won the Nobel Prize in economics seven years later. The appointment secured the place of economics in social science, though it was also a statement that it would be a different breed of the discipline than Hirschman's. There was also a move afoot, led by the young Spanish economist, Javier Santiso, to create an Albert Hirschman Chair in Latin American Political Economy at Sciences Po in Paris; this idea went nowhere.

Retirement did not mean disappearing; it accentuated a role conferred to the shrinking few as sage. Hirschman made his appearance at a conference organized by the University of Chicago historical sociologist Theda Skocpol, entitled "States and Social Structures: Research Implications of Current Theories"—which led to the landmark anthology called *Bringing the State Back In*. Convened in early 1982 at Mt. Kisco, New York, with the support of the SSRC, the event was meant to get past theoretical arguments about the nature of public power. When participants trailed into labyrinthine discussion of the state's "relative autonomy" from social and economic forces, Hirschman's commentary on the key paper by Skocpol, Peter Evans, and Rueschemeyer sliced through the controversy. The question of autonomy was so "endlessly fascinating" because it tested the validity of Marxism and "the question of reform vs. revolution [that] hinges on it." On the other hand, there were so many types of autonomous states that its explanatory stock was not very high. History pointed in diverging directions. Cases like the New Deal could be the state's "finest hour," but there were also plenty of cases where political autonomy led to history's "foulest hour." Without dissipating the cloud of personal experience that increasingly hung over his historic observations, he offered the Nazi state as "its most obvious example." Perhaps the state's own drives needed some curbs? These cautionary reminders came from the script of a "senior" scholar happily playing the typecast role of sage.[5]

The 1980s intensified a process begun earlier with the recovery of memories. The return to Berlin with his sisters, the arrival of Claus and Sabine Offe at the institute, and the subsequent translation of his works into German rekindled his interest in Europe and his origins. They were never far from the surface of his thoughts anyway. Ursula, by then renown as a crusading women's leader in Brussels, was struck suddenly in December 1975 by a cerebral hemorrhage and later aphasia, which wiped out her ability to communicate. Gone was her formidable energy. She was never her old self. Albert took the loss like a stoic, but behind the surface of control he was in agony. "Ursula: her sickness is for me like the death of my own youth and adolescence" he confided to his diary, "they are crumbling away leaving me incredibly impoverished. Perhaps one dies like that because one period after another of one's life becomes inert (Socrates' death). Persons who were close once become frozen fragments of one's past." The loss must have churned up more memories—suggesting that the allusions to history's "foulest hour" were more than academic citations. During the 1977 trip to Russia, Sarah took Albert to see a play. En route to Moscow's Taganka Theater, heavy clouds gathered overhead. The play was an avant-garde adaptation of Fyodor Abramov's *The Wooden Horses*, a tale of forced collectivization and famine and the dramatization of a family shattered by state terror. The theater was crowded. Beside Albert an elderly man sat dressed in a medaled officer's uniform with a silver silhouette of Stalin on his shirt. Albert squirmed in discomfort. When it was all over, the Hirschmans returned to their hotel. In the middle of the night, the blackness was pierced by a loud cracking sound. Albert jolted up in bed. From the penumbra of his dreams he began to mumble frantically about sabotage, connecting the play's devastating criticism to Marx's "transition from the weapon of criticism to the criticism through weapons," words recovered and recited from his fierce disputes over the fate of Weimar. Sarah consoled him: it was only a storm. In the jumble of his words she could make out his protestations, "It is terrible, isn't it terrible."[6]

Hirschman was impressively successful at masking the personal experiences informing his intellectual interventions. There remained, however, early intellectual selves to be recovered as part of his graduation to *sagesse*. One was the rediscovery of his forgotten first book. In 1975, a group of younger American political scientists called for a special issue of their flagship of the emerging trend of international political economy, *International Organization*, which was devoted to examining the economic dimensions of global power. The venture's ringleader, James Caporaso, with the encouragement of Robert Keohane, cited *National Power* as one of the pioneering books "which links the tools of foreign economic policy to the systemic structure of a state's foreign economic behavior." The special issue, which finally came out in 1978, was a signature moment in the field's development, and Caporaso was keen to get a contribution from Hirschman as an overlooked founder. Happy to contribute, and happier to accept the status as eminence, he agreed. In the course of the exchange, the idea of clearing the mothballs from *National Power* came up. Until then, no press had been interested in a book with no field. Hirschman's essay for *IO* reflected on the solitude of writing a fieldless book. Hirschman owned up to his "infinitely naïve proposals" about global power and the eclipse of national sovereignty. By the mid-70s, the world had changed. So had political science. His former Harvard student, Stephen Krasner, who regarded *National Power* as a point of reference, took up the lost book's cause. Krasner had published a field-defining essay deliberately playing on Hirschman's title, "State Power and the Structure of International Trade." When the University of California Press asked him to edit a new series for the international political economy field, Krasner seized the opportunity to bring *National Power* back into circulation; the *IO* essay was its new introduction. Not a few reviewers pointed out that it was more relevant thirty-five years later and was an appropriate anchor for the new field. Too bad the price had gone up from $3 to $16.60![7]

This was Hirschman's first retrospective exercise. As he advanced through the years, successor generations appealed for more. It testified to the breadth of the domains he had shaped that so many overtures came from so many quarters. All too often, the great-man-looking-back genre yields self-serving histories sprinkled with unknown personal detail. Hirschman never succumbed to that literary temptation, even if he did not always resist small doses of narcissism (of which he was conscious but unembarrassed). More often, his aim was to complicate and even undo earlier formulae he now found too simplistic or too mechanistic; underneath this surface, memories of a more distant past began to shape his interventions.

Only rarely did his reworkings improve on his basic insights. It is more revealing to read these as the work of an author groping to connect closely guarded personal experiences to an oeuvre meant for public consumption.

In the midst of the growing alarm over assaults on citizens' benefits in North America and Europe, Franklin Thomas, president of the Ford Foundation, asked Hirschman to join an executive panel on a large project, the "Future of the Welfare State." Hirschman had published a well-known article in *Dissent* magazine warning the welfare doomsayers that one should not confuse friction from "growing pains" with a terminal crisis. There were many more options if one could replace the preference for "structural" (and pessimistic) explanations of the malaise with "nonfundamental" diagnoses. Hirschman had been harping on this theme for years. Why not see the trouble as correctable and do something about it? Reagan's assault on "welfare bums" echoed some "earlier battles going back five or six decades," which got him thinking about the connections between conservative offensives old and new.[8]

Increasing numbers of people saw Hirschman, now in his seventies, as a walking memory willing to overturn official heroic accounts of the past. When it came to honor his old colleague Ken Galbraith in 1988,

Hirschman penned an essay that toyed with Galbraith's story of "how Keynes came to America," recast as "how Keynes was spread from America," and recounted how he witnessed as a Marshall Planner the ways in which Keynesianism became an orthodoxy in the United States, and how it became an ideological export for economic missionaries. Galbraith thanked his friend for the flattering comments, recalling that as the chief economic policy adviser in the State Department after the war "in charge of German and Japanese economic policy . . . my influence by way of the Joint Chiefs on these matters was either nil or slightly less."[9]

It was only a matter of time before these backward-looking exercises got more self-referential. If there was an occasion that brought this to full fruition it was the ritual associated with the honorary doctorate. Hirschman amassed them like trophies, and his attitude, to Sarah's chagrin, was not unlike a boy's. Sarah found the occasions a bore. But she soldiered on as Albert draped on the robes, posed severely for photographs, and gave a short lecture—usually a potted history of his connection to the institution gracing him with the doctor honoris causa. The first was from Rutgers University in 1978; Cardoso was a fellow honoree, and Albert beamed to him that he was finally going to get a respectable doctorate! Then there was a gap of eight years until the University of Southern California offered its version. Thereafter, it was a regular flow: Amherst College, Harvard, Paris, the New School, Florence, Trier, Berlin, Buenos Aires, Campinas, São Paulo . . . .[10]

Honorifics poured in. The American Academy of Arts and Sciences lauded Hirschman as a "man of letters" within the social sciences, implying he was a rare (and perhaps endangered) species. Conferring of the Talcott Parsons Prize in 1983 inaugurated a cycle of public unveiling of a hidden past. Daniel Bell, his former colleague from Harvard, presided over the ceremony and shared little-known details of Hirschman's trajectory. In 1945, Bell had been the managing editor of a magazine called *Common Sense*; its editor was Varian Fry, who must have told Bell a great deal, because he proceeded to recount the story of Neu Beginnen, Justice and Liberty, the toothpaste tubes stuffed with secret messages, and a young associate's of Fry's in Marseilles, Beamish. "I would use the phrase

Albert and Fernando Henrique Cardoso, honorary degree
recipients, Rutgers University, 1978.

'a hero of our time,'" Bell told his audience, "if not for the slight sense of
vice that applies to the character of Perchorin in the Lermontov novel."
But "Albert had few vices. And he is a hero. Varian Fry, with the help
of Albert and a few others—but very much with Albert's help, given his
skills, his languages, his knowledge and ingenuity—saved the lives of

many great figures of European culture." What Hirschman made of this outing is a mystery, though by the 1980s, he was shedding the armor of discretion—at least about that moment of his life. Other, more sickening, memories, like the Spanish Civil War, remained locked up.[11] If academics could convert their awards into the equivalent of a soldier's medals, Hirschman's uniform would have been decorated like a Soviet General's.

A career-culminating ritual for academics is the festschrift, a celebration thrown by former students, colleagues and friends, usually involving papers discussing the honoree whose best work, one presumed, was behind him and thus worthy of retrospective analysis and celebration. Hirschman had four of them, a surprise in light of his ambivalence about students, his aversion to disciples, and his determination to undo efforts to create a "Hirschman school." None of these, however, should be confused with the more nebulous "influence," which Hirschman was never reluctant to deny. Indeed, in most cases, he took advantage of the occasion to defy the presumption that retirement puts an end to cognitive activity— starting with retrospection and critiques of his own work. The first took place at the University of Notre Dame in 1984, organized by Guillermo O'Donnell, Alejandro Foxley, and Michael McPherson and which dwelled on the theme of development and democracy as South American countries were making their passage from dictatorships. What came of that event was a volume that transcended regional borders and broke into unusual disciplinary provinces, such as psychology, with a paper by Carol Gilligan on voice and exit in adolescents. Interestingly, Hirschman combed through each of the draft chapters and wrote comments, some quite extensive, for each author; Carol Gilligan got four pages of line-by-line edits. This at least ensured that an otherwise quite dispersed volume had the coherence of a subject—and a shadow voice.[12] In November 1988, the institute hosted a large event funded by the Inter-American Development Bank, "Hirschman's Work on Development and Latin America." The following year, at the occasion of his honorary degree at the University of Buenos Aires, a research center, the Instituto Torcuato Di Tella launched (with the help of the Inter-American Development Bank, the Ford Foundation, and the American Embassy) a sprawling four-day gala,

"Hirschman's Work and a New Development Strategy for Latin America." It was at this event that I, on the heels of my doctorate in economic history, got my first glimpse of someone approaching legend status. The scene conveyed something of the aura that by then surrounded him. The dozens of conferees and hundreds in attendance filled the air with expectation; when Hirschman moved, an entourage trailed him. It could not be helped that the mood was affected by what was going on outside, for Argentina was in the throes of a dramatic crisis, military unrest, hyperinflation, and a messy democratic turnover. If anything, there was a slight feeling of malaise as many of the intellectuals associated with the outgoing reformist government of Raúl Alfonsín were *Hirschmanianos*, and their turbulent final days raised—to some—questions about the viability of his brand of heterodoxy. When Albert arrived in Buenos Aires and checked into the swanky Plaza Hotel on Florida Street, he was greeted by a letter from the event organizer, Torcuato Di Tella. "Welcome to this hopeless country!" it started, not realizing that one of Hirschman's favorite quotes was Lenin's: "There is no such thing as a hopeless situation."[13]

In the blizzard of prizes that come with fame, several themes stand out. The first is Hirschman's use of the pulpit to think, speak, and write retrospectively. In the fall of 1987, he flew to Turin to receive a doctorate and recounted his "familial, personal, intellectual, and sentimental ties" he had with Italy. He warned his audience that he was averse to autobiography because "I tend to think of it as the ultimate admission to having run out of ideas" (which became something of a cliché). By now, he was repeating a refrain, which suggested that writing some kind of memoir might have been a temptation he had to suppress. So, he gave himself exception to prove his more general rule: such an endeavor could illuminate if "the autobiographical exercise serves the purpose of *recovering* an idea." In this case, it was the memory of Eugenio Colorni and the desire to prove Hamlet wrong. As Latin Americans struggled to rebuild civilian rule, he drew the arc backward to an earlier struggle and found in Colorni's example of combining participation in public affairs with intellectual openness an "ideal microfoundation of a democratic politics."[14] Retrospection, when not self-indulgent, was conversation in pursuit of a method. The final festschrift was a gathering at MIT, which prompted Hirschman to author a chronicle of his own tendency to raise doubts about his own concepts. Many of his readers often concluded that he was less interested in theory than in locating anomalies to rules, even his own. What they failed to see was that self-reflection and skepticism were aimed at adapting earlier insights to new complexities, insisting that theorizing had to account for its own historical limits. He called this practice self-subversion. Conversation was a constant; it is what he was doing with his petites idées and files of quotes and aphorisms. What changed as Hirschman became a profiled figure was that the conversations were less with the ancients and more with himself. Still, the ancients did not take a back seat: his final major book, *The Rhetoric of Reaction* (1991) was an argument with reactionaries.[15]

The second theme was the rather obvious globalization of his voice. And with globalization came a return to his European roots. With the return to Europe came the encounter with his own personal memories to reclaim forgotten legacies. The European return began in France. The translation of *The Passions and the Interests* into French brought him to the attention of a whole new public that knew little or nothing of his continental formation. To French readers, the book had clearly located *their* Enlightenment in broader European currents; this may have been obvious to non-French readers, but to the French, especially those less familiar with the narrower field of intellectual history, breaking out of the Pantheon was an eye-opener. It was this that François Furet, the celebrated historian of the French Revolution and director of the prestigious École des hautes études en sciences sociales, had in mind when he invited Hirschman to deliver the Marc Bloch Lecture in the spring of 1982. It was a kind of French coming out. Before heading to the Grand Salon de la Sorbonne, Hirschman lunched with Furet, Pierre Nora, Lucette Valensi, Jacques Julliard, and Fernando Henrique and Ruth Cardoso. Paris's intelligentsia came out en masse for the performance at the Sorbonne's Grand Amphitheatre. After Furet's introduction, Hirschman stepped to the podium and read his paper with Philippe de Champaigne's grand portrait of a stately Richelieu hanging nearby. It was as if he were born for

Delivering the Marc Bloch Lectures at the Sorbonne, 1982.

the occasion. Hirschman began by reprising his Parisian days and proceeded to braid intellectual traditions—the French Enlightenment faith in man's perfectibility, the Scots' insight into the role of unintended consequences, and the birth of a German critique of capitalism in the early nineteenth century. He was tracing the lineages of his own amalgamation. When he got to quotes of the classics, he would don a Basque beret. Midway through the lecture, he grinned and flipped the blackboard to draw graphs with chalk.

Pleased with this little trick, he argued that these conflicting "theses" about society developed largely without awareness and communication between them, leaving us with rival but disengaged views of the market. "Intimately related intellectual formations," he noted, "unfolded at great length, without ever taking cognizance of each other. Such ignoring of close kin is no doubt the price paid by ideology for the self-confidence it likes to parade." Hirschman offered a *tableau idéologique* of the rivals. In conversing with them, he drew them to the table to communicate with the other. This "democratic" approach to economic thought deprived any single argument of certainty nurtured by isolation. In staging this conversation among rival views of the market, however, Hirschman had to concede that over the course of the twentieth century the prospect of such a dialogue was getting more difficult. In fact, it could only be resurrected through his kind of historical reenactment. Ever the optimist, he suggested that this version of history should be seen as a precedent for present.[16]

At the Sorbonne, his locution had lost some of its fluency. The words were clear but laced with an unidentifiable accent whose origins were lost in a lifetime of migration and translation. One who was captivated was Annie Cot, the French historian of economic thought. Lia Rein's son, Martin Andler, arranged for them to meet, and soon Hirschman found himself on Cot's dissertation committee. Many years later, her seminar at the Sorbonne for PhD students working on the history of economic thought became baptized informally as the Séminaire Albert Hirschman.

Cliff Geertz found Hirschman's hunger for honorifics irritating and grumbled to friends that Albert was debasing himself (though it should be said that Geertz harvested his fair share, too). To some extent, he was right—it was going to Hirschman's head, but in Hirschman's own, humorously self-detaching way. His diary contains the following entry:

> When I was first in school I was told this is a bad omen for success in "life"—now that I am getting all kinds of honors while still alive I worry this is a bad omen for my fame after death.

It has been said that the hoard of honorifics was compensation for not having won *the* prize—the Nobel Prize in economics. Hirschman once quipped that he figured an honorary doctorate from Harvard was the consolation for runners up. Still: why no Nobel Prize? No question came up more often in the course of a decade's research on this book. As *Le Monde* declared in September 1997: "Hirschman, let's say it outright, should have long ago received the Nobel Prize in economic sciences."[17] Certainly, Hirschman was nominating others for the prize—including heroic organizations like the Inter-American Foundation. One reviewer noted of *Essays in Trespassing* that Hirschman was in the same league as the other founders of development economics—Arthur Lewis, Gunnar Myrdal, and Raúl Prebisch—with original thinking and many admirers. But unlike them he had no disciples. "There is nothing which could be described as a Hirschman school of development economics," noted the reviewer, and his lack of "method" explained the limits of his influence. Although Hirschman looked at the many ways in which phenomena are connected, "the connections he highlights are rarely direct or straightforward. His approach is circuitous; the most important linkages are often indirect; intellectual progress frequently requires lengthy detours and forays into seemingly unrelated areas." The reviewer drew attention to Hirschman's cherished cover of *Journeys toward Progress*, Paul Klee's painting, *Highways and Byways*, as an apt image for the content of his thinking.[18] This critique in the *Times Literary Supplement* stuck in Hirschman's craw. When he began a talk at CEBRAP in March of 1982, he despaired that his readers only saw disjointed, indirect connections.[19] Another reviewer, Alex Inkeles in the *Journal of Economic Literature*, noted that Hirschman was at his best when he connected economic relations to social and political systems; but when it came to "conventional economic analysis," a reader was left wanting. Of course, Hirschman could only reply that he never aimed to fit convention.[20]

By the late 1980s the rumors of Hirschman's nomination for the Nobel were flying fast and furious. The guessing game was becoming an autumn ritual. In 1989, Peter Passell drafted a list for the *New York Times* based on phone calls with anonymous economists. Many confirmed that there was an element of crap-shooting going on. Passell named some of the obvious contenders, like Gary Becker (who would get it in 1992), Robert Lucas (1995), Joseph Stiglitz (2001), and Ronald Coase (1991). His list was impressively accurate in retrospect. To add some drama, he added a "dark horse category." This is the "most fun" part of the whole game, he thought, as there were awardees who "would be sure to arouse controversy." At the top of this category he put Hirschman, "who has ventured deep into sociology, anthropology and philosophy to explain economic phenomena." There were others, too: Robert Fogel, Mancur Olson, Robert Mundell, and Martin Weitzman. Two of these would go on to win the prize, suggesting that dark horses could still cross the line first.[21]

To some of his fans, among them laureates, it was a mystery why he did not get the Nobel Prize. Tom Schelling argues that the arc of his life-work yielded more originality of economic thinking, and this achievement, rather than any single "theorem" or "solution," is what recommends him.[22] A common account is that Hirschman was not mathematical. Amartya Sen, Albert's nephew and a laureate, noted that in the early days most economists added math to their analytical kit bags and were recognized more for their conceptual breakthroughs; nowadays, when more and more economists start as mathematicians, this once "rare skill which Albert lacked" became increasingly notable. To Sen, this was regrettable; he considers Hirschman an uncommonly profound economic thinker. Beside, Hayek, Myrdal, and more recently Hirschman's old friend Schelling were not especially math-inclined; the lack of math was not, in itself, the spoiler.[23]

The question for many is, what did he contribute *to* the discipline? This, after all, is the metric for the award. The fact was, Hirschman's increasing breadth and originality coincided with his decreasing interest in speaking only to his discipline. His departure from Harvard Economics for the IAS in a sense represented a departure from the discipline and its fundaments. His calls to resist the grain of disciplinary specialization, to move beyond a discipline's own terms to explain social phenomena, meant that specialized practitioners were unlikely to see these injunctions as paths to further their pursuits. For this reason, Hirschman's work could not influence economic thought as it was then being envisioned—increasingly as a discipline resting on claims that had to be sharp enough to be empirically tested, followed up, developed, and refined. Economists, as Eric Maskin once told me, found it easier to operate within existing models, dissolving ambiguities and anomalies in pursuit of taut precision. Too many of Hirschman's insights did not add up to the kind of claims that could be tested in ways that yielded professional returns; by their standards, they were simply too wooly and elusive. The main exception was, paradoxically, the book that most veered him away from the discipline, *Exit, Voice, and Loyalty*, which *is* generally recognized as a work riddled with formulae waiting to be quarried. It may well be that the recent turn to examine behavioral foundations will lead some economists back to this forerunner.[24]

If this was his drift, why not acknowledge his contribution to development economics? *Strategy*, after all, was recognized as possibly the single most important book in the field. The trouble was, the field was not exactly held in high regard by the discipline. The fact that a prize had been allocated to William Arthur Lewis and Theodore Schultz in 1979 was all the recognition the subfield was going to get. According to Paul Krugman, the path it was on was leading to "an intellectual dead end." Hirschman, one should recall, was inclined to agree, though not for the same reasons. Although he never ceased to think *about* development, he worried that any proposition that the Third World required its own subfield was bound to lock economists into colonial outlooks. This concern lurked at the heart of his irritation with the big planners and "balanced growth" advocates of the 1950s and 1960s, who felt that Third World peoples need an external jolt. Rosenstein-Rodan's crack about Allende bringing the coup upon himself only confirmed Hirschman's doubts.[25] When "endogenous" theories of growth erupted on to the discipline's stage, the field flared up again, this time with technical virtuosity. But some of the circularity seemed all too familiar. In the fall of 1991, colleagues at Berkeley convened an international symposium, "Endogenous Growth," and invited Hirschman as a keynote eminence; by then, he was one of the few lucid founders left. Judging from his notes on the occasion, there was not a bit of déjà vu as a younger generation debated whether growth implied industrialization ("No!" exclaimed the seventy-six-year-old to himself) and whether "market failures" and "externalities" explained the trouble. When one economist proclaimed that "I don't have a model for that," Hirschman scribbled, "missing the point."[26]

What made Hirschman so influential beyond his discipline, speaking as an economist to social science, is what deprived him of influence within it; in the end, it was the divergence between the direction of the economics discipline—whatever one might feel about it—and Hirschman's own drift that accounts for him being passed over. He kept his disappointment to himself. Others have been vocal. "I don't know whether he was saddened," confided Sen, "by the fact that he did not get the Nobel. I am certainly saddened. Even now I don't give up the hope that he might be recognized belatedly."[27] Sen, as Hirschman's proxy, can perhaps take solace in the fact that Nobel committees often had difficulty with figures who defy easy categorization. The figure who comes to mind most readily is Jorge Luis Borges, the great Argentine short-story writer and essayist who never won the Nobel Prize for literature and left the world to question forever the wisdom of the judges. Like Borges, Hirschman could enjoy legions of readers long after some prize winners were forgotten.

With the exception of the taunting annual ritual of the Nobel Prize, Hirschman could bask in the aura as one of the world's most celebrated social scientists. It was perhaps only a matter of time before a return to Berlin, the natal city, loomed. There had been excursions with Ursula and Eva, who badgered a reluctant brother to see old sites, the ruins of their old home in the Tiergarten district, and to take walks among the lime trees. Albert generally chafed at these, for his sisters would grumble when he did not share their nostalgia. Generally, he was tight-lipped about his past. When he opened up and spoke with Claus Offe or Wolf Lepenies, their exchanges were mainly in English, which helped insulate the present from the past. Letters to and from Ursula were in French or Italian, with occasional, childlike German notes. If there was a European attraction, it was Italy and especially France. Behind his discretion, Germany summoned too many mixed emotions; Albert handled this, unsurprisingly, by keeping them at bay.

But by the 1980s, interest began to eclipse the aversion. Hirschman's reentry to Germany was paved by Claus and Sabine Offe, who had spent a year in Princeton in 1977–78, and Wolf Lepenies, who spent three years there and would turn down a permanent position to return to Berlin and help build a cousin institute there. To German social scientists, Hirschman was anything but a household name. His only translated work was *Exit, Voice, and Loyalty*, which appeared in a series better known for publishing Hayek, which branded Hirschman—identified as an American—as a conservative. Younger, left-wing social scientists ignored it. When Claus Offe arrived at Princeton, Hirschman was an unknown; it was an irony that Hirschman knew more about Offe and likened him to the critical emerging lights with whom he collaborated in Latin America. It was quite possible that this was in the back of his mind when he and Geertz arranged Offe's sojourn in Princeton. At the time, Offe was at the forefront of struggles to keep the German government from trampling on university autonomy as the Red Army Faction, a radical left-wing movement taken to kidnapping and violent attacks, stepped up its campaign. He refused to sign a special loyalty oath submitted by the minister of science and denounced the practice of isolation torture of detained Red Army members. Hirschman was fascinated, though he would not, to Offe's disappointment, be drawn into taking a public stance.

It was simply a matter of time before Hirschman's reflections on the human dilemma in all capitalist societies were marshaled to circulate in the one that was perhaps most riven by doubt. Albert and Sarah seized upon the opportunity to fly to Berlin in 1980 to visit the Offes. It was his first visit to his birthplace without his sisters, and thus he was freer to roam the city. Claus took them for a drive. Albert gazed out from the passenger seat chirping like a child in a German language that reminded Claus of his grandparents'. It was a kind of "linguistic archaeology," recalled Offe. Hirschman's tongue had been frozen in time, fluent in the anachronisms of a bygone world. Offe also noted a shift. Unlike his English voice, which was notably reticent, often mumbling, the returnee was lyrical, enthusiastic, and talkative—as if a different language brought forth a different persona. Offe would not be the first to observe the characterological shifts occasioned by Hirschman's linguistic swings. Together, Claus and Sabine Offe launched the translation of Hirschman's oeuvre into German in the mid-1980s, using their clout with a major publishing house, Suhrkamp, to reach out to broader readerships. To culminate this diffusion, Offe planned an *Autorencolloquium* to coincide with the paperback issue of *Leidenschaften und Interessen* (*The Passions and the Interests*) dedicated to discussing Hirschman's work at the University of Bielefeld in 1988. There had been one devoted to John Rawls, and then to Jürgen Habermas. Hirschman was the next eminent in line. What made this different was that the event doubled as a coming out in the form of a return for a German émigré. Offe and Bielefeld went all out and summoned a who's who of the German social sciences, with some prominent American, French, and British scholars mixed in. This was, it should be said, not quite how Hirschman saw the event. By then, his sleeves were rolled up for another book. Pleased to be celebrated and to hear others apply his work, he nonetheless receded from the discussion, his mind absorbed in *petites idées*; questions directed his way met with evasive smiles. There was a familiar sensation of him being *dans la lune*.[28]

It was thanks to Wolf Lepenies that Hirschman became a frequent visitor to his birthplace. Once Hirschman retired from the institute in Princeton, his time became more disposable; for a period, he became a de facto member of the Wissenschaftskolleg, created in 1981 and modeled in large measure on the IAS. Wolf became its second rector in 1986, overseeing its expansion and growing visibility to American scholars. By arranging for Sarah and Albert to move back and forth, he reinforced Hirschman's visibility to German social science while rekindling a bond with Berlin.

Before the decade was out, a half century of distancing was giving way; reentry pulled back the veil on his own past. When the Free University of Berlin, created in 1948 as an alternative to the Communist-controlled University of Berlin, celebrated its fortieth anniversary, it chose to award Hirschman with an honorary doctorate. Of all the awards, this one touched him most deeply. This coming out was fraught with significance. He would at last get a university degree in Berlin. As was his wont, he started his lecture with some personal recollections of being a young Berliner, recounting the conversation with his father that led to the discovery that he had no worldview. He alluded vaguely to the feebleness of Weimar democracy as a segue to a discussion of Humboldt, Rawls, and the importance of having strong but undogmatic opinions as a gauge of one's democratic personality. The possibilist, perhaps still trying to exorcise the spirits of 1933, urged his audience to explore what he called "the micro-foundations of a democratic society," the making not of Theodor Adorno's authoritarian personality, but rather a democratic one.[29]

At the festive lunch at the Chalet Suisse, he sat beside his first girlfriend, Inge, now a successful sculptress living, as befitted her family's Communist heritage, in East Berlin. On his other side was Alfred Blumenfeld, who had graduated with Albert from the Collège in March 1932 and spent the Nazi years in fear that his Jewish past would be revealed. After lunch, Inge accompanied Albert and Sarah back to their hotel, where they sat looking at photographs of her latest work. They also talked about life in the East, and Inge did not withhold her disenchantments. After several hours, she gathered her things and made way for the subway to cross to the other side. It may have been at the end of her visit that Hirschman, happening upon a good excuse for wordplay, jotted in his diary:

Communism: The dead end that justified the means.

The next day, *Der Tagesspiegel* featured a long profile of and interview with Hirschman, featuring him as the old Berliner coming home. A few days later, Wolf Lepenies, who with his wife, Annette, escorted Albert around the formalities, arranged a meeting with Jürgen Kuczynski, the son of René, whom Hirschman's father had saved in his dying days. The luncheon was planned on a frigid day at the Kolleg. Jürgen, now eighty-four years old, was frail but utterly lucid. "I have something for you, he told Albert. Out came a large envelope with the original Gerty Simon portrait of Albert's father. Kuczynski proceeded to tell a shocked Hirschman of what happened fifty-five years earlier, of Carl's hidden heroism. As Hirschman packed his bags to leave Berlin, he got a call from Henri Hempel, a high school teacher who was writing a book about the now-famous class of 1932 of the Französisches Gymnasium and wanted to interview one of its few living members.

To say that the week in Berlin was stirring would be an understatement. Certainly Hirschman had to wrestle with his customary reserve. He wrote to Claus Offe confessing an emotional tide from the Free University ceremony. But "for me the reencounter with some old friends whom I had not seen for some three or four decades was perhaps the most moving experience," which led to a reflex: "and I may even take time out to write about it."[30]

Indeed, he would.

Thus it was that as the divisions between East and West Berlin began to shudder, Hirschman would witness the closure of what he had seen open in early 1933. We can only imagine what went through his mind during the short trips in 1989 and then the four months he spent there from October 1990 to January 1991—because the notes he took from his many interviews among the fleeing easterners, followed by a ten-day trip to Leipzig and Dresden, where the decisive demonstrations had taken place against the old regime, have disappeared. To say that he recognized the epic proportions of what was going on trivializes what it represented for him personally. We can get a glimpse of the inner churning from the rushed entries in his diary of petites idées. A year after the fall of the Berlin Wall, he met with Offe at the Free University, by which time the two Germanys had hurriedly turned their backs on the past to face reconciliation in the present. Hirschman must have worried that the talk of burying old differences threatened to bleed into the intellectual milieu. "This impulse to post-bellum reconciliation," he noted, "does not exist after intellectual combat—you can't say: 'let's make sure these antagonisms haven't been argued in vain.'" It may have been that his dislike for the official way of "coping with the past" reflected the way in which he was, finally, reckoning with his own. German reunification implied a kind of internal reconnection that found characteristic expression in Hirschman's words. He scribbled a story in his diary about getting lost in the Kolleg library, until he stumbled on a librarian and said: "Ich habe mich verlaufen." These words delighted him. "This is a typically German linguistic formation of new meaning of verb laufen (run, go) by means of prefix ver—resulting in new meaning 'lose one's way . . .). I hadn't used this for some 50 years + recovered it immediately, considerable pleasure from recovering it—like finding an old friend who moreover hasn't changed or aged." He could still play in German.

By November, the outsider-insider witness to German reunification went to work, applying his model of exit and voice to an "essay in conceptual history." His rambling notes explored the varieties of artful East German exits, Dostoevsky, and currency unions. He was especially intrigued not by the hard-line party loyalist, but by the reformist Communists who worked from the inside to oppose the party line. What about them and their struggle in the name of "true Marxism-Leninism," those who lose their positions that depend on the very existence of a party line? The whole formula of voice and exit got mixed up in unexpected and therefore exciting ways. He had always thought, for instance, that loud exits were akin to the use of voice—like "banging the door upon leaving." "But it turns out that silent exit," of the type he heard testimony and witnessed in those heady weeks in Germany, "carries its own powerful message, just because of its silence, the inability to communication: with voice you can argue, with those silent AusreiBern [runaways] no discussion is possible."[31]

It is perhaps fitting that Berlin would be the scene for Hirschman's last field work; it brought out a half-century's habits. He reached for as many testimonials as possible, filling his notes with names, short quotes, and the marks of an impressionistic style one might associate with a painter's first etching. For all his gifts, Hirschman was not a systematic social historian, and the actors he described would not find themselves expressed in what was an exercise in—quite accurately—conceptual history. What he meant by conceptual history were the mutations of his own concepts. What readers could not sense, however, was the depth of personal history behind the concepts. "Having been away," he wrote a few months later,

> from Germany for well over half a century, I felt, that the con-
> cepts I had shaped could provide me with a precious point of re-
> entry. With the help of this key I might be able to open up recent
> and perhaps more remote German history and also consider, in
> turn, how much the key itself has to be re-shaped as the result of
> its encounter with a privileged historical testing ground.[32]

This historic convergence of self and history, concepts and contexts, became the themes in commentaries and interviews on German reunification in the *Frankfurter Allgemeine Zeitung* and Berlin's *Tagesspiegel*. Memories stormed back. When Peter Gourevitch accompanied Albert and Sarah to see some old sites in the spring of 1991, they walked through Potsdamer Platz. Albert pointed out where the Weimar cafés and newspaper once stood. When they reached Grunewald Station, they encountered the new memorial to Jewish Berliners deported to extermination camps. An enormous concrete block carved with the silhouettes of humans en route to their deaths led the way to the station and the infamous Track 17. Was this where his uncle had been herded? Albert was silent, but his face, recalled Peter, was defiant, as if to say "I survived. I am back. You lost."[33]

Thus it was that Hirschman oriented to two geographic poles: Latin America and Berlin. Each was going through its convulsive, and to some extent convergent, transitions, and having to deal with their respective pasts. His frequent returns to Latin America presented him with one monumental question: how could new civilian governments in Brazil and Argentina possibly solve all their problems at once—massive foreign debt, rising inflation, stagnant growth, and a woeful human rights record—without bringing the tent down on their heads? This was the mood dominating the meetings at CEBRAP in December 1985. "Dilemmas [not 'Promises'] of Democratic Transition" brought together some of the leading lights from Buenos Aires and São Paulo, including some of the veterans from *The New Authoritarianism* project. Hirschman urged his colleagues not to fall prey to pessimism. Work on what is possible, if necessary "sail against the wind"—tacking back and forth between alternating priorities; slay inflation, then consolidate democratic institutions, then focus on growth, and so forth. "I submit that it is far more constructive to think about ways in which democracy may survive and become stronger *in the face and in spite of* a series of continuing adverse situations or developments." Once again, he positioned himself as the hopeful contrarian. When Hirschman was called upon to sum up, he warned again not to get too hung up on preconditions for success; the new governments enjoyed a reservoir of legitimacy that gave them some autonomy from the past, and room for creative policy making. Upon his return to Princeton, he sent his thoughts from Brazil to Robert Silvers of the *New York Review of Books*. Given the drama of South America's democratic recovery—in contrast to the carnage of Central America and Indochina or the repression in Eastern Europe—Silvers quickly arranged to place the essay in the April 10 edition.[34]

While pressing his possibilism on Argentines and Brazilians and bolstering hopes for Chileans who still lived under Pinochet's jackboots, the trips rejuvenated Hirschman's interest in talking with colleagues and policy makers in the region. Twenty years after his paean to reformmongers, here was another round of prospects for change. In June 1985, the Alfonsín government laid out an audacious anti-inflation plan call the Plan Austral; a year later Brazilians launched one of their own, the Plan Cruzado. This was not an environment that Hirschman could keep himself from. A week later he was back in São Paulo to confer with CEBRAP people and watch the early weeks of the Cruzado take effect. He checked into the Trianon Hotel and mapped out his lecture in Portuguese. Hirschman redoubled his message to resist drawing self-fulfilling pessimistic conclusions about policies that were still in their infancy.

Back from his second trip to Brazil, Hirschman learned he had won the Kalman Silvert Award from the Latin American Studies Association

(LASA). The honor's quid pro quo was a lecture for the association's membership. Hirschman scrambled to pull something together. There was a conference in Venezuela on inflation organized by his old CEPAL friend, Aníbal Pinto, and brewing discussions in Brazil, Argentina, and Chile. Victor Urquidi, who had just stepped down as head of the Colegio de México, invited Hirschman to visit for a week and offered to help set up meetings. The Ford Foundation gave him a $5,500 travel grant to cover a seven-week whirlwind through the region with the idea of writing a series of diagnostic essays about the conjuncture. In return, the foundation asked Hirschman to share his views of the conjuncture with the organization's regional officers in Mexico, Rio, Buenos Aires, and Santiago. As deals go, this one was hardly onerous. It culminated with a flurry of Mexican meetings with Carlos Salinas de Gotari (then minister of programming and budgeting, prelude to becoming president), Jaime Serra Puche (director of the Economic Center at the Colegio de México, prelude to finance minister), Pablo González Casanova at the National University, dinner with Arturo Warman, and a large reception in his honor the evening of May 13 at the Ford Foundation headquarters. By the time he got back to Princeton, his suitcases were bulging with books, notes, and a detailed diary coded in excitement.

Excitement? The dominant mood in Latin America was anxiety and doubt! But what made many worry gave Hirschman hope. Instead of wailing about the crushing burden of the debt crisis, Hirschman observed that it was forcing policy makers to explore alternatives to the unpalatable medicine doled out by the IMF and to engage in pragmatic experimentation after many years of orthodoxy. Is this the "end of ideology in LA?" he asked himself.[35] Until about 1980, the heavy hand of structuralism and *fracasomanía* dominated perception and practice across the spectrum. Now, having delivered self-fulfilled legacies of deindustrialization, wasted oil bonanzas, and inflation and debt all around, here was an opportunity to pull possibilities out of the wreckage—Hirschman's favorite type of economic redemption act akin to that of Europe after the war. The essay, tellingly subtitled "Seven Exercises in Retrospection," was a dig at the familiar cognitive styles that dominated the Latin American social sciences and his old sparring partner, Rodolfo Stavenhagen, whose "Seven Erroneous Theses" from the 1960s was a widely read manifesto. Written in the flush of a democratic revival and the early days of heterodox shocks to stamp out inflation and tame the debt crises instead of obsessing about insoluble "fundamental" problems, his speech to LASA's membership extolled the pragmatic daring, the practical innovation, and the refusal to conform to orthodoxies. To him, this was a remarkable turn from his observations on ideology and policy making from 1950s.[36]

Hirschman was coming full circle, feeling vindicated that the dragons he'd been fighting all these years were finally slain. His idea of "retrospection" was a veiled exercise in self-redemption. The messy breakdowns of dictatorships in Latin America and the financial ruin they bequeathed reminded him that crises could also be opportunities. Stephen Holmes sent Hirschman the draft of an essay on the German legal thinker, Carl Schmitt. One might think the Nazi jurist would have made Hirschman's skin crawl. Indeed, Hirschman agreed with Holmes that the fad to rehabilitate Schmitt as a "critical" thinker was troublesome. On the other hand, Hirschman saw in the concept of crisis, of *Ausnahmezustand* (a state of exception), an insight. "I sense an odd convergence of my thought with his," he explained. "I think he was right in looking toward more exceptional situations and toward the capacity to seize them via 'decisionism' as the avenue to escape from 'the laws of motion' of both Marxist and non-Marxist (Weberian) social scientists. . . . For I have long talked of exceptional constellations that make possible the escape from vicious circles and forbidding 'prerequisites' for development or democracy . . . of course the use I make and the hopes I connect with these exceptional situations are totally different from his."[37]

If the memories of a vanquished Nazism brought out the victorious survivor, watching close friends in Latin America become the thinkers behind a new, democratic order born in crisis was a proximate elixir. Finally, in March 1990, Chileans opened a new chapter in their history. Pinochet and the military were being forced to hand over power to Patricio Aylwin and a coalition of Christian Democrats, Socialists, and others. Weeks after the Berlin Wall was torn down, Norbert Lechner of Chile's

Albert and Peter Bell at the Aylwin inauguration,
Santiago, 1990.

FLACSO, wrote to his *"estimado maestro"* inviting him to participate in
a special event to honor international colleagues who had supported academic freedom to coincide with Aylwin's inauguration. Alejandro Foxley sent a similar invitation from CIEPLAN. Hirschman could not say
no. Who knows what immediate thoughts came to mind: his friendly
conversations with Salvador Allende, his debates with Aníbal Pinto and
younger radicals at FLACSO in the late 1960s, or the fear that hung over
those who survived and stayed after 1973? The trip was clinched when
Aylwin sent a personal note asking Albert to participate in the inauguration ceremony. On the day of the swearing-in, Albert locked arms with
Peter Bell and joined the parade to the once-ruined presidential palace.

Chile's was a momentous political, as well as personal, marker. There
were some that were sheer personal pleasures, such as the Brazilian elections of 1994, which swept his long-time collaborator, Fernando Hen-

rique Cardoso, to the presidency, and José Serra, his "assistant" at the IAS to Cardoso's cabinet. Hirschman had watched Cardoso rise from senator to minister of foreign affairs and then finance minister and could not help but take pride as Cardoso and his advisors finally laid to rest the inflationary scourge. Cardoso's redemptive rhetoric—*este pais vai dar certo*, this time this country will do things right, it will succeed—moistened Hirschman's eyes. When he announced that "Brazil is no longer an underdeveloped country. It is an unjust country," it was as if Hirschman's long war against those warning of vicious cycles, binding constraints, and ineluctable traps had finally ended. Fernando Henrique asked Albert to sit with him during the inauguration on January 1 in Brasilia. Before the ceremony, Fernando Henrique had an informal lunch with his wife Ruth, Sarah, Albert, Alejandro Foxley (who was by then Chile's finance minister), and his thesis advisor from Paris, Alain Touraine. Old friends and colleagues chatted before the formalities. When they were done, someone handed a camera to a waiter, they put down their napkins and posed, the reflections of the Brazilian capital on the panes of glass being them.[38]

The "end of ideology" in Latin America highlighted something that had *not* seemed to change: the inability for the United States and Latin America to get on the same frequency. This was a conversation whose stubborn impossibility Hirschman had long lamented. In the early 1960s, Hirschman had compared US-style pragmatic reformism with Latin American quests for "fundamental" solutions and found the hemisphere "out of phase." Twenty years later, it was out of phase again. Now, the places were reversed. The Latin Americans had learned "from the spectacular miscarriage of economic policies inspired by ideology" and embraced a new experimental spirit, while in the United States whatever learning took place was thrown from the window in an effort to embrace fundamentalisms (of all sorts) and a dramatic brand of ideology. Latin Americans were open, flexible, moderate, and self-critical. American policy makers under President Reagan and the multilateral agencies they influenced were anything but. It infuriated Hirschman. He explained the problem of this *desencuentro* to readers of the *New York Review of Books*. "North Americans, so proud not long ago of their pragmatism, have taken

a distinctly ideological turn while Latin Americans have become skeptical of their former sets of certainties and 'solutions,'" he explained. Now,
with a jab at Reagan's fearmongers and the money doctors from the IMF,
Latin Americans "are naturally exasperated by the neophytes from the
North who are intent on teaching them yet another set." Returning from
Cardoso's inauguration, he asked himself, "Could it be that the torch—of
democratic freedom and social justice—has been passed from the North
to the South?"[39]

Against these European and Latin American backdrops, Hirschman
weighed in on the state of civic discourse in the United States. The triumph of Ronald Reagan and Margaret Thatcher announced an all-out
war on welfare, regulation, and the role of government in citizens' lives.
By 1988, in the middle of a vicious electoral campaign, the Republican
candidate, Vice President George H. W. Bush, hurled charges at his
hapless opponent, Michael Dukakis, for being an l-i-b-e-r-a-l. A "card-
carrying member of the ACLU," Bush snarled, as if it were an acronym for
the Communist Party. The right-wing campaign brought the vernacular
of politics to new lows. Fritz Stern, the Columbia historian, spearheaded
a campaign to defend "liberal principles and traditions," which were being
threatened by the "current political rhetoric," and enlisted Hirschman's
commitment for a large ad in the *New York Times*. In the end, Daniel
Bell, George Soros, Ken Arrow, John Hope Franklin, Donna Shalala,
Felix Rohatyn, William Styron, and others signed up. A few weeks after
the depressing election, Hirschman worked with Stern to assemble the
outraged at the Board Room Club on Park Avenue, hosted by the progressive philanthropist, Daniel Rose. That winter, upset by the degrada-
tion of American civic discourse, Hirschman labored to sort out what
was so pernicious about the opposition's talk. New York's senator Daniel
Patrick Moynihan wrote Hirschman a long and personal response to the
ad's text. "Dear Al," said Moynihan, "I write, uninvited to be sure, but not
without a sense of family, to encourage instead your hopes." He tried to
explain that the conservatives were not quite as powerful as they seemed
and that the vicious turn was not quite as new as the petitioners claimed.
The senator urged the economist to hold true to his own faith in the un-

intended blessings of opposition: perhaps the rise of conservatism could be good for liberals "as a stimulus of powerful ideas opposing them." Not without evidence, he felt that liberals basked in moral superiority and did little to rethink their principles and policies. "So far," he concluded, "all I have in the newspapers are accounts of conferences at which the losers of an eminently winnable Presidential election get together to blame the American people." So it was that Hirschman was not just alarmed by the rising tide of dogmatists from the Right, but the retreat to hermetic self-satisfaction on the Left—such a contrast to what he had witnessed in Europe and Latin America.[40]

It was alarming. Perhaps emboldened by the senator, Hirschman felt compelled to intervene. His concern about argumentation was nothing new. But it had taken a new turn. The summer of 1985 saw him reading *Considérations sur la France* by Joseph de Maistre, noting his praise for the French Revolution for devouring itself and leaving France better off for having done so. He circled back to familiar themes, like the Scottish Enlightenment and unintended consequences, Marx and romanticism. And there were the expected injunctions to open new readings, like the doctrine of Divine Providence. He sensed he was returning to the beginning of a cycle that began decades earlier in his pleas for reform. "In a sense," he noted, "I may be after something like 'Journeys Towards Reaction (or Disaster)' in counterpart to my *Journeys toward Progress*." Now, to fully understand the challenge of reform, he was finally coming face-to-face with its dialectical counterpoint. To understand why reform was so fraught, he needed "better understanding [of] why reform movements arouse resistance and passionate antagonism, why they run into decreasing returns, why there are subject to (totalitarian, etc.) dérapage." By the next summer, his ideas were crystallizing around the keyword "reaction." He was once again reading Edmund Burke.[41]

By 1988, it was time to write.

His composition began as an essay about ideologues Hirschman labeled "reactionary," those who argued that efforts at reform had the *perverse* effect of sabotaging it. Worse, reforms could move societies onto the opposite track. Some even argued that it was inevitable. Talk about unintended effects! Reform threatened to make things worse—what Hirschman called the Jeopardy Thesis, his first coinage in writing. It focused on Edmund Burke and Joseph de Maistre as the originators of the current American reactionary discourse and ended with Charles Murray, the libertarian pundit whose book, *Losing Ground: American Social Policy, 1950–1980* enjoyed near-biblical status for those eager to dismantle the welfare state for the putative good of its beneficiaries. The idea, exemplified by Murray's polemics, was that reforms guided by state policy risked undermining all progress made before the policies were implemented. They put progress in jeopardy. Hirschman plotted his ideas about this tradition of argumentation. Some old friends shared their thoughts. Offe pointed out that conservatives who believed in the bad outcomes from good intensions in politics also believed in good outcomes from bad intentions from economics: "They cherish and condemn intention-outcome discrepancies at the same time," Offe clarified. Hirschman marked this line. Skinner pointed, as one might expect, to some English precedents: "The one perfect instance of a writer who says in so many words that the drive to greater civil liberty will inevitably lead to what you call 'the perverse effect' is Hobbes in *Leviathan*." Look at the chapter "On the Office of the Sovereign" in Book 2, urged Hirschman; there you will see Hobbes' account of the *inevitable* consequence of attempted reform. And what about Fortuna, who rewards the brave for tempting her to defeat them by summoning the perverse effect? Is this not what the wheel of Fortune alludes to? The ambitious can be rewarded for their daring.[42] He put the final touches to his essay and sent it to James Fallows. In May 1989, the *Atlantic Monthly* published the long essay called "Reactionary Rhetoric," which charged the self-described "neo-conservatives" of being unwilling to argue *directly* with those who advocated reform. Instead, what they wielded were word games, a theme from *The Passions and the Interests* to chart the arguments for capitalism in its ascent. Two centuries later, with Latin American economies tearing down old restrictions and Communist verities trembling behind their walls, capitalism *was* triumphant. And yet, its apostles were deafer than ever to the voices of those who wanted it to be a little less savage.[43]

For those making transitions to market life, the essay struck a nerve. The Polish Academy of Sciences invited Hirschman to address colleagues in Warsaw to explain the Jeopardy Thesis. János Kornai and István Rév in Budapest were also eager to have him unpack the critique for Hungarians, but the rector of the crumbling Karl Marx University of Economics, eager to swap his ideological stripes for a different kind of empire, put his foot down at the idea of an honorary degree. "If you were Milton Friedman then there would be nothing to prevent your decoration," lamented an embarrassed Rév. Instead, the Hungarian Academy of Sciences would host him. Rév also wanted Hirschman to confer with opposition intellectuals, like János Kís of the Free Democrats.[44]

A volley of letters from friends and colleagues urged more. McPherson applauded the essay and especially the unmasking of Murray, adding "the only real complaint about your piece is that it isn't long enough."[45] He would get his way. To date, Hirschman's books had been outcroppings from ideas drawn from his supply of petites idées. This, his last book, *The Rhetoric of Reaction: Perversity, Futility, Jeopardy* (1991), was different. It was induced by demand to expand his critique of arguments about the self-defeatism of reform. That is, as we shall see, the core of its ambition.

There was something else at work in *Rhetoric* that did not get much play among Anglophones applauding the work. While much of the book was responding immediately to neo-conservative triumphalism in the United States and Britain, and this became the focus of readers' attentions, the events in Germany and Latin America cued him to a broader problem that transcended questions of welfare: the role of discourse in democracy. There were not just arguments on the line; there were republican values of civic life. All dogmas and "basic" logics (the inevitable crisis of capitalism, the unavoidable need for outside interventions of development planners, the intractable crisis of late industrializers, and now the ineluctable pointlessness of reform—the inventory of iron-clad certainties of the century was growing longer) had been favorite targets for decades. By definition they limited what people might consider as alternatives—and anything that limited the scope for learning from experience closed off options. But there was more at stake. Arguments that immunized them-

selves from the possibility of being wrong and from accommodating uncertainty were closed discourses that thwarted listening to others—and
this sapped democracy of its vibrancy. The major and minor keys of the
book were therefore united in a concern to address "the systematic lack of
communication between groups of citizens, such as liberals and conservatives, progressives and reactionaries."

> The resulting separateness of these large groups from one an-
> other seems more worrisome to me that the isolation of anomic
> individuals in 'mass society' of which sociologists have made so
> much.[46]

Loosening the encased certainties and the "servitudes" that flow from
them would, he believed, help restore communication. Chest-thumping
neo-cons worried him; so did the arguments coming from the progressive
side. It is important to bear this in mind because "Reaction" was read as, understandably, a position exclusively of the Right. In fact, Hirschman had in
mind all positions that *react* to the idea of reform by discounting its logical
impossibility. This is why, to the chagrin of many on the Left, Hirschman
chose to write a chapter—chapter 6—about progressive intransigencies.
This allowed him to stand above extremes to defend the space of reform
as also a disposition about *forms of arguing*. Intransigents of all stripes only
serviced a dialogue of the deaf and thus ensured that the failure of reform
was sealed from the start. The ability of a society to sustain open conversations among rivals that admitted the possibility of being wrong was a
gauge of its democratic life and its ability to promote nonprojected futures
for its citizens. Indeed, when Hirschman completed it, he asked Harvard
University Press if he could change the title from *The Rhetoric of Reaction*
to *The Rhetoric of Intransigence*. There was objection all around. Americans wouldn't understand the word and were like to mispronounce it, so
Hirschman went back to the original. But the simultaneous foreign language translations—where the question of democratic discourse was more
burning—did embrace the title change. The German, Italian, Brazilian,
Mexican editions substituted "Intransigence." The French preference for
historical narratives led to *Deux siècles de rhétorique réactionnaire*.[47]

The book, in imperceptibly powerful ways, grew in scope as readers turned the pages. Characteristically, he went back in time to the foundational arguments of the modern era. "I have a new project," he told his sister, "an "article" (or a book) on the structure of reactionary thought, inspired by the Reagan regime. But I will go back until the reaction to the French Revolution. For the first time in many years I am reading a lot of German, for instance Novalis, Schlegel, but also Schiller—did you know that the Song of the Bell is a completely anti-revolutionary poem (see the last part)—it is very pleasant to discover that my German and the feeling for the language is still there, completely intact."[48] This excavation of a tradition sired by counter-revolutionary talk gave birth to his coinage: "the perversity thesis," a foundational argument born of reactions to the French Revolution, according to which all efforts at purposeful change aggravates the condition one wants to remedy. "Everything backfires"; Le Bon argued that universal suffrage would destroy national and international order by raining the irrationality of the masses on the state, first by ramping up demands and thus augmenting public spending, and then bloating governments faced with mounting mandates, only to turn over the once-precious democracy to a class of bureaucrats. It was a formulation that presaged contemporary "public choice" theorists. One cannot help but read a lifetime's battles being poured into this "new project," including warnings that trumped-up promises of deliverance cannot help but set the stage for trumped-up declarations of absolute failure, a syndrome Hirschman cautioned a quarter of a century earlier. What had changed over the decades is that failurists no longer needed to wait for exaggerated hopes to deliver their blow. It was enough for someone ever to have bothered to think that minimum wages or safety nets might cure ills to inspire the lip-curling scorn of those who blessed themselves for having mastered the elementary sophistication of a simple paradox and turned it into a cure-all for all public policy considerations.

But how exactly did perversity unfurl its malice? The next two centuries saw the perversity thesis spawn two more: the Jeopardy Thesis and "the futility thesis." Jeopardy, as he pointed out in the *Atlantic Monthly*, insists that the costs of reform were punitive and imperiled all previous, fragile, breakthroughs. Futility argues that all efforts at change are point-less; *plus ça change plus cést la même chose* shrugged some in the wake of revolutions—French, Russian, Chinese, Cuban. Milton Friedman as-sured readers of *Time* magazine that minimum wage laws wind up driv-ing workers out of jobs while Gordon Tullock's *Welfare for the Well-to-Do* had the added virtue of boasting a title that "left nothing to the imagi-nation." At least Milton and Rose Friedman bothered to suggest there might be an option in their *Free to Choose*. There was an analogy in the futility thesis to primitive or "vulgar" Marxists—and faint echoes of the debates in Germany in 1932–33 can be heard—who argued that the state served capitalists and scorned as hypocrisy any notion that a policy might help the working class or the general interest. The Far Left had feared that a successful policy might blunt the appeal of revolutionary certainty. A half century later it was the Far Right that mocked reformers for their naïveté or idiocy for messing with a system that should, untouched, be self-equilibrating. Meddling with the market would invariably serve bet-ter the haves than the have-nots.

History turned the tables on Hirschman. Having spent so much of the 1950s and 1960s trying to get social scientists to see that unintended consequences of collective actions could yield positive side effects, trying to get them to climb down from their master plans and elaborate flow charts to see what was actually transpiring on the ground, these same side effects had been given a new, pernicious, spin. Reactionaries had claimed the power of unintended consequences for themselves and turned them into a dogma *against* change. Now Hirschman had to warn against over-claiming the power of side effects, especially those that overwhelmed the puny positive results. The posture, in the hands of the extremes, became positions of intransigence.

The Rhetoric of Reaction rolled off the presses amid a war in which overwhelming forces drove Iraqi armies from occupied Kuwait. In their wake, the American government celebrated in a fit of bravado. Everyone was talking about an article by an American pundit, Frances Fukuyama, about the end of history and the eclipse of its ideological forces. With this in the air, Hirschman's combative élan rang out of tune. Many were delighted that someone had captured what was so frustrating about the nondialogue with conservatives. The novelist Jamaica Kincaid was one of them. She read the book about the time she got her first fax machine and gave it a trial run with a short note to Hirschman. His introduction "took my breath away," she wrote. "I imagine having you for a reader."[49]

But others were not so impressed. When Hirschman returned from Berlin, he found a stack of mixed-to-hostile reviews. Some, such as those from *Critical Review* and the *Public Interest* were no surprise, although they were genuinely acknowledging of Hirschman's learned lucidity and cannot be accused of not taking the book seriously. Indeed, if Hirschman aimed to motivate a dialogue with the Right to promote more open-mindedness, his effort worked, at least in these two influential magazines. Not so with the British journalist Peter Jenkins, who was unflattering in the *New York Times*, finding the book steeped in an age riven by traditional political ideologies: "The old labels don't stick anymore," he announced with unblinking confidence. Rather immodestly, he thought Hirschman brushed reactionaries away too "lightly." After all, the French Revolution led to the Terror, and look what Marxism did, as if this had bypassed Hirschman. "The last decade of the 20th century is not a moment to mock those who have mocked such great transformational projects."[50] Thin-skinned when it came to reviews, Hirschman complained to Silvers at the *New York Review of Books* that "I cannot help feeling that some sort of concerted assault is shaping up." This was self-pity speaking. The *New Republic* and the *American Prospect* treated the book with serious enthusiasm. Still, he angled for a favorable review from Silvers, who told Hirschman he'd sent the book to two different reviewers "but was disappointed in each case." Taken aback, he turned defensive; the lectures and ripostes that ensued were self-protective, surprising given the point he was trying to make. A polemical book such as this one was bound to elicit strong reactions.[51]

The reception abroad was something else altogether, which suggests that the old contrast between a pragmatic, open-minded America and obstinate, absolutist Europe and Latin America was getting inverted. Fernando Henrique Cardoso heralded the book as a model of critical progressive thinking in a long review in *Estudos, CEBRAP* and the Argentine socialist magazine, *La Ciudad Futura*. The Mexican *Nexos* also featured, and celebrated, the defrocking of right-wing futilists. *Die Zeit* carried an extensive review by Otto Kallscheuer on October 2, 1992, noting the importance of open arguments for democratic life. But it was especially in France that Hirschman was greeted as a celebrity. Hirschman found himself besieged with overtures. The Commissariat général du Plan (fittingly, founded by Jean Monnet in 1946) asked Hirschman to speak about reactionaries and the prospects for reform. In preparation, *Alternatives Economiques*'s June 1992 issue had a cover "La grand peur des classes moyennes" with a photo below of a Los Angeles shopping mall in flames during the riots that erupted after Los Angeles police officers were acquitted for the merciless beating of Rodney King; inside was the editor Denis Clerc's profile of Albert Hirschman and an extensive Jean-Baptiste de Foucauld interview of him. So it was that a panel of French notables welcomed Hirschman at the commissariat and listened to his talk, "Progressive Rhetoric and the Reformer."[52] Reviews in *Le Monde* (by Daniel Andler, a philosopher and Lia Rein's son, as it turns out), *Le Nouvel Observateur*, and *L'Express* raved about the book and featured its author as a true *homme de lettres*.

From a European perspective, here was a European living in the United States who could finally explain all the American neo-con froth to them. There was, however, one European who took issue with the book, the eminent Sorbonne sociologist, Raymond Boudon. Pierre Nora had asked him to review *Rhetoric* for the influential, high-end magazine *Le Débat*. Unlike the American conservative reaction, which laced its criticism with deference, Boudon was downright hostile, a task facilitated by wanton misreading. Near the end of the long review Boudon charged Hirschman with knowing nothing of "the new science of rhetoric"— implying either dependence on an old style or an unscientific one. The heat seemed to reflect less an ideological dispute than a personal one, either envy (that Hirschman was getting so much attention) or resentment (that Hirschman had not made the proper genuflections; Boudon had, for instance, written about "perverse effects" and unintended consequences). Nora, to be fair and perhaps seeing the problem, asked Albert if he would like the right to reply. Hirschman's prose in *Rhetoric of Reaction* had been at times sardonic, other times playfully hard-hitting. When it came to Boudon, he poured his annoyance at his critics into an uncharacteristically acidic comment. "The objections of Raymond Boudon to my recent book," he told readers, "are so numerous and so widely scattered that I feel like the proverbial mosquito in a nudist colony: I don't know where to start."[53]

Of course, he did. Hirschman proceeded to smack his critic hard. It is possible that his riposte was fired by frustration that the popularity of *Rhetoric of Reaction* (which was so personally gratifying) had so little impact on the mood, especially in Washington (which was not). Perhaps he consoled himself that intransigents, once in position, especially positions of influence, were hardly inclined to listen to critics like Hirschman. It was not the first time he found himself at odds with an alliance of ideas and policy makers with whom he profoundly disagreed. *Rhetoric of Reaction* was an outcry; in earlier days Hirschman might have considered exit. But a century was taking its toll. He was getting too old to escape to the field or to retreat to history. Increasingly, he had to watch as others took up the challenge. As he drew the book to a close, an unusually somber tone took over; Hirschman was openly, if ambiguously, prophetic. "There remains a long and difficult road to be traveled," he concluded, "from the traditional internecine, intransigent discourse to a more 'democracy-friendly' kind of dialogue" (p. 170). In an age in which political life was being overrun by arguments conjugated to kill their opponents, it was not so easy to wish good fortune upon those disposed to doubt or to embrace the readiness to be wrong. But even this gloom could not stick. Among other things, Hirschman worried about the figure of the prophet. His diary around the same time records this:

> *Prophecy*—always a disaster
> prophet = Cassandra
> or: prophet = action-arousing
>   gloomy version?
> Ex: Malthus

Hirschman did not want to go down as a latter-day Malthus, known perhaps unfairly as the apostle of the dismal science. The point was not to predict demise. Hirschman was by then far too seasoned in his struggles against declension to give into it now. The point was to imagine a different way to argue.

Marc Chagall's Kiss

On April 7, 1995, the director of the Institute for Advanced Study, Phillip Griffiths, issued invitations to Hirschman's friends and colleagues to celebrate his eightieth birthday. There would be, as befit an eminent scholar, panels and discussion. Amartya Sen would lead a seminar on development and poverty. Ruth Cardoso, Michael McPherson, Paul Romer, Thomas Robinson, Emma Rothschild, José Serra, and James Wolfensohn planned comments. Seventy-eight people flew in from around the world. Some who could not, such as Fernando Henrique Cardoso and Wolf Lepenies, sent letters. Later that evening, over rack of lamb, gratin Dauphinois, and haricots verts, there were toasts. Finally, Albert was given the last words. "After marvelous, kind, witty messages, what remains for *me* to say?" he asked his friends. He smiled. "I am reminded" he added, "of a story about a fellow who listens to various praises and then admonishes his friends: 'Don't forget about my modesty!' It would be in the spirit of 'self-subversion' if I now undertook to refute the various claims that have been made here—but that would be tiresome. The basic fact is that I must admit to being pretty old."[1]

How to bring closure to a study about someone approaching his final years, especially when—as we shall see—each year brought him closer to death by chipping away at his life? As Hermione Lee has noted, this is often a life history's peril, where the effort to tie up the dangling threads reduces the odyssey to an essence it may never have had. We have been fascinated by exemplary deaths, or rather by deaths made exemplary, like Virginia Woolf's or Nelson's, replete with famous and mythologized dying words. We seek in the moment of death a meaning of a life.[2]

We are fortunate in at least one respect: Hirschman was aware of the dilemma. He wrote about it, often in pursuit of death's ironical features. "The longer one lives," he mused in his diary, probably in the late 1960s, "the clearer it becomes that life is short." A few years later, he asked himself: "To conquer death—how? To die smiling. Practice smiling during orgasm. Smile and laughter as the essential prologue and epilogue to having sex. Making a woman laugh = make her open up, first her mouth— the rest follows. But why is laughter also the epilogue? Do we laugh about each other or about the fact that we were precisely so *tierisch ernst* (full of animal-like seriousness) just now?" It seems likely that Ursula's illness provoked thoughts of mortality; his notebook is filled with such ruminations. Around the time of the death of his brother-in-law in May 1986, Albert almost foresaw his own biographer's problem:

> Obituary-writers love someone like Altiero with a higher & unitary mission that defines his life's meaning for them. But why should we make the life of obituary-writers easy?

The convention of using a death to sum up a life, to lend conclusive— and concluding—significance to a subject's work, is so tempting that it has become a literary parody. Ending is hard to avoid; death is impossible to, which is one reason why biographers have relied on the latter to resolve the former. But even this Hirschman knew. After all, death shadowed him from youth. The spirits of the deceased—his father, Mark Rein, Eugenio Colorni, the unmentioned relatives killed in gas chambers, the fellow volunteers in Spain—accompanied him in the way he viewed the world and in the way he wrote. What he could not know about his own ending was how to place and date it—until it was upon him. For Hirschman it took place, perhaps fittingly, in the Alps, where he had gone for the restorative powers of the mountains. It was the summer after his eightieth birthday. From 1972 onward, Albert and Sarah would visit Katia and Alain as often

Climbing near Puy St. Vincent in the Alps, 1982.

as possible, spending several weeks each summer at Puy St. Vincent in the Alps. A centerpiece of these vacations was a metronomic commitment to walking in the mountains. With each passing summer, Albert looked forward to reliving this childhood passion, all the more so as his French grandchildren joined him on outings.

Albert enforced what others regarded only half-mockingly as "the German rules": up at 6:00 a.m. sharp, an early breakfast, hit the trails by 7:00, steady walking for 50 minutes followed by 10 minute breaks. When the entourage reached the peak then the family rested and ate. It was not always easy to drill this into the occasional American tag-along, who often preferred to eat the whole way and take breaks whenever the going got tough. For Albert, it was not just the commitment to the routine and its standards, and no doubt the fond memories; he was truly inspired by the majesty of the peaks.

The visual inspirations and physical vigor were important for the days he was not walking. Part of the routine was to walk hard one day and take the next off for writing. When Albert and Sarah went to visit the Hoffmanns in their Swiss getaway near Bern, Stanley and Inge were slightly miffed that they saw so little of their guests, who were out the door at 7:30 sharp, and only after a day in the mountains would show up for dinner. At least then they could break out the wine and talk. But then the next day, Albert would hole himself up at a desk and spend hours writing on his yellow pads. This was not the shared vacation that the Hoffmanns had been looking forward to. But Stanley could not help but be impressed, though not surprised, by the work ethic.[3]

The summers thereby became reunions for Sarah and Albert with their daughters and their families. With his grandchildren as muses and surrounded by the mountain airs of his youth, he created a habitat for summer writing. This was where many of his final books were drafted. The writing of *Rhetoric of Reaction* filled those long, alternate days as he poured over his note-filled pads and read George Eliot's *Middlemarch*.[4]

Hirschman was thus a healthy man. Wolf Lepenies arranged a photo shoot of Albert and Sarah with Christa Lachenmaier during a visit to Berlin in 1994. Albert was a little nervous, but conversation with the photographer and Sarah calmed him down. The result was a portrait of serenity with old age.

Albert had occasional troubles, especially with high blood pressure and tachycardia, which hospitalized him in Toronto and Boston. He had troubles with his right eye and later suffered temporarily from zinc shortages, which briefly affected his ability to taste. In early 1988, Sarah noticed something on Albert's back. Tests revealed a nonmalignant tumor, which was later deemed dangerous sarcoma. Albert was admitted in February to the University of Pennsylvania hospital to have it removed. This was followed by seven weeks of draining radiation therapy five times each week. It was a scare, made worse because Albert fretted that he would not meet his lecturing obligations, especially in Paris in June. "This came as a big shock," he told Mike McPherson. When it was over, he breathed a sigh. "Right now I feel fine, in fact enjoying what is much like a return from the

Albert and Sarah in Berlin, 1994.
Credit: Christa Lachenmaier/Laif/Redux.

realm of the damned."[5] In 1991 he was admitted to the hospital in Berlin
for an angina pectoris angioplasty and the following year underwent radiation therapy again, this time for prostate cancer.

The occasional frights did not slow him down, but he did indulge
himself a little bit. After delivering the Patocka Memorial Lecture at the
Institute for Human Sciences in Vienna in June 1996, Hirschman decided
to splurge with part of the proceedings. He found an elegant hotel in the
Alpine town of Pontresina and invited Katia and Alain to join him and
Sarah. This was going to be a more relaxed vacation: on July 11, they made
plans to take a cable car to the peak and walk down, an unheard of extrav-
agance! Perhaps he should have stuck to his old drill, for on the descent
Albert tripped and struck his head against a rock, severely gashing his
face. It took three hours for Alain to get Albert to the bottom of the path,
by which time he was covered in blood; the whole while he kept asking
Alain if *he* was alright. A doctor cleaned him up and swathed his face
in bandages. But it was clear that the damage was more than skin-deep.
Albert's speech was slurred, more hesitant. Then his gait changed; it was
hard to keep his balance. He quickly returned to the United States, where
doctors diagnosed a cerebral hematoma, by which time Albert was having
more difficulties speaking.

He knew he was losing his grip. Benjamin Friedman, a Harvard
economist who had struck up a late but active correspondence with
Hirschman about the relations between economic growth and democra-
tization, had sent Hirschman a draft essay and list of queries. Under normal circumstances, this would have elicited a lengthy response. Instead,
he told Friedman that he found "it impossible for me to address myself
to the kind of questions you are posing." Wolf Lepenies had been planning a global colloquium on Albert's work at the Kolleg in Berlin. By the
middle of August, the effects were clear enough to someone who did not
want to refuse a return to Berlin. "I am depressed," he told Wolf, "and
have some serious doubts about our returning to the Wissenschaftskolleg
next year. I just feel that I would not be a particularly useful or productive
member."[6] Orlando Fals Borda of Colombia's National University asked
him to come to Cartagena for a conference to discuss his work on devel-

opment in Latin America. This must have been wrenching, for he had not been back to Colombia for many years. His accident "was quite a trauma," he explained to his old friend. "I am better than I was, but simply cannot now envision undertaking the trip I was much looking forward to." A concerned Fals Borda immediately responded with a fax, hoping for a speedy recovery.[7]

Being immobilized brought on depression. Doctors prescribed Prozac, then Zoloft. But there was little to arrest the steady, ineluctable decline, the deteriorating hearing and speaking, his tortuous difficulty writing, and the loss of affect or expression that had been such a subtle but important feature of his communication. Instead of reading, he spent long hours of the day asleep in his chair. Walks to the institute became prolonged shuffling excursions, which left him even more exhausted.

The Alpine tumble put an end to a long writing career. Words—the spoken and the written—that fascinated him through life became harder and harder to grasp. Their slipping epitomized an ending. As one might imagine, it was difficult to turn away the flow of invitations and solicitations. George Soros asked Hirschman to spend a weekend with him at his country home in Katonah, New York, in May to discuss "the capitalist threat" with a few friends. Unable to turn this one down, Hirschman went, but he was, by all accounts, the shadow of the sage he'd once been. His last writing effort was a short amalgamation of quotes and thoughts about the paradoxes of unintended consequences written for Soros' Open Society Institute in late 1999.[8] In September 1997, the Toynbee Prize Foundation announced that it would confer that year's prize to Hirschman for his contribution to the "health of the social sciences." He would join the likes of Raymond Aron, Jean-Paul Sartre, E. H. Carr, and others. Delighted, he accepted, and began to prepare his speech—which he decided would tackle the works of Toynbee and Gerschenkron. But it did not take long for Hirschman to realize that this was beyond his grasp. Having had a chance to reread Toynbee and a few other books, "I feel that I would be unable at this point in my life to generate the enthusiasm and energy needed to write. I hope you will forgive me," he wrote to the president of the foundation. Besides, he never liked Toynbee and likely found the exercise less exciting in practice that it was in theory.[9] In the end, arrangements were made to have Judith Tendler, John Coatsworth (the director of Harvard's Rockefeller Center for Latin American Studies), and Charles Maier step in with short speeches. Graciously, Maier took the opportunity to salute Sarah and the richness of Albert's family life that had allowed him to explore literary, philosophical, and psychological connections because he was never alone.

Several publishers moved to assemble his final essays into anthologies. Hirschman gathered his self-reflective, Montaignesque works as a commitment to self-subversion for a collection with the same title, which Harvard University Press published. Some of the essays were personal retrospections and speeches from award ceremonies about the surprising turns of a life. But there was a broader point being made, which was captured in his last serious composition, written, perhaps fittingly, for the one-hundredth session of the Bergedorfer Gesprächskreis (Discussion Circle of Bergedorfer) in Dresden. The attendees were asked to think about "how much community spirit (*Gemeinsinn*) does liberal society require?" Hirschman's answer began with a tale from Tolstoy about a peasant called Pakhom, who was obsessed with accumulating land. In his exertions to hoard, Pakhom died prematurely of exhaustion, by which time all Pakhom really needed was the plot for his grave. To Hirschman, Tolstoy's warning was "that this is the amount of land we may well end up with if we fall prey to accumulating passion." Hirschman was not denouncing greed. He was cautioning Germans against excessive calls for community spirit because it threatened to stultify necessary, but disorienting, conflicts. People had to disagree, struggle, bargain, and experiment; conflict was the real "glue and solvent." "What is actually required to make progress with the novel problems a society encounters on its road is political entrepreneurship, imagination, patience here, impatience there, and other varieties of *virtù* and *fortuna*. I do not see much point (and do see some danger) in lumping all this together by an appeal to Gemeinsinn." Closing with Machiavelli was no accident; for the Florentine, politics was an art in need of multiple activities, ranging from exit to voice to loyalty. The range thrived best when adversaries were willing to accept the uncertainty of their correctness. It withered in the face of intransigence. Hirschman's version of political economy had never been easy to model because it was not about answers, designs, or solutions in pursuit of an equilibrium or balance. To his Dresden audience he warned that the idea of a prepolitical communal identity missed the point; one's loyalty came *from* politics, its messiness and its possibilities. The third panel of his famous triptych, exit, voice, and loyalty, was now coming into relief.[10]

The book of which the essay was a part would exhibit his self-questioning at work, to show how the discovery of new meaning can come from subverting one's earlier arguments. Immediately translated into many languages, *A Propensity to Self-Subversion* (1995) consolidated Hirschman's global profile as a rare voice of learned humility and self-affirmation. Fernando Henrique Cardoso took time out from his presidential duties to write the foreword to the Portuguese edition—likening Hirschman's disguised intellectual power and ambition to Machiavelli, "nibbling" at small questions to overturn and reframe grand theories—with a warning to readers: do not mistake nibblings (Hirschman's petites idées) for fleeting interpretations. Modesty's purpose is to enhance an argument's virtue. Hirschman and the Princeton philosopher, Harry Frankfurt, struck up a correspondence about commitments to revisit one's thoughts. Frankfurt insisted that there was an important distinction between self-subversion and self-refutation; the latter he associated with Bertrand Russell or Hilary Putnam. Hirschman was doing something quite different. "The reason your work is never completed," observed Frankfurt, "is that you have a propensity to look for ways to enlarge it. What happens to you is not really that (as for Sisyphus) work you have previously done is completely undone, so that you must start again from the beginning." On the eve of the French publication of *A Propensity to Self-Subversion*, *Le Monde* featured a long *entretien* of Hirschman, all but inducting him into its Pantheon of the century's great intellectuals.[11]

Hirschman's last tome was a slender affair including a lecture in Vienna about public and private intersections and his retrospective on the Marshall Plan, capped by a long 1993 interview with Carmine Donzelli, Marta Petrusewicz, and Claudia Rusconi that had been published earlier in Italian, German, Spanish, and French at the height of the impact of *The Rhetoric of Reaction*. Hirschman fretted over the title and yearned to allude to his theme of trespassing, which entitled his 1981 anthology. In the end, he settled for *Crossing Boundaries*, though his editor at Zone Books, Ramona Nadaff exclaimed that "I still believe it is important to discuss your concept of 'trespassing' and its binding force in your thinking." He tried to oblige. By the end of 1997 it was all he could do to press himself into service to write one last paragraph for the preface.[12]

So it was that in the 1990s, the curves of history crossed. One charted the world's ascending interest in Hirschman's insights and recollections of the twentieth century as it came to a close. The other traced Hirschman's dwindling ability to summon them.

In all the recovery-mania of the post–Cold War era, one that took remarkably long to surface was the story of Varian Fry and the operation to rescue refugees from Marseilles. As long as the Fry story remained submerged, so did Albert's. Hirschman was no longer so resolutely tight-lipped about his role in the operation; it's that the rescue operation was overshadowed by the Holocaust. In 1982, Laurence Jarvik released a controversial documentary, *Who Shall Live and Who Shall Die*, exposing the United States government's and others' resistance to accepting Jews fleeing Nazi persecution. It dealt briefly with the Emergency Rescue Committee's work—and featured black-and-white footage of Hirschman's testimony to the director, filmed at his home in Princeton. The documentary chronicled the shameful Allied policies and was quickly swept up in a debate about whether more could have been done to save Jews. In this heady climate, whatever examples of saving that did take place were afterthoughts. Indeed, the footage of Hirschman, who spends the filming looking at a spot on the horizon as he recalled 1940, has him putting a damper on the ERC effort: "One tragic aspect of the story was that a great deal was accomplished and we were all very proud of what we accomplished. Perhaps everyone was so proud that"—and at this point Hirschman looked into the questioner's eyes—"they forgot about the others. Looking back on this episode, that is perhaps, to some extent, the price that we paid for getting out these few." While Hirschman was fond of unintended consequences, this self-incriminating twist—or at least what we are shown by a director keen to expose the do-nothing stance of others—merged the details of his own risks into a broader canvas of horror and complicity.[13]

It was not until the United States Holocaust Memorial Council offered Fry posthumous official recognition in 1991 that the story began to circulate. By then, the memory industry had shifted from revisionist histories of blame to a wave of public memorializing of survival. In 1996, the Yad Vashem Memorial in Jerusalem inducted Fry as one of the Righteous among the Nations. He was the first American. Varian Fry's *Surrender on Demand* was republished in 1997 with an epigram from Beamish. That year, Teri-When Damisch produced a documentary, *Marseille–New York: L'Etat de Piège ou La Filière Marseillaise*, which featured Hirschman playing the part of Fry, Beamish, and raconteur. The film also reunited Mary Jayne Gold with Beamish. Whatever reticence he felt about public speaking melted away as he clearly enjoyed acting. In 1999, an association was formed in Fry's memory in Marseilles; a French documentary filmmaker, Pierre Sauvage, also became involved in an organization called the Chambon Foundation. Hirschman's role in the rescue operation, however, remained shrouded. The Varian Fry Institute (a division of the Chambon Foundation) did not include him in its list of sacralized figures. It continues to leave him out, inexplicably. So does Paris's wall dedicated to those who helped save souls from the Holocaust, inexplicably. It was not until Sheila Isenberg's *A Hero of Our Own: The Story of Varian Fry* appeared in 2001 that the fullness of Hirschman's hidden, and hiding, hand was revealed. Her widely praised account had managed to incorporate results of her interviews with Hirschman before serious memory loss set in. The Jewish Museum hosted a remembrance of Fry's activities in December 1997. A corner of the Fry exhibition was reserved for Beamish's role. At the museum's conference, Hirschman was asked for the first time publicly to recall his part as the last living member of the Marseilles group. By that point, unfortunately, his memory was fading.[14]

There were other memorial occasions. In June 1997, the Harvard historian Charles Maier organized a symposium in honor of the fiftieth an-

Albert Hirschman as Beamish in Marseilles, 1997.

niversary of George C. Marshall's famous speech inaugurating the plan that would bear his name. It pulled together scholars and a few of the surviving planners, including some of Hirschman's oldest friends, such as Charlie Kindleberger, Lincoln Gordon, and Tom Schelling. Stanley Hoffmann was going to coordinate many of the formalities, which was to include an address by the secretary of state, Madeleine Albright. By then, Hirschman was struggling with himself. Though Maier had asked Hirschman to reflect on the European Recovery Program from his perspective as a staffer on the Federal Reserve Board, it was beyond Hirschman's capacity. Yearning to be there among old friends, however, he wrote a short reflection on the memoirs of two men with whom he worked at the time, Robert Marjolin and Richard Bissell. It was, by all accounts, a grand occasion; Hirschman was excited to have been included though he nodded through much of the proceedings.

In the meantime, tragedy struck. Lisa, by now a successful psychologist and path-breaking researcher on incest and the abuse of women in San Diego, was diagnosed with brain cancer in July 1998. She died, after extensive radiation therapy, less than a year later.

This was a death whose blows, for once, he could no longer ward off.

In the dimming of his cognitive abilities, he reached into forgotten recesses of his own life to prior losses. Lisa's dying summoned memories of his father's death at fifty-three of cancer, with children of similar ages as Lisa's Nick (seventeen, Albert's age when Carl died) and Alex (twenty-one). Over the summer of 1998, he wrote several letters to Lisa. One was about his father's commitment to brain tumor surgery. As Lisa underwent treatment and her father was powerless to intervene, he consulted some leading American surgeons, not about her cancer but about his father's surgical legacy. It motivated him to try to correct a record he felt his sister had warped. Ursula's memoir, which Albert had felt helpless to alter, passes over Carl's accomplishments and focused instead on his "career disappointments." "I myself do remember," Albert told Lisa, "that his accomplishments as a brain surgeon were important to him to the end."[15] Another letter dealt with Carl's hiding of Kuczynski in his clinic, once again Albert feeling a need to vindicate "the anti-Nazi activism my father engaged in just before his death!" As Lisa was dying (or maybe a little afterward) Albert wrote to Alex and Nick, reminding them of his own loss and his efforts to remember the redeemed, living memory of his father. The physical difficulties Hirschman was struggling with became entwined with long-gestating personal ones. When Lisa finally died after a valiant struggle, it would have been impossible to disentangle the sources of her father's grief. If he had been stoical at Carl's graveside, he was in shock beside Lisa's. He said nothing. A stricken Sarah and Katia tried to reach out and console a paralyzed, frozen husband and father. His only words anyone could recall were to Peter: "This is the worst thing that has ever happened to me," he managed to whisper.[16]

After that, Hirschman's deterioration was steady. When I interviewed him for this project during 2000–2001, after an hour's conversation in his office at the institute, he would labor to stay awake. Often, I would ask him if he wanted to continue. Part of him yearned to, but another could not. I would either drive him home after escorting him by the arm down the institute hallway, or take the pen from his hand and leave him sleeping in his desk chair.

Unable to write anymore or to read very much—one of his final books was Fernando Henrique Cardoso's memoirs, which he held with pride and admiration—he took to painting. Losing his command over words, he tried his hand at images. When his first grandson, Grégoire was about to get married in France, Katia suggested that her father paint something for the newlyweds. Off he went to the library for inspiration and came back with a book on Chagall. Did he recall that Chagall was among those saved in Marseilles? It is hard to imagine he did not, but we cannot know for sure. Either way, the image he chose suggests he was thinking less of heroic deeds than of one's passion. In this case, he fastened on the passion one feels for one's wife and of dreams a lifetime would bring together. He chose Chagall's captivating image of himself and his beloved Bella in their hometown of Vitebsk. Painted in 1915, Chagall's *The Birthday* coincided with his own, in Berlin. A romantic couple floats as if on a cloud, in the artist's dreamscape, kissing.[17]

Sailing into the Wind

Enough years have passed for Hirschman's life to enter the domain of memory, for his work and ideas to have lives of their own. Perhaps anticipating this—he was well aware that an occupational habit of intellectuals is to dream of everlasting life through one's ideas—he took great interest in reading about the uses (and sometimes the abuses) to which people put his concepts, especially if they were artful. He took special pleasure, for instance, when his friend, Arcadio Díaz Quiñones, adapted the exit, voice, and loyalty trilogy to explore how Cuban refugees cast their fates on makeshift rafts and overloaded motorboats to flee their island and revolution. Hirschman enjoyed that one less out of vanity than of appreciation for how a concept services understanding well beyond its original purpose. For others, Hirschman's was a legacy that gave courage along with inspiration. Approaching the fiftieth anniversary of the publication of *Strategy of Economic Development* in 2006, Jeffrey Sachs delivered a lecture in honor of Albert Hirschman in Mexico City. He confessed to his audience that as a crusader for the world's poorest, reading *Rhetoric of Reaction*—over and over—spared him feeling "alone in the world" as a reformer surrounded by naysayers. The next year, the Social Science Research Council in New York honored the Harvard economist Dani Rodrik as the first recipient of the Albert O. Hirschman Prize. Given in recognition of social scientists laboring in the Hirschman tradition of spanning disciplines, borders, theories, and audiences, the SSRC president, Craig Calhoun, imagined the award to honor a style of social science that had no better exemplar than Hirschman. These gestures, small and large, are signs that we no longer need him present to keep him alive. He lives on in other, and many, ways.

Albert Hirschman's odyssey of the twentieth century can be read—to borrow one of his own metaphors—as the epic of a mariner sailing ever into the wind. What he stood for, fought for, and wrote for was a proposition that humans are improvable creatures. Armed with an admixture of daring humility, they could act while being uncertain and embrace alternatives without losing sight of reality. But for much of Hirschman's century, this was heresy. There were those—from the Right and Left—who insisted that anything short of revolution either perpetuated misery or was an unromantic bore; and there were the legions of pessimists who warned that change was dangerously disordering and ran the risk of making things worse, unless entrusted to managerial savants with their multipurpose models. Faced with these headwinds, Hirschman tacked back and forth.

For many of his readers, it was often easier to see what he resisted, what he was writing or fighting against. It was not so easy to see his course. For this reason, many concluded, there was no Hirschman theory, no model. At best, he had a style, and he had style—of that there was never a doubt. Even the skeptics swooned over the prose, the illuminating metaphors, the memorable aphorisms. But a theory, a model that explains the world or one of its parts? At least in the contemporary coordinates of the human sciences, Hirschman's oeuvre seemed to fall short. In the fall of 1992, a group of MIT faculty, led by Bishwapriya Sanyal and Donald A. Schön, started a year-long Hirschman seminar using his work to reflect on the experience of economic development. It would include his former student, Judith Tendler, and friends such as Emma Rothschild, as well as sociologists such as Michael Piore and Charles Sabel and the economists Paul Krugman and Robert Picciotto. Hirschman even made an appearance and would share extensive notes on the drafts of essays that eventually appeared as *Rethinking the Development Experience: Essays Provoked by the World of Albert O. Hirschman* (1994). How does a man's work move intellectual fields forward? the volume asks. It was not a simple question, and the answers, offered in personal testimony, were hardly uniform. After one of the seminars, the group went out to a Cambodian restaurant for dinner. Krugman doubted aloud whether Hirschman had been so influential on economic theory—sparking a riposte from Amartya Sen. A serious but friendly, if inconclusive, row ensued. How *has* Hirschman shaped theories in social science? Much depends, of course, on one's definitions, and the dispute, by necessity, goes on.

Hirschman was not the first to wonder whether intellectuals were overdoing it, or at least missing some possibilities in the *rage de vouloir conclure*, as Gustave Flaubert bemoaned the affection for elegant models that explain little. A child of 1933 and that year's wreckage, Hirschman winced at grandiose proclamations and elaborate certainties like a reflex. But it would be a mistake to confuse this with lack of ambition; his was a quest that would not easily conform to the increasingly professional boundaries and norms of the academy. What he wanted was not so much a theory with predictive powers, but a way to think about societies and economies, beginning with the premise that living in the world means we cannot step out of time to divine universal laws of human motion severed from the day-to-day banalities and mysteries of existence. The intellectual is as much a creature of the world as his or her subject—and so too are his or her concepts, which are limited and liberated by the context from which they emerge. It is for this reason that experience of real life, appreciating one's place in history, was such a wellspring for Hirschman, as it was for his inspiration, Montaigne, whose last essay was "On Experience." Life, as Montaigne reminds us, is "a purpose unto itself." The excursions into real life—as struggler against European fascisms, soldier in the US Army, deep insider of the Marshall Plan, advisor to investors in Colombia, and consultant to global foundations and bankers—were never digressions for Hirschman; they were built into the purpose of observing the world to derive greater insight, and from insights invent concepts that could in turn be tested, molded, refashioned, and even discarded by the course of time.

These were the pendular swings from a contemplative life to a life of action and back again—pendular because they were codependent.

Underneath it all, Hirschman had a sense that human actions and choices were the engine of social possibilities and that any history of possible futures—is this not the script for grand theory?—starts its life as an observation of the human by another human. All categories that flowed therefrom had to be flexible and adaptive, open to the cunning of unintended consequences and side effects that were often more momentous than the original purpose. Such was the personal and moral stuff of which his vision was made, bold enough for him to dream of a unified social science. There is no shortage of ambition here. One only has to consider the concepts and keywords that he juxtaposed: the individual and the collective, private and public, markets and politics, wealth and virtue, equilibrium and disequilibrium, choice and constraint, simplicity and complexity. Fertile oppositions were not just for fun—though if there were possibilities for wordplay, Hirschman did not resist. They were meant to show how each side required the other. In this sense, the art of sailing into the wind was all about gaining speed from an oppositional force and turning it to one's advantage.

If biography is the art of the singular to illuminate a pattern, Hirschman's odyssey can be read as a journey with no particular end, the life of an idealist with no utopia because he believed that the voyage of life itself yielded enough lessons to change who we are and what we aspire to be; to require and stay on course toward an abstract destination threatened to deprive the journey of its richest possibilities. Odysseus' quest was a homecoming to Ithaca; by contrast, Hirschman's course had no destination. Once uprooted from family, home, and tradition, he became a man of our world set upon a global voyage, cherishing his origins without yearning for a return. Of course, there was a terrible, incalculable loss, and Hirschman would guard the trauma close. Yet, from the violence committed to kin and friends could come release and hope for a more humane future.

Age and ailment, however, soon withdrew Hirschman from the world, forcing him to gaze in silence from a wheelchair into the backyard where trees give life after their apparent winter death. It was in the winter of 2011 that Sarah, who comforted and accompanied an increasingly spectral husband through his decline, was diagnosed with cancer. By then, the disease had spread. For all her determination to be there until his end, the cancer would not be stopped. One January night, Katia, who had flown in from France, climbed into the hospital bed and embraced her dying mother. She sang quietly as Sarah slipped away from an afflicted body. The next morning, Katia returned to the house on Newlin Road to tell her father that Sarah was dead. Albert's head jerked up and for a moment his body shook before settling back into his remove. Alain flew from France, Peter Gourevitch and the grandchildren all arrived in time for Sarah's burial, and they made plans to move Albert to an assisted living facility outside Princeton.

It is from Albert's room at the Greenwood House that I have just returned. Almost a century after his birth, Albert's is now a life after a life. He does not communicate, and one cannot know for sure what he sees or hears. But he can feel, of that I am sure. He clasps my hand, unrecognizing but with surprising strength, and brings it to his forehead for me to caress, his eyes closed, and I tell him, "Thank you, Albert."

NOTES

ABBREVIATIONS

AOH	Albert O. Hirschman
AOHP	Albert O. Hirschman Papers, Seeley G. Mudd Manuscript Library, Princeton University, Princeton, NJ
CH	Carl Hirschmann
EC	Eugenio Colorni
EH	Eva Hirschmann
HH	Hedwig Hirschmann
KS	Katia Salomon
KSPP	Katia Salomon Personal Papers
OH	Oscar Hirschmann
PP	Private papers currently in possession of Katia Salomon
RAC	Rockefeller Foundation Archive, Rockefeller Archive Center, Sleepy Hollow, NY
RFD	Review of Foreign Developments, International Sections, Division of Research and Statistics, Federal Reserve Board, Board of Governors of the Federal Reserve System, Washington, DC
SH	Sarah Hirschman
SSRC	Social Science Research Council Archives, RAC
UH	Ursula Hirschmann
WBGA	World Bank Group Archive, Washington DC

All interviews were conducted by the author unless otherwise indicated; transcripts are in author's possession. Unless otherwise noted, all translations were by the author. Hirschman's diaries are in the possession of Katia Salomon.

INTRODUCTION: Mots Justes

1. Edward Said, "Reflections on Exile," in *Reflections on Exile and Other Essays* (Cambridge MA: Harvard University Press, 2000), pp. 173–186.

2. Lepenies' speech at Freien Universität, 3 Dec. 1988, box 1, folder 13, AOHP.

3. Eva Montefiore, interview, 16 Oct. 2006.

4. AOH to UH, June 1932, PP.

5. "Conversation with Clifford Geertz and Albert Hirschman on 'The Hungry, Crowded, Competitive World,'" IAS, 27 Jan. 1976, box 10, folder 3, AOHP.

6. AOH to Augusto Monterroso, 21 Sept. 1971, PP.

7. AOH to Daniel Bell, 15 Sept. 1993, box 76, folder 1, AOHP.

8. AOH to SH, 1 Mar. 1944, PP.

9. Quentin Skinner to AOH, 6 Oct. 1981, box 11, folder 8, AOHP.

10. Louis Menand, "Lives of Others," *New Yorker*, 6 Aug. 2007, p. 74.

11. Hermione Lee, *Virginia Woolf's Nose: Essays on Biography* (Princeton: Princeton University Press, 2005), p. 4.

CHAPTER 1: The Garden

1. CH to HH, June 1916, PP; see AOH, interview, 3 Nov. 2007.

2. Peter Gay, *My German Question: Growing up in Nazi Germany* (New Haven: Yale University Press, 1998), p. 13.

3. EH to author, 22 Dec. 2007, in author's possession.

4. Eric Weitz, *Weimar Germany: Promise and Tragedy* (Princeton: Princeton University Press, 2007).

5. Alexandra Richie provides an invaluable portrait in *Faust's Metropolis: A History of Berlin* (New York: Carrol and Graf, 1998).

6. Deborah Hertz, *How Jews Became German: The History of Conversion and Assimilation in Berlin* (New Haven: Yale University Press, 2007).

7. CH to HH, 12 June 1930, PP.

8. Hannah Arendt, "Privileged Jews," *Jewish Social Studies* 8:3–30 (Jan. 1946), p. 6; Gershom Scholem, *From Berlin to Jerusalem: Memoirs of My Youth* (New York: Schocken Books, 1980), pp. 25–27.

9. Christopher Clark, *Iron Kingdom: The Rise and Downfall of Prussia, 1600–1947* (Cambridge MA: Harvard University Press, 2006), p. 424.

10. AOH, interview, 3 Nov. 2007; EH, interview, 29 Nov. 2006; AOH, interview by Pierre-Emmanuel Dauzat, n.d., box 15, folder 4, AOHP, p. 1 (hereafter, Dauzat in-

terview); AOH, interview by Henri Jacob Hempel, Princeton April 1984 and Berlin, June 1991, PP, p. 5 (hereafter, Hempel interview).

11. AOH to KS, 25 Oct. 1982 and 18 May 1983, KSPP.

12. Hempel interview, p. 7.

13. EH, interview, 29 Nov. 2006.

14. Ursula Hirschmann, *Noi senzapatria* (Milan: Il Mulino, 1993), pp. 79–80.

15. CH to HH, 26 June 1930, PP.

16. EH, interview, 12 Dec. 2007; Weitz, *Weimar Germany*, p. 55.

17. Hempel interview, p. 4; SH, interview, 11 Oct. 2005.

18. Hempel interview, p. 3.

19. UH, *Noi senzapatria*, p. 81.

20. EH to AOH, Oct. 1936, PP.

21. AOH, interview, 6 May 2002; SH, interview, 11 Oct. 2005.

22. AOH and SH, interview, 11 Oct. 2005.

23. Fritz Stern, *Five Germanys I Have Known* (New York: Farrar, Strauss, Giroux, 2006), p. 21.

24. AOH, "Four Reencounters," in *A Propensity to Self-Subversion* (Cambridge, MA: Harvard University Press, 1995), p. 105.

25. EH, interview, 29 Nov. 2007; UH, *Noi senzapatria*, 67–69.

26. AOH, interview, 6 May 2002; AOH to Joseph Bogen, n.d., PP.

27. Hempel interview, p. 2.

28. EH, interview, 12 Nov. 2007.

29. CH to HH, 17 June 1930 and 18 June 1930, PP.

30. CH to HH, 18 June 1930, PP.

31. AOH, interview, 6 May 2002.

32. CH to AOH, 14 July 1925, PP.

33. AOH, "My Father and Weltanschauung circa 1928," in *Propensity*, p. 111.

34. Hempel interview, p. 6.

35. EH to AOH, October 1936, PP.

36. Dauzat interview, p. 5; Hempel interview, p. 1.

37. CH to HH, 5 June 1930, PP.

38. AOH to parents, 1 Jan. 1930, PP.

39. AOH to UH, 27 June 1931, PP; AOH, "Four Reencounters," in *Propensity*, p. 106; SH, interview, 8 Aug. 2005.

40. EH to AOH, Oct. 1936, PP; AOH to EH, 1 Jan. 1929, PP.

41. AOH, interview, 6 May 2002; Hempel interview, p. 27–28; UH, *Noi senzapatria*, pp. 81–83.

42. AOH to UH, 27 June 1931, PP.

43. Hempel interview, p. 3.

44. Ibid., pp. 2–3.

45. Christopher Kobrak, *National Cultures and International Competition: The Experience of Schering AG, 1851–1950* (Cambridge: Cambridge University Press, 2002), pp. 96–97.

46. AOH to parents, 14 July 1931, PP.

47. AOH to parents, 24 July 1931, PP.

48. AOH, interview, 6 May 2002.

49. CH to HH, 26 June 1930, PP; UH, *Noi senzapatria*, p. 37.

50. EH, interview, 29 Nov. 2007; Hempel interview, p. 6.

51. EH, interview, 3 Nov. 2007; Konrad Katzenellenbogen, interview, 3 Jan. 2008.

52. UH, *Noi senzapatria*, pp. 73–74.

53. Ibid., p. 52.

CHAPTER 2: Berlin Is Burning

1. Box 76, folder 18, AOHP.

2. Hempel interview, p. 12.

3. Dauzat interview, p. 18.

4. AOH, *Der Geist, die Welt der Sittlichkeit und die Vernunft in Hegels "Phänomenologie des Geistes"—Interpretation eines Abschnittes aus der Phänomenologie*, PP; Hempel interview, pp. 11–13; AOH, "On Hegel, Imperialism, and Structural Stagnation," *Essays in Trespassing: Economics to Politics and Beyond* (New York: Cambridge University Press, 1981), pp. 167–175.

5. Dauzat interview, p. 7; AOH, interview, 6 July 2002.

6. Eric Weitz, *Weimar Germany: Promise and Tragedy* (Princeton: Princeton University Press, 2007), pp. 254–256.

7. AOH to parents, 20 June 1930, PP.

8. Hempel interview, p. 16

9. Dauzat interview, p. 5.

10. Hempel interview, p. 6.

11. AOH, "Four Reencounters," in *Propensity*, p. 109.

12. SH, interview, 11 Oct. 2007.

13. AOH, interview, 6 July 2002.

14. Hempel interview, 9.

15. Donna Harsch, *German Social Democracy and the Rise of Nazism* (Chapel Hill: University of North Carolina Press, 1993); William David Jones, *The Lost Debate: German Socialist Intellectuals and Totalitarianism* (Chicago: University of Illinois Press, 1999), p. 61.

16. Hempel interview, p. 10; Dauzat interview, p. 12. Ursula also recalls an intense meeting and debate in the working-class neighborhood of Alexanderplatz with a

mysterious character with the pseudonym Miles. Later she would learn that this Miles was Richard Löwenheim. Lenin quotation from "The International Situation and the Fundamental Tasks of the Communist International," *Report to the Second Congress of the Communist International*, 19 July 1920; the quotation is cited and paraphrased often in Hirschman's writings.

17. AOH, *Crossing Boundaries*, pp. 51–52; KS to author, 16 Dec. 2003, in author's possession.

18. AOH, *Crossing Boundaries*, p. 51.

19. Weitz, *Weimar Germany*, pp. 111–113.

20. KS to author, 16 Dec. 2003.

21. CH to HH, 17 June 1930, PP.

22. Hempel interview, p. 3; EH, interview, 14 Nov. 2007; Ursula Hirschmann, *Noi senzapatria* (Milan: Il Mulino, 1993), p. 75.

23. Hempel interview, p. 33.

24. Berlin Universität transcript, 22 Feb. 1933, PP.

25. Fritz Stern, *Five Germanys I Have Known* (New York: Farrar, Strauss, Giroux, 2006), p. 105.

26. UH, *Noi senzapatria*, p. 98.

27. Ibid., p. 100.

28. Dauzat interview, p. 35.

29. AOH, interview, 20 May 2002.

30. SH, interview, 11 Oct. 2007; AOH, *Crossing Boundaries*, p. 54.

31. Jürgen Kuczynksi, *Ein treuer Rebell. Memoiren, 1994–1997* (Berlin: Aufbau-Verlag, 1998), pp. 244–245.

32. AOH, "Four Reencounters," in *Propensity*, p. 103.

33. EH, interview, 12 and 14 Nov. 2007.

34. EH, interview, 14 Nov. 2007.

35. AOH, interview, 15 May 2002.

36. Transcript from Hirschman interview, Exile Film Project Records, VC-59/8, Manuscripts and Archives, Yale University Library, New Haven, CT., p. 2.

37. AOH to HH, 28 Mar. 1934.

38. AOH to HH, 8 Sept. 1933.

CHAPTER 3: Proving Hamlet Wrong

1. SH and AOH, interview, 25 July 2005.

2. AOH, "Four Reencounters," in *Propensity*, pp. 95–96.

3. Ursula Hirschmann, *Noi senzapatria* (Milan: Il Mulino, 1993), p. 109.

4. Sabine Offe, email message to author, 26 Aug. 2011, in author's possession; UH, *Noi senzapatria*, pp. 109 and 117; Hempel interview, p. 19.

5. AOH, "Four Reencounters," in *Propensity*, p. 106.

6. Eugen Weber, *The Hollow Years: France in the 1930s* (New York: W. W. Norton, 1994), pp. 34–36.

7. AOH, interview, 2 Oct. 2003; *Crossing Boundaries*, p. 57; "My Father and Weltanschaaung, circa 1928," in *Propensity*, pp. 113–114.

8. Marc Nouschi, *Histoire et pouvoire d'une Grande École: HEC* (Paris: R. Laffont, 1988), pp. 30–31.

9. "HEC" notes, n.d., PP.

10. AOH to HH, 21 Mar. 1935, PP.

11. Hempel interview, pp. 18–19; AOH to HH, 9 Apr. 1934 and 24 Apr. 1935, PP.

12. Undated letter from R. Arasse, Entr'aide universitaire international, PP.

13. AOH to HH, 3 May 1935; EH, interviews, 12 and 14 Nov. 2007; AOH, interview, 20 May 2002.

14. AOH to HH, 24 Apr. 1935, PP.

15. Ibid.

16. Ibid.; SH, interview, 16 July 2009.

17. Elisabeth Young-Bruehl, *Hannah Arendt: For Love of the World* (New Haven: Yale University Press, 1982), p. 118.

18. AOH to Grégoire Salomon, 15 Feb. 1989, PP.

19. Hempel interview, p. 18.

20. Transcript from Hirschman interview, Exile Film Project Records, VC-59/8, Manuscripts and Archives, Yale University Library, New Haven, CT., p. 3.

21. SH, interview, 23 Sept. 2007.

22. Hempel interview, pp. 21–22; Claudie Weill, "Le Bund russe à Paris, 1898–1940," *Archives juives* 2001/2, no. 34, pp. 30–42.

23. AOH, interviews, 21 Apr. 2002 and 2 Oct. 2003; UH, *Noi senzapatria*, pp. 117–120.

24. Hempel interview, p. 21.

25. Dauzat interview, p. 13.

26. Miles [Walter Löwenheim], *Socialism's New Beginning: A Manifesto from Underground Germany* (New York: League for Industrial Democracy, 1934), pp. 48, 90, 96; Lewis Edinger, *German Exile Politics: The Social Democratic Executive Committee in the Nazi Era* (Berkeley: University of California Press, 1956), pp. 83–90.

27. Dauzat interview, p. 26.

28. AOH to HH, 9 Apr. 1934, PP; *Crossing Boundaries*, p. 58.

29. UH, *Noi senzapatria*, pp. 113–116.

30. AOH, *Crossing Boundaries*, p. 60; ibid., pp. 123–125.

31. UH to Eugenio Colorni, 3 June 1935, PP.

32. EH, interview, 29 Nov. 2007.

33. AOH and SH interview, 11 Oct. 2005.

34. AOH to UH, 27 Mar. 1957, PP.

35. AOH to UH, n.d. [early 1970s], PP.

36. Appendix to Erich Auerbach, *Mimesis: The Representation of Reality in Western Literature* (Princeton: Princeton University Press, 2003), p. 573.

37. AOH, *Crossing Boundaries*, p. 58.

38. Weber, *Hollow Years*, p. 89.

39. Stanislao Pugliese, *Carlo Rosselli: Socialist Heretic and Antifascist Exile* (Cambridge, MA: Harvard University Press, 1999), pp. 122–123.

40. UH, *Noi senzapatria*, p. 136.

41. AOH to UH, n.d. [early 1970s], PP.

42. Hempel interview, p. 26; SH, interview, 1 Aug. 2005.

43. SH, interview, 1 Aug. 2005; Hempel interview, p. 26.

44. A.O. Hirschman, interview by Franco Ferraresi, *Corriere della Sera*, 22 Oct. 1993.

45. AOH, "Doubt and Antifascist Action in Italy, 1936–1938," in *Propensity*, pp. 118–119; SH, interview, 16 Aug. 2005.

46. Carlo Rosselli, *Liberal Socialism*, Ed. Nadia Urbinatti (Princeton: Princeton University Press, 1994).

CHAPTER 4: The Hour of Courage

1. AOH, interview, 21 Apr. 2002.

2. AOH, *Crossing Boundaries*, p. 59.

3. Lionel Robbins, *An Essay on the Nature and Significance of Economic Science* (London: Macmillan, 1932), p. 15.

4. Transcript from Hirschman interview, Exile Film Project Records, VC-59/8, Manuscripts and Archives, Yale University Library, New Haven, CT., p. 7.

5. Eugen Weber, *The Hollow Years: France in the 1930s* (New York: W. W. Norton, 1994), p. 46.

6. Hempel interview, p. 18.

7. AOH, interview, 21 Apr. 2002; AOH, *Crossing Boundaries*, p. 59.

8. Dauzat interview, p. 20.

9. "The Calendar of the London School of Economics and Political Science for the Forty-First Session, 1935–36." (London, 1935), pp. 108–109.

10. AOH, interview, 21 Apr. 2002; letter of recommendation from P. Barrett Whale, reader in economics at the University of London, 27 May 1936, PP.

11. Dauzat interview, p. 22.

12. Hempel interview, p. 23.

13. Ibid.

14. Stanislao Pugliese, *Carlo Rosselli: Socialist Heretic and Antifascist Exile* (Cambridge, MA: Harvard University Press, 1999), pp. 202–203.

15. Eugenio Colorni, *La malattia della metafisica: Scritti filosofici e autobiografici* (Torino: Einaudi, 2009), p. 41.

16. Dauzat interview, p. 42.

17. Ibid., p. 22.

18. George Orwell, *Homage to Catalonia* (New York: Harcourt Inc., 1980), pp. 9–11.

19. Confidential File on Albert O Hirschman, FOIPA No. 1030518-000, Federal Bureau of Investigation, U.S. Department of Justice, Washington, DC.

20. AOH, interview, 20 May 2001.

21. Pugliese, *Carlo Rosselli*, pp. 205–206.

22. SH, interview, 16 Mar. 2006.

23. AOH, *Crossing Boundaries*, pp. 61–63.

24. AOH, interview, 20 May 2001.

25. Appendix to Sergio Bertelli, *Il gruppo: La formaziones del gruppo dirigente del PCIU, 1936–1948* (Milano: Rizzoli Editore, 1980), p. 78.

26. Hempel interview, p. 24; AOH to Ferdinando Briamonte, 25 Oct. 1978, PP.

27. UH to HH, 3 Dec. 1936, PP.

28. Ursula Hirschmann, *Noi senzapatria* (Milan: Il Mulino, 1993), pp. 147, 155.

29. Eugenio Colorni, *Scritti* (Florence: La Nuova Italia, 1975), pp. 337–38; translated version from Albert and Sarah on the occasion of the birth of their first grandson to Lisa Hirschman and Peter Gourevitch on January 1, 1978, PP.

30. O.A. Hirschmann, "Le Fecondità della Donna Italiana Secondo L'Età e il Numero dei Figli Avuti," AOHP.

31. O.A. Hirschmann, "Nota su due recent tavole di nuzialità della popolazione italiana," *Giornale degli Economisti* (January 1938), pp. 3–10.

32. "Io, detective dell'economia fascista," *Corriere della Sera*, 13 Nov. 1987, p. 3.

33. O.A. Hirschmann, "Les finances et l'économie italiennes: Situation actualle et perspectives," Société d'Etudes et d'Informations Economiques, 1 juin 1938; ibid.

34. AOH, interview, 20 May 2001; O. A. Hirschmann, "Il Franco Poincaré e la sua svalutazione," box 77, folder 1, AOHP.

35. AOH, interview by Franco Ferraresi, *Corriere della Sera*, 22 Oct. 1993.

36. SH, interview, 23 Aug. 2007.

37. AOH, interview, 29 July 2002; SH, interview, 1 Aug. 2005.

38. Michel de Montaigne, *The Complete Essays* (New York: Penguin, 1987), pp. 1132–1133.

39. AOH to UH, 23 Mar. 1966, PP.

40. Lawrence D. Kritzman, *The Fabulous Imagination: On Montaigne's Essays* (New York: Columbia University Press, 2009); Charles Rosen, "The Genius of Montaigne," *New York Review of Books*, 14 Feb. 2009; SH to author, 5 Sept. 2007.

41. AOH to Ferdinando Briamonte, 25 Oct. 1978, PP; Hempel interview, p. 25.

42. AOH, "Doubt and Antifascist Action in Italy, 1936–1938," in *Propensity*, pp. 118–119; AOH, Torino Talk, Oct. 1987, box 2, folder 3, AOHP.

43. EH, interview, 16 Oct. 2006.

44. AOH, interview, 20 May 2001.

45. EC to AOH, 3 Sept. 1938, PP; AOH, interview, 20 May 2001.

46. *New York Times*, 19 Sept. 1938.

47. Transcript from Hirschman interview, Exile Film Project Records, VC-59/8, Manuscripts and Archives, Yale University Library, New Haven, CT.

CHAPTER 5: Crossings

1. Edward Said, *Representations of the Intellectual* (New York: Vintage, 1994), pp. 48–52.

2. Eugen Weber, *The Hollow Years: France in the 1930s* (New York: W. W. Norton, 1994), pp. 102–103.

3. Vicki Caron, *Uneasy Asylum: France and the Jewish Refugee Crisis, 1933–1942* (Stanford: Stanford University Press, 1999), pp. 163–181; Timothy P. Maga, "Closing the Door: The French Government and Refugee Policy, 1933–1939," *French Historical Studies*, 12:3 (Spring 1982), p. 140.

4. AOH to HH, 23 May 1940, PP; EH, interview, 16 Oct. 2006.

5. EC to AOH, January 1939.

6. Hempel interview, p. 30.

7. AOH to Max Ascoli, 4 dic 1938, Ascoli Papers, Boston University.

8. AOH to Max Ascoli, 30 dic 1938, Ascoli Papers, Boston University.

9. OH to Max Ascoli, 25 May 1939, Ascoli Papers, Boston University.

10. AOH to UH, 21 Feb. 1940, PP.

11. Hempel interview, p. 30.

12. Ibid.

13. O.A. Hirschmann, *L'Activité economique*, 16–31 Janvier 1939, p. 354.

14. Transcript from Hirschman interview, Exile Film Project Records, VC-59/8, Manuscripts and Archives, Yale University Library, New Haven, CT.

15. AOH, interview, 15 Apr. 2002.

16. AOH to Ascoli, 4 dic 1938, Ascoli Papers, Boston University; O.A. Hirschmann, "Étude statistique sur la tendance du commerce extérieur vers l'équilibre et le bilatéralisme," 1939, box 77, folder 2, AOHP.

17. O.A. Hirschmann, "Memoire sur le control des changes en Italie," 1939, p. 82, box 56, folder 3, AOHP.

18. Ibid., pp. 66, 83.

19. AOH, interview, 28 May 2002.

20. Ibid.; Caron, *Uneasy Asylum*, pp. 163–181; Maga, "Closing the Door," p. 140.

21. AOH to HH, 18 Sept. 1939, PP.

22. AOH, interview, 28 May 2002.

23. AOH to UH, 14 Mar. 1940, PP.

24. Marc Bloch, *Strange Defeat: A Statement of Evidence Written in 1940* (New York: W.W. Norton, 1968), p. 8.

25. AOH to HH, 11 June 1940, PP.

26. AOH to HH, 23 May 1940, PP.

27. Hannah Diamond, *Fleeing Hitler: France, 1940* (Oxford: Oxford University Press, 2007), p. 83.

28. Michael R. Marrus and Robert O. Paxton, *Vichy France and the Jews* (Stanford: Stanford University Press, 1981).

29. AOH, "Four Reencounters," in *Propensity*, p. 97; Dauzat interview, p. 33.

30. AOH, interview, 28 May 2002.

31. AOH, "L'atmosphère à Merseille en 1940," Colloque Varian Fry, Mars 1999, PP; Andy Marino, *A Quiet American: The Secret War of Varian Fry* (New York: St Martin's, 1999), pp. 120–121.

32. Transcript from Hirschman interview, Exile Film Project Records, VC-59/8, Manuscripts and Archives, Yale University Library, New Haven, CT.

33. Mary Jayne Gold, *Crossroads Marseilles, 1940* (Garden City: Doubleday, 1980), p. 155.

34. Varian Fry, *Surrender on Demand* (Boulder, CO: Johnson Books, 1997), orig. pub. 1945, pp. 24–25.

35. Donald Carroll, "Escape from Vichy," *American Heritage* (June/July 1983), p. 88.

36. Lisa Fittko, *Escape through the Pyrenees* (Evanston, IL: Northwestern University Press, 1991), pp. 101, 117.

37. Transcript from Hirschman interview, Exile Film Project Records, VC-59/8, Manuscripts and Archives, Yale University Library, New Haven, CT.

38. Gold, *Crossroads*, p. 160.

39. Ibid., p. 158.

40. Fry, *Surrender*, pp. 46–47.

41. Gold, *Crossroads*, pp. 160–161.

42. Ibid., pp. 209–211.

43. Fry, *Surrender*, p. 89; Gold, *Crossroads*, p. 228.

44. Transcript from Hirschman interview, Exile Film Project Records, VHS-5/2, Manuscripts and Archives, Yale University Library, New Haven, CT; Fry, *Surrender*, p. 150.

45. Sheila Isenberg, *A Hero of Our Own: The Story of Varian Fry* (New York: Random House, 2001), pp. 152–153.

46. OH to Max Ascoli, 25 Sept. 1940, Ascoli Papers, Boston University.

47. Max Ascoli to OH, 27 Sept. 1940, Ascoli Papers, Boston University.

48. Max Ascoli to OH, 4 Oct. 1940, Ascoli Papers, Boston University.

49. OH to Max Ascoli, 2 Oct. 1940, Ascoli Papers, Boston University; Alexander Stevenson, interview, 17 Oct. 2003; Diaries, Alexander Makinsky, 1 Nov. 1940, RG 12.1, RAC.

50. Fry, *Surrender*, p. 151.

51. AOH Interview, 15 Apr. 2002.

52. Diaries, Alexander Makinsky, 1940–42, 26 Dec. 1940, RG 12-1, RAC.

53. Cited in www.varianfry.org/fittko_en.htm

54. AOH to HH, 8 Feb. 1941, PP.

55. AOH to HH, 13 Feb. 1941, PP.

CHAPTER 6: Of Guns and Butter

1. Andy Marino, *A Quiet American: The Secret War of Varian Fry* (New York: St Martin's, 1999), p. 257.

2. "Fellowship Card, Otto Albert Hirschmann," Series US-HSS, RAC.

3. AOH, interview, 15 Apr. and 11 June 2002.

4. AOH to UH, 23 Mar. 1941, PP.

5. AOH and SH interview, 11 Oct. 2005; Transcript from Hirschman interview, Exile Film Project Records, VC-60/1-2, Manuscripts and Archives, Yale University Library, New Haven, CT.

6. Ezra Suleiman to SH, n.d., box 20, folder 5, AOHP.

7. "Fellowship Card, Otto Albert Hirschmann," Series US-HSS, RAC.

8. AOH to UH, 21 July 1941, PP.

9. UH to AOH, 3 July 1941, PP.

10. AOH and SH interview, 11 Oct. 2005.

11. Transcript from Hirschman interview, Exile Film Project Records, VC-60/4, Manuscripts and Archives, Yale University Library, New Haven, CT.

12. AOH to UH, 21 July 1941, PP.

13. AOH to SH, 21 May 1941, PP.

14. SH, interview, 14 Apr. 2006.

15. AOH to SH, May 1941, PP; AOH and SH, interview, 19 Apr. 2005.

16. AOH to UH, 3 Nov. 1941, PP.

17. AOH to UH, 2 Sept. and 5 Oct. 1941.

18. AOH to UH, 21 July 1941, PP; AOH and SH interview, 11 Oct. 2005.

19. AOH to SH, May 1941, PP.

20. AOH to UH, 21 July 1941, PP.

21. AOH, interview, 11 Mar. 2002.

22. Transcript from Hirschman interview, Exile Film Project Records, VC-60/5-6, Manuscripts and Archives, Yale University Library, New Haven, CT.

23. J.B. Condliffe, *The Reconstruction of World Trade: A Survey of International Economic Relations* (New York: W.W. Norton, 1940).

24. AOH, interview, 11 June 2002; AOH to UH, 21 July and 9 Aug. 1941, PP; AOH, "On Measures of Dispersion for a Finite Distribution," *Journal of the American Statistical Association* (September 1943); AOH, "The Commodity Structure of World Trade," *Quarterly Journal of Economics* (August 1943).

25. Alexander Gerschenkron, *Bread and Democracy in Germany* (Ithaca: Cornell University Press, 1989).

26. AOH, interview, 11 June 2002; Sandy Stevenson interview, 17 Oct. 2003; Nicholas Davidoff, *The Fly Swatter: Portrait of an Exceptional Character* (New York: Vintage, 2002), pp. 121–125.

27. "Fellowship Card, Otto Albert Hirschmann," Series US-HSS, RAC.

28. AOH, interview, 11 June 2002.

29. Ibid.

30. SH, interview, 25 July 2005.

31. AOH Interview, 11 June 2002; AOH, *National Power and the Structure of Foreign Trade* (Berkeley, CA: University of California Press, 1980 ed.), p. 3.

32. Philip Buck, *Annals of the American Academy*, March 1946, p. 222; Henry Oliver, *Southern Economic Journal* (Jan. 1946), p. 304; Michael Florinski, *Political Science Quarterly* 61, p. 272.

33. AOH, "Beyond Asymmetry: Critical Notes on Myself as a Young Man and Some Other Old Friends," *International Organization* 32:1 (February 1978), pp. 45–50, republished in *Essays in Trespassing*, pp. 27–34.

34. AOH, "The Paternity of an Index," *American Economic Review* 54:5 (September 1964), p.762.

CHAPTER 7: The Last Battle

1. Fellowship Card, Otto Albert Hirschmann," Series US-HSS, RAC.

2. Ibid.

3. AOH to Adjutant General of the United States Army, 13 Feb. 1942, PP.

4. Fellowship Card, Otto Albert Hirschmann," Series US-HSS, RAC.

5. Ibid.

6. AOH, interview, 24 June 2002; Barry M. Katz, *Foreign Intelligence: Research and Analysis in the Office of Strategic Services, 1942–1945* (Cambridge MA: Harvard University Press), pp. 8–10.

7. AOH and SH interview, 11 Oct. 2005.

8. Ibid.

9. AOH to SH, 15 Feb. 1944.

10. Max Corvo, *The OSS in Italy, 1942–1945* (New York: Praeger, 1990), pp. 90–99; George C. Chalou, *The Secret War: The Office of Strategic Services in World War II* (Washington: National Archives and Records Administration, 1992), pp. 184–185.

11. AOH to SH, 18 Mar. 1944; Brown Notebook, n.d., PP.

12. Katz, *Foreign Intelligence*, pp. 23–24.

13. AOH to SH, 30 Mar. 1944, PP.

14. AOH to SH, 23 Apr. 1944, PP.

15. AOH to SH, 30 Mar. 1944, PP.

16. AOH to SH, 1 June 1944, PP.

17. AOH to SH, 11 May 1944, PP.

18. AOH to SH, 28 Feb. 1944, PP.

19. Eugenio Corloni, "Ventone Manifesto," in *Documents on the History of European Integration*, ed. Walter Lipgens (Berlin: Walter de Gruyter, 1985), vol. 1, p. 473.

20. John Pinder, "Spinelli and the Ventotene Manifesto," *The Federalist Debate* 14:3 (November 2001), pp. 12–14.

21. AOH to SH, 14 May 1944, PP.

22. Eugenio Colorni, "Character of the European Federation," in *Documents on the History of European Integration*, ed. Walter Lipgens (Berlin: Walter de Gruyter, 1985), vol. 1, p. 507; Klaus Voigt, "Ideas of the Italian Resistance on the Postwar Order in Europe," in ibid., pp. 463–465, quotation on p. 466.

23. Frank Rosengarten, *The Italian Anti-Fascist Press (1919–1945)* (Cleveland: Case Western University Press, 1968), p. 100.

24. AOH to SH, 22 and 25 June 1944, PP.

25. Hempel, p. 29; Brown Notebook, entry 23 June (n.yr.), PP.

26. Brown Notebook, n.d.; AOH to UH, 30 Apr. 1945 and 27 Aug. 1969, PP.

27. AOH to SH, 27 June 1944, PP.

28. AOH to SH, 10 July 1944, PP.

29. AOH to SH, 25 July 1944, PP.

30. AOH to SH, 9 Aug. 1944, PP.

31. AOH to SH, 12 Sept. 1944, PP.

32. AOH to SH, 5 Oct. 1944 and 22 May, 1944, PP.

33. AOH to SH, 14 Jan. 1945, PP.

34. AOH to SH, 21 Oct. 1944, PP.

35. AOH to SH, 30 Nov. 1944, PP.

36. AOH to SH, 15 Mar. 1945, PP.

37. AOH to SH, 7 Oct. 1945, PP.

38. AOH to SH, 21 and 26 Dec. 1944, PP.

39. AOH to SH, 12 Jan. 1945, PP.

40. Saba poem quoted in AOH, *Exit, Voice, and Loyalty*, p. 113, fn 10.

41. AOH, interview, 24 June 2002; SH to author, "Group in Siena," letter, n.d., in author's possession.

42. AOH to SH, 10 Feb. 1945, PP.

43. AOH to SH, 12 Apr. 1945, PP.

44. AOH to SH, 10 Feb. 1945, PP.

45. AOH to SH, 25 Feb. 1945, PP.

46. AOH to SH, 30 Sept. 1945, PP.

47. F.A. Hayek, *The Road to Serfdom* (Chicago: University of Chicago Press, 1994), p. 223.

48. Manlio Cancogni, "Historic Eulogy to the Black Market in Italy during the Twentieth Century" [in Italian], trans. AOH, box 69, folder 14, AOHP.

49. AOH to SH, 23 July, 1945, PP.

50. AOH to SH, 27 Mar. 1945, PP.

51. AOH to SH, 10 Mar. 1944, PP.

52. AOH to SH, 10 June and 9 Aug. 1944, PP.

53. AOH to SH, 13 Oct. 1944, PP.

54. AOH to SH, 19 Oct. 1944, PP.

55. AOH to SH, 15 Aug. 1945, PP.

56. AOH to SH, 4 Feb. 1945, PP.

57. AOH to SH, 15 and 19 Aug. 1945, PP.

58. AOH to SH, 21 Apr. 1945, PP.

59. AOH to SH, 28 Nov. 1945, PP.

60. AOH to SH, 5 May 1945; AOH to UH, 29 May 1945, PP.

61. AOH to SH, 12 Dec. 1945, PP.

62. AOH to UH, 27 May 1945, PP.

63. AOH to SH, 22 June and 12 Dec. 1945, PP.

64. See the superb Kerstin von Lingen, *Kesselring's Last Battle: War Crimes Trials and Cold War Politics, 1945–1960* (Lawrence, University of Kansas Press, 2009).

65. AOH to SH, 7 Oct. 1945, PP.

66. AOH to SH, 10 Oct. 1945, PP.

67. AOH to SH, 14 Oct. 1945, PP; Richard Raiber, *Anatomy of Perjury: Field Marshal Albert Kesselring, Via Rasella, and the Ginny Mission* (Newark DE: University of Delaware Press, 2008), chap. 5.

68. Virginia Lee Warren, "Dostler Sentenced to Die for Shooting of OSS Men," *New York Times*, 13 Oct. 1945, p. 1.

69. SH, interview, 14 Apr. 2006.

70. AOH to SH, 26 Oct. and 2 Nov. 1945, PP.

71. AOH to SH, 11 Dec. 1945, PP.

72. Ibid.

73. AOH to SH, n.d., PP.

CHAPTER 8: The Anthill

1. AOH to UH, 13 Jan. 1946, PP.

2. AOH to UH, 2 Feb. 1946, PP.

3. AOH to UH, 13 Jan. 1946, PP.

4. AOH to UH, 24 Apr. 1946, PP.

5. SH, interviews, 15 Sept. and 16 Aug. 2005.

6. AOH and SH interview, 11 Oct. 2005.

7. AOH to UH, 13 Oct. 1946, PP.

8. Ibid.

9. US National Archives, declassified FBI file, in author's possession.

10. AOH to UH, 14 June 1946, PP.

11. AOH, interview, 31 June 2002; AOH to UH, n.d. [fall 1946], PP.

12. "M. Schuman's Devaluation Paradox," RFD, 31 Dec. 1946, pp. 6–8.

13. AOH to UH, 22 Dec. 1946, PP.

14. "Higher interest rates and the credit shortage in France," RFD, 28 Jan. 1947, pp. 10–13; "Exchange Control in Italy," RFD, 11 Mar. 1947.

15. AOH, interview, 31 June 2002.

16. AOH to UH, 21 Apr. 1947, PP.

17. AOH, "France and Italy: Patterns of Reconstruction," *Federal Reserve Bulletin* 33:4 (April 1947), pp. 353–366.

18. AOH, "Public Finance, Money Markets, and Inflation in France," RFD, 29 July 1947.

19. Greg Behrman, *The Most Noble Adventure: The Marshall Plan and How Americans Helped Rebuild Europe* (New York: Free Press, 2007), p. 43.

20. "Trade Structure of the Marshall Plan Countries," RFD, 12 Aug. 1947, pp. 7–12; "Trade and Credit Arrangements Between the 'Marshall Plan Countries,'" RFD, 26 Aug. 1947, pp. 8–11.

21. "Italian Exchange Rate Policy," RFD, 16 Dec. 1947; AOH, "Inflation and Deflation in Italy," *American Economic Review* 38:4 (September 1948), pp. 598–606; "French Exports and the Franc," RFD, 23 Sept. 1947.

22. Richard Bissell, *Reflections of a Cold Warrior: From Yalta to the Bay of Pigs* (New Haven: Yale University Press, 1996), p. 38; AOH to UH, 24 Nov. 1947.

23. AOH, interview, 11 Mar. 2002.

24. AOH to Altiero Spinelli, 1 Aug. 1948, PP.

25. SH, interview, 16 Aug. 2005.

26. AOH to Altiero Spinelli, 1 Aug. 1948, PP.

27. "The OEEC 'Interim Report on the European Recovery Program'—A Summary," RFD, 8 Feb. 1949.

28. Bissell, *Reflections*, p. 54.

29. AOH to UH, 21 Dec. 1947, PP.

30. "Some Recent Developments in French Finance and Credit Policy," RFD, 19 Oct. 1948; "Credit Controls in the Postwar Economy of France," RFD, 8 Mar. 1949; AOH, "Postwar Credit Controls in France," *Federal Reserve Bulletin* (April 1949), pp. 1–13.

31. "Economic and Financial Conditions in Italy," RFD, 14 Dec. 1948.

32. "Inflation and Balance of Payments Deficit," RFD, 24 Aug. 1948; these thoughts induced him to write a more formal arithmetic model that would explain the multicausal relationship between devaluation and trade balances, "Devaluation and the Trade Balance: A Note," *The Review of Economics and Statistics* 31:1 (February 1949), pp. 50–53; Charles P. Kindleberger to AOH, box 65, folder 7, AOHP.

33. AOH, "Disinflation, Discrimination, and the Dollar Shortage," *American Economic Review* 38:5 (December 1948), pp. 886–892.

34. "International Aspects of a Recession," RFD, 7 June 1949; "The US Recession and the Dollar Position of the OEEC Countries," RFD, 27 Sept. 1949.

35. Alan S. Milward, *The Reconstruction of Postwar Europe, 1945–1951* (Berkeley: University of California Press, 1984), p. 278.

36. "The New Intra-European Payments Scheme," RFD, 19 July 1949.

37. AOH to UH, 22 Sept. 1947, PP.

38. Bissell, *Reflections*, p. 66; AOH, "Proposal for a European Monetary Authority," 2 Nov. 1949, Program Secretary, ECA, box 65, folder 7, AOHP; AOH, "Proposal for the Establishment of a European Monetary Authority," marked "Secret", box 65, folder 7, AOHP.

39. "European Payments Union—A Possible Basis for Agreement," RFD, 28 Feb. 1950; "Multilateralism and European Integration," RFD, 25 Apr. 1950.

40. Bissell, *Reflections*, p. 57.

41. AOH, "Approaches to Multilateralism and European Integration," Department of State, Foreign Service Institute, Washington DC, 1950, box 65, folder 9, AOHP.

42. Behrman, *Most Noble Adventure*, pp. 290–327.

43. AOH to UH, 17 Aug. 1949, PP.

44. SH, interview, 8 Aug. 2005; AOH to UH, 24 Feb. 1946, PP.

45. AOH, interview, 31 June 2002.

46. KS, interview, 11 May 2007.

47. SH, interview, 8 Aug. 2005.

48. Ibid.

49. David M. Oshinsky, *A Conspiracy So Immense: The World of Joe McCarthy* (New York: Oxford University press, 2005).

50. AOH to UH, 2 Feb. 1948; AOH to UH, n.d. [summer 1948], PP.

51. AOH, "Criteria, Timing, and Revision of US Economic Aid to Western Europe," 15 June 1951, box 66, folder 1, AOHP.

52. "The Problem of the Belgian Surplus in the EPU," RFD, 25 Sept. 1951.

53. AOH to UH, 20 Jan. 1951, PP.

54. AOH to Tommy Tomlinson, 13 July, 1951, box 65, folder 7, AOHP.

55. AOH to UH, n.d. [early 1951], PP.

56. AOH to HH, 10 Apr. 1951, PP.

57. AOH to UH, 22 Dec. 1951, PP; AOH, interview, 11 Mar. 2002.

58. Sandy Stevenson, interview, 17 Oct. 2003.

59. AOH, interview, 11 Mar. 2002.

60. SH, interview, 16 Aug. 2005.

61. Robert Triffin to AOH, 19 May 1952 and Howard Ellis to AOH, 12 May 1952, box 39, folder 1, AOHP.

62. Brown Notebook, n.d., PP.

CHAPTER 9: The Biography of a File

1. Confidential File on Albert O Hirschman, FOIPA No. 1030518-000, Federal Bureau of Investigation, U.S. Department of Justice, Washington, DC. Unless otherwise noted, all quotations are from this document.

2. "Fellowship Card, Otto Albert Hirschmann," Series US-HSS, RAC.

3. AOH to UH, 13 Jan. 1946, PP.

4. Dauzat interview, p. 49.

CHAPTER 10: Colombia Years

1. Richard Bird, interview, 5 Aug. 2009.

2. Cited in Michele Alacevich, *The Political Economy of the World Bank: The Early Years* (Stanford: SUP, 2009), p. 13; Amy L.S. Staples, *The Birth of Development: How the World Bank, Food and Agriculture Organization, and the World Health Organization Changed the World, 1945-1965* (Kent, OH: Kent State University Press, 2006), pp. 24–30; Mary S. Morgan, "'On a Mission' with Mutable Mobiles," Work-

ing Paper on the Nature of Evidence, London School of Economics, August 2008, pp. 5–6.

3. Edward Mason and Robert E. Asher, *The World Bank Since Bretton Woods* (Washington: Brookings Institution, 1973), pp. 161–163.

4. On Currie, see Roger J. Sandilands, *The Life and Political Economy of Lauchlin Currie* (Durham NC: Duke University Press, 1990); Federal Bureau of Investigation, Investigative Report 101-3616, US National Archives.

5. *The Basis of a Development Program for Colombia*, Report of a Mission Headed by Lauchlin Currie (Washington DC: IBRD, 1950).

6. Eugene R. Black to President Ospina Pérez, 27 July 1950, Currie Mission Files, WBGA. There had been some grumbling. One bank official wondered whether the mission hadn't missed some rather obvious complexities. Foremost among them were the effects of the civil war, which threatened to undermine the whole effort, or at the very least shake the confidence in the figures upon which the grand plan was premised. Others worried about more technical matters, like the scant attention to the private sector and investors inside Colombia. Was the private sector really so inert and deprived of funds? There were doubts about the balance of payments estimates—the very concern that had motivated so much of Hirschman's dissenting reports about Europe's "dollar gap" when he was working for the Fed. Currie himself worried in a confidential letter to the vice president of the World Bank that the civil strife in the country posed awkward questions about the prospects of good government, without adding that in large swaths of the country there was no government at all. But in public, and in light of the haste with which the chief sought to publish his report, little room was made for doubt or alternatives. When some Colombians sought input on the report, Currie batted them down; any study could be indefinite. Under the circumstances "I must be content in doing the best job I can in the limited time available." Lauchlin Currie to Juan de Dios Ceballos, 14 Feb. 1950 and Currie to Robert Garner, 5 Sept. 1950, Currie Mission Files, WBGA.

7. *Development Program for Colombia*, pp. 356 and 593.

8. AOH to Emilio Toro, 11 Apr. 1952, box 39, folder,1, AOHP; Alacevich, *Political Economy*, p. 53.

9. AOH to Burke Knapp, 18 Sept. 1952, box 39, folder 1, AOHP.

10. Sandilands, *Lauchlin Currie*, p. 175; Alacevich, *Political Economy*, p. 56.

11. AOH, "The Effects of Industrialization on the Markets of Industrial Countries," in *The Progress of Underdeveloped Areas*, ed. Bert Hoselitz (Chicago: University of Chicago Press, 1952), pp. 270–283; AOH, interview, 11 Mar. 2002.

12. Alexander Gerschenkron, "Economic Backwardness in Historical Perspective," in ibid.

13. SH to Helen Jaszi, Saturday, 1952, PP.

14. SH to Helen Jaszi, 11 Aug. 1952, PP.

15. AOH, "Lisa's Questions," p. 6, PP.

16. Howard Ellis to AOH, 12 May 1952, box 39, folder 1, AOHP.

17. Alacevich, *Political Economy*, p. 85.

18. Informe Anual del Consejo Nacional, p. 37; Roger Sandilands to Osvaldo Feinstein, 9 Mar. 2003, in author's possession.

19. Jacques Torfs, *The Basis of a Development Program for Colombia*, Appendix A, National Accounts (Washington DC: IBRD, n.d.); "Informe Annual del Consejo Nacional de Planificación" (1953), p. 6, Banco de la Republica Archives; AOH, interview, 24 Mar. 2002; Burke Knapp to AOH, 7 Nov. 1952, box 39, folder 1, AOHP; AOH to Burke Knapp, 1 May 1954, box 39, folder 1, AOHP; "Conversation with Clifford Geertz and Albert Hirschman," IAS, 27 Jan. 1976, box 10, folder 3, AOHP; AOH, "A Dissenter's Confession: The Strategy of Economic Development Revisited," in *Rival Views of the Market and Other Recent Essays* (New York: Viking, 1986), pp. 90–91.

20. AOH to Howard Ellis, 18 Apr. 1953, box 39, folder 1, AOHP.

21. AOH to Burke Knapp, 20 Nov. 1952, box 39, folder 1, AOHP.

22. Research Project, "Case Studies of Instances of Successful Economic Development in Colombia," 8 Mar. 1954, box 36, folder 4, AOHP.

23. AOH to Knapp, 16 Sept. 1953, box 39, folder 1, AOHP.

24. AOH, interview, 11 Mar. 2002.

25. Memo, 15 May 1954, box 39, folder 3, AOHP.

26. Burke Knapp to AOH, 10 May 1954, box 39, folder 1, AOHP; SH to Helen Jaszi, 14 Apr. 1954, PP; SH, interview, 8 Aug. 2005.

27. AOH to George Jaszi, n.d., PP.

28. AOH to UH, 2 Sept. 1953 and SH to Helen Jaszi, 4 Feb. 1954, PP.

29. SH to Helen Jaszi, 5 July 1954, PP.

30. "The Market for Pulp and Paper in Colombia," 15 June 1956, box 37, folder 2, AOHP.

31. "Colombia: Highlights of a Developing Economy"; "Present and Prospective Fiscal Position of the Empresas Municipales de Cali," box 36, folder 6, AOHP.

32. Dauzat interview, p. 17; SH to Helen Jaszi, 12 Jan. 1956, PP.

33. AOH to George Jaszi, n.d., PP; 4 Feb. 1956 Entry by Montague Yudelman, folder 282, box 43, series 200, RG 2, RAC.

34. "Nicaragua Notes," Sunday, 28 Mar., box 36, folder 4, AOHP; SH to Helen Jaszi, 15 May 1955, PP.

35. SH to Helen Jaszi, Saturday, 1952, PP.

36. KS to author, 5 Oct. 2008, in author's possession.

37. Dauzat interview, p. 12.

38. Lore Friedman, interview, 6 July 2004; SH to Helen Jaszi, 3 Sept. 1953, PP.

39. SH, interview, 3 Mar. 2004.

40. Lore Friedman, interview, 6 July 2004.

41. SH, interview, 8 Aug. 2005.

42. HH to AOH, 17 Sept. 1956, PP.

43. AOH to George Jaszi, n.d., 1954, PP.

44. Nils Gilman, *Mandarins of the Future: Modernization Theory in Cold War America* (Baltimore: Johns Hopkins University Press, 2003), pp. 161–165.

45. "Economics and Investment Planning," in *Investment Criteria and Economic Growth* mimeo (Cambridge, MA: Center for International Studies, M.I.T., 1954); published by Asia Publishing House, New York, 1961, p. 41.

46. "Economic Policy in Underdeveloped Countries," *Economic Development and Cultural Change* 5:4 (July 1957), pp. 362–370.

47. SH to Helen Jaszi, 14 Feb. 1956, PP.

CHAPTER 11: Following My Truth

1. SH to Helen Jaszi, 9 Nov. 1952, PP; KS to author, 21 Aug. 2007, in author's possession.

2. AOH, interview, 6 July 2002, Lloyd Reynolds to AOH, 13 July 1956, and Tom Schelling to AOH, 6 Aug. 1956, Filename: Yale 1956–58, box 83, AOHP.

3. AOH to Lloyd Reynolds, 7 Jan. 1981, box 11, folder 8, AOHP.

4. Nils Gilman, *Mandarins of the Future: Modernization Theory in Cold War America* (Baltimore: Johns Hopkins University Press, 2003), pp. 190–197.

5. AOH, interview, 6 July 2002; Thomas Schelling, interview, 2 Oct. 2008.

6. Norman S. Buchanan to AOH, 28 Mar. 1957, folder 5196, box 607, series 200, RG 1.2, RAC; AOH to UH, 7 Apr. 1957.

7. "Some Suggestions for Social Science and Economic Research in Latin America," May 1958, folder 120, box 15, series 300, RG 1.2, RAC; "Albert O. Hirschman Diary, Brazil and Colombia, Aug. 12–Sept 12, 1957," folder 336, box 46, series 300, RG 6 (1957), RAC.

8. Alexandre Kafka, "The Theoretical Interpretation of Latin American Economic Development," in *Economic development for Latin America*, ed. Howard Ellis (New York: Macmillan, 1961), p. 1; AOH, interview 15 July 2002.

9. Albert O Hirschman Diary, Brazil and Colombia, folder 336, box 46, series 300, RG 6 (1957), RAC.

10. AOH to UH, 12 Jan. 1957, PP.

11. SH, interview, 16 Aug. 2005.

12. AOH to UH, 12 Jan. 1957, PP; Some basic principles of *Strategy* can be found in "Investment Policies and 'Dualism' in Underdeveloped Countries," *American Economic Review* 47:5 (September 1957), pp. 550–570.

13. AOH to UH, 27 Jan. 1958, PP.

14. "Outline of a Proposed Study, 1957–1958," 1 Apr. 1957, folder 5196, box 607, series 200, RG 1.2, RAC.

15. Strategy Notes, file 1, box 80, folder, 16, AOHP; Burke, *Letter to the Sheriffs of Bristol*, in *The Works of the Right Honourable Edmund Burke* (London: Henry G. Bohn), vol. 2, p. 29.

16. Strategy Notes, file 2, box 80, folder 16, AOHP.

17. Ibid.

18. Ibid.

19. Ibid.

20. Ibid.

21. Quotes from "For Lisa, 6 June 1967," PP.

22. AOH to UH, 19 Oct. 1957, PP.

23. AOH, "Three Basic Ideas from My Book to Be Developed," box 8, folder 13, AOHP.

24. AOH, "The Economics of Development Planning," Institute on ICA Development Programming, 15 May 1959, Strategy Notes, file 2, box 80, folder 16, AOHP. This paper would later appear as the preface of the 1961 paperback edition.

25. AOH to UH, 23 Aug. 1958, PP.

26. AOH to J.R. Hicks, 12 Aug. 1959, *Strategy* Fan Mail, box 80, folder 14, AOHP.

27. Roy Harrod to AOH, 8 June 1963, *Strategy* Fan Mail, box 80, folder 14, AOHP.

28. Hollis B. Chenery, *American Economic Review* 49:5 (December 1959), pp. 1063–1065.

29. AOH to Coos Polak, 20 Aug. 1959, *Strategy* Fan Mail, box 80, folder 14, AOHP; AOH to Hollis Chenery, 8 Aug. 1959, *Strategy* Corresp., box 80, folder 12, AOHP.

30. Amartya Sen, *Economic Journal* 70 (September 1960), p. 590–594; Amartya Sen, interview, 3 June 2010.

31. C.P. Kindleberger, *Yale Review* 48 (Spring 1959), pp. 440–442.

32. AOH to Paul Streeten, 5 May 1958, *Strategy* Corresp., box 80, folder 12, AOHP.

CHAPTER 12: The Empirical Lantern

1. AOH to UH, 19 Oct. 1957, PP.

2. Kathryn Sikkink, *Ideas and Institutions: Developmentalism in Brazil and Argentina* (Ithaca: Cornell University Press, 1991); Peter Hall, ed., *The Political Power of Economic Ideas: Keynesianism across Nations* (Princeton: Princeton University Press, 1989).

3. AOH, "Some Suggestions for Social Science and Economic Research in Latin America," May 1958, folder 120, box 15, series 300, RG 1.2, RAC.

4. AOH to Leland C. De Vinney, 20 June 1958, folder 5196, box 607, series 200, RG 1.2, RAC.

5. AOH, "Some Suggestions for Social Science and Economic Research on Latin America," folder 120, box 15, series 300, RG 1.2, RAC; AOH to De Vinney, 23 July 1958, folder 5196, box 607, series 200, RG 1.2, RAC. I am grateful to conversations with Mary Morgan on these points. For more on "the field," see Henrika Kuklick and Robert E. Kohler, introduction to *Science in the Field, Osiris,* vol. 11 (1986), pp. 1–10.

6. Alex Abella, *Soldiers of Reason: The RAND Corporation and the Rise of the American Empire* (New York: Harcourt, 2008), p. 49; Saul Friedman, "The RAND Corporation and Our Policy Makers," *Atlantic* (September 1963), 63; Joseph Kraft, "RAND: Arsenal for Ideas," *Harper's Magazine* (July 1960), 74; Bruce L. R. Smith, *The Rand Corporation: Case Study of a Nonprofit Advisory Corporation* (Cambridge, Mass.: Harvard University Press, 1966), 125–126.

7. G. Marine, "'Think Factory' De Luxe – The Air Force's Project RAND," *Nation* 188 (1959), pp. 131–135.

8. Friedman, "The RAND Corporation," 63; Kraft, "RAND: Arsenal for Ideas," 74.

9. Charles Lindblom, memo to Hirschman, n.d., p. 8, box 68, folder 15, AOHP.

10. AOH and SH, interview, 1 Aug. 2005; "Economic Development, Research and Development, and Policy Making: Some Converging Views," in *Bias for Hope: Essays on Development and Latin America* (New Haven: Yale University Press, 1971), pp. 63–84.

11. Charles Lindblom, memo to Hirschman, n.d., box 68, folder 15, AOHP.

12. AOH, interview, 15 July 2002.

13. "Soviet Bloc–Latin American Economic Relations and United States Policy," Project RAND Research Memorandum, 28 Sept. 1959, box 80, folder 8, AOHP.

14. AOH to Altiero Spinelli, 31 Mar. 1962, PP.

15. AOH, "Second Thoughts on the Alliance for Progress," *The Reporter*, 25 May 1961, reprinted in *Bias for Hope*, pp. 175–182.

16. AOH, interview, 15 July 2002.

17. AOH to UH, 14 June 1958 and 23 Aug. 1958, PP.

18. AOH, interview, 29 July 2002.

19. Economics 1 Lecture on Economic Development, June 1968, box 71, folder 3, AOHP.

20. Colin Bradford, interview, 7 Aug. 2009.

21. Richard Bird, interview 5 Aug. 2009; Peter Kenen, interview 10 Mar. 2010; Judith Tendler, interview, 2 Aug. 2009.

22. Robert Picciotto to AOH, 7 Oct. 1985, AOH to Robert Picciotto, 14 Oct. 1985, box 59, folder 2, AOHP.

23. Dauzat interview.

24. "Staff Report, Annual Meeting of the Board, 1959," Century Fund Archives, New York.

25. Notes on "Draft Memorandum by AOH," Century Fund Archives.

26. AOH, interview, 22 July 2002.

27. AOH, "Memorandum on Twentieth Century Fund Study on Latin America," 24 Nov. 1959, box 69, folder 8, AOHP.

28. AOH, "Ideologies of Development in Latin America," in AOH (ed.), *Latin American Issues* (New York: Twentieth Century Fund, 1961), esp. p. 36.

29. *1960 Annual Report* (NY: Twentieth Century Fund, 1960), pp. 31–32.

30. "Some Notes by the Author," box 69, folder 3, AOHP.

31. Enrique Peñalosa to AOH, 29 Oct. 1962, box 68, folder 13, AOHP.

32. AOH and SH, interview, 1 Aug. 2005.

33. *1962 Annual Report* (NY: Twentieth Century Fund, 1962), p. 35.

34. Ibid.

35. Enrique Peñalosa to AOH, 3 Dec. 1962, box 68, folder 13, AOHP.

36. AOH, interview, 22 July 2002; Celso Furtado to AOH, 29 Jan. 1962, box 68, folder 13, AOHP.

37. Lincoln Gordon to AOH, 29 Jan. 1962, box 69, folder 1, AOHP.

38. "Fals Borda," n.d.; Carlos Lleras Restrepo, box 40, folder 7, AOHP.

39. "Albert O. Hirschman Diary, Brazil and Colombia, Aug. 12–Sept 12, 1957," folder 336, box 46, series 300, RG 6 (1957), RAC.

40. Fals-Borda, *El Hombre y La Tierra en Boyacá: Bases Socio-Históricas para una Reforma* Agraria (Bogotá: Documentos Cololmbianos, 1957); SH, email to author, 12 Sept. 2007.

41. "Brazil," box 39, folder 12, AOHP.

42. Clotario Blest, Eduardo Frei, Salvador Allende, interviews by AOH, box 40, folder 3, AOHP.

43. AOH, "Some Notes by the Author on Journeys Towards Progress," p. 4, box 69, folder 3, AOHP.

44. Lincoln Gordon to AOH, 3 Sept. 1963, box 68, folder 9, AOHP.

45. AOH, interview, 29 July 2002; AOH, "Obstacles to Development," box 10, folder 16, AOHP; "Obstacles to Development: A Classification and a Quasi-Vanishing Act," *Economic Development and Cultural Change* 13:2 (July 1965), pp. 385–393.

CHAPTER 13: Sing the Epic

1. F. Champion Ward to AOH, 6 Dec. 1963, General Correspondence, 1963, C-1453, Ford Foundation Archives, New York.

2. AOH to UH, 15 Mar. 1964, PP; Andrew W. Cordier to AOH, 23 Mar. 1964, PP.

3. AOH to UH, 20 June 1964, PP.

4. AOH to J. Burke Knapp, 14 Mar. 1963, Projects Evaluation—Professor Albert O. Hirschman—Vol. 1, Series No. 4225: Operations Policy Files, Projects and Studies—General 1946–68, WBGA–Hirschman Vol. 1; see also Michele Alacevich, "Albert O. Hirschman and Project Evaluation at the World Bank," unpublished ms. in author's possession.

5. Alexander Stevenson, interview, 17 Oct. 2003; Robert E. Asher to Robert D. Calkins, memorandum, 18 Apr. 1964, WBGA–Hirschman Vol. 1.

6. Alexander Stevenson to Escott Reid, office memorandum, 3 Mar. 1964, WBGA–Hirschman Vol. 1.

7. Robert F. Skillings to Syed S. Husain, 26 Feb. 1964, WBGA–Hirschman Vol. 1.

8. AOH to UH, 20 June 1964.

9. Francine R. Frankel, *India's Political Economy, 1947–1977: The Gradual Revolution* (Princeton: Princeton University Press, 1978), pp. 201–216.

10. "India DVC," DPO file, box 57, folder 2, AOHP.

11. AOH to UH, 10 July 1965, PP.

12. AOH, "Nigeria Notes," DPO file, box 57, folder 2, AOHP.

13. AOH, "Ideas-Miscellaneous," DPO file, box 57, folder 2, AOHP.

14. AOH, INDIA-DVC, p. 1, DPO file, box 57, folder 2, AOHP.

15. Ibid., p. 4.

16. AOH to UH, 4 Feb. 1965, PP.

17. AOH, "Ideas-Miscellaneous, DPO file, box 57, folder 2, AOHP.

18. AOH, "Uganda Notes," DPO file, box 57, folder 2, AOHP.

19. "AOH, "A Study of Selected World Bank Projects—Some Interim Observations," August 1965, WBGA–Hirschman Vol. 1.

20. Hans Adler, "Comments on Professor Hirschman," 22 Sept. 1965; Mario Piccagli to H.B. Ripman, 22 Sept. 1965, WBGA–Hirschman Vol. 1.

21. AOH to Kenneth Bohr, 18 Oct. 1965, WBGA–Hirschman Vol. 1.

22. AOH to UH, 29 Sept. 1966, PP.

23. AOH, "Thailand Notes," DPO file, box 57, folder 2, AOHP.

24. Ibid.; AOH to Walter Salant, 7 Feb. 1967, box 57, folder 1, AOHP.

25. AOH, review of W. A. Lewis, *Political Sciences Quarterly* 82:1 (March 1967); "Out of Phase," *Encounter* (September 1965), pp. 21–23.

26. Sandy Stevenson to AOH, 29 Dec. 1967, box 10, folder 4, AOHP.

27. Herman G. van der Tak to AOH, 20 Dec. 1966, box 57, folder 1, AOHP. Kenneth A. Bohr to AOH, 14 July 1966, AOH to Herman G. van der Tak, 27 Dec. 1966, Raihan Sharif, "Draft Check List of Points for Examining Project Design and Economic Evaluation of Projects," 17 July 1967, WBGA–Hirschman Vol. 2.

28. AOH to Tom Schelling, 27 July 1966, box 57, folder 15, AOHP.

29. Walter Salant to AOH, 1 June 1966, WBGA–Hirschman Vol. 2; Nathan Rosenberg to AOH, 19 Jan. 1967 and AOH to Walter Salant, 7 Feb. 1967, box 57, folder 1, AOHP.

30. Irving Kristol to AOH, 26 July 1966 and Goran Ohlin to OH, 13 Aug. 1966, box 57, folder 2, AOHP; Andrew Kamarck to AOH, 28 Oct. 1966, WBGA–Hirschman Vol. 2.

31. AOH to Hans Singer, 9 Dec. 1968, box 57, folder 14, AOHP.

32. Edward S. Mason and Robert E. Asher, *The World Bank since Bretton Woods* (Washington: Brookings Institution, 1973), p. 250.

33. AOH, interview, 4 Aug. 2002.

34. AOH to Theodore Moran, 2 Jan. 1973, box 68, folder 9, AOHP.

35. AOH to UH, 3 July 1966; Alain Salomon, interview, 13 Apr. 2010.

36. AOH to UH, 2 July and 3 Sept. 1967, PP.

37. Fernando Henrique Cardoso, interview, 6 July 2012.

38. AOH, "A Dissenter's Confession: The Strategy of Economic Development Revisted," in *Rival Views*, p. 104.

39. AOH, "The Political Economy of Import-Substituting Industrialization in Latin America," *Quarterly Journal of Economics* 82 (February 1968), pp. 2–32, reprinted in *Bias for Hope*, pp. 85–123; for more on fundamental vs. nonfundamental see AOH, "The Welfare State in Trouble," in *Rival Views*, pp. 163–168; Fernando Henrique Cardoso, interview, 6 July 2012.

40. Ibid.

41. "Underdevelopment, Obstacles to the Perception of Change, and Leadership," *Daedalus* 97:3 (Summer 1968), pp. 925–937.

42. Richard Bird, interview, 5 Aug. 2009.

43. AOH, "Foreign Aid: A Critique and a Proposal," *Princeton Essays in International Finance*, 69 (July 1969), reprinted in *Bias for Hope*, pp. 197–224; Sandy Stevenson to AOH, 29 Dec. 1967, box 10, folder 4, AOHP.

CHAPTER 14: The God Who Helped

1. AOH to Sam Bowles, 21 Jan. 1970, box 67, folder 1, AOHP.

2. AOH to UH, n.d. and 2 July 1967, PP.

3. Stanley Hoffmann, interview, 7 Nov. 2009.

4. Sam Bowles, interview, 7 Oct. 2008.

5. "Hirschman Receives Littauer Chair," *Harvard Crimson*, 31 Mar. 1967.

6. Richard Bird, interview, 5 Aug. 2009.

7. "Faculty Radicals," *Harvard Crimson*, 18 Nov. 1974.

8. Peter Gourevitch, interview, 21 July 2011.

9. AOH to UH, 14 Sept. 1965, PP.

10. AOH to UH, 2 Sept. 1966, PP.

11. SH, interview, 25 July 2005.

12. Parmar Inderjeet, *Foundations of the American Century: The Ford, Carnegie, and Rockefeller Foundations in the Rise of American Power* (New York: Columbia University Press, 2012), pp. 200–208; AOH to Kalman Silvert, 3 Dec. 1967, General Correspondence, GEN-72, Ford Foundation Archives.

13. "Competition vs Monopoly," November 1967, box 60, folder 5, AOHP.

14. Kenneth Arrow, interview, 6 Aug. 2009.

15. Alexander Gerschenkron to AOH, 9 Nov. 1966, box 60, folder 6, AOHP.

16. AOH to UH, 9 Dec. 1967, PP.

17. Kalman Silvert to AOH, 15 Jan. 1968, General Correspondence, GEN-72, Ford Foundation Archives.

18. AOH, *Exit, Voice, and Loyalty: Responses to Decline in Firms, Organizations, and States* (Cambridge MA: Harvard University Press, 1970), p. 105.

19. AOH to UH, 10 July and 8 Sept. 1968, PP; *Exit, Voice, and Loyalty*, p. 101.

20. AOH to UH, 20 Oct. 1968, PP.

21. David C. Atkinson, *In Theory and in Practice: Harvard's Center for International Affairs* (Cambridge MA: Center for International Affairs, 2007), p. 137.

22. Roger Rosenblatt, *Coming Apart: A Memoir of the Harvard Wars of 1969* (New York: Little Brown, 1997).

23. AOH to UH, 8 Sept. 1968, PP.

24. SH to UH, 21 Feb. 1969, PP.

25. SH to UH, 9 June 1969, PP.

26. Cited in *Exit, Voice, and Loyalty*, p. 27, fn. 7.

27. Ralph Nader to AOH, 7 Apr. 1969, box 60, folder 12, AOHP.

28. AOH to UH, 8 Sept. 1968, PP.

29. AOH, "Why EVS?" n.d., box 60, folder 2, AOHP.

30. AOH, "Introduction: Political Economics and Possibilism," *Bias for Hope*, p. 27.

31. Oscar Oszlak, interview, 4 June 2011.

32. AOH, "The Search for Paradigms as a Hindrance to Understanding," *World Politics* 22:3 (March 1970), pp. 329–343, reprinted in *Bias for Hope*, pp. 342–360, quotation from p. 342.

33. Notes on Payne and Womack, box 54, folder 9, AOHP; AOH, "Search for Paradigms."

34. Notes on Payne and Womack, box 54, folder 9, AOHP.

35. AOH to UH, 20 June 1964, PP.

36. Leon Festinger to AOH, 10 Apr. 1964, box 10, folder 16, AOHP; AOH, "Obstacles to Development: A Classification and a Quasi-Vanishing Act," *Economic*

Development and Cultural Change 13 (July 1965), pp. 385–393, reprinted in *Bias for Hope*, pp. 312–327.

37. Philip Zimbardo to AOH, 17 Feb. 1971, box 10, folder 9, AOHP; Philip Zimbardo, interview, 11 Aug. 2009.

38. *Exit, Voice, and Loyalty*, p. 126.

39. AOH, "Center Seminar," December 1968, box 60, folder 5, AOHP.

40. Stanford talk, January 1968, box 71, folder 3, AOHP.

41. *Exit, Voice, and Loyalty*, pp. 109–110.

42. AOH to Ernest May, 11 Dec. 1968, box 11, folder 13, AOHP.

43. AOH to UH, 22 July and 27 Aug. 1969, PP.

44. AOH to UH, 27 Aug. 1969, PP.

45. *Exit, Voice, and Loyalty*, pp. 78–79.

46. AOH, "Exit, Voice and Loyalty: Further Reflections and a Survey of Recent Contributions," *Social Science Information* 13 (1974), pp. 7–26, reprinted in *Essays in Trespassing*, pp. 213–235.

47. AOH, "Exit and Voice: An Expanding Sphere of Influence," in *Rival Views*, pp. 76–77.

48. Kenneth Boulding to Max Hall, 15 May 1969, box 11, folder 8, AOHP.

49. Ibid.

50. *Exit, Voice, and Loyalty*, pp. 76–79.

51. Joseph Reid Jr., review of *Exit, Voice, and Loyalty*, *Journal of Political Economy* (July–August 1973), pp. 1042–1045.

52. Roger Hansen, *American Political Science Review* 67 (September 1973), pp. 1110–1111.

53. AOH to Ken Galbraith, 1 Oct. 1971, box 58, folder 24, AOHP.

54. Gordon Tullock, review of *Exit, Voice, and Loyalty*, *Journal of Finance* 25:5 (December 1970), pp. 1194–1195.

55. Mancur Olson to AOH, 20 Feb. 1973, and AOH to Olson, 5 Mar. 1973, box 11, folder 8, AOHP.

56. William Olson to Ralph Richardson, 17 June 1973, A 78, box R1369, series 120, RG 2, RAC.

57. Brian Barry, "Review Article: Exit, Voice, and Loyalty," *British Journal of Political Science* 4:1 (January 1974), pp. 79–107.

58. David Riesman to Herbert Kelman and Everett Mendelsohn, 24 Mar. 1971, box 11, folder 8, AOHP.

59. *Exit, Voice, and Loyalty*, p. 103.

60. Henry Kissinger to AOH, 13 May 1970, box 58, folder 24, AOHP.

61. AOH to UH, n.d., PP.

62. Richard Bird, interview, 5 Aug. 2009; Tom Schelling to AOH, 6 Oct. 1970, box 9, folder 13, AOHP.

63. John Marshall Note, 15 July 1970, folder 528, box 91, series 900, RG 3.2, RAC.

64. AOH, "Bias notes," box 54, folder 9, AOHP; AOH, "Defense of Possibilism," in *Rival Views*, p. 171; Seymour Martin Lipset, "Some Social Requisites of Democracy: Economic Development and Political Legitimacy," *American Political Science Review* 53:1 (March 1959), pp. 69–105.

65. AOH, "Bias notes," box 54, folder 9, AOHP.

66. Ibid.

67. AOH, "Political Economics and Possibilism," in *Bias for Hope*, pp. 1–37.

CHAPTER 15: The Cold Monster

1. Colegio de Mexico 1971 file, box 24, folder 10, AOHP; Notebook Argentina 1971, box 24, folder 10, AOHP; AOH to Katia Solomon, 17 Dec. 1971, KSPP.

2. Daniel Rodgers, *The Age of Fracture* (Cambridge MA; Harvard University Press, 2011), p. 49.

3. Schelling to Hirschman, 18 July 1972, box 11, folder 7, AOHP.

4. AOH to KS, 20 May 1970 and 31 Dec. 1972, KSPP.

5. AOH to KS, 20 May 1972, KSPP; Stanley Hoffmann, interview, 7 Nov. 2009.

6. AOH to KS, 10 May 1972, KSPP.

7. Tom Schelling, interview, 2 Oct. 2008; Henry Rosovsky, interview, 9 Oct. 2008.

8. Herb Gintis, interview, 6 Aug. 2009; AOH, "Notes on Changing Tolerance" and "Lexicographic Ordering," box 54, folder 17, AOHP.

9. Michael Rothschild, interview, 21 Sept. 2009; AOH to KS, 1 Dec. 1971, KSPP.

10. Michael Rothschild, interview, 21 Sept. 2009.

11. AOH to KS, 24 Feb. 1973 and 28 Sept. 1973, KSPP.

12. AOH to Carl Kaysen, 3 Nov. 1971, box 10, folder 9, AOHP.

13. Income Distribution Speech, Oct. 1973, box 71, folder 3, AOHP.

14. AOH to Charles Lindblom, 27 Jan. 1975, box 11, folder 4, AOHP.

15. AOH, "The Changing Tolerance for Income Inequality in the Course of Economic Development," IAS, October 1972, box 71, folder 3, AOHP.

16. AOH to KS, 1 Dec. 1971, KSPP.

17. AOH, "Some Political and Economic Responses to Income Inequality," manuscript, February 1974 talk at Harvard, box 71, folder 3, AOHP.

18. Ibid.

19. AOH, "The Changing Tolerance for Income Inequality"; IAS, October 1972, box 71, folder 3, AOHP; Clifford Geertz to AOH, 8 Nov. 1973, box 54, folder 16, AOHP; Quentin Skinner to AOH, 6 Oct. 1981, box 11, folder 8, AOHP.

20. *Plural*, December 1972, box 54, folder 18, AOHP; Guillermo O'Donnell to AOH, 27 Feb. 1973, Box 58, folder 24, AOHP.

21. Fernando Henrique Cardoso, *The Accidental President of Brazil: A Memoir* (New York: Public Affairs, 2006), pp.112–113.

22. Fernando Henrique Cardoso, interview, 6 July 2012.

23. Louis Goodman, interview, 3 Oct. 2008.

24. AOH to KS, 28 Sept. 1973, KSPP.

25. AOH to Guillermo O'Donnell, 26 Sept. 1973, box 9, folder 17, AOHP; AOH, "Policymaking and Policy Analysis in Latin America—A Return Journey," 1974, in *Essays in Trespassing*, pp. 142–166.

26. AOH to KS, n.d. [May 1974], KSPP.

27. Louis Goodman, interview, 3 Oct. 2008.

28. AOH to Carl Kaysen, 19 Nov. and 17 Dec. 1971, box 10, folder 9, AOHP; AOH to KS, 5 Mar. 1972, KSPP; AOH to Fernando Henrique Cardoso, 13 Feb. 1973, box 9, folder 16, AOHP; AOH to KS, 24 Feb. 1973, KSPP.

29. Charles Lindblom to AOH, 27 Jan. 1975 (referring to a trip in 1973), box 11, folder 4, AOHP.

30. Douglas Chalmers to Fernando Henrique Cardoso and Julio Cotler, JCLAS (Joint Committee on Latin American Studies) Memorandum, 8 Mar. 1974, SSRC, RG Acc 1, box 102, folder 550, and Acc 2, box 290, folder 3515, RAC.

31. Guillermo O'Donnell and Philippe Schmitter, "Work Plan for the Study of Public Policy in Latin America," August 1974; AOH, JCLAS, 19 Sept. 1974, RG Acc 1, box 102, folder 552, RAC.

32. AOH to KS, 26 Sept. 1975, KSPP; loose notes, n.d., box 8, folder 20, AOHP; Fernando Henrique Cardoso, interview, 6 July 2012.

33. David Collier to AOH, 7 Oct. 1974, box 9, folder 17, AOHP; AOH to Philippe Schmitter, 15 Oct. 1974, box 9, folder 17, AOHP; Philippe Schmitter, interview, 5 July 2012; Louis Goodman, interview, 30 Oct. 2008.

34. AOH to Harry Woolf and Clifford Geertz, 6 June 1977, box 11, folder 8, AOHP.

35. Fernando Henrique Cardoso to Carl Kaysen, 27 Apr. 1976, Members Report, Box 8, 1975–76, The Shelby White and Leon Levy Archive Center, Institute for Advanced Study, Princeton, New Jersey.

36. Louis Goodman to David Collier, 21 Oct. 1975, SSRC, RG Acc 1, box 102, folder 552, RAC; O'Donnell to Collier, 3 Nov. 1975, SSRC, RG Acc 2, box 290, folder 3515, RAC.

37. AOH to Guillermo O'Donnell, 27 Oct. 1975, box 8, folder 19, AOHP. On micro-Marxism, see his "A Generalized Linkage Approach to Development, with Special Reference to Staples," in *Essays in Trespassing*, pp. 59–97.

38. Shlomo Avineri to AOH, 30 Apr. 1973, box 11, folder 2, AOHP. The quotes from Hirschman are from "On Hegel, Imperialism, and Structural Stagnation," 1976, in *Essays in Trespassing*, pp. 167–176.

39. "Reflexiones sobre las tendencias generals del cambio en el Estado Burocrático-autoritario" was printed as the first CEDES working paper in August 1975; AOH to Guillermo O'Donnell, 14 Oct. 1975; Guillermo O'Donnell to AOH, 7 Nov. 1975, box 8, folder 19, AOHP.

40. Working Group on the State and Public Policy, Progress Report on Phase I and Proposal for Phase II, February 1978, SSRC, RG Acc 1, box 102, folder 552, RAC; David Collier to AOH, Fernando Henrique Cardoso, and José Serra, 21 Jan. 1978, box 8, folder 19, AOHP.

41. Guillermo O'Donnell to AOH, 3 Nov. 1975, box 58, folder 24, AOHP.

42. AOH to David Collier, 26 Apr. 1976, box 8, folder 19, AOHP.

43. AOH, "Notes on LA Trip," box 9, folder 7, AOHP.

44. Cardoso, *Accidental President*, pp. 125–127; Fernando Henrique Cardoso, interview, 6 July 2012.

45. AOH to KS, 6 Dec. 1976, KSPP.

46. AOH to Gert Rosenthal, 16 Mar. 1977, box 9, folder 1, AOHP.

47. AOH, "The Turn to Authoritarianism in Latin America and the Search for its Economic Determinants," 1979, in *Essays in Trespassing*, p. 135.

48. AOH, "A Generalized Linkage Approach to Development, with Special Reference to Staples," 1977, in *Essays in Trespassing*, pp. 59–96.

49. Juan Gabriel Valdés, *Pinochet's Economists: The Chicago School in Chile* (New York: Cambridge University Press, 1995).

50. AOH, *Strategy*, p. 24; "The Turn to Authoritarianism," pp. 98–135.

51. AOH to McGeorge Bundy, 5 Feb. 1976, box 10, folder 3, AOHP.

52. "Conversation with Clifford Geertz and Albert Hirschman on 'The Hungry, Crowded, Competitive World,'" IAS, 27 Jan. 1976, box 10, folder 3, AOHP.

53. Ibid.

54. Ibid.

CHAPTER 16: Man, the Stage

1. Elizabeth Jelin, interview, 4 June 2011.

2. AOH, "Talk on Prince and Machiavelli," IAS, October 1976, box 69, folder 12, AOHP.

3. AOH to Katia Solomon, 13 Oct. 1975, KSPP.

4. See John M. Najemy, *Between Friends: Discourses of Power and Desire in the Machiavelli–Vettori Letters of 1513–1515* (Princeton: Princeton University Press, 1994) for more detail.

5. AOH to KS, 26 Sept. 1976, KSPP.

6. AOH, "Talk on Prince and Machiavelli," IAS, October 1976, box 69, folder 12, AOHP.

7. AOH to Katia Hirschman, 25 Mar. 1973, KSPP.

8. Flexner quoted in Clifford Geertz, *After the Fact: Two Countries, Four Decades, One Anthropologist* (Cambridge MA: Harvard University Press, 1995), p. 122.

9. Report to Carl Kaysen, n.d., box 10, folder 9, AOHP.

10. Sir John Elliott, interview, 2 Apr. 2010.

11. Israel Shenker, "Foes at the Institute Dig in for a Fight," *New York Times*, 4 Mar. 1973; "Economic Development Lectures," Woodrow Wilson School, March 1973, box 71, folder 3, AOHP; AOH to KS, 25 Mar. 1973, KSPP.

12. Geertz, *After the Fact*, p. 125.

13. Alexander Gerschenkron to John W. Milnor, 10 Dec. 1973, Albert O. Hirschman File, The Shelby White and Leon Levy Archive Center, Institute for Advanced Study, Princeton, New Jersey.

14. Carl Kaysen, interview, 25 Aug. 2009; Albert O. Hirschman File, The Shelby White and Leon Levy Archive Center, Institute for Advanced Study, Princeton, New Jersey.

15. Kenneth Arrow, interview, 7 Sept. 2009.

16. "Economic Development in Latin America," 1974, Box 9, folder 9, AOHP.

17. AOH to KS, 6 Aug. 1974, KSPP.

18. AOH to KS, 26 Sept. 1974, KSPP.

19. Stanley Hoffmann, interview, 7 Nov. 2009.

20. AOH to KS, 18 May 1974, KSPP.

21. AOH to KS, 18 Sept. 1974, KSPP.

22. Donald Winch, interview, 1 Apr. 2010; Susan James, interview, 19 May 2010; Joan W Scott, interview, 2 Apr. 2011.

23. AOH to KS, 27 Sept. 1972, KSPP.

24. Robert Darnton, interview, 12 Apr. 2010; Clifford Geertz to AOH, 8 Nov. 1973, box 54, folder16, AOHP.

25. "Member Lists," Box 4, folder 7, AOHP.

26. AOH, "Eighteenth-Century Hopes and Twentieth-Century Realities," MIT lecture, 1977, box 8, folder 17, AOHP. The lecture was his first draft of what would later be his essay for the Collier anthology *The New Authoritarianism in Latin America*.

27. AOH, interview, 9 Sept. 2002.

28. AOH, "Notebook Argentina 1971," box 24, folder 10, AOHP.

29. AOH, "Introductory Note," *Essays in Trespassing*, p. 288.

30. AOH to KS, 25 June 1972 and before Thanksgiving 1972, KSPP; José Serra, interview, 31 Oct. 2011.

31. Robert Darnton, "Intellectual and Cultural History," in *The Past Before Us*, ed. Michael Kamen (Ithaca: Cornell University Press, 1980), pp. 339–340.

32. Donald Winch, interview 1 Apr. 2010; Joan W. Scott, interview, 2 Apr. 2011.

33. Donald Winch to AOH, 30 Apr. 1975, box 71, folder 1, AOHP; Donald Winch, interview, 1 Apr. 2010.

34. Quentin Skinner to AOH, n.d. [probably spring 1975], box 71, folder 1, AOHP.

35. AOH, "Reasons for Undertaking this Project," n.d. [probably 1975], box 71, folder 7, AOHP.

36. Ibid.

37. Ibid.

38. Ibid.

39. AOH to KS, 13 Apr. 1973, KSPP.

40. AOH, *The Passions and the Interests: Political Arguments for Capitalism before Its Triumph* (Princeton: Princeton University Press, 1977).

41. "The Concept of Interest: From Euphemism to Tautology," in *Rival Views*, p. 36.

42. AOH to KS, 13 Apr. 1973, KSPP.

43. AOH, "The Concept of Interest," p. 41, n 5.

44. AOH, *Passion and the Interests*, pp. 43–44.

45. Ibid., pp. 104, 111.

46. AOH, "The Concept of Interest," p. 51.

47. Nannerl Keohane to AOH, 12 Sept. 1977 and AOH to Nannerl Keohane 10 Oct. 1977, box 11, folder 8, AOHP.

48. Bruce Cummings to AOH, 13 June 1977, box 11, folder 8, AOHP.

49. AOH to KS, 3 Feb. 1974, KSPP.

CHAPTER 17: Body Parts

1. AOH, "Favorite Quotes," box 5, folder 8, AOHP.

2. Robert Darnton, interview, 12 Apr. 2010.

CHAPTER 18: Disappointment

1. "Trip to Russia—June, 18–28 Diary," box 9, folder 2, AOHP.

2. AOH to McGeorge Bundy, 5 Feb. 1976, box 10, folder 3, AOHP.

3. Alejandro Foxley to AOH, 9 Aug. 1976, box 9, folder 3, AOHP.

4. Private goods are excludable—one person can prevent another from enjoying it—and rivalrous—one person's benefit affects another's. Public goods are neither.

5. AOH, "The Concept of Interest," in *Rival Views*, p. 48.

6. Brian Barry's review article of *Exit, Voice, and Loyalty* in *British Journal of Political Science* 4:1 (February 1974), pp. 79–104. Hirschman would have his riposte in *Shifting Involvements*, p. 78.

7. AOH, "Olson and Collective Action," December 1977, box 86, folder 2, AOHP.

8. Ibid.

9. Herbert Gintis, interview, 6 Aug. 2009.

10. AOH, "Olson and Collective Action," December 1977, box 86, folder2, AOHP.

11. AOH, "Exit, Voice, and the State," 1977, in *Essays in Trespassing*, pp. 246–265; Robert Keohane to AOH, 24 Oct. 1977, box 4, folder 5, AOHP.

12. Clifford Geertz to AOH, 28 Sept. 1978, box 4, folder 5, AOHP; Sir John Elliott, interview, 2 Apr. 2010.

13. Clifford Geertz to AOH, 3 Nov. 1978, box 4, folder 5, AOHP.

14. AOH to Clifford Geertz, 27 Apr. 1979, box 4, folder 5, AOHP.

15. Clifford Geertz, *After the Fact: Two Countries, Four Decades, One Anthropologist* (Cambridge MA: Harvard University Press, 1995), p. 127.

16. Paul Rabinow and William M. Sullivan, "The Interpretive Turn: A Second Look," in *Interpretive Social Science: A Second Look*, ed. Rabinow and Sullivan (Berkeley and Los Angeles: University of California Press, 1987), pp. 1–31.

17. AOH, "Our View of Social Science," box 4, folder 12, AOHP.

18. AOH to KS, 26 Sept. 1975, KSPP.

19. AOH, "Self-Perception, Mutual Perception, and Historical Development," 13 Oct. 1977, box 77, folder 5, AOHP; Sir John Elliott, interview, 2 Apr. 2010; David Cannadine, interview, 25 May 2010.

20. AOH to Mark Gersovitz, 22 Feb. 1980, box 76, folder 5, AOHP.

21. AOH, "The Rise and Decline of Development Economics," 1981, *Essays in Trespassing*, pp. 1–24; David Cannadine, interview, 25 May 2010.

22. "Professor A Hirschman's Comments on the Final Draft of Science and Technology in the New Socio-Economic Context," box 8, folder 12, AOHP.

23. AOH, "Welfare State in Trouble: Systemic Crisis or Growing Pains?" manuscript, box 7, folder 7, AOHP, and final publication in *American Economic Review* 70:2 (May 1980), p. 113–116.

24. Michael McPherson, interview, 4 Aug. 2009.

25. AOH, "Private and Public Happiness: Pursuits and Disappointments," The Eliot Janeway Lectures on Historical Economics in Honor of Joseph Schumpeter, Princeton University, December 1979, box 72, folder 11, AOHP.

26. AOH, "Public vs Private" (summer 1978), box 80, folder 3, AOHP; Amartya Sen, interview, 7 Apr. 2010.

27. AOH to KS, 25 Nov. 1979, KSPP.

28. The quote from Cervantes is in *Shifting Involvements: Private Interest and Public Action* (Princeton: Princeton University Press, 1982), pp. 23–24.

29. AOH, "Private and Public Happiness," Janeway Lectures, December 1979, box 72, folder 11, AOHP.

30. Ibid.

31. Ibid.

32. Robert Keohane to AOH, 11 Apr. 1979, box 77, folder 8, AOHP.

33. AOH, "Private and Public Happiness," Janeway Lectures, December 1979, box 72, folder 11, AOHP.

34. AOH to KS, 19 Aug. 1981, KSPP.

35. AOH, *Shifting Involvements*, p. xvi.

36. Quentin Skinner to AOH, 17 Dec. 1979, box 80, folder 3, AOHP.

37. Judith Tendler to AOH, 9 July 1979, box 77, folder 8, AOHP.

38. Lisa Hirschman to AOH, February 1979, box 77, folder 8, AOHP.

39. Robert Lane to Sandford Thatcher, 6 May 1981, box 78, folder 5, AOHP.

40. Joan Scottto AOH, 22 Feb. 1979, box 77, folder 8, AOHP.

41. George Akerlof review, 4 June 1981, box 78, folder 5, AOHP.

42. AOH to Claus Offe, 19 Dec. 1979, box 77, folder 8, AOHP.

43. AOH to Sanford Thatcher, 27 May 1981, box 78, folder 5, AOHP.

44. Ibid.

45. George Akerlof to AOH, 14 May 1981, box 78, folder 5, AOHP.

46. AOH, "Comment," Smygehus Sweden, 20–23 Sept. 1982, box 7, folder 18, AOHP; Steven Maser, *American Political Science Review*, vol. 78 (1984), p. 590; Jan Smith, *American Journal of Sociology* 89 (July 1983), p. 228; Robert Heilbroner, "The Way of All Flesh," *New York Review of Books*, 24 June 1982, pp. 44–46; Jon Elster, "Trespasser," *London Review of Books*, 16 Sept–6 Oct. 1982; Quentin Skinner to AOH, 2 Feb. 1983, box 5, folder 7, AOHP.

47. Lewis Coser, "America's Eclectic Economist," *New Republic*, 19 and 26 July 1982, pp. 40–42; Peter L. Berger, "History as a Disappointment Machine, *New York Times Book Review*, 18 April 1982, p. 9; AOH to KS, 19 Apr. 1982, KSPP; Michel Massenet, "Les deceptions de la démocratie," *Le Figaro*, 6 Jan. 1983, p. 17; David Reisman to AOH 2 May 1982, box 77, folder 10, AOHP.

48. AOH, "Remarks at Berkeley Conference, March 1980," box 8, folder 6, AOHP.

49. AOH to David Reisman, 12 Dec. 1983, box 77, folder 8, AOHP.

CHAPTER 19: Social Science for Our Grandchildren

1. "Remarks at Berkeley Conference, March 1980," box 8, folder 6, AOHP; Michael McPherson, interview, 4 Aug. 2009.

2. AOH to Wolf Lepenies, 18 Aug. 1980, box 8, folder 6, AOHP.

3. Published later in *Essays in Trespassing*, pp. 294–306.

4. Daniel Bell to AOH, 14 Dec. 1980 and AOH to DB, 8 Jan. 1981, box 1, folder 8, AOHP.

5. AOH to Robert Solow, 2 Jan. 1980, box 1, folder 8, AOHP.

6. Kenneth Arrow to AOH, 12 Jan. 1981, box 1, folder 8, AOHP.

7. AOH, "Morality and the Social Sciences," n.d., box 8, folder 6, AOHP.

8. Quentin Skinner to AOH, n.d. and Henry Ehrmann to AOH, 20 Dec. 1980, box 8, folder 6, AOHP.

9. Dennis Thompson to AOH, n.d. and AOH to Michael McPherson, 31 July 1980, box 8, folder 6, AOHP.

10. AOH, "Morality and the Social Sciences: A Durable Tension," in *Essays in Trespassing*, p. 306.

11. AOH, "University Activities Abroad and Human Rights Violations: Exit, Voice, or Business as Usual," *Human Rights Quarterly* 6 (February 1984).

12. Richard Lyman to AOH, 18 Mar. 1982, box 7, folder 19, AOHP.

13. AOH, "A Dissenter's Confession," in *Pioneers in Development*, ed. Gerald M. Meier and Dudley Seers (Washington, DC: World Bank/Oxford University Press, 1984), pp. 87–111.

14. Terry Karl, interview, 5 July 2012.

15. Peter Hakim, interview, 26 May 2010.

16. Steve Vetter to AOH, 3 Jan. 1982, box 38, folder 1, AOHP.

17. María del Carmen Feijoó and Sarah Hirschman, *Gente y Cuentos: educación popular y literatura* (Buenos Aires: CEDES, 1984); Maria del Carmen Feijoo, interview, 6 Aug. 2012.

18. Memorandum, Anne B. Ternes to Robert Mashek, 2 June 1983, box 37, folder 8, AOHP; Unidentified Citadel Notebook, n.d., box 24, folder 10, AOHP; Elizabeth Jelin, interview, 1 June 2011.

19. AOH Note Book, R.D., Col., Peru, Chile, box 24, folder 10, p. 55, AOHP.

20. AOH Note Book DR, Col., Peru, Chile, box 24, folder 10, pp. 77–78, AOHP.

21. Peter Hakim, interview, 26 May 2010; Sheldon Annis, interview, 29 May 2012; Peter Bell, interview, 26 July 2011.

22. Peter Hakim, interview, 26 May 2010.

23. IAS Talk, January 1984, box 66, folder 9, AOHP.

24. AOH Note Book, R.D., Col., Peru, Chile, box 24, folder 10, pp. 8–9, AOHP.

25. AOH, *Getting Ahead Collectively: Grassroots Experiences in Latin America* (New York: Pergamon Press, 1984), p. 101.

26. Michael McPherson, interview, 4 Aug. 2009.

27. AOH to Paul Streeten, 6 Oct. 1983 and AOH, "Reply to Readers," box 24, folder 10, AOHP.

28. Dominican Republic Notebook I, box 24, folder 10, p. 107, AOHP.

29. AOH Note Book, R.D., Col., Peru, Chile, p. 7 and Colombia Notebook II, box 24, folder 10, pp. 256, 312, AOHP.

30. Colombia II Notebook, box 24, folder 10, p. 152, AOHP.

31. Latin America 1983 Trip file, undated note on IAF stationery, box 7, folder 11, AOHP.

32. AOH Note Book, R.D., Col., Peru, Chile, box 24, folder 10, pp. 8–9, AOHP.

33. SH, Dominican Republic Notebook I, box 24, folder 10, p. 107, AOHP.

34. SH, Dominican Republic Notebook I, box 24, folder 10, pp. 76, 91, AOHP.

35. From Latin America 1983 Trip file, IAF letterhead n.d., box 7, folder 11, AOHP.

36. AOH, *Getting Ahead Collectively*, p. 94.

37. Mitchell Denburg, interview, 25 May 2012.

38. AOH Note Book R.D., Col., Peru, Chile, box 24, folder 10, p. 33, AOHP.

39. Peter Hakim, interview, 26 May 2010.

40. AOH, "Self-Inflicted Wound," *New Republic* 190:1/2 (January 1984), p. 9.

41. Peter Bell to AOH, 1 Jan. 1984, box 66, folder 12, AOHP.

42. "Brown University, Oct., 1984" notes for UN, box 66, folder 7, AOHP.

43. William Klausner, "Reflections on Bellagio Conference," 20 Sept. 1985, RF, Unprocessed (A 96), box R2931, series 120, RG 2, RAC.

44. "For Peter Hakim," January 1985, and Louis Emmerij to AOH, 11 Aug. 1986, box 66, folder 7, AOHP.

45. Patricio Meller, interview, 4 June, 2011.

CHAPTER 20: Reliving the Present

1. Quentin Skinner to AOH, 22 Dec. 1984, box 7, folder 11, AOHP.

2. Anthony Marx, interview, 5 Aug. 2009; Elizabeth Jelin, interview, 1 June 2011.

3. Cliff Geertz, "AOH Talk," PP.

4. Adele Simmons to AOH, 18 Jan. 1996, box 20, folder 5, AOHP.

5. AOH, "States and Social Structures," February 1982, box 8, folder 10, AOHP.

6. "Trip to Russia," box 9, folder 2, p. 24, AOHP.

7. Stephen Krasner, interview, 16 Dec. 2009; James Caporaso, "Guidelines for Writing the Papers," 19 May 1975, and AOH to Caporaso, 16 Dec. 1975, box 9, folder 14, AOHP; Benjamin J. Cohen, *International Political Economy: An Intellectual History* (Princeton: Princeton University Press, 2008).

8. AOH, "The Welfare State in Trouble," *Dissent* (Winter 1981), reprinted in *Rival Views*, pp. 163–170; "Reflections on *The Rhetoric of Reaction*," paper presented to the Society for Philosophy and Public Affairs, New York, 12 Nov. 1991, box 75, folder 2, AOHP.

9. John Kenneth Galbraith to AOH, 28 Dec. 1988, box 66, folder 17, AOHP; AOH, "How Keynes Was Spread from America," *Challenge*, November–December

1988, and an expanded version "How the Keynesian Revolution Was Exported from the United States, and Other Comments," in *The Political Power of Economic Ideas: Keynesianism across Nations*, ed. Peter Hall (Princeton: Princeton University press, 1989), pp. 347–360.

10. The awards, prizes, and medals rolled in. Here's an abbreviated catalogue. The American Economic Association named him Distinguished Fellow in 1984. The American Philosophical Society gave him the Thomas Jefferson Medal. The University of Michigan hosted him for the Tanner Lectures; the Academy of Sciences at the University of Budapest also hosted him for a lecture. The government of Argentina decorated him with the Orden de May al Mérito; Brazil's awarded him its highest honor, the Ordem do Cruzeiro do Sul (this one had special meaning because it came straight from Fernando Henrique Cardoso, by then the country's president); and Colombia's government gave Hirschman the Orden de San Carlos. The University of Köln gave him the Fritz-Thyssen Prize.

11. Daniel Bell, Speech to American Academy of Arts and Sciences for the Talcott Parsons Prize, 14 Mar. 1984, box 2, folder 22, AOHP; AOH, "Against Parsimony: Three Easy Ways of Complicating Some Categories of Economic Discourse," in *Rival Views*, pp. 142–162.

12. Alejandro Foxley, Michael S. McPherson, Guillermo O'Donnell, eds., *Development, Democracy, and the Art of Trespassing: Essays in Honor of Albert O. Hirschman* (Notre Dame, IN: University of Notre Dame Press, 1986).

13. Torcuato di Tella to AOH, 26 Oct. 1989, box 55, folder 56, AOHP; Simón Teitel, ed., *Towards a New Development Strategy for Latin America: Pathways from Hirschman's Thought* (Washington, DC: IDB, 1992); Lloyd Rodwin and Donald A. Schön, eds., *Rethinking the Development Experience: Essays Provoked by the Work of Albert O. Hirschman* (Washington, DC and Cambridge, MA: The Brookings Institution and Lincoln Institute of Land Policy, 1994).

14. AOH, Torino Talk, October 1987, box, folder 3, AOHP.

15. "A Propensity to Self-Subversion" was originally in Rodwin and Schön, *Rethinking*, and subsequently became the anchor essay of *A Propensity to Self-Subversion*.

16. AOH, "Rival Views of the Market," in *Rival Views*, pp. 105–141.

17. Philippe Simonnot, "Les mots et les choses," *Le Monde*, 12 Sept. 1997, p. 12.

18. Keith Griffin, "An Economist Abroad," *Times Literary Supplement*, 19 Feb. 1982, pp. 9–10.

19. AOH, "Linkage Approach to Development, Some Further reflections," March 1982, São Paulo Conference), box 7, folder 23, AOHP.

20. Alex Inkeles, *Journal of Economic Literature* 21 (March 1983), pp. 79–80.

21. Peter Passell, "The Morning Line on the Next Nobel," *New York Times*, 18 Oct. 1989, p. D2.

22. Thomas Schelling, interview, 2 Oct. 2008.

23. Amartya Sen, interview, 21 Apr. 2006; Kenneth Arrow, interview, 7 Sept. 2009.

24. Eric Maskin, interview, 29 Nov. 2011.

25. "Salvador Allende died not because he was a socialist, but because he was an incompetent," from "Why Allende Failed," *Challenge*, vol. 17 (May–June 1974), pp. 1–14.

26. AOH, "Endogenous Growth Workshop Notes," October 1991, box 6, folder 1, AOHP.

27. Amartya Sen, interview, 21 Apr. 2006.

28. Sabine Offe, interview, 17 Aug. 2011; Claus Offe, interview, 24 Oct. 2009; AOH to Claus Offe, 24 June 1987, box 6, folder 1, AOHP.

29. Berlin Festvortrag, 21 Nov. 1988, box 54, folder 7, AOHP.

30. AOH to Claus Offe, 12 Dec. 1988, box 1, folder 13, AOHP; AOH, "Four Re-encounters," in *Propensity*, pp. 101–105.

31. AOH, "Exit, Voice, and the Fate of the German Democratic Republic," in *Propensity*, pp. 9–44.

32. AOH, "Report on Academic Activities," June 1991, box 5, folder 13, AOHP.

33. Peter Gourevitch, interview, 21 July 2011.

34. AOH, "Closing Comments," box 5, folder 17, AOHP; "On Democracy in Latin America," *New York Review of Books* 10 Apr. 1986, pp. 23–26.

35. AOH, "LA Diary," box 5, folder 19, AOHP.

36. AOH, "The Political Economy of Latin American Development: Seven Essays in Retrospection," *Latin American Research Review* 22:3 (1987), pp. 7–36.

37. AOH to Stephen Holmes, 29 Mar. 1988, box 54, folder 5, AOHP.

38. Alejandro Foxley, interview, 4 June 2011.

39. AOH, "Out of Phase Again," *New York Review of Books* 18 Dec. 1986; "Social Democracy Moves South," manuscript, box 5, folder 19, AOHP.

40. Daniel Patrick Moynihan to AOH, 25 Jan. 1989, box 6, folder 5, AOHP.

41. AOH, Notes—Summer, 1985; Notes—Summer 1986, box 56, folder 10, AOHP.

42. Claus Offe to AOH, 14 Jan. 1988; Michael McPherson to AOH, 6 Feb. 1988; Quentin Skinner to AOH, 3 Jan. 1988 and 7 Mar. 1988; AOH to Skinner, 25 Mar. 1988, box 75, folder 4, AOHP.

43. AOH, "Reactionary Rhetoric," *Atlantic Monthly* (May 1989), pp. 63–70.

44. István Rév to AOH, 25 Apr. 1991, box 75, folder 4, AOHP.

45. McPherson to AOH, 6 Feb. 1988, box 75, folder 4, AOHP.

46. AOH, *The Rhetoric of Reaction: Perversity, Futility, Jeopardy* (Cambridge MA: Harvard University Press, 1991), pp. ix–xi.

47. AOH, "Harvard Lecture" n.d. [probably 1991], box 75, folder 4, AOHP.

48. AOH to UH, 12 Apr. 1987.

49. Jamaica Kincaid to AOH, 18 Oct. 1991, box 75, folder 3, AOHP.

50. Peter Jenkins, "Conservatives' Progress," *New York Times Book Review*, 5 Dec. 1991, p. 3.

51. AOH to Robert Silvers, 17 Sept. 1991, box 75, folder 3, AOHP.

52. Peter Gourevitch to AOH, 10 Oct. 1992, box 75, folder 2, AOHP.

53. See the exchange in *Le Débat*, 69 (March–April 1992), pp. 92–109.

CONCLUSION: Marc Chagall's Kiss

1. AOH, "Talk," 7 Apr. 1995, Box 1, folder 1, AOHP.

2. Hermione Lee, "How to End it All," *Virginia Wolf's Nose: Essays on Biography* (Princeton: Princeton University Press, 2005), p. 95.

3. Stanley Hoffmann, interview, 7 Nov. 2009.

4. SH, interview 18 Feb. 2006.

5. AOH to Michael McPherson, 14 Mar. 1988, box 75, folder 14, AOHP.

6. AOH to Benjamin Friedman, 9 Aug. 1996 and AOH to Wolf Lepenies, 16 Aug. 1996, box 5, folder 10, AOHP.

7. AOH to Orlando Fals-Borda, 22 Oct. 1996, box 20, folder 8, AOHP.

8. AOH, "The Paradoxes of Unintended Consequences," 23 Nov. 1999, box 80, folder 10, AOHP.

9. AOH to Bruce Mazlish, n.d, box 2, folder 24, AOHP.

10. AOH, "Social Conflicts as Pillars of Democratic Market Societies," *Political Theory*, vol. 22 (May 1994), pp. 203–218, reprinted in *Propensity*, pp. 231–248.

11. Harry Frankfurt to AOH, 25 Mar. 1993, box 72, folder 12, AOHP; "L'Oeuvre revisitée," *Le Monde*, 28 Apr. 1995.

12. Ramona Nadaff to AOH, 19 Dec. 1997, box 56, folder 6, AOHP.

13. *Who Shall Live and Who Shall Die*, directed by Laurence Jarvik, 1982.

14. "Fry Story," 2 Dec. 1997, box 3, folder 8, AOHP.

15. AOH to Lisa Hirschman, 13 July 1998, PP.

16. Peter Gourevitch, interview, 12 Feb. 2011.

17. AOH to KS, 14 Mar. 2003, box 3, folder 4, AOHP.

Albert O. Hirschman's long life of writing ranged over an astonishing array of disciplines, themes, and genres. What follows is a bibliography of his publications.

Published Works of Albert O. Hirschman

AUTHORED BOOKS

National Power and the Structure of Foreign Trade (Berkeley and Los Angeles: University of California Press, 1945; reprinted 1969; paperback edition with new introduction, 1980); translated into Spanish.

The Strategy of Economic Development (New Haven, CT: Yale University Press, 1958; reprinted 1978 by W. W. Norton; in 1988 by Westview Press); translated into French, German, Italian, Spanish, Portuguese, Swedish, Japanese, Indonesian, Bengali, and Korean.

Journeys toward Progress: Studies of Economic Policy-Making in Latin America (New York: Twentieth Century Fund, 1963; reprinted 1973 by W. W. Norton with a new preface); translated into Spanish and Portuguese.

Development Projects Observed (Washington, DC: Brookings Institution, 1967); translated into Spanish, Portuguese, Italian, Japanese; reedited, with a new preface by the author, by the Brookings Institution, 1995.

Exit, Voice, and Loyalty: Responses to Decline in Firms, Organizations, and States (Cambridge, MA: Harvard University Press, 1970); translated into Spanish, Portuguese, French, German, Italian, Swedish, Japanese, and Hungarian.

A Bias for Hope: Essays on Development and Latin America (New Haven, CT: Yale University Press, 1971; reprinted 1985 by Westview Press); translated into Spanish.

The Passions and the Interests: Political Arguments for Capitalism before Its Triumph (Princeton, NJ: Princeton University Press, 1977); translated into Spanish, Portuguese, French, German, Italian, and Japanese. Twentieth Anniversary Edition, 1997, by Princeton University Press, with a foreword by Amartya Sen and a second preface by the author.

Essays in Trespassing: Economics to Politics and Beyond (New York: Cambridge University Press, 1981); translated into Spanish.

Shifting Involvements: Private Interest and Public Action (Princeton, NJ: Princeton University Press, 1982); translated into French, Italian, German, Spanish, and Portuguese; being translated into Japanese.

Getting Ahead Collectively: Grassroots Experiences in Latin America (New York: Pergamon Press, 1984); translated into Spanish and Portuguese.

Rival Views of Market Society and Other Recent Essays (New York: Viking/Penguin, 1986; paperback edition, with new preface, Harvard University Press, 1992); translated into Spanish and Portuguese.

The Rhetoric of Reaction: Perversity, Futility, Jeopardy (Cambridge, MA: Belknap Press of Harvard University Press, 1991); translated into French, Spanish, Italian, German, Portuguese, and Japanese.

A Propensity to Self-Subversion (Cambridge, MA: Harvard University Press, 1995); translated into French, Spanish, Italian, Portuguese, German, and Japanese.

Crossing Boundaries: Selected Writings and an Interview (New York: Zone Books, 1998).

EDITED BOOKS

Latin American Issues: Essays and Comments (New York: Twentieth Century Fund, 1961); translated into Spanish, Portuguese, and Italian.

BOOKS IN OTHER LANGUAGES
(IN ADDITION TO ABOVE NOTED TRANSLATIONS):

Ascesa e declino dell'economia dello sviluppo (Torino: Rosenberg and Sellier, 1983); a collection of essays edited and with an introduction by Andrea Ginzburg.

L'économie comme science morale et politique (Paris: Gallimard/Le Seuil, 1984); a collection of essays, with an introduction by François Furet; Italian translation with introduction by Luca Meldolesi; translated into Portuguese.

Vers une économie politique élargie (Paris: Editions de Minuit, 1986); lectures given at the Collège de France in 1985.

Potenza nazionale e commercio estero: Gli anni trenta. l'Italia e la ricostruzione (Bologna: Il Mulino, 1987); translation of parts of *National Power and the Structure of Foreign Trade* and of articles on the Italian economy written in the 1930s and

'40s, edited and with an introduction by Pier Francesco Asso and Marcello de Cecco.

Come complicare l'economia (Bologna: II Mulino, 1989); selected articles and book chapters for series "I grandi economisti contemporanei," edited and with an introduction by Luca Meldolesi.

Entwicklung, Markt und Moral: Abweichende Betrachtungen (Munich: Carl Hanser, 1989); selected essays from 1969 to 1988.

Come far passare le riforme (Bologna: 11 Mulino, 1990); selected articles and book chapters edited and with an introduction by Luca Meldolesi.

ARTICLES

* Articles are included in *A Bias for Hope: Essays on Development and Latin America.*
\# Articles are included in *Essays in Trespassing: Economics to Politics and Beyond.*
** Articles are included in *Rival Views of Market Society and Other Recent Essays.*
\+ Articles are included in *A Propensity to Self-Subversion.*
++Articles are included in *Crossing Boundaries: Selected Writings and an Interview.*

"Nota su due recenti tavole di nuzialità della popolazione italiana," *Giornale delli Economisti*, January 1938.

"The Commodity Structure of World Trade," *Quarterly Journal of Economics*, August 1943.

"On Measures of Dispersion for a Finite Distribution," *Journal of the American Statistical Association*, September 1943.

"Inflation and Deflation in Italy," *American Economic Review*, September 1948.

"Disinflation, Discrimination, and the Dollar Shortage," *American Economic Review*, December 1948.

"Devaluation and the Trade Balance: A Note," *Review of Economics and Statistics*, February 1949.

"Postwar Credit Controls in France" (with Robert V. Roosa), *Federal Reserve Bulletin*, April 1949.

"Movement toward Balance in International Transactions of the United States" (with Lewis N. Dembitz), *Federal Reserve Bulletin*, April 1949.

"International Aspects of a Recession," *American Economic Review*, December 1949.

"The European Payments Union—Negotiations and Issues," *Review of Economics and Statistics*, February 1951.

"Types of Convertibility," *Review of Economics and Statistics*, February 1951.

"Industrial Nations and Industrialization of Under-Developed Countries," *Economia Internazionale*, August 1951.

"Effects of Industrialization on the Market of Industrial Countries," in *Progress of Underdeveloped Areas*, ed. Bert F. Hoselitz, (University of Chicago Press, 1952).

"Guia para el análisis y la confección de recomendaciones sobre la situación monetaria," *Economia Colombiana*, October 1954.

*"Economics and Investment Planning: Reflections Based on Experience in Colombia," in *Investment Criteria and Economic Growth* mimeo (Cambridge, MA: Center for International Studies, M.I.T., 1954); published by Asia Publishing House, New York, 1961.

"Colombia: Highlights of a Developing Economy" (with George Kalmanoff), booklet (Bogota: Banco de la República Press, 1955).

"Demanda de energía electrica para la C.V.C." (with George Kalmanoff), *Economía Colombiana*, June 1956.

*"Economic Policy in Underdeveloped Countries," *Economic Development and Cultural Change*, July 1957.

"Investment Policies and 'Dualism' in Underdeveloped Countries," *American Economic Review*, September 1957.

"Investment Criteria and Capital Intensity Once Again" (with Gerald Sirkin), *Quarterly Journal of Economics*, August 1958.

*"Primary Products and Substitutes: Should Technological Progress Be Policed?" *Kyklos*, August 1959.

"The Strategy of Economic Development," *Farm Policy Forum*, vol. 12, 1959–60.

"Invitation to Theorizing about the Dollar Glut," *Review of Economics and Statistics*, February 1960.

"Exchange Controls and Economic Development: Comments," in *Economic Development for Latin America*, ed. H.S. Ellis (New York: St. Martin's Press, 1961).

* "Second Thoughts on the 'Alliance for Progress,'" *The Reporter*, May 25, 1961.

* "Ideologies of Economic Development in Latin America," in *Latin American Issues: Essays and Comments*, ed. A.O. Hirschman (New York: Twentieth Century Fund, 1961).

* "Abrazo vs. Co-existence: Comments on Ypsilon's Paper," in *Latin American Issues—Essays and Comments*, ed. A.O. Hirschman (New York: Twentieth Century Fund, 1961).

* "Analyzing Economic Growth: A Comment," in *Development of the Emerging Countries*, ed. Robert E. Asher et al. (Washington, DC: Brookings Institution, 1962).

* "Economic Development, Research and Development, Policy-Making: Some Converging Views" (with Charles E. Lindblom), *Behavioral Science*, April 1962.

"Models of Reformmongering," *Quarterly Journal of Economics*, May 1963.

* "The Stability of Neutralism: A Geometrical Note," *American Economic Review*, March 1964.

* "Obstacles to Development: A Classification and a Quasi-Vanishing Act," *Economic Development and Cultural Change*, July 1965.

"Out of Phase," *Encounter*, September 1965 (special issue on Latin America).

"The Principle of the Hiding Hand," *The Public Interest*, Winter 1967.

* "The Political Economy of Import-Substituting Industrialization in Latin America," *Quarterly Journal of Economics*, February 1968.

* "Foreign Aid: A Critique and Proposal" (with Richard M. Bird), *Princeton Essays in International Finance*, July 1968.

* "Underdevelopment, Obstacles to the Perception of Change, and Leadership," *Daedalus*, Summer 1968.

* "Industrial Development in the Brazilian Northeast and the Tax Credit Scheme of Article 34/18," *The Journal of Development Studies*, October 1968.

* "How to Divest in Latin America, and Why," *Princeton Essays in International Finance*, November 1969.

* "The Search for Paradigms as a Hindrance to Understanding," *World Politics*, March 1970; also in *Interpretive Social Science: A Reader*, ed. P. Rabinow and W. M. Sullivan (Berkeley: University of California Press, 1979).

* "Ideology or Nessus Shirt?" in *Comparison of Economic Systems: Theoretical and Methodological Approaches*, ed. Alexander Eckstein (Berkeley: University of California Press, 1971).

\# "The Changing Tolerance for Income Inequality in the Course of Economic Development" (with a mathematical appendix by Michael Rothschild), *Quarterly Journal of Economics*, November 1973.

\# "An Alternative Explanation of Contemporary Harriedness," *Quarterly Journal of Economics*, November 1973.

\# "Exit, Voice, and Loyalty: Further Reflections and a Survey of Recent Contributions," *Social Science Information*, February 1974.

\# "Policy Making and Policy Analysis in Latin America—A Return Journey," *Policy Sciences*, December 1975.

\# "On Hegel, Imperialism, and Structural Stagnation," *Journal of Development Economics*, March 1976.

\# "Exit, Voice, and Loyalty—Comments," *American Economic Review. Papers and Proceedings*, May 1976.

\# "A Generalized Linkage Approach to Development, with Special Reference to Staples," *Economic Development and Cultural Change*, vol. 25 supplement, 1977 (Essays in honor of Bert F. Hoselitz).

"Beyond Asymmetry: Critical Notes on Myself as a Young Man and on Some Other Old Friends," *International Organization*, Winter 1978.

"Exit, Voice, and the State," *World Politics*, October 1978.

"The Turn to Authoritarianism in Latin America and the Search for Its Economic Determinants," in *The New Authoritarianism in Latin America*, ed. David Collier (Princeton, NJ: Princeton University Press, 1979).

** "The Welfare State in Trouble: Systemic Crisis or Growing Pains?" *American Economic Review. Papers and Proceedings*, May 1980. Reprinted with slight changes in *Dissent*, Winter 1981.

"The Rise and Decline of Development Economics," in *The Theory and Experience of Economic Development: Essays in Honor of Sir W. Arthur Lewis*, ed. Mark Gersovitz et. al. (London: Allen and Unwin, 1982).

"Morality and the Social Sciences: A Durable Tension," acceptance paper, The Frank E. Seidman Distinguished Award in Political Economy, P. K. Seidman Foundation, Memphis, TN, October 1980; also in *Social Science as Moral Inquiry*, ed. Norma Haan et al. (New York: Columbia University Press, 1983).

** "Rival Interpretations of Market Society: Civilizing, Destructive, or Feeble?" *Journal of Economic Literature*, December 1982.

"The Principle of Conservation and Mutation of Social Energy," *Grassroots Development* (Journal of the Inter-American Foundation) vol. 7, no. 2, 1983.

"University Activities Abroad and Human Rights Violations: Exit, Voice, or Business as Usual?" *Human Rights Quarterly*, February 1984.

** "A Dissenter's Confession: Revisiting the Strategy of Economic Development," in *Pioneers in Development*, ed. Gerald M. Meier and Dudley Seers (Oxford: Oxford University Press, 1984).

"Inflation: Reflections on the Latin American Experience," in *The Politics of Inflation and Economic Stagnation*, ed. L. N. Lindberg and C. S. Maier (Washington, DC: Brookings Institution, 1985).

* "Against Parsimony: Three Easy Ways of Complicating Some Categories of Economic Discourse," *American Economic Review*, May 1984; expanded versions in the *Bulletin of the American Academy of Arts and Sciences*, May 1984, and in *Economics and Philosophy*, vol. 1, 1985.

"Grassroots Change in Latin America," *Challenge*, September/October 1984.

** "In difesa del possibilismo" (In Defense of Possibilism), in *I limiti della democrazia*, ed. R. Scartezzini (Naples: Liguori 1985).

** "On Democracy in Latin America," *New York Review of Books*, April 10, 1986.

"Out of Phase Again," *New York Review of Books*, December 18, 1986.

+ "The Political Economy of Latin American Development: Seven Exercises in Retrospection," *Latin American Research Review* vol. 22, no. 3, 1987.

"How the Keynesian Revolution Was Exported from America," *Challenge*, November/December 1988, and in *Unconventional Wisdom: Essays in Honor of John Kenneth Galbraith*, ed. Samuel Bowles et. al. (Boston: Houghton Mifflin, 1989).

+ "How the Keynesian Revolution Was Exported from the United States, and Other Comments," in *The Political Power of Economic Ideas: Keynesianism across Nations*, ed. Peter A. Hall (Princeton, NJ: Princeton University Press, 1989).

+ "Having Opinions—One of the Elements of Well-Being?" *American Economic Review*, May 1989.

"Opinionated Opinions and Democracy," *Dissent*, Summer 1989.

"Reactionary Rhetoric," *The Atlantic*, May 1989.

"Two Hundred Years of Reactionary Rhetoric: The Case of the Perverse Effect," *Tanner Lectures in Human Values*, vol. 10 (Salt Lake City: University of Utah Press, 1989).

+ "The Case against 'One Thing at a Time,'" *World Development*, August 1990.

+ "Good News Is Not Bad News," *New York Review of Books*, October 11, 1990. Also published in Spanish as "Es un Desastre para el Tercer Mundo el Fin de la Guerra Fria?" *Pensamiento lberoaroericano* no. 18, 1990.

"L'argument intransigeant comme idée reçue. En guise de réponse a Raymond Boudon," *Le Débat*, March–April 1992. A reply to Raymond Boudon's critique of *The Rhetoric of Reaction* that appears in the same issue of *Le Débat* under the title "La rhétorique est-elle réactionnaire?"

+ "Industrialization and Its Manifold Discontents: West, East, and South," *World Development*, September 1992 (Original German version in *Geschichte und Gesellschaft*, Spring 1992).

+ "Exit, Voice, and the Fate of the German Democratic Republic: An Essay in Conceptual History," *World Politics*, January 1993.

"La rhetorique progressiste et le reformateur," *Commentaire*, Summer 1993.

+ "The Rhetoric of Reaction—Two Years Later," *Government and Opposition*, Summer 1993.

+ "The On-And-Off Connection between Political and Economic Progress," *American Economic Review*, May 1994.

+ "Social Conflicts as Pillars of Democratic Market Society," *Political Theory*, May 1994.

+ "A Hidden Ambition," preface to new edition of *Development Projects Observed* (Washington, DC: Brookings Institution, 1994).

+ "A Propensity to Self-Subversion," in *Rethinking the Development Experience: Essays Provoked by the Work of Albert O. Hirschman*, ed. Lloyd Rodwin and Donald A. Schon (Washington, DC: Brookings, 1994).

"Social Democracy Moves South," (on the election of President Fernando Henrique Cardoso in Brazil), *Dissent*, Spring 1995.

++ "Melding the Public and Private Spheres: Taking Commensality Seriously," *Critical Review*, Fall 1996.

++ "Fifty Years after the Marshall Plan: Two Posthumous Memoirs and Some Personal Recollections," *French Politics and Society*, Summer 1997.

Further Reading

BOOKS ON OR ABOUT ALBERT O. HIRSCHMAN

Alejandro Foxley, Michael S. McPherson, Guillermo O'Donnell, eds., *Development, Democracy, and the Art of Trespassing: Essays in Honor of Albert O. Hirschman* (Notre Dame, IN: University of Notre Dame Press, 1986).

Ludovic Frobert and Cyrille Ferraton, *L'enquête inachevée: Introduction à l'économie politique d'Albert O. Hirschman* (Paris: Presses Universitaires, 2003).

Luca Meldolesi, *Discovering the Possible: The Surprising World of Albert O. Hirschman* (Notre Dame, IN: University of Notre Dame Press, 1995).

Lloyd Rodwin and Donald A. Schön, eds., *Rethinking the Development Experience: Essays Provoked by the Work of Albert O. Hirschman* (Washington, DC: Brookings Institution, 1994).

Simón Teitel, ed., *Towards a New Development Strategy for Latin America: Pathways from Hirschman's Thought* (Washington, DC: Inter-American Development Bank, 1992).

Following the course of such an itinerant and productive life invariably means the biographer is plunged into an equally varied set of literatures. Rather than submit the reader to an exhaustive list of the books and articles I used along the way, I have chosen instead to direct readers to a selection of texts.

GERMANY

Michael Brenner and Derek J. Penslar, eds. *In Search of Jewish Community: Jewish Identities in Germany and Austria, 1918–1933* (Bloomington: University of Indiana Press, 1998).

Michael Brenner, *The Renaissance of Jewish Culture in Weimar Germany* (New Haven, CT: Yale University Press, 1996).

Christopher Clark, *Iron Kingdom: The Rise and Downfall of Prussia* (Cambridge, MA: Harvard University Press, 2006).

Donna Harsch, *German Social Democracy and the Rise of Nazism* (Chapel Hill: University of North Carolina Press, 1993).

William David Jones, *The Lost Debate: German Socialist Intellectuals and Totalitarianism* (Urbana: University of Illinois Press, 1999).

Pamela E. Swett, *Neighbors and Enemies: The Culture of Radicalism in Berlin, 1929–1933* (New York: Cambridge University Press, 2004).

Eric Weitz, *Weimar Germany: Promise and Tragedy* (Princeton, NJ: Princeton University Press, 2007).

INTERWAR EUROPE

R.J.B. Bosworth, *Mussolini's Italy: Life under the Fascist Dictatorship, 1915–1945* (New York: Penguin, 2006).

Hanna Diamond, *Fleeing Hitler: France, 1940* (New York: Oxford University Press, 2007).

Lisa Fittko, *Escape through the Pyrenees* (Evanston, IL: Northwestern University Press, 1991).

Sheila Isenberg, *A Hero of Our Own: The Story of Varian Fry* (New York: Random House, 2001).

Julian Jackson, *The Fall of France: The Nazi Invasion of 1940* (New York: Oxford University Press, 2003).

Rosemary Sullivan, *Villa Air-Bel: World War II, Escape, and a House in Marseille* (New York: Harper Collins, 2006).

Eugen Weber, *The Hollow Years: France in the 1930s* (New York: W. W. Norton, 1994).

HISTORY OF SOCIAL SCIENCES

David C. Atkinson, *In Theory and in Practice: Harvard's Center for International Affairs* (Cambridge, MA: Weatherhead Center for International Affairs, 2007).

Volker R. Berghahn, *America and the Intellectual Cold Wars in Europe* (Princeton, NJ: Princeton University Press, 2001).

Lewis A. Coser, *Refugee Scholars in America: Their Impact and Their Experiences* (New Haven, CT: Yale University Press, 1984).

Martin Jay, *Permanent Exiles: Essays on the Intellectual Migration from Germany to America* (New York: Columbia University Press, 1986).

Gerardo Munck and Richard Snyder, eds. *Passion, Craft, and Method in Comparative Politics* (Baltimore: Johns Hopkins University Press, 2007).

Sylvia Nasar, *Grand Pursuit: The Story of Economic Genius* (New York: Simon and Schuster, 2011).

Richard Parker, *John Kenneth Galbraith: His Life, His Politics, His Economics* (New York: Farrar, Straus, and Giroux, 2005).

WAR AND RECONSTRUCTION

Greg Behrman, *The Most Noble Adventure: The Marshall Plan and How America Helped Rebuild Europe* (New York: Free Press, 2007).

François Duchêne, *Jean Monnet: The First Statesman of Interdependence* (New York: W. W. Norton, 1994).

Barry M. Katz, *Foreign Intelligence: Research and Analysis in the Office of Strategic Services, 1942–1945* (Cambridge, MA: Harvard University Press, 1989).

Joseph E. Persico, *Roosevelt's Secret War: FDR and World War II Espionage* (New York: Random House, 2002).

DEVELOPMENT, LATIN AMERICA, AND POLITICAL ECONOMY

Michele Alacevich, *The Political Economy of the World Bank: The Early Years* (Stanford, CA: Stanford University Press, 2009).

Edgar J. Dosman, *The Life and Times of Raúl Prebisch, 1901–1986* (Montreal: McGill-Queens University Press, 2008).

David Ekbladh, *The Great American Mission: Modernization and the Construction of an American World Order* (Princeton, NJ: Princeton University Press, 2010).

Nils Gilman, *Mandarins of the Future: Modernization Theory in Cold War America* (Baltimore: Johns Hopkins University Press, 2003).

Michael E. Latham, *Modernization as Ideology: American Social Science and "Nation Building" in the Kennedy Era* (Chapel Hill: University of North Carolina Press, 2000).

Inderjeet Parmar, *Foundations of the American Century: The Ford, Carnegie, and Rockefeller Foundations in the Rise of American Power* (New York: Columbia University Press, 2012).

Robert L. Tignor, *W. Arthur Lewis and the Birth of Development Economics* (Princeton, NJ: Princeton University Press, 2006).

INDEX

Notes: Page numbers in italic type indicate photographs or illustrations.